Community Organizing and Development

SECOND EDITION

HERBERT J. RUBIN
Northern Illinois University

IRENE S. RUBIN
Northern Illinois University

Macmillan Publishing Company
New York

Maxwell Macmillan Canada
Toronto

Maxwell Macmillan International
New York   Oxford   Singapore   Sydney

Cover photo: Thom Clark, *Neighborhood Works*
Editor: Linda James Scharp, MSW
Production Editor: Regina Sanford
Art Coordinator: Vincent A. Smith
Text Designer: Debra A. Fargo
Production Buyer: Pamela D. Bennett

This book was set in Clearface by Carlisle Communications, Ltd. and was printed and bound by Book Press, Inc., a Quebecor America Book Group Company. The cover was printed by New England Book Components.

Macmillan Publishing Company
866 Third Avenue
New York, NY 10022

Macmillan Publishing Company is part of the
Maxwell Communication Group of Companies.

Maxwell Macmillan Canada, Inc.
1200 Eglinton Avenue East, Suite 200
Don Mills, Ontario M3C 3N1

Library of Congress Cataloging-in-Publication Data
Rubin, Herbert J.
    Community organizing and development / Herbert J. Rubin, Irene
  Rubin. — 2nd ed.
        p.   cm.
    Includes bibliographical references and index.
    ISBN 0-675-21235-9
    1. Community development—United States. 2. Community
  organization—United States. 3. Social action—United States.
    4. Community power—United States.   I. Rubin, Irene.   II. Title.
HN90.C6R73   1992
307.1′4′0973 —dc20   91–22943
                                                                                CIP

Printing: 4   5   6   7   8   9   Year: 4   5

Photo Credits: pp. xii, 108, Courtesy of Department of Housing and Urban Development; p. 42, Courtesy of Cleveland Neighborhood Development Corporation; p. 188, Copyright by Bill Dobbs, 1985, and Northland Poster Collective; p. 242, Courtesy of Fred Wright, UE News, United Electrical, Radio, and Machine Workers of America; p. 348, King Schoenfield.

Preface

C ommunity organizing means mobilizing people to solve their own problems. Through community organizing, people learn that their problems have social causes and that fighting back is a more reasonable, dignified approach than passive acceptance and personal alienation. Community organizing enhances knowledge of how to pressure government and business, enables people to set up their own locally controlled organizations, and increases political power. As people learn that working together in progressive organizations is successful, they gain confidence that they can fight and win and that, collectively, they can resolve many of their problems.

This book is for people who have decided to spend their energy in community organizing. It is not intended to substitute for experience but to alert future organizers to needed skills, options, and possible problems. We offer a variety of principles, organizing models, and patterns for development as well as examples of successful organizations and those that have failed.

An organizer's job is demanding, whether the person works full-time with neighbors in rebuilding a community or part-time with an environmental organization to prevent dumping poisonous chemicals. The job of organizing requires patience, knowledge, and experience. The results may be long in coming and the glory transitory. So, why do people do it? How do they become involved?

The touchstone of community organizing is the existence of a problem, for which the victims typically are blamed. They are pressured to accept their situation rather than to fight it. The bitterness that results from being told to accept what is to someone else's advantage may motivate a lifetime desire to battle oppression through community organizing.

Individuals may be motivated to work through community organizing by their own experience or empathy for the experience of others. Consider a woman who works and leaves her child with a neighbor. The child is hurt in a fire. The mother is told she is a bad parent and is forced to bear the guilt of a situation she cannot resolve. But the accident was not really her fault. Inadequate daycare facilities and discrimination against women make it difficult to earn enough money to pay for child care. Her problem is socially caused and susceptible to collective solution. The injustice of blaming individuals who are the victims of socially caused problems creates a slow-burning anger that keeps community organizers at their task.

In this book we present an approach to organizing in changing political and social settings. We try to bridge the gap between the first-hand experiences of organizers and academic knowledge about community change, social mobilization, and organizations. We call attention to the choices—the tradeoffs—that community organizers are likely to meet during their careers.

We balance descriptions of stirring protest actions with the day-in–day-out activities necessary for the continual success of an organization. Action campaigns are the dramatic, visible side of community organizing. We all have images of protesters chaining themselves to bulldozers to block the destruction of a historic building. We can picture students sitting in at their university's administrative center. We can imagine Saul Alinsky's scheme of a "bathroom-in," in which protesters tie up the restroom at a public airport until their demands are met.

Protests are important tactics in organizing, but successful community organizers need more than a flair for dramatic action. The newsworthy social action campaign is the culmination of many months of daily effort in building an organization and mastering the political environment. Organizers must run complicated and changing organizations while dealing with politicians and bureaucrats. Building an organization is hard work, requiring competence with many separate tools: mobilizing the membership, following a budget, raising funds, running meetings, and reaching democratic decisions among people with diverse interests. Once mastered, these skills provide a basis for accomplishing longer-term development projects, so that people working together can do things for themselves, such as organizing a food cooperative to purchase higher-quality food at lower cost, providing job training for new skills, or maintaining a network in which the elderly help each other.

CHANGES IN THE SECOND EDITION

In this second edition, we have provided a tighter flow of the chapters and updated examples. We pay more attention to social action campaigns, coalition formation, and problems facing the organizers, and less attention to the technical tools of social research. We contrast separate models for organizing and examine contending philosophies of direct action. Three new chapters have been added: the historic context of progressive organizing, community-based economic development, and the future of organizing. In addition, the second edition reflects three changes in perspective:

- *Progressive Organizations.* We have increased the emphasis on issue-based organizations concerned with civil rights, feminism, environmentalism, housing, economic development, and public interest groups working to achieve openness in government. In these conservative times, it is impossible to separate problems in neighborhoods and communities from broader social issues.
- *The History of Organizing.* We pay greater attention to the historical continuity of community work. Future organizers should find the slow but steady progress of

community organizing energizing and the vitality and ability of community organizing to rebound from defeats encouraging.

- *Community Organizers and the Professionalization of Social Work.* In this day of computers, community-business partnerships, and complexity in governmental social programs, professional knowledge is vital. In this edition we emphasize the contribution of professionally trained social workers as teachers, supporters, and resource persons for community organizations. Professional education in community organizing must communicate a respect for others, a respect that enables organizers with formal training to work with those less educated without imposing their own values. Training in organizing must teach flexibility in approaching problems and dealing with changing circumstances. And, most important, learning professional skills involves developing empathy for others.

THE CONTENTS OF THE BOOK

This book contains six parts. The first presents our approach to community organizing, along with its history. In Part II, we discuss how collective actions can increase personal empowerment, describe progressive organizations in different community setting, and examine the organizer's role in bringing about needed changes.

Part III provides background on the political and social environment in which organizing takes place and describes tools for finding out about the problems facing particular communities. Part IV presents techniques for mobilization and then explains how organizational meetings become a tool for encouraging collective involvement.

In Part V, we discuss protest and pressure tactics to compel government and businesses to accommodate community needs. In Part VI, we turn to the developmental model to examine how progressive organizations run their own community-based programs. Particular attention is paid to using the tools of organizing to bring about economic development for social change.

In the epilogue, we present our hopes for organizing and development and our concerns about future problems. This concluding chapter communicates our philosophy that organizing is an ongoing and adaptive process that survives because it reflects the needs of people in a changing society.

ACKNOWLEDGEMENTS

We would like to thank the following reviewers of our second edition: David M. Austin, University of Texas–Austin; Daniel L. Soss, Washington State University; Meredith Minkler, University of California–Berkeley; Edwin Simon, New York Technical College–Brooklyn; William E. Buffum, University of Houston; Donald Cooney, Western Michigan University; William H. Whitaker, University of Maine; Michael Seipel, Brigham Young University; and Elizabeth Piccard, Florida State University.

Contents

I | The Historic Goals of Organizing

C ommunity organizing is a search for social power and an effort to combat perceived helplessness through learning that what appears personal is often political. Organizing is a way of collectively solving problems like unemployment, deteriorated housing, or sexism and racism. The message of organizing is that a better world is achievable if people work together as a community.

In the first part of the book, we place current goals and values of community organizing in their historic traditions. Chapter 1 introduces our definition of community development. Chapter 2 recounts the history of community organizing. The history of organizing provides a source for optimism, with its numerous illustrations of the success of the downtrodden against the dominant, and the poor against the rich.

1 The Goals of Community Organizing

A lone Greenpeace rower challenges a nuclear ship; neighborhood groups pressure city hall for affordable housing; grandmothers, mothers, and daughters march on Washington to protest court decisions on abortion rights; residents demand recompense for homes and health lost to toxic wastes; environmentalists strive to protect the trees and hills in the Northwest from clear cuts. Community actions are part of our daily lives, a part of the evening news.

Community organizing has the power to transform society. Successful grass-roots movements of blacks, workers, feminists, and gays have secured and implemented legal rights. Community organizations address problems such as a lack of affordable housing, drug abuse, discrimination, and lack of access to health care. Organizing helps develop people's skills, their sense of efficacy and competence, and their sense of self-worth. Community organizing creates a capacity for democracy and for sustained social change. It can make society more adaptable and governments more accountable.

PEOPLE, PROBLEMS, AND POWER

Community organizing means bringing people together to combat shared problems and to increase their say about decisions that affect their lives. *Community development* occurs when people form their own organizations to provide a long-term capacity for problem solving.

People face a variety of socially caused problems. Urban renewal programs may destroy housing for the poor. Gangs may terrorize the elderly. Housing discrimination may concentrate the poor and minorities in neighborhoods served by inadequate school systems. The combined burdens of child rearing and earning a living are falling increasingly on women, but women have more difficulty getting jobs that pay enough to support a family. Many industries are leaving communities, causing widespread unemployment. These and many other problems can motivate community action.

3

Community organizing helps people overcome the feeling that they face problems alone or that they are to blame for their problems. Community organizing combats the sense of helplessness people feel in dealing with the problems that confront them.

Why People Feel Helpless

We expect people to feel helpless in authoritarian regimes, but people may feel intimidated and helpless even in a democracy. Although they perceive injustice and seethe with resentment, people may feel so powerless they don't think about coming together to solve shared problems.

People feel powerless because their problems are complex and require knowledge they often lack. Whom do you fight when a city development agency, working with national real estate promoters, destroys neighborhood housing to build a shopping mall made accessible by a highway funded by a state agency? What happens if a chemical company chooses a site for a toxic waste disposal near a town's supply of clean water, or if the public hospital is deluged with acquired immune deficiency syndrome (AIDS) victims, or if the economically dispossessed mix with the mentally handicapped to form a new and highly visible group of homeless people? Feeling helpless is natural when faced with such overwhelming problems.

Some people feel helpless because they blame themselves for problems they did not cause. Though newly unemployed steelworkers know a distant corporation shut their mill, many of them blame themselves for their misfortunes: "If only I were more deserving or worked elsewhere or had a different set of skills, this would not have happened." Battered women and victims of rape often react in a similar way. "If I had been a better wife, prepared tastier foods, or looked prettier, perhaps he would not have hit me." Or, "Maybe my clothes were too provocative; the police said I shouldn't have been walking by that park at night."

It is to the perpetrator's advantage when victims blame themselves. Self-blame among women allows abusive men to avoid the consequences of their actions. These violent men avoid divorce, avoid thinking of themselves as violent, and avoid imprisonment when they have done real damage. Similarly, unemployed workers who blame themselves allow companies that shut plants to continue to wreak havoc on the communities that have provided them with a home and labor force. Blaming themselves for circumstances they did not cause makes many people helpless, because they cannot respond constructively until they admit that someone or something else is at fault.

Fear of retaliation is a powerful explanation for why many people do not raise their voices in protest. People who marched for civil rights had to face hostile police, who dispersed them with water cannons and set dogs to attack them. Their homes were bombed and their lives threatened. Bosses sometimes fire people who are identified as troublemakers. The impact of such firings is not lost on those who remain. Retaliation may include arrests of those provoked into violence, planting false evidence, disseminating harmful rumors, and blackballing—that is, circulating lists of known "troublemakers" to employers, to prevent the person from being hired.

In part, the reason people suffer in silence and fail to protest is that they have been taught that those in authority must be right and questioning authority is wrong. Those in charge, whether government officials or business leaders, maintain their positions by claiming they represent legitimate authority and cannot and should not be challenged. As Piven and Cloward describe:

> An elaborate system of beliefs and ritual behaviors . . . defines for people what is right and what is wrong and why; what is possible and what is impossible. . . . Because this superstructure of beliefs and rituals is evolved in the context of unequal power, it is inevitable that beliefs and rituals reinforce inequality, by rendering the powerful divine and the challengers evil. (Piven & Cloward, 1977, p. 1)

Even when people earnestly want to protest the conditions they live under and solve the problems they face, they often don't know how. People have little experience with or information about the process of protest—making posters, putting out newsletters, contacting the press, handling permits, and the like. The traditions of protest are downplayed in the schools to avoid threatening "the superstructure of beliefs and rituals" that support those in power.

Another reason why people feel helpless is that they are often dependent on precisely those that are causing them harm. Citizens understand that their families are being poisoned by dirty air, undrinkable water, and tainted food. They worry about the effects of industrial wastes on their health but are unwilling to antagonize the companies that provide their jobs. Wives who are abused stay in a marriage because they cannot figure out how to support themselves and their children without their husband's income.

This state of perceived helplessness is reinforced by the continuing de-skilling of the labor force, which is a product of industrialization and urbanization. As people took routine jobs in factories, they gradually lost the skills that made them self-sufficient on farms—repairing machinery, making furniture, doing bookkeeping, nursing animals and people, canning, and designing and sewing clothes and shoes. When factory workers are thrown out of work, they have few skills to offer a labor market.

Finally, isolation often keeps people from organizing. People feel vulnerable when they feel alone; they feel ineffective as long as they are the only ones complaining. One person can accomplish too little, and an isolated individual is easy for the opposition to pick off, defuse, or ignore. Sometimes it is geographic isolation that causes the problem, as occurs among the handicapped, or environmentalists, or even housewives. More often, it is social space that isolates people, the social distance between poor black women and middle-class white women, between blue-collar and white-collar labor, between those educated at school and those educated through life's experiences, between ethnic groups, and between status categories.

For all these reasons, then, even in a democracy, people feel powerless, and their lack of protest is misconstrued as consent or approval. Community organizing combats these sources of powerlessness.

COMMUNITY ORGANIZING IS A SEARCH FOR POWER

Community organizing increases people's capacity to solve problems, by building democratic organizations that focus and multiply the power of many individuals.

Community development involves local empowerment through organized groups of people acting collectively to control decisions, projects, programs and policies that affect them as a community.

Community organizing resolves many of the sources of powerlessness. It works to end people's isolation, to get them to recognize shared problems as political rather than personal; it confronts the myth that decision makers are right because they are in power. Community organizing strives to build both the skills for democracy and the capacity for economic betterment. It helps protect organization members from intimidation and reprisal. Community organizations gather and focus information, pressure government agencies, and demonstrate that popular protest can be successful. Each successful group activity makes community members feel more confident and competent about solving their problems.

Community organizing involves a struggle for power, often between the "haves" and the "have-nots" (Alinsky, 1969):

Power is the ability to affect decisions that shape social outcomes.

Individuals and groups struggle over who has power to make decisions on questions as broad as the future direction of society and as specific as who benefits and who pays for particular government services. Community-controlled businesses, such as food cooperatives or day-care centers, demonstrate power because they enable people to declare their independence from the marketplace and government, to make their own decisions. Organizations that cope with deprivation and alienation demonstrate power because they reallocate resources and decision-making authority.

The power goals of the community movement signified in a demonstration. (Courtesy Allen Zak)

How Community Organizations Gain Power

Community organizations gain power by taking control of the public agenda, by using legal actions, expertise, and the threat of force, and by harnessing the energies of committed people. They question authority, and their successes build more power. Asking questions and debating policies imply that authorities do not have legitimate and exclusive control. To prevent such threats to their power, authorities attempt to keep many issues of interest to community organizations off the public agenda. Issues can be kept from public discussion by obscuring them or by redefining social problems as personal ones.

Controlling the Agenda.   People in authority try to control the public agenda by "non-decision making." Non-decision making means that crucial questions are not contested because they do not come under public scrutiny. Unlike open conflicts, in which sides are clear and issues clearly laid out,

> non-decision making is the practice of limiting the scope of actual decision making to "safe" issues by manipulating the dominant community values, myths, and political institutions and procedures. (Bachrach & Baratz, 1963, p. 632)

Typically, the issues people agree on are laid out clearly; other issues are obscured.

Until recently, few contested the right of a business to move from one community to another to increase its profits. Society's right to impose sanctions on such businesses remained a non-decision. It was a cultural premise that profit maximization was not to be questioned, and so the issue was never raised.

Community organizations determine the issues to be discussed publicly, turning non-decisions into contested issues. Community organizations gain power by calling attention to problems. Few politicians or bureaucrats advocate poor housing, destruction of neighborhoods, ignoring the homeless, isolating the elderly, or polluting the environment. These are problems that politicians agree *should* be solved; yet, they do not see it as in their interests to spend public money to solve them, when they can spend the money on other things instead, or keep tax rates low. Community organizations can focus public attention on social issues and shame those in authority for their indifference. Setting an agenda does not ensure a victory, but it does deprive authorities of the power they gain from determining which issues will be discussed.

Combating Personalization.   Personalization is another way those in power control the public agenda. They argue that *they* represent the general interest and that members of community organizations, by contrast, are concerned only with their personal interests. A request for company-sponsored day care is described as a selfish attempt on the part of women (not men) to have someone else take over their responsibilities. The legitimacy of the need to work and to ensure the health and safety of one's child is denied.

The first step in combating personalization is *consciousness raising*. It involves a sharing of experiences to learn that what appears personal is really political. The concept has been popularized in the feminist literature as a way of getting one's "personal" problems into the open not in order to adjust but to discover that the problems are, in fact, social and require a collective solution. (Deckard, 1983, p. 330)

Consciousness raising is applicable in many other settings. It is the reason why organizers call meetings in which people discuss their problems to learn that many of them are shared. Discovering that a problem is shared and socially caused rather than a personal inadequacy is the first step in gaining power.

Legal Authority, Expertise, and the Threat of Force.   Community organizations can gain power through legal actions, expertise, and the threat of force. Bringing suit to stop dumping of toxic material is the use of legal authority; learning how to read budgets of government agencies to make sure programs targeted at the poor do benefit the poor is a form of expert power. Community organizations create power when they use disruption, such as public demonstrations, sit-ins, picketing, and other public displays. But disruption achieves power only under certain conditions. As Piven and Cloward point out:

The amount of leverage that a group gains by applying . . . negative sanctions is widely variable. Influence depends, first of all, on whether or not the contribution withheld is crucial to others; second, on whether or not those who have been affected by the disruption have resources to be conceded; and third, on whether or not the obstructionist group can protect itself adequately from reprisal. (Piven & Cloward, 1977, p. 25)

The use of force—disruption—is dangerous for a community group unless it is able to protect its members from the use of counterforce. Sometimes it is better to try to affect behavior through the hint of possible disruption, rather than actually doing the deed. As Alinsky (1971, p. 127) described, "power is not only what you have but what the enemy thinks you have."

Power Created by Committed Members.   The main source of power for most community organizations is the number of members they attract and the skills, enthusiasm, and persistent dedication of the membership. Business groups may have more money, but when the goal is to influence government, it is people with votes that count. The enthusiasm and seriousness of ordinary people acting together makes a good impression on the public, on the media, and on politicians. Community organizations can often achieve a great deal with little financial support because community members volunteer their time and energy and risk their physical safety. In a democratic society, when many people show dramatically that they feel intensely on an issue, they are hard to ignore.

Building Power Gradually

Power is gained step by step. The first step is to increase people's awareness that they share problems and that the solutions are collective rather than individual. The community organization then addresses the problems faced by its members. As the organization becomes more visible and associated with the successful application of power, more and more individuals join. They learn skills, generate enthusiasm, and contribute to future successes that enhance organizational power.

Participation in community organizations helps make people more politically sensitive and more effective political actors. As Krauss argues, participation in protest leads to politicization.

> Through such protests . . . ordinary people construct a broader analysis of politics: they shift from a non-ideological stance to an ideological stance, from defining themselves as non-political to defining themselves as political, from having a deep faith in the established political system to developing a critical political analysis. This critical perspective . . . creates the potential for grass-root activists to play a more active and militant role. (Krauss, 1988, p. 259)

The more people participate in community action, the greater the future capacity to solve community problems through political action.

An organization need not win each campaign or each issue to enhance its power. A community organization might fight city hall on a zoning issue and lose but gain a lot of publicity and become a recognized interest on zoning cases. In the future, the city may consult with the organization at the planning stage, and perhaps the organization may be influential in convincing a developer to include a home for the elderly in a downtown redevelopment project.

In short, from small beginnings, community organizations overcome the sense of powerlessness that prevents many citizens from effectively mobilizing to solve problems.

THE GOALS OF COMMUNITY ORGANIZING

What will the society look like if many community organizations achieve their goals? Organizers should have a vision of a better society that will result from the sum of their smaller and more local efforts. We present here one such vision, but readers may wish to substitute their own. Our aim is not to present an orthodoxy but to argue for the need to have a vision that is broader than achieving the immediate objectives of their own community organizations. Even Alinsky, who emphasized pragmatic approaches to immediate problems, espoused visionary goals about community creation and the importance of gaining power for the "have-nots" (Reitzes & Reitzes, 1982). Organizers need to formulate their goals in specific terms, because if they don't have a clear idea of what the goals of organizing are, they can get involved in efforts that lead to a less progressive rather than more progressive society.

Critics of neopopulism have warned about this danger. Neopopulism merges the goals of empowerment and cooperation with more traditional values. Neopopulists advocate voluntarism, attack materialism, and support merging religious values into political action (Members of the Project 2000, 1987). Neopopulist movements have accomplished much by providing services in place of government, fighting to provide healthier working conditions, and defending communities against changes imposed from outside (Boyte, 1980, 1984; Boyte, Booth, & Max, 1986). But critics suggest that the neopopulist movement may lead to a less tolerant, less open, less equal society. For example, neopopulists may fight to preserve the neighborhood against governmental efforts to build more affordable housing or integrate the schools, even though such actions have racist implications. Moreover, neopopulism may be sexist and anti-intellectual (S. N. Miller, 1985).

To make such contradictions apparent, community organizers must present their visions openly and think about their current efforts in light of their larger goals. They must ask themselves whether, if their movements are successful, the outcome will be a society in which they would like to live. Such visions of the broader goals provide the motivation for long-term efforts for community organizing and development.

The Goals of Community Organizing and Development

For us, successful community development is intended to achieve five goals. The first is the improvement of the quality of life, through the resolution of shared problems. Reduction in the level of social inequities caused by poverty, racism, and sexism constitutes our second goal.

The third goal is to exercise and preserve democratic values, as part of the process of organizing and as an outcome of community development. Our fourth goal is enabling people to achieve their potential as individuals. Our fifth goal is the creation of a sense of community, in which people can feel more efficacious, not only as individuals, but as part of a broader society toward which they are contributing.

Accomplishing one of the goals at the sacrifice of another is questionable. For example, we feel that a more equitable distribution of wealth and power is desirable, but it should be obtained democratically through local organizations in which people make the decisions that affect them. We *don't* advocate a centralized socialistic state even if the leaders of such a state fairly allocated wealth to all. Under a state socialist solution, even if poverty is temporarily eliminated, local control will be lost, and eventually inequality will be restored. A two-tiered society—whether one of workers and capitalists or one of workers and bureaucrats—has no appeal to us.

The means of accomplishing the goals must be consistent with the ends desired. It matters not only what we try to accomplish, but how we try to accomplish it. There cannot be racism or sexism in the process of organizing if we hope to achieve a more equal society. Authoritarian decision making in organizations fighting to achieve a more democratic government not only sounds contradictory, it is unlikely to work. One cannot achieve a democratic community by ignoring the contributions of individuals.

The Solution of Problems

We believe that ordinary people can learn to cope with the many problems affecting their lives. But they may lack knowledge of how to do so, or they may not believe that the status quo can be changed. They have been taught that the government has experts and that ordinary citizens are not well enough informed to offer a challenge. Similarly, business leaders must know something, or how else could they be rich? By working together in community organizations, people can acquire knowledge and power.

In solving problems, community organizations play *mediating* roles; that is, they provide a link between individuals and larger or more formidable institutions, so that individuals need not confront GM or the White House or city hall by themselves. Mediation is an antidote to social alienation. A new widow feels isolated until she joins a self-help group for the newly bereaved, which through its mediating role, helps her reestablish ties to the broader society.

Community organizations gain power by aggregating individual concerns and fragmented complaints and targeting them to those responsible. An individual might want the senate to support increased funding for food stamps. Senators often respond to personal letters with a form acknowledgment. But if the individual belongs to a neighborhood organization, which in turn is a member of the National Association of Neighborhoods, the national association can lobby for a food stamp program. Then, the senator is likely to pay attention.

Community organizations sometimes solve problems by linking them together. Burghardt and Fabricant describe a community-based construction company that

> addresses the multiple needs of the homeless through a single program. In effect, homeless people are trained to build and renovate housing. Just as important, this new housing is set aside for the needs of the homeless. (Burghardt & Fabricant, 1987, p. 40)

Community organizations address many different quality-of-life issues. A successful community-development movement would bring about better housing, safer streets, better child care, better health care, and improved social relations. It would help bring in local businesses and local jobs, and it would help ensure clean air and drinkable water.

Eliminating Inequities in the Distribution of Wealth and Power

Another goal of community organizing is a more equitable distribution of wealth and power in the society. We are dismayed that in this country 2.5% of all adults own 28% of the wealth (Beeghley, 1989, p. 190) and that the richest fifth of all families had an average income of $76,310 in 1986 compared to $8,033 for the poorest of all families (Harrison & Bluestone 1988, p. 131).

We are angered that, in recent years, the situation is becoming worse. "For more than a decade, the United States has been evolving as an increasingly unequal society" (Harrison & Bluestone, 1988, p. 131). The income of the richest fifth of all families increased 7.9% from 1968 to 1986, while the income of the poorest fifth has decreased in real terms by 17.9% (Harrison & Bluestone, 1988, p. 131). Women and minority group members still earn less than others, even when they have the same educational attainments. Black men with a college degree earn almost $10,000 a year less than do Anglo men; Hispanic females with 8 years of education still earn $4,600 a year less than do Hispanic males (Beeghley, 1989, p. 275).

Many legal changes have taken place that reduce ethnic and gender-based discrimination, but there are still major problems. Job and housing discrimination continue to hamper the economic and social opportunities of minorities. The disproportionate

Wealth is far from fairly shared. (Courtesy of TTB)

responsibility of women for child rearing and the lack of adequate day-care resources and socially imposed interruptions to a woman's career help maintain the gender imbalance in income. Working to end ethnic and gender discrimination should be an important goal of community organizing.

As people who have been blocked from participation in the battle over power and wealth gain the ability to fight as equals in the political process, the outcome will be greater equity. Community organizations should help bring about more fair distribution of wealth and power in American society by making that participation possible and effective.

The Exercise and Enhancement of Democratic Values and Practices

Our third goal of community development is to improve democracy through increasing the shared involvement of people in making decisions that affect their lives. Alinsky stated the ideal well.

> Every conceivable effort must be made to rekindle the fire of democracy. . . . A people can participate only if they have both the opportunity to formulate their program, which is the reason for participation, and a medium through which they can express and achieve their program. . . . The universal premise of any people's program is "We the people will work out our own destiny." . . . *Can there be a more fundamental democratic*

program than a democratically minded and participating people? (Alinsky, 1969, pp. 196–197)

Democracy involves the informed participation of a large number of people in decisions that affect them. Democracy requires that public decision making be accessible to all and that policy issues are clearly stated and widely disseminated.

Democracy implies a level of conflict, because differing interests are expressed, fought out, and resolved by majority vote, often with a secret ballot. But as a sense of community is built, other systems of democratic decision making can emerge. Democratic decisions can then be made through face-to-face contact among people with common interests, who have developed a respect for one another. These procedures emphasize building consensus (Mansbridge, 1980, p. 5).

The ideals of a democratic movement must be carried out within community organizations. Leaders must strive to remain responsive to their members. Though a limited number of activists might actually implement policies, the membership at large, acting democratically, should determine general policies.

Democracy is fragile. What destroys it most easily is lack of use. If people feel alienated and powerless—and thereby do not use the democratic rights they have and do not try to direct the system to their own needs—the system ceases to be democratic. People who do not believe they can exercise power will not fight against infringements of their rights or the rights of others. If they do not believe the system ever worked, they will not fight to preserve it. Successful community organizing gives the widest number of people possible a stake in preserving democracy and should create a stable democratic society, formally and actually open to all.

Achieving the Potential of Individuals

Community development helps people achieve their potential by improving their daily lives and expanding their sense of efficacy. Community organizations can help remove barriers caused by discrimination against gays, women, blacks, Hispanics, the elderly, and the handicapped. The provision of day-care facilities helps women with children get off welfare and work for a living, making them providers rather than recipients of public funds. Cleanup and fix-up campaigns make neighborhoods more attractive and make people feel better about who they are and where they live.

Through involvement with community organizations, people learn to feel more competent and more effective. Successful organizing can lead people away from attributing success and failure exclusively to individual effort toward a belief in the importance of collective solutions for societally caused problems. People who control their own work life or who battle banks or fight city hall and win must have a different and better image of themselves than people who are certain it cannot be done.

Involvement in collective, community organizing activity can make people feel good about themselves. For people whose lives are otherwise dull or empty of special accomplishments, or whose education and experiences may be limited, organizing offers a new opportunity for excitement and for a sense of belonging. It provides an opportunity to learn and to be of service. Community organizations can reduce alienation and bring people into fuller participation in society.

Community organizing helps people achieve their capacity by teaching them to do things they never thought they could do or never had the opportunity to try: fund raising, public relations, negotiations, coalition building, public speaking, dealing with officials, designing public programs, repairing housing, managing an office, or writing a press release. These are skills that not only make people feel more competent; they allow freer expression of talents people may never have known they had. They are useful not only in community organizing but also in the world at large. Active membership in a community organization may be a passport to respect and possibly employment in the society at large.

Strengthening Community

Building a successful organization is a means of creating a sense of community in which people work together to accomplish collective goals. Community building involves a change in attitudes of individuals, a change that says people can be important and powerful and effective as members of an organized community. It is an antidote to the American myth of "rugged individualism," which claims that an individual who strives hard can accomplish whatever he or she wants.

The myth of rugged individualism prevents people without power from questioning social and political inequities. As Fox-Genovese argues,

> The American myth of individualism has probably stood as the single most important barrier to Americans' perceptions of the class relations in which they are enmeshed (Fox-Genovese, 1986, p. 344).

Concrete illustrations of how this process works are seen in observations of those newly unemployed as a result of plant shutdowns:

> Although they do not necessarily feel that their joblessness is their own fault, they retain other individualistic reactions. For example, they feel that going out to look for work for themselves is more effective than group political activity in their own behalf and that of their jobless colleagues. Being particularly vulnerable to feelings of worthlessness and depression, the unemployed feel an unusually strong need to be self-reliant and thus have a further reason to go out personally to seek work. The irony is that in communities of mass unemployment few jobs are to be found, thus increasing people's emotional vulnerability and eventual frustration. (Gans, 1988, p. 78)

The myth is that an individual is free and not dependent on others. In practice, such a sense of freedom prevents people from seeing their dependence on corporations and the state. There is

> an ideal of freedom that leaves Americans with a stubborn fear of acknowledging structures of power and interdependence in a technologically complex society dominated by giant corporations and an increasingly powerful state. (Bellah, Madsen, Sullivan, Swidler, & Tipton, 1985, p. 25)

People do not make all their own problems; many are created for them by the society. The solution to many of these problems is a group solution. If one can see sexism as a structural problem, a problem that a woman or girl suffers because she is a member of a group, one can shape appropriate strategies of response, including pressing class action suits and demanding state and federal laws against sexism. Such solutions cannot occur unless organizing has created a sense of community, a sense of shared problems, and at least a minimum amount of mutual trust.

Successful community development is the means to achieve our vision of what American society can and should be. In this vision, people solve their problems together through democratic means; wealth and power are more fairly distributed; the obstacles to a more just society, such as poverty, racism, and sexism, are eliminated; and people develop a sense of their own capacity as part of a broader community willing to act collectively. This vision may be a dream, but it is an achievable dream. We know it is achievable, because community organizing has already made much progress toward these goals.

The way has not been easy, especially for the community organizer. The role of the organizer is a difficult one, because building progressive community organizations requires a lot of knowledge and experience and an ability to handle occasional setbacks and to learn from experience. This book is intended as an aid to ease the path. It combines information about the political and social environments in which organizers

Join together to battle social problems. (Courtesy of *City Limits*/Sian Roderick)

work with knowledge about group psychology, administrative skills, and conventional and unconventional political tactics. It also provides examples of the experiences of others in community organizing. By examining what community organizing has been historically, the book provides the reader with a background and lessons for future practice. There is no way to avoid mistakes, but we hope that this book will help reduce the number of defeats and speed the way to learning from them.

2 | Organizing Is as American as Apple Pie: Lessons from History

WHY STUDY HISTORY?

Because organizing is a here-and-now activity to empower people who face present-day problems, why should one stop to look backward? First, we examine history because the community organizer inherits a grand tradition from the organizers of the past. The courage of the civil rights protesters, the feminists, and the early labor organizers, and their successes in changing society, form a legacy to future generations. Organizers should feel some of the greatness that comes from continuing this tradition.

Second, history lends us patience while teaching us persistence. When defeats crush us, or authorities take vengeance, imprisoning, blacklisting, or even killing our members, we need to remember that past community organizations have been successful against similar obstacles. David can and will knock out Goliath. Organizers need to know that there are lean days, times when recruiting is difficult and funds scarce, but there are also better days. There is an ebb and flow, and slow times do not mean the death of an ideal.

Third, history explores what is possible. It provides concrete lessons on tactics and strategies so that each generation need not learn everything from scratch. The legendary antics of Saul Alinsky remind us of the role of humor in protest. The nonviolence of Dr. Martin Luther King, Jr., motivates us with the knowledge that a subject people can confront armed might and win. We can learn from failure, too, as we examine why the women's movement lost the fight for the Equal Rights Amendment and why the organized poor have failed to keep city hospitals open.

In the history of organizing, many of the same questions of strategy, tactics, and moral justification appear repeatedly. Is violence as a protest tactic ever appropriate? How far can community organizations trust government officials and big business when they offer support? Which models work for mobilizing people from apathy into action and under what circumstances? What is the role of expertise and, by extension, the community organizer? How much effort should go into solving immediate problems and how much into the longer-term effort of community building?

In short, history sensitizes us to issues, provides concrete advice, and gives us hope and pride.

THE ERAS IN COMMUNITY ORGANIZING

The five major eras in organizing parallel broader changes in American society (Fisher, 1984). The first, social welfare neighborhood organizing, overlaps with the Progressive Era, from approximately 1895 to 1920. Radical neighborhood organizing arrived during the Great Depression of the 1930s. The period following the Second World War until the end of the Eisenhower administration, the late 1940s and 1950s, was characterized by more conservative neighborhood organizing. In the 1960s, organizing was reinvigorated, as issues of poverty and racism merged with more traditional neighborhood organizing. From the 1970s to the present, organizing on issues—the homeless, the elderly, the environment, and the unemployed—became as important as traditional neighborhood-based efforts.

Social Welfare Neighborhood Organizing

At the end of the 19th century, organizing took place in the overcrowded neighborhoods that housed recent immigrants. One approach was to open settlement houses, such as Jane Addams's Hull House, in which reformers set up community-based social service centers. Most settlement-house workers, as well as those working in the parallel community-center movement, were drawn from upper-class families. For them, helping the new immigrants meant teaching them middle-class values. Though the settlement houses provided needed services, especially to improve the health of their clients, in their efforts to Americanize the immigrant, the settlement house programs discouraged ethnic pride and ignored social class divisions.

The International Institutes, originally affiliated with the Young Women's Christian Association (YWCA) in 1909, worked out a more pluralistic view of organizing. This movement encouraged and celebrated ethnic traditions but with the intent to encourage mutual respect among ethnic groups. The International Institutes considered a solid ethnic identity as a basis for social work but also saw such identity as the basis for group and community interests. The approach continued into the 1930s and 1940s, during which the Institutes encouraged ethnic communities to hold and take pride in folk festivals (Betten & Austin, 1990, p. 57).

Toward the end of the Progressive Era, the Cincinnati Social Unit Plan (1918–1920) began. The purpose of the plan was to provide social services, especially cooperative health services and child-care services, to the poor (Melvin, 1987). This social experiment combined elements of the paternalistic help-the-poor attitude characteristic of the period with facets of community participation and control.

The unit was democratically run, operated primarily by block workers, who lived in the neighborhoods and regularly visited all the families in their block. These block

The Hull House. (Courtesy of the Chicago Public Library)

workers formed a policy-making council. There were also a series of occupational councils, made up mostly of professionals who lived in the neighborhood, to design and provide services, with input from the community. The local health efforts were very successful, and the program was very popular in the neighborhood.

The apparent success of the experiment roused opposition. Doctors opposed it, fearing it would cut into their income; the mayor opposed it, calling it Bolshevik; and government agencies opposed it because it set up a government within a government. Local businessmen opposed it, fearing neighborhood members would choose to buy collectively in bulk, threatening their business. None of this political opposition was anticipated, and leaders of the experiment did not put enough effort into organizing the community to defend the experiment and neglected to get the support of the churches (Betten & Austin, 1990, pp. 35–53).

For community organizing, the progressive era displayed mixed themes. To some extent, the altruistic middle class sought to do things for the poor, without allowing them to threaten the status quo. Some social workers sought to Americanize the foreigners, while others worked to preserve their ethnic heritage and to encourage democratic participation as an important and realizable dream. Yet, efforts to combine local control with professional expertise were opposed by those in power who saw and feared the radical possibilities. Fledgling community organizations were not yet prepared to deal with such opposition.

Radical Neighborhood Organizing

The 1920s was a period of relative prosperity, ending abruptly with the Great Depression in 1929. This Depression threw a third of the population out of work and cast doubts on the viability of the American economic system. After considerable delay, the federal government assumed some responsibility for providing social services. During this time of nationwide stress, three interdependent neighborhood organizing efforts appeared. The Communist party worked to organize unemployed workers at home. Radical social workers, a small portion of the large number of newly employed social workers who staffed the programs started under the New Deal, tried to promote militant actions among their clients. Saul Alinsky organized direct-action movements demanding neighborhood power.

The Communist party tried to capitalize on Depression-Era fears by organizing unemployed workers (Fisher, 1984, pp. 34–46). In addition, the party established neighborhood workers' councils, which could modify tactics and demands according to local needs. Such councils organized protests in Cleveland, Los Angeles, and eventually nationally, demanding relief provided by government agencies. Yet, even with a neighborhood base, the movement remained centralized and under party control (Fisher, 1984, p. 39).

Working with socialist organizations, the Communist party organized sit-ins at relief offices, defended tenants evicted from apartments, and organized black communities to promote interracial cooperation. These efforts were weakened by two factors. When working in a coalition with the Congress of Industrial Organizations, an industrial labor union, party attention drifted from the neighborhoods to the factories, and not so incidentally, away from promoting interracial harmony. Also, as world tensions increased, the party concentrated more attention on opposing fascism and less on domestic issues.

In response to pressures from the left, and in reaction to the very real suffering of the American public, the Roosevelt administration under the rubric of the New Deal began to construct the modern welfare state. Relief programs for businesses, farmers, and ultimately the unemployed followed one another. Social security, Aid to Families with Dependent Children, and capital projects to stimulate economic growth were initiated. As part of the expansion of the welfare programs, the number of social workers rose dramatically, though most of the Roosevelt social workers had scant education in the field (J. H. Ehrenreich, 1985, pp. 43–102).

A radical faction of social workers organized the Rank and File Movement (Wenocur & Reisch, 1989, pp. 182–207). Its philosophy was to equate the oppression felt by clients with that felt by poorly paid social workers.

> Social workers fought to unionize and fought along with "clients" as tenants or as demonstrators themselves, not as a separate movement but as part of a growing movement organized along class lines. In this period, young caseworkers did not see a separation between themselves and their clients. (Wagner, 1989, p. 267)

The Rank and File lost much of its momentum as the expansion of social welfare programs under Roosevelt co-opted the movement (Wenocur & Reisch, 1989, pp. 197–199).

The most important influence of the radical era on present-day organizing was the advent of the Alinsky approach to neighborhood organizing (Reitzes & Reitzes, 1987).

Influenced both by the sociological perspective that social problems have a community basis and the militant labor organizing tactics of John Lewis, Saul Alinsky built problem-oriented community organizations.

The basic characteristics of the Alinsky model of organizing included creating an umbrella coalition from local groups, working to strengthen community attachment, and choosing issues on the basis of immediate felt needs. Alinsky is mainly remembered for organizing dramatic public protests, such as masses of the poor entering upper-status department stores, or protesters depositing the garbage of neighborhoods with infrequent pickups on the lawns of politicians. However, underlying his dramatic tactics was a coherent model for organizing collective action on a neighborhood level. The goal was to show the "have-nots" that they could gain power against the "haves." As the organization solved immediate problems, such as access to jobs in a department store or better enforcement of housing standards, people learned that power came from collective action.

The Back of the Yards Neighborhood Council (R. Slayton, 1986a), formed in the area surrounding the stockyards in Chicago, illustrates the Alinsky approach. Before Alinsky began his work, the community was already in ferment from left-wing organizing efforts at the meat-packing plants. Alinsky argued with Catholic clergy, who feared the ideological left, that they should help form a nonideological organization to solve local economic problems. The church provided funding and a way of bridging the gap between the many ethnic and neighborhood groups in that part of Chicago. The support of the church, when combined with common employment in the stockyards,

Early community meeting involving children in Back of the Yards neighborhood. (Courtesy of Back of the Yards Council)

provided a sufficient base so that Alinsky was able to convene the first neighborhood council in 1939.

The council was a coalition of church-based, social and ethnic organizations that shared a common territory. Meetings were democratically run. The council focused on issues that affected the self-interest of community members, in areas such as improved employment or deteriorating housing. To attract members to the organization and to show its effectiveness, neighborhood organizers tried a variety of nonviolent tactics. Through publicity-seeking protests or humorous attacks on opponents, they gained small victories, such as the rerouting of garbage trucks, the installation of stop signs, and the provision of local health stations. These protests kept interest alive, enabling the community to build a permanent organization that could pressure government on longer-term issues such as maintaining housing conditions. Community pride and integration were emphasized, which helped give people a sense of attachment to place.

For Alinsky, a professional community organizer was the trigger for local action. However, the organizer had to have community support. Alinsky organizers had to be invited into the community by community members and would not begin work until sufficient funds were available to permit a sustained effort. The goal was for the organizer to work himself or herself out of a job, as neighborhood people developed their own skills.

Post-Second World War Conservative Neighborhood Organizing

From 1945 to 1960 the United States experienced economic growth, rapid suburbanization, and social and political conservatism. With the Cold War dominating the political agenda, problems of poverty and racism were ignored or bulldozed away. Urban renewal programs tore down the housing of the poor and hid the sight of poverty from the well-to-do, while new highways allowed the middle and upper classes to drive through these areas on their way to suburban homes.

Some liberal issue-oriented social movements were active, and Alinsky organizations continued to build, but the dominant form of local organizing was an effort to preserve social status. The prevailing conservative ethos considered community development a way of promoting democratic capitalism. For example, established social welfare agencies set up the United Community Defense Services (UCDS), a centralized organization that sent organizers into communities to talk to business elites and welfare officials about local problems. The UCDS officials "fundamentally accepted the existing system and sought, within the limits of that system, to ameliorate social inequalities in support of the objectives of those in power" (Fisher, 1984, p. 71). Funding was slight and accomplishments minimal.

In response to the opening up of new suburbs, conservative neighborhood improvement associations proliferated. As Fisher argues "the association serves to protect property values and community homogeneity by opposing commercial development and excluding members of lower classes and racial minorities" (Fisher, 1984, p. 73). Neighborhood improvement associations attempted to keep out the poor and minorities, often relying on restrictive covenants, provisions put into the deeds of homeowners that forbade selling homes to minority group members. After the Supreme Court ruled such covenants illegal, neighborhood associations switched tactics, pressuring suburban governments to adopt zoning and building codes that made houses prohibitively expensive (Danielson, 1976). To supplement such tactics, real estate agents steered minorities away from protected neighborhoods; minority group members who persisted were subject to physical attacks and harassment.

The Drama of the 1960s

In the 1960s, organizing efforts led to unprecedented successes. The tactical approaches to progressive problem solving that emerged influenced a generation of protest leaders who are now middle-aged (Gitlin, 1989; J. Miller, 1987). The "old left" with its moribund, European, labor-oriented, socialist views was replaced by a "new left," vibrant with American ideals of promoting social justice, yet concerned with preserving individualism. It was the era in which racism and sexism were redefined as societal and institutional problems.

The federal government was both devil and angel, the devil that repressed protest and the angel that provided funds for some community-based efforts. During the 1950s, inner cities continued to decay, leaving the poor and minorities in wretched ghettos. In much of the country, especially the South, Jim Crow laws kept black people in subservient positions, deprived of wealth and basic civil rights. In the 1960s, with the recognition of poverty and racism by Presidents Kennedy and Johnson—a consciousness made dramatic by urban demonstrations and terrifying, destructive riots—the problems could no longer be ignored.

Organizing efforts in the 1960s were influenced by the courageous protests of the civil rights movement in the mid- and late 1950s—in the Montgomery bus boycott to integrate public transportation, the sit-ins to desegregate public facilities throughout the South, and later, the voter-registration drives that resulted in the deaths of black and white organizers alike. Led by black ministers and young black activists in the Southern Christian Leadership Conference (SCLC), the Congress of Race Equality (CORE) and the Student Non-Violent Coordinating Committee (SNCC), these protests called attention to racial inequality and discrimination and brought federal promises to protect civil rights against state-level oppression.

Besides the successes of the civil rights movement, two other factors came into play. The first was the invigoration of the activist left among the mostly college-educated population who joined such organizations as the Students for a Democratic Society (SDS). Early SDS activists, most of whom were white and middle class, worked in the South with the civil rights movement and then shifted their efforts to community organizing in northern cities and in Appalachia. In actions such as the Economic Research and Education Project (ERAP), SDS organizers worked to build democratic, self-help programs among the poor.

These organizers were hampered by several factors. Few of them had personal experiences in ghetto life; the work was educational to the organizers, but the effect on

Early civil rights march, 1965. (Courtesy Allen Zak)

the communities they tried to organize was minimal. In addition, SDS refused to impose either tight organization or directive leadership in these projects. In many cases, no one was in charge.

The second major change was the election of a more liberal President, John F. Kennedy. He was appalled by rural southern poverty, awakened by Harrington's (1962) *The Other America: Poverty in the United States,* and politically grateful for black votes in a very close election. He promised a government more concerned with promoting social justice, but in spite of promises, little happened.

As problems continued, the poor rioted in many northern cities in protest against horrible living conditions. The riots were intensified by the assassination of Dr. Martin Luther King, Jr. Partly in response to black protests and partly to carry out the promises left unfulfilled on the assassination of President Kennedy, the Johnson administration supported a series of welfare and community-based programs for the poor.

The federal government sponsored a "War on Poverty" and a Model Cities program and established the Office of Economic Opportunity (OEO) as institutional scaffolding for action programs to aid the poor. The government funded housing programs, Project Headstart to help the preschool poor, and food programs for the hungry. Community Action Agencies distributed federal urban development funds. Federal law required city officials to work with neighborhood organizations on priorities for spending those funds in ways that would benefit the poor. Concurrently, federal dollars were provided for other programs — the community mental health program, community health agencies, and community development agencies — to help the needy and the poor at the community level. Though funding was large by historic standards, the overall sums were still modest.

At least in public declarations, government supported community power and control. Federal dollars were to be spent only after "maximum feasible participation" by those affected by the programs (Brilliant, 1986, p. 574). Community Action Agencies, using federal money, could hire organizers to work with the poor. Volunteers, many of whom later became organizers, got first-hand experience with poverty through Volunteers in Service to America (VISTA), while attorneys from the federal Legal Services Corporation acted as advocates for the poor.

Hundreds of smaller neighborhood organizations grew up to combat problems that hurt the poor. Some opposed federal highways threatening to destroy inner-city neighborhoods to facilitate the trip to suburbia. These battles showed the devil and angel balance in federal programs, as OEO-funded community groups battled programs sponsored by the Federal Highway Administration. In larger cities like New York, neighborhood organizations battled for local control over school systems with centralized bureaucracies. In Chicago, The Woodlawn Organization (TWO), an Alinsky organization, moved from a militant organization that demonstrated for increases in social services to an organization spending federal funds on its own development projects. It appeared for a while as if neighborhood organizations would have an effective say in controlling poverty programs.

The prevailing ethos legitimated protest and demonstrations. Using protest tactics, Alinsky organizations such as FIGHT in Rochester, New York, successfully demanded jobs for poor minorities while former civil rights workers organized welfare clients into local chapters of the National Welfare Rights Organization (NWRO). The NWRO used direct action, marches, and sit-ins to successfully demand additional benefits for the welfare poor.

The Alinsky movement spread to Hispanic communities in the West and the Southwest. Cesar Chavez organized a farmer workers' union, by contacting laborers both in their home and in their places of work. To pressure the owners of the farms to recognize the unions, Chavez organized a nationwide boycott of farm products.

Dramatic confrontations and progress by the poor and disenfranchised created a strong counterreaction. State and local governments responded to the NWRO by changing rules to make localities less vulnerable to protest tactics. Mayors complained to the President and Congress about power delegated to Community Action Agencies. Regulations were modified, giving local elected officials, who were often responsive to the industrial and commercial redevelopment community, the final say in the choice of projects.

Concurrent with domestic protests to improve the lot of the poor and minorities, the war in Vietnam escalated dramatically, pulling federal resources and attention away from poverty programs. Organizers began to question whether social control, rather than helping the poor, was the goal of many federal programs, because, for example, the federal Law Enforcement Assistance Administration provided the local police riot gear and vehicles to suppress social protests.

Students for a Democratic Society and other campus groups redirected their focus from poverty and civil rights to efforts to end the carnage in Southeast Asia. Claiming domestic security concerns, state and federal officials spied on protesters, both those engaged in antiwar efforts and those fighting for civil rights. Protesters who had been working hard to enfranchise minorities began to distrust the electoral system. Democratic party conventions became the scene of conflict between the establishment and protesters.

By the end of the decade, internal contradictions in the ideologies of the movement became apparent. Reformist and radical organizations were having difficulty practicing the goals they had expressed. Full-time organizers sometimes became arrogant and learned to manipulate organization members to reach decisions the organizers wanted. Organizers preached equality, people died to promote equality, but within the movement, women were exploited as second-class citizens. Many activists became disillusioned and dropped out (Gitlin, 1989, p. 424).

The 1970s Until the Present

Since the 1970s, grass-roots efforts have been widely accepted both by those supporting as well as those opposing progressive causes. Four trends in organizing have become apparent since the early 1970s. First, the emphasis today is less on neighborhood work and more on forming specialized organizations to focus on specific issues. Second, community organizations pay far more attention to problems of economic development as decent-paying jobs in heavy manufacturing have moved overseas. The third trend has been an increased emphasis on direct, electoral, political actions. Though the 1960s ended with a rejection of government, many progressive groups are now involved in the electoral process, sometimes even putting forward candidates for office. The fourth trend is an effort to incorporate neopopulist and feminist ideologies within other organizing models.

The First Trend: Increased Attention to Issue-Based Organizing.   Recent decades have seen an increase in numbers of locally based organizations that focus on a specialized issue, or at most a cluster of closely related issues, without a concern for establishing a multipurpose neighborhood organization. The women's movement is an example of local organizing around a series of related issues, as are national coalitions to build housing for the poor or find shelter for the homeless.

Most special-interest organizations gain political strength through national coalitions. Local organizations of the physically handicapped help their members develop independent life-styles, while working as part of a national coalition to promote laws that guarantee ease of access to public facilities for the handicapped. On the local level, anti–drunk-driving organizations teach people to avoid drinking and driving, while on the state level, they pressure legislators to increase enforcement and penalties for drunk driving. Nationally known leaders of gay and lesbian movements work to provide an atmosphere of pride among their constituents, while local-level activists work to prevent discrimination in housing and jobs.

In many ways, the increase in special-interest community-based organizations blurs the distinction between neighborhood organizations and national progressive organizations. For example, the environmental movement originated as an upper-class recreational movement whose pressure activities—for example, to create national parks—were carried out by professional staff at the national level. Today, these organizations are far more active in working with and supporting state and community chapters on issues of immediate, local concern. Controlling the environment has become a local empowerment issue.

Even the Alinsky model has changed. Alinsky organizations rely more on national coalitions and put greater emphasis on solving specific problems. Associations of Community Organizations for Reform Now (ACORN) and National People's Action (NPA) are national coalitions that continue the Alinsky tradition of working to benefit the poor, by pressing utility companies to reduce rates or by stopping cities from destroying homes and replacing them with hotels and office buildings. The founder of NPA, Gale Cincotta, is most famous for her work to require banks to disclose where they are investing their money. The law the NPA helped pass—the Community Reinvestment Act—has been a powerful tool to combat banks' tendencies to disinvest from poor or black neighborhoods. Other neo-Alinsky organizations are now involved in programs to preserve needed housing or construct housing for the poor.

The Second Trend: Emphasizing Community-Based Economic Development.　Older, inner-city neighborhood organizations have moved from protest and toward economic and housing development work. In Baltimore, the Southeast Community Organization (SECO) provided social services to its members and pressured government for programs for the poor, but its primary claim to fame is housing redevelopment (Crenson, 1983). The Woodlawn Organization, previously a militant Alinsky organization, works to develop local businesses and renew and manage housing (Fisk, 1973, p. 294).

Recently, local groups—both descendants of older neighborhood organizations and newer groups set up specifically to provide economic development—have started Community Development Corporations (CDCs) to run or finance local businesses and housing. Among many other projects, CDCs have built or rehabilitated housing for poor and moderate-income families, established and managed neighborhood shopping centers, and worked to establish local businesses. Such businesses have included conventional ones such as shoe factories and more creative enterprises such as greenhouses in the South Bronx to produce fancy herbs for Manhattan restaurants (Neal Peirce & Steinbach, 1987; Task Force on Community Based Development, 1987). Community Development Corporations represent "community on the way" and a hope for self-sufficiency, or at least economic improvement, among the poor (D. Perry, 1987).

Local economic development organizations attempt to break the cycle of problems that so often confronts poorer neighborhoods. Deterioration, especially in housing, creates a lack of community pride and contributes to a feeling that nothing can be done to improve the neighborhood. Capital flees from the visibly deteriorating neighborhoods, exacerbating the deterioration of housing and removing jobs, the very jobs that provide the income and skills people need to pull themselves out of poverty and improve the neighborhood. Community Development Corporations try to break this downward trend by teaching people marketable skills.

Community Development Corporations are just one of many forms of alternative economic enterprise that show concern for equity, for neighborhood preservation, and for personal capacity building. There are worker-owned cooperatives in businesses, neighborhood-owned and -managed banks, alternative forms of community finance, and many forms of local self-reliance, such as recycling and local food production. They strive to promote an ethos of progressive development and empowerment while competing in a capitalist economy.

The Third Trend: Becoming a Permanent Political Actor.   Since the 1970s, the trend has been toward more permanent and stable relationships with governments. In some cases, the community organizations have become part of an informal government that controls or directs policy in key areas of interest. In other cases, community organizations have become more involved in elections. Neighborhood organizations, such as COPS—Communities Organized for Public Services—are now regular political actors who are consulted before local governments take actions that affect the local community. In Santa Monica, California, people who formed a middle-class tenant's organization captured the city council (Kann, 1986). Other cities—such as Hartford, Connecticut; Cleveland, Ohio; Burlington, Vermont; and Berkeley, California—have had mayors or council members whose electoral base was from the neighborhood movement (Clavel, 1986).

In other cases, to gain political power, progressive organizations had to work to change the political structure.

> [The Oakland Community Organization (OCO)] mobilized local residents and through their coordinated actions won passage of an ordinance restructuring the Council into local districts. Not only has OCO found a much more responsive Council since 1981 but has also succeeded in placing its members and other candidates with strong ties to local areas on the council. (Reitzes & Reitzes, 1987, p. 190)

In addition to these efforts at the local level, coalitions of community organizations maintain a continuing lobbying effort at both the state and national governments. One outcome of successful long-term lobbying was the Community Reinvestment Act, which requires banks to make public where they are investing their funds and thus helps prevent banks from disinvesting in poor communities.

In addition to lobbying, direct involvement of community organizations in state and national electoral politics has become far more common. As one type of electoral strategy, feminist and environmentalist organizations point out to their membership which elected officials have been and have not been supportive of their organizations' causes.

The Fourth Trend: New Ideological Emphases.   Recent organizing efforts have been influenced by ideological beliefs prevalent within the neopopulist and feminist movements. For example, underlying neopopulist ideology is a belief that the distribution of wealth in this country is antagonistic to creating a more democratic polity.

> Real populism recognizes that the biggest problem in America is that too few people hold too much economic and political power. . . . As the late Supreme Court Justice Louis Brandeis once said: "We can either have democracy in this country or we can have great wealth concentrated in the hands of a few, but we can't have both." (Boyte et al., 1986, p. x)

Such beliefs emphasize the importance of organizing to bring about economic change. This perspective has become widely shared among community organizations, even those that would not necessarily think of themselves as neopopulist. For example, the civil rights movement has gradually shifted its focus more to issues of jobs and economic justice. Dr. Martin Luther King, Jr. is reported to have said it "made no sense to be able to sit down and order a hamburger if you could not afford one" (G. Delgado, 1986, p. 18).

Neopopulists directly oppose large corporations. The movement also is supportive of the trend toward worker-owned businesses, customer-owned banks, and community-owned land. The goal here, however, is not simply to change who owns the wealth but to redirect the ownership of wealth to solving problems that the market has shown it cannot handle, such as housing for the poor and massive unemployment. The vision underlying these efforts includes creating more self-sufficient communities while blending capitalistic self-interest with compassion on a community-wide basis.

The second major influence on the underlying values of community organizing has come from the feminist movement. Feminists have brought into question the ways that male values of competition and dominance operate in community organizing. They recommend less hierarchical, more consensual decision making while suggesting that success be defined more collectively and less individualistically. Their writings emphasize that there can be no sharp distinction between means and ends, especially in community organizing, where the democratic process of solving problems is part of the goal (Deutschmann, 1988; Garland, 1988; Hooks, 1989; Iannello, 1988; Katzenstein, 1987; Nes & Iadicola, 1989; Rothschild, 1987).

LESSONS FROM HISTORY FOR THE PRESENT-DAY ORGANIZER

What can organizers learn from this summary history? Three themes seem apparent. First, organizing ebbs and flows. Knowing that defeats can become victories conveys patience and helps motivate organizers through hard times. Knowing that successes can become defeats helps frame strategies to lock in successes and anticipate sources of opposition. Second, organizers are always observing, reacting, and inventing. Community organizing has survived and flourished because organizers learn and adapt, remaining flexible and nonideological. Organizing has responded to the spirit of the times. Third, today's organizers can take a shortcut to victories by examining which strategies and tactics that have been used in the past are most likely to lead to long-term successes.

The Ebb and Flow of Community Organizing

Community organizing has had periods of greater and lesser successes, but the achievements of the more successful eras last and help organizing in the more difficult times. Organizers can build on past victories: Unions are legal, minority group members can vote, community-based programs provide social services, and progressive organizations have broad access to the political arena. Some tenants are organized, and some manage their own buildings. Industry faces opposition when it despoils the environment. The civil rights movement resulted in legislation protecting voter rights and in integrated public transportation and accommodations. Being fed up with fetching the coffee was translated into laws to eliminate gender barriers to good jobs. Fighting for a fair share of federal funds to be spent in their community ultimately empowered the Hispanic membership of COPS in San Antonio politics. These contributions last and help organizers get over the bad times when people focus more exclusively on the achievement of immediate material gains.

To some extent, there is a natural progression from good times for organizing to bad times. Individuals who have benefited from collective actions deny that they have gained from the community movement. It is more comfortable for educated middle- and upper-middle-class minorities to attribute their gains to their individual merit, forgetting that before the civil rights movement, the same level of ability and effort would have gotten them nowhere. Similarly, young women who have experienced equal educational opportunities, have advanced in business, and who are now allowed some control over their reproductive capacities, sometimes forget that these gains are but a generation old and are still contested.

Success breeds failure in another way. As in the Cincinnati experiment, the victories of community organizations may threaten city officials, professionals, and merchants. Part of the reason for the failure of the maximum feasible participation requirement of the War on Poverty was that it bypassed city officials and threatened their power. When community organizing works, it threatens oppressors and limits their freedom; they are likely to strike back. The more successful the organization, the more profound the changes it makes, the more energy and force, legal and otherwise, the opponents are likely to use.

In part, the ebb and flow of success in the community movement stems from alternating periods of conservative and liberal public opinion. During more liberal periods, the problems of the poor are more likely to be blamed on broad social factors, such as the changing international economy or urban decline. During more conservative periods, the poor are more likely to be blamed for their own problems. J. H. Ehrenreich has argued as follows:

> Very crudely, in the last decades of the nineteenth century, the 1920s, the 1940s and 1950s, and the present time, the more individual orientation has predominated (and along with it, despair as to the possibility of reform and disdain for social action). Conversely, in the years before World War I, the 1930s and the 1960s, community action and social reform dominated the attention of social workers and planners, and casework fell into a degree of disrepute. (J. H. Ehrenreich, 1985, p. 12)

The level of support for reform through organizing has varied with the temper of the times. One cannot easily imagine Gay Pride parades in the 1920s or the 1950s, but in the 1960s they were, if not common, at least expected (Adam, 1987). Social climates do change, sometimes quite quickly. When the Equal Rights Amendment was passed by the U.S. Congress, it appeared that feminist organizers only needed to maintain their momentum to gain state support and complete the amendment process. Yet, in the following years, the climate had changed, so the amendment failed to get the necessary support.

Community organizing ebbs and flows in part because of the actions and beliefs of elected government officials, though whether such officials lead or follow the public is debatable. Under Attorney General Palmer, infamous for leading the Palmer raids in 1919 against leftists, and again in the late 1940s and 1950s, federal officials repressed the activities of progressive organizers. In contrast, both community organizations and organizers received direct federal payments as part of the Kennedy–Johnson era.

Government actions have sometimes been hurtful to community organizing while at other times helpful. Sometimes city governments have failed to support agreements between tenants and landlords when the agreements came to court, but later the same local governments supported rent control and helped pass enabling legislation allowing rent strikes. At the state level, tenants' organizing in Santa Monica, California, was eased as California passed state enabling laws. And, crucial breakthroughs for Chavez's farm workers union occurred when a progressive state labor board ruled that organizing near work sites of farm laborers was permissible. Until the ruling, it had been difficult to gain access to talk to workers who were on the private property of the commercial farmers.

Community organizing ebbs and flows for a variety of reasons, including changes in the economy, increased opposition, shifts in national mood, and the actions of government officials. But knowing that these changes will occur suggests approaches that an organizer can take.

When organizations solve the immediate problems they were set up to address, people they helped might lose interest. One approach to this problem is to avoid defining the problems too narrowly and to show how problems are linked. Even NIMBY (not in my backyard) movements can be broadened, if the choice of site for a garbage dump is linked with the community role in long-term planning. Another approach is to shift the definition of the problem as the original problem gets solved. Thus, as the women's movement helped women get better educations and better jobs, some women lost interest in the movement. Goals then shifted to solving problems faced by working women, such as day care for children or elderly parents and equal work for equal pay.

As community organizations succeed, they often rouse increasing opposition. The trick to dealing with opposition is to anticipate it. Figure out who is likely to be opposed and why. Then disarm them. Sometimes the opposition can be bought off or co-opted, that is, brought on board so that their opinion can be heard while they are learning about and becoming more sympathetic to the group and its goals. Sometimes the enemy needs to be isolated, and the organization may need to set up in advance a strong enough coalition to overwhelm them.

Organizing during conservative times presents particular difficulties. Because there is a tendency at such times to blame the victims, be careful in picking issues. Instead of choosing to organize around the issue of unwed mothers, pick the issue of infant mortality. It is difficult even in conservative times to blame a baby for dying. Ironically, in conservative times, getting the poor to help themselves may sound cost-effective and might gain more support than at other times. A strategy for getting support for day care might be to argue that it takes women off the welfare roles and puts them in a productive position in the economy and makes them taxpayers.

Organizing in the face of government opposition can be extremely difficult, but even in this case, some planning can be helpful. Always assume the possibility that an agent provocateur might be present and that phones might be tapped. Such assumptions may seem paranoid, but historically, such tactics have been used often enough to make the possibility realistic. A wise strategy is to have a number of people trained to take over as leader if one or more leaders are imprisoned. Even when governments are not out to destroy community organizations, they can renege on past agreements or not enforce laws already passed.

More generally, progressive organizations need to lock in the gains they have won as solidly and tightly as possible when they are at the peak of their power and the height of their visibility. Organizers need to make it as hard as possible to reverse previously won benefits. That may mean that agreements are formalized into enforceable contracts, or it may mean that cases are brought to court to set precedents. It means that working out a bargain is not left until later, when the spotlight of publicity has gone elsewhere. If organizers pay enough attention to locking in successes during good periods, they can make the bad periods much easier.

Community Organizing Has Evolved

Approaches taken by one organizer or group are learned by others, who then go on to add to the body of knowledge and the list of successful strategies. Success stories inspire other organizers to try the same techniques, and organizers spread new ideas when they move from one group to another. The Reitzes and Reitzes history of Alinsky (1987) sounds almost biblical with its "begats": Alinsky, influenced by the labor organizer John Lewis, taught Fred Ross and Ernesto Cortes, who in turn inspired Cesar Chavez. After being inspired by civil rights activists, SDSers Tom Hayden and Steve Max became leading advocates of neopopulism. Populists such as Harry Boyte had extensive experience in the civil rights movement, as did the founders of ACORN (Fisher, 1984, p. 128).

Organizations themselves have traceable lineages. The NWRO bridged the civil rights movement and neighborhood organizing (Adamson & Borgos, 1984, p. 113). Alinsky's Woodlawn Organization at its early stages was intimately linked with CORE. Chavez's farm workers received help and guidance from progressive labor unions. And many of the CDCs that today run community-oriented businesses are direct spinoffs of previous direct-action community organizations.

The Evolution of Models for Organizing.   Students of organizing often hear the phrase "organizing model," for instance, the Alinsky model, the Boston model or the ACORN model.

> *An organizing model is a series of tactics for how to activate individuals to work in a community organization.*

A model perpetuates itself through a system of training for organizers. Organizing models sometimes provide different answers to the following questions:

1. What are the appropriate issues on which to base an organizing effort?
2. How is contact made with potential members? Is contact made one on one, through existing groups, or through other means?
3. What stages does an organization go through as it is being built?
4. What are the respective responsibilities and powers of local leaders, outside organizers, and, for larger organizations, paid staff?
5. What types of action agendas are appropriate, and in particular, when is militant direct action a correct strategy?

The answers to these questions differed as political and social environments changed. For many years, the Alinsky model of organizing—having a professional organizer work with existing local organizations and focusing in a nonideological way on issues of interest to community members—was *the* model for organizing. As environmental circumstances changed, major adaptations occurred in the Alinsky approach. In the Boston model, welfare clients were organized one by one through a door-knocking campaign (Staples, 1984); an implication of this approach is that issues mentioned had to immediately appeal to the self-interests of potential members. Ross, while working in Hispanic communities, introduced the idea of the house meeting, in which small groups of neighbors and kin met together to discuss their (collective) idea of local problems, long before calling an organizational meeting.

The ACORN model combined features of the Alinsky model and the Boston model and added a more explicit political element. From the Alinsky model, ACORN took the idea of forming a long-term multi-issue organization; from the Boston model, it took the idea of recruiting individuals directly, rather than organizations. The leaders of ACORN then added a direct political role to the older models.

Organizing models are not locked in stone; they emerge and evolve depending on changing historic circumstances. For example, the Industrial Areas Foundation (IAF), the most direct descendent of Alinsky groups, has upgraded the status of organizers and provided them with far more training than Alinsky felt appropriate. Unlike Alinsky, who argued for the need to break contact with local organizations once they were set up, IAF maintains a more permanent, if somewhat distant linkage.

National People's Action, also a descendent of Alinsky groups, works with a loosely linked national network of neighborhood organizations.

> [NPA works] to try to help local groups confront common issues. Its educational mission is to disseminate information about national policies or programs that may help or hinder local communities, as well as to collect information about successful tactics and programs used by local community organization. (Reitzes & Reitzes, 1987, p. 181)

National People's Action, similar to other newly formed institutions for training community organizers, finds information for local action and provides expertise that enables neighborhood organizations to more quickly accomplish their goals. Heather Booth, trained through IAF and a leader in the populist organization Citizen Action, changed the model more dramatically by pushing for direct electoral involvement (Reitzes & Reitzes, 1987, p. 151).

Booth appealed to people's distrust of utilities and other governmentally supervised organizations; this set of issues required direct political action. Thus, as organizing shifted from neighborhoods to more issue-based efforts, the techniques for recruitment had to change; as the times became more conservative and neopopulist issues more prominent, more direct political involvement became an acceptable and necessary strategy.

Different organizing models reflect not only the time and the specific group and issue involved but also the ideology of its founders. Alinsky's pragmatism, which was often emulated by ACORN, reflects a belief in the possibility of long-term systemic reform. The more strident confrontations endemic to George Wiley's approach in organizing the NWRO movement reflects a revolutionary philosophy in which organization is the means for stimulating social revolution and not an institution for guiding more gradual improvement.

The lesson from the evolution of these models is that organizers need to pay attention to the spirit of the times, as well as to the group and issues they are involved with, and to choose the most appropriate, while adapting, adjusting, and inventing new approaches. Organizers learn from each other, but they also adapt to a changing environment, and they invent new responses. There is no room for orthodoxy, in the sense of adopting a model and not allowing it to change.

Varieties of Strategies From Which to Choose

The history of organizing is marked by enormous variety in causes, philosophies, and strategies. When organizers are trying to figure out what to do, what will work best, they can sometimes look back and see what has worked in similar circumstances, or what has not worked that should be avoided. We shall describe both the legacies and lessons of three major social movements—civil rights, the women's movement, and populism—on which organizers can build.

We turn first to the black civil rights movement because it has been one of the most successful in organizing history. That is not to argue that African-Americans have achieved all they set out to achieve, or that some of their gains may not be eroded in the future. But because of its long and successful history, the black civil rights movement has much to offer in teaching organizers about what works and about the choices of strategies available.

One of the most important lessons from the civil rights movement is that society can systematically ignore injustices that are generations old. People tolerated the two-class society of black and white and blithely ignored the costs of a second-class education, employment, and political rights for African-Americans. Those who benefit from injustice often learn not to see it. Sometimes the role of the organizers is to force people to see injustices that they have blinded themselves to. Sometimes this means exploding comfortable myths, such as the myth of natural inferiority of blacks; sometimes it means making the invisible visible, by widely publicizing personalized accounts of socially caused suffering.

The black civil rights movement had to make choices between different strategies, choices that still confront organizer's today. Let's review what these choices were and some of the implications of each one.

Integration Versus Separatism.   The civil rights movement has alternated between separatist and integrative strategies. Separatist strategies sought to make the black community self-sufficient, supporting black colleges, black businesses, and sometimes an independent black nation. Marcus Garvey's Back to Africa movement was an early separatist effort; more recently, separatist ideology has been espoused by the Black Panthers and the Nation of Islam. The Black Muslims' emphasize separate black capitalism. Other black groups, such as the National Association for the Advancement of Colored People (NAACP) and the Southern Christian Leadership conference, have worked toward integration in the larger society through ending segregation in public schools, ensuring voting rights for blacks, and reducing discrimination in hiring.

There is no simple answer for which is the better strategy. Complete isolation, especially when bolstered by force and buttressed by the rhetoric of hatred, is probably not effective organizing. It invites destruction by force before it can have accomplished much of use, and it wastes too much energy in rage. Moreover, as a vision of the desirable society, it falls short; dividing society into armed and hateful camps doesn't sound like a very good long-term solution. Nevertheless, separatism as a strategy short of militarism may be not only viable but helpful in building self-worth, capacity, and empowerment. Many ethnic groups have helped themselves by remaining distinct and supporting local businesses of their own ethnicity. Giving minority entrepreneurs a base of customers may provide the chance to learn skills and possibilities for advancement that are blocked in the wider society.

Community organizations have to pick strategies somewhere along the continuum from total isolation to full integration. The appropriate answer should revolve around several considerations. Will separatist movements be so threatening to the broader society that they bring immediate and forceful repression? Can the groups being organized compete successfully in the wider society, or do they need temporarily reduced competition to learn skills and confidence? Will organization members learn more from mixing freely with the main society or separating themselves out? Full integration may mean loss of separate identity and be no more desirable than full isolation, but there are many choices between the two extremes.

Accommodation Versus Opposition.   For much of its history, the NAACP followed an accommodation strategy, working through the courts, working with the government, making slow but steady progress. The SCLC campaigns to desegregate southern bus systems, CORE's sit-ins at lunch counters, or SCLC's voter registration drives were more oppositional and intended to force changes. The urban riots of the late 1960s represent an uncontrolled oppositional response. The relative importance of each of these activities in securing the federal voting rights acts, important civil rights acts, or the social programs of the 1960s is debatable.

Whether an accommodation strategy is appropriate depends in part on the level of desperation of the group being organized. If a group is striving to improve economic conditions that have been dismal for years, then maybe a long-term effort is appropriate. If one is organizing the homeless, or people with acquired immune deficiency syndrome (AIDS), time may be of the essence, and slow legal strategies or persuasion of government officials may take too long to be effective. It is hard to channel moral outrage into slow accommodationist strategies, and hence these strategies may not be the best choice for building community organizations. On the other hand, when organizing in conservative times, confrontation tactics may be met with immediate repression, which ordinary members may not wish to face.

The civil rights movement has shown that multiple strategies simultaneously followed by different groups can be effective. If one group can call attention to problems with dramatic confrontations while another shepherds court cases through the legal system, the total effect may be more powerful than either alone.

Passive Resistance, Active Defense, and Violence.   Civil rights activists demonstrated the importance of pacifistic courage. The black movement has always been threatened by violence, including violence by the government. The genius of Dr. Martin Luther King, Jr., was to turn this weakness into a strength, by adopting and demonstrating the courage of nonviolent resistance. Being jailed became an honor and both a personal and, more importantly, a public demonstration of courage against injustice.

Techniques of passive resistance can be extraordinarily important when a movement is threatened by violent repression. More aggressive responses are likely to be seen as the excuse for sharper and ever more violent repression, which may deplete the membership and scare off sympathizers. But waiting to have one's head bashed with a night stick is not for everyone, even if it is an effective tactic, especially when photographed and displayed by national media.

Preemptive violence has not been a successful tactic in the black civil rights movement, and there are very few instances in which it would make a reasonable community organizing strategy. We argue that the ends do not in fact justify the means, that the means must be commensurate with and contribute to the achievement of the ends. When one talks about armed aggression, one is talking about revolution, not community organizing or community action. Generally, one does not achieve a peaceful and equal society by killing people, even when the people one is killing are themselves violent; one substitutes one group of killers for another.

To summarize, the civil rights movement teaches organizers the importance of bringing injustices to public awareness and offers a variety of strategies to choose from, including separatism and integration, cooperation and confrontation, and passive resistance and violence. It also helps suggest when each of these strategies might be best used, if at all.

The women's movement has also been a highly successful and highly varied approach for social change. The women's movement began in the 1800s as a civil rights quest for access to the vote and the right to maintain property. Later, concerns about equality in the work force emerged as women worked in offices and factories during both World Wars and afterward were told to return home or work at lower-status jobs at lower pay than men. The resurgence of the women's movement in the 1960s continued to focus on passing laws to guarantee equal access to education and equal pay for equal work.

The women's movement has contributed two very important lessons that apply to current organizing. The first is that, in organizing, *the personal is the political.* The second is that issue-based organizing can cut across existing class and race boundaries, creating new problems and new solutions for community organizing.

The Personal Is the Political. At the turn of the century, long before the phrase "the personal is the political" became a rhetorical device, women activists for reproductive rights, such as Margaret Sanger, understood that political repression of women was maintained by denying women control over their own bodies. Recent battles—over sex education, abortion, day care, the recognition of rape as a crime not a sex act, and protective housing for battered women—all link the personal to the political.

The principle that the personal is political applies much more broadly in organizing. For example, problems like high death rates for infants in the United States are not just the personal problem of women who bear premature children but social problems that stem from inadequate numbers of public health nurses, closing public hospitals in poor areas, and inadequate education in ghetto neighborhoods. Problems of unemployment are not just those of the person who is fired but are collective problems having to do with weaknesses in the economy, inability to compete with Japan and Germany, and weaknesses in the educational system. Unemployment also results from tax laws that encourage businesses to move and to swallow each other up, and from public programs that pay companies to locate here or there, rather than concentrating on developing a flexible and skilled labor force to attract them. The lesson is that even things that have been treated as extremely personal, and even embarrassing, such as birth control or rape, may reflect social causes of powerlessness and may be appropriate organizing targets.

Crossing Class and Racial Lines. In addition to emphasizing how political personal issues are, the women's movement called attention to the need to cross both racial and class lines in organizing. Women might share some problems, but they may not feel any solidarity across class and ethnic lines. To what extent can a wealthy, educated, white woman feel disempowered and join in struggle with a poor, ill-educated, Hispanic, migrant woman?

The women's movement suggests that one approach to this problem is to concentrate on common problems. A white middle-class woman may have a chance to become a doctor while a poor ghetto black woman may not have a chance to get any job at all, but both may be intimidated by fears of rape by strangers, lovers, or their own husbands. While one may have a private physician and the other may go to a public clinic, both have to deal with doctors who tend to patronize women and often assume their ills are psychological. Women, regardless of race and class, are likely to be victims in a divorce and to have lower incomes after a divorce than before.

Concentrating on the common problems is one approach, but progress can also be made if organizing focuses on the subgroups where solidarity is likely to be greater or the number of shared problems greater. For example, concentrating on employed women gives a range of problems to organize around, including equal pay, equal promotion possibilities, pregnancy leaves, insurance coverage for pregnancy, and so on. Inside an organization, a women's group may want to call separate meetings with clerical and professional staff, because their problems may be different or because each may be threatened by being treated the same as the other. When working women come to admit that some of their problems are political rather than personal, and that they have problems because they are women, they may become more comfortable about dealing with women's problems more generally. Then a larger and more unified group may be created in steps through coalitions.

The women's movement provides insights into how to organize across class, status groups, and ethnicity. These insights apply to many other issue-based groups, such as gays or the handicapped, where there is a diversity in income, education, and ethnicity and a wide range of problems to face.

Strategies from populism also affect present-day organizing. Populism rallies ordinary folk to oppose the depredations of big business. The early populist movement was an effort by farmers to organize against the shippers and the granaries. Its early successes, around the turn of the century, resulted in farmer-owned cooperatives. In the cities, populist reformers such as Hazen Pingree in Detroit (who became mayor in 1890) pushed for municipal ownership of electric production and low fares for street cars (Holli, 1969). The demise of the first phase of populism occurred at the time of the Bolshevik revolution, as a period of xenophobic nationalism swept across the country and provided a basis for discrediting populism.

There has been a recent resurgence in populism, whose tactics provide important lessons for organizers. Anticorporate movements based in states and localities, such as the Illinois Public Action Council or Massachusetts Fair Share, organize individuals to control the rates of utilities and insurance companies. Fair Share, headed by Michael Ansara, an old SDSer, lost a major referendum to make industries pay the same electric rate as individuals but won a number of issues like street repairs, housing rehabilitation, playgrounds, and schools (Boyte, 1980, pp. 98–99). Organizers mobilize individuals because of their irritation at big businesses.

The populist movement reminds organizers to pay attention to both the scope of what they are trying to accomplish and to whether their actions will result in successful empowerment of the public. The neopopulists have been reluctant to advocate large-scale alterations in the economic system. Are their goals big enough? While one community organization may not be able to change an economic system, one has to ask whether the goal, when achieved, will be too small or too limited to be worth all the effort. A way of thinking about this problem may be to start small, but think big, be ready to capitalize on successes and expand programs, to other neighborhoods, to nonmembers, to other services. Opposing utilities should lead to questioning why government tolerates monopolies at all.

The neopopulist movement also provides insights into what empowerment really means. To what extent does building a counterforce to big business imply empowerment? If a grass-roots organization can influence the rates charged by large companies, there is some empowerment, but if the arguments are all technical, and require the hiring of professional staff to do studies and lawyers to make the arguments, the organizational members may not be actively involved and may not be learning much. In the end, they may not feel that they have done much to achieve the rollback or stabilization of rates. On the other hand, if community organizations combat chain food stores and organized medicine and the public school bureaucracy by providing their own food coops, their own health-information centers, and their own alternative schools, and they participate in the design and delivery of these services, the members may be truly empowered. Community organizers need to pay attention not only to the outcomes—controlling big business—but also to the process, to ensure that empowerment takes place.

To summarize, a study of the history of community organizing sensitizes the organizer to the ebb and flow of organizing, to what it means to organize during a conservative era. History suggests the adaptations that have occurred as the field has matured and the range of alternative strategies that have been used. By examining instances in which these strategies have been used, inexperienced organizers can get a feel for when these strategies might be most effective and when they should be avoided.

COMMUNITY ORGANIZING AND SOCIAL WORK

The history of community organizing makes us more aware of community organizing as a career. That orientation shifts the focus to where and how organizers learn what they know. While much learning about community organizing goes on in the neighborhoods and in specialized workshops and institutes, community organizing has long been associated with social work and been taught in schools of social work. Yet the relationship between community organizing and social work has not always been a smooth one.

Community organizing grew out of social work of the Progressive Era, a social work that was primarily middle and upper class in origin and that focused on improving health and sanitation conditions for the poor. Progressive reformers at the time generally believed that technical skills could solve many major problems but opposed developing the capacity of the poor or the oppressed to solve their own problems.

As community organizing emerged from social work, it emphasized creating and fostering solidarity and encouraging ethnic identity as a basis for social work. It minimized the gap between the social worker and the client to the extent possible. And, it focused increasingly on giving people the capacity to fight their own battles and solve their own problems. The community-organizing model, of encouraging participation and sharing an expanding expertise with people, has been out of step with the professionalization of social work, which has emphasized the expertise of social workers and regarded people with problems as clients.

Through adopting psychiatric and psychoanalytical models as part of the professional knowledge base, the status and professionalism of social workers has increased. However, such models almost inevitably see problems as the result of individuals' maladaptation. Such a perspective can be useful, for example, in dealing with abusive men or abused women, but it is antagonistic to the perspective that the personal is political. As social work has increased its emphasis on psychological counseling, it has expanded its client base to include the entire population, not only the poor. Thus community organizing and social work have drawn further apart.

In addition, it has been difficult for many social workers, working for government agencies, to stimulate opposition to government. Even under the Poverty Programs of the 1960s, when government funding was used to hire organizers, the organizers found themselves under serious stress when they tried to force their own agencies to be more responsive to the poor (Lipsitz, 1988). The recent attempts to eviscerate and terminate the Legal Services Corporation epitomize the problem: Government does not want its employees to stimulate lawsuits against the government.

Historically, there have been strong reactions against social work's rejection of an activist tradition. Alinksy left social work in rebellion; outstanding figures in social work education such as Mary Richmond or Bertha Reynolds are used as exemplars for a more activist approach. Yet even during the activist 1960s, social work education moved only slightly toward a community-organizing orientation. Though there were many community activists during this period, social work agencies "contrary to expectations failed to promote social change and used the federal poverty funds to expand their traditional casework services" (J. H. Ehrenreich, 1985, p. 179). Wenocur and Reisch describe the era in more detail:

> Although the social work enterprise remained preoccupied with issues pertinent to professionalization . . . the political turmoil of the 1960s—the social movement for peace, civil rights, women's liberation, an end to poverty, welfare reform and the government's expansion of the welfare state—did shake it from its absorption with matters of "function" for a short time. . . . The social ferment in and around social work pushed the enterprise as in the 1930s, to reexamine its commitment to helping the disadvantaged and correcting social injustices through institutional reform. With the return to social equilibrium and conservatism in the mid-1970s and 1980s, social workers again turned to their preoccupation with "function," initiated a new cycle of emphasis on individually oriented clinical social work. (Wenocur & Reisch, 1989, p. 268)

Much of this individually oriented clinical social work involves an increase in private practice, made more remunerative through insurance payments.

At present, there is still movement for an activist-oriented community organizing approach in schools of social work. The calls for near revolution from Frances Fox Piven and Richard Cloward (Piven & Cloward, 1977, 1978) emerged from schools of social work. Some of the activists of the 1960s, many of whom are still working as organizers, are now mid-career educators in schools of social work trying, with various degrees of success, to inculcate a community focus in their students. This group of activist–educators has tried to bridge the gap between professionalism and activism by maintaining a socially progressive world view while founding professional organizations supportive of community practice, such as the Community Organization and Social Administration section within the Council of Social Work Education.

The idea of encouraging advocacy for radical social work emerged as a compromise between neighborhood organizing and casework. With this approach, caseworkers, as government bureaucrats, attempt to change the orientation of their agency and their clients. They become advocates for the clients and encourage activism as a form of self-help, while trying to impart a social mission to the agency (J. H. Ehrenreich, 1985, p. 201; Fabricant, 1988; Fabricant & Epstein, 1984).

While the two models, that of community organizing and social work, have grown apart, there is still hope that they can be supportive rather than hostile. While community organizing sometimes attacks government, that is not its only focus; in recent years, the focus has been more on participation with government rather than demonstrating against it. Organizing to build capacity is a tremendously cost-effective way to address social problems that have defied traditional governmental approaches. Paying for unemployment and welfare is much more expensive than helping people learn new skills and start their own businesses. The goals of capacity building and creating empowerment will influence mainstream social work, not because they are democratic, but because they might be a cost-effective solution that both liberals and conservatives can agree on.

And, as this chapter has shown, mastering psychological and psychiatric approaches are not the only way to achieve professional status. Inheriting the traditions of Dr. Martin Luther King, Jr., Margaret Sanger, Hazen Pingree, and Michael Ansara also provides professional status.

II The Components of Community Development

What's a city without neighborhoods?

As our definition states

> *Community development involves local* **empowerment** *through* **organized** *groups of people* **acting collectively** *to* **control** *decisions, projects, programs, and policies that affect them as a* **community**.

The five bold terms jointly provide a bridge between the individual and collective aspects of community development as shown below.

Working with people to help them gain power in organized communities is the responsibility of the community organizer. In Chapter 3, we discuss the roles and skills of the successful community organizer.

Empowerment is the feeling that they can succeed that occurs when people *control* their everyday environment. Control is the flip side of being dominated by others. *Collective actions* are the means through which individuals overcome feelings of helplessness. These social–psychological parts of our definition are examined in Chapter 4.

In Chapter 5, we examine communities and organizations as the building blocks for social change. Belonging to a community and fighting together in an organization are a better way of approaching problems than the individualistic and submissive approaches that those in power prefer. Community organizations are an antidote to the economic, political, and bureaucratic organizations that support those in power.

But such organizations must be set up in ways that emphasize the democratic, participatory, empowering goals of development.

Participatory organizations not only run effective campaigns but also illustrate that democratic involvement can succeed.

3 Community Organizers: Professional Activists and Activist Professionals

The community-organizing movement has survived and succeeded in spite of opposition because many organizers believed deeply enough in the goal of an empowered and more equal society to dedicate their lives to its achievement. Today, a wide variety of individuals are involved in organizing work.

Some are neighborhood residents agitating for immediate change, possibly to rid their neighborhood of prostitutes or drug dealers. Others are trained community organizers from ACORN, Citizen Action, or the Industrial Areas Foundation, who work to solve problems while teaching others the techniques of collective community action. More recently, those motivated by community-development ideals have joined public interest organizations to influence public policies on the environment or to aid the homeless.

Some organizers provide a link between grass-roots movements and social services. These individuals work in agencies to help abused women, to bring about local economic development, or to provide technical assistance to people as they upgrade their neighborhoods. What distinguishes these individuals from conventional social service providers is their belief that their work is empowering people by helping them solve their own problems.

The incredible variety of tasks performed by organizers can be seen in an examination of actual advertisements for jobs in progressive community organizations.

> **Community Organizer:** Recruit members. Identify and research issues; development; direct action strategy on issues.
>
> **Field Campaign Coordinator:** Plan and implement campaign strategy on local and statewide level; work with press; advocate before legislatures.
>
> **Executive Director:** Promote a broad agenda . . . oversee operation of organization; recruit and coordinate volunteers.
>
> **Fundraiser:** Annual appeals, direct mail, and special events.

Community Organizer: Work with organization that brings together tenants, homeowners, church people, youth, and merchants to organize for change in the Bronx.

Community Development: Work as a liaison with the Brooklyn business community.

Activists: Fight pollution and get paid for it; canvass; petition, raise funds, manage campaigns.

Environmental Advocate: Strong research and public speaking skills; commitment to environmental protection and public interest advocacy; policy development and/or campaign experience helpful.
(From various issues of *Community Jobs* and *City Limits*)

Overall, of 313 jobs examined, 89 had the title *organizer* and 52 had the title *director* or *executive director*. The other 170 positions were scattered among 70 or so different titles such as researcher, fund raiser, activist, and lawyer. The 313 advertisements presented in Table 3–1 show the variety of organizations for which organizing skills are seen as important.

Traditional organizing positions in neighborhood groups, working with low- and moderate-income people and fighting to obtain better housing, are still important, representing almost a third of the jobs. Many of the economic development positions are neighborhood-organizing positions that are meant to focus on job issues. Farm and rural organizing is primarily targeted at small family farmers threatened with loss of ownership. Other positions are as staff members for issue networks such as those for feminism, peace, the elderly, and human and civil rights. Work in energy and environmentally related issues has become important, with almost 20% of the advertisements in this area, though many of these positions are in environmental research organizations rather than direct-action groups.

Such variability shows the difficulty of describing precisely what an organizer does. Imagine preparing one broad job description for the entire field. The beginning of the advertisement would be easy enough to write, although it probably would not attract too many people.

Wanted: A Community Organizer. Willing to work long and inconvenient hours at less pay than could be earned elsewhere. Must have the patience of Job and a hide thick enough to withstand constant criticism. Must be willing to accept the blame for failures. Must not try to claim personal credit for successes.

But how does the advertisement continue? What are the responsibilities of the community organizer? And how do these responsibilities differ from position to position? What skills are required to be successful?

To answer these questions, we first describe the different types of people and different positions involved in bringing about progressive social change. Organizing is done both by concerned individuals with no special background or preparation and those who have received specialized training in community-organizing tactics and techniques, either at organizer institutions or schools of social work. We'll discuss the skills organizers use and provide some information on where they can be obtained, paying

TABLE 3–1
Types and Numbers of Organizations Advertising in *Community Jobs*

Organization Type	Number
Environment, energy, hazardous waste	58
Neighborhood organizations	41
Low- and moderate-income support, legal services for low and moderate income, church-based coalitions for the poor	34
Peace/anti-nuclear war, Central American peace	25
Economic development—new jobs, unemployment, cooperatives, plant closings	20
Housing	19
Consumer and consumer advocacy	17
Farm and rural issues	16
Newspapers, mass media of progressive views	13
Feminist	11
Human rights/civil rights	11
Health	10
Union organizing	9
Public interest research groups (emphasis not specified)	7
Homelessness	6
Children—alternative schools	5
Elderly	4
Granting agencies and foundations	4
College student issues	4
Mental illness	3
Training institutes for organizers	3

Source: Jobs advertised in *Community Jobs* March, July, September 1989 and June, September, December 1988.

particular attention to the pros and cons of professional training in organizing. Regardless of their particular background or training, organizers play four important roles—as catalysts, teachers, facilitators, and linking persons.

ORGANIZERS IN ACTION

Organizers differ by background, by how they started organizing, by their degree of professional training, and by their outlook. People move from position to position and from task to task; they learn from experience and from specialized training.

Some professional organizers receive training from academies run by ACORN or the Industrial Areas Foundations and then find communities in which organizing would be of help. Others receive instruction as student trainees in courses in social work

taught by people who themselves go back and forth between the teaching and organizing roles. For example, Mike Fabricant works to organize the homeless while teaching and writing about organizing. His students will learn about organizing from someone who is doing it, and then they will go out and try it themselves. This way of combining experience and training is called *praxis*.

Many organizers get their feet wet in a local campaign and only afterward seek out special training from organizing academies. For them, organizing begins as an immediate reaction to a problem. Charles Buffum joined with his neighbors to combat the crack epidemic in Midtown Manhattan (Buffum, 1989); Michael Herz is organizing a pollution patrol to try to preserve San Francisco harbor (J. Gross, 1989). These are people who were so mad they could not take it anymore and set out to solve a problem by organizing others with similar beliefs.

Ordinary people are empowered as they learn the organizer role. *A Life in the Struggle: Ivory Perry and the Culture of Opposition* (Lipsitz, 1988) is a fascinating biographical view of a working person, a poor black man who, responding to the adverse circumstances he and others like him faced, led a life of struggle for community causes. His actions were courageous and often dangerous—facing brutality in the civil rights drive in the South or blocking traffic with his body in St. Louis. He went door to door to increase black power in the South, fight poverty in St. Louis, combat unjust land-lords, and agitate against lead-based paint, which was poisoning children. Often, he worked on his own or with other black activist groups, though during the War on Poverty era, he was an employee of a poverty agency. As one informant described:

> The interesting thing about Ivory Perry was that he didn't shoot for the limelight. You'd always see him in a secondary role getting the job done. Ivory was always there, and I always understood that, well, this guy's legitimate. He's there because there's a mission to be accomplished and he's not hogging the headlines. (Lipsitz, 1988, p. 74)

There are uncounted numbers of people who are there "because there is a mission to accomplish." Maggie Kuhn founded the Gray Panthers, a loosely structured militant group of the elderly; Lois Gibbs, the leader of the Love Canal Homeowner's Association, fought and won against the poisoning of her neighborhood by Hooker Chemical. They both became well-known and professional organizers, but at first, they were everyday people upset by problems that affected them and those around them. When ordinary people take the lead in confronting problems, they are empowered.

Some literature on organizing contrasts the professionally trained, often university-educated organizers with local activists such as Ivory Perry, who educated himself. The distinction made is between *organizers,* especially those from outside the community and *local leaders,* who, as longtime residents of an area, influence others in the community, while learning tactics and techniques from professional organizers. But the distinction between organizer and local leader can be overblown and creates a wrong tone:

> For the most part, there was no leader/organizer dichotomy in the early days of either the labor movement or the civil rights movement. The twin roles were actually developed in the early community organizations to address the question of the role of "social work" professionals in ghetto communities. (G. Delgado, 1986, p. 185)

The dichotomy is a reflection of the wide gap in class, race, education, sex, and age between the outside organizer and the local activist, a gap that can cause discomfiture on both sides. To the extent that the organizer–leadership dichotomy emphasizes the teaching role of the professional organizer, it creates no problems. It emphasizes that those with college education who enter organizing as a career need a firm understanding that their role is not to be boss, not to determine, not even really to lead, but to empower, to inform, and to encourage. But when the dichotomy reflects the emphasis on professionalization in social work, it suggests a distance between organizers and the people with whom they work that may be inappropriate and paralyzing.

In concrete ways, there is another gap between the organizer and the local leader. Professional organizers are paid and can work full-time at it, while local leaders are often volunteers who work full-time at something else. Organizers for ACORN receive a nominal $7,800 a year, but salaries for other organizers are better. For example, of the 313 jobs examined in *Community Jobs,* 237 mentioned salaries. The average salary was $19,747, nothing like what a skilled college graduate could earn, but a lot higher than the poverty level.

Another way of classifying organizers is found in the distinction between what has been termed the *empowerment models* and *administrative models* (M. Williams, 1984). The empowerment model focuses on a kind of freelance organizer, who comes into a community to help find and develop leadership and help build the capacity to solve problems. The goal is to teach empowerment to others and then move on. The administrative model involves the provisions of social services, such as mental health or spouse-abuse shelters and counseling but with a community-oriented and capacity-building focus.

Many trained professionals follow the empowerment model. Lee Staples, like other ACORN organizers, organized welfare clients in Boston and worked to establish Massachusetts Fair Share, an organization meant as a counterbalance to business interests in Massachusetts (Boyte, 1980, p. 97). Steve Burghardt has been involved in community organizing in the South Bronx (Burghardt, 1982a, 1982b).

An alternative approach, especially important for the college-trained organizer, is the administrative model, in which organizers working out of a social service agency attempt to solve problems while expanding the problem-solving capacity of the community. An example is the work of William Berkowitz (1982), who used a community mental health facility as a home base, to establish community-based programs such as a cooperative education program. Consistent with the community-development ideal, local people chose and controlled the classes offered. In this model, organizers tend to focus on a narrow range of problems and spend more time building the administrative and organizational capacity to run such programs.

At the present time, organizers following the administrative model are often involved in community-based economic development work. For example, the historically important Back of the Yards Neighborhood Council sponsors projects for job creation in the neighborhood. The developmental organizer is Paul Ladniak, whose training is in public administration rather than in organizing.

The administrative model provides a bridge between conventional social work training (and social science education in general) and a more activist, community-based approach in which administrative skills and knowledge are put to good use in helping people find empowerment and solve problems. This role is not restricted to professionally trained social workers. For example, Lois Ahrens (Ecklein, 1984) and others like her have worked to establish and maintain shelters for battered women and rape victims. They initiated such action to take control over a hostile environment, yet as work progressed, they had to devote more time to the administrative details of funding, staffing, and running such centers.

TABLE 3–2
Types of Community Organizers

Primary Model	Form of Training	
	Professional Training	Experiential Training
Empowerment	Staples, Burghardt, Fabricant, Delgado	Perry, Kuhn, Herz, Buffum
Advocacy	Dolbeare	Gibbs
Administrative	Berkowitz, Ladniak	Ahrens

There is a position between the empowerment and administrative model, called the *advocacy role.* An advocate, such as Cushing Dolbeare, founder of the National Low Income Housing Coalition, is an individual who works *for* people with problems, often, people who are extremely difficult to organize, such as the homeless. Other advocates work in the National Congress for Community Economic Development to support programs that aid the homeless and community-based developers. Lois Gibbs, who originally became an activist in her community to combat the toxic waste at Love Canal, is now a Washington-based advocate for those facing similar problems. Much of the advocate's work is to push for programs that enable people with problems, the ill housed, or the unemployed, to have the resources they need to solve their own problems, an empowerment concept.

Table 3–2 summarizes the six types of organizer and highlights the actions an organizer is taking at a particular moment, but organizing is never stagnant. People move from type to type as their experience changes and the issues they confront vary. Tom Hayden, one of the founders of Students for a Democratic Society (SDS), was a theorist of the empowerment model developed during the 1960s. In later roles, as both an activist and elected official, he worked as an advocate for the poor and for consumers. As agencies were established to benefit the downtrodden, he worked in the administrative model.

THE SKILLS OF THE ORGANIZER

Organizers require an unusual mix of skills. Alinsky described the job of an organizer in fine rhetorical style:

> It is the job of building broad, deep Peoples' Organizations which are all-inclusive of both the people and their many organizations. It is the job of uniting, through a common interest which far transcends individual differences, all the institutions and agencies representative of the people. It is the job of building a People's Organization so that people will have faith in themselves and in their fellow men [sic]. It is the job of educating our people so they will be informed to the point of being able to exercise an intelligent critical choice as to what is true and what is false. (Alinsky, 1969, p. 202)

Teaching people to have faith in themselves is necessary for successful organizing. To actually carry out the job, Alinsky outlined a number of technical skills, including how to build, maintain, and activate an organization. Much of the rest of this book focuses on such skills, including fund raising, budgeting, and doing background research on problems, as well as a variety of political and direct action tactics.

Job advertisements for progressive organizations reflect this mix of narrow technical skills and knowledge of broader approaches to social action campaigns. In the longer ads, the word *organizer* assumes an ability to meet and talk with people, so these are not always listed as specific job skills. Table 3–3 lists the number of times different technical job skills were mentioned in the 313 advertisements from *Community Jobs.*

But organizers are more than people who believe in community development and have a set of technical skills. Successful organizers empathize with other people, ex-

TABLE 3–3
Job Skills Mentioned in *Community Jobs*

Job Skill	Frequency Mentioned
Fund raising, grant writing	126
Publicity, public relations, action pamphlets	75
Canvassing, recruiting, mobilization	70
Research, action research	68
Office or staff supervision	66
Interorganization coalitions, networks (excluding government)	58
Action campaigns, campaign strategies	45
Leadership development, training	42
Budgeting, fiscal management	39
Government relations, working with agencies, lobbying, policy design	37
Project planning, goal choices, issue development	36
Multilingual skills (usually Spanish and English)	31
Community education, grass-roots education	28
Organizational development and skill development	18
Computer skills, handling data bases	17
Conventional business and business development skills	15
Litigation or helping with litigation	14
Running meetings and conferences	13
Specific technical knowledge (such as knowledge of toxic wastes)	13
Working with volunteers	12
Voter registration	8
Advocacy	6

Source: Coding of jobs advertised in *Community Jobs,* June, September, December 1988, and March, July, September 1989.

emplify the movement in their own actions, and have the self-awareness to learn from their own actions.

Organizers must *empathize* with people, that is, understand what people are feeling and why. Empathetic understanding, that is, comprehending and accepting beliefs held by others, makes it easier to bring people together to discuss problems and goals. Empathy enables people to listen to one another, even when they have strongly held, different opinions, such as often occurs at a meeting with other members of a community organization or while negotiating with possible allies or opponents of the community organization.

An organizer must *exemplify* the empowering, democratic processes that bring about community development. Exemplification occurs by respecting people's opinions, showing concern about the time commitments of others when scheduling meetings, and helping others increase their responsibilities within the organization. It means being willing to learn from others, to seek out what community members can teach them, so that learning is not always one way.

Organizers have to live their values in a visible way, which means that those values have to be deeply felt and naturally expressed. And, organizers must not forget they are always on display, which means even in their leisure time, they have to avoid playing status games, acting as the boss, or favoring one group or faction.

Organizing is about democracy, and democracy is exemplified through full and open debate among organizers and members of community organizations. Organizers need to be able to structure discussions so everyone gets a chance to air their opinions without turning the organization into a debating society.

Exemplification also occurs whenever a movement is personified through a charismatic leader, the *symbolic organizer.* Symbolic organizers (who are also involved in the more ordinary organizing activities) exemplify commitment to the cause through their own courageous actions. As symbolic leaders, they can, through their own actions, change the definition of events.

Cesar Chavez became a symbolic leader in his acceptance of arrest and in his hunger strikes. Dr. Martin Luther King, Jr. exemplified a belief in pacifism by accepting jailing in a dignified manner. King redefined jailing in the black community from humiliation to pride (Branch, 1988) and provided a model that could be carried out by others. Ivory Perry reported:

> If he could be picked up and jailed for a crime he did not commit, he might as well go to jail for a cause. In that way he could turn an indignity into a badge of honor, transforming incarceration from a random blow of fate into a conscious strategy to undermine the power of those seeking to intimidate him. (Lipsitz, 1988, p. 80)

Using episodes in their own lives, symbolic leaders create a language of political communication, giving prior repression a new and more positive meaning, one that speaks to the experience of the poor but also dramatically communicates with the rest of society.

Symbolic leaders give voice and image where there was noise; they define humiliation as collective experience and transform that experience into political energy for change.

Cesar Chavez. (Courtesy TTB)

There is a danger that some symbolic organizers seek out publicity that is self-aggrandizing, rather than exemplary for the organization. To avoid such problems, organizers need to develop the ability to step back and analyze the meaning and consequences of their actions and to learn from their mistakes.

When organizers can think critically about their own behavior, they are more likely to see themselves as a product of the political and social climate and hence be more aware of their own prejudices and class-based perspectives. If organizers can recognize these weaknesses and learn to handle these problems, they will be more sensitive to the problems that other people have in dealing with prejudice and will be better able to act as examples for others in the organization. Burghardt's comments on how an organizer can cope with racism, classism, and sexism are worth examining:

> Developing a methodology that actively deals with the not-so-hidden realities of racism, classism, and sexism means more than adopting some pat formula. . . . An effective method . . . seeks to resolve them over time in a flexible, open, and tactically self-aware manner. Some of these elements are:
>
> 1. A belief that social problems like racism, sexism and classism hurt yourself and not just others.
> 2. A willingness to view your own often unconscious prejudices as an inevitable part of daily life [and] stay open to ways in which one can minimize their influence over your behavior.
> 3. The use of your own experiences of oppression, however minor, as a vehicle to identify the ways in which others may be reacting to actual and perceived experiences of oppression. (Burghardt, 1982b, p. 134)

The Organic Intellectual

The skills of the organizer are a combination of technical knowledge, personal attitudes, as well as an ability to learn from experience. Underlying these skills is an ability to translate what is often perceived as personal into collective political action. Gramsci, a Marxist theoretician, described people who had such skills, but lacked formal intellectual credentials as *organic intellectuals.*

> Organic intellectuals try to understand and change society at the same time. They conduct their intellectual inquiries through the practical activities of social contestation; they measure their own efforts more by their effect on changing society than by their correspondence to preestablished standards of eloquence and originality. (Gramsci cited in Lipsitz, 1988, pp. 10–11)

Gramsci distinguishes organic intellectuals from the academic variety. But the attributes of Gramsci's organic intellectual—learning from experience, reflecting on the meaning of action, and moving easily back and forth between theory and action—are core characteristics of any organizer, regardless of the formality of his education. If an organizer is empathetic and willing to learn from observations, then even a relative lack of prior experiences in a community can be overcome. One college-educated organizer working in a poor community described how she learned from experience:

> "I discovered the welfare line," she recalls. . . . "Here every Tuesday . . . was a long line of people. As an organizer, I knew immediately that this was an ideal place. We had a captive audience, they were standing in line, having to wait for their welfare check, being humiliated—they *loved* having somebody to talk to." (J. Miller, 1987, p. 203)

To the welfare poor, such experience was familiar. It was new to the college-educated organizer, but she sensed its importance. Through observation and conversation, she figured out who would be good community activists, who had the ability and initiative, who was there every day in the community (J. Miller, 1987, p. 203).

Organizers become organic intellectuals as they respond to problems, get into the middle of things, and then step back to analyze the situation and figure out what to do. Dr. King's organizing skills grew as he responded to changing events during the Montgomery bus boycott. He went from event to event, learning how to organize until he got enough mastery to be able to create and plan events and protests. His strengths were the ability to learn from the situation and articulate needs in moving and eloquent language.

Many women activists have been ordinary people who faced a personal problem and, through working to solve the problem, learned about its political nature (Garland, 1988). Having discovered the political nature of the problem, these people then articulated the problem in ways others could understand. For Cathy Hinds, the bad reaction of her children to local water created questions that were not answered by doctors or public authorities. She discovered that such problems were shared by her neighbors and learned how to get water analyzed. The movement from the personal to the political followed the pattern of the organic intellectual.

> The whole experience transformed Cathy, an otherwise reticent woman, into an outspoken advocate for her rights. . . . In early 1979, Cathy and Cheryl watched a television documentary . . . which covered the Love Canal tragedy and other toxic waste problems around the country. Suddenly they knew they weren't alone . . . Cathy and Cheryl were so upset by what they found that they initiated their own press conference. (Garland, 1988, pp. 94, 96, 97)

They got neighbors together and pressured governmental agencies about the problem. They spoke about the dangers of toxic waste, inspiring others to act. Her house was purchased by the Superfund (government money for cleaning up toxic waste).

> Cathy didn't declare victory for herself and her family and start taking it easy—instead, she broadened her involvement. She had developed into an expert on the issue of toxic wastes . . . and was respected by the press as articulate and reliable. [She] got involved with organizations on a statewide, and then [on a] national level. (Garland, 1988, p. 102)

More Formal Training of Organizers

Though organizers learn by being in the middle of events, figuring out how to deal with them, and reflecting on that learning, organizers do seek more formal training, at training centers and at schools of social work. Training centers are normally for short courses, while the programs at schools of social work are longer.

Training Academies.   There are numerous training academies, usually associated with networks of community organizations that provide specific skills to organizers. The Industrial Areas Foundation works with a network of organizers that provides technical training on specific issues during short sessions, in an effort to provide neighborhood people with more specific information.

> [The] training sessions offer local leaders an introduction to community development, organizational structure, and community power, as well as some of the techniques and skills necessary for effective leadership. The training also is designed to instill in community leaders a sense of esteem, confidence, and pride in themselves and their organizations. (Reitzes & Reitzes, 1987, p. 101)

Training centers such as the Midwest Academy directly stimulate and coordinate community actions. Literally thousands of people have received the short 5-day courses, and many others have participated in weekend retreats. Technical issues of "recruitment of members, issue selection, investigative research, and grass-roots fund raising, as well as more general background on the purpose of community organization, the dynamics of power and coalition building" are covered (Reitzes & Reitzes, 1987, p. 154).

There are many other such training organizations usually associated with action coalitions. Organizers Shel Trapp and Gail Cincotta set up training programs under the National Training and Information Center (NTIC), associated with the National People's Action (NPA). Training focuses on specific issues of immediate import to people in the field. Many of the major points have been summarized in Trapp's pamphlet *Dynamics of Organizing* (1976b).

Most such training centers emphasize the particular model or perspective of the sponsoring organization. For example, training centers associated with Citizen Action are more likely to emphasize tactics of political participation while those associated with the Industrial Areas Foundation are more likely to shun political work and focus attention on coalition building (Reitzes & Reitzes, 1987, p. 155).

The variety of training enables philosophies and approaches to organizing to evolve, to accommodate to new environments and changing times. Such a variety of training and approaches is useful in combating the attitude that one's own approach is the only possible way to get something done. In addition, these training schools are in constant touch with organizers and what is happening in the trenches and are able to continually interpret that information and reformulate what will work, and what the appropriate skills and techniques are.

Schools of Social Work.   Training centers are the lifeblood of the community-based organizing movement; they hone the skills of people combating immediate problems. Even college-educated organizers who focus on organizing theory are well-advised to read the pamphlets of these centers or to attend the sessions.

Still, the training is of necessity brief and often experiential. It tends to focus primarily on one model. An alternative educational path is the longer, more formalized programs in schools of social work. Such programs can teach a range of models and suggest when each one has been used or might be used most effectively. The longer curriculum allows time to reflect on the broader goals of organizing and time to learn a larger number of technical skills. These programs can teach explicitly the self-awareness that we have already described.

Programs in social work schools can teach the context, the background for social issues, the history of poverty, of unemployment, of industrialization, and the deskilling of the labor force. These programs present the history of organizing, helping organizers realize their place in a proud and successful tradition and teaching proportion and patience. Social work curricula can help compensate for the lack of experience of many college-educated students, by describing the experiences of women, gays, the unemployed, and the elderly.

In recent years, there has been an increasing emphasis on building a feminist agenda into community-organizing curricula.

> Feminist social workers focus considerable attention on the convergence of social work values and feminist values. . . . Values and goals within this common ground include: self-determination and self-help, individual dignity, person–environment interaction, non-discrimination, individual and group empowerment, interdisciplinary knowledge base, and commitment to social welfare and social justice. (Hyde, 1987, p. 2)

In short, training academies and university curricula do different things. They both emphasize particular skills, and they both have a practical problem-solving approach, but the academies are likely to be in the midst of practice, evolving a particular approach and set of answers. The universities are more likely to emphasize a broader approach, including the context of community organizing, its history, and different approaches to choose from. People from the community in the midst of organizing have plenty of experience but need some specific tools that they can pick up at the training academies; college students who have never organized may be desperately lacking experiences and the empathy that comes with personal knowledge of how other people live. They can pick up some of that knowledge at the university, and they can learn to accept and be more alert to their own biases. Ultimately, it doesn't matter where organizers learn what they need to know: They can learn it gradually from doing it and from watching other organizers; they can learn it from training academies; or they can learn it in schools of social work. And, no matter where they first learn organizing, they have to continue to learn from experience.

THE ROLES OF THE COMMUNITY ORGANIZER

Let us return to our discussion of how to complete the job ad for the generic community organizer. In part, the successful organizer requires many technical skills including analyzing problems, planning, budgeting, fund raising, bargaining, and evaluating. But organizing is more than simply learning skills; it is applying these skills in the separate roles that enhance the community-development ideology.

Community organizers play four roles: As catalysts, they stimulate others to take action on problems they face; as teachers, they develop people's capacity to solve their own problems; as facilitators, they provide information and do many of the important routine organizational tasks; and as links, they connect community organizations to information, allies, skills, and power structures outside the organization.

Organizers as Catalysts

The organizer is *catalyst,* making changes by stimulating actions in others. Organizers start community organizations by helping community members identify problems they feel are important, bringing together people who may not know each other, or working to create a sense of community that becomes the basis for organizing. Organizers try to target initial actions so that they bring about victories to keep people interested and active. Organizers gradually enlarge people's visions of what is possible and thereby get them active on a range of issues.

Organizers as Teachers

The goal of increasing human capacity to handle new problems is basic to development. To encourage this goal, the organizer becomes a *teacher.* The organizer is a particular sort of teacher, however. This teacher must respect the students, understanding that in many areas the students know more than the teacher. An organizer should be able to switch easily from being the teacher and talker to being the learner and listener. In this sense, teaching is teaching people to respect themselves and to learn from one another.

> [The organizer as an] organic intellectual [is] a manipulator of signs and symbols, an educator and an agitator rationally translating the needs and aspirations of [the] commu-

nity into effective action. . . . In order to succeed, organic intellectuals rely on collective memory—shared experiences and perceptions about the past that legitimate action in the present—and on social learning—experiences with contestation in the present that transform values and goals for the future. (Lipsitz, 1988, p. 228)

As a teacher, the organizer encourages local leaders to directly confront authorities.

Building capacity is teaching people that they can be leaders.

Organizers as Facilitators

Too often, community actions fail because activists lack the experience or patience or time to keep an organization going. Probably, more organizations fail from lack of follow through than from lack of enthusiasm. As a *facilitator,* the community organizer keeps an organization going and ensures follow-through.

Organizers may become staff members for an ongoing organization. As staff members, facilitators do the less glamorous, routine tasks involved in running the organization that make the rest of the effort successful. They work with members to plan a campaign that will maximize the chance of victory and increase member involvement and motivation. They make suggestions based on technical skills or knowledge. For example, they can advise the group on how to approach a bank for loans or can suggest to the group which corporations might donate funds. The organizer may do preliminary research, keep records, and provide information required for good decision making. The organizer can have managerial responsibilities, to stretch every dollar and arrange the work so that each person's contribution will have the maximum payoff. As a staff member, the organizer does not set policy or overall direction of the group. To do so flies in the face of community development ideals.

Acting in this way, organizers are *team coordinators* who harmonize the preferences of others. They handle the background details that enable routine office work to be accomplished smoothly. They run meetings and teach others to run meetings so that everyone's opinions are heard. Organizers balance organizational detail and group enthusiasm.

Without enthusiasm, there is no organizing; but without concern for administrative detail, there is no organization.

Organizers in a Linking Role

Another role for the organizer is as a *link* between the community organization in which he works and other community organizations, funding agencies, and the press. Sometimes, linking involves a broad search for information. What is the political climate? How much support will the group receive for its cause? And how can this support be obtained from politically potent allies? At other times, linking is limited to a very specific task. For example, one person in a women's rape-counseling center may work as a liaison with police to discuss testimony, protection, or police training to deal with victims.

Dr. Martin Luther King Jr. inspired many other civil rights organizers. (Courtesy Cleveland Public Library Photographic Collection, from the *Cleveland Plain Dealer*)

A linking role is often played by a person working for a government agency or in an advocacy organization. The community organizer in this position might be hired by a police department or a human relations department at city hall and aid government agencies to work better with community groups. A linking person working for the police department might encourage community organizations to augment traditional police functions (calling police when a crime is in progress) or advise group members on how to protect themselves. An advocacy person for the handicapped will provide local organizations with advice on when to target which legislators to support needed legislative changes.

Catalyst, teacher, facilitator, and link person are all roles of the organizer. In addition, from a personality perspective, it helps if the community organizers have confidence in themselves and little need to prove themselves or take the limelight. It helps if the organizer understands people's problems and wants to help people solve them. It helps if the organizer is a good communicator, open with community members about what is going on and how it is happening. A certain amount of enthusiasm and a vision of what is possible are useful to rouse people. A community organizer should be at least somewhat analytical, to diagnose problems, help plan effective strategies, and link personal and social problems. An organizer should also be sufficiently self-aware to sense the need to balance the symbolic and emotional aspects of organizing with the technical aspects.

Organizers must recognize their own potential for growth and development. They must recognize that they can learn from the people they work with and from the tasks they attempt. They must reflect in their own actions the confidence that people can learn enough to do what is required to control their own lives.

With these characteristics in mind, the advertisement at the beginning of the chapter can now be completed.

WANTED: A Community Organizer. Willing to work long and inconvenient hours at less pay than could be earned elsewhere. Must have the patience of Job and a hide thick enough to withstand constant criticism. Must be willing to accept the blame for failures. Must not try to claim personal credit for successes. Must be willing to learn new skills and grow with the people in the organization to bring about a democratic community of constantly increasing capacity. The work involves mobilizing others into action. It requires teaching others, facilitating action, and linking community members to a broader society. Good communication and analytical skills desirable. Warm and empathetic personality a plus.

4 | Empowerment, Control, and Collective Action

T he first three terms in the definition of community organizing are *empowerment, control,* and *collective action.* Empowerment occurs when people realize they have the capacity to solve problems they face, while control is having an effective say in decisions that affect their lives. Collective action describes working together to solve shared problems.

EMPOWERMENT

Empowerment is the sense of efficacy that occurs when people realize they can solve the problems they face and have the right to contest unjust conditions. Without empowerment, people grant those in high governmental or business positions undue deference, assuming that those in positions of authority ought to be making decisions for others. In granting such deference, people fail to realize that authorities might make it even more difficult to solve the problems of ordinary people. This capitulation to hierarchy creates a cultural illness in which "a society . . . is robbed of the will to understand its own pain, sickness, suffering and dying" (Rappaport, 1985, p. 15). People lack the will to see that the problems they experience are widely shared and socially caused. To achieve empowerment, people must learn that they are neither helpless nor dependent on bosses, government, and business.

In an empowered society, people act together to control their own lives. Empowerment is the process of gaining control over different forms of social power. Empowerment occurs in the struggles over who is going to make larger political decisions. It also occurs when people gain skills and feel more confident. In tenant-managed public housing, tenants, or at least the activists among them, are more empowered than are clients of a city or county housing bureaucracy. The process of learning to manage housing expands the experiences and background of participants. By taking trips to observe tenant-managed properties in St. Louis and Washington, DC, poor people in a newly formed housing management committee discovered that their ideas were as good as those of people already managing public housing (L. E. Wright, 1989). Now in a position to make decisions, the tenant-managers began looking around for answers to how things were supposed to work, how they could work, and what goes wrong when they don't work. As they find more information, they can make better decisions and have more confidence in their skills. Learning confidence creates empowerment.

Central to empowerment is a willingness to challenge formal authority and to escape dependency on those in power. Challenges to formal authority rarely involve dramatic confrontations or revolutionary actions. Increased self-confidence and independence can occur gradually and "take advantage of the cracks in the system to win victories and demonstrate that authority can be challenged and that people can generate power" (Perlman in Cox et al., 1979, p. 423). Empowerment gained through one small victory belies the belief that it is impossible to contest those now in power.

People demonstrate empowerment when they pressure businesses or government to change their practices. Fair Share in Massachusetts lobbied to set utility rates with less concern for profits and more for social equity. Communities Organized for Public Service (COPS) in San Antonio worked to change the voting system from one that discouraged Hispanics from voting to one that encouraged them to vote. After COPS successfully worked to introduce district elections, Hispanics elected their own representatives from the predominantly Spanish-speaking district in which they lived. Success showed the possibility for further success.

Empowerment is working out your own destiny; an early theme of the Back of the Yards Council. (Courtesy Back of the Yards Council)

To succeed politically is to feel better about oneself and reduce the fear of failure in other endeavors. People are empowered when they work together to handle neighborhood problems that authorities have failed to solve. Organized members of the Fairlawn community in Washington, DC joined together to harass and drive out the drug hustlers from their community. "Today, children are playing again on the sidewalks and in the yards of Fairlawn. People can walk to the market or stand at the bus stop without encountering whispering young men consummating drug deals" (Ayres, 1989, p. 14).

Empowerment links the personal and the political. Among those who are dominated or exploited, private fears are reinforced by bureaucrats in unemployment offices, by doctors in public clinics and hospitals, and by bankers, newspaper publishers, and almost every business person with whom they have contact. Empowerment bridges the gap between the personal and the political and reduces the humiliation that keeps people powerless.

This goal of combating disempowerment by linking public action with private feelings is expressed by Bell Hooks, as she reflected on the domination of women and minorities:

> I see how deeply connected that split [between personal and political] is to ongoing practices of domination (especially thinking about intimate relationships, ways racism, sexism and class exploitation work in our daily lives, in those private spaces—that it is there that we are often most wounded, hurt, dehumanized; there that ourselves are most taken away, terrorized, and broken). The public reality and institutional structures of domination make the private space for oppression and exploitation concrete—real. That's why I think it crucial to talk about the points where the public and private meet, to connect the two. (Hooks, 1989, p. 2)

Disempowerment occurs because society is structured in such a way that those who are in dominated groups, who are less successful, end up blaming themselves and accepting the situation. The hurt, the lack of success, become personal humiliations that are difficult to talk about and keep those who are hurt from joining together or fighting back. A disempowered handicapped person hides his or her handicap because it is treated as embarrassing. He or she is unlikely to join a group of handicapped people because that would call attention to the handicap. The social manipulation is to make people who are handicapped feel embarrassed by their problems. To achieve empowerment is to recognize that the personal hurt is socially caused and remediable through joint action, "to talk about the points where the public and private meet" (Hooks, 1989, p. 2).

Disempowerment also occurs because people *learn inefficacy.* People may take from the public mythology the idea that only experts or those with money or degrees can build profitable businesses, and so they do not even try to learn the skills to be financially successful. By believing they will fail, they fail.

People are taught that if they try to fight back, to make decisions for themselves, they will not succeed. For example, people may be taught that access to power is difficult or that contacting government requires expensive lawyers or arcane knowledge of bureaucratic and legislative procedures. Or they may feel that to address a city council means risking mockery or harassment.

People learn not to challenge government. Sometimes an official may make sarcastic statements to a citizen, the story of which may be widely circulated among

Disempowerment occurs by not fighting back when faced with a problem. (Bill Goodell/ *City Limits*)

friends, and passed on to children. People are taught by teachers or newspapers that wealthy business interests have disproportionate influence, and they conclude ordinary citizens do not have a chance, so why even try? People learn from a single experience that government cannot be trusted; they do not give each new set of officials they meet a chance to prove themselves.

Public schools teach students that if they have no natural talent for something they should not do it at all. Art, math, and athletics are treated as gifts that you either have or do not have, not things that can be learned. Rather than a place where people learn confidence in their ability to learn new things, school becomes a series of narrowed possibilities, a list of things one is supposedly not good at and should not do. Trying would only bring humiliation.

Society reinforces some of this learned inefficacy when it tells women that they will not be good politicians because they lack the biological aggressiveness of males, or that they cannot be effective lobbyists, because they will not be accepted by old-boy politicians. Rather than trying to redefine roles that have needlessly been cast in racist or sexist terms, employers discourage would-be applicants and teach people what they ought not try to do. Underlying this pattern is the notion that whatever one wishes to do is limited by biology—one must be white or male or of a certain age, size, strength, intelligence, or have some natural skill or ability. The model does not allow for learning or becoming; nor does it allow for a redefinition of the skills or talents required. This model of discouragement, of learned inefficacy, is intended to reduce competition and gradually force people into acceptance of their lower status and career accomplishments.

Television reinforces the elimination of possibilities by showing the poor and stigmatized in a negative way. They show blacks being arrested for drug dealing; they air footage of shoot-outs in the poorest parts of town. They show gays in drag at an annual ball. The news highlights financial irregularities in a community organization. They don't tell stories about people who were unemployed getting a job or single mothers getting a degree a course at a time at a local community college. They don't give examples of all the successful gays who have contributed to society. This is not a plot by the media to make people feel bad about themselves, reporters are just trying to sell stories, but the result is that people with socially caused problems see their groups portrayed as lower on the social scale or less acceptable than they really are, which may reinforce their sense of limited possibilities.

Sometimes authorities convince the disempowered not to act by arguing that protests are against the interests of the disempowered. Being disempowered is thus for *their own good.* For years, factory owners have convinced workers that pollution means jobs; to fight to breathe or to avoid cancer is to ask for unemployment. If a plant closes or moves away, the authorities blame the workers, not only for the loss of their own jobs, but also for the loss of their neighbors' and friends' jobs. This is a form of *blame shifting.* Instead of the factory owners being responsible for poisoning people, they create the widely accepted argument that those who oppose the carnage are guilty of causing unemployment.

Blaming the victim is a widespread cause of disempowerment that takes a variety of forms. The classical case is blaming the raped woman for "asking for it" by dressing sexily or going to a man's apartment. When a woman is beaten by a man, the first question many people ask, is what did she do to provoke him? The arguments can be more subtle and sound reasonable at first glance. For example, in one university, students who forged permits to get into closed classes were blamed and threatened with expulsion; but the problem occurred because the university set requirements for the students and then did not provide enough sections for students to meet the requirements, forcing them to stay an extra year to complete their degrees. The students who were determined to graduate in 4 years then forged permits that would enable them to graduate on time. Blaming the victim shifts the focus from the perpetrator to the victim and simultaneously burdens the victim with shame that helps prevent a collective response.

Making people ashamed of problems they did not cause, teaching them what they should not attempt to do, arguing that continued dominance by others is for their own good, and blaming the victim each involve intentional manipulations by those in positions of power to maintain social control. Organizers must combat the acceptance of self-blame among the oppressed and needy because it prevents them from taking action to help themselves. Paolo Friere has argued that those who are oppressed accept the legitimacy of their oppression, through having a "fear of freedom" (Friere, 1990, p. 20).

> The oppressed, having internalized the image of the oppressor and adopted his guidelines, are fearful of freedom. Freedom would require them to eject this image and replace it with autonomy and responsibility. (Friere, 1990, p. 31)

When people accept their exploitation, they sometimes identify with the dominators and adopt their ideology. Rather than working to improve their own lot, people sometimes idealize the life-style of others who have more than they do. Television shows that exaggerate the flamboyant life-styles of the rich and famous make this pastime easier. When those who should be struggling to make changes in their lives and neighborhoods identify with their oppressors, wishing they were the oppressors instead of the oppressed, it is very difficult to organize them. Dope peddlers in disadvantaged neighborhoods use their organizing ability to ape the life-style of wealthy people instead of building their own communities. When you want to be the landlord, you don't think about rent strikes. Instead, you become the landlord's assistant and collect the rent, while fantasizing about owning the building.

Part of the reason that many people accept their exploitation is that "the dominated are kept largely unaware and unable to collectivize" (Adam, 1978, p. 55). A response is to revamp school curricula so that they are more racially and gender sensitive. For example, including a more accurate and complete history of Native Americans in history textbooks not only allows Native Americans to see the commonality of their problems but also conveys the point to others that the society can cause individuals and groups to suffer and that government can make terribly damaging mistakes. It is virtually impossible to read about the history of Indians in this country and not begin to root for them instead of the cavalry.

In empowering people, organizers work to reduce the shame that keeps people from publicly expressing their needs or joining an organization that will fight for them. Organizers try to increase people's understanding of the social causes of their problems, so they are less likely to accept their problems as either personal or deserved and less likely to identify with their oppressors and try to become like them.

For example, returning to the problems of battered women, victims often believe that their problems are personal and would prefer to hide what has happened to them rather than agitate for collective solutions. An objective of the battered women's movement is to show victims they are innocent of provoking abuse (Schillinger, 1988, p. 469). Community organizations publicize the availability of shelters and let victims know that many others face the same problem. This feeling of commonality can be translated into community and can be the basis for organizing.

Capacity Building

Personal empowerment is learned by discovering that even those labeled as poor or disadvantaged or otherwise socially incapacitated can win, can improve their own lot. We term this process *capacity building,* the creation of an ability to accomplish and succeed through one's own actions.

Individual capacity can be bolstered in a variety of ways. Community organizations can fight for better schools or training programs that give individuals more marketable skills; they can also give individuals assignments in community organizations that build skills and confidence. These efforts not only build confidence but also enhance political activism. For example, many organizations for the handicapped have established education programs that

> helped disabled citizens develop skills in planning and organizing. It has helped them to view themselves as a political unit, represent their interests in public proceedings, and affect the quality of services. (Checkoway & Norsman, 1986, pp. 274–275)

Individual capacity can also be enhanced by membership in community organizations that can mobilize resources in ways that individuals cannot do alone. An individual in an organization has the support of fellow members, so issues can be fought as a group. The group can raise funds to carry out projects an individual could not afford to try. A community organization can help reverse the unfavorable images of the disempowered in the mass media. With good publicity, organization members can see positive images of their group and opportunities to accomplish instead of negative images of drugs, crimes, and despair.

Individual capacity is increased when people belong to a community group that can and has succeeded. As Friere has cogently argued, "the oppressed must be their own example in the struggle for their redemption" (1990, p. 39). Tenant organizations and housing advocacy groups give people greater confidence in the availability, affordability, and livability of their housing, as members learn that by working together they can fight slumlords (Lawson, 1986). Sometimes community economic development organizations succeed in providing jobs in areas in which traditional, capitalistic firms have failed, which creates a tremendous feeling of control and increased capacity to solve problems.

Progressive organizations build individual capacity by directly addressing learned inefficacy. For example, as one member of an organization for the disabled described:

> Before the project I felt helpless about the decisions that were affecting my life. But then we visited our legislators at the Capitol and learned that letters and phone calls are taken seriously and can be effective in decisions. (Checkoway & Norsman, 1986, p. 270)

Such efforts attack the mystical proceduralism that is so often disempowering.

Building individuals' capacity is an important goal but does not always lead to community development. People learn that they can gain a sense of control over their environment. But if they then focus only on the personal rather than building a base for longer run political and social change, the result is what Hooks has termed *narcissism* (Hooks, 1989, p. 105). This criticism has been made of self-help groups that teach empowerment through consciousness-raising activities and that then refuse to attack the social bases for the problems (Hicks & Borkman, 1988).

Linking Capacity Building to Successful Organizing

If successful community organizing is to occur, capacity building has to be linked to a broader three-step process. First, individuals must come to see the connection between individual problems and solutions and social and political causes of these problems. Second, individuals must assert themselves, either directly combating those in power or at least symbolically declaring their willingness to do battle. Third, small successes lead to a willingness to attempt bigger problems.

Consciousness Raising.   The first stage of personal empowerment requires the escape from the manipulated guilt in which people blame themselves for their own difficulties. People share experiences with one another and learn that what they thought was intensely personal is also political. This stage is called *consciousness raising*. Consciousness raising was originally a feminist term for recognizing the effects of sexism on one's life, but it applies whenever people learn the social basis for problems about which they have remained silent because of embarrassment or guilt.

As a personal example, in our city, many homes suffer from disgusting sewer backups caused because of inadequately sized sewer pipes that provided profit for some builder in the past. Yet, people have been reluctant to combat the problem: Having human waste in their basement is considered embarrassing, and not to be discussed in public. Clearly, consciousness raising was called for. We made a symbolic, humorous protest to publicize the problem, to make others aware that they shared the problem, could discuss it, and perhaps find a solution. By discussing the issue in public in a humorous way, by our willingness to use our names and our pictures brushing our teeth at city hall because we could not use our bathrooms, we made it possible for others to see the issue as a public one, a political one, rather than a personal embarrassment. In this case, learning that the personal is political involved a public education process focused on making people aware of the shared nature and political causes of problems and the potential political solutions.

Self-Assertion.   The second stage of linking enhanced capacity to community development is encouraging self-assertion through which people give vent to their anger, through public declarations, and by acting against those causing the problem. To avoid narcissistic behavior, the attacks must be linked to collective and not simply individual solutions to problems. Talking back to a landlord and getting a better apartment is a form of self-assertion; it is narcissistic, unless it is part of a broader effort to improve housing conditions, hold down rents, or organize tenants.

Personal resistance, even if it is primarily symbolic, is an important step because "stories of resistance are . . . assertions of self-respect" (Dill, 1988, p. 43). Resistance can involve individual acts of disobedience: An employee publicly insists that a boss clearly set forth job responsibilities; individuals demand information from banks about where housing loans are being made; shoppers argue with merchants over shoddy merchandise. Such actions take courage; carrying them out is an empowering experience.

Organizers work hard to encourage participants in community actions, to speak in public, to find one's voice, and talk back (Hooks, 1989). For the dominated, to speak in public is often a new and scary experience. It teaches a new skill, itself an empowering act; it may convince others to act, and most important, is a sign of self-assertion. The act of arguing back is courageous as individuals try to force those who have power over them to obey the law or improve conditions.

"Jail-house lawyers" who use their knowledge of law and civil rights to speak up for prisoners are an illustration of people gaining confidence through talking back (J. Thomas, 1988). The possibility of prison administrators trying to get even in these circumstances is a powerful threat and normally would cause passive acceptance. But some inmates are courageous enough to fight back even under these conditions. Further, fighting back requires research, as jailhouse lawyers connect their own experiences to a corpus of law. And, in so doing, they learn that even technical matters such as the law do not require outside experts. Prisoners, who are in an extreme position of subordination, can learn to use the law to defend their rights against their custodians. Preparing for the act of self-assertion is itself empowering.

Bootstrapping.   Community organizations are built by steps, with incentives for individual participation at each step. Organizers usually begin with small projects that will succeed and use the sense of achievement to build the empowering belief that joint action is possible and successful. This process is called *bootstrapping.* Fair Share, in Massachusetts, illustrates the bootstrapping process:

> Fair Share concentrated on small victories at the local level: tax abatements in Dorchester, bridge repairs in East Boston, a dump relocation in Worcester. These issues . . . engage people in work that teaches them something about power. . . . The actions were picked to be winnable. (Zald & McCarthy, 1979, p. 30)

Bootstrapping involves two stages. The first is to carry out an activity that has low costs to community members yet yields a victory. For example, the organization gets a politician who has avoided constituents to show up at a meeting or gets community members to sign a petition for a new stop sign, and the sign is put in place by the city. People learn that collective effort creates power that they lack as individuals and that group involvement is empowering.

The second stage is to encourage people to move from small victories to larger issues that require more resources and effort. If a small effort obtained a stop sign, maybe a larger effort would get the attention of the city rat catchers. Maybe if we can pool our money, we can set up a walk-in health clinic. To bootstrap successfully, organizers must initially choose issues that can be won with minimal commitment yet are important enough so people are willing to put out more effort for the next issue.

People who participate in successful bootstrapping activities emerge with a sense of *"we-ness"* that reinforces the willingness to collectively combat shared problems. This feeling of "we-ness" is a necessary antidote to the isolation and individualism that perpetuates disempowerment. People come to realize that even if they don't immediately get personal benefit from each action, they will eventually benefit from community improvement.

To summarize, organizers should first pick simple goals that are easy to achieve yet emphasize personal efficacy. These successes encourage people to stay involved.

CONTROL

The search for control is a quest for the means to determine decisions that affect community members. But why must special efforts be made to obtain community control? Don't we live in a democracy, and doesn't democracy mean that people have control? Yes, but only to a limited extent. We elect public officials, but interest groups donate to politicians' campaigns, earning a loyalty from the politician and influencing decisions more than citizens in general. Though we elect a new mayor and city council, the sections of the city with company headquarters or large stores continue to receive redevelopment funds while residential neighborhoods are relatively neglected. To the extent to which we do not control the outcome of decision making, we are not empowered.

Under the community development model, people control their own neighborhoods, workplaces, social services, and other aspects of the environment that influence their daily lives. Ideally, community members working together define problems, pose resolutions, find ways of paying for these solutions, and assure that such solutions are achieved. However, control is not an all-or-nothing state; those making decisions don't have to do everything themselves.

For members of community organizations to gain control over the decisions, projects, programs, and policies that affect them as a community, they must alter the mechanisms through which those in power maintain dominance. Sometimes this means organizing to change laws and social customs; sometimes it means curtailing or disabling the force through which power maintains itself. The use of force has been an effective mechanism for control.

With widespread and organized popular support, such power can be curtailed. Unions provide some protection to employees against dismissals without notice; the civil rights movement has helped reduce lynchings to almost zero; and women's groups have been successful in training police to deal more equitably with domestic violence. Not all the problems have been solved, certainly, and government can still rely on police force, but police civilian review boards and improved recruitment processes have reduced the number of violent police officers, and improved training has reduced the amount of force typically used against demonstrators.

System Bias

As the history of organizing shows, force and violence have been used to maintain social control, especially in the repression of minority group members. However, for authorities, force and violence are costly; a regime dependent on such tools must engage in continual repression, lest the tools of brutality be turned on them. Control is more often maintained less expensively in less overt ways. Some of the ways this is achieved include teaching people that they don't have the knowledge to challenge officials, blaming the victim, and putting shame on those who might protest. Even more subtle is a tendency on the part of government officials to make access to decision making easier for business leaders than for community members. Such a tilt has been labeled *system bias.*

System bias or the more encompassing concept of *ecological power* (Stone, 1976, 1989) is the way in which "the power-wielder is effective without having to engage in direct action to prevail over opposition or to prevent opposition from developing" (Stone, 1976, p. 105). Businesses gain an advantage over community and neighborhood groups because it is simpler and more bureaucratically advantageous for public officials to work with the business community. Stone explains:

> First, and most obviously, a group could achieve a positional advantage through the se-lection of spokesmen [sic] to serve its interest in strategically vital offices. . . . Second, a group might enjoy a positional advantage by virtue of the fact that the occupants of im-portant places in the governmental system share the group's perspective on leading pol-icy questions. Third, a group might possess an advantage in that their leaders have infor-mal ties to and enjoy the respect of major officeholders. Since their views are expressed in a relationship of mutual trust, the group leaders can expect a sympathetic hearing. (Stone, 1976, pp. 18–19)

The history of the city manager form of government shows how a city can be structured to reflect disproportionately businesses' view of public interest. From the history of urban reform, we learn the following:

> Most business structuralists . . . were not promoting the new reform as a revitalization of popular government. Democratic ideology, involving equitable representation to all social classes and geographic areas of the city, received little emphasis in their programs. What they sought was the replacement of the ward system . . . with a centralized administra-tion that would organize municipal services according to the business view of what was good for the community. City manager government promised to accomplish all of this. Businessmen could then reduce the influence of lower-class groups in city government and advance their own notions of public policy. (Scheisl, 1977, p. 176)

Sometimes system bias is intentional and reasonably obvious, as when a business group puts together a slate of candidates to draw up a city charter that will favor business and work against lower-class groups. But system bias can also result from the sum of many small decisions rather than one or two dramatic changes. For example, many of a city's transactions with the business community are kept secret, with the justification that business won't deal with the city if its negotiations are made public. In reality, "lower visibility provides a protective cover under which advocacy could take place relatively free from the sanctions of unfavored groups" (Stone, 1976, p. 197).

Part of the reason that business is more successful than neighborhood groups is that the business community often has a well-worked out agenda and is in a position to maintain a continuing presence at city hall, to keep its agenda in the forefront. To combat system bias, community organizations need to press for the structural changes that result in increased likelihood of their members being elected to office; establish their own, ongoing organizations that continually interact with governmental officials; and create their own agendas of issues that they put forward at every opportunity. There is nothing that businesses have done that community organizations cannot also do, although they may substitute their numbers and votes for campaign contributions.

The Social-Psychology of Control

Those in power often thwart the efforts of community members to gain control over decisions that affect them. At the most subtle level, the disempowered do not know they need to strive for control because power is maintained through nondecisions. Who benefits is never raised. It is hard to fight a decision that is never publicly made, merely assumed.

In addition, those in power may control decisions through interpersonal contacts and social networks or through a variety of psychological manipulations, including the organization of consent, the embedded obscurity of power relationships, and the perception that power and control are necessarily zero-sum concepts. Each is a way of keeping the disempowered from taking control of decision making.

Organization of Consent.   The *organization of consent* is a technique through which capitalists manage to gain labor's cooperation by getting dominated groups to compete with one another rather than oppose owners. It has been best described in the workplace, but the idea applies to other situations in which small-scale accommodations between those in power and those dominated distract from more fundamental issues. With the organization of consent,

> the control of the labor process by capital involves the cooperation of workers . . . consent is generated and sustained [by] . . . the seductive practice of fulfilling quotas and getting assigned work done with the least amount of effort . . . even the most antagonistic workers [participate] in the interest of achievement, piece-rates, and promotion. . . . This form of pragmatic acceptance of capitalist domination on the part of workers disperses conflict laterally (between workers) instead of vertically (between workers and capitalists), muting class antagonisms. (Isaac, 1987, pp. 131–132)

The organization of consent focuses on how fairly individuals think they are being treated in contrast to their colleagues and distracts from broader questions of the legitimacy of the power structure.

As another example, those in positions of control argue that success is attributable primarily to individual hard work, and that failure is a personal fault. They call attention to the exceptional individual among the disempowered who does succeed, rather than the social obstacles to that success. A brilliant child of a migrant farm laborer might become the chief of staff of a major research hospital, but this powerful position is far more likely to be held by the son (sexism intentional) of a person already in such a dominant position. Most farm laborers' children could never get the education that could open such a door and would be completely unfamiliar with the steps to such a career, no matter how hard they worked.

The widely accepted belief that success is possible through competitive achievement ends up as a way of preserving the present structure of control. As long as people think that if they work hard they will succeed, and that lack of success results from laziness, they will not be motivated to protest against the system, or even to think it unfair, and they are unlikely to be sympathetic to others who are unemployed, homeless, or broke. After all, they are in competition with these less fortunate folks, whose failure signifies that they themselves are better, more successful people.

To combat the organization of consent, organizers must search for the beliefs, such as the belief that hard work yields success, that maintain present control structures. Organizers must then demonstrate that the game is fixed, that the level of success is limited, and that there are institutional barriers that need to be removed. Gaining control is not simply changing those who occupy decision-making positions; it involves questioning the structure that allows only some people to be in positions of power while others are systematically blocked from the same positions.

The Embedded Obscurity of Power Relationships.   People relate to each other differently, depending on their gender, race, ethnicity, and class. Society sets up a status hierarchy based on these (and other) categories: male over female, light-skinned over dark, northern European ethnic groups over others, and rich over poor. Although people pay attention to these characteristics, they often pretend that they do not, making it difficult to challenge the resulting inequities. Pretending to greater equality than actually exists strengthens the advantages of the socially favored.

What may happen during collective actions is that protesters mistakenly accept the myth of social and political equality and assume they are legitimate contenders on the particular issue under dispute. They offer reasons, information, and evidence on which they believe the outcome should depend, yet the outcome may not turn on any such argumentation. Authorities feel justified in ignoring the entire argument merely because the protestors, as members of a dominated group, are seen as having little legitimacy.

Until activists admit to themselves that the battle is in part based on assumptions about their low status, it is difficult for them to devise appropriate strategies and easier for authorities to maintain dominance. The first step in responding to these often-hidden assumptions is to unmask or *deconstruct* the bases of dominance. That is, they must learn how authorities justify that they do not have to listen to the arguments of those in opposition.

Sometimes the authorities make it easy to figure out what they are thinking along these lines because in the heat of the moment they come right out and say it. An example of this kind of revelation occurred in a battle by poor minority women to maintain a women's health clinic in a hospital. During the battle, the spokespeople for the hospital attacked the demands of the protesters in such a way that their low view of the status of the protesters was obvious. They tried to shut the protesters up, telling them, "You don't 'demand' of doctors. You wouldn't make demands of your husbands" (Morgen, 1988, p. 105). The hospital representatives did not argue on substantive grounds but labeled the protesters patients or wives, two subservient roles whose protest was illegitimate, regardless of the merits of the case.

> What had begun as a feeling of being denied access to the decision to close the clinics was transformed through direct contact with the doctors and the hospital into a recognition . . . that "they think we are stupid and unworthy of having our views taken seriously." (Morgen, 1988, p. 104)

In the case of the battle for the clinic, the put-downs were so obvious that the protesters could easily deconstruct the situation and understand the mechanisms of control. Though those in authority may frequently think this way, they seldom state it so baldly. Deconstructing the arguments may take some thought and possibly even some provocation.

More generally, the obscurity of power relationships makes it difficult to see when dominance based on low status is denying a group legitimacy in a bargaining situation. Suppose a housing agency staff has an image of poor minority group members as lacking managerial skills. They are unlikely to air such views in public, but their negotiations with tenants about cleaning buildings, achieving social order, and maintaining elevators may be influenced by these assumptions. The real issues might not be those on the table but the fact that the staff looks down on the tenants. In such circumstances, activists should develop "conceptual frameworks that capture the complex ways that gender, race, ethnicity and class become politically meaningful" (Morgen, 1988, p. 113).

There are other bases of social status that can function in similar ways, such as being a student, an outsider, childless, or a communist. If protestors can be put in these categories, they can be defined as having no legitimate voice so that their issues need not be addressed. What is especially interesting about these categories is that they are not necessarily verifiable facts and can be attributed incorrectly to a group or individual to avoid facing their arguments. Thus, the Federal Bureau of Investigation (FBI) struggled for years to give the impression that Martin Luther King, Jr. was either a communist or a communist dupe.

Once the nature of these status put-downs has been figured out, the community group needs to work out a counter strategy. Ignoring the negative perception of the group and pretending that the outcomes will be determined on the basis of the evidence generally do not work, though sometimes just bringing the authorities' negative assumptions into the open can create enough embarrassment to force a change. Headlines that read, "Doctors Call Women Subservient" might well bring about public denials and new negotiations, as well as increase the respect of hospital officials for the political skills of the organization. Another tactic is to emphasize broader principles—for example, that all citizens have a legitimate voice that must be taken seriously.

In combating hidden bases of power, the spokesperson for the group needs to be carefully selected. It is easy to imagine making a plea for parents to watch their children for signs of drugs, and the whole effort falling apart when a parent in the audience asks, "are you a parent?" and the speaker stutters a "no, but . . ." Once the group has been put in a category that does not need to be taken seriously, there is no hope that the argument will be listened to. It may be wiser to anticipate the problem and choose a parent for such a presentation.

In short, the obscurity of power relationships begins with a polite agreement to pretend that race, class, and ethnicity are not accepted bases for social dominance. And then, when people collectively cease to see the bases of dominance, the disempowered often cannot understand what it is that is hurting them and hence cannot react in an appropriate way. One goal of community organizing should be to make these power relations visible and help devise appropriate strategies to increase the legitimacy of dominated groups in political discourse.

Zero-Sum Situations.   Another psychological manipulation that maintains the present structures of control is the belief that control is *zero-sum;* that is, gains in control by one group or individual come at the expense of losses for another group or individual. People in authority then feel that any gains made by community organizations will directly reduce their own control and so fight that much harder against any form of community empowerment.

Too often, members of progressive organizations handicap themselves by accepting the zero-sum definition. They want to keep the present control structures but simply reverse who it is that makes decisions. Or they consider any weakening of authorities as important and focus strategies on discomforting power holders, rather than achieving ends that better serve everyone.

The acceptance of a zero-sum model is in part based on a mistaken belief that control is power over someone or something, rather than the power to accomplish a beneficial outcome (Deutschman, 1988). For example, a group concerned with improving the availability of healthy, affordable foods need not eliminate the local chain supermarket. The supermarket does provide canned goods more efficiently and less expensively than smaller, community-controlled cooperatives. The community group should focus on building a cooperative that supplies healthy fruits, vegetables, and grains, a task for which it is better suited than a chain because it can buy in moderate quantities on a local market.

The zero-sum model encourages individuals to try to get their own piece, rather than to build toward a collective effort to expand the pie. It encourages contention rather than cooperation, especially between ethnic and racial groups, where cooperation would benefit most if not all. The zero-sum image was one of many reasons for the virulence of racism among poor southern whites, whose economic lot was only slightly better than the blacks. Each group was persuaded that the economic gain of one was at the cost of the other. People of wealth and power encouraged the poor to believe that the amount of wealth was limited, so that they would have to fight with one another over available resources.

Authorities maintain control through system bias or through the more subtle psychological mechanisms of the organization of consent, the embedded obscurity of power relationships, and the mistaken zero-sum image of control. Despite these mechanisms, dominated groups can increase their sense of control. Community organizations that emphasize horizontal solidarity can offset the competitiveness between groups that is the mainspring of the consent to be dominated. Worker-owned firms and community enterprises can help workers escape from the problems of the zero-sum model by expanding the pie and sharing control widely. Community-based political organizations that have their own agendas and fight for them over time are one answer to problems of system bias.

The DARE Criteria

Control is situational, evolving, and non-zero sum. Degrees of control are possible. How much control a group has at any time can be ascertained by asking:

Who Determines the goals?

Who Acts to achieve the goals?

Who Receives the benefits from the actions?

Who Evaluates the actions?

We call these four measures the DARE criteria. The more that people in their own organizations determine the goals, act together to achieve the goals, directly receive benefits, and evaluate whether or not the action was worthwhile, the more the control for the previously disempowered.

A neighborhood food cooperative in which participants decide to save money on fresh produce, buy the produce themselves, eat the food, and determine if the coop is worth the effort it takes, clearly illustrates that community members can gain control on each of the four aspects of DARE. On the other hand, if politicians determine that business profits are more important than health and safety, tell bureaucrats not to inspect waste sites, and hide their actions so no one can evaluate them, the result is a negative on each of the DARE criteria.

Most situations are in between. Local activists might decide that a community organization rather than a government agency should direct the redevelopment of a neighborhood. The organization may hire technicians to carry out the work. Under these circumstances, many community members will be unaware of what is happening. Because the organization has limited resources, only a handful of buildings can be rehabilitated, and few in the community will benefit. Even though such a situation represents limited empowerment, it probably provides greater local control than if the development had been entirely run by a city government. The city might have leveled the entire neighborhood and turned over the land to a developer to build a shopping center.

Working to meet the DARE criteria need not mean antagonism between community members and education, social service, business, and government agencies. Control, as we have argued, is not zero sum. People, institutions, and government can work together to provide empowerment while enhancing local control.

For example, suppose neighborhood people form a not-for-profit development corporation to purchase and rehabilitate houses. The corporation may obtain funds from local banks and community foundations, while pressuring government to make it easier to buy deteriorated houses by insuring mortgages. Government inspectors work with the organization to assure the quality of housing. This type of activity has been the basis of the Neighborhood Housing Services program, in which community organizations,

The DARE criteria in action: Mayor Dinkins of New York joins a community crime patrol.
(Courtesy Office of the Mayor, City of New York; photographer, Edward Reed)

banks, foundations and government agencies work together to upgrade the quality of life in poor but stable neighborhoods.

In large cities with expanding downtowns, neighborhood groups, businesses, and government have set up deals that might benefit both the downtown and neighborhoods. For example, in Boston, investors have obtained government support and funding for large office or commercial projects, such as the huge Copley Square redevelopment project. As part of the agreement for gaining government support, these business investors contribute money to a fund from which neighborhood organizations receive grants for improving residential communities, especially those of the poor.

Joint action between issue-based organizations and progressive government agencies can satisfy the DARE criteria by expanding resources. For example, environmental groups purchase crucial parcels of land that they feel should be used for parks or left in a natural state. They then work with park districts, forest districts, or governmental agencies to buy the land from them, at cost, and use the legal authority of government to preserve it. Their logic is that government can rarely act quickly enough to purchase these parcels of land before developers build homes or businesses on them, so the environmental groups should protect the land in the interim. The resulting cooperative arrangement permits the environmental group to use and reuse the same limited funds in purchasing land, giving them more control over which parcels of land are to be acquired and when.

ACTING COLLECTIVELY

Acting collectively means more than working on a project together or within the same organization. It means understanding that there is a collective responsibility and collective ability to accomplish goals. It means that individuals develop strength from the successes of community organizations and understand that community is a result of collective actions. Individuals learn to think of themselves not as cases or clients but as members of a collectivity and members of a class of individuals sharing common problems and similar disempowerments.

Community development occurs when many people recognize they have similar problems and these problems can be overcome through working together. A person in subsidized housing is only a client, 1,000 living in one building can form a tenant management team, and 10,000 working together may be a successful group lobbying for better housing conditions. Three hundred poorly kept houses are a slum, but an organization of 300 homeowners can work to stop banks from ignoring the area and work to improve housing conditions.

Many Americans cherish a belief that individuals succeed or fail through their own efforts and shortcomings. Because many people have bought this myth of rugged individualism, demonstrating the need for collective action is a major difficulty for the community organizer. Those in authority perpetuate the image of the self-reliant person while *they* preserve their own positions through control of their collective organizations, such as business associations, political parties, and lobbying groups. The organizer must work with people until they understand that their problems will not be solved as long as they act in isolation.

To motivate collective action, the community organizer must try to get people involved in solving the problems of most immediate interest to community members. Then, gradually, as successes occur, the organizer can approach other issues and build successes in those areas as well. This bootstrapping approach causes community members to recognize the importance of the collective approach as the way to solve problems. An organizer might start first with a crime-watch detail. As people meet together to talk about crime, they learn they share other problems, such as a need for inexpensive loans to fix up deteriorating houses.

An organizer turns personal concerns into group actions. People usually don't join an organization out of a belief in the importance of collective action; they join because they or a friend got mugged. They don't join because they philosophically disagree with the city redevelopment program; they join because a gentrified shopping mall is being built in their backyard, creating traffic dangers as their children walk to school. Working to oppose crime or to assure the safety of neighborhood children teaches people that they can work together and see the results.

Collective actions build on each other, creating positive cycles of improvement. A safe block from a crime-patrol program means that more people will be out on the street at night, which in turn further increases safety. A neighborhood with a reputation of being a little bit safer than others has a greater demand for apartments, and landlords may be willing to spend a little more money on paint and cleanup. A community-organized fix-up program may increase property values, making banks more willing to lend money for housing rehabilitation, further improving the neighborhood and increasing property values.

The willingness to work collectively is increased as people learn that collective action can increase individual self-confidence. In women's organizations, self-confidence and collective actions go hand in hand:

> It is for these reasons that when women were asked . . . how collective work changed them, they speak of developing new competencies, becoming more self-confident, more willing to express opinions and more tolerant of others' views. (Rothschild, 1987, p. 9)

Individual growth and collective action are mutually supportive.

Acting collectively is the mechanism for solving disempowerment and lack of control. It derives its fundamental power from the fact that individuals can achieve goals together that they cannot achieve alone, and might not even think of trying. When they form groups that decide on agendas and use their political skills, people can counteract system bias. They can solve social problems and enhance their individual skills and sense of self-worth. They can learn to increase their control over their lives and communities.

Through acting collectively, people learn the political nature of dominance and become empowered, giving reality to democracy. They come to understand what a neighborhood is, what city government is like, what social and systematic problems mean. They learn tolerance and cooperation with others. Ultimately, people learn to see the world around them in terms other than self- or family interest and develop a sense of responsibility for the collectivity. For all these reasons, a society with active progressive organizations is a better place to live, not only for the disempowered, but also for the empowered.

5 | Community and Organizations

B oth community and organizations are products of the social solidarity that enable people to work together to combat shared problems. *Community* refers to the bonds that link people, while *democratic organizations* are the means through which people focus power to bring about changes.

CREATING SOCIAL AND POLITICAL SOLIDARITY

Social solidarity is the feeling of mutual support and shared identity that evolves from common membership in a group, organization, or social movement. It is the human "connectedness" that provides the strength and the sense of safety that encourage both social interaction and political engagement (Morgen & Bookman, 1988, p. 19).

Social solidarity can be based on shared religion, ethnicity, or common ancestry. These *ascriptive* characteristics, the personal background that people acquire when they are born into a particular group, provide a base for organizing. People join African-American, Hispanic, Jewish, Catholic, and Polish groups simply because they are African-American, Hispanic, Jewish, Catholic, or Polish.

In building solidarity, these ascriptive factors are important, but ascriptive solidarity is not a necessary precondition for building political solidarity.

The process of being involved in collective action brings about social solidarity from the pleasures of interpersonal encounters or the sense of obligation that people acquire to a group that has benefited them. For example, Hirsch (1986) describes how solidarity develops in block associations. People initially join the associations for their own material self-interest yet, once they have benefited from the group's actions, many stay involved. Why?

Hirsch argues that people who receive help from others feel an obligation to reciprocate and work on issues beyond their immediate concern. A quote from a participant illuminates this idea:

> As long as my conscience lets me, I will help whomever helps me. I have to say that about my conscience, because my head [self-interest] and my heart [generalized participation] might want to do different things. (Hirsch, 1986, p. 378)

Further, when people do work together, they learn that the group can achieve solutions they, as individuals, cannot. The process of working together in an organization increases the bonds of solidarity (in this case, through the norms of reciprocity), consistent with the bootstrapping process. It creates an *emergent solidarity*, a togetherness brought about through sharing experiences (Hirsch, 1986, p. 374).

In discussing labor organizing, Fantasia (1988) explores how emergent solidarity developed among workers as they took action against authorities:

> The organization and maintenance of flying squadrons, food distribution centers, clinics, and communication networks and the mobilization of family members, union and non-union workers . . . were all emergent institutions . . . that at once created and expressed solidarity. (Fantasia, 1988, pp. 21–22)

Later Fantasia describes that

> the workers had defied company authority, at its highest levels, and a strong sense of solidarity had emerged, growing strong at each phase of the action. Solidarity among the workers was not an a priori "fact," but grew out of this interactive process of negotiation between workers in their confrontations with authority. (Fantasia, 1988, p. 88)

Just as it does for union members, struggling together provides solidarity by enabling the poor, the dispossessed, or the disempowered to gain common identity through the act of resistance.

People in solidarity groups invent *symbols* that members in the group understand and that others outside learn to associate with the group. Sometimes these symbols are physical, such as a church or civic center. Sometimes the symbols are actions, such as shared rituals in a religious community. Alternatively, symbols may be slogans or logos that represent the message of the group.

To summarize, solidarity can be found within preexisting social, ethnic, or symbolic communities, or it can be created through the shared experiences of struggling together. In either case, it provides the basis on which both community and organization are built.

COMMUNITY

Community refers both to the place in which organizing occurs and to the group among which organizing is happening. Thus, one can talk about the Westside Community (place) or the community of gays. In either case, community implies *social integration,* that is, the issues and bonds that link people together.

Sociologists describe social integration as based on either *affect (sentiment)* or *interests*. Examples of affective linkages include ethnic ties, nationality, religion of birth, and neighborhood or village ties. Ties based on interest result from individual choices such as with whom to socialize, in which bank to put money, and what hobby to adopt. People are linked by both affect and interest, but the mixture may vary from setting to setting (Fischer, 1977, 1984).

Ties based on interest are shaped, in part, by affective linkages. For example, in a society with ethnic or racial discrimination, affectively linked ethnic groups share an interest in obtaining fair allocation of housing or job opportunities. And the reverse holds, as shown by the emotional bonding of those who have shared a common fight—against a firm, or a redevelopment company, or a noncooperative city government—that brings about an affective sense of group loyalty that far surpasses in scope and intensity the initial shared interest.

By examining different ways people are linked through affect and interest, sociologists have called attention to five major kinds of communities, as well as three important variations. The five types—neighborhoods, solidarity communities, social classes, networks, and communities of interest—differ not only in the extent to which each is based on affect or interest but also whether people must live near one another to be within the community. Strategies for organizing—the particular issues chosen and the possibility for forming coalitions with other community groups—depend on which type of community is involved.

Each type of community provides different problems for organizers and requires different strategies for organizing (A. Hunter & Riger, 1986). We'll first describe these five types of community and their variants and then discuss in more detail how organizing strategies differ in neighborhoods, solidarity communities, and social networks (Table 5-1).

Five Community Types

The first type of community is the *neighborhood,* a connected physical territory. Ties in a neighborhood are based on sharing a life-style, though these ties are often reinforced by common ethnic or cultural backgrounds. People in neighborhoods face similar problems (e.g., toxic waste affects everyone who lives nearby) and have comparable resources (because people who live near one another tend to have similar incomes, education, and jobs).

People can easily leave one neighborhood for a new one. They may not live in a place long enough to develop loyalty to it or a willingness to fight shared problems. People feel less loyalty to their neighborhood than they do to their work, churches, college, sports teams, and relatives. Such areas have been termed *communities of limited liability.* In such communities:

> The individual . . . is likely to demand more from the community than he [sic] will invest. But more significantly, his relation to the community is such that when the community fails to serve his needs, he will withdraw. (Janowitz, 1967, pp. 211–212)

Still, individuals in communities of limited liability may participate in their neighborhoods on an issue-by-issue basis, if their interests are directly affected.

The second type of community is a *solidarity community*. Solidarity communities involve firm, permanent bonds, though whether or not such bonds can be evoked for collective action is uncertain. Solidarity communities come about when people of a common heritage, ethnicity, religion, or language choose to remain together and by definition exclude those of other ethnic or religious groups. Members of a solidarity community define themselves as belonging to that group and feel emotional loyalty to it.

The bonds in solidarity communities are strengthened when its members live in the same neighborhoods because churches and religious schools reinforce communal ties. But solidarity communities can exist over wider territories if people keep up ties through frequent communications, visits, and shared institutions, such as foreign language newspapers, ethnic restaurants, grocery stores, and churches.

TABLE 5–1
Contrasting Forms of Social Integration

Form of Community	Types of Social and Geographic Integration	Bases for Membership	Examples
Neighborhood	Integration based on geographic proximity and on issues facing people within one geographic area	Membership determined by place of residency	Mission District in San Francisco, Hyde Park in Chicago, Adams-Morgan in Washington, DC—city areas that share a primary school and a shopping area
Community of limited liability	People live near one another, but that rarely is sufficient to create social bonds	People who live nearby choose to join together on issues that particularly benefit them	People protesting busing to a neighborhood school; members of a homeowners' association involved in a zoning fight
Solidarity community	People who share a common heritage whether ethnic, national, cultural or religious, that promotes shared values	People are born into solidarity communities, though the degree of identification varies by individual	A Hispanic barrio in Los Angeles, the Greek Orthodox in the Chicago area, Hasidic Jews throughout the world
Traditional community	A solidarity community where people are co-resident so social control is possible	People are born into such communities; opting out often requires moving away	A traditional rural village before urbanization of a society and the introduction of mass communications
Social class	Integration based on common life circumstances as defined by income and ownership of property	Economic and work status determine class membership	Upper class—those with several generations of inherited wealth Working class—individuals who earn their living without owning the means of production

TABLE 5–1
continued

Form of Community	Types of Social and Geographic Integration	Bases for Membership	Examples
Social network	Integration based on shared interests	Individuals choose to be involved, but personal background factors influence the possibilities to choose from	The aging network—people throughout the country working to improve conditions for the elderly
			Environmental networks—those individuals who work on environmental issues
Latent interest group	People who share common problems or interests but who are not yet linked together	Individuals must be made aware of the common problems they face	People adversely affected by environmental pollution who are not yet fighting polluters; white- and pink-collar workers not yet unionized
Community of interest	Integration based on a shared understanding of the importance of collective action	Individuals choose involvement after understanding an issue	Successful community and progressive organizations

Solidarity communities are defined by shared customs, holidays, traditions, and food tastes. (Courtesy Department of Housing and Urban Development)

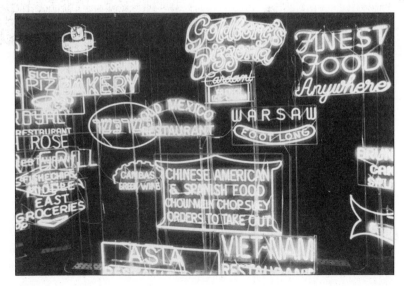

In some cases, social solidarity is imposed on a group by others. For example, the most important forms of solidarity communities today are those based on ethnicity and race, defined by surname and color. A person of color with an African origin is treated as ethnically and racially black, no matter whether the person's family was originally from Kenya, South Africa, Haiti, Jamaica, or elsewhere.

Sometimes people come to accept the designations given to them. Different Slavic groups, who were antagonistic to one another in Europe, accepted a common Slavic identity in the United States (Kornblum, 1974). Today, it is possible that a common Spanish language will create a solidarity community among the highly divergent groups from Cuba, Mexico, Puerto Rico, and other Spanish-speaking countries.

A traditional community is a variant of a solidarity community in which people are linked by affective bonds strongly reinforced by shared residential locations. Membership occurs because people are born in a particular place, have generations of common kinship ties, and share cultural and religious beliefs. With the possible exceptions of isolated villages in the American Southwest or Alaska, traditional communities are not important for present-day organizing. In fact, organizing efforts can be weakened by a belief in the myth of the utopian traditional community in which everyone knows everyone else and everyone is willing to share and help. In reality, traditional communities are often stultifying to personal growth and capacity building because the group rigidly defines how individuals should respond to varying social situations.

The third type of community is *social class*. Social class is more a potential than an actual basis for integration in the United States, as studies show that most Americans deny class distinctions and consider themselves middle class. Social class is primarily based on how income is earned and whether an individual owns more than a trivial amount of property. Membership in a common social class yields similar attitudes and levels of power for its members.

Social class also defines many important conditions of one's life. For example, there is a marked reduction in life expectancy for those in lower classes, reflecting differences in the heaviness of work, the danger of occupations, the increased impact of crime, and poorer health care. Social class perpetuates itself because members develop shared understandings about the importance of education, what types of jobs people can reasonably expect to get, and the appropriateness of participating in public or collective activities (Beeghley, 1989; Gilbert & Kahl, 1982).

Social class would appear to provide a basis for organizing because working class people share diminished life opportunities and must undertake dangerous labor. To the extent that working class people have union experience, they may have worked together to solve common problems. Yet, there is a gap—a *trench*—between work, which primarily defines social class, and home, which provides the setting for broader political and social participation. This trench has made it difficult for workers to perceive how class issues affect their home life (Katznelson, 1981).

Fortunately for organizers, people do recognize specialized linkages within *social networks,* the fourth type of community. A network is a pattern of linked relationships across which help and information flow on a particular issue. Network ties can be based on either shared affect or shared interest or both. Childhood friends who share similar interests are more likely to maintain contact than old friends whose interests have grown apart.

A plant closing united labor and community members in different solidarity groupings to defend an economically threatened neighborhood. (Thom Clark)

A network can be formal, in the sense that the names of members are publicly announced and the network lasts over time. Sometimes, however, networks can be informal, coming together only when needed, with no stable or announced membership. For example, a support network may form among old friends and relatives to help someone who is unemployed. In between in formality, duration, and publicness are networks of people such as those who suffer from acquired immune deficiency syndrome (AIDS) or who have an alcoholic spouse.

Networks usually link people to people, but sometimes they also link organizations through those individuals in each organization who know each other. Social service agencies are often connected this way to provide assistance to each other and to clients in a particular issue area.

Networks based on shared interests are often easier to organize than those based on affect. Networks composed of individuals who want to save the whales, or reduce utility rates, or achieve safe shelters for battered women are natural communities, often eager to take some collective action. They may need some additional information or advice, but they do not need to be shown that they have common interests. Not all people who share interests know that they do. Latent interest groups are potential communities. Bringing together members of latent interest groups is no easy task. The organizer's role is to help people see their shared interests and the possibilities for joint action.

A quandary faces organizers when people do not articulate their beliefs or interests. Should an organizer work to bring about ends that he or she thinks are in people's interest (Isaac, 1987, p. 97)? Imposing outcomes on people, even for their own good, is clearly not an empowering procedure. Organizers should create environments that encourage open discussion of group interests but refrain from manipulating people to follow the organizers' beliefs about the interests of the group.

The fifth type of community is as much a goal as an existing type. In a *community of interest* people recognize a range of shared problems and act together to resolve them. Working together increases affective bonds, strengthening the willingness and ability of group members to continue joint actions. A community of interest is the product of community organizing.

Organizing in Neighborhoods and Solidarity Communities

Of the five types of community, three are especially important for organizing efforts— namely, neighborhood, solidarity community, and network. People living near each other face common problems, solidarity linkages allow the organizer to build on pre-existing bonds, while social networks link individuals with shared interests that can provide a base for collective actions.

Neighborhoods.   The urban neighborhood, the historic site for community work, remains an active forum for organizing activities. Though all neighborhoods are small areas where people live within easy walking distance of each other, neighborhoods serve different needs for their residents. For example, in Detroit (D. Warren 1975, 1977) six different types of neighborhoods served distinct needs for their inhabitants (see Table 5–2).

The possibilities for organizing differ depending both on what type of neighborhood it is as well as the extent to which people recognize the neighborhood as an identifiable place. Status communities are more likely to organize for the purpose of denying access to the poor or minorities, an activity that progressive organizers should avoid. Mutual aid communities provide an active base for developing organizations that carry out social service functions. To the extent that people try to use a neighborhood as a forum for interpersonal influence, it is more likely that one can find leaders and activists willing to carry out collective activities. When people see a neighborhood as a place for social activities, they may be willing to organize block parties or create a place for teens to gather. Being able to get together for social activities provides a base for sharing felt needs that could lead to subsequent organizing.

Sociological studies show that in large cities there is only modest contact between neighbors and limited knowledge about neighbors, a finding that questions the neighborhood as a basis for organizing. However, potential local leaders are not necessarily those with the highest degree of affective integration into the community. People who are culturally and socially integrated into neighborhoods are less likely to become politically involved (Crenson, 1980, 1983). Frequent interaction with neighbors and warm interpersonal relations are often not the basis for building community organization.

Fortunately for organizing, some neighborhoods do provide a base for organizing. First, neighborhoods that have a history of active, collective activity attract people who

TABLE 5–2
Neighborhoods and Their Function

Neighborhood Type	Functions Served by the Neighborhood
Status arena	Through the choice of a physical neighborhood, people assert their social status. For example, the rich live in exclusive enclaves that sometimes are entered only through private guarded roads.
Interpersonal influence	Neighborhoods are social arenas in which communication of information takes place orally. A neighbor who is "in the know" finds out "what is happening," then discusses this with others.
Mutual aid	Help is given to people who live nearby. Such help is usually restricted to small exchanges such as advice on yard work, a loan of a hammer, or in emergencies rushing someone to a hospital.
Organizational base	The neighborhood provides the setting in which people interested in organizational participation have a chance to become involved.
Interaction arena	Through visiting and other forms of socializing, people try to overcome the depersonalizing aspects of the city.
Social context	The neighborhood provides individuals with reference groups. That is, people learn what behaviors are expected through observing and imitating others.

Sources: Adapted from Warren 1975, 1977.

wish to follow such a life-style. For example, one such area is the Five Oaks neighborhood in Dayton, Ohio. Active community organizations form

> an "ideological community". . . . That is, residents choose the neighborhood in part because of its urbaness and diversity and because they consciously seek a neighborhood that will serve as a community. (T. J. Majka & Donnelly, 1988, p. 158)

Organizers can find a ready base for collective activity in such communities.

Second, older, inner-city black communities used to provide a fertile base for organizing activity. Racially imposed isolation and poverty made people more dependent on each other. A generation ago, studies showed that black neighborhoods were both socially and politically integrated.

More recently, the situation appears to be changing for the worse (Wacquant & Wilson, 1989; Wilson, 1987). Upper-income minorities move out of the poorer ghettos. Black neighborhoods in the city have split into two types of residential community. The first is an economically poor but not destitute area that remains rich in networks and associations, though cut off from the outside society. This area provides a rich base for organizing. The second is a *hyperghetto,* which has been emptied out of traditional organizations and institutions. A hyperghetto is a black neighborhood that has lost much of its organizational strength—the "pulpit and the press," for instance, have virtually collapsed as collective agencies—as it has become increasingly marginal economically; its activities are no longer structured around an internal and relatively autonomous social space that duplicates the institutional structure of the larger society and provides basic minimal resources for social mobility. (Wacquant & Wilson, 1989, p. 15)

These communities most in need of collective actions to combat shared problems provide the least basis for organizing.

From the organizer's perspective, urban neighborhoods are difficult but not impossible to organize. First, such neighborhoods may contain many social networks based on shared interest that provide a motivation for getting people to work together, even if neighbors do not know each other. Second, it is often the alienated rather than the socially integrated who are the leaders of local political action. As Crenson describes:

The residents who do make these contributions are often people who exhibit some of the symptoms of the loss of community . . . informal deliberations about matters of community concern occur in an atmosphere of neighborly tension, not neighborly solidarity. (Crenson, 1983, p. 154)

The same process of emergent solidarity that builds worker solidarity occurs in neighborhoods, as people start working together in an interest-based cause. Geographic propinquity makes it easy for people with shared interests to work together. As they work together, they create the missing solidarity.

As an example, Crenshaw and St. John (1989) examined neighborhoods whose residents were not personally close but were collectively facing extensive housing renovation programs. People joined organizations to protect their housing investment (a shared interest), leading to a reinforcing cycle of organization building and neighborhood identification. "Expending time, energy, and money for a neighborhood cause and developing a sense of collective identity should induce strong allegiance" (Crenshaw & St. John, 1989, p. 417).

Organizers need to focus on helping to motivate a few dedicated activists who can get the initial activities going. Once underway, community action can create collective neighborhood identity and make further organizing easier.

Solidarity Communities.   Solidarity communities are based on ethnic or racial groups that share ties of history, culture, language, and religion. Organizing in solidarity communities has advantages and disadvantages. On the positive side, cultural pride and ethnic identity keep people involved in community organizations even when they are unlikely to obtain immediate material benefits. Another plus is that religious and ethnic groups can use their own history and culture to forge symbols that can boost pride and facilitate organizing. On the negative side, solidarity communities are often conservative and may be hostile to outsiders. Solidarity communities may organize to preserve a church or the physical integrity of the neighborhood, but the goal of organizing in solidarity communities is often to exclude or denigrate people of different beliefs and backgrounds. Building community on ethnic pride makes it very difficult to carry actions over into the broader, multiethnic, multiracial society. A society where all the solidarity communities were organized might consist of warring ethnicities and races, rather than cooperative and empowered neighborhoods.

If members of a solidarity community show interest in issues other than hostility to other groups, they can be easier to organize than other groups. Solidarity groups create shared symbols from a set of dramatic historic events—pogroms in Russia and the Diaspora for the Jews, slavery and the civil rights movement for African Americans, Wounded Knee and forced migrations for Native Americans—that act to reinforce identity with the community. Organizers can use these symbols that reflect the shared history and suffering of a group to communicate that experience to the rest of the world. Traditions can be molded to translate the crippling humiliation of the past into a feeling of self-respect. It is the role of the organizer to encourage stories and art that make a history of injustice comprehensible to the descendants of those who suffered, while suggesting what needs to be done now to improve the group's circumstances.

Many groups need to define their cultural solidarity in opposition to the dominant culture. Padilla describes the development of Puerto Rican ideology of cultural difference as an approach to building such solidarity:

> An essential feature of this ideology is the rejection of "white definitions" and myths of subordination, and their replacement by Puerto Rican definitions. . . . This ideology defines Puerto Ricans as possessing precisely those human qualities in which dominant white America is so morally deficient, and some of the very qualities by which white America defines this subordinate group are transformed from denigration to approbation. (Padilla, 1987, p. 65)

Symbols and traditions of solidarity can be used directly to help organizing. By forcing museums to return the skeletons of ancestors and cultural artifacts, Native Americans have combined cultural symbolism with organized power. Their successful protests convey that white society has treated them badly in the past and that that time is over. Cultural solidarity became a tool of empowerment.

Traditional communities can be relatively easy to organize on the affective issues that define community membership but very difficult to get moving on broader social problems. A study of the Chinese community in New York city shows the relative ease of organizing a solidarity community on issues that threaten the whole community but the difficulty of getting any significant attention to other issues.

> The CCBA [Chinese Community Business Association] decided that the community should protest the city's closing of the local police Fifth Precinct. An order went out; every store in the main Chinatown area was closed, and 20,000 Chinese turned out for the demonstration. As a result, the city government quickly rescinded the decision. (Kwong, 1987, p. 93)

But Kwong argues that under this same informal political structure, "working people will not get a fair settlement: in a labor/management dispute, the Chinese elite will side with management" (Kwong, 1987, p. 95).

Another example of the strengths and weaknesses of relying on solidarity linkages for organizing is found in the role of the black church. The church has been a core part of black communities and black identity and has been a crucially important part of the civil rights movement. At the same time, precisely because it is a church, it is sometimes acts in ways that are antiprogressive. Many preachers, for example, have taken stands against gay rights (Hooks, 1989, p. 123).

Solidarity organizing can also encourage racial and ethnic exclusiveness:

> Many neighborhoods that have been successfully organized are segregated and racist.
> When white neighborhoods fight blockbusters and panic peddlers they often do so not
> only to preserve neighborhood stability, but also to keep minorities out. (Peterman,
> 1988, p. 8)

For example, in Chicago, Save our Neighborhood/Save our City (SON/SOC) developed as a coalition of white ethnic organizations that build parish-based, church-linked community groups (P. M. Green 1988). The organization works to preserve the quality of the neighborhood, fight crime, end real estate abuses, and assure that downtown development also benefits the residential communities. Despite these laudable goals, the group has been accused of building white ethnic and neighborhood solidarity based on racial antagonisms (P. M. Green, 1988, p. 25).

A second problem is that it is difficult to extend organizing based on one ethnic group to another. For example, the United Neighborhood Organization (UNO) has organized Mexican Hispanics in the Pilsen neighborhood in Chicago (Cruz, 1988, p. 18). But UNO has been unable to extend the model from Mexicans to Puerto Ricans.

> In 1985 UNO did try to organize Puerto Ricans and form another parish-based UNO chapter in the Puerto Rican neighborhoods. . . . But Puerto Rican leaders vehemently complained that UNO was an outsider. (Cruz, 1988, p. 19)

There are many possible approaches to dealing with the special difficulties posed by organizing within solidarity communities. One is to reinterpret the traditions so that a broader social response to problems is possible. A second is to refocus racist issues on more constructive projects.

The first approach is helping to reinterpret the tradition so that broader social and political responses are possible. For example, when clergy argue that the bible condemns homosexuals, activists can emphasize other elements of the tradition, such as supporting the outcast or loving all of God's creation. Mutual aid associations are an important part of Hispanic culture. Such groups provide help in emergencies or contribute financially to important religious and cultural ceremonies. An organizer can reinterpret this tradition to provide a base for broader, collective actions, for example, combating economic inequality.

A second possible strategy is to link issues such as housing, which may be based on a desire to keep other groups out, with neighborhood revitalization, which is less likely to provoke racial polarization. Instead of moving from one racial issue to another, a group can go from housing, to rehabilitation, to neighborhood redevelopment, just as logical a progression. The organizer can show members who are interested in housing the implications for neighborhood revitalization. Many different groups live in areas facing neighborhood decline, so linkages between such groups may become necessary and possible (Peterman, 1988, p. 1).

To summarize, organizing within solidarity communities can create special problems that might defeat progressive goals. If organizing reinforces a traditional structure that does not allow widespread participation, or facilitates organizing in one community for the purpose of keeping out other groups, the organizing cannot be considered successful. But when organizing within solidarity communities works, it can transform alienated and depressed groups into dynamic community organizations. The translation of historical experience into acceptable symbols can make people feel better about themselves and less willing to accept the negative images that others impose on them. These are important steps toward empowerment.

Organizing Along Social Networks

The primary way of building an action organization today is to organize among people who share a common problem, whether filling potholes in the streets, housing the homeless, or keeping drinking water uncontaminated.

Thinking about networks forces an organizer to determine which issues cause what people to join together. Rather than assume that neighbors care about crime, an organizer learns which neighbors have talked with, worked with, or otherwise interacted with whom on this issue. Network analysis enables one to locate those with shared interests in such issues as environmentalism, ageism, and feminism across neighborhood boundaries and solidarity groupings.

An organizer needs to pay attention to both issue networks and liberated networks. *Issue networks* link persons interested in a particular topic, almost irrespective of their feelings on other topics. Groups that focus on feminist issues, environmental preservation, or problems of the elderly or the handicapped are examples of issue networks. In contrast, *liberated networks* involve a range of relationships between people, some based on issues, others based on kinship, friendship, work, or church ties. Liberated networks are the interpersonal social ties along which help, information, or support might flow.

People who share beliefs on specific issues are called into action along issue networks. For example, after the Supreme Court ruling that weakened abortion rights, organizations like Planned Parenthood, the National Abortion Rights Action League, People for the American Way, and the American Civil Liberties Union sent out mailings to individuals throughout the country to activate issue networks to support freedom of choice.

Networks also provide the contacts through which people help one another on more immediate problems. For example, cooperative workplaces, such as artist cooperatives and feminist firms, communicate with networks of progressive economic organizations that loan money only to projects that are consistent with a progressive ideology. The potential support from such networks is seen in the worker-owned manufacturing cooperatives in the Basque region in Spain that have competed successfully in a capitalist world, in part because they provide each other knowledge and capital, as well as purchase goods and services from one another (Whyte & Whyte, 1988).

Issue networks need not have a geographic focus, but sometimes they do. For example, in San Francisco, networks among gays linked people concerned with gay rights and those who understood the local political structure. The result was a community organization that was very effective at the local level (Castells, 1983, p. 140).

Sometimes people may share common problems but be unwilling to take an active role because powerlessness and a feeling of shame breed a denial of the problem rather than a willingness to join in issue networks.

> To be perceived as disabled is typically to be seen as helpless and incompetent, and many individuals with physical impairments seek to disassociate themselves from disability. (Scotch, 1988, p. 161)

To create an issue network among the disabled, a change in perception was required.

> A redefinition of disability was required—one that treated disability as a label for a group of people who had the potential for political action and who were unfairly excluded from mainstream social institutions on the basis of their physical or mental impairments. (Scotch, 1988, p. 163)

The issue that linked those in the networks was not the disability itself but, rather, the unfair exclusion from everyday activities of those capable of participating.

Issue networks are important especially as they link together the original activist core in a progressive organization. But how do you reach out to others to expand power, gain resources, or in general learn about problems? Part of the answer is to use liberated networks, the interpersonal bonds that exist even in a modern metropolis in which neighbors do not know one another (Wellman & Leighton, 1979). Liberated networks are found

> in the extensive informal helping networks, in the ad hoc development of coalitions for local purposes, in the strength of sociometric ties, in the meaningful associations within a religious group, an ethnic group, or other groups with common bonds of interest. (R. Warren, 1978, p. 419)

Membership in liberated networks enables people to solve problems by working with others with whom they have no direct connection. A person may need counseling for a child in trouble and have no knowledge of how to get help. Talking to people at church or in a bowling league, he or she learns the name of an organized support group. Networks empower people by putting the connections of other people at the disposal of those in need.

Liberated networks emphasize the variety of ties that connect people, either loose, with few linkages, or tight, with many shared interests. People who are tightly linked through common background, education, or membership in solidarity communities are likely to share skills and knowledge. As a result, they tend to know the same people and repeat the same solutions, whether or not they work.

Sometimes for successful development, people need to escape the confines of their immediate social networks and make contact with others who have different approaches and different skills. These connections can be made through casual acquaintances, the loose ties of social networks (Granovetter, 1973). People in working class communities are unlikely to understand how to block leveraged buy outs, but the friend of a cousin who is an investment banker may be able to provide the information needed to combat this threat to their livelihood.

Community organizations can use liberated networks to announce meetings or get additional funds for the organization. If a small core of members activate their networks, at the Parent–Teacher Association (PTA), at work, at church, and at sports meets, information spreads very quickly. Similar networks can be used to collect contributions or sell shopping bags, cookies, or other items.

Networks generally link individuals, but sometimes they link organizations. Newspapers may be linked with stores that discriminate in hiring, because they accept ads from these businesses and are afraid to offend them by covering stories about pressures for equal opportunity hiring. Banks, insurance companies, and realtors may cooperate with each other in withdrawing resources from communities they have decided are not good risks. The insurance company stops writing fire policies; the bank stops issuing mortgages and business loans; and real estate agents steer customers to other neighborhoods. Such cooperation is enhanced if one business has a representative on the board of trustees of the other business. Alternatively, business owners may meet through the Chamber of Commerce or social clubs and decide to cooperate (Feagin, 1988; Galaskiewicz, 1979; F. Hunter, 1980; Turk, 1977). Facing this wall of opposition to investing in the neighborhood, community businesses may fail, and neighborhood deterioration may accelerate.

Understanding the linkages between organizations that oppose community organizing can be helpful in devising strategies. If a newspaper depends on local businesses for advertising, the community group should not depend on them for a publicity campaign. If the organizer discovers a link between realtors, bankers, and insurers that is harming the neighborhood, the organization might pressure the weakest link, assuming that the organization that is being pressured can successfully pressure the other two.

We have discussed five major concepts of community and some of the strategies of organizing that are associated with each. Beyond specific strategies, what do these different and overlapping concepts mean to the organizer?

First, organizers can build on the existing community. For example, the linkages that hold together solidarity communities might create enough trust to enable people to work together. An ethnically based church provides a good location to begin organizing in a solidarity community because people already trust the church and see it as a collective property. If well-developed networks are already in place, community organizations can use them to recruit members and to publicize events.

Second, community provides a target to work toward. If a community lacks helping networks that focus on individual problems, community organizations can help build such networks. Community organizers try to develop a community among potential activists where the initial level of solidarity is too low to encourage collective action or where the group involved needs to reinterpret its past to create some group pride that will facilitate empowerment. A primary activity of organizers is to make neighbors aware of shared problems, turning latent communities into communities of interest.

However, social integration is a means to bring about change and not an end in itself.

ORGANIZATION

Working in progressive organizations is a way to combat helplessness and disempowerment. Progressive organizations provide the continuity of opposition that is lacking in spontaneous collective actions. A riot and burning (unorganized collective action) might convince a city government that housing conditions are poor. The official response might be a promise to build better housing. But only through a permanent organization that can continually lobby city hall for better housing, check existing housing for violations, and run a housing rehabilitation program will there be long-term positive outcomes for the collectivity.

But what are organizations? To paraphrase sociological definitions, "organizations are goal-directed, boundary maintaining activity systems that exist on a relatively continuous basis" (Aldrich 1979, pp. 4–5; R. Hall, 1982, p. 33). *Goal directed* means that the organization has a purpose and a technology (the knowledge base) for accomplishing that purpose. *Boundary maintaining* means that there are membership criteria. An *activity system* is the means for accomplishing a collective purpose, whether manufacturing a product or coordinating people to demonstrate in front of the offices of a company that is polluting the environment. Finally, organizations should be long lasting, even if that means maintaining a skeleton form to provide continuity between major, collective activities (Milofsky, 1988, pp. 202–203). Community organizations are a way of translating solidarity into action for community change.

What Organizations Do for Community Organizing

Organizations make community action more effective for many reasons: They create power, they provide continuity, they amass and use expertise, and they can react quickly to changing events or negotiations. They can sustain a battle over a period of months or even years.

Organizations Create Power.   To the authorities, organizations represent power because they can gather resources and use them and because public officials respect large numbers of committed voters concerned about a particular issue. At the same time, organizations help individuals who might be intimidated to stand up and fight back. It might seem difficult for an individual to fight city hall, but a group of individuals can make a real battle.

Organizations Provide Continuity.   Organizations can sustain action over a period of time, either providing services or keeping pressure on authorities. To assure that neighborhoods receive their share of development funds (and not simply promises), someone must monitor fund dispersal over time; to run a day-care center, someone must take care of children every day; to provide jobs for people who have not received appropriate education, someone must run a job retraining program while maintaining contact with employers. To fight housing discrimination, someone must be ready to receive complaints and act on them, whether the action is to attend a hearing or to organize a rent strike.

Organizational continuity allows for long-term projects and ongoing services. Long-lived organizations can negotiate for changes and monitor and implement the results. They can close the power gap between business and community organizations by continual pressure to set the public agenda. Continuity allows for planning, for anticipation of new projects, and for quick response to changing situations.

Organizations Garner Expertise.   Organizations accumulate the expertise and experience needed to accomplish locally determined goals, especially when individual members might not have the time to do so. Many working people cannot afford the time to monitor government meetings, to learn how to set up a detailed budget, or to shop for the best prices for the cooperative. Organizations collect enough resources so that members can also hire experts when needed. In this sense, a professional community organizer is one of those experts, a person hired to do the tasks others would do if they had the time.

Expertise is also acquired through experience that can be shared among people to allow them to avoid the mistakes of their predecessors. Describing poor people's movements in St. Louis, Lipsitz argues:

> Those drawn into . . . protests provided the cadre organization for other struggles. They engaged in . . . "organizational learning"—a process of struggle in which each stage of contestation creates new resources for the next one. Individuals and groups adapt to events and crises on the basis of immediate needs and interests, but they also draw on the lessons of the past, on the ways their previous encounters with politics educated them about what to do in the present. (Lipsitz, 1988, p. 165)

Organizational members share a history that guides current actions. This expertise is acquired "on the job" as people work in and for the organization.

Organizations React Quickly.   Sometimes the power of an organization becomes apparent by the speed with which it enables people to respond to problems. Neighborhoods with existing organizations react quickly to problems that would be ignored elsewhere (Henig, 1982, p. 170). Issue-based organizations respond quickly to persuade the president, the governor, the mayor, or representatives to take the action they want. Sometimes, organizations must bring pressure to bear immediately by contacting their members to mount a letter, telephone, or telegram campaign while the issue is hot. The power of the American Association of Retired People lies in its ability to quickly get members all over the country to write or phone their representatives.

The Variety of Community and Progressive Organizations

Over the years, there have been an incredible variety of community organizations. The lives of some have been brief, while others have lasted for generations. Some focus on building a sense of community in a particular geographic area; others deal with issues that confront people throughout the nation. Most people are familiar with community organizations that are noisy and conflict oriented. These gain the headlines, but the majority of community organizations work quietly to produce services.

A Classification of Community Organizations.   The great variety of community organizations makes more sense if similar organizations are grouped together. To do that, we categorize organizations according to two criteria. The first is the type of problems they face; the second is the importance of government as it affects the strategies of the organization.

The problems faced by community organizations vary from very specific, concrete matters of personal or economic interest to the more abstract, though equally important, concerns of civil rights, civil liberties, or social justice. Demands made by members of a tenants' union for keeping rents within reason in one apartment building illustrate the concrete, economic end of this continuum. At the other extreme might be the actions taken by the American Civil Liberties Union to protect civil liberties by defending the symbolic speech of a flag burner. In practice, distinctions between concrete issues of self-interest and more abstract issues of civil rights and social justice are rarely this clear. A group seeking to end sexism on campus may also be working for social justice, but in doing so improve the chance of female students to get scholarships and recommendations to better jobs.

How much or how little it interacts with government is a major defining characteristic of any community organization. At one extreme, there are progressive community organizations such as in Santa Monica, California, that have themselves become the government through winning elections. At the other extreme, communitarian organizations that try to achieve economic self-sufficiency in some isolated mountain area are mostly independent of governmental agencies. The level of government involvement may vary from issue to issue or from one set of tasks to another. A neighborhood housing organization might seek a grant from local government to help it improve the conditions of local apartment buildings, though most of its time is spent in managing its properties, regardless of governmental action.

There are distinctions among organizations that deal with government. *Pressure* organizations work within conventional rules to persuade politicians and bureaucrats to change their policies. In contrast, *protest* organizations work outside of the conventional rules, because they question the legitimacy of the rules. A sit-in for civil rights is a form of protest; lobbying to strengthen the law preserving endangered species is a form of pressure. Organizations that provide services in conjunction with government are divided into coproduction and partnership organizations.

Coproduction organizations perform public services but generally accept the agendas proposed by others. For example, during the era of the community mental health movement, organizations worked with government to provide needed services on a local level. In *partnership* organizations, community members define what problems to deal with; that is, they set the agenda but work with government, particularly to obtain funds. Neighborhood housing organizations that decide which properties to repair typify partnership organizations. Government might provide the capital, but the task is determined and managed by the organization's members.

Putting the characteristics of community organizations—the issue focus and the relationship toward government—together into one classification scheme, leads to four types of community organizations: social equity, self-help, community identity, and social justice (Table 5–3).

Social Equity Organizations. *Social equity* organizations pressure governmental agencies to provide individualized benefits to their members. Welfare rights organizations sought during the 1960s and 1970s to pressure government to provide adequate

TABLE 5–3
Typology of Community and
Progressive Organizations

Importance of government	Issue Focus	
	More abstract—Social justice, civil rights, and liberties	More concrete personal benefits, economic gains
High importance	Social justice	Social equity
Less importance	Community identity	Self-help

social welfare payments. Organizations of the aged, from the Gray Panther movement to the American Association of Retired Persons, have worked to gain economic benefits for the elderly such as improvements in social security and Medicare.

Self-Help.   *Self-help* organizations, too, attempt to provide economic benefits to their membership, but here the role of government is much less. Cooperatively owned housing or not-for-profit or cooperative businesses are self-help organizations that tend to have little to do with government. Some community-controlled health facilities are independent, such as women's health cooperatives.

Some self-help groups provide social rather than economic benefits. Some deal with spouse or alcohol abuse, others provide support groups for those with cancer or heart disease. Such groups typically have little to do with government.

Community Identity.   The goal of *community identity* organizations is to work with people to develop a sense of collective identity or pride, which later provides a basis for more concrete actions. The folk and food festivals put on by neighborhood organizations, such as the Hill in St. Louis (Schoenberg, 1980) or ethnic art fairs at local cultural centers (Adams & Goldbard, 1980) typify such activities. Though most neighborhood organizations are stimulated by specific problems such as the marked decline in property values that preceded the formation of the Edgewater Association in Chicago (Marciniak, 1981), an early step in building any neighborhood organization is getting people to identify with the locale.

The basis of much of the subsequent political activity of Hispanic groups in the Southwest was a strong identity as an oppressed minority. The early homosexual rights movement was focused on creating a sense of community identity and pride: The process of "coming out of the closet" represents the development of a prideful identity, which was later the basis of successful community organizing.

Social Justice.   *Social justice* organizations pressure government on broader issues that affect many people at once such as increasing civil rights and civil liberties or protecting the environment. Civil rights groups that protested to gain equal access to public facilities, equal opportunity for education, and the right to vote without threat or harassment is one good example of social justice organization.

Effective organizations grow out of community bonds. Recognizing this relationship, a development organization in a Hispanic community celebrates community with wall art. (Courtesy TTB)

The individuals involved in most of these protests were seeking the rights for themselves, but social justice organizations often take on symbolic cases that have benefits for many others who may not be members of the progressive organizations. The lobbying and litigation carried out by Ralph Nader's organizations, Common Cause, or the American Civil Liberties Union to make government information generally available or to defend the political speech rights of radicals, provide social justice for all, not just for members.

Though at one time an organization is probably performing either a social justice, social equity, community identity, or self-help task, the focus of organizations moves from one category to another. Self-help efforts turn into quests for social justice. For example, organizations of the handicapped formed to provide needed services then pressured Congress to change laws to guarantee civil rights for the disabled. Community organizations evolve and have to remain flexible to continue as a force for progressive change.

What Can Go Wrong?

Community organizations are indispensable. They leverage political power and provide some permanence, expertise, and rapid response. But they can go seriously awry and not accomplish anything. The experts hired by the organization can end up determining its policies, thus defeating the empowerment ideal. The organization can become a forum in which members ventilate their anger at the establishment, then do nothing. Worse yet, leaders may express their opinions independent of community needs or membership beliefs. If an organization does not reflect the needs of community members in providing answers to everyday problems, organizing efforts are wasted.

Balancing Mass Participation and Effectiveness.   In building community organizations, there are choices made that involve balancing contradictory goals. Organizers want their organizations to be effective, but they also want large numbers of people to participate in the decision making. Professional organizers, consultants, and other experts can aid an organization and make it appear more successful, but democratic development cannot take place if professionals, even professional organizers, do the work for the community. If they take too large a role, community members will attribute success to the leadership and not to their own efforts. On the other hand, successful development is unlikely if people in the community lack the knowledge to take appropriate and timely action and bring in no assistance.

Part of the reason that the tension between participation and effectiveness occurs is that early organizational successes increase the chance of broader community participation, but early successes are most likely when organizations are controlled by experts. A second reason the problem occurs is that active community organizations can be led by a few concerned individuals who work hard on the issues and care the most about the outcome. They bring an intensity and concern that others might lack. However, the harder they work, the greater their tendency to make many of the decisions by themselves.

In the short run, concentration of power makes the organization appear successful. Limiting information about protest tactics to a few leaders can prevent leaks and stop the target from planning effective counter measures. When bargaining with business or government agencies has reached a stage of mutual accommodation, a limited number of people working one-on-one can make the best progress. A mass organizational meeting can spend all night arguing points that a few people can quickly settle.

There is a need to balance participation with effectiveness and to encourage dedication in organizational leaders but avoid the egoism of leadership.

The egoism of leadership occurs when leaders hold a mistaken belief that sincere concern and dedication gives them the right to decide for the organization. For example, Brill (1971) describes how leaders of a rent strike virtually ignored the tenants in planning their actions. These leaders strongly felt the need for the strike, feared that some tenants would not cooperate, but lacked enough respect for the very people for whom the organization had been created to consult with them. As a consequence, the strike failed.

In addition to reducing participation and leading to the failure of particular campaigns, the egoism of leadership can lead to the demise of the organization itself. If the original leaders of an organization take too much of the decision making and implementation on themselves, once these founders lose interest, the organization collapses.

Progressive organizations are not owned by their founders.

Yet the reality of most organizational life, especially in voluntary organizations, is that a limited number of people do much of the work. How can those who founded the organization have sufficient self-confidence to try to motivate others into action and attack established authority without at the same time developing the belief that they are always right?

Professional organizers, like organizational leaders, have to avoid taking a dominant role. Instead, they need to teach community members how to organize and provide advice on tactics. This may be difficult, because the professional organizer is most active in the early stages of organizational action, when community people must be convinced that the organization can do something before they will participate. Without immediate successes, the organization and the idea of organizing lose credibility. The danger is that early successes of the organization will be attributed to the organizers's skills and thereby fail to lead to a sense of increased community empowerment. To combat this problem, training schools for organizers emphasize how to work behind the scenes and teach local leaders to take active roles. Yet even here, there is a thin line between unobtrusive guidance and subtle, undemocratic manipulation.

A skillful organizer has to learn to move in and out of the expert role, being the teacher sometimes and the student at other times. An organizer has to be able to present technical material in a convincing way without creating the impression that the technical material cannot be questioned and analyzed. If an organizer argues that community members must question authority, then resents members' challenges to him or herself, the membership will not learn to question authority.

If the local organization determines the goals and the organizer helps to implement them, what happens if the goals are antithetical to the values and beliefs of the organizer? If the organizer feels that housing conditions are a more central problem than crime, but community members of the organization are more concerned about crime, the organizer should defer to the beliefs of the membership.

An organization however, can have more fundamental value conflicts with the organizer on issues such as racial, ethnic, or sexual equality. Some of these problems can be dealt with in the original contract hiring the organizer. For example, ACORN organizers must "inform the ACORN board that a problem exists" if "any leadership action [leads to] racial, ethnic, sexual or other exclusion" (Staples, 1984, p. 13). We think that the organizer should be prepared to quit the position and move on. In the 1930s, Alinsky could work in the Back of the Yards in Chicago to organize among poor blue-collar workers. In a later era, the same organization was seen as encouraging racial exclusion; we highly doubt that during that later period Alinsky would return to the community.

The Collectivist-Democratic Solution

If community organizations pattern their structures and decision making carefully, they can generally avoid many of the problems that arise from the tension between the need for success and the need for membership involvement. Collectivist-democratic structures help build democratic participation without making a community organization ineffective (Rothschild, 1979; Rothschild & Whitt, 1986).

The crucial characteristics of collectivist-democratic organizations are that authority belongs to the whole group not just the administrators or officers; they have few rules, although personal ethics are important; people are seen as valued individuals, rather than as cogs in a machine; they have less hierarchy of positions and minimal career advancement; people belong because of emotional attachment, excitement, and belief in the organization's goals, not for money. And in the collectivist-democratic organization, deference to expertise is played down, as people learn many different responsibilities; the role of the amateur and the generalist is highly valued. Table 5–4 contrasts the characteristics of collectivist-democratic organizations with more conventional bureaucratic forms.

Democratic-collectivist organizations reconcile a democratic orientation with the continuity and knowledge needed to accomplish goals. They do this by choosing a structure that preserves democracy while maintaining adaptability and the possibility of quick and effective action. They reject the radical position that opposes all organizational structure. Experience under the no-structure model showed the following:

> There was a kind of *"tyranny of structurelessness"* in that lack of structure gave way to the development of informal leaders—individuals who gained power due to media attention or personal characteristics. Such leaders were not chosen by the group and thus could not be removed by the group. (Iannello, 1988, pp. 4–5)

Lack of structure does not necessarily mean democracy.

Both the Students for a Democratic Society (SDS) and the Gray Panthers illustrate problems caused by lack of organizational structure. The SDS rigidly maintained that there should be full participation in all discussion and minimal routinization of activity. Because of this fear of routinization, SDS activity turned into talk rather than action (Gitlin, 1989; J. Miller, 1987). The Gray Panthers showed a "free wheeling individualism" (R. Jacobs, 1980, p. 97) that was originally opposed to many organizational constraints, for example the payment of dues. However, as the organization needed more resources and realized that its aging leadership, especially its founder Maggie Kuhn, would not live forever, greater structure was introduced.

Democratic-collectivist organizations can develop structures that preserve democratic ideals, yet permit goals to be achieved (Iannello, 1988; Milofsky, 1988). For example, rather than fighting to maintain the importance of organizational boundaries, alternative organizations reach out to work with other groups of similar beliefs. Coalition building replaces turf battles. When expertise is needed, experts are not treated as distant, almost sacred leaders. Alternative organizations recognize "ability or expertise within the membership" (Iannello, 1988, p. 21) and distinguish between the ordinary knowledge needed to keep an organization going from day to day and the special knowledge involved in crisis decision making. To avoid hierarchical decision making, democratic-collectivist organizations emphasize a consensual structure in which "control rests ultimately and overwhelmingly with the member-employees-owners, regardless of the particular legal framework through which this is achieved" (Rothschild-Whitt, 1986, p. 2).

Compatibility of Strategies and Structures.   To help ensure that community organizations are effective, yet remain democratic, they must be built thoughtfully, with an eye to matching the organization's structure to its task. Structure should never determine tasks; the goals and strategies should determine structure.

Organizational structure consists of relatively permanent patterns of behavior in an organization. This structure includes the selection of leaders, the recruitment of members, and the frequency of meetings. It also includes patterns of staffing, including the relative authority of members and leaders to hire staff. It includes the degree to which coordination within and between organizations is achieved informally or by rules.

TABLE 5–4
Comparison of Two Ideal Types of Organization

Dimensions	Bureaucratic Organization	Collectivist-Democratic Organization
1. Authority	1. Authority resides in individuals by virtue of incumbency in office and/or expertise; hierarchical organization of offices. Compliance is to universal fixed rules as these are implemented by office incumbents.	1. Authority resides in the collectivity as a whole; delegated, if at all, only temporarily and subject to recall. Compliance is to the consensus of the collectivity, which is always fluid and open to negotiation.
2. Rules	2. Formalization of fixed and universalistic rules; calculability and appeal of decisions on the basis of correspondence to the formal, written law.	2. Minimal stipulated rules; primacy of ad hoc, individuated decisions; some calculability possible on the basis of knowing the substantive ethics involved in the situation.
3. Social Control	3. Organizational behavior is subject to social control, primarily through direct supervision or standardized rules and sanctions, secondarily through the selection of homogeneous personnel especially at top levels.	3. Social controls are primarily based on personalistic or moralistic appeals and the selection of homogeneous personnel.
4. Social Relations	4. Ideal of impersonality. Relations are to be role-based, segmental and instrumental.	4. Ideal of community. Relations are to be wholistic, personal, of value in themselves.

The structure of a community organization should depend on the strategy adopted. Members of an organization decide what to do and how to accomplish it, then gradually design an organization that will fit the tasks. Organizations that deal with routine tasks ought to have different structures than those facing unusual tasks. For example, a food cooperative probably performs some tasks week after week, such as picking up groceries, shelving them, and selling them. A co-op ought to be able to create routines and divide the work among volunteers in a regular way. A drug-abuse counseling center handles more varied problems with much less predictability. It is impossible to foresee all the problems that can come up, so the organization cannot create rules that cover every situation. New members have to learn by watching and trying to deduce general principles. Then they can create a new response to each situation.

TABLE 5–4
continued

Dimensions	Bureaucratic Organization	Collectivist-Democratic Organization
5. Recruitment and Advancement	5a. Employment based on specialized training and formal certification.	5a. Employment based on friends, social-political values, personality attributes, and informally assessed knowledge and skills.
	5b. Employment constitutes a career; advancement based on seniority or achievement.	5b. Concept of career advancement not meaningful; no hierarchy of positions.
6. Incentive Structure	6. Remunerative incentives are primary.	6. Normative and solidarity incentives are primary; material incentives are secondary.
7. Social Stratification	7. Isomorphic distribution of prestige, privilege, and power; i.e., differential rewards by office; hierarchy justifies inequality.	7. Egalitarian; reward differentials, if any, are strictly limited by the collectivity.
8. Differentiation	8a. Maximal division of labor; dichotomy between intellectual work and manual work and between administrative tasks and performance tasks.	8a. Minimal division of labor; administration is combined with performance tasks; division between intellectual work and manual work is reduced.
	8b. Maximal specialization of jobs and functions; segmented roles. Technical expertise is exclusively held; ideal is the specialist-expert.	8b. Generalization of jobs and functions; wholistic roles. Demystification of expertise; ideal of the amateur factotum.

Note. From "The Collectivist Organization" by Joyce Rothschild-Whitt, 1979, *American Sociological Review, 44*(4), p. 519. Copyright 1979 by *American Sociological Review.* Reprinted with permission.

It is easy to see that if people create organizations in which structure does not match the activity, they won't be able to get anything done effectively. If community members are undertaking actions that require the organization to work as a single unit, a formal hierarchy may be needed. In a march or a demonstration, where discipline is important, members may agree to abide by a strict hierarchy for the duration of the demonstration. A demonstration in which everyone does their own thing is not going to be a successful demonstration. There will be individualized slogans, instead of one theme, and the press will get a confused image of what members are protesting.

The mismatch is just as serious if a volunteer who has to deal with emergencies and make on-the-spot judgments has to clear everything with a bureaucratic superior. A counselor cannot be expected to wait for advice from a supervisor when a caller threatens suicide. Authority and discretion (and hence personal empowerment) must be given to the organization member who answers the phone, and the person must be trained to know what to do.

Achieving a match between goals and structure is not that hard if community members develop the organization slowly, as they carry out its tasks. Skillful organizers let rules emerge gradually on the basis of experience, so that people know how often events will recur, and they do not set up too many rules for events that don't happen often. For example, if meetings generate a lot of controversy, then the organization must set up rules to facilitate discussion without acrimony; if meetings are straightforward, such rules unnecessarily handicap discussion.

In general, rules should be kept to a minimum, so most collectivist-democratic organizations start with almost none, to see how few are actually required. Over a period of a year or two, an organizational structure emerges that suits the strategies of the members and the tasks to be performed. As Weick (1979, p. 147) argues, organizations are "enactments" of underlying values.

As strategies and goals change, so do structures. Without such changes, there is the danger that organizations will rigidify. Beginning in a period of great ferment, an organization starts with a flexible structure. Everyone contributes ideas and there are few routines; everything is discovery. But as the organization learns that certain solutions work, it builds routines to ensure that these solutions are used when the problem occurs. As long as the same problems keep recurring, the new rigidity increases organizational effectiveness. A day-care center need not reformulate its goals and mission every month, so long as community members monitor the center to ensure that it helps children grow emotionally, socially, and intellectually. However, if the organizational structure becomes more rigid even though the problems continue to change, the inability to adapt to changing circumstances becomes a problem. A protest organization using the tactics of the 1960s in the political environment of the 1990s will be ignored rather than effective.

Too much organizational structure can create problems, especially because it discourages personal empowerment. Shelters for battered women are particularly prone to such difficulties. The goal of many shelters is to protect women while they develop sufficient self-confidence and resources to become empowered and take up a less threatened life. The concern with teaching women self-reliance is consistent with a free-floating organizational form that provides the women autonomy. Yet, concerns for the physical security of its inhabitants and the need to provide order and harmony in what is almost always an overcrowded facility, necessitate rules that the battered women might find constraining (Wharton, 1987). Such tradeoffs are not easy to make.

One answer to the tendency to create more rules and become inflexible over time is to foment an organizational culture in which democratic values take on a high priority. An organization culture is

> the deeper level of *basic assumptions* and *beliefs* that are shared by members of an organization, that operate unconsciously, and that define in a basic "taken-for-granted" fashion an organization's view of itself and its environment. (Schein, 1985, p. 6)

In an organization with a democratic culture, members habitually question the need for new rules, their scope, and duration. They check the tendency to make rules that apply to everyone when one person has had a problem, and they help prevent rule making that applies to one bad situation that is unlikely to occur again.

Organizational founders and leaders are often able to pass democratic beliefs on to other members, initially because they influence how events are interpreted, and later, because their belief in democratic operations has been embodied in the organizational culture, the set of unquestioned ways of doing things. These beliefs show up in a variety of ways. Members of democratic organizations assume that criticism of the organizations and each other is good, as long as it is not couched roughly or hurtfully (Rothschild & Whitt, 1986, p. 84). Such organizations are likely to structure themselves to get regular input from membership on emerging policy issues, so that decisions that occur too quickly for extended consultation or deliberation can be guided by members' policies. The need for speed and the need for participation are thus blended (Rothschild & Whitt, 1986, p. 91).

Finally, democracy is strongest when organizations are part of a broader struggle. Knowing that other organizations are out there fighting permits local activists to maintain their idealism: if their particular group doesn't achieve its goals in a democratic fashion, another similar organization will. It is better for the organization to die than to sacrifice its democratic nature to survive (Rothschild & Whitt, 1986, p. 129).

III | Learning About the Action Environment

M any of the problems communities face result from economic and social changes impacting the larger society. In Chapter 6 we examine these changes as well as government's responses to them. Because of the importance of government as a supporter of progressive programs and as a target for campaigns, Chapter 7 describes what government does and how it is politically and administratively structured. In Chapter 8, we describe how organizers learn from community members which problems bother them and how strongly they feel about these problems. What difficulties do people face? Are there shared beliefs about the causes of these problems?

By examining felt needs, community structures, and governmental responses, the organizer learns about the action environment for planning a campaign. Following is an example of the action environment for a neighborhood revitalization organization. An action environment portrays a realistic assessment of the problems facing a group and the resources available to combat these problems. The information to construct such a picture is obtained through the research described in this section of the book.

The Action Environment of a Neighborhood Revitalization Organization

---

Perceptions of Community Members

Felt Needs	Affordable housing to preserve a working class neighborhood adjacent to manufacturing plants
Problem Definition	City supports displacement of working class to provide housing for white-collar workers in new office jobs

The Action Environment of a Neighborhood Revitalization Organization, *continued*

Community Context	Organizational Linkages
Economic: High unemployment; industry migrating out of the area	*Political support:* Similar organizations in other transitional neighborhoods near central business district
Social: Multiethnic community with interethnic rivalries	*Knowledge support:* Both local and national organizations provide needed information
Social Integration: Strong issue-based networking on housing among neighbors	*Economic support:* Funds from Neighborhood Housing Services; Local Initiatives Support Corporation
Organizational density: Block clubs in wealthier areas; clubs missing in poorer areas; active local church	
Agency involvement: Social service agencies try to move the poor to distant working class neighborhood	
How others perceive community: Seen as a slum suitable for gentrification because of closeness to central business district	

Local Government Context	State Government Context
Political structure: Strong mayor/weak council; at-large elections	*Political structure:* Long-term governor; more professional legislature
Electoral process: Elections dominated by a good government group	*Electoral process:* Costly and competitive; campaign contributions by developers
Agency activity: Has rival housing and economic development agencies	*Agency activities:* No housing agency; has large economic development staff
Redistributive policies: Limited budgets, but housing funds target the poor neighborhoods	*Redistributive policies:* Money to business interests; belief in "trickle-down" effects
Goals: Mixed; wants jobs for all, but most efforts are to lure young professionals back to central city	*Goals:* Lure in international firms

National Political and Economic Climate

Economic Climate	Recession ending, but job improvement primarily in service and not manufacturing industries
Political Climate	Conservative administration opposed to social programs
Agency Resources	Housing agency in administrative disarray
Problem Climate	Strong ideological belief in individualism, reduction in size of government, and privatization of government services

6 | Problem Solving in a Changing Society

F inding problems is not difficult for organizers. In poor neighborhoods, unemployed adult men hang around street corners; long lines of people wait outside blood banks to sell their blood, because they have no other way of earning money. Each morning people line up outside day-labor offices, hoping for temporary, often back-breaking work. Drug deals take place in the open. Tired looking buildings alternate with tire-strewn lots and burned out, boarded up housing. In the downtown, the homeless sleep in doorways and on park benches, some begging from passersby. In the old manufacturing towns, large plants stand empty, and for-sale signs are everywhere. Many stores are empty or closed; people have moved away, and those who stay behind have little money to spend.

Bottled water is widely advertised and sold in grocery stores, because toxic wastes have infiltrated the water supply. On hot days, city people stay inside or flock to air-conditioned public buildings, because the air is so loaded with pollutants it is not breathable. In the Northwest, the once-lush hills have the stubbled look of newly shorn marines. There are few animals, because there is no place for them to hide.

The newspapers report stories of children beaten by their parents, and aging parents abused by their children. Signs in women's rooms offer respite to women beaten by their men. Blacks and whites clash on campuses, and the number of racially motivated beatings is increasing. Subway riders shoot their assailants and shove overly aggressive beggars. Ideologues contradict their own values, as right-to-lifers bomb abortion clinics and state legislators encourage hooligans to beat up anyone who shows disrespect for the flag.

It is easy to imagine the personal impact of these problems. One feels for the middle-aged breadwinner who is thrown out of his decent-paying job because of a corporate takeover, who looks for years for another job, and ends up taking a menial job at half the pay. One can imagine the turmoil of a pregnant teenager who has reluctantly decided on an abortion, is terrified and alone, and accosted by right-to-lifers showing her pictures of aborted fetuses. It's not hard to empathize with single parents trying to hold down a job, maintain a home, and bring up children, with low incomes, unsafe

111

neighborhoods, and little medical care. Watching the wheelchair bound or blind nego-tiating the streets, one thinks, "I hope that never happens to me."

Organizers have to be sensitive to the personal impact of social problems as people join together on the basis of their personal experience of these social problems. But the organizer's understanding has to go beyond empathy with the victims. By analyzing the social causes of problems and the opportunities their solutions present, organizers can come up with possible remedies that are collectively empowering. The newly unem-ployed manufacturing worker is a victim of the continued inability of the United States to compete with the more robust economies of Germany and Japan. If a plant was closed because owners felt they could make a larger profit elsewhere, then potential solutions include more worker ownership and management. If a local market has been aban-doned, the solution should emphasize starting small-scale businesses owned by com-munity members. The goal is to alleviate personal suffering, but the solutions will be more effective if based on a sound understanding of the nature of the social cause of the person's suffering.

To illustrate the connection between broader social problems and their personal consequences, we describe several problems that have motivated contemporary orga-nizing. We also trace the recent history of government programs in these areas to suggest the extent to which government has addressed these problems, the areas in which government should be pressured, and the obligations on which government has turned it back, abandoning the field to the community activists.

SOCIAL PROBLEMS AND CONTEMPORARY ORGANIZING

As a consequence of more than 10 years of conservative national politics, five clusters of problems stand out, demanding action by progressive and community groups. The first is that the poor have become poorer. The second is that with suburbanization the middle class and middle-class jobs have deserted the central city, leaving behind in-creasing concentrations of the poor, elderly, and unemployed. Third, as company own-ers try to maximize their short-term profits, they move plants (even plants still making money), regardless of the impact on the community. The fourth problem is that envi-ronmental protection has bumped head on into the desire to increase or maintain the number of jobs. Fifth, and compounding the other four cluster of problems, is that government is far less concerned with solving what ails the society.

Each of the five problem areas shows the near impossibility of separating public from private solutions. The abrupt departure of an industry from a community puts enormous stresses on public social services. New jobs in the private sector can alleviate many of these problems but only if the jobs are available to the unskilled and undered-ucated. Providing both jobs and skills requires cooperation between businesses, the federal government, and the community.

The five issue clusters demonstrate the connections between problem areas. For example, reductions in federal programs such as Aid to Families With Dependent Chil-dren (AFDC), Medicaid, food stamps, and school lunches, aggravate the problems facing the poor. The migration of wealthy people and jobs to the suburbs has exacerbated the unemployment problems of the inner cities, which resulted from the loss of heavy industry. With a smaller resource base, inner-city schools deteriorate, further encouraging the middle class to flee, taking shops and businesses with them. The reduction in the number of blue-collar jobs exacerbates the conflict between the environment and economic growth. If there were plenty of alternative jobs, closing a polluting or dangerous plant would not be so threatening to workers.

Part of the community organizer's job is to recognize patterns of decline and to design programs that break up negative cycles. To help the organizer get a handle on these dynamics, and to help maintain the sense of outrage that motivates many organizers, the following section discusses these social problems in more detail.

Poverty Is Increasing

Over the past 15 years, the rich have gotten richer while the poor have fallen further behind.

> Large numbers of Americans are falling over the abyss into the most acute forms of poverty witnessed in this country since the Great Depression. Marked increases in homelessness, hunger and chronic unemployment among former blue collar workers and minority youth have not abated, but rather have expanded substantially in the 1980s. (Burghardt & Fabricant, 1987, p. 11)

Between 1979 and 1986, the poorest 20% of the population lost 9.8% of their income (including inflation) while the richest 20% gained 15.6% (Changing Shares, 1988). By 1990, the richest 1% had combined incomes matching the bottom third.

Moreover, wealth and poverty are increasingly concentrated, by geographic area, by ethnicity, and by gender. While suburbanites are the richest and least likely to be unemployed, poverty is concentrated

> in certain areas of central cities, especially cities in the older regions of the country. . . . This growing poverty is occurring even in command-and-control cities with improving economies, like New York and Boston, indicating that economic growth alone is not sufficient to improve the situation. (McGreary & Lynn, 1988, pp. 5–6)

Blacks are poorer than whites, and women are poorer than men, especially when the women are bringing up children by themselves. In 1985, 44% of all black children lived in poor households, compared to 16% of white children. Similar differences occur between white and other minority groups, especially Spanish speakers (Jaynes & Williams, 1989, p. 279). It is not just that blacks are poorer than whites but that extremely poor blacks are living in areas in central cities in which poverty is just one of many associated problems.

The number of poor, female-headed households has increased considerably in recent years, resulting in a feminization of poverty. "Women head over half of all poor families and over half the children of female-headed households are poor" (Burghardt & Fabricant, 1987, p. 94). The situation is even more extreme among black women to the extent that "economic hardship has become almost synonymous with black female-headed families" (Wilson, 1987, p. 27). The children in female-headed families are likely to remain poor as they grow up.

> Research shows that children from female-headed families are more likely to drop out of school, to have low-status jobs, and to have out-of-wedlock births. (McGeary & Lynn, 1988, p. 22)

The number of female-headed households increases the demand for day-care facilities, but mothers earning low salaries cannot afford expensive facilities, and there are not enough at a reasonable cost. Children may be unsupervised for part of the day. Or people may choose welfare over working because they cannot afford to pay for child care.

Poverty has become so extreme that recent years have witnessed an increase in the number of homeless people. Though some of the homeless are mentally handicapped, many are simply broke. And, according to Robert Hayes, counsel for the National Coalition for the Homeless, "three fourths of the newly homeless in America are families with children" (Kozol, 1988, p. 8).

Despite the increase in homelessness, some cities have been reducing their commitment to the homeless. In Philadelphia:

> Scores of homeless people and their advocates jammed the City Chamber here today, waving placards and chanting slogans to protest the city's 50% cut in money for programs for the homeless this year. (Hinds, 1989, p. 8)

Government's inability to provide affordable housing has contributed to the problem.

> For public housing . . . the waiting list contains 200,000 names. There are only 175,000 public housing units in New York. Manhattan borough President David Dinkins calculates the waiting time at eighteen years. (Kozol, 1988, p. 17)

Poverty means living in housing that is cold in winter, hot in summer, often rat and roach infested, located in dangerous neighborhoods; it means a poor diet, few doctor visits, continuing high levels of stress, and lower resistance to infections. All these contribute to higher rates of illness, which means that more medical care is needed for precisely those individuals least able to afford it. People who work may have poor attendance records because of ill health and, hence, be more likely to lose their jobs.

All these problems—chronic illness, homelessness, unemployment, violent crime, drug addiction, female-headed families, lack of marketable skills, and welfare dependency—cluster in poor areas. The result is *hyperghettoization,* neighborhoods so stressed by multiple problems that even the potential for rebuilding them has been called into question. As a result of the combination of problems

> One segment of our population has become increasingly immobilized in culturally and economically isolated inner-city areas of decline. Without jobs and without much hope for jobs, the "new immobiles" are caught in a downward socioeconomic spiral that is unprecedented for urban dwellers in this country. (J. D. Kasarda, 1988, p. 198)

Many people who are poor are poor only temporarily, during an illness, between jobs, or after a divorce. They may believe (correctly) that they can get out of poverty on their own, given a little time. Those living in hyperghettos may accept their poverty as permanent. This feeling of defeatism makes organizing particularly difficult. In working with the demoralized poor, the strategy of starting with limited activities that produce small but immediate successes is important for building a sense of the possible.

Working with the poor means dealing with urgent human need. Community organizers should help support social service programs that alleviate suffering. The focus of their own work, however, should not be short-term relief but efforts to reduce the causes of poverty and homelessness.

> The tremendous urgency that human-service workers feel to help the homeless, feed the hungry, and assist the increasingly impoverished disabled should not blind them to the responsibility to create services that not only help individuals but carry with them the seeds of lasting change. (Burghardt & Fabricant, 1987, p. 9)

A Class-Based Restructuring of Urban Regions

Problems of poverty are exacerbated by population and job migration within metropolitan regions. People, jobs, and wealth have moved to the suburbs as metropolitan areas become increasingly racially segregated. For example, in the Detroit metropolitan area, the segregation index (in which 0 means no segregation, 100 total segregation) has increased from 17 in 1940 to 75 in 1980, and the trend is still up (Darden, 1987, p. 78). The result is a higher concentration of blacks and minority groups in the inner cities, allowing minority members to increase their political power. But the local economic base has deteriorated, making cities more dependent on decisions made by distant corporations. As a consequence, "the modern city has become politically democratic, but economically dependent" (Kantor, 1988, p. 5).

Population and Job Shifts.   Population and jobs have dramatically shifted from the central city to the suburban fringes. A higher proportion of the total jobs in metropolitan regions is located in the suburban ring. In the last 25 years, Detroit's share of total metropolitan employment declined from 55.6% to 22.4%. Similar figures can be found in other metropolitan areas. For example, in 1947 Chicago had 70% of the area's manufacturing jobs, while in 1982 it had about 33% (Squires et al., 1987, p. 26). Overall employment in the central city has declined 20% in the last 10 years (Squires et al., 1987, p. 35).

The poor, the elderly, and the handicapped without adequate transportation cannot follow the jobs to suburbia, thereby increasing central city unemployment and poverty (Knox, 1982, p. 177). Those who do manage to get jobs in the suburbs face further difficulties if they are minority group members likely to face housing discrimination (Danielson, 1976). And, because they cannot find housing in the white suburbs where the jobs are, blacks have to commute further to work than whites. Among the employed in suburban Washington, DC, poorly educated whites commute 32 minutes, while blacks, regardless of education level, commute 75 minutes (J. Kasarda, 1989, p. 41).

People who flee to the suburbs deny responsibility for central city problems. One suburbanite expressed these feelings trenchantly:

> It is ridiculous to suppose that those of us in suburbs have any responsibility to help in the current Philadelphia school crisis. We did not create the problems of the inner city and we are not obligated to help in their solution. (Jackson, 1985, p. 278)

Factories abandon the cities while jobs open up in suburban areas. (Courtesy TTB)

While wealth and jobs have been fleeing to the suburbs, the nature of the jobs left in the central cities has been changing. The number of good-paying semiskilled and unskilled manufacturing jobs decreased, while the number of jobs requiring more education has increased. In the decade ending in 1980, blue-collar jobs declined by 62,000 in Boston, 118,000 in Chicago, 34,000 in Cleveland, and 171,500 in New York. Jobs requiring a high school education or less rapidly decreased. Yet, for college graduates, there were 58,000 new jobs in Boston, 112,500 in Chicago, 16,000 in Cleveland, and 266,000 in New York (J. Kasarda, 1989, pp. 30–31). The poor cannot step into these new jobs. Many have not completed high school, and even those who manage to graduate from high school still lack skills and cannot compete successfully for a diminishing number of jobs. Training programs increase skill levels, but they do not increase the number of jobs available in the inner city.

Favoring the Business Class.   Partly because of their dwindling tax bases, cities have concentrated on subsidizing businesses that supposedly will provide jobs (M. P. Smith, 1988, p. 3). Planning for economic development is done by boards that are dominated by business, bankers, and others in the establishment, with little representation from the poor (H. J. Rubin, 1986). As a consequence

> Various urban policies . . . have sought to restore the property value of urban space by using tax incentives to stimulate private reinvestment in urban land. Where they have succeeded in this objective they have destroyed hundreds of thousands of available low rent housing units. (M. P. Smith, 1988, p. 43)

The elimination of housing for the poor as part of economic development is common in older declining cities, as "downtown rebuilding has taken precedence over neighborhood maintenance" (Squires et al., 1987, p. 92). New housing is sometimes provided for those displaced, but the small businesses, churches, and social organizations that provided a modicum of community solidarity are destroyed. For example, General Motors threatened to abandon Detroit unless the city cleared hundreds of acres for a factory in Poletown. In response, "city officials had to acquire nearly seventeen hundred pieces of property, relocate more than thirty-five hundred residents, [and] demolish fifteen hundred residential and commercial structures" (B. Jones, Bachelor, & Wilson, 1986, p. 84). Similar examples have occurred in New York, Chicago, and other large cities.

Gentrification. The class-based battles over urban change are most apparent in neighborhoods undergoing *gentrification,* in which richer people move into previously deteriorating central city neighborhoods located near the central business district (CBD). Gentrification receives support from cities that are trying to reduce the exodus of the middle class to the suburbs.

Their success in doing so, however, is uncertain. On the positive side, residents of gentrifying areas are often young, professional couples, both black and white, with incomes higher than the previous inhabitants, who buy old homes and refurbish them. In studies of Washington, DC, gentrified neighborhoods were losing population less quickly than other areas, and residents had higher educations and more prestigious jobs (Gale, 1987, pp. 67–73). However, most inhabitants of the gentrified neighborhoods are not people returning from the suburbs but those moving from other parts of the city (Goldfield, 1980, p. 456).

In gentrifying neighborhoods, housing costs escalate dramatically, sometimes from under $10,000 to hundreds of thousands of dollars. As a consequence, while housing quality visibly improves, the previous inhabitants can no longer afford to live there. Gentrification has led to a further concentration of poverty. "Large drops in poverty rates often accompanied gentrification near the CBD, but poverty rates then rose farther away from the core" (Nelson, 1988, p. 152).

Sometimes its not just housing that is threatened but the few remaining factories that provided jobs to middle- and lower-class workers. For example, a central corridor of older factories in Chicago is threatened by an expansion of upscale housing.

> Businesses . . . have fled the industrial district. . . . The trend was set off by a wave of new residential development that has spilled over from the upscale Lincoln Park neighborhood. . . . Residents and manufacturers have been at logger heads for years. The problem is the population, garbage, truck traffic, noise and bad smells that accompany manufacturing zones. Factory owners see the encroaching yuppie development as fuel to a long ranging fire. (George, 1987, p. 3)

Upscale housing is incompatible with blue collar employment.

Gentrification is something that happens *to* a poor neighborhood, when the neighborhood is in a convenient location and the housing is basically attractive, if dilapidated. Upgrading by gentrification is to the advantage of real estate people, contractors, decorators, bankers, and city officials but not to the poor who live in that neighborhood.

There are many different community-based approaches to encourage the preservation of neighborhoods that do not displace the residents. In one such approach, *incumbent upgrading,* organizers work with people in deteriorating neighborhoods to help them preserve the quality of the housing.

Incumbent upgrading can best be understood by considering Pittsburgh's Neighborhood Housing Services (PNHS). . . . PNHS began with Ford Foundation funded grass roots organizing to build neighborhood confidence, fight encroaching large-scale absentee owners, and challenge the private sector to offer credit. . . . An imaginative special loan fund was created . . . to assist those who could not afford conventional loans for home improvement, while the code enforcement process was tailored so that renovation was within the financial grasp of the majority of area residents. . . . Property values appreciated appropriately, making recovery of the outlays from the special loan fund possible when the properties of households on restricted incomes are eventually sold. (Goetze, 1979, p. 104)

Incumbent upgrading maintains the attractive old housing stock, stabilizes neighborhoods, attracts investment from banks, and increases assessed valuation. By preventing neighborhoods from becoming completely blighted, it reduces the tremendous risks and potential financial windfalls of many traditional gentrification projects.

Commodification of Labor

The problems within central cities have been exaggerated by major structural changes in the U.S. economy, away from manufacturing and toward service industries. These changes are

traceable mainly to deeper structural causes: the increasingly vulnerable position of the United States in the volatile global economic system, the particular strategies adopted by corporate managers to reduce the cost of labor in an effort to cope with the profit squeeze engendered by this heightened competition, and the many ways in which the U. S. government has encouraged those corporate experiments in restructuring. (Harrison & Bluestone, 1988, p. 137)

There has been a large reduction in the numbers of blue-collar jobs as heavy industry has declined. Family income has held steady only because there are more two-career families; for many families with only one wage earner, the income situation has worsened. In addition, while the number of better paying blue-collar jobs has decreased, there has been an increase in the poorer paying service and non-unionized manufacturing jobs. As a result, many full-time workers can barely make ends meet (Levitan & Shapiro, 1987). At the same time, the number of high-paying white-collar jobs for educated people has increased, exacerbating income inequality (Timberlake, 1987, p. 48).

The problem is most severe in central city areas where the mismatch is acute between the education provided and the educational level needed for employment. Describing the nation's capital, Gale argues

the problem of unemployment is linked not to the rather robust growth in employment in the advanced services but, instead, to the loss of jobs in unskilled and semiskilled blue-collar fields or to lagging growth in skilled trades and lower-level clerical and technical occupations. (Gale, 1987, p. 24)

There has been a dramatic drop in jobs for those with less than a high school education in precisely those cities that have the nation's highest dropout rates (J. D. Kasarda, 1988; Wilson, 1987, p. 39). The situation is particularly dramatic in blue-collar communities whose manufacturing plants have closed. Since the mid-1970s, about 16 million jobs were eliminated (Perrucci et al., 1988, p. 22).

About 60% of the *displaced workers* (those losing their jobs because of the elimination of manufacturing jobs) have been reemployed but often in positions paying less than half of what their previous jobs paid; about 14% have become discouraged and stopped looking for work (Burghardt & Fabricant, 1987, p. 141; Perrucci et al., 1988, p. 70).

Plant shutdowns are dramatic and very threatening events. As a result, plant owners have been able to use the threat of a shutdown to reduce wages and benefits and to break the unions. Owners also weaken unions by moving plants to parts of the country that have less of a tradition of unionization. Reduction in the proportion of the work force that is unionized has been facilitated by the shift into service work, because service work has been traditionally nonunionized.

This shift in the labor market has implications for community organizing. Unemployment is most likely to be a problem in blue-collar, central city communities that have been the traditional focus of neighborhood organizing. Organizing efforts must help direct the alienation and anger that workers feel into constructive channels.

Though depressed about the future (Perrucci et al., 1988, p. 107), workers understand that they need to respond collectively (Perrucci et al., 1988, p. 98). They know that a problem was inflicted on them, which may "leave them less likely to blame themselves and more likely to locate the source and solution to their discontent in existing social institutions" (Perrucci et al., 1988, p. 101). The result in some cities has been a greater willingness to experiment with worker ownership and control of the workplace.

GOVERNMENTAL RESPONSE AND COMMUNITY PROBLEMS

Community organizations need to be cautious in dealing with government, but they cannot reasonably ignore its effects. Since 1960, governmental responses to social problems have ranged from indifference to active involvement in three key areas that affect community organizing: antipoverty programs, housing, and economic development. Government sponsors social programs, yet governmental policies have supported business interests and objected to radical changes. Community organizations can help formulate the policies that government carries out and can make sure that the voice of the community is heard when solutions are being examined.

Federal Antipoverty Programs

The federal role in antipoverty programs began in the Great Depression, with a variety of programs to provide emergency funds to the multitudes of unemployed people. The income support programs created under Social Security have continued, growing in a variety of ways, with expansion of existing social service programs and the addition of new ones particularly rapid in the 1960s and 1970s, during the Kennedy and Johnson administrations. In the 1980s, under Presidents Reagan and Bush, federal involvement declined precipitously.

The Kennedy–Johnson-era antipoverty programs, including Head Start, the Job Corps, and the Food Stamp Program, were called the *War on Poverty*. These antipoverty programs were located in the newly created federal Office of Economic Opportunity. At the local level, cities set up Community Action Agencies to receive money and carry out programs.

Other locally controlled antipoverty efforts were started, including community medical clinics to provide free or low-cost medical care, and Community Development Corporations (CDCs) to encourage locally controlled economic development. The War on Poverty provided funds for Legal Service attorneys, to help the poor gain access to the legal system. Community organizations and welfare-advocacy organizations worked with legal services attorneys to bring class-action suits that had the potential of improving conditions for a whole class of people, such as those dependent on welfare. Just before President Kennedy's assassination in 1963, the Community Mental Health Centers Act was passed, which bypassed state and local governments and specifically required the participation of community members on the boards.

In theory, citizen boards controlled Community Action Agencies, Community Development Corporations, Community Mental Health Centers, and Community Health Agencies. However, the quality of citizen participation was not always very good, and government officials or members of the local establishment often captured leadership positions. Some agencies became arenas for struggles over patronage and control. Though these programs were not fully successful in empowering local communities, they created a tradition of community participation and leadership that outlasted the federally funded Community Action Program (Fainstein et al., 1983, p. 18).

President Johnson supported the Older Americans Act (OAA), which authorized funds to pay public or nonprofit agencies to work with the elderly. Amendments to the OAA during the Nixon administration authorized the funding of community groups to set up multipurpose senior centers (Meenaghan & Washington, 1980).

The thrust of the Republican Nixon and Ford administrations (1968–1976) was to weaken the community basis of federal social service programs, though the overall level of funding was only marginally reduced. The Office of Economic Opportunity was broken up, and many of its functions delegated to other governmental departments, ending a lobby group for the poor. Federal programs were again run as welfare-oriented services, over which recipients had little control.

To provide the poor with the needed job skills, the Nixon administration sponsored the Comprehensive Employment Training Act (CETA). There is little evidence that the program created many new jobs for poorer people, although it did create some temporary and entry-level jobs in local government. The program affected community organizing, however, because local governments often used CETA funds to hire personnel for community-based social services.

The Carter administration tried to re-orient poverty programs more toward directly benefiting the poor and minorities and increased the funding for many social service programs, including the food stamp program. Cities were allowed to use some money from the Community Development Block Grant for social service activities. Carter appointed community activists to the Office of Neighborhoods in the Department of Housing and Urban Development, expanded the Law Enforcement Assistance Agency's Community Anti-Crime Program, and encouraged neighborhood organizations to carefully monitor federal programs for compliance with requirements to benefit the poor.

Under President Reagan, funding for many social service programs was reduced, with especially serious consequences for the working poor. For example, even ignoring the effects of inflation, early in the Reagan administration, AFDC dropped 6%, food and nutrition assistance went up only 1.4%, and employment and training funds were halved (Weicher, 1984, p. 9).

Efforts were made to obscure the size of cuts by combining programs into state-administered block grants. These block grants combined several social service programs, ostensibly to allow states to decide which particular programs they preferred or needed most. The Social Services Block Grant, which included AFDC, was redesigned so that states need not target all the money at the extremely poor; in addition, in real dollars the federal funding was approximately 70% of what it had been in 1979. Fortunately, many states increased the share of state money going to the extremely poor, though often at the cost of reducing funding for such programs as energy assistance (U.S. Conference of Mayors, 1986, pp. 177–178).

The states did compensate for federal reductions in welfare. However, when the Community Services Block Grant was cut by 50%, state governments not only did not pick up the slack, they spread the money more widely, further reducing the sizes of the grants. In effect, such block grants set one needy group against another, especially as overall funding decreased.

In employment programs, CETA was replaced by the Manpower Job Training Partnership Act, which turned over job training to business councils, while sharply limiting the involvement of government and not-for-profit organizations. In addition, the administration encouraged states to require AFDC recipients to work or attend job training or else their aid would be cut off. Such programs do not make sense in states where there are few low-skilled jobs, few tax-supported training programs, and little if any state-supported child care. The work stipulation provides an excuse to cut the welfare roles.

Federal cutbacks in social programs emphasize the need to maintain active lobbying efforts to stem the loss of funds. Community organizations can highlight the deception involved in requirements that recipients of welfare work, when they cannot afford training programs or day care for their children, and cannot risk taking a job that doesn't provide the health benefits they get on welfare.

Housing and Urban Development Programs

An examination of the last 30 years of federally funded urban renewal and housing programs shows a tremendous variety in the amount of funding available, in the ways in which programs were targeted, and in the extent of control maintained by the federal, state, and local governments, as well as community groups. In recent years, the pattern has been one of federal neglect, resulting in increased demands on neighborhood organizations to try to undo some of the harm.

The middle class and business, rather than the poor and poor neighborhoods, have been the primary beneficiaries of federal efforts at urban renewal. Early urban redevelopment efforts, after the Second World War, were primarily for slum clearance. The federal government paid to tear down blighted homes, often the only places in which the poor could afford to live, to make way for expansion of central business districts. Because so many of the poor neighborhoods that were torn down were primarily black, renewal was often referred to as "black removal." Displacement was high; for example, in New Haven 20% of the people in the city were moved, and overall "four dwelling units have been destroyed by renewal for every one built" (M. P. Smith, 1979, p. 241).

Some of those displaced ended up in federally financed public housing, but far fewer units of public housing were built than the government tore down. Builders benefited more from some of the housing projects than the poor because the construction was often shoddy (M. Mayer, 1978). Bluntly stated, the goals of renewal programs were to

> bring back the white middle class, remove lower-income and minority households from the central business districts, maintain and reestablish racial and class territorial segregation through locational decisions involving clearance, zoning, public facilities (especially schools), transportation routes, and publicly subsidized housing and encapsulate the lower classes in peripheral locations. (Fainstein et al., 1983, p. 253)

Downtown redevelopment often ignores housing problems. (Courtesy Department of Housing and Urban Development)

But while the federal government was engaging in urban renewal, it was aiding the middle-class flight to suburbia through subsidized mortgages, a trend that was to have devastating and long-term effects on central cities. Federally subsidized suburban housing far outstripped public housing for the poor. For example, the

> total volume of public housing production between 1949 and 1960 (about 280,000 units) was about the same as the average annual volume of single-family FHA mortgage housing. (Struyk et al., 1988, p. 62)

In the inner cities, people with multiple economic and social problems were concentrated in one or several public housing buildings without adequate schools, playgrounds, or security. The Pruitt-Igoe housing project in St. Louis became so unmanageable because of crime that it had to be torn down a short time later.

In reaction to the failure of urban renewal to serve the poor and in response to the increasing unrest in urban areas, Presidents Kennedy and Johnson initiated the Model Cities program. The objective of Model Cities was to encourage community participation in activities that would bring together both social planning and neighborhood rehabilitation. The original purpose was to target money to a limited number of cities, and, within these cities, to neighborhoods with the greatest need for social and physical revitalization. The impact of the Model Cities Program was greatly weakened, however, as Congress insisted that a large number of cities receive some of the small amount of money appropriated and as mayors within these cities successfully demanded that they, and not community groups, make program decisions.

The impact on community organizing was mixed. Some organizations, such as the Mission Coalition in San Francisco, were able to provide social services for people but were unable to build a long-lasting empowered political force (Castells, 1983). The tendency was for groups to start out militantly, obtain community involvement, and then lose the empowerment ideal. The history of PUNC, a government-sponsored community development organization in Los Angeles, is typical as it "moved from militant advocacy, with broad community participation, to community development directed largely by professionals, with substantially reduced involvement from community residents" (T. Cooper, 1980, p. 411).

The evolution of these less militant community groups reflected a demand for professionalism from the federal government and pressures from local politicians to reduce community control. These organizations were financially dependent on the federal government, so that when program funding was severely reduced under the Nixon administration, the organizations could no longer function effectively. The positive legacy is that many present-day organizers got their street training during this period.

During the 1960s, public housing produced about 27,000 units a year. Government changed from direct payment for construction, ownership, and management of public housing to indirect subsidy programs that were intended to encourage private construction of low-rent apartments and less expensive homes. Many of the subsidized homes were shoddily built and then sold to people with incomes inadequate to pay the mortgage or maintain the property.

Under Presidents Nixon and Ford, the remnants of different urban renewal and redevelopment programs were combined into the Community Development Block Grant (CDBG). Under the grant, cities can spend money on street repairs, sewer construction, housing, urban planning, community services, restoring or maintaining historic buildings, or encouraging economic development. Money for CDBG is allocated by formula to several thousand local governments.

CDBG grants require community participation, but it has been unclear how much say community organizations have in the programs. A variety of interest groups, including city governments and community organizations, have fought about what proportion of the grant should directly benefit the poor, and whether or not community groups can directly receive funds. Poorer cities received more funds, but during the Nixon and Ford administrations, many local governments used CDBG funds to supplement their regular budgets with little concern about who benefited. Some of the grant money was used to finance a walking path for horses; another outrageous CDBG project improved a sports facility, displacing the poor (National Citizens' Monitoring Project, 1981b).

During the Carter administration, neighborhood organizations monitored the CDBG programs while federal officials used their review authority to insist that poor individuals benefit from CDBG programs. During President Carter's administration, changes were made in the CDBG program so that 75% of the benefits of CDBG programs were required to go to people with low and moderate incomes. In addition, efforts were made to target program funds to the most needy neighborhoods. The Department of Housing and Urban Development directly funded neighborhood organizations through the Office of Neighborhoods. In many cities, a certain percentage of the CDBG was automatically allocated to these groups for neighborhood-based programs.

The Urban Development Action Grant (UDAG) was also a Carter initiative. This controversial program enabled governments in fiscally stressed cities to loan money at low interest rates to businesses that would increase employment among the poor. There is real doubt about how effective UDAGs have been. New jobs may have been created without the UDAG subsidies, and many of the jobs created for the poor were dead-end positions, such as maids in urban hotels (U.S.D.H.D., 1982).

On occasion, city governments feigned giving into neighborhood pressures to share CDBG funding by providing small sums to competing neighborhood groups, while spending larger amounts on business-oriented projects. In Detroit, only about 10% of the grant money was guaranteed for neighborhood projects in the Neighborhood Opportunity Fund (NOF).

> Allowing citizens control over this small sum of money diverts the attention of community groups from how the rest of the funds are allocated and ensures that citizen preferences opposed to the city's overall development plans will have relatively little impact. (Bachelor & Jones, 1981, p. 535)

For housing and urban development programs, the Reagan years were disastrous. Funding dropped precipitously, and requirements for community participation were drastically reduced. President Reagan also persuaded Congress to terminate the UDAG program.

Funds for the CDBGs were cut back, and control over allocation of some of the funds was given to the states. At its peak in 1978, CDBG was funded at about $2.25 billion (in 1988 dollars). By 1988, funding had dropped to less than $1 billion, correcting for inflation. The percentage of the grant that was to be targeted at the poor was reduced from 75% to 60%. The states have responded to local pressures, distributing the portion they control to many different jurisdictions rather than concentrating on places with the most poverty and unemployment. In addition, states increasingly emphasize business-oriented projects rather than housing activities.

Under Reagan, the poor were required to spend 30% of their income on rent in subsidized housing (up from the previous 25%), while there has been a dramatic drop in federal support for housing. Combining all forms of housing assistance to the poor, in 1977 the federal government aided about 500,000 units, a figure that had been reduced to 200,000 by 1985 and was continuing to decline. These cutbacks in housing supply are undoubtedly contributing to the number of homeless people. Because one of the most significant housing subsidies (tax reductions for mortgage interest) goes disproportionately to middle-and upper-class homeowners, more than 50% of all federal money for housing is received by households with an income over $50,000.

Community organizations have taken a number of creative approaches to dealing with the federal cutbacks in housing. They have supported resident-managed public housing, an initiative that was welcomed by the Secretary of the Department of Housing and Urban Development. Advocates of the homeless have done everything from building inexpensive shelters from cast-off materials to opening armories and public buildings in cold weather. Emphasis on inexpensive home-repair loans and grants for housing rehabilitation combine well with job training for carpentry, plumbing, painting, and electrical work. Building their own shelter can give people a sense of competence as well as the ability to maintain a house or apartment.

In late 1990, community efforts to increase support for housing resulted in Congress passing the National Affordable Housing Act. The law replaces many separate federal housing programs with a lump sum payment to localities and reinstates the requirement that 70% of community development block grant funds go to low and moderate income communities. The act authorized (allowed for) a large increase in federal funding, but sufficient money to pay for such housing has not yet been appropriated (made available).

The new law mandates that at least 15% of housing funds be set aside for projects developed by non-profit, community based organizations. In addition, localities will not receive funds until the federal government approves their Comprehensive Housing Affordability Strategy (CHAS) that details how the money is to be spent. To ensure that funds are spent to benefit the poor, community groups should get involved in preparing the CHAS document (Housing Bill 1991).

With a little imagination, community organizations can ensure that this new law benefits the homeless and the ill-housed. Previous failures of public housing policy, symbolized by the construction and destruction of the Pruitt-Igoe Housing, to some extent were failures of public imagination. When imagination worked, as in rent subsidy plans, programs were so seriously underfunded and poorly implemented that they were no more than scams. Community organizations need to monitor federal programs to see that grant money is spent on poor and moderate-income people. Equally important, they need to ensure that clever and empowering programs are funded rather than those that create crumbly bricks and mortar for the benefit of construction firms and politicians who can claim they have created construction jobs.

State and Local Economic Development Programs

Many of the problems affecting local communities and poor people stem from the rapidly changing economy. Yet the federal government has been reluctant to formulate an overall economic development strategy. It sponsors job training and provides a small amount of aid to workers who lose their jobs because of international competition. Despite these scattered efforts, economic development programs have been primarily state and local efforts.

State and local economic development programs often offer incentives to encourage business to move from one area to another, so that one locality's gain is another's loss. There is little evidence that such programs do more than transfer public wealth to businesses (H. J. Rubin, 1988, 1989, 1990). Despite the lack of favorable evidence, officials generally assume that economic development is good because businesses create jobs and expand the tax base (Rubin & Rubin, 1987).

To promote economic development, public officials work closely with the business community, often without labor or neighborhood participation (H. J. Rubin, 1986). In Baltimore, a shadow government of business and political leaders directs economic development policies, making it hard to trace out who is responsible for decisions.

> Major industrial development efforts are channeled through the Baltimore Economic Development Corporation . . . outside the normal flow of policy making, thus making it quite difficult to track policy. Expenditures are typically "off-budget." (Hula, 1989, p. 16)

Much of what passes as economic development is only an expensive ritual meant to assuage the fears of the populace about a declining local economy. Officials offer fiscal incentives, such as tax reductions for new construction, to make it look like they are doing something about the economy (Swanstrom, 1985, pp. 149–150), and "if firms do move into the community, even if the fiscal incentives are not a motivating factor, the prior offering of incentives provides politicians [the chance] to take credit for the event . . ." (Wolman, 1988, p. 25).

In a more constructive approach, states such as Pennyslvania have set up incubator programs in which businesses and universities work together to create new products and jobs. Unlike the incentive programs in which one city's gain is another's loss, these programs seek to expand the pie by helping to create new businesses. In more progressive cities, governments work with neighborhood-based CDCs (Giloth, 1988; Neal Peirce & Steinbach, 1987; S. Perry, 1987) whose

> chief goal is to generate employment and business ownership opportunities and a positive cash flow in low-income areas. Such groups may launch new enterprises and assist others in expanding; develop commercial real estate; plan and market industrial sites; create job training and placement programs. (Task Force on Community Based Development, 1987, p. 7)

In recent years, CDCs have been used as a tool for community-controlled economic development.

Organizers need to be familiar with the rapidly changing policies of states and cities in the area of economic development. Because so much of the decision making goes on deliberately out of the hearing of community groups whose members might be adversely affected, it can be difficult to get direct access to the decision making. There are several possible strategies of influence, however.

One strategy is to get organized labor included in the discussions and to support their demands for training, local hiring, and where appropriate, closed (union) shops. Another approach is to develop an alternative economic development plan that includes minorities, neighborhood groups, and social service providers and that argues for affordable housing and an educated labor pool. The alternative plan should be widely aired, getting input and approval from the community.

A third strategy to influence economic development plans is to play on the divisions within the business community. Older businesses in the community that have paid taxes for years tend to resent newcomers who get tax breaks. The community organization might be able to get considerable business support for a proposal that came close to paying for itself, as opposed to one with massive subsidies for a limited number of businesses at public expense.

Staying Informed.   In each of these problem areas—poverty, urban redevelopment and economic development—it is difficult to predict governmental policies. We recommend that community organizers stay informed through reading newspapers, especially the *New York Times* and the *Washington Post.* Changes in federal regulations governing how a program will be administered, or changes in the percentage of a grant that must be spent on the poor, are published in the *Federal Register.* Specialty newspapers such as Crain's *City & State* provide good coverage of changing state and local policies, while *Industrial Development* provides information on state-level economic development incentives.

We especially recommend *Community Change,* a quarterly publication put out by the Center for Community Change in Washington, DC. This periodical traces the implications of changes in governmental policies for community organizations and progressive advocacy organizations. Recent issues have focused on housing, block grant programs, and worker displacement. *Neighborhood Works* and *City Limits* provide parallel city level information for Chicago and New York.

LESSONS FOR ORGANIZING

This material on social problems and governmental responses suggests five themes that should influence how organizers and community groups approach solving major social problems:

1. Local problems reflect national action.
2. Social problems compound.

3. Government often does not want to solve social problems; instead it rationalizes them away.
4. What is a social problem emerges from a collective definition.
5. Organizers need to understand the causes of social problems.

Local Problems Reflect National Action

It is very difficult to deal with local problems such as unemployment or lack of adequate housing without understanding their national context. It is not only that the problems are of national scope but also that federal programs and laws, by what they do and what they don't do, frame and to some extent cause local problems. Federal housing policy has increased the number of homeless; federal water subsidies and permits to graze animals and cut wood on public lands have had major impact on the environment.

Funding reductions in federal programs have had major impacts on cities and on community organizations dependent on those funds. When the federal government sneezes, many localities, especially those heavily involved in social programs, catch pneumonia. The city of Chicago reports

> the annual level of federal funds to the City has plummeted $166 million or 32.8% in just five years. . . . As a result, disruption will be caused in the myriad programs provided by both the City and its contracted community organizations. (City of Chicago, 1989, pp. i–ii)

Many local governments used General Revenue Sharing to pay for social services. When Revenue Sharing was terminated, many cities reduced or eliminated those social services. And, as the Chicago report suggested, much of the impact of reduction in federal funding fell on the not-for-profits that were providing these social services through contracts to local governments. Many of them suddenly found survival problematic and had to spend more time on fund raising, and less on providing services for the poor or building local capacity (Randall & Wilson, 1989, p. 13).

The end result has been that the cutbacks of federal programs have fallen most heavily on the working poor.

> In Rochester, as in cities across the nation, the effects of the federal budget retrenchment were most directly and deeply felt by the working poor. Cuts in funding for social services, coupled with changes in eligibility for AFDC, were translated into losses of supplements to earned income and of subsidies for day care. (Liebschutz & Taddiken, 1986, pp. 152–151)

Suddenly certain problems become much worse, the federal government is not acting to solve the problems, and community organizations are more likely to get involved. The problems may be more difficult to resolve because of the loss of funding, but the need to find additional funds helps to link grass roots organizations to their constituencies, and ultimately strengthens local organizations. The funding crunch in some ways is a stimulus to more radical solutions than would be considered otherwise.

The federal Department of Housing and Urban Development has supported resident-managed public housing, for example, as funds for housing have declined.

The impact of government on these social problems strongly suggests that purely local solutions are not enough, that coalitions of progressive organizations have to concern themselves with analyzing the causes and solutions to the larger problems and lobby for these solutions. For example, in some cities, abandoned housing can be sold by the federal government for $1 to future residents who are taught by city staff how to fix them up. Materials may be contributed by foundations or charities. The private charity Habitat, which builds low-income housing, sometimes involves local community groups in construction. Such projects stabilize neighborhoods and build capacity.

Social Problems Compound

Problems cluster. A solution for an individual problem, such as job training to overcome inadequate preparation at school, will not by itself rectify a cluster of problems, such as the lack of jobs, poor health, and the lack of reasonably priced day-care facilities.

Multiple problems magnify the effect of each of the separate problems. Unemployment in the central city is a serious problem because jobs have moved to the suburbs

Social problems compound.
(Catherine Green)

where there is little affordable housing. Without the ability to get to available work, the unemployed are less likely to try to get new job skills. Those who are homeless and have acquired immune deficiency syndrome (AIDS) or who are battered women with no place to stay are extreme cases of one problem compounding another.

Neighborhoods with high unemployment have higher crime rates, especially in areas of concentrated public housing. Scattered site housing reduces the concentration of public housing, but it creates new problems. The "fear of crime is significantly lower in deconcentrated public housing, but economic isolation is significantly higher" (Burby & Rohe, 1989, p. 127).

The implications for organizing are that a whole set of problems must be viewed together, and the possible consequences of particular solutions examined carefully, lest one problem be substituted for another. Transportation may have to be combined with job training, to get the unemployed to the work sites if they don't own cars, can't afford insurance, or don't qualify for driver's licenses. Perhaps employers can be persuaded to provide day care, or the job training can include teaching some of the unemployed how to work in day-care centers, and the organization can set up its own day-care facilities associated with the job-training center.

Some solutions address high school dropout rates and high unemployment simultaneously. In some cities, students who work in part-time jobs while they are in high school are promised full-time jobs if they graduate. Given the shrinking number of jobs that require less than a high school education, such programs are to be encouraged. Solutions require an understanding of the context of the problem—where the jobs are, what the educational requirements for existing jobs are—and what the other problems are that the target group may confront that have to be simultaneously addressed.

Officials Sometimes Don't Want to Solve Problems

Government isn't always committed to solving social problems. Public officials who field a lot of resentment against environmental controls, affirmative action, and welfare may support these programs half-heartedly and may cut back on funding or enforcement. Those who oppose social programs, in and out of government, sometimes frame a problem so that its solution creates resentment against government action. Thus, clean air is posed against economic development, so that efforts to clean the air are blamed for the loss of jobs, pitting workers against environmentalists and against their own interests in breathing. Moreover, attention is drawn away from one of the real causes of job loss, namely, that businesses close down profitable plants because more profit can be produced elsewhere. A similar problem occurs with affirmative action programs. The issue is framed in such a way that hiring women or minorities is said to make unemployment worse for white men. All men who feel they have been overlooked for promotion, or did not get the job they wanted, build resentment against affirmative action, when the real problem is the limited number of jobs for people with a given education. Attention is successfully diverted from the real problem and hence from any possibility of solution.

Because of this structured backlash, the more successful environmental and affirmative action programs are, the more pressure the affected public puts on public officials to dismantle or disable the programs. Public officials sometimes react to such pressures by supporting the appearance of doing something but ensuring such lax enforcement that opponents are relieved.

That some government programs fail provides a second kind of rationale for withdrawing effort from social problem solving, even when the evidence of failure is quite weak. Charles Murray, in his nefarious book *Losing Ground,* argues that as social programs increased, unemployment also increased, so government efforts were harmful. In spite of mistaken logic, the argument provided an excuse to cut back on governmental services. Many people point to failures in the administration of welfare to show that the program does not work. It is not the deserving poor, but the undeserving poor, they claim, who collect welfare, so why should we all pay taxes to support the welfare system?

Another strategy is to point out the exception who has succeeded and to blame those who are left behind as being somehow at fault for not matching the exceptional behavior. Today successful women are better off than ever before; the elderly who have pensions are wealthier than many younger families; and college-educated, married black couples are economically indistinguishable from their white counterparts. Such examples are held up to show that those who want to can succeed. These arguments ignore the increasing number of poor, female-headed households; they ignore that most blacks are not college educated and are not living in intact families; and they ignore the number of elderly people who are totally dependent on social security for their sustenance.

Progressive activists must fight the false dichotomies that lead to government inaction. The problems have to be reframed and the public educated into a more reasonable view of the problem, so that anger and effort is directed more constructively. Organizers can, for example, show that clean air and beautiful countryside are an economic asset, as the rapid growth in cities like Seattle testifies; being known for polluting chemicals and poisoned drinking water is hardly an advertisement likely to attract new residents and new businesses. Or the economic benefits of recycling can provide a basis for setting up new businesses in the community. There is no reason for environment and economic growth to be antagonistic.

A strategy for dealing with the argument that government programs don't work is first to debunk the arguments factually. Not only is it unlikely, for example, that welfare causes unemployment, but welfare includes a variety of programs, many of which work quite well. Sometimes it helps to remind people that private sector organizations also make mistakes, or in some cases have stopped trying altogether. How can one leave housing the poor to the private sector when builders generally do not find low-income housing profitable and hence do not build any? Sometimes government programs flounder because they have the tough problems that the private sector has refused to deal with.

To counter the image of the undeserving poor, organizers can find and publicize stories of families in homeless shelters or describe the lives and fears of the elderly poor who are trying to live off their social security checks. Organizers need to get across not only that the needs are real and legitimate but that public programs are not "us paying for them," but a safety net for everyone. Long-term unemployment, disabilities, and prejudice can happen to anyone, including white men, especially as they age.

The argument that government programs are unnecessary because some people can save themselves, and that those that don't are undeserving, can be addressed in several ways. One is to point out the variety of advantages that those who have made it "on their own" have had. Going to college is a lot easier in an intact family where someone is earning an income and can help support the student. Attending state-supported schools with low tuition requirements also helps. In fact, most of those who succeed did not do it "on their own"; they had extensive help from family and the public. A parallel argument is to show how difficult it is to pull yourself out of poverty when you face multiple problems.

What Is a Social Problem Emerges From a Collective Definition

How society collectively defines a problem is often more important in determining its outcome than the seriousness of the problem. For example, the battle over abortion is a battle over the shared definition of the problem. Is there a human being in the womb that has rights? If the answer is yes, then abortion is murder. Looked at differently, abortion represents a woman's right to control her own reproductive system, and the public's right to make reproductive decisions without the interference of the state. Different sides of the issue struggle to determine how the public will perceive the matter.

Perceptions of what causes social problems vary with the political climate. When society wishes to ignore a problem, it blames the victim as the cause of the problem, because of either laziness or craziness. At other times, society has been more willing to look at the societal causes of behavior. In general,

> in politically conservative times, psychological theory and practice tend to view individuals as the source of their own mental health problems, whereas during more politically liberal eras the environment is more often seen to be at fault. (Seidman & Rappaport, 1986, p. 2)

For the organizer, the problem is less that the broader society misdefines the causes of social problems and more that many of the victims accept such definitions and are unwilling to combat them.

For the activist the fight is to frame the issues and set the policy agenda so as to define a problem in ways compatible with progressive, collective action. As an example, the problem of battering women has been redefined over time and by different groups.

> Feminists have argued that the control of intimate violence depends on fundamental re-structuring of gender relations and the empowerment of women. Mental health professionals have promoted therapeutic intervention for offenders and victims of domestic violence. . . . Past research shows that police did not arrest men who battered their wives, even when victims were in serious danger and directly asked officers to arrest. . . . Activ-

ists in the battered women's movement saw failure to arrest as tacit support for batter-ing, contributing to the inability of women to escape violent relationships and in the escalation of abuse to domestic homicides. (Ferraro, 1989, p. 61)

Is battering a private domestic problem, as many police officers believed? Or is it a crime, as many women's groups contend? Is it cured through individual therapy, as the psychologists argue? Or is it biological and inevitable? Is the solution to arrest the perpetrators to protect the women? Or can the problem be solved by redefining the role of men and women in society?

From the perspective of community organizing, some of these perspectives work much better than others. Defining the problem as a private domestic problem or a biological or psychological problem is not useful for organizing. Defining abuse as a crime has some organizing potential and has the advantage of providing the possibility of enhanced safety and small victories; it also fits more into the spirit of the times, which is punitive, rather than flexible and exploratory about male and female roles.

Fashionable problems come and go, often at the behest of decision-making elites who have access to the mass media. According to President Bush, current U.S. problems are crime, drug abuse, and the lack of respect for the flag. This definition of societal problems distracts attention from the homeless, the accumulation of the poor in the inner cities, rising health-care costs, the AIDS epidemic, and the federal bail out of the savings and loan industry.

Progressive organizations can often get their issues on the public agenda by ap-proaching the problems in ways that get public attention. Such a problem must have drama and novelty and must be formulated in ways compatible with the needs of the government and volunteer agencies, legislators, and other groups that will have to deal with the problem (Hilgartner & Bosk, 1988).

Drunken driving has long been recognized as an important problem, but move-ments to confront this problem failed to capture public attention until Mothers Against Drunk Drivers (MADD) focused on the victims (Reinarman, 1988). In a short time, MADD had created an organization with over a half a million members and a budget in the tens of millions of dollars. The group was successful in many states in getting stronger DUI (driving under the influence of alcohol) laws passed (Reinarman, 1988, p. 92).

MADD worked with the liquor industry and was in agreement with the industry that promoting alcohol consumption was not bad and took "a narrow focus on the drunk driver—on the individual deviant" (Reinarman, 1988, p. 102). They might have had a more difficult time getting their issue on the agenda if they had tried to ban alcohol or liquor advertising. But MADD grew out of a political climate that argued for victim's rights, severe penalties for criminals, and minimizing the role of broader economic and structural conditions in creating social problems. MADD succeeded because it had a dramatic issue and framed it in a way that was compatible with the climate of the times.

Organizers have to recognize the importance of the spirit of the times but do not have to accept the opponents' framing of the issues. Organizers can help influence the public perception of a problem by framing the problem in ways that lead toward collective and empowering solutions.

Organizers Need to Understand the Causes of Social Problems

A sense of why a problem is occurring can help in choosing appropriate tactics and targets. Most organizers work with a tacit theory that it is the broader society rather than individual failings that create social problems. They do not believe in a hidden hand that justly, or at least dispassionately, creates economic inequality. Beyond such common themes, each organizer should work out for himself or herself explanations of why such severe social problems are occurring in a wealthy society and why particular problems are becoming more severe.

A useful theory of the causes of social problems can emphasize biological, political, psychological, or economic factors. In the example of battered women, the problem can be looked at biologically and deterministically; does male sexuality include violence? It can be looked at politically and psychologically, in terms of the balance of decision-making power in group settings. It can also be looked at economically, in terms of the role of women in the economy and in the family, and the degree of dependence of the woman on the man, especially during the childbearing years.

A theory of the source of social problems ideally should be broad enough to encompass several issues at the same time. Efforts to solve minority unemployment by promoting minority entrepreneurship ignore the problem of inadequate education. The homeless cannot be sheltered successfully without dealing with the issue of treatment for the insane, drug counseling for addicts, and job training for those whose skills no longer match existing jobs. What initially seems to be one problem often turns out to be a cluster of problems caused by multiple sources.

An organizer's theory must come to grips with what government can be pressed to do and how closely progressive organizations can work with government without losing their soul. Government sometimes solves but sometimes creates problems. Government programs provide money, housing, job training, and education for families with low or moderate incomes; but they also encourage corporate mergers that displace workers and offer incentives to businesses to relocate from one state to another. Government spends money to arrest drug dealers on the street, pays for the construction of prisons, pays to feed and keep those dealers behind bars, while long waiting lists accumulate for the nation's few drug rehabilitation centers, that cannot find money to help people restore their lives. Without governmental resources, damage to individuals from pollution is difficult to halt and impossible to reverse; yet, as a frequent ally of business, government too often looks the other way.

An organizer's theory of the causes of social problems emphasizes that individuals' problems are caused by changes in broad social and economic factors. But organizers aren't working with distant structures or abstract social forces. They are working with people in small groups in which individuality counts and is encouraged. Organizers have to merge empathy for people's problems with an understanding of the structural basis of where the problems come from and how they can be resolved. The purpose of organizing is to solve problems and to change a society; but it also is to benefit the individual who suffers from these problems.

7 | Learning About the Governmental Environment

The relationship between government and community organizing can be a complicated one. Government is the enemy when it works for business instead of ordinary people or when it opposes community power in local decision making. But, when pressured by community organizations, government may become a force for progressive change. Governmental agencies provide housing for the poor and elderly, hospitals for the medically indigent, and shelters for the homeless. Sometimes government agencies engage in community-development projects and provide funds for community organizations. Whether friend or enemy, government's effects on community organizations are pervasive.

This chapter describes some of what organizers need to know about government. It lists the functions governments perform, suggesting how community organizations can influence each of these functions. Second, the chapter sketches the structures of the national, state, and local government, so community members will know where to put pressure. The chapter concludes with an overview of the policy process, to help community organizations influence the decisions governments make.

GOVERNMENT FUNCTIONS AND COMMUNITY ORGANIZING

What does government do? An organizer can grasp the extent of governmental impact by taking a visual inventory in a typical middle-sized city. There is a city hall, a post office, an unemployment office, a jail, and a court house. There is a police and fire station and public housing. A community may have ambulances, public hospitals, community mental health centers, day-care centers, and a social security office. City trucks pick up garbage, and work crews repair streets and water pipes. Children play in neighborhood parks. Storefront offices serve as outreach centers for city council members and state representatives.

The observer may also see a shuttle service for the elderly or a sign announcing what number to call as an abused spouse. There might be a site for a future hotel, convention, and business complex, funded, in part, by state economic development programs. Or, there might be an elegant old building that escaped redevelopment after its owners petitioned government agencies to designate it a historic landmark.

Government activities are easy to categorize by programs—welfare, employment, parks, courts, and so on—but such distinctions do not tell the organizer much. It is more meaningful to divide government activities into a series of tasks and show how they can be influenced by community organizations. For this purpose, we divided government activities into 10 tasks: designing programs, allocating funds, providing services for citizens, building projects, awarding and supervising contracts, determining and enforcing laws, making and enforcing regulations, negotiating agreements, mediating disputes, and planning for the community.

Program Design

Community organizations can work with governmental agencies to design programs to help those in need. Advocacy organizations testify before state and federal legislative bodies about the need for new or recommended programs. At the local level, community organizations may pressure the health department to figure out better rat control programs and improved housing inspections for lead-based paint or may work with the police department to set up neighborhood watch programs. Housing organizations pressure city building inspection departments to enforce building codes and safety standards. Environmental organizations work with planning departments to draw up ordinances that will curb construction in flood plains.

Program Funding and Allocation of Resources

Community organizations work to pressure governmental agencies to provide the funds for the projects supported by community groups. For example, community groups have successfully convinced city governments to spend some of their economic development budget on neighborhood projects.

Another way for community groups to influence fund allocation is to monitor the activities of state and local government to make sure that grant funds are spent the way they were intended to be spent. For example, in the past, money intended to provide job training for the poor was diverted to pay for regular local government positions.

Provide Direct Services for Citizens

State and local governments provide services such as education, police and fire protection, sewage treatment, water, and street repairs. Some provide hospital care and public health facilities and occasionally run airports and golf courses and maintain parks. State and local housing authorities administer public housing programs.

The inadequacies of local services often make citizens angry and provide good issues for organizing. Community groups may complain about police brutality and slow response time, sewage backups and floods, broken pavement, driveways blocked by snow plows, streets that were never plowed, or cars that were towed and disappeared. Poor neighborhoods might note whether they receive a fair share of services and agitate for more. Or, neighborhood groups might work with government to provide services, that is, engage in co-production. For example, community groups might patrol their neighborhoods, using technical support and equipment provided by the city.

The federal government provides few direct services, though it does maintain a national police and court system and collects information on population, housing, business, and local government finances. This population information is important because federal and state grants, especially social service grants, are often allocated by population size or the number of poor. Yet, the poor and homeless are most likely to be undercounted in a census, so that cities that need the most social service funding may receive less than is due them. Community groups have pressured the census bureau to reduce the undercount of the poor and homeless.

In addition to information, the federal government provides police and judicial services. Both the Federal Bureau of Investigation (FBI) and the Attorney General's office share responsibility for investigating civil rights violations, and federal marshals have been involved in implementing school desegregation decisions. Federal attorneys also investigate accusations of corruption. Community organizations sometimes launch voter registration drives, campaign for school desegregation, or monitor grant spending, activities that might require the assistance of federal officials.

Building Projects

Governments build highways, hospitals, and housing. Public agencies may construct prisons, old age homes, transit facilities, or gymnasiums, auditoriums, or convention centers. Construction creates temporary jobs. Community organizations may want to help determine who gets the jobs, to assure minority group participation, or to assure that female-headed firms get some of the work.

Concern about the type and location of projects can stimulate community action. A large public building can provide a spark for redevelopment in a declining neighborhood. The location of a new facility or a new highway may raise questions of social equity. Who will it serve? Whose neighborhood will be torn down to make way for it?

Government indirectly supports construction projects through grant and subsidy programs. Community groups should question why government is subsidizing new offices and apartment buildings that provide homes and jobs for the upper class while displacing the poor. Or community groups can insist that governmental aid to business development be contingent on the businesses' showing concern about the social impacts of their projects.

Awarding and Supervising Contracts

Government offers some services indirectly by issuing contracts to private companies or not-for-profit organizations to carry out the work. Contracting sometimes presents opportunities for community organizations. For example, local governments contract with community organizations to provide job training programs including finding the unemployed who might be employable, bringing them into the programs, evaluating their skills, giving them job training, and placing them in jobs. Community organizations receive state contracts to provide day care, home nursing care, and refuge for abused spouses. Contracts provide revenue to the community organization, while allowing it to perform vital services with a personal rather than a bureaucratic spirit.

Community organizations may also want to monitor government contracts, especially for services that are sloppily performed or performed without regard to the rights of the people involved. Sometimes contracts to provide these services are awarded to political allies, or awarded in ways that evade state laws, or are much too expensive for the quality of services received. If a community organization observes any irregularities in the process of letting contracts, it may be able to improve programs or at least use that information to get opponents out of office.

Making and Enforcing Laws

All levels of government pass laws (on the local level often called *ordinances*). Community organizations can agitate for the passage of particular ordinances or argue for stricter enforcement of some existing laws. Community organizations might want to encourage the city to establish an effective Human Relations Board, while national advocacy groups have succeeded in getting laws passed to end discrimination against the handicapped.

Getting a law passed or ordinance promulgated is but the first step. Too often, social legislation is passed without teeth; that is, it has no real penalties or even a mechanism for catching offenders. The purpose is to reduce pressure from progressive organizations, without really rocking the boat. Community organizations need to guard against legislation of this type.

Environmental organizations got a major law passed to protect endangered species, and then they worked to make sure the law was enforced. They spend time documenting which species are endangered and which construction projects or commercial uses threaten them, pressing the government to enforce the law. Most environmental organizations are not strong enough to stop those who would destroy the environment for economic gain, but once the laws are on the books, the battle can become one between government and industry, a far more even battle.

Regulations

The government does not just pass laws, it also creates regulations. The word *regulation* means two different things, both of which are central to community actions. First, *regulation* refers to the standards established by government to protect the public from harm. Second, it means the rules established by government agencies that translate laws into workable programs.

In the first sense of the word, the federal government is deeply involved in regulation. It sets minimum standards for clean water, clean air, automobile safety, nuclear power plant construction, food purity, and drug safety. For example, the Environmental Protection Agency can deny a city permission to dump untreated sewage into rivers or streams, fine industrial polluters, or cut off federal highway funds to cities that do not inspect automobiles for pollution. It can force plant owners to clean up hazardous waste dumps that threaten community health.

Any kind of ecological disaster, such as chemical pollution of drinking water, makes a good organizing issue because people are immediately threatened by it. The need is to make government take action to enforce already-existing regulations. Chemical pollutants may threaten food supplies, in which case, the federal Food and Drug Administration may be involved. The Occupational Health and Safety Administration deals with dangerous work environments. The Nuclear Regulatory Commission oversees the nuclear power industry and can withdraw or deny a power company permission to open a nuclear plant. Though these agencies have legal authority to protect the citizenry, community organizations must pressure them to do so. Lackadaisical regulatory enforcement is probably worse than none at all, because it creates the illusion of protection and hence hinders grass-roots organizing.

Community organizations can use federal regulatory agencies in several ways. They can threaten polluters or electric companies or city governments that they will report the problem to the appropriate federal agency, which may be enough to force compliance. Or, community organizations can collect information about violations of federal regulations and forward the information to sympathetic bureaucrats in the regulatory agencies.

State and local governments are also involved in a parallel form of regulation to protect health and safety. They establish minimum standards for housing quality, maximum levels of building density, and restrictions on land use. They also set standards for the cleanliness of restaurants, the healthfulness of food, and the honesty of scales and gasoline pumps. To reverse the deterioration of housing, community groups have pressured government to create and enforce housing standards.

Zoning is the regulatory authority through which cities can determine what types of buildings, for what purposes, can be constructed where in the city. Zoning is intended to reduce overcrowding and problems of health and safety, for example, by preventing dangerous industrial plants from locating too close to residential housing or schools. Though cities can't arbitrarily change the zoning of land to the detriment of property owners, within limits they can regulate whether property will be used for single-family homes or apartment buildings, or for industrial or commercial use.

Block associations and neighborhood organizations often get involved in zoning disputes. If a neighborhood is zoned for residential use and developers want to build a commercial center, they must request permission to change the zoning to permit the new and more intense use. If the neighbors view this as a threat to the residential character of the neighborhood, they can put pressure on city hall to deny the builder's request. Unfortunately, the same tactics are used to deny permission to build less expensive housing, needed by the poor, in suburban areas.

The term *regulation* also refers to the rules that agencies establish to implement laws. Laws passed by Congress or state legislators usually are written in general terms, so that the agencies that carry them out have considerable discretion, for example, in determining who is eligible for support from social service programs or how much money should go to particular neighborhoods. For example, for years there were battles over regulations for spending development funds designated for the poor. Builders wanted the regulations to allow constructing a hotel in a poor neighborhood even if the hotel destroyed local housing, while the community organizations insisted the money directly benefit poor people.

Negotiation and Persuasion

Negotiations are discussions in which governmental agencies try to persuade one another to make particular decisions. The White House negotiates with agencies over the levels of budget and staffing for programs while legislators negotiate with interest groups and with the chief executive (the President, the Governor, and the Mayor) about the wording of legislative proposals. For example, in describing how taxation gets decided, a recent study indicates:

> The politics of taxation is not a politics of coercion, it is a politics of persuasion. When public officials plan to raise a tax . . . they spend time gathering opinion, publicizing need, crafting deals that will gain political support. (I.S. Rubin, 1990, p. 53)

If a community organization is concerned with the location of a redevelopment site, or about how much housing will be destroyed and how much replaced, or how many jobs will be created for neighborhood people, the community organization's representative needs to be involved in the negotiations from the start. If a community organization is concerned about population growth, density, traffic flow, or the type of housing or commercial or industrial development in the city, the time to take definitive action is while the city is negotiating with builders. In general, many governmental decisions emerge out of such piecemeal negotiations. Community organizations must be involved in the process.

Adjudication and Mediation

Governments on all levels support judicial and quasi-judicial bodies that can affect community actions. For example, if a community organization believes there is a violation of civil rights, the group can bring the case to a federal court. The federal Equal Employment Opportunity Commission (EEOC) handles problems concerning age, sexual, and racial discrimination in employment. City human relations boards hear cases on job, housing, or age discrimination. The boards generally have no power to punish the offending party, so their role involves fact finding and persuasion. Community organizations can watch for instances of housing, sexual, or employment discrimination, refer them to the commissions, and provide support for the complainants. Recently, neighborhood mediation centers have been established to allow local dispute settlement without the intervention of the court system. When people are afraid of the court system, community organizations can help set up such mediation centers.

Planning

Planners estimate future need for physical facilities—new water mains and roads, recreational open space, and industrial parks—and try to lay out what they visualize as the best use of land within and adjacent to a city. Social planners anticipate which social and governmental services will be required based on changes in the size, age composition, and economic status of the population. They estimate future needs for public transportation, hospitals and nursing homes, and schools and libraries.

Working with planners can be helpful in getting needed background data and defining issues. In addition, community organizations should talk to planners to make them more sensitive to the social agenda, especially because planners tend to focus on economic development or land use concerns rather than on the people affected. By getting involved in planning, community groups can make their case to politicians for an increased amount of open space, better public transportation, or more housing for moderate-income families.

But be wary of too much effort on planning. Politicians, fearing to deny a request from a community group, yet not wanting to grant the request, will often set up a planning study to postpone action. In this case, planning is a waste of time.

In summary, governments perform a variety of tasks of import to community organizers. Community groups can agitate for new laws or better enforcement of current laws, design new programs, defend programs that have benefited their constituency, or pressure city governments to relocate proposed physical facilities that threaten neighborhoods. They can monitor local government programs for compliance with federal regulations. In a less oppositional vein, community organizations can supplement city services through coproduction, use the mediation and conciliation services of government, or obtain contracts from governments to deliver service.

To be effective in dealing with government requires knowledge of the structure of federal, state, and local government. Community groups have to know where to put their pressure.

THE STRUCTURE OF GOVERNMENT

To successfully pressure government, community organizers must know which agency at what level of government has responsibility for the programs and decisions they are interested in. Unfortunately, the answer is not simple.

National, state, and local governments have different but often overlapping responsibilities with no simple hierarchy of power. For some problems, the federal government is dominant; for others, the state and local governments are more important. State governments can delegate responsibility to a local government or not, as they choose.

There are about 82,000 different governmental bodies including the federal government, the states, counties, municipalities, towns and townships, and special districts. Some of these units overlap, so people can live in several different jurisdictions at the same time. Because there are so many special- and general-purpose governments at the local level, power is fragmented and government jurisdictions often overlap in authority. Table 7–1 lists the government bodies with legal authority in one suburban area of Illinois.

A compensating feature for this complexity is that there are often multiple access points to government. If a group fails to get support at one level of government, it can try again at another level.

Governmental Specialization

One way to get a sense of how functions are divided among the levels of government is to examine the areas in which federal, state, and local government specialize. The federal government has primary responsibility for foreign affairs and defense and for maintaining the minimum requirements for commerce, that is, a postal system, standards for weights and measures, and a monetary system. The federal government has also assumed the primary responsibility for civil rights of citizens. In addition, the federal government funds a number of social programs, most of which are administered by state and local governments.

State governments play major roles in law enforcement and increasingly in economic development policy. State governments play important roles in education and mental health. The states delegate responsibility for primary and secondary public education to local governments. More activist states have programs to aid the elderly or

TABLE 7–1

Government Units in One City in Suburban Dupage County, Illinois

General-Purpose Nonlocal Government	General-Purpose Local Government	Special-Purpose Local Governments
U.S. Federal Government	City of Naperville	Dupage Airport District
State Government of Illinois	Dupage County	Dupage Forest Preserve Districts
	Naperville Township	Dupage Water Commission
	Lisle Township	Naperville Library District
		Naperville Park District
		Edward Hospital
		School District 203
		Community College District 502

Source: Dupage County Clerk's Report, Tax Codes 1988.

defend consumer rights. State governments typically regulate the insurance industry and electric companies and hence influence rates.

For a number of years, the states and the federal government have shared major responsibility for social welfare programs. With some limits, the state governments determine welfare policies, the administrative requirements for eligibility, and the amount of assistance while the federal government provided much of the money on a matching basis.

Local governments concentrate on delivering services: police, fire, sanitation, streets, and water. They often provide other direct services as well, such as education, recreation, libraries, housing code enforcement, and parking. Some local government services are provided by special districts, such as park districts or sanitary districts.

Though each level of government specializes in some activities, there is often overlap of responsibility between different levels of government. State, federal, and local agencies sometimes work together in particular programmatic areas. To add to the complexity, changing federal policies affect the relative responsibilities and independence of federal, state, and local governments. One of the major changes brought about by President Reagan's "New Federalism" was to decentralize more federal authority to the states.

Picket Fence Federalism.   Political scientists metaphorically describe cooperative relationships between levels of government as a picket fence that ties together officials at different levels of government who are working on the same problems. As an example, in dealing with wetlands, someone from the national Army Corps of Engineers might work with a state conservation officer and a city planner. Under picket fence federalism, the interpersonal and working relationships up and down a particular program picket are closer than between pickets for separate activities. For example, public works officials at the local level who work on highways are often more involved with state highway officials than with city community development officials, even though the former might work in the state capital and the latter on the next floor.

Under picket fence federalism, decisions on one level of government have personnel and action implications for another level.

> A federal rent subsidy program . . . prompted state governments to hire new employees to . . . complete reports showing state eligibility for funds. Still other state employees . . . determine which families qualified for the federal assistance. State inspectors were required, moreover, to certify that participating housing units met minimum standards of safety and sanitation and that rents fell within the "fair market" criteria established by the federal Department of Housing and Urban Development. (Dresang & Gosling, 1989, p. 96)

Because of the large number of government units in the United States, the complexity of the division of responsibility among them, and the resulting pattern of interaction, it is not a simple matter to figure out which government unit or units is responsible for a particular program or policy.

The first step in successful interaction with government is to find out what level of government has primary responsibility for the program or policy of concern. The second step is to map out the decision-making process at the level of government

Housing programs are intergovernmental endeavors. Here, former President Carter and Mrs. Carter meet with Chicago's Mayor Washington to encourage housing rehab programs. (Thom Clark)

responsible for the decision or policy. Who has power over decision making? Who initiates ideas? Who determines funding levels? And who controls implementation?

The Federal Structure and Community Action

Because the federal government funds many social and urban programs, it has been the key level of government for many progressive organizations. To influence federal policy, some knowledge of federal structure is required. Fortunately, the basic structure of the federal government is familiar to most people.

There are three branches, the executive, the legislative, and the judicial. The executive branch includes the President and the White House staff, the executive departments (whose heads are the Cabinet Secretaries), and a number of independent agencies that are loosely under presidential control. The legislative branch consists of Congress, with its supporting staff, and a small number of agencies that provide information or undertake investigations for Congress. The federal court system, including the Supreme Court, constitutes the judicial branch.

In theory, Congress prepares and approves laws, the executive enforces and implements them, while the judiciary provides legal interpretations and clarifies disputes on the meaning and constitutionality of laws. In practice, the situation is more complicated, with each branch of government taking on activities nominally assigned to another. Because of the overlap in roles, community organizations can press the same issue in the executive branch and in Congress and bring cases to court.

All three branches are formally open to input, although Congress is perhaps most open. Legislators hire professional staff to help them gather and analyze information, draw up legislation, and maintain contact with constituents and lobbyists. The staff members are informed about pending issues and are more accessible than members of Congress. They are good contact points for community organizations. The courts hear cases, but it may be difficult and take years to get a case before the Supreme Court. The executive branch, bound by the Administrative Procedures Act, must provide advance public notice on changes in procedures or regulations, and solicit public input.

Technically, all policy proposals are introduced by legislators, but in fact much legislation is suggested by executive agencies. Congress approves the federal budget, designs new programs, reviews ongoing programs, and suggests priorities. Members of Congress modify legislative proposals based on public hearings and individual lobbying efforts. Community organizations can testify to Congress about the impacts of existing legislation and propose changes in the legislation. Advocacy organizations, public interest groups, and community organizations provide information to legislators on their evaluation of needs and point out problems that require special legislative attention.

Although the passage of a bill into law requires action by the entire membership of both the Senate and the House of Representatives, most of the work in preparing legislation is done in small committees or subcommittees. Given the size of the federal government, the number of separate programs and policy areas, and the size of the budget, no Congressperson can develop the expertise to follow all the issues; accordingly, specialized committees are established. These committees hold hearings about problems, propose laws, revise their proposals during what are known as *markup* sessions and make recommendations to the whole Senate or House that are usually sustained by the whole body when it votes. Hence, the most logical members of Congress to contact are the members, especially the chairs, of the committees and subcommittees working on legislation of particular interest to the membership of the progressive organization.

Committees that work on particular legislation to design programs for particular policy areas are known as *authorizing committees*. Funding for many programs is considered by *subcommittees* of the *appropriation committee.* Authorizing committees and appropriation subcommittees in the House and the Senate each specialize in particular substantive areas, such as defense, foreign policy, transportation, or housing. In addition, *finance committees* in each house specialize in taxation, determining how tax burdens are allocated between the rich and the poor, between individual citizens and companies. The finance committees also have jurisdiction over social programs. Authorizing, appropriation, and revenue committees do their work independently of each other, and sometimes a committee in the House works independently of its counterpart in the Senate. Different bills may be introduced and referred to committees in each house, the differences to be worked out later.

Community groups often have two opportunities to introduce their ideas into the discussion. The House Banking and Housing Committee and its Senate counterpart consider whether or not to target programs to poor cities through the Community Development Block Grant or various federal housing programs. They also suggest the rules and regulations for carrying out such programs. More liberal members want money to be targeted to poor people, and more conservative members approve more discretion for localities. Meanwhile, the House Appropriations Committee and its Senate counterpart consider how much money will be spent on the particular programs. It is possible to have a well-thought-out program with limited funds or a poorly conceived program with large amounts of money. If a program is badly designed, community groups should pressure the authorizing committees to amend the legislation; if the program is severely underfunded, they should pressure the appropriations subcommittees.

The legislative process has become more complicated since the passage of the Gramm-Rudman-Hollings legislation that requires a continual reduction in the size of the federal deficit, either by legislative action or automatic formula. Gramm-Rudman-Hollings was amended in 1990. Discretionary spending—that must be approved regularly by Congress—is divided into three categories: defense, international, and domestic. Each has a separate target to limit spending. Entitlement programs—that automatically continue from year to year without new approval—are required to "pay as they go." That means that any increase in entitlement spending has to be made up by a reduction in discretionary spending or by increased taxes. The new law will make it very difficult to introduce new social service programs or to expand existing ones without making tradeoffs between them, at least through 1993.

Both the executive agencies, such as the Department of Health and Human Services and the Defense Department, and the independent agencies, such as the Nuclear Regulatory Agency and the Environmental Protection Agency, carry out programs passed by Congress. A peace organization might focus on the Department of State or the Defense Department, while organizations wanting to promote innovative job training and education programs for inner-city students might target the Department of Education and the Department of Labor.

Departments and agencies issue regulations stating how programs are to be implemented. If they are going to make any changes in these regulations, they have to make a public announcement and solicit opinions from the public. Community groups need to respond to these requests for opinions and try to shape regulations that help achieve community objectives.

Bureaucratic experts in executive branch agencies and on the White House staff propose new laws and new programs. The Treasury Department drew up the original proposal for tax reform that passed in 1986; the Department of Labor helped design the Job Training Partnership Act, which replaced CETA. Proposals for new or amended programs that arise in executive branch departments and agencies have to be approved by the Office of Management and Budget (OMB), in the Executive Office of the President, before they are referred to Congress for approval. The OMB is considerably less accessible to community organizations than are the departments and regulatory agencies.

The courts judge cases in which federal laws are contested or that involve conflicts between the states. At the pinnacle of the federal judiciary, the Supreme Court judges on the constitutionality of laws and can invalidate them. By determining which issues it will rule on, the Supreme Court sets part of the policy agenda for the federal government. Sometimes in interpreting the laws, the Supreme Court actually sets policy. For example, decisions of the court may state that women may (or may not) have abortions, that prayer in the schools is (or is not) legal, or that forced admissions of guilt are (or are not) permitted as evidence in court. These are issues that are of central concern to progressive organizations, and a clear-cut Supreme Court ruling, while perhaps not the end of the issue, can be a crucial step in changing or establishing policy.

State Government and Community Action

In recent years the states have become more important actors in making and implementing social policy.

> States are better equipped today to assume leadership than at any time before. Executive branch reforms have strengthened the ability of governors to set policy agendas . . . Gubernatorial staff have increased . . . Legislators have also become more professional and better staffed in their own right. (Dresang & Gosling, 1989, p. 22)

In the early 1980s, the Reagan administration provided states with increased responsibility for many social programs formerly run by the federal government. As a result even though the money is provided by the federal government, much of the discretion in running the programs is now at the state level.

In spite of the increase in their importance, less is known about the state government than about government at either the federal or local levels. Structurally, state governments appear to parallel the federal government with an executive branch, a two-house legislature in most states (Nebraska has only one house), and a judiciary. Looked at more closely, state government structures differ from one another and from the federal government. Organizers must examine each state individually to learn where power lies and how it can be influenced.

Most states have strong governors with power over appointments, the ability to propose a budget, and the right to veto specific parts of legislation. Strong governors have a major say in what will be funded as the federal government funnels its grant programs primarily through the governor's office (Dresang & Gosling, 1989, p. 36). Only a few states, Rhode Island, Mississippi, and Texas, still have weak executives (Burns et al., 1981, p. 123). The implication is that funding from the state usually requires the governor's support (Dresang & Gosling, 1989, p. 71).

As part of the growth in the state role and in executive power, the bureaucracy has expanded. As of the mid-1980s, state agencies and commissions, including universities, employed approximately 4 million people (Dresang & Gosling, 1989, p. 88) within a chaotically organized bureaucracy. With a vast array of state agencies and authorities, some of which are only quasi-public and not easily accessible to community groups, it is not always clear which agency or program reports to whom, or even to what branch of government. Adding to the confusion, state governments often reorganize, shuffling programs among departments and agencies to give more power to officials currently in favor. As a result, the location of programs may appear illogical, as when a neighborhood program is placed in an economic development agency.

A second reason for reorganizations is to enhance the policy-making power of the governor. As more of the smaller agencies have been brought together in larger departments under direct gubernatorial control, governors have been better able to coordinate programs and influence their direction. That arrangement makes the bureaucratic structure more logical, but it reduces the ability of a community organization to do an end run around the governor. Community organizations do not normally involve themselves in reorganizations, but they need to keep tabs on where their programs are and who has power and resources.

In addition to the cabinet agencies, most states have numerous quasi-independent agencies, often appointed by the governor, that have separate legal authority. These agencies do such things as set utility rates or provide funding for building projects. It is important to pressure such agencies, because they often control resources and set policies of interest to community groups.

In a number of states, some important officials are elected independently of the governor. For example, the state attorney general is often an independently elected officer and can choose his or her own enforcement actions without reference to the governor's agenda. In fact, many state's attorneys have been more aggressive in enforcing environmental laws than their governors, and some have acted as consumer advocates (Dresang & Gosling, 1989, p. 133).

Legislative power has increased as state lawmakers have become more professional. Nowadays legislators are more likely to work at the job full-time and to employ a professional staff that can provide information independent of lobbyists (Dresang & Gosling, 1989, pp. 111–118). This increase in professionalism has encouraged legislators to come up with their own policy initiatives. For community organizations this is a marked advantage, because it increases the likelihood that their legislators will be willing to work on community issues.

Citizens have more direct power at the state level than they do at the national level. In some states, citizens can propose legislation, called *initiatives,* pass a binding or nonbinding advisory to legislators on a current issue, called a *referendum,* and kick a sitting elected official out of office, through a *recall* election. In California, citizens imposed a severe limitation on local property taxes and voted to reduce the cost of insurance. In addition,

> California voters defeated a proposal aimed at quarantining AIDS victims, placed restrictions on toxic discharges into drinking water, and required notice of exposure to toxins; Oregonians chose not to restrict public funding of abortions. (Dresang & Gosling, 1989, p. 189)

Twenty-two states have powers of initiative and referendum (Dresang & Gosling, 1989, p. 175).

Initiatives and referenda are potentially powerful tools of citizen organizations, so long as the citizen groups are organized enough to conduct a state wide signature campaign. We'll discuss these tools more fully in Chapter 12.

Local Government Structures

The structures of local government differ from state to state, and within states, from place to place. Fortunately, local governments vary along a limited number of defined paths. They differ in their scope of responsibility, in their degree of autonomy from state authority, in the relative power of the executive and the legislative, and in the degree to which they are reformed or run by machines.

The scope of powers and responsibilities of *general-purpose local governments*— municipalities, counties and townships—differ depending on the state, and within states, by size. A broad-scope local government might be responsible for almost all local services, such as police, fire, sanitation, social services, welfare programs, community development, job training, planning and zoning, economic development, education, parks, and recreation. A narrow-scope local government might control only the police or zoning. In some states, like New York, townships are very important, while other states don't even have this form of government. The respective power of cities and counties differs by state. In some places, the city and county have completely merged, and in a few, the county and city are joined for certain governmental functions but remain independent for others.

Special Districts.   In addition to general-purpose governments, such as cities, there are also single-purpose, or *special-purpose* local governments. In many places education is the responsibility of school districts. Other special districts maintain parks and provide recreation, eliminate mosquitoes, maintain sewer systems, and support community hospitals.

A special kind of governmental district—a taxing or service district—might be set up in very small areas inside a city, when a particular street or neighborhood wants additional services that the rest of the city should not have to pay for. For example, one neighborhood might want to maintain its old brick streets, at a higher cost than other neighborhoods' blacktop surfacing. If they are willing to pay the difference themselves, the city may set up a special service area. Depending on state laws, extra policing in particular areas can be paid for this way, too.

Most special-purpose governments are governed by an elected board, though the boards might be appointed by mayors or other elected officials. Turnout for elections for special districts has been very low, because it is difficult for people to stay informed about the many different issues facing each of these separate districts. As a result, many special districts are easily dominated by small groups of interested people, which may make them a good target for concentrated community action.

General-Purpose Local Governments.   Most often it is not the special-purpose governments that are targets for community organizations but the general-purpose governments, the cities, towns, and counties. Their ability to carry out demands differs, depending on the degree of discretion they are permitted by the separate states.

Local governments might or might not have *home-rule* powers. Home-rule municipalities can undertake almost any local government activity not specifically limited by state law; for example, they can contract debt, they can initiate and carry out development projects, and they can increase taxes to pay for social services. Municipalities lacking home-rule powers can only undertake functions explicitly permitted by state law; without home rule, city hall might not have the discretion to take the actions a community organization wants it to take.

General-purpose governments are governed by elected officials on a council, an elected executive (county board chairperson, for example, or a mayor) and administered either directly by the executive or by an appointed administrator. Policy making is divided among the council members, the executive, and the administrator.

The structures of municipal government vary considerably, especially in terms of the power of the mayor, city council members, and the professional administrative staff. There are four basic types of city government: the strong mayor–council form, the weak mayor–council form, the commission form, and the council–manager form.

In the strong mayor form, the mayor has the primary power over the budget and can appoint the heads of city departments, the members of citizen advisory boards, and, on occasion, the boards for special districts that are controlled by the city. In the weak mayor form, appointment and budget-making powers are shared with the council; the mayor has little more power than any other council member. In the commission form, commissioners who are elected officials serve both as council members and as administrative heads of the separate departments such as police, fire, or public works. Finally, in the council–manager form, the council sets general policy and hires a professional city manager to supervise the departments, prepare budget recommendations, and run the city on a day-to-day basis.

The structure of local government is a good indicator of the extent to which it will display a more political or more a managerial orientation. The strong mayor form tends to be more political; the council–manager form has more managerial power. The structure also suggests the degree of power the local government has, who has discretion, and therefore, who community organizations should seek to pressure to get their case across. Do professional staff have sufficient discretion to make decisions without political consultation? Is a coalition of support needed on the council, or will support from a single member provide an entry to decision making?

Reform or Machine Control.   The present forms of local government structure emerged out of historic battles between *reform governments* and *political machines*. Machine governments are those that are dominated by a coherent political group, often a political party, which systematically delivers blocs of votes for chosen (slated) candidates. Machines typically pay off supporters with positions at city hall, to further cement their political coalitions. Professional administrators may be hired, but their power is curtailed by close political supervision.

Reform governments are dominated by professional managers, who think of cities as systems of problems that can be resolved through technical or managerial rather than political skills. Reform governments are often nonpartisan, that is, candidates run without party labels. Ideally, reform governments are less concerned with pleasing interest groups and more focused on providing services to individual citizens. In practice, most reformed governments tilt toward business.

Political machines with colorful bosses are now primarily a thing of the past because the basis for them is largely gone. The massive immigration that fed the machines has long since been reduced to a trickle; social services are provided by governmental agencies without regard to party loyalty. Though the powerful political machines have passed their peak, there is still a residue of the past that creates two different types of city administration.

The "unreformed" cities are likely to have a strong mayor with a city council consisting of members elected by districts. The mayor, who is elected at large and has a citywide constituency, often based on a coalition of ethnic groups, is more powerful than the council members, who have only the support of a single district. Even though individual council members don't wield much power, because they are district based, they provide neighborhoods with representatives who are likely to be responsive to local demands.

Reform governments are those that try to discourage the use of government resources to build political machines. "Reformed" cities are more likely to be characterized by a "weak mayor" and a strong council, often with the council members elected from the city as a whole, or some from the city as a whole and some from districts. Sometimes the mayor is chosen from among the council members and has little more authority or power than other council members.

Such cities hire city managers, who are trained professionals, to carry out the technical aspects of administration. The manager is responsible for preparing a balanced budget, handles routine administrative activities, and often has authority to hire and fire department heads. A number of cities have civil service-type hiring systems that reduce the control of politicians over hiring of staff.

In less reformed cities, the political process is more open to electing representatives of organized minorities, especially those clustered in a single election district. But the decision-making process itself may be difficult to dominate because most elected representatives do not wield much power. Decision making is more likely to be centralized in the person of the mayor. Agreements and deals may be kept secret, and council meetings, though open to the public, may reveal nothing because the decisions have already been made.

The reformed city is almost the opposite. It is more difficult to get representatives of specific neighborhoods on the council, but the council tends to be smaller and usually has more say in the decision-making process. Decisions are generally made in full view, and individuals are given more opportunity to speak before the council.

Though reformed and unreformed city governments seem far apart, real cities tend to lie between these poles. In reformed cities, city managers do defer to political pressure from the mayor and council, and even in unreformed cities, technical advice from staff has an impact. Community organizers have to study the structures of individual city governments and evaluate their strategies depending where the city falls on the reformed–unreformed continuum.

THE POLICY PROCESS AND GOVERNMENTAL DECISION MAKING

The reason that organizers study government structures is so they can better influence the policy process. For any particular issue, the number of programs and points of access may be numerous. For example, in antipoverty programs:

> The maze of programs is formidable. A 1986 White House report identified 59 "major public assistance programs," 31 "other low income grant programs," [and] 11 "low income loan programs." Two years later the Congressional Research Service listed 25 antipoverty programs. Eighteen congressional committees authorize and appropriate funds for these programs and 12 federal departments administer them. Most programs have administrative counterparts at the state and local level, each with its own eligibility rules and distribution formula. (Levitan et al., 1989, p. 6)

Policy advocacy groups have to know the details of such programs and who has decision-making control over each one. But almost any community group may find it strategic at some point to influence government policy. Having a general sense of how policy is made can be helpful in bringing community influence to bear.

> *Policy making in government takes place in four stages: putting a problem on the agenda, designing alternative solutions, promoting passage of legislation, and influencing implementation.*

Progressive organizations and their opponents try to influence each stage. To have input at one stage and not another is often to miss shaping programs for community needs.

The first stage is getting an issue on the policy agenda; that is, calling the attention of politicians to the issue and its importance. Politicians—at least those that get reelected—listen to people, read newspapers, and keep their eyes open to see what issues have to be addressed. Sometimes, they react to a problem because of a dramatic event, such as a fatal restaurant fire that publicly demonstrates inadequacies in the building codes. At other times a book such as Rachel Carson's *Silent Spring* (about the dangers of insecticide) or Michael Harrington's *The Other America* (about poverty in the United States) stimulates politicians to adopt an issue as their own. Bureaucrats sometimes place topics on the agenda, because they see better ways of solving problems or as a means for expanding the importance or budget of their agency.

Attentive people at a public hearing affecting neighborhood housing programs in Cleveland. (Courtesy Donn R. Nottage/City of Cleveland)

Community and progressive organizations get their issues on the policy agenda by creating a political cost to those who ignore the problems. At a minimum, this only requires showing up at city council or legislative hearings and making a case. When these tactics fail, a demonstration, sit-in, or other of the protest tactics described in Chapter 13 are required to get the issue on the agenda.

The next stage in the policy process is to generate possible solutions to problems. Elected officials and professional staff search for solutions through professional knowledge, they ask their peers at conventions what they are doing about similar problems, and they look to lobbyists for suggestions. At this stage, before laws are proposed, community organizations can propose and circulate ideas on how to handle a problem.

Legislators are often highly receptive to ideas that make them look active, creative, and useful. It is strategic to let legislators claim credit for the group's proposal. While

Friends in government can help a community group get its issues on the agenda. Chris Warren, former neighborhood activist, is now Community Development Chief in Cleveland. (Courtesy Donn R. Nottage/City of Cleveland)

the organization's membership will know who thought of the idea, ideas are more likely to turn into active legislation if others have a stake in its passage. Most solutions to social problems are widely circulated and modified; by the time they are passed, their origins are often forgotten. There is no harm in this so long as an appropriate policy is adopted.

The third stage in the policy process is the passage of a law or an ordinance. For the organization, this stage involves traditional lobbying: contacting legislators or council members, writing letters, making phone calls, and testifying before committees. Knowing when to approach an authorization committee, when to pressure the appropriations committee, when to speak to the mayor, or whether to try to influence the city manager is vital to the success or failure of this stage.

Passing a law is a time-consuming, multistage process involving many separate committees and both the legislative and executive branch of government. Getting a bill introduced is not enough because legislators might introduce the legislation to please the organization, knowing full well it will receive no support. Before a bill is introduced, the organization must learn who in each branch will pay serious attention to it. To gain such preliminary support often requires negotiation and compromise on the content of the bill before it is even considered (Dresang & Gosling, 1989, pp. 152–156).

Getting laws passed is an *iterative* process. That is, proposed laws are negotiated as they go back and forth between committees, between the executive and the legislature, and between interested citizen groups and government. From the community group's perspective, progress is made, then undone, and then made again. A bill or an ordinance will be proposed and defeated because it has one or two features that a pressure group strongly objects to; it may be reintroduced in a form that eliminates those features. Many of the ideas supported by progressive organizations are considered too radical to be passed as is. But even a fairly radical program may get governmental support if it is proposed as an experiment or trial that can be expanded if successful. Proposals have to be modified to get sufficient support to pass, but they should not be modified so much that they no longer serve the group's purpose. It is better to let such a watered down proposal die; otherwise, it will be difficult to introduce better legislation on the same subject.

The passage of a law or bill is not the end of the process. The fourth stage of the policy process entails influencing the implementation of a law or a regulation. This may mean that the progressive organization presses for more enforcement of a law, or equal enforcement of a law, or a more favorable interpretation of a law.

Figure 7–1 summarizes the policy process. In this figure, the policy process is viewed in terms of inputs, decisions, and outputs. The inputs include the policy makers' perceptions of the problem, and the pressure put on them by community or progressive organizations. The decision process includes the bureaucratic and political decision makers and the constraints on them. The outcomes include policies, programs, and the ways in which such policies and programs are implemented.

In short, policy making varies from one issue area to another, but a general pattern guides what to do next. That pattern includes getting issues on the agenda, designing alternative solutions, getting laws passed, and getting them implemented. Community

FIGURE 7–1

Summary of the Policy Process

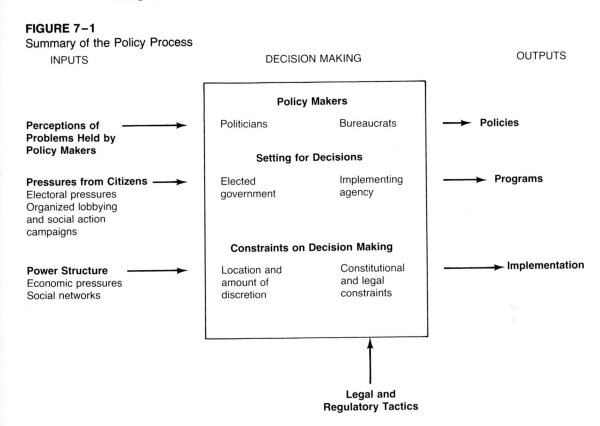

organizations can play an appropriate role in influencing policy at each of these stages. Social action campaigns help get issues on the agenda; action research helps to find appropriate solutions; pressure tactics help influence the passage of legislation; and monitoring and pressure tactics can influence regulations and implementation.

8 | Information for Mobilization and Social Action

C ommunity activists have to be good at finding out things. They have to learn what problems people feel are most important, because those are the issues people will take action on. Activists look for information about the community in which the problems occur to plan mobilization tactics. Organization members hunt for solutions that are most likely to work in their community, because successes build capacity. *Action research,* as this process is called, not only finds out what community members feel the problems are, but what in particular about the problems disturb them, and what they hope to accomplish by solving them.

Action research occurs at every step of organizing, from initial surveys of the community to working out the most likely solutions to the problems found (Biklen, 1983; Fear et al., 1985; Seidman, 1983). It describes the level of social integration and points out community antagonisms. It helps sort out who has power in a community and hence whom to pressure. Information from action research can help win campaigns by describing targets' vulnerabilities or outlining the negative impacts of proposed projects. And finally, action research can find out what solutions have been tried and failed and what works elsewhere.

> Action research *is the systematic gathering of information by people who are both affected by a problem and who want to solve that problem. It is a fact-gathering endeavor as people learn about the problem, a mobilization endeavor as people learn they share the problem, and a capacity-building endeavor as people work to solve the problem.*

It is empowering for organization members to learn research skills and to bring about changes based on the information they found by themselves.

Action research doesn't mean that group members have to do all the research themselves. They can read and use studies prepared by other groups and individuals interested in similar issues. Rachel Carson's *Silent Spring* (1962) helped environmental groups work to ban DDT; Jessica Mitford's (1963) investigation of scandals in the funeral industry helped increase regulation of morticians; and Ralph Nader's *Unsafe at Any Speed* (1972) spawned the consumer movement.

The Center for Community Change in Washington, DC, produces a newsletter on neighborhood and urban problems that summarizes research needed by progressive organizations. Recent issues document a decline in quality rental housing and discuss the question of whether government subsidies for businesses provide jobs for the poor. Newsletters of the Sierra Club, Greenpeace, the Nature Conservancy, Public Citizen, Common Cause, and other groups document many issues suitable for organizing.

Regardless of whether a group starts from scratch in gathering its own information or begins with data already collected by other organizations, action research is a way of building capacity. The Love Canal situation demonstrates that information from action research becomes the power needed to force change (A. Levine, 1982).

After filling up Love Canal with noxious chemicals, Hooker Chemical covered it over; later, it was surrounded by residential housing. Potential health problems were ignored until local residents were shocked into action by poisons leaking into their basements. They formed the Love Canal Homeowners Association, led by Lois Gibbs, a local housewife turned organizer. The association pressured government authorities to tell them what was happening and help them. After denying there was a problem, public agencies prepared reports, but these reports minimized the health problems. The more minor the consequences and the fewer people affected, the less expensive reparations would be for both government and business.

The homeowners conducted action research to learn about the effects of the chemicals; that research included a reexamination of the data collected by the government agencies. This new analysis showed extremely negative health consequences on those living near the dump. When the extent of the health threat was presented to the news media, the pressure was sufficient to turn around governmental health authorities and convince them they had to declare an emergency. After a long fight, the association prevailed, and its members received money for resettlement.

The homeowners' ability to document the harm of the chemicals was the key to success. When people who are affected by a problem develop the skills to learn about it, they are empowered. And getting the information is the type of group activity that helps create solidarity. Action research provides an antidote to reliance on experts who, through technical research skills, might define the problem for community members and set their action agenda. It also helps counteract cynicism toward official data, "because people are more likely to trust findings if they help conduct the research" (Fear et al., 1985, p. 199).

Because the data collected is meant to guide action, the information needs to be accurate. If the information is biased, an organization might spend time on problems people don't really care about; if it is incomplete, the organization might attempt solutions that have failed elsewhere. When information is being gathered for public presentation in the midst of controversy, it must be accurate. Opponents will try hard to discredit the community group's research to weaken its public impact.

The rest of this chapter outlines how to do action research. We describe how to find out what problems are of concern to community members and how to document these problems, as well as how to describe the community in which actions will take place.

At the end of the chapter, we give some pointers on how to summarize and present the results, emphasizing the importance of turning research into collective actions.

LEARNING ABOUT FELT NEEDS AND INDIVIDUAL BELIEFS

Felt Needs as Problem Definition

No matter how hard an organizer tries to document a problem, people won't work to solve the problem unless they feel it is important. The first step in action research is to learn what problems people want to solve and how community members interpret given problems.

Different interpretations of a problem might lead to different actions.

Suppose people indicate that one of their felt needs is to eliminate a pornographic book store next to the high school, but the interpretations they give for why the store is there vary markedly. Religious groups may explain the problem as a sign of moral decay and be willing to picket the store and try to zone it out of existence. Those more concerned about economic deterioration might interpret the opening of the store as a result of economic decline, because other stores don't want to locate in that neighborhood. Their response might be to work on rehabbing some of the property and making it more attractive to other businesses.

If organizers incorrectly assume that they understand what a problem means to community members and then jump in and try to organize, they could make serious mistakes. For example, if people say they want to stabilize the community, organizers might at first believe that people are concerned about changing housing conditions when in actuality residents fear the changing racial composition of the neighborhood. Working to find a source of funding for good-quality racially integrated housing will not solve the problem as seen by community members.

Knowledge about how people interpret problems is used in designing action campaigns. For example, through their research, prochoice organizations learned that people were nervous about supporting abortion on moral grounds but were willing to accept that abortion represented an issue on the privacy rights of women. The subsequent campaign was based on this understanding of the issue.

The simplest and most direct way of collecting data about what people feel they need is to ask. First, meet people on an informal basis, in laundromats, at bars, at restaurants with counters, on park benches—any place comfortable to hang around and listen. Attend community meetings or go to neighborhood social clubs and listen to people's complaints and learn how they view the world.

To obtain more systematic information about felt needs and people's understanding of problems, two research procedures are appropriate. Surveys ascertain felt needs from a large number of people, though with little depth. Focused in-depth interviewing is more suited to uncovering how a smaller number of people understand problems and what they think the causes and possible remedies might be.

Focused Interviews

In a *focused interview*, people discuss in detail their feelings about a problem or their experiences with the problem or attempted solutions. For example, community members might complain that police routinely pick up minorities on the street and intimidate them into confessing to crimes. Or community members might express concern that when a mother is arrested insufficient effort is made to care for her children. Black or Hispanic interviewees might want more police protection, arguing that police pay attention only to crimes against white Anglos.

Focused interviews should be conducted with local leaders, members of citizen boards, or knowledgeable clergy or social workers. Find out who heads various block associations, merchant groups, and service clubs, and talk to them. If crime is a problem, the action researcher might want to talk to victims, the victims' family, the police, and legal assistance attorneys to get one side, and the defendants, their families and attorneys, as well as probation officers and judges to get a second and third point of view.

Researchers can ask the people they interview to suggest others with whom they should talk. Finding people this way is termed *snowball sampling*. Be cautious of this technique, because people are likely to suggest others who share their opinions, which limits the range of views the researchers can discover. To increase the range of opinions gathered, action researchers might go around the neighborhood, knocking on doors and interviewing people house by house. Alternatively, the researcher can ask informants to provide names of people who disagree with them. In any case, the researcher should select interviewees who logically ought to take a different position, such as a factory owner, a union representative, and blue- and white-collar workers.

An in-depth interview is like a conversation but a conversation that focuses on only a limited number of topics. To do it right takes some practice. First, to encourage people to talk openly and fully, assure them that their opinions will not be revealed to others or otherwise misused. Ask about people's experiences—asking when they complained to city hall is almost always better than asking their general opinions, such as do they think city hall cares? Then, once they begin a story, pay close attention, and encourage them to provide details. Notice when people hesitate before answering a question, and try to figure out whether they were uninformed or whether the question was somehow too sensitive to answer.

Interviewers need to keep the respondents focused on a topic yet avoid leading them to answer in any particular way. This is a real challenge for many activists, because they want to make changes and are unlikely to show enthusiasm when people praise the status quo. But during the information-gathering stage, activists need to curb their enthusiasm in order to collect unbiased answers about what community members want.

Focus Groups and Information Gathering.   Often it is easier to conduct focused interviews among small groups of friends and neighbors in restaurants, bars or places of work, or in home meetings. Shy people who may not respond to direct questions from an organizer may be more willing to talk in a group setting because they are among their friends. In conducting group interviews, the organizer tosses out a general question about community problems and then steps back and lets group members present their views.

The general experience is for people in the group to talk for a while and then converge on a topic that creates great enthusiasm. The organizer should listen to such discussions and then after everyone has had a say, delicately suggest moving on to another topic. "You've all had some inconveniences with day care, but nobody mentioned how to pay for it. Is that a problem?"

People in group interviews have to express their opinions openly, or the technique has little value, but once a strong opinion has been expressed, others are less likely to express their disagreement. To prevent this follow-the-leader pattern from occurring, participants should initially be provided an opportunity to present their opinions without responses being made by others.

In addition, a skillful organizer can learn about problems by watching how people interact with one another in the focus group (Morgan, 1988). For example, suppose the subject matter is day care, and there is little excitement in the group when people discuss the types of toys the day-care center needs. But when describing how late the center is to be open, the men and women start strongly disagreeing. It is possible that community members are not in agreement on the sexual division of labor. To fully understand how the community feels about day care, this hint should be followed up with direct questions later. Observations of group discussions might highlight the tensions within a community group early enough to prevent future problems.

In-depth interviews are vital to identify how people interpret community problems. But because the organizer cannot talk to very many people at great length, it is difficult to determine what the majority of community members feel or what the priorities of the organization should be. This is accomplished through surveys.

Community and National Surveys

Information about preferences and perceptions of the whole community or an entire membership of an organization can be obtained from surveys in which the same questions are asked to everyone. In a survey questionnaire, the depth of response of a focused interview is sacrificed to obtain a broad representation of the opinions of many people.

For state and national organizations, a survey might be the only practical way of finding out about the feelings of the organization's widely scattered membership. For example, the Sierra Club, an environmentalist organization, conducted a survey to find out if its membership wanted the organization to oppose nuclear testing. Did the membership consider nuclear war the ultimate environmental threat, or were issues of war and peace too far from the perceived mission of the Club?

Needs-assessment surveys question community members on issues that in-depth interviews indicated are troublesome to many people in the area, such as fear of crime, unemployment, and the condition of housing. Most needs-assessment surveys also include a question about people's willingness to work with a community organization to solve the problems they have ranked as very important to them. Table 8–1 shows the variety of information that can be found on a needs-assessment survey.

TABLE 8–1

Types of Questions on Needs-Assessment Surveys

Purpose of Question	Examples
To determine overall living conditions within a particular community	1. Overall, how would you rate the quality of life within South Side? Good Fair Poor Very Bad 2. What do you especially like about South Side?
To determine action priorities	1. People have described different problems South Side faces. Of the following four problems, which do you think is most important, second most important, third most important, and least important? The garbage in the streets and alleys The condition of the apartment buildings on South Main Street The lack of recreation programs for teenagers The lack of housing for the elderly 2. In your own words, what are the most important problems facing South Side?
To determine action priorities within a specific problem area	1. How concerned are you about the following transportation issues? Amount of Concern: Severe Moderate Low The amount of traffic The cost of public transit The frequency of bus service
To learn why people think that problems occur	1. Do you agree or disagree with the following statements? The crime rate is high in South Side because the police tend to ignore the community. Agree Disagree The crime rate is high in South Side because teenagers run wild without any supervision. Agree Disagree The crime rate is high in South Side because strangers can just walk around. Agree Disagree
To find out personal background such as family size, education, employment history, income, job experience	1. Please compare your earnings to what they were before the steel mill closed. I'm still unemployed. I'm earning way less than I did before. I'm earning about the same. I'm earning more than I did before.

Preparing Questions.   It is worth spending a little time to construct a survey questionnaire correctly; in fact, national organizations often hire professional firms to design their surveys, though this might be somewhat disempowering. It is also disempowering, however, if volunteers collect information from a poorly prepared survey instrument and then cannot interpret the findings. For advice in preparing the instrument, organizers should read one of the standard textbooks that include descriptions of questionnaire construction (Babbie, 1989; Dillman, 1978; H. J. Rubin, 1983). Minimally, in preparing the questions, keep the following in mind:

1. *Questions should make sense to the respondents and seem important to them.* It makes sense to ask subscribers to an environmental magazine how they feel about disappearing rain forests, especially right after the publicity of Earth Day. In neighborhood surveys, questions should focus directly on specific problems in the community and experiences people have had in trying to solve these problems. Questions should only be written after talking with people in the community, or looking around and reading local newsletters and newspapers.

2. *Don't collect more information than is needed.* Keep the instrument as short as possible and make sure the answers are necessary in planning action. If working on improving community facilities for the elderly, information on the number of elderly in a household and their medical coverage would be relevant, whereas attitudes about social security or Medicare are unlikely to be important. Many background questions, such as the level of the respondent's education, might be unimportant for subsequent action, and need not be asked.

3. *Word questions carefully.* Language should be simple, direct, and familiar to the respondents. Asking someone if they have been mugged is better than asking if they have been the victim of a felonious assault.

Avoid questions that are either loaded or double barreled. A loaded question virtually forces a given answer, for example, "Do you oppose dumping of toxic chemicals?" A double-barreled question asks two items in one question, such as "Do you want to tear down existing housing and build a home for the elderly?" People who do not want to tear down housing still might want to support housing for the elderly. How should they respond? Answers to loaded or double-barreled questions are not interpretable.

4. *Keep the answer categories fairly simple.* Survey questions ask people for short answers or for answers that do not require explanations. For most items, the survey should provide a short list of clear choices for people to choose from. Questions that provide a short list of alternatives to pick from are called *fixed format questions.*

The survey might ask people which is more important: housing improvement, crime fighting, street cleaning, or day care. Don't ask people to put more than five or six items in priority order, and try to make sure items are roughly comparable in effort or difficulty. Getting a needed stop-sign should not be compared with working to promote neighborhood incumbent upgrading.

5. *Decide whether or not to have open-ended questions along with the fixed format questions.* Table 8–1 has both fixed format (those questions numbered 1) and open-ended questions (those questions numbered 2) for various topics. Rather than force people into fixed categories, open-ended questions allow people to provide answers they think of themselves. The purpose of open-ended questions is to explore an issue or learn

about a problem that those designing the survey missed. It's okay to have one or two open-ended questions, but more than that means that those designing the survey probably did not do their homework in talking with people. Open-ended questions are not a substitute for in-depth interviews in which issues are explored in detail.

Choosing a Sample.   With standardized survey instruments, it is feasible to ask community members the same questions and find out what the typical community member thinks about particular problems. However, if action researchers ask the survey questions to the first few people they find, they will probably end up talking to more aggressive people or to their own friends, who are likely to have similar ideas to themselves and be more willing to participate in organizational activities than other people. Such untypical respondents might lead to an exaggerated sense of the level of community support and mistaken ideas about what issues are important to the membership.

Instead, action researchers can use scientific sampling procedures, which allow answers given by a few hundred randomly chosen people to provide the basis for accurately judging the opinions of all people in the neighborhood or the entire organizational membership in a national group. Scientific sampling can get somewhat complicated, but as long as three basic principles are followed, the results will tend to be accurate (H. J. Rubin, 1983, pp. 131–162).

First, action researchers decide whose opinions are of interest, that is, who is in the population of interest. If the organizer wants to know about needs and problems in a neighborhood, the population might be all adults in the community. In this case, a couple living with their two college-aged children is treated as four separate members of the population. If the organization is interested in measuring housing blight, each dwelling unit is treated as one member of the population (of housing units), no matter whether it is empty or three families are sharing it.

In national organizations, organizers need to decide whether they want the opinions of all members of the organization or only those who have indicated they want to participate in political activities. In groups such as the Audubon Society or Sierra Club that mix people interested in outdoor recreation with those interested in environmental activism, such distinctions are important.

Once the population is specified, the researcher prepares a system for uniquely identifying each member of the population. For a national membership group, the membership number of each person is such an identifier. If the organizer wants opinions of voters in a precinct, a list of registered voters can be obtained from the Board of Elections. If the population consists of dwelling units, a listing of addresses can be obtained by walking around the block or by using a city directory.

Sometimes, lists aren't available but the researcher can prepare a substitute that is just as good. Even the homeless have been "listed" by clever researchers working for advocacy groups. One team of researchers mapped out a city to locate alleys, doorways, and other places the homeless might sleep and conducted a survey of these locations in the early hours of the morning (P. Rossi, & Wright, 1989). Another team used as the "list" people in shelters at any particular time. They did a second survey to enable them to estimate how often people who were in the shelters on one night stayed on the streets on another night. Through some rather elaborate calculations, they converted the data to be representative of street people (Burnham & Koegel, 1988).

Once a list has been prepared describing the population, the researcher wants to choose people (or buildings) from the list that represent the broader population. Information from people chosen in this way represents (with some error) the information from the whole group so long as the people are chosen from the lists randomly.

Random in this case does not mean hopping and skipping down the list; rather, it means working in a way in which every element on the list has an equal chance of being chosen, but which elements will be chosen is not known. For example, to get information from half the people, they can be chosen randomly by flipping a coin. If the coin comes up heads, talk to that person. If it comes up tails, go on to the next name, and flip again. Usually, flipping coins is an awkward way of picking a random sample, so a scientifically prepared table of random numbers is used. (For information on how to use a table of random numbers to choose a sample, see H. J. Rubin, 1983.)

Carefully describing a population and picking people randomly from that population are the first two steps in making sure survey sampling is done correctly. A third stage is ensuring that most of the people randomly chosen actually answer the questionnaire. People who are missed or refuse to answer tend to have different opinions from those who are more easily found. Certain people are almost never home when an action researcher calls, yet, it is dangerous to assume that the answers from people who are at home are typical. Or, if only the most cooperative community members provide answers, the sample is probably biased.

If only a few people are missed by the random selection from a listing of the population, the answers on a survey from a small sample will represent the entire population. Some mathematics are involved in interpreting the results, so community researchers might want to work with someone from a neighboring university who is trained in doing sampling.

LEARNING ABOUT THE COMMUNITY—ITS NETWORKS AND PROBLEMS

To effectively mobilize people, organizers need background information about the community. For example, they need to know the degree of social integration. How important are the solidarity communities? Are people loyal to and proud of their neighborhoods? They also need to find visible indications of community problems to provide evidence of problems that community members share.

Community analysis is a form of action research that examines the relationship between people and problems within a geographic setting. In focused interviews, residents might complain about a decrease in their sense of physical safety. Action researchers then take a walking tour and try to find out some of the causes of this feeling of insecurity. Are there teens or adult gangs hanging around parked cars, drinking and bantering with passersby? Are the street lights out, creating dark corners and shadows? Are there long blocks with buildings that are shut at night, so that no residents can look out windows to see an attack and call police? Do panhandlers accost pedestrians? Are purse snatchings common?

Community analysis also ascertains the degree of social integration. In a community with good support networks, someone who is unemployed can get help putting food on the table and is unlikely to leave the community to look for work. Someone without such support networks might be quicker to look for work elsewhere. Or a person in a solidarity community might be able to borrow from relatives to start a small business, while a person living in a community without strong social networks would have no resources and see no possibilities of improving his or her situation. Community analysis is more than simply understanding the physical setting of problems, it is understanding how the social environment affects people's perceptions.

Information for community analysis can be obtained through ethnographic and network approaches as well as from available data.

Ethnographic Approaches

Ethnographic researchers walk about, observe, and ask people about their community and their problems. They write down nearly everything they hear, look it over for inconsistencies or puzzles, and then go out to ask more questions and observe some more to try to unravel the puzzles.

To observe the sense of neighborhood identity, one might start by looking for natural boundaries, such as a major highway, a river, or perhaps a large park. The ethnographer would also look for a part of the community that might provide it with an identity or a name such as a small shopping center, primary school, church, or community center. The researcher can observe the conditions of front porches or stoops, and front yards, as well as the condition of the streets and other public areas. Are sidewalks tidy? Are there plantings that show community pride? Is there a neighborhood or community newspaper?

To check on the existence and strength of solidarity communities, look for signs of ethnic or cultural affinity. Learn about the churches in the community and the ethnic background of the priests and ministers. Are there stores in which foreign languages are spoken and, if so, what languages are spoken? Are there other signs of cultural identity, such as Italian pastry shops or kosher butchers? Are there private schools with clear ethnic or religious identity? Is there a local foreign language paper?

An ethnographic researcher will try to find out what holds the community together. Have there been protests or collective actions led by other community organizations? Do people know their neighbors? What holidays are important in the community? Are there local festivals that celebrate contributions of different ethnic or cultural groups? Even simpler, can people give a name to the part of the city in which they live (Crenson, 1983, p. 40)?

Sometimes, what seems to be one ethnic neighborhood may be several, an important complicating factor in organizing efforts. For example, a neighborhood with Chinese stores and Chinese language signs may appear to be one solidarity community. In fact, it most likely houses a variety of Asian immigrants, only some of whom are Chinese. Even the Chinese immigrants may be from different countries, from The People's Republic of China, Taiwan, Hong Kong, and Singapore. Reading local papers and talking to local leaders will often reveal whether there are many ethnic groups living in that neighborhood.

Ethnographic Procedures and Community Problems.   An ethnographic approach makes community problems and needs visible. For example, to measure the intensity of police patrol, an observer can stand at one corner for several hours and count the number of times a squad car passes by. To find out about garbage service, organization members can walk through the streets the day after garbage has been picked up and note what was missed. To understand medical needs, members can go to the emergency room of the community hospital, which often is the primary source of medical aid for the poor, and measure how long people have to wait for service. Environmentalists can count dead animals in polluted watersheds or walk along waterways and note illegal dumping of industrial waste. Ethnographers use a camera to document problems and

In convincing people, pictures are often worth a thousand words. Early photo used by Back of the Yards Council to show horrible conditions of rooming homes. (Courtesy Back of the Yards Council)

encourage people to talk about whatever is being photographed. The picture can be used in leaflets to encourage people to join an organization to solve the problem.

As part of an ethnographic walking tour, the community researcher can note what is located in each lot—a house, apartment building, store, service station, park, dump—then observe whether each structure is dilapidated or unpainted, or if windows are broken. A visual survey of the neighborhood will reveal such problems as broken sidewalks, unpaved or chip-and-seal roads, and gaping potholes. Poor drainage will show up in flooded underpasses; sewer backups will be apparent through their stench, especially after a heavy rain. If the community has many homeless people, they will be on the streets, pushing supermarket carts with their belongings and sleeping on park benches and in doorways. Trees on the parkways may be dead, or there may be no green anywhere. Or there may be weeds and small trees pushing up through broken pavement, suggesting the length of time since the last major repair. Each of these observations documents a community problem.

On a walking survey, community researchers may also see teenagers hanging around street corners or game rooms or see the spray-painted names of street gangs on the walls of buildings. They may watch people catching the bus after a long wait in rain or snow. They may note that food prices are outrageously high in comparison to other parts of the city. Or, they may see people hurrying home at dusk, trying not to be caught out alone after dark.

A visual needs assessment should also include an inventory of community services. For example, are there parks? Do they seem to be in continuous use? Are there public swimming pools, basketball courts, or a golf course? Is there a community mental health facility or walk-in medical clinic? Are these facilities being used? Are there half-way houses for those released from mental institutions, for rehabilitated drug users or recovering alcoholics? Are there sheltered workshops for the retarded? Are there hospices for the terminally ill? Is there a van that transports the elderly to clinics or shopping? Is there a home for the elderly? Is it located within easy walking distance of stores or recreation? Is there low-income public housing? If so, what does it look like? How old are the school buildings? Do they have playgrounds?

Notices on public bulletin boards, such as in supermarkets or laundermats, may indicate community problems. If many of them are people looking for odd jobs, it suggests something about the employment and skills levels; if many of the notes indicate used furniture for sale, it suggests lots of turnover, people moving into and out of the neighborhood.

The presence of other community organizations and community activities can be noted on a walking tour. Community groups often maintain storefront operations, and posters may announce forthcoming community activities. An art fair suggests a particular kind of community; notices of a revival meeting suggest a different kind of community. A poster for an informational meeting on the community development block grant budget provides a different message about community integration than posters for a community play, though both suggest a form of community solidarity.

Researchers can document economic problems in the community using ethnographic methods. Many day-labor employment offices suggest that the community contains a number of people with low skill levels who want to work. A lot of empty storefronts suggest a limited economy, and a lot of "leakage"; that is, money spent in the community quickly leaves to make outsiders better off. Poor communities often have no banks, only money exchanges, that cash welfare and social security checks for a fee. The businesses that do exist may have small capital investments, like barbers or beauty salons. There may be many shops that sell pornographic materials or drug paraphernalia. These are unhealthy signs.

Action researchers can also document problems through ethnographic experiments. For example, in testing whether there is housing discrimination, couples with different racial and ethnic backgrounds but with similar incomes try to rent apartments. Action researchers compare how often dominant-group and minority couples are shown apartments in choice locations and whether the minority couple is shown apartments only in minority neighborhoods.

This list of things to look for and actions to take to document community problems is only suggestive. As action researchers learn to pay detailed attention to the community, they will undoubtedly find evidence of problems not listed here.

Ethnographic Approaches and Decisional Power.   Ethnographic approaches provide information on governmental decision making. At the national level, observers can watch (or read the transcripts of) hearings, paying attention to which organizations present what ideas, and then later examine the legislation that is proposed, to see whose ideas were accepted and whose ideas were ignored. At the local level, observers can see which witnesses are questioned intently and which ones only routinely. The observations can be supplemented by interviews to find out who initiated which ideas that were subsequently adopted.

Sometimes those with the most influence over government never appear at hearings, because the outcomes they prefer have been reached in private. If a series of decisions benefit a particular builder or a bank, and representatives from those businesses never show up at hearings, that ought to rouse the action researcher's curiosity and prompt some interviews to track down the level of influence of the absent parties.

Observing Corruption, Openness, and Fairness.   Strategies for action campaigns vary depending on the honesty and openness of governmental agencies. A community organization does not want to spend much time working with or lobbying city hall if many of the agencies are corrupt or if city hall is closed to public input. To bid on a service contract when the process is fixed is a waste of time. To serve on advisory boards that do little distracts from more important efforts.

Information about openness, fairness, and honesty can be gathered using *participant observation,* in which researchers become part of the process they are observing. To find out how the unemployment insurance system treats people in a neighborhood, a participant observer can stand in line, listen to the requests and responses of those in front, and when his or her turn comes, ask questions about benefits or eligibility. The observer would note how long people had to wait in line, the level of courtesy, the clarity of the information, and whether similar cases seemed to receive similar benefits.

Sometimes participant observation can be very similar to police undercover work. For example, the Better Government Association (BGA) of Chicago used undercover techniques to document rumors of government corruption. The BGA bought a bar and managed it, to see if city inspectors would request bribes. They did, and the BGA recorded the evidence. On another occasion, BGA members got involved in an investigation of the Chicago Housing Authority, documented corruption, and brought about much-needed changes.

> In the aftermath of a BGA-*Chicago Tribune* investigation of the Chicago Housing Authority (CHA) which found obvious mismanagement and a serious conflict of interest on the part of the Authority's chairman, the federal government ordered the CHA to transfer funds it had deposited in interest free accounts to accounts where interest would accrue. Consequently, the public agency now earns interest on over $20 million that once sat idle. (Manikas, 1979)

Less dramatic forms of observation are equally important. During the Carter administration, the National Citizens Monitoring Project of the Working Group for Community Development Reform systematically monitored the CDBG program. They observed meetings to ensure that citizens were given the right to speak and that money was allocated to projects that benefited the poor and poorer areas. They documented violations of federal regulations on the allocation of funds and reported them to the Department of Housing and Urban Development.

Relatively simple observational techniques can be used to determine the level of openness and honesty at the local level. For example, attend public meetings and look for the following indicators:

Is there a consent agenda? To speed up meetings city councils will group minor items together in a single vote that is passed without discussion. Check to make sure that major items have not been slipped into the consent agenda.

Is the city accepting the lowest bids for goods and services from qualified merchants and contractors? If not, it may indicate favoritism or even bribes. If the organization thinks this may be happening, members can ask disappointed contractors to evaluate the bidding process and provide confirmation or disconfirmation. This procedure isn't always accurate, but it is usually helpful.

Are public meetings held at times convenient for citizens to attend? Does the council seem to meet very frequently in executive session, that is, behind closed doors? Or, are meetings held during a working day or with little notice? If the council doesn't make its decisions in public, there are grounds for suspicions.

Do citizen boards have any power? Citizen boards give recommendations to the city or county government for action. Is their advice followed or ignored most of the time? For example, we attended meetings of citizen advisory boards on community development budgetary allocations. These meetings were open: people had plenty of time to talk; arguments and counter arguments were made; officials responded to questions. The problem was the budget allocations were determined before the hearing, as we found out by interviewing governmental officials.

A difficulty with participant observation is that community activists want to be part of the action rather than just observers. If this is the case, send several people to a meeting, so some can actively participate and make short speeches, while the others observe. New members of the organization might find such observational tasks doubly illuminating: They can learn how local government works while watching how organization members participate in public meetings.

Network Analysis

Community analysis also involves learning about the relations—the network linkages—between people and between organizations. Is a neighborhood simply a group of strangers living near one another or an integrated social grouping? The answer influences mobilization strategies and choice of projects and goals.

Personal Networks.   When talking with people, find out how many friends they have living nearby and whom they talk to about problems. From whom do they learn about job opportunities? Whose advice is sought on how to vote? Do people know many others in the area or do they go elsewhere for friendship? If they have been involved in community actions, find out with whom.

Discovering the strength of social networks affects organizing strategies. Its easy to spread the word about upcoming events if people know each other, but more formal means, like letters or posters are required if people are strangers. In neighborhoods with low social integration, organizers have to bring people together informally before they can begin community actions.

Pay particular attention to how people in different issue networks relate to one another. Is there overlap of the people involved in women's rights, day care, environmental preservation, civil liberties, and community job creation? If so, the possibility of cooperative activities or coalitions between organizations is good, so a community organization can consider projects that require more political clout or larger numbers of people or resources. Are there separate cliques of people who have little to do with each other? If so, organizers have to be careful not to inadvertently antagonize one group by locating a meeting in the territory of another group.

Organization Sets.   The success of action campaigns depends to some extent on the responses of other organizations. An *organization set* is composed of those organizations whose actions influence a particular organization. It includes possible members, allies, government agencies, rival organizations, and targets. Figure 8–1 illustrates an organization set for a neighborhood revitalization organization.

Though organization sets differ depending on the particular issues, the categories remain relatively fixed. First, there are *potential partisans,* those who might join the organization and become active. Next, there are *local allies,* such as sympathetic church groups or local sources of funds, and *external allies,* such as Local Initiatives Support Corporation (LISC), a major source of redevelopment money.

FIGURE 8–1
The Organization Set of a Neighborhood Revitalization Organization

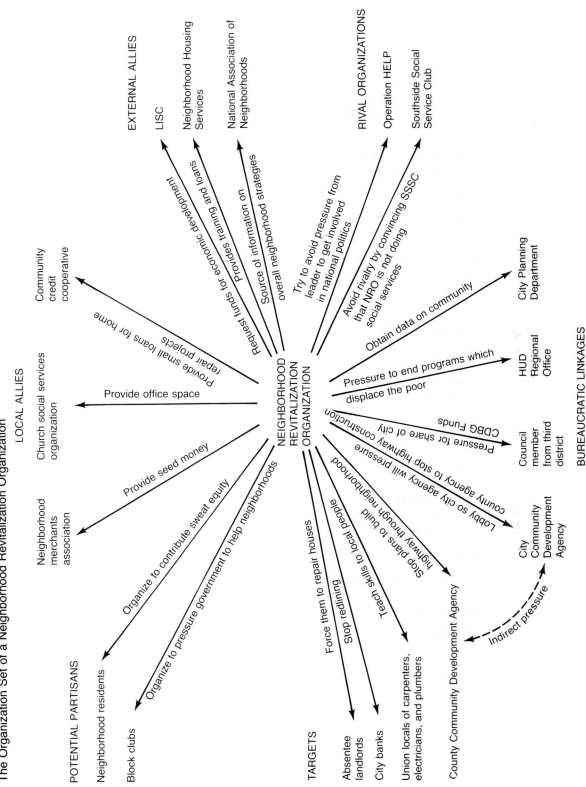

Bureaucratic linkages include supporters within the city council, the city community development agency, and the regional office of the federal Department of Housing and Urban Development. *Rival organizations* include the older and less effective Southside Social Service Club. The *targets* of this housing rehabilitation organization include local banks, absentee landlords, some union locals, and the county community development agency.

An organization set traces out the linkages between organizations that might affect the success of the community group. For example, the city community development department (an ally of the neighborhood group) might pressure the county development department to provide needed road repairs.

Quantitative Data That Describe Communities and Document Community Problems

Ethnographic techniques provide needed information in planning a campaign, as well as in strategies of mobilization. Unfortunately, public officials may treat ethnographic data as unsystematic or only as exaggerated personal accounts. To document the extent of a problem, ethnographic data need to be supplemented with numbers that authorities will believe.

A report by a feminist organization that women feel they are discouraged from applying for supervisory positions might be discounted as too soft, but data on the number of women at different ranks by age, education, and experience may raise a few eyebrows. Environmentalists concerned with an odd taste in the water can document their suspicions by looking up local figures on hospital admissions for diarrhea and vomiting; they can also check the figures from the local water plant on how much coliform bacteria is being found in the water.

When a community group needs to document the extent of a problem or changing social or economic conditions, it can draw on available data, that is, descriptive information about communities and neighborhoods collected by government and private agencies and made accessible to others. Such data have to be used cautiously, because they are not always accurate and were collected to make a different kind of argument than the community group now intends. But official data have credibility with politicians precisely because they were not collected for the organization's purposes and are seen as less likely to be biased toward the organization.

The U.S. Census.   The major source of available data is from the Bureau of the Census, whose decennial population and housing reports describe the number of people who live in each community, their age, family income, race and ethnic background, gender, education, employment status, commute to work, and the type, quality and expense of housing they live in. A separate report provides descriptive data on local government finances. National population data are updated through an annual survey, but the data are not detailed enough for individual communities. The census bureau studies housing in larger metropolitan areas on a frequent basis.

Population and housing data are released by census tracts, units of approximately 4,000 respondents. In larger cities, the census bureau will try to provide tract data that match neighborhoods, at least as the city officially defines neighborhoods. Otherwise, action researchers have to combine tract data to find out about their neighborhood, an awkward and not always accurate process.

Census data can help document community problems by showing how poor a neighborhood is or how poorly educated its residents are. Census data show the increasing numbers of female-headed households and can demonstrate the relationship of poverty and female-headed households. The census routinely documents the difference in family income between blacks, whites, and Hispanics, and the changes in the number of poor over time.

Action researchers tie needs shown in census data to campaign goals. An increase in female-headed households is an argument for quality day-care facilities. Figures showing low educational attainment cry out for efforts to improve community schools. A picture of a rat in a decaying apartment combined with statistics about housing age and condition makes effective propaganda for upgrading housing.

Some census data can be used as is, but more convincing arguments can be made with a little analysis of the data. Some of the analysis is just making comparisons, between neighborhoods or groups, or between time periods. If one community is substantially worse off than others, politicians may be willing to target programs to areas in need. With a little analysis, census data on where blacks and whites live can show the extent to which residential segregation is increasing in large cities.

In preparing action reports, census data can be combined with other figures descriptive of how federal grants are spent. Under many state and federal programs, areas that appear economically troubled should receive a higher proportion of projects and project dollars. By combining census figures that describe social need by geographic area and proposed city projects by neighborhood, action researchers can examine the fairness of expenditure decisions made by local government.

Other Forms of Available Data. Many other sources of available data can help document economic problems. State employment offices prepare unemployment estimates, private commercial surveys describe vacancies in stores and apartments, and private financial services distribute data on the fiscal health of cities. Other sources supply information on the quality and distribution of government services. Local government agencies maintain information on schools' dropout rates, the need for public transportation, the amount of crime, and housing conditions.

Available Data on Economic Problems

A key piece of economic data to measure public hardship is the unemployment rate, though interpreting the rate can be difficult. Unemployment data are reported on a countywide basis, which may make it difficult to find out the figures for a particular city neighborhood. Official unemployment figures measure only those currently unemployed who are looking for work. The numbers do not include those who were recently unemployed but now have a far worse job or those who have given up looking for work. If a group is trying to document *under*employment—the number of people working for less than a full year against their own desires or working at positions far less than their education warrants—official figures are not very useful.

Private commercial surveys, such as those by Dun & Bradstreet, contain information about turnover in local businesses, vacancies in office buildings, capitalization of businesses, and other figures that suggest where economic problems might occur. Also of use in sketching the economic life of a community is the *Polk Directory,* which is prepared by a commercial company to supplement and update census material. The directory lists types of buildings by address, the number of inhabitants, and the occupations of the inhabitants. It is not that accurate in describing the people in a neighborhood, but it does provide a quick way of learning which buildings have been added or torn down.

Information on the financial status of cities can be found in Standard and Poor's or Moody's directories of municipal bonds, which are guides for investors. Among other information, they report the proportion of property taxes levied that a city actually collected. When that figure is less than about 95%, there is usually some kind of serious problem. Maybe the elderly on fixed incomes cannot afford to pay the increased taxes as property values rise, or maybe absentee landlords are trying to increase their profits by not paying taxes. In either case, there is a problem that community organizations might want to pursue.

Available Data on Social Conditions

Local government offices collect information that action researchers can use to document community problems, such as crime rates by location, traffic accidents by intersection, housing complaints against particular building owners, the number of road repair projects in different parts of the city, and the emergency response time for police, fire, and ambulance.

Police records on crimes by location might show a need for increased patrol or a citizen crime-watch program. Fire department records on the locations of fires can be useful data demonstrating the need for building improvements such as sprinkler systems, improved fire alarms, and new wiring. Action researchers can combine information from school districts on dropout rates and classroom expenditures with census material on neighborhood poverty to show how underfunding of education hurts the poor.

A good place to find community data is the city planning or community development offices because these offices sometimes collect information on the location of troubled neighborhoods, changes in poverty levels, and the amount of deteriorated housing needed for grant applications. Planners' data can also help document a variety of other problems.

For example, planners collect descriptive data on land use and zoning changes. Increasing numbers of rezonings from residential to commercial uses might indicate that the city is so hungry for economic development that it is not protecting residential neighborhoods from strip development or obnoxious uses. A zoning change to permit office construction in an area of lower income housing is a warning of problems requiring community action.

Local agencies conduct special studies on city problems, such as the condition of streets or the need for moderate-income housing. Sometimes cities hire outside consultants to study local needs. Not only do these studies contain useful information, but they can be important weapons if community groups point out the discrepancies between what consulting firms recommended and what the city actually did or did not do.

Available Data on Public Spending

Another source of available data that can often be used to document unfilled social needs is the city budget. Budget documents are the plans for government expenditures and revenues and usually include the actual expenditures of the previous year. Most often, municipal budgets are broken down into three categories: general government, such as police and fire; public enterprises, or businesses that bring in their own revenue; and capital spending for permanent structures and equipment.

Members of a community organization might compare changes in the amount of money spent on police with the amount spent on social services or housing to determine city priorities. In doing this analysis, look carefully at whether the city transfers state or federal money for social programs to other programs. How much is drained off for administration? (More than 10% should raise eyebrows.) Do the police receive social service money for work at public housing? If the budget document is not clear enough on this topic, ask the finance or budget director.

The budget also provides information on city or county contributions to public facilities, such as public hospitals, nursing homes, animal shelters, and airports. Suppose a community organization is working to improve public health. It might want to check whether the city or county contribution to the local hospital has increased or decreased over time. In St. Louis, the city shut down the public hospitals to save money, and contracted for a joint facility with the county, over the vociferous protests of the local community. The protesters needed to follow up their arguments by looking at the city budget to see how much the city actually saved by such an arrangement.

Some city budgets have a section called a *capital improvement plan*. This plan lists the location and approximate cost of each proposed public improvement, such as street and sewer repairs, park equipment replacement, improved drainage, and additional lighting. Organizers can use these plans to document city neglect of particular neighborhoods.

Available data is generally fairly easy to get, though some may require a little effort. Census summaries are kept in many libraries. Commercial services can provide, at some cost, answers to questions from the census beyond the material published by the bureau. Unemployment rates are published at regular intervals and usually are printed in the newspaper. Budgets are easy to get from the city finance director or the city clerk. Data from city departments and consultant reports can be more difficult to obtain, especially if the city doesn't keep the data on the computer, or feels that the release of the information violates citizens' right to privacy. Many cities and counties don't keep good records and may not be able to find needed information.

There may be other ways to obtain departmental and consulting reports even when a city isn't cooperating or cannot find materials. Sometimes the League of Women Voters saves copies of reports. The national *Index to Current Urban Documents* locates consulting reports and studies prepared by city departments, assuming the departments sent a copy to this document archive. The *Index* guides the reader around a microfiche collection that is based on documents submitted by a pool of up to 250 cities (Durrance, 1984, p. 92). Fiches are on sale from Greenwood Press, and sometimes they can be borrowed on interlibrary loan. Using the index, researchers can look for documents from their own city but can also check to see if some other cities have done studies on the need for shelters for the homeless or drug rehabilitation centers or other pressing problems.

Generally, when a local government refuses to give a community organization some document, it is because it can't find it. But if organization members discover that the information is being intentionally withheld because officials fear the community organization might make trouble, researchers can try to get the information by threatening to use the Freedom of Information Act (FOIA) or the local equivalent.

On the federal level, the FOIA requires most forms of nonclassified information to be made available to people on request and at nominal cost. For example, an environmental organization learned the dangers of radioactive contamination around the Hanford Reactor only after using an FOIA court suit. The FOIA should be a last recourse, though, because government officials can stall and then try to swamp the organization with reams of unanalyzed data such as traffic counts or building inspections and charge the organization for photocopying.

Help is available in gaining access to government information from the Freedom of Information Clearing House, part of Public Citizen. The organization provides legal advice on how to get governmental information and will bring suit if necessary (Durrance, 1984, p. 99).

ACTION RESEARCH AND CAMPAIGN STRATEGIES

Action research is the tool to find out what the key issues are, how people understand them, and what the best strategies are for mobilizing the community. Once in a campaign, community organizations become hungry for information on how to conduct the campaign. Effective action campaigns are based on information about potential targets, while developmental efforts need information on how to solve problems.

Available Data on the Targets of Campaigns

From available data, community organizations can learn about the background of economic and political leaders, who are often the target of campaigns. For example, action researchers might need to know the names of corporation or bank presidents or the names of people who own slum housing. Who is the owner of the toxic waste site that is polluting the stream? Such information can be found by digging in libraries and sifting government documents.

Public libraries with business sections, business libraries, and government libraries each contain sources of information useful in campaigns against corporations or government officials. Company annual reports describe their overall financial status, while more detailed profit and loss statements for companies traded on a stock exchange become public data when filed at the Securities and Exchange Commission. Information on the largest stockholders of the companies can also be found here. Names of corporate officers can be located in *Poor's Registry of Executives and Directors*.

Background material on politicians is even easier to track down, for example, in *Who's Who in American Politics*. The names of campaign contributors (above a nominal amount) are kept on file at election bureaus. For national officials and increasingly for many state and local officials, conflict of interest laws require candidates to publish statements on their financial worth and investment holdings.

Who to target depends on how politicians voted. At the national level, organizations such as the Americans for Democratic Action keep records on how legislators voted on key issues, and other organizations, such as environmental groups and women's groups, keep records of how elected officials voted on their issues. At the local level, city clerks keep council minutes that go back many years and record each vote.

Organization members can find, by digging through public government records, information on local community power structures. Suppose action researchers want to learn who owns some property and whether or not taxes are paid on it. Tax and ownership records are public data, though it is possible for property to be owned by a "blind" (without a name) trust. It is particularly important to learn the owners of slum property and the people whose property will increase in value as a result of public construction, such as a renewal project or a highway.

Property ownership data are usually kept at the county seat. In some areas, an address is sufficient to find who owns the property. Cities usually keep information about building code violations. By merging code violations by address and ownership records, the action researcher can locate the landlords who allow property to deteriorate. Because mortgages are also listed in public records, the organization can also find out which banks are providing the funds for slum lords and put pressure on them too.

If a bank is federally chartered, regulatory agencies require the bank to provide information on where it is investing its money, information the action organization can use to find out if redlining is occurring. By combining this information with the previous research on who owns particular buildings, action researchers might be able to show that the same bank that is redlining a poor community is funding the downtown development projects of a friend of the mayor.

Available Data and Impact Assessment. Sometimes a community organization opposes a project, such as an eight-lane highway that will raze large parts of a neighborhood. To block such a project, the group generally has to convince others who don't live in the neighborhood that the project is a mistake. To do that, the group has to develop information on the impact of the project, especially the real costs and real benefits of the highway.

Determining direct financial costs is straightforward. There is the dollar cost of building the road, that is, labor, supplies, machinery rental, insurance, and inspection; there is the cost of acquiring the right of way and tearing down existing structures. There may be a cost of resettling displaced people. Action researchers add to these official figures other costs that are often ignored by public authorities, such as the number of people who will have to move to lesser quarters at higher rent levels, in neighborhoods removed from their helping networks.

The important nonmonetary costs and benefits created by the highway construction should be described. For example, these costs include the anguish of the elderly forced to move from homes they are familiar with and neighbors they know or the possibility that the highway will physically split a socially integrated community, making future community actions that much harder. Other costs include the emotional effects of the noise of squealing cars on the people who live along the highway. Also, there are figures about impact of various levels of automobile emissions on the health of those who must breath the fumes.

A good impact analysis goes beyond assessing direct and indirect financial costs and benefits. There are also questions concerning who would benefit (middle-class suburbanites who do not pay city taxes) and who would suffer (working class neighbors who do pay city taxes.) Others who potentially benefit are politicians who get credit for the construction jobs and who may get campaign support in return for awarding the contract to a particular construction company.

If a community organization wants to oppose a newly proposed residential development, they can use financial impact assessment techniques to figure out how much burden the new development will put on schools. Planners follow fairly standard techniques to estimate the revenues produced by new housing developments as well as the costs to the school system. With these data in hand, community organizations can figure, at least roughly, whether the school system will come out ahead or behind, and by how much. Financial evaluations can provide strong arguments to oppose projects that a city wants to impose on a community.

Information for Problem Solving

As action researchers get a better grasp on the nature of the problems the community confronts, they need to focus more on figuring out ways to solve them. To begin, the researchers should ask community members what solutions have been tried already, and which ones have succeeded or failed.

Suppose, for example, that an organizer wants to find out whether a neighborhood association should adopt a crime-watch program to help reduce crime rates while making people feel more secure. From focused interviews, action researchers find out that such a program was tried once but dropped. The researchers need to find out what the program was like and what happened to it. Was it carried out poorly? Was it designed in such a way that people did not really feel they were participating? Have circumstances changed to make a crime watch more appropriate now? Does its prior failure indicate that this is not a good approach for a particular community?

To find the answers, the action researchers should talk to people who were associated with the program. They can check newspapers to find stories about the program and see if any of the people mentioned in the stories are still around. Alternatively, the researchers might start with the police, and ask for anyone who was involved with the neighborhood-watch program and then begin a snowball sample of participants.

In addition, action researchers might want to learn how other communities have handled similar problems. It is empowering to learn that other communities, with no greater resources, were able to succeed. Such information is readily available, in community newsletters and publications of progressive national organizations. For example, activists routinely publish how they handled problems in periodicals like *The Neighborhood Works* or *City Limits*. These articles usually give the names of contact people who are willing to help other groups with similar problems.

The publication *Community Change* focuses on two or three problems an issue and catalogues publications of other groups on how they faced problems. A recent issue listed:

> *The National Technical Assistance Directory. Coalition on Human Needs*. 1000 Wisconsin Ave, NW, Washington, DC, 20007 ($3, free for low-income individuals and groups). This guide is intended for low-income advocates and service providers who want to know more about national technical assistance and public policy organizations. (*Community Change*, 1989, p. 10)

The community movement is linked by numerous newsletters. (Courtesy TTB)

Another handy reference source is

> *Getting Organized: A Directory of Action Alliances, Publications, and Information Services* [It] lists nearly 500 organizations that provide practical advice on developing health services, fighting a landlord, obtaining legal rights, etc. (Durrance, 1984, p. 101)

For more detailed information on particular ways problems have been solved, action researchers need access to publications of other progressive organizations. Many of these are listed in indexes prepared by Alternative Press Center Inc., P.O. Box 33109, Baltimore, MD, 21218–6401. Or contact the organizations described in Table 8–2.

Useful information can be also found in popular and specialized journals. Popular journals are indexed, that is, listed by title and subject in the *Reader's Guide to Periodical Literature*. More specialized journals can be found through the *Social Science Index* while *Public Affairs Information Service* describes government programs and political problems. For articles on urban problems, consult *Urban Affairs Abstracts,*

TABLE 8–2
Some Sources of Information on Community Problems and Problem Solving, by Issue Area

Community Organizing in General

    ACORN Research
    1605 Connecticut Ave
    Washington, DC 20009

    National People's Action
    810 N. Milwaukee Ave.
    Chicago, IL 60607

    National Center for Policy Alternatives
    2000 Florida Ave, NW
    Washington, DC 20009

Housing and Neighborhoods

    Center for Community Change
    1000 Wisconsin Ave, NW
    Washington, DC 20007

    The Center for Neighborhood Technology
    2125 W. North Ave.
    Chicago, IL 60647

Plant Closings and Economic Development

    Midwest Center for Labor Research
    3411 West Diversey Ave, Suite 14
    Chicago, IL 60647

    National Congress for Community Economic Development
    1612 K St. NW, Suite 510
    Washington, DC 20006

UIC Center for Urban Economic Development
The University of Illinois at Chicago
815 W. Van Buren, Suite 500
Chicago, IL 60607

Community Information Exchange
1120 G. St. NW, Suite 900
Washington, DC 20005

Fund Raising

    The Foundation Center
    79 Fifth Avenue
    New York, NY 10003

Environment

    Concern, Inc.
    1947 Columbia Rd. NW
    Washington, DC 20009

    Environmental Action Foundation
    1525 New Hampshire Ave, NW
    Washington, DC 20036

    Environmental Defense Fund
    257 Park Avenue South
    New York, NY 10010

Co-ops

    Co-op America
    2100 M. St, NW, Suite 310
    Washington, DC 20063

Urban Studies Abstracts, and *Public Administration Abstracts.* Most university libraries have these indices and abstracts, which can be quickly searched by computer.

Larger city libraries might have *"Recent Publications on Governmental Problems* [which] is published every two weeks by the Merriam Center Library . . . Chicago Illinois" (Durrance, 1984, p. 92). This is an index of publications on city problems in broad categories, such as poverty, housing, and unemployment. Libraries that lack such resources are often computer linked to larger university and state libraries.

PRESENTING ACTION DATA FOR MAXIMUM EFFECTIVENESS

To have any impact, information has to be made public in a dramatic way. Some problems are so self-evident that highlighting them through a photograph or video is enough to stimulate action, especially if newspapers publish the photos prominently. Most of the time, however, pictures are just a start. The community group has to figure

FIGURE 8–2
Sample Graph *(Source: Darden, Hill, Thomas, & Thomas, 1987)*

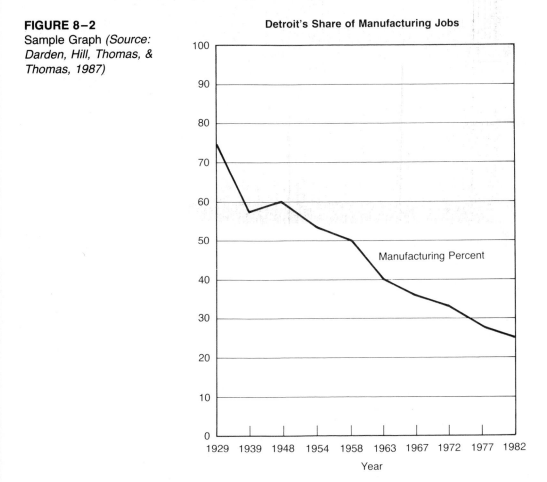

out an effective way of presenting the results of its action research in ways that are understandable, persuasive and, point to future actions.

It is important to think about what makes a report credible. It helps to use reliable data from sources that people trust. Local government officials have a hard time ignoring data collected by their own planners. Multiple sources of data are more convincing than a single source. The vividness of ethnographic data compensates for the dryness of available statistical data; both are needed.

Numeric data are best presented in graphic or pictoral form, so that even people with little understanding of mathematics can get the picture. Figures 8–2 to 8–9 illustrate some simple and clear graphic presentations of problems. Using standard data presentation packages and portable computers, a group can prepare a demonstration that vividly compares social data for one area of a city with another.

Maps are good for showing the extent and location of problems. Maps take on special importance when dealing with elected public officials who think in terms of

FIGURE 8–3
Sample Graph *(Source: Lauer, 1989)*

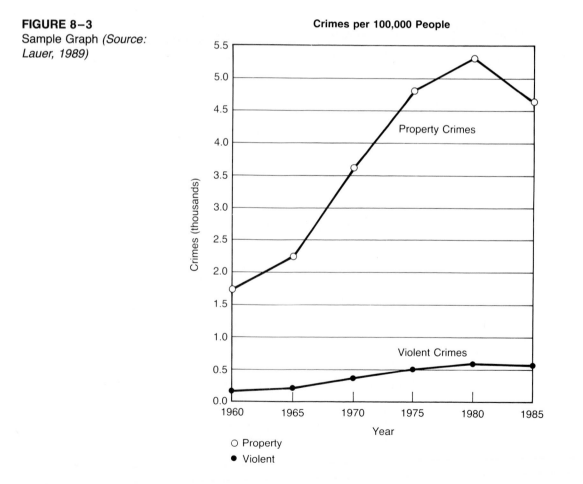

FIGURE 8–4
Sample Graph Using Color to
Emphasize Impact *(Source:
Lauer, 1989)*

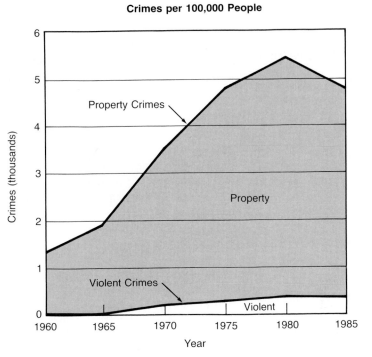

Crimes per 100,000 People

FIGURE 8–5
Sample Pie Chart *(Source:
City of Chicago, 1989)*

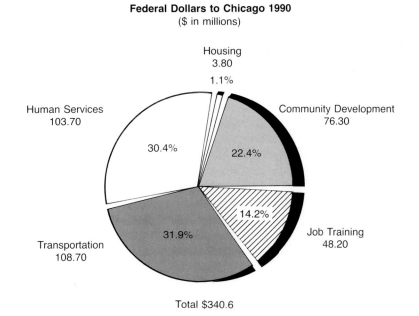

Federal Dollars to Chicago 1990
($ in millions)

FIGURE 8-6
Sample Pie Chart *(Source: U.S. Department of Housing and Urban Development)*

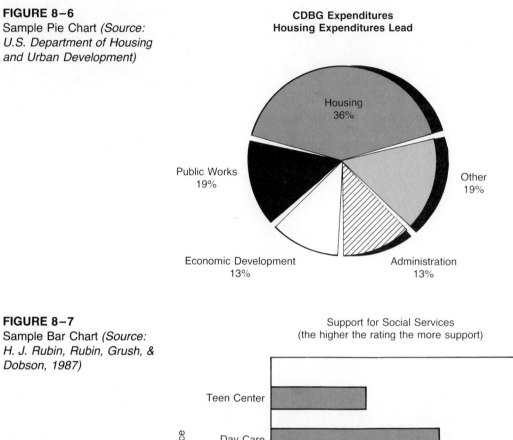

**CDBG Expenditures
Housing Expenditures Lead**

Housing 36%

Other 19%

Administration 13%

Economic Development 13%

Public Works 19%

FIGURE 8-7
Sample Bar Chart *(Source: H. J. Rubin, Rubin, Grush, & Dobson, 1987)*

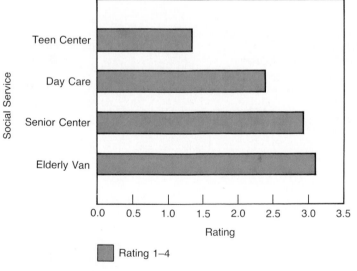

Support for Social Services
(the higher the rating the more support)

Social Service

Teen Center
Day Care
Senior Center
Elderly Van

Rating

Rating 1-4

FIGURE 8–8
Sample Bar Chart *(Source: Kasarda, 1988)*

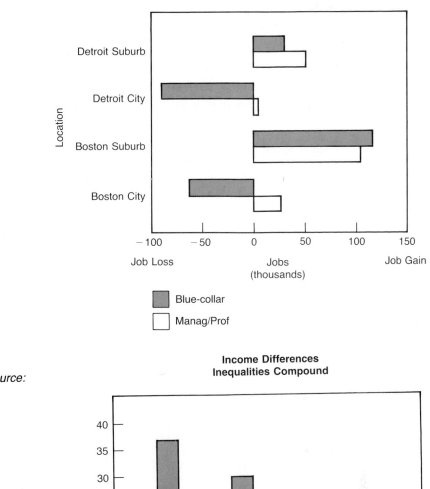

**Job Changes by Skill Level
Blue Collar Workers in Trouble**

FIGURE 8–9
Sample Bar Chart *(Source: Beeghley, 1989)*

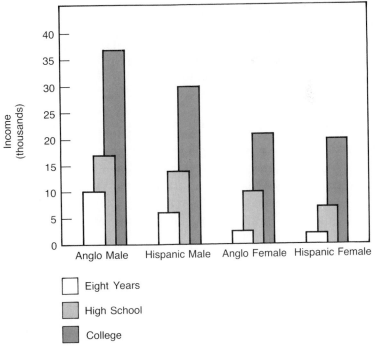

**Income Differences
Inequalities Compound**

voting districts, especially when computer presentations are prepared that let the politicians see the extent of a problem in their election districts.

Finally, in both the oral presentation and written reports, recommendations for actions should be made explicit.

It is not enough to document a problem; action researchers must link information to goals and to future action, as in the following examples:

Conclusion of Report on Health Care in Southside

[Goal] To improve the health conditions in Southside, [information on the problem] in which 15% of the children show below-normal growth patterns resulting from protein deficiency, [action] Southside community organization strongly advocates establishing a combination day-care and food cooperative that [information on resources for action] can be paid for using money from the Social Services Block Grant.

Conclusion of the Report on Housing Conditions in Southside

[Information on the problem] Having ascertained that 60% of the housing is owner occupied by lower-middle-income people, yet two thirds of this housing needs repairs, [action] Southside Neighborhood Housing Services will set up a revolving loan program. [Information on resources for action] In part, the funds will be obtained from the Engulf Trust Company, which has promised to double the amount of money lent to homeowners in Southside. [Goal] This work will improve the overall quality of housing in Southside for the people presently resident in the community.

Action research is an appropriate and necessary activity for community organizations. It involves many members, it is empowering, and it can be extraordinarily useful at almost every stage of a campaign. Action research discovers community problems and how people feel about them; it helps to design campaigns, because it can provide information about community integration, openness and honesty in government, and about the targets of a campaign. Information on the likely impacts of projects can be part of a campaign to oppose highways, downtown developments, strip mines, or gambling casinos, though information about who benefits from a project may be more useful than whether benefits outweigh costs. Action research also sorts through solutions to community projects to find the ones most likely to work in the local environment.

Whether action research is used to design a development campaign, as ammunition to knock out an opponent, or as a red flag to rouse a community to take action, people must understand the findings. The results of action research have to be presented in a convincing way. The data must appear sound, and the report must be written in a lively and easy to understand manner. Most important, the report has to include what the group proposes to do to solve community problems.

IV | Mobilization and Meetings

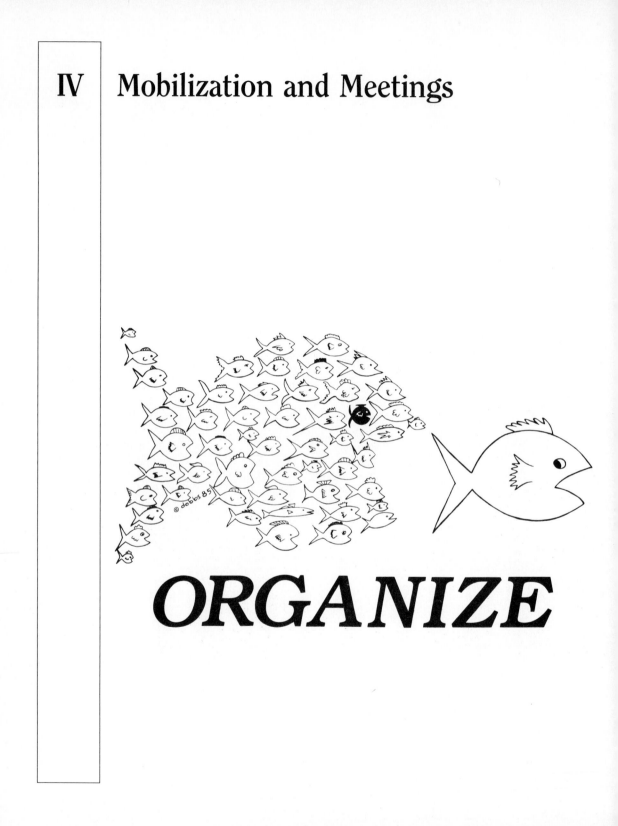

ORGANIZE

O rganizers help turn indignation at shared problems into organizational action. To do that, they have to involve people in collective actions.

Chapter 9 discusses mobilization tactics. Some of the barriers to mobilizing people appear daunting—the low level of political participation of poor people, for example. Yet, the message of this chapter is upbeat: Once people believe they can satisfy felt needs, the possibility of future successes provides a powerful motivation for continued effort.

Meetings build cohesion so that people who face shared problems can work together. In Chapter 10, we describe three forms of meetings: the membership meeting, the decision-making meeting, and training sessions. The aims of these meetings include creating a sense of "we-ness," determination of the action goals, and passing on skills needed for success.

9 | Mobilizing for Action

Action research is the first step in organizing during which people express their felt needs. The next step is one of political *mobilization,* that is, convincing people that their felt needs are shared by others and that they should work together to bring about needed changes. As mobilization progresses, people move from apathy to passive support for a cause and gradually become more active in community organizations.

Mobilization is the process of moving personal grievances to the realm of collective action.

Mobilization is stimulated by "click" events (*click* as when a light turns on). The click highlights the persistence of unjust dominance structures. A male attorney insists that the female attorneys fetch the coffee, or a boss threatens to fire a worker who is trying to eliminate dangerous working conditions. Blinders are suddenly removed, and people experience a particularly blatant abuse that stimulates grass-roots protests.

These grass-root protests spring from "practical" matters which cause fear and anger in people's lives, such as parents' horror when they find out that their children have been drinking water polluted by toxic chemicals. (Krauss, 1988, p. 260)

Mobilization occurs when those who have experienced such clicks join together to take action on their grievances. The experiences that make a person aware of a problem are the trigger events that move people from apathy to action.

Mobilization campaigns rarely try to change people's values and beliefs. Organizers would not try to recruit a white racist to a black community organization or a finance capitalist into a workers' cooperative. Instead, the purpose of mobilization campaigns is to turn passive supporters into active participants and motivate those who would benefit from social changes to work to bring about those changes.

Mobilization might involve building an organization from scratch. People gradually create organizations that focus their efforts and magnify their political and economic clout. More often, the organization already exists, so the mobilizing effort is focused on getting people to participate. Mobilization might involve seeking support from existing

191

organizations that in turn try to involve their own membership. For example, Alinsky-style organizers persuade established neighborhood organizations such as churches, homeowners' associations, and social clubs to join in progressive causes.

Sometimes people don't participate in progressive organizations because they think they can get the benefits of organizational actions without putting in the work or the time. Why get involved in a neighborhood cleanup effort when lots of other people will do the work? *Free riders,* those who want to benefit but want others to do the work, will join the effort only after seeing that the job will not get done without everyone's participation.

Even when they realize they are victims of problems, some people are still unwilling to get involved. Culturally imposed beliefs that they cannot succeed and that it is wrong to participate in collective action make it difficult for them to join community organizations. Mobilization has to undo a sense of learned inefficacy.

MOBILIZATION BOOTSTRAPS

Refusals to participate in collective action can be frustrating. But when mobilization efforts are even somewhat successful the process can take off. Once an organization is

Community members deciding whether or not to hire Alinsky for organizing work. (Courtesy Cleveland Public Library photographic collection from *Cleveland Plain Dealer*)

seen to satisfy felt needs, the commitment of individuals to work together increases. By working together, people learn that they can solve common problems and become more willing to articulate other felt needs.

As shown in Figure 9–1, mobilization leads to organizational success, and success increases mobilization.

Furthermore, collective participation in conflictual activity strengthens social bonds among group members and can make additional actions easier. Conflict increases solidarity. During labor struggles with management and with the police and strike breakers,

> An emergent culture is created in which new values are incubated, new forms of activity generated, and an associational bond of a new type formed. . . . Not only was the commitment of each activist sustained . . . but a collective identity was formed as well. (Fantasia, 1988, p. 174)

Having battled together once, people are more willing to work for the good of the group without always asking "What is in it for me?"

Community organizations with early successes are more likely to mobilize new members; even after apparent failure, mobilization efforts can succeed whenever a trigger event transforms personal grievances into collective explosions. After decades of passivity, much of Eastern Europe is in ferment, as people work collectively to liberalize their political systems. In the United States, gains in civil rights and sexual equality have come in bursts after years of apparent lull.

When such explosions occur, organizers may find themselves pushed by the momentum of a movement. For example, civil rights organizing in the Woodlawn Community in Chicago had been going slowly until the Woodlawn Organization hosted a civil rights rally for returning Freedom Riders (people who worked for voting rights in the South). The rally itself was the trigger as "Woodlawn had turned out en masse for the Freedom Riders" (Horwitt, 1989, p. 400). Nicholas von Hoffman, the Alinsky organizer who was working in the community, described the explosion to Alinsky:

> I think we should toss out everything we are doing organizationally and work on the premise that this is the moment of the whirlwind, that we are no longer organizing but guiding a social movement. (Horwitt, 1989, p. 401)

Motivating these explosions of involvement is the social-psychology of bootstrapping, in which people are more likely to become involved if they expect a movement to succeed (Klandermans, 1988). Demonstrating the potential for success and creating optimistic expectations about the willingness of others to be involved can create the increased involvement that leads to success.

FIGURE 9–1
The Mobilization Cycle

Felt Needs → Legitimate Building → Organization

Organization → Provides Opportunity to Satisfy → Felt Needs

Satisfying Felt Needs → Reinforces the Original Commitment → To Build Organization

---

With skill and luck, community organizations outlast their defeats. During periods of relative inactivity, a core cadre keeps the organization alive, awaiting the triggers that lead to widespread mobilization. When the political climate permits, these core activists can call on other like-minded individuals to become involved. Anti-war groups often function in this way, maintaining a small cadre during inactive periods, who activate others to join protests during crises like invasions of countries.

Not only can community organizations survive defeats and slow periods, sometimes apparent defeats can lead to increased mobilization, as the overreactions of authorities brings new people into the battle. Eric Hirsch describes a protest at Columbia University in which students demanded that the administration divest the university of investments in South Africa. When the administration ignored the student demands as well as the faculty support for divestment, a demonstration was called, but mobilization was haphazard. When the administration tried to expel students who had participated, the students welded together, facing the collective threat of expulsion (Hirsch, 1990, p. 249). With this new unity, students were energized and were able to force the university to give into their demands.

MOBILIZATION: THEORY AND FINDINGS

Who should organizers try to recruit? What proportion of the potential community should an organizer aim to bring in and activate? What makes organizing easy, what makes it more difficult, and why? What trigger events are there that might stimulate the explosions of successful community action described here? Fortunately, there is a large literature from political science (called *political participation*) and sociology (called *resource mobilization theory*) that can guide mobilization campaigns.

Studies of Political Participation

One way of looking at the question of who to try to bring into community organizations is to examine who generally gets involved in what kinds of political activities. Milbrath (1977) classified citizens into four levels of political participation that we'll apply to potential members of a community organization: apathetics, spectators, foot soldiers, and gladiators.

Apathetics are politically and socially inactive. Organizers focus very little effort on apathetics because they have usually dropped out of the political process or never entered it in the first place. Unfortunately, apathetics are the largest group. Political *spectators* are a little more active. They support particular organizations or issues and can be convinced to join the organization and participate in mass activities such as appearing at a public rally or voting for the organization's candidate for city council. Such people are reached through door-to-door canvassing, publicity efforts, and meetings.

More active still are the *foot soldiers,* who routinely show up at meetings, hand out flyers, lick stamps, and demonstrate in support of community issues. These individuals care deeply about the issues or feel they can benefit from the organization but for personal reasons are unwilling or unable to play a leadership role. The personal involvement of foot soldiers increases their sense of efficacy. The *gladiators* are highly involved individuals, who lead confrontations, spend many hours on organizational activities, and if necessary, subject themselves to arrest to publicize organizational goals. The gladiators provide leadership and hence are the most visible members of any community organization.

Organizers turn spectators into foot soldiers, that is, convince people who have compatible beliefs to get active in the community organization. Organizers also help recruit local leaders (the gladiators) and channel their energy into effective leadership of the organization. Studies of political participation suggest realistic targets for the proportion of the population that can be mobilized. Such studies also suggest which groups of people will be easy or hard to mobilize and to some extent how to rouse people from a spectator status.

The number of people who can be expected to get involved in community actions depends on what is expected from them. Almost a third of the people claim to have been active in some political activity (Milbrath, 1977, p. 22). About 8% of the population is involved in some community organization (defined quite broadly), about 14% contacts government officials, 30% works with others on local problems, while only a handful, 3%, claims it would participate in public demonstrations (Milbrath, 1977, pp. 18–19). Studies of federally sponsored community development organizations report that 13% to 14% of the population claims some sort of involvement (Steggert, 1975, pp. 4, 11), while Alinsky organizations tend to attract about 5% of the community.

More people express verbal support for an issue than actually participate in collective actions like marches or demonstrations on that same issue. A suggestive study of participation in peace demonstrations in Europe shows the difference between supportive opinions and final action. At the top of Figure 9–2, 74% of those asked agreed with the goals of the demonstrations. Most of that 74% had been the target of a mobilization attempt, but of those who had been reached by the mobilization campaign, only a small proportion expressed the intention to participate. In the end, only 4% of the sample actually went to the demonstrations, even though 74% agreed with the organizers' aims. These results suggest that organizers should be cautious about expecting large turnouts for demonstrations.

Organizing is easier among those who are already more empowered: the well-educated participate more than the poorly educated; majority-group members participate more than minority-group members; the wealthy participate more than the poor; and people in professional occupations participate more than blue-collar workers (D. H. Smith, Macaulay, & Associates, 1980, pp. 156–158; D. H. Smith, Reddy, & Baldwin, 1972, p. 214; Steggert, 1975, pp. 13–15).

Furthermore, people who feel alienated and inefficacious do not undertake political action (Milbrath, 1977, pp. 7, 66). At first, such findings appear discouraging for those seeking to work in poorer or minority neighborhoods. But other research offers more hope.

Participation among the deprived appears to be low because many of the national issues that involve people from upper-income communities are less salient in lower-income communities. Fortunately,

FIGURE 9–2

Participation in Peace Demonstrations in Europe *(From "Potentials, Networks, Motivations, and Barriers: Steps Towards Participation in Social Movements" by B. Klandermans and D. Oegema, 1987,* American Sociological Review, 52, *p. 524. Copyright 1987 by* American Sociological Review. *Reprinted by permission.)*

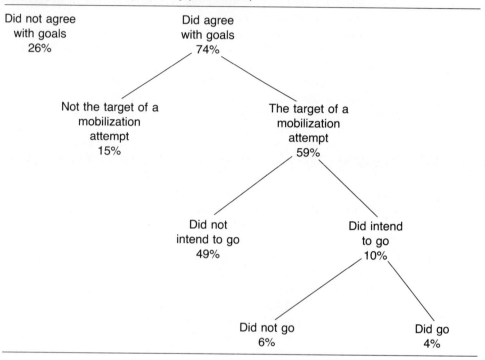

Did not agree with goals 26%

Did agree with goals 74%

Not the target of a mobilization attempt 15%

The target of a mobilization attempt 59%

Did not intend to go 49%

Did intend to go 10%

Did not go 6%

Did go 4%

recent research indicates that social background loses much or most of its explanatory power in predicting participation in voluntary associations when intervening attitudes, personality and situational variables are controlled statistically. It is possible, for instance, that those groups who avoid participation in the larger social fabric because of their perceived inefficacy, will respond to an arena of concrete, visible concerns such as their own block. (Wandersman, 1981, p. 37)

When people are interested in particular local problems, they may participate regardless of class or race. They may not feel competent to deal with the arms race, but they may be willing to try to influence the quality and frequency of police patrol.

In addition, regardless of the economic status of an area, the more stable the population, the higher the social participation. Residential longevity, an indication of personal integration into a neighborhood, increases participation (D. H. Smith, Reddy, & Baldwin, 1972, p. 219). For example, more stable communities have an easier time establishing crime patrols (Lewis, Grant, & Rosenbaum, 1988). This increase in participation can occur no matter how people are linked into their communities. Even being a client of a neighborhood service organization increases involvement in other local organizations (J. C. Thomas, 1986).

In stable, socially integrated neighborhoods, people are likely to belong to some organization. And, generally, when people belong to one organization, it is easier to persuade them to join other organizations or to work on community tasks (Podolefsky & DuBow, 1981). For example, overall participation in neighborhood anticrime activities is quite low; only about 10% of the people participate in such activities. But of people already involved in any neighborhood group, over 50% participate in anticrime activities (Podolefsky & Dubow, 1981, p. 111).

Cultural or ethnic identification, as a member of a solidarity community or identification with a geographic area, increases political participation:

> Persons who exhibit strong group identification, participate more actively. . . . blacks generally are somewhat less likely to participate than whites in politics . . . but if one considers those blacks who regard their "blackness" as salient [i.e., identify as a member of a solidarity community] they are more likely to participate. Although higher socioeconomic blacks tend to be more conscious of their black identity, the relationship between group feeling and political participation seems to be independent of the influence of socioeconomic factors. (Milbrath, 1977, p. 57)

Prime targets for organizing are people in socially integrated communities who strongly identify with the neighborhood yet are highly dissatisfied with city services (Ahlbrandt & Cunningham, 1979, p. 51; Crenson, 1980). They are motivated to act by their sense of dissatisfaction. And, because they identify with the community, they prefer to act to improve their community rather than flee to other neighborhoods.

If the neighborhood is small or poor, mobilization may be easier than expected, as people once active feel more empowered. Research findings suggest:

> Relatively isolated . . . local communities are more likely to mobilize members in local organizations; but more significantly, they are less capable of mobilizing financial resources for their local organization, which in turn makes them more likely to engage in political action . . . and more directly challenge existing authorities. (A. Hunter & Staggenborg, 1986, p. 179)

When mobilized neighborhoods lack resources, they substitute people power for money, which is the essence of community organizing.

To summarize, the research on political participation can be boiled down to three lessons for organizers. First, don't expect everyone to join the organization. Be happy if there are enough foot soldiers to make a credible presentation of organizational demands.

Second, those already involved in community activities are most likely to be joiners. That means that building community integration is a step toward mobilization. In poorer communities, tighter social integration can lead to increased political involvement, enabling the disempowered to substitute numbers of people for dollars in gaining political access.

Third, people who identify with their locality yet are dissatisfied with how their neighborhood is treated by city officials are most likely to be active. This principle can probably be generalized to people who identify with groups such as gays, the handicapped, or veterans, and who believe that society or government agencies are not treating them right. Setting up networks between people who feel loyal to a group and mistreated is a useful mobilization strategy.

Resource Mobilization Theory

The sociology of collective behavior examines why mass movements occur when they do. One of the theories of collective behavior, resource mobilization theory, has important implications for those engaged in organizing work. The central premise of this theory is that there is always sufficient discontent in any society to generate collective political action, so that mobilization does not depend on broader political or economic changes. Instead resource mobilization theorists argue that action occurs after someone intentionally creates a trigger event.

For the trigger event to be effective in creating mass mobilization, money, material, and communication networks first have to be present. These resources are provided by what the theorists call *social mobilization organizations* that are awaiting opportunities for action. But what gets the original organizations going in the first place? In resource mobilization theory, the answer is professional organizers who are either ideologically or financially (or both) committed to the issues of their organization. Unlike many community members who are tangentially affected by the issues, the major activity of these organizers is promoting the cause.

Resource mobilization theory emphasizes that many social mobilization organizations start with funds donated by "conscience constituencies," that is, wealthier people who feel guilty about a problem and provide money to combat it. Thus, the foundations that provided support for the Alinsky groups or the national environmental groups that become involved in local toxic waste activities are funded by people concerned about problems, yet unable or unwilling to commit their bodies (rather than their purses) to the action.

The theory calls attention (possibly too much attention) to the importance of having support from people who themselves are not immediately trapped by cycles of deprivation. A college-educated community organizer working out of a school of social work, or an Alinsky organizer being indirectly funded through foundation money, has a staying power that a working class person dependent on his or her immediate income might lack. For example, Martin Luther King, Jr. was from an upper-status ministerial family, while early in his career Alinsky was supported by foundation funds funneled through universities. During the model cities era, organizers received direct salaries from federal programs.

Though the theory calls attention to advantages of relying on outsiders, there are also some dangers. The organizations may be overly influenced by the people who fund them and end up not empowering ordinary participants. If, for example, the Ford Foundation funds a block-watch program, community organizations that might have chosen other crime-control techniques may be constrained to try a block watch, draining energy and enthusiasm from other more popular projects. When funders are foundations or government agencies, they are unlikely to sponsor programs that seriously criticize them or oppose the capitalist system (Jenkins, 1989; Jenkins & Eckert, 1986).

According to resource mobilization theory, people always have problems, and resources to deal with them are often available. A core of committed organizers is within reach. What is often missing is a trigger that brings about mass mobilization. The trigger may be an event or series of events that symbolize the failure of government, the administration, or the boss to cope with a problem. In the Columbia University divestment protest, the trigger was the administration's unilateral voiding of the university senate's decision to divest. Downtown economic development programs that displace the poor and destroy housing act as a trigger for activation of organizations concerned with neighborhood revitalization and racial justice. Police brutality often has been the trigger to groups concerned with civil rights and liberties.

Sometimes the trigger is an outside organizer or group that provides resources or support. The company doctors of the coal and textile industries obscured the occupationally caused lung diseases of employees, such as black lung (in the coal industry) and brown lung (in the textile industry). The trigger was provided by outside physicians drawing support from the United Church of Christ and the (Catholic) Campaign for Human Development. Cesar Chavez's farm-organizing efforts were helped by liberal groups that helped place sympathetic people in positions in state agencies dealing with labor relations.

Implications for Organizing

Combining the sociological insights from resource mobilization theory and the political science literature on who becomes active suggests how trigger events can overcome a reluctance to participate and that poverty need not be an obstacle to activism.

Trigger events that have an immediate impact on people can mobilize even those who are less ideologically committed to a cause. For example, after the near disaster at the Three Mile Island nuclear reactor, people in adjacent areas who were immediately (and dramatically) threatened by the possible melt down became active against nuclear energy, even if they did not feel strongly about nuclear energy before the accident. In cities further away, individuals who already were working to oppose nuclear energy were able to involve others who had some nervousness about nuclear energy to become involved (Walsh & Warland, 1983). The lesson for organizers is that the more immediate a problem, the easier it is to shift people from an inactive to an active participant role. Trigger events can mobilize even those with less strong ideological commitments.

The resource mobilization literature and the political science literature on activism suggest that while upper-income areas are more likely to mobilize than are poor areas, poverty itself does not preclude mobilization. Activism is low in poor neighborhoods because they are unstable, lacking in shared institutions, and because residents within them lack confidence in their ability to bring about change. In poor but stable areas in which social integration has been maintained and in poor areas in which people feel that can succeed, activism is as high as it is in wealthier places. Poverty itself is not the reason for lack of mobilization (Mohai, 1985).

The suggested response is for organizers to work to encourage solidarity, build networks, celebrate ethnicity, and help build community pride. If the barrier to organizing is lack of confidence in the possibility of success, then the organizer needs to convince people that the organization can succeed, and that their participation will contribute to the success. Organizers must break into the cycle in which poverty makes people feel ineffective by showing them that they can succeed. In poor and unstable communities, organizers must try to bootstrap small initial successes so people feel more confident about the possibility of long-run success.

MODELS OF MOBILIZATION

Organizers tend to follow one of four models of community mobilization: the Alinsky model, the house-meeting variant of the Alinsky model, the Boston model, and the ACORN model. Each model is based on a philosophy of social action that prescribes how best to recruit members to a social action organization. For example, the Alinsky approach builds an action coalition by persuading leaders of existing organizations to join together; in contrast, the Boston model forms a direct membership organization by appealing to individual community members. Though these models differ in many specific ways, in practice, organizers borrow liberally (and appropriately) from several models.

The Alinsky Model

An Alinsky organization is a coalition of existing neighborhood organizations including religious groups, social organizations, tenants' associations, and a variety of others. Though the organizations gain supporters by working to solve immediate problems, their purpose is the long-term goal of teaching people that they have the capacity to solve problems by joining together in a democratic, participatory organization.

Alinsky organizers are invited into a community by local organizations usually after these groups have obtained enough funds to support long-term organizing efforts. Once in the community, Alinsky organizers learn about its physical, ethnic, and cultural structures through informal conversations, walking tours, and other techniques described in Chapter 8.

As part of this familiarization period, the Alinsky organizer maintains contact with the leaders of the organizations that invited him or her into the community and pays special attention to meeting with ministers and priests of progressive churches. Together with the organizer, these local leaders come up with a preliminary list about community problems and obstacles to solving these problems. They form a temporary steering committee for the community organization (to which the organizer acts as an adviser), and a convention is called of representatives of the separate organizations. The convention forms a neighborhood council that undertakes community actions and sets up a governing board. In theory, though rarely in practice, the organizer withdraws from active work as local leaders take over.

The House Meeting

Alinsky organizations assume there is enough community solidarity to form the ethnic, neighborhood, religious, and other groupings that compose the coalition. Ross devised the house-meeting model, as a procedure to build social solidarity when it is lacking. As Ross described

> First, I'd hold small house meetings for three weeks, building up to the big organizing meeting when we'd set up temporary offices. Then we'd organize through house meetings for several more weeks before the second organizing meeting. (J. Levy, 1975, p. 100)

The mass organizational meeting grows out of the many smaller house meetings that bring together people within social networks. Meetings are scheduled at the homes of volunteers, who are asked to invite friends. Meetings are kept small with the hope that people will not be embarrassed about saying what is really on their minds. At the meetings, people share grievances and discuss common problems while the organizer appeals to the need for ethnic solidarity and tries to persuade people that they can accomplish their goals through collective action.

Cesar Chavez, the farm-worker organizer, organized primarily through such house meetings.

> Cesar opened with a few introductory remarks and then, suddenly leaning forward as though about to confide some marvelous secret, asked softly if they had heard of the new organization he was building in the valley—the Farm Workers Association. None of them had, of course, nor was he all that familiar with it himself, having just that day decided on the name. But the words held magic, because heads came straining forward.
>
> He sat in silence, letting the suspense mount before he went on. It was a movement, he said, in which farm workers could struggle to free themselves from the injustice of the job, the government, and life in general. There was no ready-made plan, he assured them. That was one of the reasons he was meeting with them and other workers—to gradually put together ideas based upon what they wanted, along with some of his own. . . . He then passed around some self-addressed three-by-five cards with lines on the back for the name and address of the worker, and for what the worker considered a just hourly wage.
>
> The idea was an instant hit. Always before, one worker said, others had decided what he deserved. Now he, himself, was being consulted. "It's like letting us vote," he said, "on what we think." . . .
>
> Cesar called for more questions and other issues were raised—the use of Mexican braceros who took the jobs away from local people, the many times they had been cheated by labor contractors, the lack of toilets and clean, cold water in the fields.
>
> They could have gone on all night, but Cesar cut in, explaining that when the workers had their own Association, many of these things would be changed. They would be able to stand up to the growers, he told them, and demand an end to the injustices they had been suffering for so many years. (J. Levy, 1975, p. xxi–xxii)

This is a wonderful example of how to use a house meeting, eliciting common complaints while suggesting a collective solution.

The Boston Model

The Boston model entails direct recruiting of individuals who share a common problem into a new organization meant to solve that particular problem. The model is focused on a problem and aims to recruit individuals through several stages of action.

> The organizer first talks with key "gatekeepers" in the community, who, once convinced of the merits of the organizing effort, provide a "contact list" of potential members for the organizer to visit. The organizer then meets with those contacts (adding new ones in snowball fashion as s/he goes along) and pulls together an organizing committee that provides the initial core group for the organizing drive. (Staples, 1984, p. 20)

The major use of the Boston model has been to build single-issue organizations whose primary goal is solving that problem. The Massachusetts Welfare Rights Organization is the prominent example of the Boston model.

The ACORN Model

The ACORN model combines individual recruitment (from the Boston model) with a goal of building a long-term, multiple-issue organization (as suggested by Alinsky).

> In building ACORN, Rathke hoped to keep what he perceived as good in his welfare rights experience (the membership base, the use of a replicable model, and the strategic manipulation of the press), while incorporating some parts of the old Alinsky model (strong ties with such existing organizations as unions and churches) and experimenting with electoral politics as a way to consolidate organizational victories. (G. Delgado, 1986, p. 46)

While the Alinsky model was primarily focused on neighborhoods and, at least in its early days, avoided electoral politics, "ACORN planned to build a nationwide organization of affiliated neighborhood groups" (Stein, 1986, p. 102). It sought to be independent from existing political and social structures by funding itself directly from membership fees rather than from foundation or church contributions. And, instead of accommodating to the political structure, "ACORN favored direct action and sought to experiment with electoral politics as a way to consolidate organizational victories" (Stein, 1986, p. 102).

A Mobilizing Model for National Progressive Organizations

The strategies for recruitment into national, progressive organizations differ markedly from neighborhood-based models. There is less individual persuasion, because people join in response to mail or newspaper solicitations. People learn about these organizations when one progressive group shares its mailing list with another, which then begins a mail membership drive. Such organizations define issues based on the felt needs of a limited number of people and then try to find other people who support their cause. For national progressive organizations, mobilization and action campaigns are often run simultaneously because people only learn about such groups when they are in the midst of a well-publicized campaign.

There are two kinds of such national progressive organizations. One type is based on issues, either single issues or clusters of them, such as peace or civil liberties; and the other type is based on advocacy of the rights or benefits of some particular group, such as welfare mothers, gays, or the victims of crime.

Public interest organizations concerned with issues like peace or civil liberties are very dependent on ideological support from conscience constituencies, people who support such groups with dues without becoming active (McCann, 1986). These organizations use trigger events to motivate people to join the group. Gun control organizations may use a shooting of a public figure, or environmentalists may use an oil spill. People for the American Way, an anticensorship group, monitors instances of book burning, school-board censorship of books, and libraries spying on readers. When times are worst, these organizations have the easiest time mobilizing, because they can show their membership that the problems about which they have expressed deep concern have come back in a new virulent form and need to be controlled. Most of their actions are accomplished through coalitions of similar groups that lobby Congress on specific issues.

Advocacy organizations recruit primarily by suggesting they will obtain specific benefits for their members. The membership itself may not feel much solidarity among themselves—consumers may not feel much bond with other consumers, for example—so advocacy groups may spend time building solidarity either at the same time or before planning collective activities. Advocacy organizations offer a variety of incentives to potential members; housing advocacy organizations can offer improved and less expensive housing; environmental organizations can provide technical information about poisons; and human rights advocacy groups, such as gay rights groups, can offer an end to personal isolation and stigma.

Table 9–1 summarizes some of the distinctions between the separate models of mobilization.

Three of the four community-based models focus primarily on building capacity for longer-term problem solving, though markedly different appeals are made to potential

TABLE 9–1
People, Organizations, and
Models of Mobilization

	Emphasis on Organization as Capacity Building	Emphasis on Organization as Problem Solving
Recruit Individuals	ACORN	Boston model
Build Solidarities	House meeting	National advocacy organizations
Merge Organizations	Alinsky	Public interest groups

members. Of the community models, only the Boston model primarily concentrates on immediate problem solving. National progressive organizations also emphasize their ability to solve problems. They have to develop enough capacity to be a politically viable player, but capacity building of the membership is rarely a separate goal because most members are too far away from Washington, DC, where most of the work is done.

There are, however, some similarities between the national progressive organizations and the community-based models. Like the Alinsky model, liberal public interest groups often form coalitions. For example, the American Civil Liberties Union and the National Organization for Women (NOW) work as a coalition on prochoice issues. National advocacy groups, like neighborhood groups in fragmented communities, sometimes have to build solidarity among potential members—the homeless, the disabled, or homosexuals—before working to solve specific problems.

MOBILIZING TACTICS WITH ORGANIZATIONS, NETWORKS, AND INDIVIDUALS

Three tactics of organizing involve working with other organizations, pulling together networks, or recruiting individuals. In practice, all three often occur simultaneously.

Mobilizing With Organizations

One of the quickest ways to mobilize people is to bring together established community groups. The organizer talks with leaders of church groups, social organizations, block associations, merchants, athletic associations, youth and labor groups, and other relevant groups. He or she tries to convince these individuals to have their organizations join in a community conference. When successful, this technique is fast. One organizer noted,

> Organizing individuals . . . is "the slowest way to hell." It was by recruiting groups, not individuals, that the coalition was able to build as quickly and strongly as it did. (Henig, 1982, p. 88)

Part of what makes this an effective way to recruit members is that people who are members of one organization are more likely to join others.

These organizations need not be action groups, so long as the organizer can show their leaders and members that they share a common interest in a community problem. For example, an organizer working on issues affecting the elderly might approach groups that provide social and recreational activities for the old (Kleyman, 1974, p. 38). Community crime patrols can be set up through shared interests between block clubs and organized groups of teenagers.

The Alinsky tactic was to gain support by associating with respected community organizations, especially churches with reform-minded clergy. A well-liked and respected priest or minister provides good will and credibility for the organization, and the physical permanence of a church building provides the group an image of stability. Churches sometimes serve Alinsky groups as a home base and, through their association with funding sources such as the Catholic Charities, provide a financial start for the organization. Alinsky's first organization, the Back of the Yards, was housed for some time in the offices of a local park, after Alinsky secured the support of Joe Meegan, the Park Director and a community leader.

The strategy of affiliating with existing organizations has its dangers. In communities with competing ethnic or religious groups, it is difficult to choose which ethnically based organization to use as an organizational home without so offending members of other ethnic or cultural groups that they will actively oppose the action organization. This problem can be handled. In South Chicago, Alinsky made sure that the community organization not only had white ethnic Catholic churches but also some black Protestant church membership. In Rochester, New York, the Alinsky organization FIGHT was built primarily from black Protestant churches. White organizations formed a separate group called Friends of FIGHT to support the black community organization.

The key to setting up such coalition organizations is to search for coincidences of interest between the organizations and then build on these shared interests. An organizer can persuade a merchants' association that their business is likely to increase if they work with senior citizen groups. Sometimes, quite diverse groups might share interests. In one case, a clever organizer tried to build a group based on senior power and black power. Seniors were afraid to go out at night, and the black power groups wanted to show that they had power to enforce the law-abiding norms of the community (Kleyman, 1974).

These local organizations are often the power base of local leaders. For the organizer, the local leader becomes a consultant who can tell the organizer what arguments others will accept and which issues are likely to evoke community support. Local leaders can open doors and facilitate talking to community members. These community leaders are central to communication networks and can reach many other people quickly.

Mobilizing With Networks

Networks are extremely important to organizers, who have to know how to locate them, how to recruit from them, and how to strengthen them. Networks make recruitment quicker. People who have been affected by a plant closing or other shared problems often seek each other out along issue networks. Networks provide a basis of solidarity that is necessary for organizing, while they are the route by which information comes into and is interpreted by the community.

Studies in public opinion and persuasion show that facts and opinions about the outside world enter a community through a two-step flow. An opinion leader learns information from first-hand experience, from network linkages to other communities, from the mass media, or from attendance at informational meetings. When other people in the community want to learn about this subject, they seek out the opinion leaders.

However, a person recognized as knowledgeable about current events will not necessarily be equally knowledgeable about local gossip or economic problems in the neighborhood. An organizer locates opinion leaders on an issue-by-issue basis.

> *Opinion leaders are leaders because they are good followers. They are energetic, informed and willing to make efforts, but they are leaders because they accurately reflect the sentiments of other group members.*

That means that opinion leaders are sources of information for the community, but an organizer cannot feed such a person information radically at odds with what the community thinks or knows and expect the new message to be forwarded and accepted.

Networks describe connections between people who share a problem. The members of these networks already know they are widowed, or have family troubles, or have no one to talk to when they feel depressed. The organizer works to convince people who are already linked together to take action.

In addition, an organizer can bring together networks with overlapping interests. For example, a community might contain many self-help groups, each working independently on the same problem area, whose efforts can be combined (Lieberman et al., 1979). Parents without Partners may already be linked to Big Brothers and Big Sisters, an organization that seeks volunteers to be role models and companions to children in single-parent homes. But perhaps both of those groups could be linked to a self-help network of the newly bereaved.

Often, people with interest in one problem area know each other, and perhaps help each other on a case-by-case basis, but have not yet formed an organization. For example, many communities have "helping networks" or "community support networks."

> In neighborhoods and communities throughout the U.S., a vast array of informal or lay support systems exists. These systems include the help provided by friends, neighbors, clergy, natural helpers, mutual aid/self-help groups, ethnic, fraternal, and social organizations, co-workers, etc. (Naparstek, Beigel, & Spiro, 1982, p. 74)

These community support networks contain individuals who can be future leaders for community action, especially if an organizer puts these people in contact with each other. In doing so, the organizer provides people with an opportunity to take action that they want to take anyway, a crucial step in empowerment.

Network connections also facilitate participation in social action campaigns because linkages to others are often as important as beliefs in motivating action (Eckberg, 1988). Who you know influences who will talk to you about particular issues or campaigns and who will ask you to sign a petition or go to a meeting. Eckberg, in a study of why physicians signed a "prolife" statement, learned that activism stemmed as much from whom people knew in the prolife movement as it did their own beliefs on the issue (Eckberg, 1988, p. 388).

Sometimes the level of stability and solidarity in a community is too low to sustain many networks, formal or informal. This makes it difficult to recruit leaders or members and makes it hard to disseminate information. The role of the organizer in this case may be to help build the networks.

When organizers are going door to door talking to people, and they find several individuals with similar problems, they can put the individuals in contact with one another. This should probably be done even if the people are concerned about issues other than the ones immediately confronting the organization. Capacity is developed by solving virtually any problem, even if it is not the one the organizer started with, and enhanced networks may be useful later for organizing on other issues.

A second way to encourage neighborhood networks is to create a setting for sharing common concerns. An organizer can encourage parties, bring in speakers, and arrange festivals in which people get to know one another.

> The Monaberry Heights Neighborhood Association in University City, Missouri, for example, "recruits" residents through informal neighbor to neighbor interaction, emphasizes the social aspects of its monthly meetings and sponsors a neighborhood picnic and other social events. (E. Sharp, 1978, p. 47)

To summarize, a community that has good networks and to which people feel strong loyalty is usually easier to organize, but organizers might have to create networks before trying more ambitious collective action. They may need to start a newsletter, or encourage special events in which local people interact, or find other ways to let people know they are part of a potential community. They may need to invite neighbors who do not know each other to a house meeting, discuss common problems, and help form a network.

Mobilizing With Individuals

No matter whether the underlying organizing model involves first working with existing organizations or directly appealing to people, organizers end up trying to persuade individuals that collective action can accomplish individual goals. Persuasion is not about changing peoples' minds about goals or values. Arguing with people who disagree with the values of the organization is inefficient and might convince those opposed to work against the goals of the organization. Moreover, if too much effort is made to change people's minds, organizers may be violating the democratic ethos of community development. Instead, organizers find people who are in general agreement about problems and convince them to work together. Persuasion involves *reinforcing* the beliefs people already have and then showing people that what they want can be achieved through collective action.

An important part of mobilization involves a one-on-one effort in which the organizer persuades spectators to toss off the shackles of indifference and join in collective activities. In *canvassing* efforts—one-on-one conversations that come about by knocking on doors—activists meet community members and listen. The organizer need not be a high-powered salesperson, nor need he or she get involved in philosophical debate about the nature of the just society or the equity of social service programs. The goal is to learn which problems people feel are important and to learn whether or not people are willing to act to solve them.

Felt needs are learned through careful listening. (Courtesy VISTA)

Many potential organizers are shy about intruding on someone else's life. However, a required step in building an organization is to talk to people who face similar problems. As Kahn points out:

> Person-to-person contacts build organizations where people feel equally valued. When someone takes the trouble to visit to you and talk with you about his or her organization, it means something, especially when you know that the person is not being paid to hustle you. (Kahn, 1982, p. 110)

Talking to people is easy if a person is dealing with his or her immediate friends or neighbors, so we'll restrict our advice to situations in which an organizer is meeting strangers.

If the person doing the recruiting is working in his or her own neighborhood, the canvasser should let people know that. Organizers from outside a community shouldn't pretend to be local people. Highly educated college graduates who pretend to be poor people—just one of the folks—come across as hypocrites. Organizers show they care about the community by being involved, not by copying mannerisms of speech and dress.

People distrust anyone who seems too enthusiastic; boisterous enthusiasm is interpreted as a hustle rather than as persuasion. Casualness is reinforced by meeting people informally. Organizers can meet people at shopping centers, coffee shops, or sports events. Or they can meet people at home, at the laundromat, or other places that people gather.

The organizer should start with people he or she knows and then move on to strangers. When working in a new neighborhood, organizers introduce themselves to local leaders such as politicians, heads of other community organizations, religious leaders, and employees of social service agencies. If the organizer can gain the support of such leaders, they'll introduce him or her to others in the community. If the organizer fails to get their support, there will probably be some trouble, but at least that will be learned quickly. For example, in Albuquerque, New Mexico, members of a Hispanic neighborhood association chased Anglo organizers from ACORN out of the community (Cunningham & Kotler, 1983, p. 49).

When organizing people on an issue, such as spouse abuse or homelessness, the organizer has to locate somebody in the community affected by the problem and ask for referrals along the network. If a personal introduction is not possible, the organizer should at least be able to point out a common acquaintance. It is even better if the organizer can state that a friend of the person to whom he or she is referred has already joined the organization. The Gay Alliances in San Francisco were built this way (Castells, 1983).

A good organizer is a good listener. Organizers find out about the problems people feel strongly about by listening.

> By encouraging people to talk about their lives, their hopes, their dreams, the way things used to be, the way things could be. Most people are wonderful talkers, given the chance. Leaders should be wonderful listeners. (Kahn, 1982, p. 93)

Rather than telling people what their problem is, the organizer asks them what they feel is the problem. This is courteous, shows interest and respect, and is an effective way of making people begin to commit themselves. The organizer then makes an appeal to join the organization based on their expressed needs. Obtaining contributions of ideas from people is both consistent with the community development ideology and a pragmatic method for mobilization:

> Long experience with organizing has shown that people tend to support decisions they feel involved in making. When they feel they were not consulted, that they did not have a part in the decision-making process, they tend to vote with their feet and walk in the other direction. (Kahn, 1982, p. 69)

When talking to people about their problems, the organizer should remember that the problems people describe come from their experiences with everyday life. People don't think about income distributions; they think about whether they earn enough. People don't think about urban planning, but they care if too much traffic goes by their house or their kids have to cross busy streets.

The issue need not be a federal case. As one activist put it, "At the local level, you organize around dog shit, stop signs, whatever people are talking about." (Cassidy, 1980, p. 72)

Organizers persuade by finding out what people are thinking and then showing them how collective action can lead to solutions to their problems.

An organizer has to maintain a balance between describing a problem, so the potential recruit knows what the subject is, and encouraging the person to provide his or her opinions.

ORGANIZER: Hello, I'm Herb Rubin from around the corner on Wilson Place, and I'm working with Waste Water. You've probably heard of the work we have done; we shut down the dump in the park that was polluting the city wells.

RECRUIT: Yeah.

ORGANIZER: Well, we're trying to get some people together to do something about water pollution. How do you feel about the water in Columbia?

RECRUIT: Well for one thing, it's too expensive, and during the summer the pressure is too low.

The organizer encouraged the person to talk about water-related problems. The needs expressed were not about pollution. The organizer may find very few people concerned about pollution. The organizer can then either expand the issue to include the concerns of a larger group of people or work with those few for whom pollution is a real concern. In either case, the organizer cannot go far from the expressed needs of the people he or she talks to.

There is always a danger in such conversations that people will reflect back the opinions of the organizer rather than present their own.

> *Organizers must try to find out if they are really hearing the needs expressed of community members or if they are only hearing echoes of their own beliefs.*

Though an organizer should try not to impose his or her own beliefs, good listening is **not** a passive process. People might be unwilling to express their true feelings, especially to strangers or neighborhood "troublemakers." Organizers have to find ways to encourage people to talk openly but without putting words in their mouths. If potential recruits echo back the words of the organizer, when push comes to shove, they won't act on them.

In one-on-one meetings, potential activists may make false excuses for inaction. The real reason for not joining the action might be that they fear they will anger someone in authority. People probably will not express such feelings; who wants to appear cowardly? Instead, they may rationalize, "I am too busy to go down to city hall." People may claim that they are too busy to work on an anticrime patrol even though they recognize that crime is a problem. But what they are really saying is that they don't want to get involved with the police under any circumstances. To handle such situations learn to search out the rationalizations, treat them as rationalizations, and break through. Do not make the mistake of locking yourself up in conflict with them as if they were the issues or problem with which you are trying to engage the local people. (Alinsky, 1971, p. 112)

Organizers listen to the excuses people give and try to determine their real objections to participation. They formulate ideas of what they think people's real objections are and test these ideas with community members with whom they can talk openly. Then organizers and local leaders figure out ways of responding to the real objections, such as that the fear of the police is greater than the fear of crime, or that being involved chances being harassed.

Once organizers understand the objections to action, they are better prepared to suggest ideas that people can accept. For example, community crime prevention programs can be arranged so people do not have to deal alone with the authorities. Members of the community crime prevention patrol can talk to the police together. Or, as in the Edgewater neighborhood in Chicago, community members can go together when one of them has to go to court as a witness in a criminal case. Going together lessens the fear of standing out alone against the accused (Marciniak, 1981).

Organizers should focus on the problems individuals face and not on the mechanics of organizing. No one will join if they think the organizer is just building an organization for the sake of organization building. People want solutions; they don't want organizational gobbledygook. Organization is the **means** for solving a problem and the tool for focusing power, not a set of offices, jobs, and ranks.

Incentives for Participation.   Regardless of whether one is mobilizing organizations, networks, or individuals, one has to think about the potential rewards of participation. Researchers tell us that people will work for organizations if they feel they get something out of it, if they can contribute to the direction the organization takes, and if they believe that the organizational leaders really represent the community (Jenkins & Perrow, 1977; Knoke & Wood, 1981; Kweit & Kweit, 1981).

Successful mobilizing requires organizers to show community members how acting together provides personal advantages to them.

Collective mobilization . . . happens because individuals . . . believe or hope that mobilization will make them (or someone they care for) better off. Failure of a neighborhood to mount a viable speedy response may, therefore, be due to the strategic failure of those who perceive and evaluate the threat facing the neighborhood to provide the amount and kind of incentives that facilitate collective action. (Henig, 1982, p. 192)

Organizations can rely on a variety of incentives, including material incentives like improved income or better housing, solidarity incentives such as the enjoyment of belonging to the group, and expressive incentives including the excitement and satisfaction of articulating opinions and values. Perhaps most important, the success of the organization can be an incentive.

Individualized and Material Incentives.   "*Material incentives* are those involving the provision of some good or service or the means to obtain them, e.g. day care, job counselling or other social services, group insurance and the like [emphasis added]" (E.

Sharp, 1981, p. 419). Material incentives have obvious economic value and are the easiest to demonstrate to individuals. We know that people who have the largest investment to protect in communities (homeowners) and those who receive the most services from communities (heavy users of service agencies) are most likely to participate in organizational activities (J. C. Thomas, 1986). They are aware of the value of the community to them and are willing to work to protect these individualized goods. For working parents, day care for their children is of individual value; homeowners benefit from programs that renovate housing and increase the value of their homes.

Showing individuals evidence that they can achieve personal goals by participating is more effective than general statements about community welfare. To get people to clean out junk from empty lots to build vest-pocket parks, organizers don't wax eloquent on the advantages of social solidarity, they talk about junk harboring rats that bite children and vest-pocket parks that provide a place for the elderly to meet.

The individual incentives for joining a group need not be the same for everyone. Some people join a block association to fight boredom, others join to preserve property values, still others to keep an eye out for strangers. Organizers learn the different objectives people have and use them as incentives to encourage people to work with the organization. Organizers **meld** a large number of personal incentives for involvement into a collective action. A sense of community solidarity can emerge from community efforts to satisfy separate goals.

However, it is possible to go so far in individualizing incentives that the possibility of developing a sense of community and collective responsibility is reduced. For example, the collapse of the Massachusetts Welfare Rights Organization (MWRO) occurred because benefits of increased funds for furniture and other necessities were so individualized that participants in MWRO never saw any reason to join longer-term efforts.

> MWRO organizers were able to promise welfare recipients that if they participated in welfare rights activities, they would soon be rewarded by supplementary welfare grants. . . .
> With the passage of time . . . many of the general membership gained enough confidence to make demands of the welfare office personnel without belonging to a group, others soon found that after a few major supplementary welfare checks had been won, there was little more that the group could continue to offer them.
>
> Thus all components in the welfare rights movement—members, organizers, and leaders—began to lose interest in maintaining the local affiliates and the groups began to fade away. (Bailis, 1974, p. 3)

Pure individualization of incentives builds neither community nor organization.

Service organizations—such as those providing day care or economic assistance—face this danger of incentives that are so individualized they do not encourage a sense of community. However, with careful planning, services can be provided in such a way that people are encouraged to participate in broader social action programs:

> Some direct action organizations have started to experiment with service projects as benefits to members. Food co-ops in low income areas are one example. The organization maintains a direct action program. Its members may join the organization's co-op as a privilege of membership. . . . The key element is that the direct action program is set up

before the service component, and that membership is required to participate in the action program of the organization as *well* as in the service component (Midwest Academy, 1977, p. 69)

Solidarity and Expressive Incentives.   While people might want to know what they will gain from collective participation, such gains need not be purely materialistic. Individuals can also be motivated by feelings of belonging to a group or by the opportunity to express their opinions in a public setting.

Solidarity incentives "derive in the main from the acts of associating and include such rewards as socializing, congeniality, the sense of group membership and identification, the status resulting from membership, fun, conviviality and so on." (Clark & Wilson quoted in E. Sharp, 1981, p. 419)

Expressive sentiments are those which accrue from the opportunity to express commitment to important values, "ideological" organizations are exemplars of the expressive incentives. (E. Sharp, 1981, p. 419)

A feeling of belonging to a solidarity community can encourage participation, as can the pleasure of comradeship, amusement at a bit of mockery, or a funny protest tactic. Organizational commitment increases if collective actions provide excitement, enjoyment, and good fellowship. Having fun, as Alinsky taught, is important in getting people to participate in organizational actions.

Here's an example of how to put fun in your fight. "When we first started the antiredlining battle, the local bank president told us that the bank didn't make loans in our area because it was a slum," recalls Shel Trapp. "Needless to say, people got mad about that. But what could they do? We had only $36,000 in deposits in that bank. . . . We tried picketing. Nothing. We kept picketing. No results. They just ignored us and went on with business."

Then one of our ladies said "Let's have a bank-in!" We said, "Great idea!" Then we asked, "What the hell's a bank-in?"

The next day, we had our bank-in. We put five of our people at each of the windows. They would each withdraw a dollar. Then they'd deposit a dollar. Then they'd ask for change. We even tied up the drive-in windows. And we sent in a racially mixed couple to get a loan.

Then Josephine . . . dropped two dollars in pennies on the floor. All the guards came rushing over to pick the money up. She thanked them, and dropped the coins again. Finally, the bank president came running out to the office asking what we wanted. We told him we wanted a meeting with the bank's board of directors that afternoon at two o'clock. But all the directors live in the suburbs! he bellowed. Right we said, that's the problem—they live in the suburbs and won't make loans in the city.

Well, we got our meeting, and we got a $4 million loan commitment, a review of all previously turned-down loans *and* a $1,000 contribution to the community organization. (Cassidy, 1980, pp. 80–81)

Having fun creates group solidarity. In a somewhat different approach, the organizer builds on the solidarity or neighborhood sentiments to encourage participation. "If the highway goes through here, the Armenian [Greek, Turkish . . .] Church will be unable to keep its social program. Your kids will marry outside of the fold. Don't you think you should join the Stop the Highway Organization?"

In making such appeals, the organization plays on the importance of friends, family, kin, and church to make what are termed *value-based* appeals. Value-based appeals bridge the gap between the individual and the collectivity by showing how self-interest can be achieved through collective actions that build the solidarity community. This tactic is now part of the Industrial Areas Foundation (IAF) strategy. As a result,

> "self-interest" as a concept became considerably richer and broader. IAF training began to combine the two earlier Alinsky themes of listening to community culture and individual self-interest to gain a different view of what motivates individuals. It began to distinguish between "self-interest" and "selfishness," arguing that people's basic concerns are not only for themselves in an immediate, short-term sense . . . people . . . evidence a strong interest in the intangibles of their lives—their families' well-being, their own sense of contribution and dignity, their core beliefs, their friends and closest associates, and their sense of efficacy in the world. (Boyte, 1989a, p. 89)

With value-based mobilization, the struggle for empowerment for an individual merges into a sense of belonging to a community whose values the individual shares.

Further, there is strong evidence that the importance of (shared community) values increases as people participate more in organizational activities. The movement from foot soldier to gladiator is often a movement from more specific personal incentives to a broader sense of working for communal values. As Hirsch describes for activists in block associations:

> Those who come to block clubs and tenant unions to attempt to find a solution for a narrow economic problem often quickly stop participating once that issue has been resolved one way or the other. Very active block club members may be motivated primarily by social i.e. solidary incentives. Reciprocity may be the crucial motivator for those who make the jump to community-wide work. And the most active leaders may be motivated primarily . . . by commitment to the collective goals of the group. (Hirsch, 1986, p. 384)

This understanding of the relationship between values, incentives, and community provides an optimistic extension to the mobilization cycle (Figure 9–3).

Care is required that the solidarity values used to build a sense of common identity are not inherently exclusionary. The increasing inability of members of separate minority communities to work with each other to solve common problems is an indication

FIGURE 9–3
The Mobilization Cycle

Felt Needs → Legitimate Building → Organization

Organization → Provides Opportunity to Satisfy → Felt Needs

Satisfying Felt Needs → Reinforces the Original Commitment → To Build Organization

Building Organizations → Legitimates the Values Underlying Community

Valuing Community → Encourages Collective Actions

---

of this intensifying problem. Black is beautiful not because it isn't white, but because African Americans share a common heritage of problems and suffering, of victories and triumphs.

Success as a Sustaining Incentive.   Another incentive for continued participation grows out of seeing the possibilities for success. While the more active individuals participate because of their ideological beliefs, less ideologically committed people need constant reinforcement or rewards to stay interested and active over longer periods of time. The immediacy of the protests undertaken by ACORN or the humorous tactics suggested by Alinsky are forms of such reinforcement. Other types of rewards can increase commitment and grow out of carefully planned organizational activities.

First is the reward of participating in a successful campaign, which involves delight in the exercise of power and the improved quality of life that results. Second is the sense of accomplishment that comes from doing a task as a member of a well-run organization. Part of this sense of accomplishment occurs as organization members learn to express their opinions and find that other group members take their opinions seriously.

Commitment is increased as participants see immediate rewards for their actions. Though organizations should have long-term goals, it is unwise to base organizational survival on all-or-nothing grand victories. This advice has been expressed by organizers.

> Regardless of strategy, it is important that an organization's early efforts result in a few successes, even if they are minor ones. . . . Some early success is vital to encourage the new cadre, and help it expand. (Cunningham & Kotler, 1983, p. 20)

Nothing encourages participation better than being on a winning team. People might want to achieve the long-run goal of better houses, streets and parks, but in the short run, organizations should focus on smaller activities, such as improving a building or corner. Success at the smaller task increases commitment of organization members to the larger and more distant accomplishments.

In protests, each time the enemy is discomforted can be defined as a victory on the way to the larger objective. Alinsky advised organizers to "personalize the issue," that is, identify the problem with a politician, banker, an interfering federal judge or bureaucrat. In part, such a tactic makes an issue appear more manageable. Equally important, it defines actions in terms of small, easily accomplished activities such as contacting and arguing with the individual target.

Organizations need not succeed on every issue once people have developed some commitment to the group. Any loyalist to a losing baseball team that *sometimes* beats the league leader demonstrates this principle. *Intermittent reinforcement*—that is, an occasional success—is sufficient to maintain loyalty to the organization. If an action fails, quickly attempt another one. For those people with prior commitment to the organization, a small success will wipe out the taste of a larger failure.

Being part of a well-run organization can also provide a continuing incentive to participate. The routine steps of organizing can reinforce people's commitment. More people showing up at a meeting is a victory, an increase in paid membership is a victory, getting the newsletter out is a victory, having a politician come to the group's meetings is a victory. With some people, successful performance of any of the routine tasks of maintaining an organization—keeping a budget, distributing flyers—can reinforce their willingness to stick with the group over the long haul. Within reason, the larger the number of routine tasks accomplished, especially tasks that are new to those undertaking them, the better. Success in maintaining a phone tree, preparing a block directory, or obtaining a room for a meeting can reinforce commitment to the organization.

In small organizations, such as a block club or a neighborhood food cooperative, almost everyone has a chance to participate, and through such participation, reinforce their original decision to become involved. In larger organizations, to create such a sense of involvement, many active committees should be set up. These committees will improve organizational performance while giving people a chance to participate, thus reinforcing their decision to join in the first place.

An organizational newspaper or newsletter plays an important role in reinforcing organizational commitment. First, people working on it have a sense of success, an expanded capacity, as each issue is produced. Second, the newspaper can play up each success of the group or describe the collective struggle so that members not directly involved can learn what is happening.

National progressive organizations try to reinforce members' commitment through stories in newsletters and action alerts. The newsletters describe the accomplishments of the organization, mentioning specific victories, to reinforce the member's belief that the organization is doing good things and is winning on a variety of fronts. Action alerts also describe particular campaigns urging members to take action, such as phoning or writing to legislators. Through newsletters and action alerts, the organization presents itself as successful and well run and brings in the members to participate in the success.

10 | Participatory Meetings and Democratic Leadership: The Path From Mobilization to Action

Participatory meetings turn personal indignation into focused collective action by providing the confidence that the organization can solve problems. Though meetings can produce effective and creative decisions, there is a tension between holding successful meetings and running meetings in a democratic fashion. The role of leadership is to ensure that tasks are accomplished, while encouraging broad-scale involvement.

At meetings, the leader provides inspiration and direction for the group while inculcating a *democratic organizational culture* in which people feel willing, able, and obligated to participate. To do so, the leader can interpret the organization's past and its present environment in a positive way and help pass on skills needed for self-confidence and organizational success. Leaders can structure meetings to reduce intimidation so that people will contribute their ideas.

The actions of leaders must symbolically represent the possibility of people working together, inspiring the membership. Yet the leaders have to avoid becoming charismatic, attracting members who want to do things for the leader rather than for themselves and the group. Charismatic leaders inspire members but expect them to be followers, an inappropriate pattern for a community organization.

MEETINGS: INDIVIDUAL GROWTH WITHIN COLLECTIVE ACTIONS

Meetings create a commitment to action by creating a shared interest in a problem, democratically determining collective solutions, and building the skills required to carry out the decisions made by the group. At full-membership meetings, leaders guide discussions of problems facing the community so that individuals can see the possibilities for collective action. Membership meetings may also be the forum at which major policies of an organization are determined and overall priorities for organizational action are hashed out. More specific decisions are made at smaller committee meetings, especially at meetings of an elected steering committee that guides the organization when the overall membership cannot get together. At small, informal meetings people get to know each other and try to reach decisions on specific plans of actions.

No matter what the format or purpose of the meeting, certain skills are required to make it go well. A badly run meeting can negate all the work that has been done in mobilizing people and can thwart any effective community action. A good meeting moves toward accomplishing goals, whether setting up a community day-care center or leading a protest against a Fortune 500 company. A good meeting not only shows the potential for success by getting things done, it makes people feel influential as they see how their ideas affect group choices.

Characteristics of Good Meetings

The first step in learning how to run successful meetings is to recognize the characteristics of good and bad meetings. Bad meetings are long and boring. They alienate people, who sit there but don't really feel part of what is going on. **Nothing** is accomplished. They are often chaotic, and decisions are made even when needed information is missing. Bad meetings make individuals feel inadequate and angry. Perhaps most important, they create a sense of the impossible: How can we defeat them, if we can't even run a simple meeting?

Good meetings are exhilarating. They flow from issue to issue in a fast-paced, logical progression. Information is available in time to make decisions. Members interact and increase their sense of competence through participation. Such meetings create an increased sense of unity and possibility. How can anyone stand in our way when we are so strong together?

A well-run meeting is marked by broad participation. Establishing an agenda, anticipating problems, and skillfully handling conflicts permit more people to participate effectively. The more people participate, the more likely they are to feel that they **own** the decisions reached. The chairperson of a good meeting simultaneously keeps the meeting orderly and flowing and ensures democratic participation.

Preparation for Successful Meetings

Good meetings require preparation both in creating a setting that motivates participation and encouraging people to attend. Preparations include decisions about where to hold the meeting, the size of the room, the layout of the furniture, and when and whether to serve food. Once these decisions are made, the organizer reserves the room and arranges for podiums, blackboards, speaker systems, and coffee or other refreshments.

Participants need to know that the meeting will take place, so thought must be given to how best to announce it. Going door to door to announce a meeting can both increase attendance and provide another opportunity for recruiting. Alternatively, members can make posters printed with felt-tip marker and tack them to bulletin boards in a housing development, tape them on store windows, or slip them under people's doors. These posters announce the subject, the time, the place, and the speakers. In addition, the group can draw up a press release to be read on the radio or printed in the newspaper in the community events section. The widespread informal announcement of a meeting is meant to communicate its openness and convey a sense of spontaneity.

Preliminary arrangements can affect the tone of the meeting. Is the meeting site in a neutral enough location to attract individuals from different factions within the community? Some people might be uncomfortable at the Catholic Church meeting hall, others might be bothered by meeting at the Hispanic Center. Even meeting at organizational headquarters can discourage newcomers from participating. Sometimes, it's worth renting a room so the meeting place is not identified with any particular faction or ideology and is easy and safe to get to.

The size of the meeting room as well as the arrangement of the furniture can affect what goes on. For small meetings, having a single table everyone can sit around will add to the feeling of solidarity. If there are two rows, one at the table and one behind, those behind may feel left out. The room should look full, so take away any extra chairs. Making the room look full is especially important for a membership meeting, so that the organization can impress reporters with the turnout.

When a large crowd is expected at a membership meeting, a raised platform and lit podium might be necessary. A wider, shallower room is better than a long narrow room to minimize the distance between the speaker and the audience. If the physical setting communicates an image of elitism, counteract the setting by ensuring that the speakers represent a wide variety of organization members.

Don't underestimate the importance of the physical environment. Some meetings are dreadful just because it is difficult to hear or understand the speaker. Too many hard surfaces and too many corners create an echo that makes speech sound noisy and indistinct. Instead, look for a room with acoustical tiles or carpeting. However, too much softness just swallows sound. In some cases, the organizers can overcome sound problems with a public address system, but make sure to check out the equipment before the meeting starts.

Different room arrangements affect social interaction. A coffee table with space around it encourages people to gossip and share experiences and impressions. Sitting opposite each other tends to make people more antagonistic in their arguments; sitting next to each other enhances a more cooperative attitude. Arrange furniture so people who might have opposing views are sitting side by side. Light, movable furniture is necessary in training sessions, so people can break up into smaller groups or to go off into a corner to discuss strategy with a team.

If the meeting is going to last for a while, plan the schedule to encourage sociability. Start off the meeting at breakfast with coffee and a little bit of pleasant chatter. Have frequent breaks, and make sure coffee is available at break time. If possible, try to arrange that people have the opportunity to eat together sometime during the meeting; don't let everyone go off on their own for lunch; and try not to let people go off together in cliques. Conversations can defuse potential antagonisms.

Membership Meetings: How Much Structure?
How Much Participation?

Membership meetings can continue the mobilization process by reinforcing interest in the cause. People can meet others who are interested in the same issues. Those not yet in the organization can see how powerful the organization has become and decide that they want to join. For example, at the 10th annual membership meeting of **BUILD**, a Baltimore-based, Alinsky-style coalition,

> the heart of the meeting was called "Empowering the **BUILD** Agenda," an exchange between **BUILD** leaders . . . and public actors in the city. Their presence, more than anything said, made visible **BUILD**'s power. (Boyte, 1989a, p. 113)

Membership meetings demonstrate progress in the midst of a campaign, rally members to the cause, and report to the broader community what has occurred. If reporters are expected, prepare a written statement for them, and have the membership discuss the progress that has been made. The primary purpose of meetings during campaigns is to keep the momentum going.

Another purpose of a membership meeting is to provide overall focus to a group and prevent early enthusiasm from degenerating into chaos. At initial membership meetings, people work out overall goals of the organization and choose (temporary) officers and members of a steering committee. In an ongoing organization, membership meetings are held regularly to discuss progress and difficulties, choose new officers, and consider the effectiveness of the steering committee. Such meetings reinforce the idea

Gale Cincotta addresses national meeting of National People's Action. (Courtesy National People's Action)

that the membership **owns** the organization and is responsible for its actions. Regular meetings also pressure those in leadership positions to accomplish something lest people stop attending if nothing has been achieved.

One important tactic is for leaders to hold a post meeting evaluation session, to examine the issues raised at the membership meeting and the way the meeting was held. The leaders review the questions raised, examine whether the organization has gotten off the track, and explore whether members' suggestions can be implemented. The leaders also examine whether the meeting succeeded in promoting the democratic, participatory ideology of the organization, and if it didn't, what should be changed for the next time.

In larger organizations, membership meetings can be complicated affairs, so while it is important to have a tone of informality, it is necessary to maintain some order through the use of agendas, bylaws, and rules of procedure. The skill is in creating sufficient informality to encourage participation but not so much as to lead to chaos, where everyone speaks at once and few know what decisions have been reached.

At the first organizational meeting, leaders from the community and professional organizers should introduce themselves and describe the problems they see. People discuss the problems they face and select committee members, especially for the steering committee. It is also important to collect dues. The organization needs money, and paying dues reinforces identity with the organization.

Balance is required between communicating information efficiently and letting people build their enthusiasm. A brief, written agenda may be all that is needed to ensure information is presented. Some people worry that agendas and rules of procedure hamper democratic participation, because more active, aggressive, or experienced members manipulate the rules to dominate decision making. But as long as the rules make it easy for every member of the organization to add items for discussion, following an agenda is democratic.

Bylaws and rules of procedure provide both order and fairness yet can be loosely enforced when members are caught up in the enthusiasm of the moment. Rules of procedure are meant to preserve democracy by limiting the domination of loudmouths and verbal bullies. Bylaws permit the organization to anticipate conflict and establish procedures for handling them. There is a difference between healthy debates on the issues at hand and unnecessary confrontations caused by ambiguous rules for reaching decisions.

One problem that should be resolved in the bylaws is the definition of who is a voting member of the organization. For example, if the organization has a hired staff, who are members of committees ex officio (i.e., who are on the committees because their work requires them to know what is going on, not because they are elected), it is important to specify whether or not they can vote. Usually the answer is no. If members are concerned that inactive people who do not understand the issues, or who have been inspired to attend the meeting by a particular faction, may come to a meeting and swamp it, specify that only those who have paid their dues may vote. Bylaws can permit true democratic representation, while preventing a small faction from taking over the organization and ramming unpopular decisions down the throats of the membership.

If major disagreements affect large portions of the membership, the issues must be discussed and some accommodation reached. But if a very small group feels strongly that its opinions must prevail and disrupts discussion, making every meeting tense, such factionalism is harmful and preventable. To reduce the tyranny of a small minority, specify in the bylaws a minimum number of members that must be present before business can take place—a quorum—and set the minimum number larger than the size of small factional groups. Ideally, the size of the quorum should be small enough that business can be transacted at most meetings but large enough to prevent a small faction of the organization from making decisions for everyone else.

Another way to deal with factionalism is to state in the bylaws that all business meetings must be announced a reasonable time in advance and that notices must be sent ahead of time, reminding members of the meeting. If this rule is observed, there ought to be no last-minute meetings of the organization with only one faction represented.

Bylaws can reduce the chance of meetings being so contentious that members don't get a chance to discuss things or listen to each other's arguments. The most common set of bylaws adopted by organizations is called *Robert's Rules of Order* (Robert, 1984), though most organizations simplify these rules.

Rules help keep order at meetings, while permitting full and open discussions. They specify that the chairperson has a right to call on people and that unless recognized by the chair, people should not speak, except to clarify procedures. *Motions* are made in which one or two people first suggest what they think should be done. *Discussion* is then limited to the content of the motions, preventing issues from getting too complicated for everyone to understand, though some modifications can be suggested. Unless the organization makes decisions by consensus, after the discussion someone calls for a vote, and then the meeting moves on to the next topic.

Rules are meant to facilitate not to limit and need not be followed rigidly. In fact, small organizations need not adopt rules for meetings unless keeping meetings running smoothly and giving everyone who wants it time to speak is clearly becoming a problem. Formal voting rules are not appropriate for discussion and brain-storming sessions.

While not exactly a rule, a useful tradition is to leave time at most meetings for expressing general grievances, perhaps toward the end after agenda items have been discussed. During the gripe sessions, few limits should be placed on the time spent on any one issue. If an issue seems important enough, establish a committee to study it, hold informal meetings to discuss it, and then report it back as an item on the agenda of a membership meeting.

In smaller organizations, membership meetings and decision-making meetings blur into each other. For larger organizations, there is an important difference. The overall strategy and set of goals of an organization must be arrived at during the general membership meeting. But detailed decision making—planning of tactics, careful analysis of problems—is better done in smaller meetings of democratically chosen action committees.

Different ways of choosing committee members include open nominations followed by votes of the membership, assignment of people by lottery, or rotation of everyone into key positions over time. Any procedure is okay if it assures fair representation and the inclusion of less dominant members.

In new organizations, recruitment committees and committees to organize the next meeting must be quickly established. But the membership might not be familiar with the people who want to serve on committees and might end up choosing people from the original group of organizers, reducing the involvement of others. On the other hand, waiting too long can cause the organization to drift as the urgency that motivated people to attend the meeting disappears. There are two ways around this problem. One way is to have several informal meetings in the homes of community members, so people can get to know each other before selecting committee members. The second way is to elect temporary committees for 3 to 6 months, then elect more permanent bodies.

The person who chairs a membership meeting, usually the group leader or president, must have good speaking skills, a touch of humor, and an ability to play on emotions. The chair needs to show vision and portray goals that the members understand and approve and needs to instill a sense that the goal can be accomplished. To do so, the chair can be dramatic, recounting recent battles and earlier victories of the organization vividly, so that those who were not there can participate in the shared experience.

The organization's leader becomes a role model and, therefore, needs to radiate competence, confidence, and loyalty to the organization's goals. Sometimes, humorous references to long hours spent working for the organization can set a tone for hard work. The leader can build confidence by describing clever tactics that were successful in the past and outlining future campaigns.

Even with safeguards to maintain an open process, formal meetings may seem too hierarchical for a democratically run organization. Some people are sorted out as leaders and sit on a raised platform, while others, defined as members, sit below. Those upset by this symbolism may advocate participatory democracy models that obtain the involvement of as many people as possible by shunning structure, avoiding agendas, and setting no time limit on discussions. The meeting continues until total consensus is obtained. Encouraging participation is considered more important than the decisions reached to solve the problems at hand.

When participatory democracy is fully implemented, it results in dysfunctional levels of disorder. The history of the Students for Democratic Society (Gitlin 1989; J. Miller 1987) shows that such meetings collapse under their own weight. Even more damning, feminist literature points out that the participatory democratic model did not work to provide everyone access, especially because women had far less opportunity to speak than men. The goal of maximum participation is a good one for community organizations, but complete lack of structure excludes the less aggressive.

A more efficient approach to increasing participation is to adopt some of the practices associated with participatory democracy but not all of them. One useful idea is to divide the responsibility of the chair into two roles, a *facilitator* who handles problems when they arise and a *traveling chair.*

> The *traveling chair* can be used in conjunction with a regular facilitator. In this method, the person who has been talking is responsible for calling on the next participant. She or he speaks and then calls on someone else who has indicated a desire to contribute.

This process shares the responsibility and power of recognizing speakers, distributes the awareness of recognizing members who don't talk much, and generally increases participation, commitment and involvement. (Avery et al., 1981)

While this procedure need not be followed exactly, the idea of giving a variety of people experience as chair (and setting up a system to preclude only socially dominant people from taking that position) has merit.

Decision-Making Meetings

Though decisions on overall goals are set forth and ratified at membership meetings, the details are often worked out at smaller group meetings. A large group can't discuss issues and explore options the way a small group can. A large group is unlikely to read background material so its decision making is likely to be less informed. And large groups can discuss complicated issues only with the adoption of formal rules that limit the time each speaker can talk, which makes for awkward discussions.

Small decision-making groups should be no larger than 12 people. With more than a dozen people, discussions become awkward, and if everyone participates, the meetings become overly long. The decision-making group can be elected from the membership, or it can be appointed with a view to representing different constituencies in the organization. The decisions of the smaller group can be referred back to the full membership for a vote.

Decision-making meetings should facilitate creative solutions, encourage democratic involvement, and avoid many of the dysfunctions—dominance by upper status males, unwillingness to express dissent—that plague small groups. Small decision-making groups are good for open-ended tasks that require a division of labor among group members with different skills and knowledge (Kowitz & Knutson, 1980).

Community Development planning session sponsored by Kenwood Oakland Community Organization. (Thom Clark)

Many problems facing community organizations satisfy these criteria. They tend to be open-ended, that is, the problems have many different interpretations and no single correct answer. The variety of tasks encourages a division of labor. These tasks include learning about the problem, fund raising, publicity, running meetings, and managing community businesses or housing.

Structuring Good Decision-Making Meetings. The structure of effective decision-making groups emerges slowly over time (Kowitz & Knutson, 1980, p. 34). In the first stage, *orientation,* group members learn each other's personalities, strengths, and weaknesses. Next, in the *formation* stage, the roles of individuals are resolved, some group members may be expected to keep harmony in the group; some may be expected to provide technical information or information about the organization's history and experience. In the third stage, *coordination,* negotiations occur between group members over the meaning and importance of information and group goals. Finally, in the *formalization* stage, the group determines a course of action and tries to create within itself harmonious support for the action.

If formal rules are imposed too early, people lack enough time to successfully complete the orientation stage. On the other hand, if rules are incorporated too late, groups can drift and never really reach the formalization stage. Group meetings should be structured enough to encourage people to contribute ideas but not so structured that the rules or procedures, rather than the ideas themselves, become the focus.

Preparation for a decision-making meeting should include an agenda and supporting materials. An agenda lists items to be discussed so that they will be handled. Each item on the agenda should be briefly and clearly described. If supporting or explanatory materials are included for any item, this should be noted on the agenda, and the supporting material should be numbered to match the item on the agenda. For example, if item 4 is "alternative march routes," maps displaying different routes should be labeled "supporting materials for item 4" and should be included with the agenda.

The agenda should be prepared and distributed in time for people to think about the issues that are coming up for discussion. The agenda should be sent to committee members and also posted in the organization office and circulated in the newsletter, so that others not on the particular committee can see what the committee is doing. One way of promoting full discussion on a topic is to describe the topic in a provocative way on the agenda. People are going to show up at a meeting with ideas in mind if they see an agenda item like "handling the increased sexism in the organization."

Agendas not only inform people of upcoming issues and allow them to prepare for a meeting, they also regulate its flow by scheduling when each issue will be discussed or announced. An agenda contains different kinds of items, such as the formalities of carrying on meetings (e.g., setting a time for the next meeting); reports on projects or investigations in progress; the business of the organization itself (such as paying bills); and the decisions that have to be made at the meeting. Here are several recommendations for arranging an agenda:

- Place some routine business or announcements first. Read brief reports, if there are any.

- Place the important decisions about 15 to 20 minutes after the start. People tend to be most alert at this point.
- Wrap up with some noncontroversial items in a consent agenda, the list of routine business items that don't involve any discussion.
- Don't crowd the agenda with long, complicated items. Try to estimate the time each item will take to discuss. The convener might even want to put the estimated, or targeted, time for discussion on the agenda. Aim for a total length of an hour and a half or less. If the meeting goes much more than 2 hours, people will start to leave.
- Don't let discussions on the routine issues take time away from the more thorough discussions on difficult issues. With controversial issues, hold separate meetings to discuss different options and then bring back decisions to the next meeting for ratification.

Even if the work of preparing an agenda is done by paid staff, at decision-making meetings, staff should be largely silent. The executive director of a local environmental group pointed out dangers of domination by staff:

> I have expressed . . . my fear about the Defenders becoming a staff-run organization. . . . I have seen enough environmental organizations that have started out as a grassroots movement become so structured and top heavy with staff they lost touch with the roots and eventually withered and sometimes died. (McHenry County Defenders, 1987)

The staff, often professional organizers, may answer questions addressed to them, such as requests for information. Occasionally, they may intervene to suggest a technical solution or give advice about the legality of what is being suggested. But basically, the staff should not run or direct the meeting. Members can learn to handle the mechanics of decision-making meetings themselves.

What organizers in their role as staff can do is help structure decision making to ensure progress and encourage people to present their own ideas:

1. Keep groups small enough so that individuals are willing to participate. It is better to form several subcommittees than to have too large a committee.
2. Physically symbolize equality between group members. Sit in circles rather than at a table with a head.
3. Run meetings with an agenda, even if it is informal. Setting up the agenda forces people to think about the issues that ought to be covered, and getting through the agenda gives people a sense of progress.
4. Don't try to accomplish everything in one meeting. The first meetings of small groups are spent in establishing interpersonal relations and learning about each other's areas of competence. Such understandings are vital for making decisions later on. Effective groups share a history.
5. Leave the time before and after meetings for conversation. Personal familiarity promotes effective group actions.
6. When the group has decided on actions, be sure to assign follow-up responsibilities. It is frustrating to call another meeting and then learn that no one obtained the needed information.

(Adapted from S. E. Jones, Barnlund & Haimun 1980; Kowitz & Knutson 1980).

Table 10–1 portrays the balance required between maintaining order and efficiency while encouraging contribution and providing satisfaction.

Creating and Stimulating Ideas.   Democratic decision-making groups aim to come up with ideas that solve shared problems. The purpose, though, is more than solving the problems. It is getting people involved and learning from their own success that they have the capacity to devise solutions.

There are different techniques for stimulating group ideas. Some involve a leader who knows how to elicit the opinions from other group members. Others build on formal techniques designed to encourage shy people to contribute their ideas.

The leader of a decision-making group can play a variety of functions in a meeting, including provoking original thoughts in others, helping to evaluate ideas that are on the table for discussion, clarifying and summarizing points that are being made, and suggesting items that require further discussion and need to be put on the agenda for the next meeting (S. E. Jones, Barnlund, & Haiman, 1980). Different leaders should emerge, depending on the task. A reporter in the group will probably have more suggestions about public relations than an electrician. The reverse is true if the topic is building-code violators.

Leaders must be able to provide order and coherence to discussions of decision-making groups without forcing their own ideas on the group. A leader may be able to summarize a discussion, listing alternatives that have been raised, and add a few ideas that haven't been mentioned yet, before going down the list to evaluate feasibility or look for weaknesses. The discussion leader must be careful about expressing his or her ideas, because others are likely to defer to them whether they agree with them or not. Leaders' ideas must be subject to the same scrutiny as anyone else's.

TABLE 10–1
Decision-Making Meetings Require Careful Balance

	STRUCTURE	
With too much structure, talking is inhibited because people are afraid of making a procedural error.		With too little structure, people defer to others and fear to talk.
	LEADERSHIP	
Too strong a leadership makes group members fear to contribute.		Too weak a leadership makes discussions lose their focus.
	COHESION	
With too much emphasis on cohesion, people defer to the majority opinion.		With too little cohesion, people are afraid to present their ideas.
	CONFLICT	
Constant conflict leads to disruptive power struggles.		Without conflict, weaker ideas go untested.

It is important for the leader of a decision-making group to be tactful. The leader should not put people down roughly, no matter how bad the idea or how poorly expressed.

> When defining an issue or problem always define it as shared. Responsibility for a conflict never lies with just one person or faction. Say, "We do not agree about the distribution of office space," *not,* "Jack refuses to share his desk." Say, "Mary and Tom have a problem coordinating their work schedules," *not* "Tom is never around when Mary needs to consult with him." (Avery et al., 1981)

The leader should never yell back at people who get excited or rude but should politely ask them to tone down the discussion. Continued courtesy in the face of rudeness encourages people to respect each other's ideas and moves away from personality conflicts. However, sometimes it may be impossible to carry on business because the issues are so controversial. In such circumstances, the leader should call a recess or terminate the meeting.

To elicit the contribution of ideas by group members, the most important trait of a good leader is the ability to listen, that is, to indicate to others that he or she is paying attention to what they are saying. The leader, as the one who is moderating the discussion, must remain neutral and not slant the discussion in one direction or another (S. E. Jones et al., 1980 p. 83).

Leaders should indicate the direction a discussion is taking and summarize or refine the suggestions that others make. Leaders listen carefully and then encourage others to clarify and summarize their own argument. For example, a discussion leader might say, "I understand the first part of what you said, but I'm not sure what you think we ought to do after the boycott."

The leader then brings the discussion to a head by formulating a position that reflects the sentiment of the group. Often, this is not a position stated in so many words by any one individual, so it takes a bit of imagination and practice to do this well. The chair pieces together partially formed ideas suggested by different people. One person argues for getting front-page publicity while another describes the frustration of community members ignored by city hall. The leader combines the ideas to suggest a well-publicized sit-in at the city plaza.

For the quality of decision making, for the unity of the group, and for the acceptability of the committee's decision to the membership, it is also important that everyone have a chance to speak. Only by so doing will all sides of an issue be explored and alternative actions examined. This means that the chairperson needs to keep in mind who has spoken and who has not. The chairperson can say, "Dick, you have been pretty quiet so far. What do you think about all this?" Be sure the ones most likely to be swayed by the responses of others are called on first.

The chairperson should not rush to get the group to agree to a new idea. Even in the most effective, harmonious groups, ideas are born, discarded, and reborn. Time is required for a good idea to simmer in a group until it has been refined. By letting an idea sit on the back burner for a while, it becomes group property and not simply Mary's pet scheme; egoism is replaced with collective ownership. Social psychologists term this process of letting an idea simmer *decision modification,* during which old ideas are "reborn" often in modified form; that is, the first time a solution is suggested it is likely to draw some opposition, or else the topic may be simply dropped. Later the idea may reappear, usually in altered form if there are objections to the idea the first time it was brought up. The same basic solution may go through a number of such transformations before it is accepted. Ideas which do not continue to reemerge in new form do not survive. (S. E. Jones et al., 1980, p. 166)

Good leadership encourages the cycling of ideas until they become group property.

To do all these things requires both experience and forethought. It is a good idea, therefore, to provide some kind of training for new committee members. They might feel insulted if the training were too basic, but a thoughtful presentation may work. As one approach, organizers can write a handbook for running meetings that contains restatements of the organization's bylaws relevant to meetings. Beneath the excerpt from the bylaws could be examples of what to do. For example, there could be a statement on the responsibilities of the chairperson, with examples. Another approach might be to start each new committee with a summary of the issues decided by its predecessor and a discussion of the strengths and weaknesses of the process over the past year or two. Such a presentation should refresh continuing members and interest new members, while laying groundwork for improved decision making.

Increasing the Variety of Ideas.   Skillful group leaders can increase the number of ideas suggested. But other techniques are required to get people to contribute ideas, especially those who fear that by making suggestions they will appear foolish. One such technique is *brainstorming.* Brainstorming is

> a procedure wherein members are encouraged to suggest any idea about the problem that comes to mind. The ideas are written on a blackboard or flip chart, and no positive or negative evaluation of the ideas is permitted, including scowls, groans, sighs or gestures. (Yukl, 1989, p. 250)

Occasionally, when this process is begun people will spark off each other, and one good idea will suggest another. The dynamics of the situation encourage people to participate.

Another way of brainstorming is to place an idea on a blackboard and have people shout out its pros and cons, while someone writes them down. The pros and cons are then discussed individually. This pattern sets up an environment that encourages talking by everyone.

If a group has a tendency to adopt new ideas without a thorough examination of their implications, creativity should be accompanied by selecting one or more *devil's advocates.* The role of the devil's advocate is to look for weaknesses in an important idea, after the original meeting is completed (Yukl, 1989, p. 255). Creative ideas occur in a reinforcing group context, while critical evaluation of the idea occurs outside the group. This way, somebody doesn't propose an idea only to have it publicly and perhaps humiliatingly shot down. The enthusiasm of the moment is preserved, but the chance of going off half-cocked is reduced.

The problem of settling too quickly on a single idea occurs frequently because people tend to be conformists. If the early suggestions all go in one direction, those speaking later will not feel free to suggest something different. One way to avoid this problem is to have people write down their ideas, collect them, and read them to the group anonymously, discussing the possibilities in each one. That way everyone gets their ideas in before they hear anyone else's. The second advantage of this technique is that if people know their ideas won't be attributed to them—no one can laugh at them—they are likely to be more creative.

A related procedure is called *round-robin* (C. M. Moore, 1987). In this case, somebody suggests an idea, and it is put down on a pad. The pad is circulated, and everyone is required to add or cross out a statement but to somehow build on the original idea. The obligation forces people to contribute, and because no emendations are signed, anonymity is preserved. Round-robin tends to work once somebody formulates the original goal or policy idea. Unfortunately, such ideas are more likely to come from people already in more dominant positions.

Social-psychological research has shown that in public settings, individuals who are less shy and more dynamic, but not necessarily better informed, are able to impose their ideas on a group. Especially during early meetings of decision-making committees, systematic procedures are required to get people, often strangers to one another, to express their priorities. One such procedure, known as *nominal group techniques* (NGTs) (from Delbecq, Van de Ven, & Gustafson, 1975; revised by C. M. Moore, 1987), aims at getting people to describe their ideas in ways in which they will not be embarrassed then has the entire group discuss and set priorities among the different ideas.

The use of NGT can be relatively complicated and conceivably could tie up meeting time and bore group members. The following modified version, however, should work with smaller groups.

1. At the meeting, the chair or the original organizers talk about the overall problems and possible goals to be accomplished. Ideas are placed on a board.
2. Discussion is requested from other people, and their ideas are added to those on the board.
3. For groups of better-educated individuals, people are asked to write down their suggestions for the problems confronting the community or organization.
4. For groups of people less comfortable with writing, the meeting breaks up into small cells of two or three people each. Collectively, these people produce suggestions concerning the problems confronting the community or organization.
5. The lists of items are then combined and placed on the blackboard. No names are associated with the ideas. Members of the entire group discuss and attempt to rank the importance of the items. Depending on the size, education, and formality of the group, such ranking can be accomplished through formal voting or through consensus.

It is not important to follow NGT step-by-step. It is, however, vital to get the active involvement of most committee members in making key decisions. The acceptability of the committee's decision to the whole membership may depend on having worked out a solution acceptable to each of the constituencies. If not all the committee members participated, the constituencies those members represent may feel left out or tricked.

Problems of Cohesion, Satisfaction, and Groupthink.   Individuals tend to be most satisfied working in cohesive groups that maintain a sense of camaraderie and group harmony. In cohesive groups, people participate more, present their ideas more readily, and are more willing to accept group outcomes as their own while working for the good of the group. In addition, in cohesive groups, people are more likely to make riskier and more innovative decisions than the members would individually, in part because group members share responsibility and no one gets blamed if the tactic doesn't work (Chell, 1985, p. 141). Making such risky decisions may be the only way to succeed when community organizations are fighting from a position of weakness and the opponent seems to have all the power.

Unfortunately, cohesiveness can become the goal of a meeting, rather than the means for accomplishing work. If having a harmonious discussion becomes the goal, members may feel they have made progress because they have attended a socially satisfying meeting. Remember

> member satisfaction and group cohesiveness are useful tools to assist a group in develop-ing a decision proposal only if they are used to that end. . . . Do not let your group be-come *too* cohesive or your members too satisfied without working on your task. (Kowitz & Knutson, 1980, p. 116)

Too much concern for group cohesiveness can contribute to poor decision making, if individuals search only for information that supports the group's stated (and shared) beliefs (Kowitz & Knutson, 1980, p. 53). Irving Janis has called the resulting biased evaluation of an alternative *groupthink*.

> "groupthink" [is] a mode of thinking that people engage in when they are deeply involved in a cohesive group, when the members' strivings for unanimity override their motivation to realistically appraise alternative courses of action. . . . Groupthink refers to a deteriora-tion of mental efficiency, reality testing, and moral judgement that results from in-group pressures. (Janis, 1982, p. 9)

When groupthink occurs, members of a group feel more powerful than they are, are unwilling to search out evidence contradictory to their beliefs, and apply strong pres-sure on anyone who dissents (Janis, 1982, pp. 174–175). With groupthink, groups may believe that they can do no wrong, ignoring the ethical consequences of their action. A small leadership group might suggest making political deals that are kept secret from the membership. Such strategic choices thwart the democratic ideals of community organizations.

Or, the sense of invulnerability that sometimes occurs in overly cohesive groups may lead members to underestimate the strength of opponents. For example, in plan-ning a demonstration, the tactics committee may be so caught up in their own clev-erness that they forget that the authorities control the police and that the target of the demonstration owns the local newspaper.

Finally, if groupthink prevails, dissenters are discouraged from speaking. This de-nies the group contrary views and may cause some members to opt out of community actions. For example, organizations in the women's movement lost members by ignoring the demands of lesbians (Deckard, 1983).

The dangers of groupthink are clearly present when building community organizations. People join such organizations because they care about issues and believe that something can be accomplished yet their enthusiasm can lead to a cockiness about the organization's power. The enemy is seen as evil, information necessary for effective action is not sought, and dissenters are either ignored or more likely excluded from the group. In the end, the organization fails, because it underestimated the enemy and refused to listen to alternative plans.

To avoid groupthink, decision-making groups should include people who are willing to present different ideas. The devil's advocate approach, making someone responsible for coming up with objections to plans, is useful here. Alternative ideas should be solicited, and dissent should be encouraged. One doesn't want the group to fall apart from excessive conflict, but a healthy amount of dissent is a sign of good decision making.

Group Conflict and Consensus Decision Making.   A group can develop cohesion while avoiding groupthink if it learns how to handle conflict. The need to handle conflict extends far beyond the problem of groupthink because good-quality decisions depend on the presentation and discussion of alternative viewpoints that might create conflict. Conflict can be disruptive to effective group decision-making if it involves a clash of personality over and above disagreement on the issues. But as long as personality conflicts are avoided and fundamental value conflicts do not exist, disagreement increases participation and improves the quality of decisions.

Conflict can be a constructive way of motivating people to present their ideas on the problems facing the community or interpretations of controversial issues:

> Conflict . . . ordinarily contributes to group effectiveness by getting participants involved, providing a safety valve for frustrations, strengthening bonds after the expression of disagreement, testing ideas and insuring a fair hearing for innovative points of view. The risk in conflict is that it is time-consuming and can lead to group disintegration. . . . It is easier to handle when it concerns means rather than goals. . . . Especially difficult is the situation in which "hidden agendas" of personality or status conflicts emerge as ideational disputes. (S. E. Jones et al., 1980, pp. 153–154)

Groups that know how to handle conflicts produce better decisions, generate more alternative solutions, increase interest and the willingness of people to participate, and force group members to be specific about the information needed to resolve problems facing the group (Kowitz & Knutson, 1980, pp. 171–175).

Rather than simply let an idea pass uncontradicted, leaders of groups should encourage dissent on proposals. But they should try to ensure that disagreements focus on the issues and not on personalities. When people disagree sincerely on policies, the group leader should clarify differences and point out where more information is needed. In running such discussions, leaders should keep in mind the types of conflict that are likely to occur and the strategies for handling each (S. E. Jones et al., 1980, p. 146–147).

Individuals can disagree on *assertions,* that is, untested statements of personal preference or belief. For example, in a multiracial neighborhood, someone might simply state that members of X group are incapable of working together. To handle disagreements on assertions, particularize the situation: Rather than argue that the general assertion is incorrect, choose cases in which the statement is false. "Do you think you can work with Mr. Y (a member of group X)?" "Of course I can, Mr. Y is an exception." At that point, don't worry about the broader questions of prejudice. Just get on with the job.

Individuals can disagree on *reasoning,* that is, how they go from their understanding of the facts of the situation to the conclusions. If this occurs, ask people why they believe as they do. Perhaps people disagree on factual premises that can be bridged. At least the arguments become clearer to other group members, who themselves can then join in. For example, a member might argue, "I am against the building of a shelter for the homeless in this city." Inquiries might uncover the rest of the argument namely, "If we build a shelter, homeless from other areas will come here, and we will have to pay for them." The new information opens up the possibility of discussion of whether there are many homeless in neighboring towns, and whether other towns may wish to contribute financially to a shelter we build. Someone might ask if it much matters whose homeless are being sheltered. Someone else might question whether the homeless travel from town to town to find shelters. This question offers the possibility of getting some information from directors of shelters in other cities. If any of the links in the argument are weak, the conclusion may not follow.

Disagreements can occur on factual matters of *evidence.* For example, if someone argues, "We can't target Exxon to clean up the river, it will cost too much, and one industry will never pay that much." One might want to know how much it costs to clean up a river polluted by an important industry, and has a single large corporation ever been successfully forced to clean up a river? Set up a subcommittee, with individuals from both sides of the argument, to examine the evidence.

The most difficult conflicts are those on *values,* fundamental beliefs about what should be. Debates over fundamental values such as free speech, nonviolence, or abortion should not occur within most progressive or community organizations. Such disagreements represent a gulf too wide to easily bridge; when fundamental values are in conflict, several groups should be spun off.

Some organizations adopt *consensus decision making* as a way of handling conflict while demonstrating a belief in the importance of member equality. Under consensus decision making, actions are not taken unless there is total agreement among the participants. This model of decision making is radically antihierarchical and presupposes a *unitary model of democracy* (Mansbridge, 1980), in which decisions are taken only after shared interests emerge as people reason and compromise together in group meetings.

A belief in consensus is seductive because it is consistent with the participatory ethos that turns potential conflict into a search for common belief. For example, at meetings of the antinuclear Clamshell alliance

> the emphasis was on accommodation, as explained by a Clamshell member at a training workshop: "Under majority rule, when you and I disagree I try to convince you that I am right and you are wrong; under the consensus process, I try to accommodate myself to your objection." (Downey, 1986, p. 368)

Yet, there are problems.

"Consensus" voting, where people discuss an issue until a formulation is reached with which everyone agrees is . . . both elitist and undemocratic. It is elitist because consensus meetings can go on for hours—hours that working people and parents do not have. It is undemocratic because it assumes that disagreement is a sign of group weakness rather than actual strength. (Burghardt, 1982a, p. 54)

Consensus voting can be sabotaged or become increasingly difficult. One observer reported:

The increasing size of the organization made a consensus more elusive, for the area of common agreement became smaller as the group grew larger. The larger size also increased the potential that a single disruptive individual or *agent provocateur* would immobilize the entire group by simply expressing disagreement, which happened, in fact, on several occasions. (Downey, 1986, p. 368)

Other studies question how well consensus decision making works. An analysis of the American version of the Green (proenvironment) political party indicates further difficulties with consensus decision making. Requiring consensus makes it harder to delegate work to special committees if their decisions require ratification by the whole group. It leads to questions of whether a new member has an equal say to older members, makes it difficult to send delegated representatives to meetings of coalitions, and in practice, is not free from the manipulation of rules that plague more conventional decision-making procedures (Zisk, 1989, p. 10). It is important to encourage group participation and demonstrate respect for the opinions of others, but requiring consensus is not usually the best way of doing this.

Fortunately, consensus decision making can be modified to reduce or eliminate many of its drawbacks. For example, some community groups increase the proportion who have to agree with a proposal beyond a simple majority, to 60% or more, without requiring 100% agreement. Clamshell revised its voting procedures to require an 80% agreement rather than total consensus. To handle immediate decisions without seeking complete consensus, some Greens create small empowered subcommittees and then rotate the membership of such committees frequently.

The Center for Conflict Resolution, a proponent of consensus decision making, suggests that if a group fails to achieve consensus, members should ask those who oppose the decision if they could live with the dominant opinion. The principle respects the opinions of others while recognizing that when there is strong disagreement that precludes a consensus that the group would be well-advised to explore the issue further (Avery, 1981).

Training Meetings

At training sessions, members of the organization learn specific skills that enhance their sense of competence. People learn how to run meetings, raise funds, prepare press releases, arrange rallies, make budgets, or virtually any other action of a community organization. As members develop these skills and use them to promote collective purposes, the group becomes more successful, and the individual's commitment to the ideals of community development is increased.

Training sessions vary in size. Sometimes more formal lectures can be given to large groups, while at other times small workshops are needed. An effective procedure is to have a larger meeting, during which general principles are discussed, and then to break up quickly into smaller workshops or practice sessions, at which individuals try their hand at whatever is being taught.

Training sessions should be run with a light touch. Training sessions must balance the need to communicate specific skills with the requirement to create an environment that makes people feel comfortable learning those skills. People should not feel like they are back in school.

Effective training sessions require preparation to make sure information and skills are communicated in the allotted time. The trainer orchestrates a program by listing speakers in order and scheduling workshop and break times. From 1 to 2 PM, group one should do this; from 3 to 4 PM it should do that. Support materials should be presented at the training sessions. One way to do this is to use plastic binders with tabs, each tab indicating material for a different time slot. If the first speaker is talking about legal constraints on door-to-door solicitations, the first tab could be a copy of the state laws on the solicitation of funds. These printed materials will reinforce what has been said after the speaker has left and will free group members from the need to take detailed notes.

The role of the trainer differs from that of the chair at membership or decision-making meetings. The leader of the training session is a knowledgeable person, sharing experiences and values with the trainees. It is best to find trainers who are also members of the organization or of sister organizations. If the trainer in protest tactics becomes the trainee in how to budget funds, expertise in one field is less likely to translate into being a boss.

The personality and speaking skills of the trainer are important. It helps to use a bit of humor and to indicate not only that the speaker has been there before—led a demonstration, been audited, or arrested, or petitioned city hall—but also was successful. Equally important, the trainer must indicate that there is nothing he or she has done that the trainee cannot also do. "Here is how it works, now you do it," ought to be the basic message of the training.

To get across the idea that the trainee can do whatever the trainer has done, the trainer should have as similar a background as possible to the people being trained. He or she ought to be able to say "Five years ago I was sitting where you are now." If the trainer dresses and talks like the trainees and draws on shared values, the impression of being the same kind of people will be strengthened. Otherwise, organizational members might feel that the trainer succeeded because he or she is better educated or has a different background and that what is being proposed cannot be done. "That's all right for you, you are rich or you are college educated, but I can't do that."

Effective training relies on references and examples familiar to others. A person teaching about budgets should use the organization's own budget or one from a similar group. If the training session concerns ways of running effective meetings, the trainer can analyze the last meeting of the organization and then hold a mock session.

In general, trainers have four responsibilities: they should build skills; integrate philosophy with skills; help set realistic goals for trainees; and generate enthusiasm and loyalty.

Build Skills.   At the training sessions, have people practice, no matter what is being taught. Don't let people leave until they demonstrate at some level not only that they understand what has been said but that they can do it. In training for fund raising, the group can practice soliciting funds from each other. The trainer can ask the group to write opening lines, then collect and read them (anonymously) to the group, pick the best (not the worst), and comment on why they are good. Work at it until the whole group can recognize the effective appeals. Let members take the role of the citizen being solicited, while the trainer asks for money. Though role-playing teaches, it can be very funny and helps people have a good time. Just imagine the mockery involved in playing the president of a large bank in a training session on pressuring business.

Integrate Philosophy With Skills.   The ethos of training sessions is to show that everyone can learn skills. Many technical skills, though, are not meaningful unless placed in the broader philosophy out of which they grow. For example, in training for civil disobedience, people learn how to accept arrest passively or how to act as a dead weight when the police cart them out of a building. But these skills are meaningful only when the philosophy of nonviolence is understood. You have to know not only what to do in the circumstances but also why you are supposed to do it. Unless members both understand the tactic and believe in the philosophy, when push comes to shove, push is likely to be the response to shove. Before both the civil rights demonstrations led by Martin Luther King, Jr. (Branch, 1988), and sits-ins to protest nuclear reactors, hours of training were spent in combining tactics with the philosophy of nonviolence (Downey, 1986).

Be Realistic.   Give trainees realistic goals for both time spent and money collected. Otherwise, people will become discouraged as soon as the enthusiasm generated by the training session wears off. If the trainer is teaching fund raising, let the trainees know that some people won't let them in the house or, if they do, will insist on talking about a recent operation rather than community problems. Be realistic, too, about the dangers of canvassing in some neighborhoods (two members together might be better than one going alone) and the difficulty of gaining trust where the organization member is white and the community is black or vice versa.

Build Enthusiasm and Loyalty.   Enthusiasm is contagious. The trainer should be both enthusiastic and loyal to the program. The trainer should concentrate on what is possible, what is desirable, and what this group can achieve. The trainer needs to focus on how important the contributions of the trainees will be.

The trainer can instill enthusiasm in several ways. One is to ensure that the training doesn't get dull. Choose new and unusual situations to keep peoples' interest up. Let them find the errors in a poorly constructed budget and laugh at them rather than simply learning by rote the rules for making a budget. People tend to find simulations—acting out real-world scenarios—fun and informative. Divide the group into a bargaining team for the neighborhood and one for the city. Watch how seriously all involved treat their roles; people will pay close attention to the trainer's analysis of the game later on. Discussing what they did during the negotiations is far more effective than an abstract lecture on negotiating tactics.

Psychologists argue that people believe something after they have acted on these values. If trainees act enthusiastic, they are more likely to feel enthusiastic. Getting people to sing loudly and with energy—this won't always be possible—increases the chances that they will be more enthusiastic about the whole enterprise than if they sing with reserve. If the group trainer is natural and uninhibited, the trainees will probably be less inhibited too. To summarize, the trainer should

- Share experiences and values with trainees
- Build skills
- Provide a philosophical basis for the skills
- Give trainees a realistic picture of what they can expect
- Build enthusiasm, which increases loyalty to the group

THE DILEMMAS OF DEMOCRATIC LEADERSHIP

Throughout the discussion on meetings, we have emphasized the importance of the leadership in ensuring true group involvement in the choice of goals. Only a thin line separates a leader who guides community members to achieving their goals from one who dominates them through personality, experience, or ability to dramatize an issue.

These problems of the leader's role in meetings reflect a broader dilemma in community organizing: An organization needs a leader to give it guidance, but the members need to participate and set the direction of the group.

An organization without an obvious leader has difficulty in gaining public attention and often will lack focus in its actions. But when there is a leader who has public recognition, the organization can become an extension of the personality of the leader. The purposes of the organization may be blurred with the public persona of its leader: Martin Luther King, Jr., with the Southern Christian Leadership Conference, Cesar Chavez with the Farm Workers, Ralph Nader with Public Citizen, or Maggie Kuhn with the Gray Panthers.

Personality cult organizations can support progressive causes and are effective in showing the need to bring about changes yet fail to encourage democratic participation and do little to establish longer-term structures for capacity building. Charismatic leaders can satisfy their followership because much of what they advocate appears to be, and often is, for the good of their followers. But they teach that success occurs by following the decisions of the capable leader and not through building self-confidence. To the extent that charismatic leaders ignore organizational mandates or autonomously set goals, such leadership is not appropriate for community organizations.

The dangers of dominance by a charismatic leader cannot be ignored. Yet there is a parallel danger of being so afraid of leadership that the more enthused are discouraged from participating, the more persuasive do not become active, and the organization drifts rather than develops the concentrated focus needed for success. Having a person labeled as leader, or having a chair or facilitator of a meeting, is not inherently contradictory to active membership participation. As Zisk argues

> The near-paranoid way some Greens view their leaders, is best solved by changing that attitude, i.e. for Greens to learn to distinguish between creative leadership that is empowering for all vs. the sort of power-grabbing style they fear. (Zisk, 1989b, p. 14)

Sometimes leaders become public figures for doing what they ought to be doing for the organization, playing the gadfly, typifying the experiences of the group, and symbolizing the problems and solutions the organization is proposing. As a *gadfly,* a leader may bring a civil suit to enforce environmental laws when those in power refuse to bring criminal charges. Such actions highlight the ability of people to tweak the establishment. The jailings of civil rights leaders such as Martin Luther King, Jr. created public awareness of the mistreatment that less well-known black people face in their everyday lives. For the public, he typified the problem; they never would have seen the problem, and in fact had ignored it for many years, until someone of Martin Luther King's status showed them in his person, through his vulnerability, what was going on. For both members of organizations and their opponents, organization leaders become symbols of ability, courage, and determination.

As gadflies, typifiers, and symbolizers, leaders receive much publicity, but to the extent that they are viewed as representatives of the organization and are doing what the members want and agreed to, these roles of the leader are not inconsistent with community organizing ideals. The leaders may show to others the possibility of action and the potential for success, a most constructive activity.

Though some of the activities of leaders put them in the public eye, leaders are more than glory seekers. They undertake mechanical, administrative tasks that can be delegated with minimal loss of participatory control. Somebody must call a meeting, for example, or make sure many of the preparations for successful meetings are accomplished. Ongoing organizations maintain records, prepare budgets, and do other important housekeeping functions. A leader can keep track of this vital, yet ordinary activity, without denying power to the membership.

Leaders coordinate complicated social action campaigns in which many activities have to be sequenced and adjustments quickly made to changing events. While the goals of the campaign and the guiding philosophy of action (e.g., will the group undertake civil disobedience?) must be decided through democratic involvement of the group, the delegation of the coordination function to an elected leader involves minimal loss of member involvement.

Leadership and community development philosophy are compatible when leaders' actions are interpretive of basic directions given by the membership. But when the leadership is playing a visible symbolic role, the leaders must be cautious and the membership alert lest charismatic leaders arrogate to themselves the policy decision making that must belong to the membership.

Leaders of community organizations are and ideally should be more than neutral chairs of decision-making meetings. And they do more than symbolize the organization's history in their actions. They take on an active and creative role that aids rather than challenges the democratic model of decision making. The most creative part of their jobs is to show the potential for organizational members to take the actions needed for their own empowerment. They combat the desempowering belief in helplessness that destroys collective actions. They do this through interpreting the experiences of the group and the meaning of the environment.

> In this sense, community organizers [as leaders] are social reconstructionists. Their role is to develop the ability of people to understand the world so that they can act in it. (G. Delgado, 1986, p. 89)

A second creative and positive part of leadership in community organizations is to help motivate people to do more than they might otherwise. Leaders help *transform* their followers:

> Followers feel trust, admiration, loyalty, and respect toward the leader, and they are motivated to do more than originally expected to do. A leader can transform followers by: (1) making them more aware of the importance of the task outcomes, (2) inducing them to transcend their own self interest for the sake of the organization or team, and (3) activating their higher order needs. . . . Transformation leaders influence followers by arousing strong emotions and identification with the leader, but they may also transform followers by serving as a coach, teacher, and mentor. (Yukl, 1989, p. 211)

Leaders help create and reinforce the values that are part of the organizational culture and help bring people into the culture. Through their actions, they define for the membership the importance of involvement and community. They focus the attention of organizational members on participatory values and behaviors, for example, by fully recognizing and respecting the opinions of others. They react to crises in ways that show the possibility of learning from experience, by regrouping alliances, and by immediately coming back with different ways of attacking problems when the first approach fails. As role models, leaders seek agreements, never imposing major decisions. They reinforce values through the allocation of rewards, for example, by praising those who contribute to the best of their own ability. And they select for special assignments or attention or praise those who show skills and dedication to organizational values (modified from Schein, 1985).

Leaders help shape meanings by building a democratic organizational culture that teaches newcomers what the important values are; they also shape meanings directly by taking action that others can see exemplifies the values and capacity of the organization. They help shape the myths, the stories, the elaborated versions of past history that teach newcomers in a concrete way what can be done and how it can be done. In addition, a leader gives definition to the direction the members of the organization are taking, by finding out which way the group is going and by summarizing those directions to the group, to the press, and to the public. Leaders often take symbolic steps to suggest determination to quickly implement the group's choices, which helps get members going. Leaders in community organizations ideally play one other role. They introduce people to each other, linking people with different and complementary skills needed for organizational success. (P. B. Smith & Peterson, 1988, p. 69).

An effective leader in a progressive, democratic organization moves people along the paths the membership has chosen to achieve collectively determined goals. By shaping meanings and sharing such shaped meanings, leaders teach the potentials for democratic development. By acting as an example to others, by bringing particular people together, and by prodding others to go in ways they have said they wanted to go, leaders enable people to succeed through democratic action. The possibility of effective, minimally hierarchical leadership is demonstrated through effective and democratic membership, decision making, and training meetings.

V | Social Action Campaigns

C ommunity organizations can follow two different kinds of strategies. They can
devise social action campaigns, which call attention to problems and compel government or business to make the needed changes. Or they can provide services, housing, or employment for their members, that is, they can pursue the developmental
model. In this section, we focus on social action campaigns, and in Part VI we examine
development efforts.

The two approaches should be complementary. Community groups picket city hall
to call attention to inadequate housing or crime-ridden neighborhoods. Other community organizations provide housing, organize neighborhood crime patrols, and even
establish community shopping markets. The developmental organization often relies on
assistance from government and business that they would not have been able to get
without social action campaigns.

Chapter 11 introduces a philosophy toward action campaigns. Winning an action
campaign is important, but the victory might be hollow if it lessens people's respect for
the rights of others or belies democratic values. Action campaigns should be empowering to people, enable them to better solve problems on their own, and lead to an
expanded sense of democratic involvement. Social action campaigns question the legitimacy of those in power, while gaining a say for the poor, the dispossessed, and the
abandoned. To be effective, action tactics must be accepted by the broader society, must
effectively symbolize the issue under dispute, and must ensure that campaign issues are
placed on the public agenda.

In Chapter 12, we discuss political pressure tactics including petitioning government, lobbying efforts, and running for office. Political pressure campaigns accept the
rules of the game but are intended to change the outcomes to favor community goals.
In Chapter 13, we describe social confrontations and direct-action campaigns in which
people ignore the accepted rules of the game to fight against personal, economic, and
political oppression. Tactics may include massive civil disobedience that invites authorities to publicly abuse their power and discredit themselves. In Chapter 13 we also
discuss legal actions that provide a bridge between pressure and confrontations. In

Chapter 14, we discuss how to extend the organization's power beyond its own members, by working in coalitions, by bringing public opinion to its side, and by using effective bargaining and negotiating tactics.

11 | An Introduction to Social Action Campaigns

Through social action campaigns, members of community organizations dispute decisions made by authorities, challenge the structures of inequality that limit life opportunities, and alter the beliefs of people who, through lack of understanding, allow social injustices to persist. The targets of social action campaigns include landlords, businesses, banks, hospitals, and government institutions. Rather than quietly accept decisions that hurt people, community organizations fight back.

> *Social action campaigns DOCUMENT a problem, choose as a TARGET those who can effect a solution, SYMBOLIZE the issue, take PRESSUREFUL actions and try to ensure the IMPLEMENTATION of promised changes.*

To illustrate, a neighborhood group concerned about the safety of schoolchildren documents the high accident rate at a particular corner. They target the city council as the group that can put in a stop sign. To symbolize the problem, they circulate a picture of an injured child. The group appears at a city council meeting to argue for the stop sign. When the plan is approved, group members check that the stop sign has been installed.

Social action campaigns vary from one-shot efforts to solve immediate problems like a missing stop sign, to massive movements for social justice such as the civil rights campaign. Some campaigns are international in scope, such as those for disarmament or environmentalism, while others stay within a city block. Despite their variety, many issues are common to social action campaigns. We will first discuss some of the similarities in social action campaigns and then describe the choice of tactics available for different campaigns.

COMMON ISSUES IN SOCIAL ACTION CAMPAIGNS

Five concerns should be thought about before commencing any social action campaigns:

City demolition projects have inspired many protest movements. (Courtesy Department of Housing and Urban Development)

1. How does an organization obtain the power needed to overcome opponents?
2. What tactics can the organization follow so that its activities will be viewed as legitimate?
3. What symbols allow community organizations to get their issues high on the political agenda?
4. How can community organizations affect bargaining to increase the chances of victory?
5. Since social action campaigns confront overwhelming social power, what can organizations do to maintain morale until victories occur?

Power

Social action campaigns are battles in which the disempowered contend with people in authority to create the power they need. As Alinsky argued, "The building of a People's Organization is the building of a new power group" (Alinsky, 1969, p. 132). Power can be built on many different bases, ranging from physical force, prestige, and information to the ability to manipulate images of what is right and wrong. Skillful campaign tacticians determine the power base appropriate for the immediate campaign, a power base that weakens the opponent while building capacity for future action.

Power can be obtained by circulating information about the problem, influencing the agenda for public discussion. A community organization holds a rally or a demonstration to make people aware of a problem and displays power by making the issue salient. City council members are less likely to tolerate overpriced apartments with rodents once the problem has been shown on television. The squeaky wheel, or perhaps squeaky rat, gets the attention.

Information campaigns create power because they can force the establishment to live up to its definitions of right and wrong. If politicians believe that it is wrong to leave the elderly with no place to live, and a community organization documents that the city is pushing many elderly people out of their homes, the information is likely to force action. Using information on corruption to make an opponent resign or back down is another way to translate information into power. A community group may be able to block a downtown development that will tear down single-room occupancy housing by discovering that the costs of the project were increased by rigged bidding.

By increasing the cost of the opponents' actions, community organizations create a second possible base of power. For example, builders and contractors normally operate on large sums of borrowed money, and city grants usually have to be spent within fixed periods of time. Each day of delay in tearing down old buildings or putting in sewers costs opponents money they cannot easily recover. If a community organization can force a delay, by questioning building permits, by demonstrating at the site, or through court injunctions, the organization may be able to force the target to negotiate on outstanding problems.

Once it is clear that the organization can cause havoc, the mere threat to do so—the potential for disruption—becomes a source of power. The threat is often more effective than actually causing the disruption, because the public response to an actual disturbance may be negative. If an organization stops traffic on freeways in Los Angeles to protest lack of adequate public transit, the group demonstrates power but infuriates hundreds of thousands of people, possibly harming the campaign. The awareness that the organization is willing to create traffic chaos, though, might be sufficient to pressure a city council.

A fourth source of power is humiliation or embarrassment. For example, publicity about a government agency's failure to stop tainted milk from being marketed can embarrass bureaucrats to take action. Similarly, calling attention to the illogical or impossible aspects of administrative procedures will often bring about changes. Publicizing a case of a man living in a car who was denied welfare because he had no permanent address mocks an agency by showing that the rule defeats the purpose of the government program. In the face of such mockery, the agency is likely to change the rule. Tactics of embarrassment also can be effective when focused on individual business leaders or slumlords by making their troubles apparent to their friends and neighbors. Picketing the home of the head of a corporation that discriminates might be more effective than picketing outside his or her place of business.

A fifth source of power, the potential to mobilize people in large numbers, is central to organizational tactics. Slumlords recognize that their tenants know they are living in bad housing; what they worry about is that people will organize and refuse to pay their rent. Community organizations have numbers on their side, and collective actions such as public demonstrations, picketing, and rent strikes threaten a target. In addition, politicians are sensitive to the ability of an organization to mobilize a bloc of voters. The more support that a community organization can demonstrate, the greater the power of the organization to persuade politicians to yield on the issue.

Generally speaking, it is not sensible for community organizations to use violence as a part of a campaign, because those in power control far more physical force. When large numbers of angry people gather in a protest, there is always the possibility of violence. If marchers taunt police or provoke incidents, opponents may overreact and have police disperse the march. Demonstrators may be hurt or even killed. Social actions are targeted at opponents' weak spots not at their strengths.

Examine the Organization's Strengths and Opponent's Vulnerabilities.   Community organizations design their campaigns to take advantage of the target's weaknesses and the organization's strengths. The vulnerabilities of opponents change over time and require analysis during each campaign. Answers to the following questions on opponent's vulnerabilities can guide campaign strategies and tactics:

1. **Can the opponent grant the demands made by the community organization?** An opponent that lacks the discretion to satisfy demands is totally invulnerable to any demands that are made. Targets of campaigns must be able to effect a solution.
2. **What are the least secure resources of the opponent?** Is their strength based on corporate wealth or a razor-thin electoral victory? A national boycott might threaten an opponent backed by corporate wealth, and a signature campaign followed by phone calls might elicit a response from a politician dependent on a scant electoral margin.
3. **How willing and able are the opponents to strike back?** Has the city arrested people during demonstrations, or have they kept the police away for fear of provoking a violent confrontation? Landlords can seek support from the court by getting eviction notices, but have the courts shown a willingness to serve such notices during a rent strike?
4. **Are your opponents susceptible to pressure from their own supporters, and if so, from whom?** Business interests often support "reformed" local government and vice versa. If government won't capitulate to the organization's demands, pressure the business community and let them pressure city hall for you.
5. **For what sorts of community actions are the opponents prepared?** Campaigns are chess games where each side anticipates the actions of the others and where victories occur by capitalizing on the lack of preparedness of the opponent. If the opponents lack lawyers, sue them. If the building they own is open and has little security, a sit-in is a possibility, especially if they are too concerned with public opinion to arrest those sitting-in.
6. **Is your opponent vulnerable to moral persuasion?** Church groups and government agencies are more likely to respond to charges that they are unfair to individuals in need. Argue for an end to hunger or shelter for the homeless or education for children. Businesses are much less likely to respond to abstract ideals. They are more sensitive to a campaign that can threaten their market for goods or services or call into question the economic value of the company.

To answer these questions, study opponents before beginning a campaign. Ask other progressive organizations about their experiences with different targets of the campaign. Read newspaper accounts of how the targets responded under attack. Read minutes of government organizations. Look at voting returns. Check the balance sheets of corporations. Find out names of campaign contributors or recipients of large government contracts. Information is power.

While studying the opponent, leaders must also examine their own organization to see what can be learned about its strengths and weaknesses. Is it vulnerable to counterattack? Can the opposition break apart a coalition of action organizations by playing different organizations against each other? Does the action organization have the financial and membership resources to sustain a long struggle?

Determine the organization's *knowledge base;* find out what its members know about the issues and the skills they have that can be useful in running campaigns. Does someone in the organization know how to measure toxic wastes in water when health inspectors deny that there are any? Do some of the members have experience in running electoral campaigns to make credible a threat to oppose a recalcitrant politician? Are there allies or sympathizers who work for the target who are willing to provide information or show where skeletons are buried?

The skills and resources of the organization may make some strategies more feasible. Having articulate members who have suffered from the problem makes a public information campaign possible. A volunteer lawyer may make a court injunction less expensive and, hence, more desirable. A cadre of dedicated individuals who are willing to risk arrest make sit-ins possible.

A community organization can enhance its power by matching its tactics to the organization's strengths and the opponents' weaknesses. Suppose the organization is trying to stop a downtown development project until dwellings for the homeless are found. If the project is about to commence, a court injunction might cause delay, or building a tent city on the site might work. The choice of which to use depends on the resources of the organization and the perceived vulnerability of the target. Do organization members know how to file an injunction? If the target has a team of on-call attorneys, then the tent city strategy might work better. Even if the target can control the police department and plans to wreck the tents, the organization might get some good publicity and the target some bad publicity if the organization can take pictures of police smashing the tent city. With more lead time, and some detective work, the organization can find out if the developer has violated city regulations in other projects. If the answer is yes, the organization may be able to cause a delay.

To summarize, to overcome their opponents, community organizations need to select the appropriate source of power and choose tactics that build on the organization's strengths and target the opponent's weaknesses. The appropriate form of power depends on the specific situation that confronts the organization. And organizations must design flexible campaigns in which the base of power and specific tactics change as the campaign evolves.

Legitimacy

Effective power is gained when people accept their right to get and use power. The right to power is termed *legitimacy* and is obtained when people believe the outcomes are just, the means morally correct, and that those pushing for change have a right to do so. The crux of many social action campaigns is the determination of whether it is legitimate to rock the boat, to ask questions, to try to change the outcomes. Campaigns are lost unless people feel that it is appropriate to combat the inequalities they face.

> Excluded groups are always objectively deprived but this does not mean that they will uniformly perceive these conditions as socially unjust and alterable. . . . Objective social inequalities have to be collectively redefined as the source of social injustices that can be remedied by collective action. (Jenkins, 1985, p. 5)

To get involved, organizational members have to believe in the legitimate right of collective dissent.

The definition of the legitimacy of a particular social action campaign is fought over and manipulated by both sides. For example, religious leaders and protesters against U.S. policies in Latin America banded together to offer sanctuary to political refugees, especially from El Salvador. The U.S. government wanted those providing sanctuary to be convicted for aiding illegal immigrants. Protesters argued they were defending religious and political freedom. If the sanctuary movement can define the issues as broad and important matters—religious and political freedom—they can legitimate what would otherwise be perceived as breaking the law.

Part of the action campaign involves getting the public to accept the community group's definition of the problem they face. Protest leaders may argue that their organizations are seeking justice on vital questions of collective importance, while their opponents claim that the community organizations are acting militantly to obtain selfish ends. In the 1960s, welfare rights organizations considered militant tactics part of a fight to humanize bureaucratic procedures and to end hunger and cold among the poor; their opponents accused them of using force to cheat the honest taxpayer (Bailis, 1974; West, 1981).

Different interpretations of what it means to own property have affected disputes about urban redevelopment programs. To progressive groups, the value of property is measured through its *use,* the social and psychological value to people who live there. To business people, property is considered only in terms of its *exchange value,* its dollar cost when it is bought and sold (Logan & Molotch, 1987). Community-based organizations fight to preserve use values. They

> challenge the conception of the city as a vehicle for the production and maximization of profit. To define the city as a use value is to define it in terms of what amenities it can provide rather than in terms of profit and accumulation. For example, residents may lobby for a new park to provide a place for leisure activities and have no interest in whether the park would contribute to the profitability of capital. (Shelton & Feagin, 1987, p. 4)

Is it legitimate to view the value of apartments (or open space) as worth more than the dollars they would bring if sold to profit making businesses? Part of the struggle of progressive organizations is in convincing people that such a perspective is appropriate.

The Legitimacy of Social Actions.   It is not simply outcomes that need to be legitimated but the tactics used in achieving these outcomes. Almost any tactic might prevail

Minorities fight back against displacement. (H. Fuentes/*City Limits*)

in the short run, but to use a shockingly inappropriate tactic may lose the support of the broader society (plus many of the organization's own members). Permanent victories depend on the larger society's accepting the legitimacy of the organization's actions.

Unfortunately, the legitimacy of tactics is often defined by the establishment. Appeals, petitions, and other types of suppliant actions are almost always considered legitimate. More militant actions, consistent with the form and style of American protest, such as picketing, boycotts, or sit-ins, are considered appropriate if the issues being fought are seen as extremely important. To picket city hall over a parking ticket is illegitimate; no broader issue is being raised. But if the organization pickets city hall, claiming parking tickets are issued disproportionately in poor neighborhoods, then a larger issue is raised, and the organization is seen as justified in its use of more militant tactics.

Seeking broad, public consensus on the importance of the issues at stake should be an early concern of an organization engaged in protest or pressure tactics. If some members of the establishment admit that the issues raised are important, or based on moral commitment, it is easier to legitimize the use of protest tactics (Jenkins & Perrow, 1977). Getting major political figures to speak in favor of civil rights helped legitimize sit-ins, marches, and other protest tactics. Much was accomplished for the United Farm Workers when Senator Robert Kennedy flew to the West Coast to wish Cesar Chavez well on the conclusion of one of his protest fasts.

There is a danger that an organization could go too far in seeking legitimation, reject all tools and tactics that might create disapproval, and only seek moderate changes. A middle path is required in which the organization tries to achieve social legitimation through matching the choice of tactics to its aims.

Means and Ends.   It is not necessary to limit an organization's tactics to only those considered legitimate by the establishment. But some tactics that might be effective in the short run should be ruled out as illegal or harmful to people. Power obtained through intimidation is not compatible with a democracy that respects the rights of individuals.

Organizations constantly choose between the effectiveness of a tactic and the ethical implications of relying on it: What means are appropriate for which ends? In a classic argument on means and ends, Alinsky claims that whether the ends justify the means always depends on the situation:

1. One's concerns with the ethics of means and ends varies inversely with one's personal interest in the issue.
2. The judgement of the ethics of means is dependent upon the political position of those sitting in judgement.
3. In war the end justifies almost any means.
4. Judgement must be made in the context of the times in which the action occurred and not from any other chronological vantage point.
5. Concern with ethics increases with the number of means available and vice versa.
6. The less important the end to be desired, the more one can afford to engage in ethical evaluation of means.
7. Generally, success or failure is a mighty determinant of ethics.
8. The morality of means depends upon whether the means is being employed at a time of imminent defeat or imminent victory.
9. Any effective means is automatically judged by the opposition as being unethical.
10. You do what you can with what you have and clothe it with moral garments.
11. Goals must be phrased in general terms like "Liberty, Equality, Fraternity," "Of the Common Welfare," "Pursuit of Happiness," or "Bread and Peace." (Alinsky, 1971, pp. 24–47)

Alinsky argues that the establishment tries to make social action organizations adhere to a level of morality that will curtail their actions; this pressure from the opponent is a manipulative tactic that should be resisted. He also argues that ethics are often situational, meaning that they are not right or wrong in themselves but depend on the context.

While Alinsky's points are well taken, caution is required in their application. Especially in confrontations, organizers should not be so concerned with accomplishing a short-term end that they justify means that will undermine long-term community empowerment. If the means used in campaigns offends the members of the organization or makes them feel less idealistic, the tactic might win a particular battle but lose the war.

Those contemplating illegal actions must face this means–end dilemma. It is simply wrong to trick members of a group into joining illegal actions. For example, a leader of an animal rights organization convinces members that they are setting up an informational picket outside of a fur store, knowing that some militants are planning on breaking windows and splattering paint on fur coats. This action gets media coverage, but because members of the organization were not informed, it weakens the democratic nature of the group.

Are illegal actions justifiable if the members are willing to participate?

When it is an unjust law itself that is the target of confrontations, illegal actions almost are a necessity.

To protest legally enforced segregation in public facilities, civil right workers had to disobey the unjust law.

Peaceful and public illegal actions in which group members are willing to accept arrest are a vital tactic in demonstrating commitment to bring about social change.

These tactics of *nonviolent civil disobedience* are used when organization members put their bodies on the line against a visible target of protest—a nuclear reactor or a factory producing war goods. Here, illegal action becomes the symbol that highlights the injustice.

What happens though, when the illegal action is meant to directly stop the injustice and those undertaking the illegality intend to get away? Sitting in and being arrested in a bank lobby to symbolize the bank's unwillingness to provide mortgages is one thing; robbing the bank, even if the money is to be redistributed Robin Hood style, is another. For example, radical environmental groups put metal stakes inside trees, making them impossible to harvest. In the short run, such tactics work, but the possibility of injuring a working person is likely to alienate people, making the ultimate goal, public support for preserving forests, harder to achieve. When those who staked the trees seek to avoid arrest, capturing them can become the issue, distracting from concern with environmental protection.

The Tactics of Violence.   When is violence an appropriate means in social action campaigns? This is far from a theoretical question. The history of labor relations is a history of picketers fighting scabs and public or private police. During antiwar protests, street demonstrations turned into street fights as taunts turned into fisticuffs. Anti-abortion militants have bombed abortion clinics, and "eco-saboteurs" (D. Russell, 1987) have destroyed property of those creating environmental damage. Civil rights workers were beaten and shot, and many died.

Most movements for social change in the United States are philosophically divided on the question of violence. The Students for a Democratic Society grew out of pacifistic movements, yet the Weather Faction split off partly because of the failure of nonviolent means to stop the war in Vietnam. They believed that only by violently bringing home the costs of the war, through sabotage, could they get the attention of the establishment. In the civil rights movement, the nonviolent leadership of Martin Luther King, Jr. stands in sharp contrast to the advocacy of militancy and violent self-defense philosophies of Malcolm X or "Rap" Brown. But even militants see violence as a desperate last resort, necessitated by the inability of less dramatic tactics to work. Advocacy of violence among militants in the civil rights movement was often symbolic posturing, a threat of violence, if change did not occur.

Violence can occur if people believe that the laudable goals justify violent means. Or it might emerge almost accidentally during confrontation tactics provoked by hotheads in either the progressive organization or the establishment. Having the police walking too close to demonstrators at a rally is asking for pushing and eventual club swinging. Because active nonviolence often provokes violence in others, it may be tinged with some violence of its own. Is the pacifistic sit-down an act of violence when it is intended to create a violent reaction?

We are strongly opposed to situations in which violent encounters are intentionally sought.

There is an inherent contradiction between tactics of violence and the respect for human dignity and autonomy that underlies community development. As Chavez argues:

> If we had used violence we would have won contracts a long time ago but they wouldn't have been lasting because we wouldn't have won respect. Wages are not the main issue in the strike. . . . No what is at stake is human dignity. If a man is not accorded respect, he cannot respect himself and if he does not respect himself, he cannot demand it. (Chavez quoted in Ecklein, 1984, p. 15)

More pragmatically, even if organizers do not have an aversion to violence for its own sake, violence is inexpedient. Members of progressive organizations simply do not control the means of violence.

Nonviolent tactics are **not** a capitulation to power. Rather, the practice of nonviolence is a means for controlling political power (G. Sharp, 1973, p. 7). The many tactics of nonviolence vary from giving speeches to quietly courting arrest. Each is based on the assumption that power comes about when people refuse to obey. Power is gained from nonviolence through political *jiu-jitsu.*

> An extensive, determined and skillful application of nonviolent action will cause the opponent very special problems, which will disturb or frustrate the effective utilization of his own forces. The actionists will then be able to apply something like *jiu-jitsu* to their opponent, throwing him off balance politically, causing his repression to rebound against his position, and weakening his power. (G. Sharp, 1973, p. 110)

Active nonviolence is based on building a crescendo of protest, from voicing opposition to active militant sit-downs, always hoping the opponent will concede.

The intent of nonviolent tactics is to create a favorable moral image of the organization among a wide audience while highlighting the extent of repressive tactics of the opponents. It takes moral tenacity to maintain a belief in nonviolence, especially when change occurs so slowly, but acting morally is an important end that violent means destroys.

Martin Luther King, Jr. was frustrated at the slowness of change, but in contrast to Alinsky, King continued to believe that means are as important as the ends, because ends are inherent in the means.

[King] invited them to contemplate the potential of a system that embraced no inherently repugnant means. . . . "And this is where nonviolence breaks with . . . any other system that would argue that the end justifies the means, *for in the long run the end is pre-existent in the means, and the means represents the ideal in the making and the end in process."* (emphasis added, Branch, 1988, p. 871)

Nonviolence is a way of gaining legitimacy for the organization's tactics. But more important, as King's philosophy of nonviolence reminds us, in community organizing, the process to a large extent is an outcome. Earning legitimacy for social action campaigns is more than a way of winning campaigns, it means empowerment for organization members, it means it's okay to fight to improve your situation. So, while Alinsky is correct that ethics are situational and organization members should not allow themselves to be manipulated by the opponents' labeling of ethical and unethical behavior, community organizations need to carefully develop their own long-run sense of fair play that goes beyond winning in the short run.

Symbols and Agenda Setting

Social action campaigns are battles over the symbols that create an agenda for societal action. A *symbol* is a word, phrase, image, icon, or person that stands for deeper, more complicated ideas. In groups that share a common culture, people assign affect—both positive and negative—to shared symbols. For most "mother," "God," "love," and "free enterprise" are considered positive symbols while "whore," "devil," "hate," and "communism" are seen as negative symbols. Actions in support of positive symbols are legitimate, and actions that oppose negative symbols are laudatory. If an organization devises appropriate symbols, it can increase its legitimacy, get a lot of public attention, and press its issues onto the public agenda.

Symbols offer simplified explanations and solutions for problems. They present reality in ways that have profound ideological import. To many, the flag is a symbol of patriotism, love of country, and, perhaps, obedience to authority. To some, law and order symbolizes order and harmony, to others repression and control.

When using existing symbols, a group has to pick ones that are relatively unambiguous. As shared symbols, myths and metaphors explain simply why a problem occurred. Most people prefer and respond to such simple explanations.

> The causes and remedies of the depression, inflations, wars, and riots . . . are complex and hinge upon the small and large decisions of vast numbers of people. Myths and metaphors permit men [sic] to live in a world in which the causes are simple and neat and the remedies are apparent. (Edelman, 1971, p. 83)

Social action campaigns often involve battles between such metaphors, each of which is a shorthand for a political ideology. For example, public officials may argue that villainous drug peddlers cause the problems associated with narcotics and can be battled through police action. The symbol "drug peddler" suggests an individual with no morals, an object of legitimate hate, who has no rights. The symbol evokes the solution, "put the scum in jail." A community organization might make a very different interpretation, that drug problems are caused by lack of job opportunities, symbolized by pictures of closed factories. When people cannot see a legitimate way to earn a living and improve themselves they search for profitable, albeit illegal, economic niches. The symbol in this case suggests the need for more fundamental changes, including better schools, more jobs, and less discrimination. Any symbol that focuses on the individual as a cause of the problem distracts from the identification of structures that disadvantage the poor, old, handicapped, or rejected.

Social action campaigns labor to associate positive cultural symbols with the goals of the campaign and to create new and compelling symbols that support the cause of social change, while preventing those in power from identifying the progressive group with negative symbols. A community organization might portray its demonstrations as an attempt to "redress grievances," a term that echoes the demands of the colonists in the Declaration of Independence (a positive symbol), while government officials portray the same demonstrations as "disorderly," "lawless," and "outside of proper channels." Those in power who opposed feminists developed the symbol of "bra burner"—people without respect for social proprieties. A much more positive symbol is "women's liberation" suggesting freedom from enslavement and hinting at left-wing national political movements. There is nothing conventional or passive about this symbol, and it says nothing one way or the other about social conventions. Rather, it suggests the seriousness of the issues and compares them in importance to battles against political dictators in oppressive regimes.

How can progressive community organizations create symbols to support their causes? We suggest four approaches to the use of symbols, each of which recognizes that a symbol must simultaneously communicate to those in the organization as well as appeal to the wider population.

Create and Portray Unity Through Organizational Symbols. Community organizations need to symbolize the "we-ness" in a community in ways that the broader society will interpret in a positive fashion. This is not always easy, because what works well within the group may to the outside suggest threat, for example, symbols of ethnic pride such as "Black Power." Similarly,

> the term *Chicano* increasingly became the symbol of self-identification for many activities. . . . For many people Chicano connoted a militant stance, confrontation actions and intense pride associated with the movement for brown identity and power. (Hammerback et al., 1985, p. 5)

But when cultural pride is symbolized through fairs, festivities, and other glorification in which people outside of the group can identify and to some extent participate, the tone of the symbol can be softened (Padilla, 1987).

Symbols as Catchy Typifications. When possible, campaign symbols should typify the problem itself in a simple, easily communicable fashion. The pro-choice and pro-life movements both have such powerful symbols with the coat-hanger and the partially formed fetus. Pictures of cooling towers of nuclear reactors communicate the danger of present-day nuclear technology.

A symbol can both create a typification of the problem as well as build solidarity within a social protest group. For example, students protesting apartheid in South Africa have constructed shanty-towns on the lawns of universities (Fordham, 1986). The shanty-towns are visible representations of the horrible living standards facing black South Africans. The willingness of student protesters to live in them personalizes and adds poignancy to the issue.

Songs and their titles (e.g.,"We Shall Overcome") create powerful symbols of an issue, while providing a simple way of identifying with a group. The sentiment expressed by Pete Seeger in the introduction to a book of grass-roots songs, *Rise Up Singing,* expresses the power of song.

> You'll find some songs are best for certain places and certain times . . . at a meeting . . . or at a demonstration. . . . And when strangers meet and find they like the same song, then there is one more connect made for the future world network. . . . A singing movement is a winning movement. (Seeger quoted in Blood-Patterson, 1988, p. iii)

And, songs can provide unity to a movement while portraying the issues under dispute.

> If one examines just the lyrics of protest songs associated with social movements, one can find many examples of diagnoses of what is wrong with the present order of things. . . . In addition . . . a second important function of music is in the development of social solidarity among group members and potential members. (G. Lewis, 1987, pp. 169–170)

This occurred, for example, among Hawaiians who were concerned that tourism was destroying their cultural heritage. In protest, they promoted traditional Hawaiian music with lyrics that lamented the destruction of the older society.

Even the tactics of social action campaigns take on symbolic meaning. As an action tactic, environmentalists work together to maintain open spaces and repair areas others have damaged. The act of cleaning up areas that people have despoiled—as pictured in news stories—becomes a living symbol of the potential for human–environmental harmony.

Protest symbols are most effective if they can evoke broader societal values. The image of civil rights workers facing the police dogs both shows the nature of the oppression and the bravery (a valued symbol) of the activists. When Greenpeace surrounds nuclear naval vessels with its small dinghies, the image is of David taking on Goliath. The action can have the immediate effect of stopping testing while the symbolism reinforces the idea of the power of the small but brave.

Personalize the Symbol.   Those in power try to find symbols that portray problems as being the fault of individuals. The symbol of the welfare queen bleeding the system dry or the unemployed bum are personalizations of the message that the poor are not worthy, there is no need for social change. Community organizers combat this false level of explanation, but the image of the individual as personally responsible is still powerful and far more easily communicable than more subtle societal forces. To cope, in social action campaigns, activists personalize the symbols of those harmed by the problem.

A powerful personalized symbol for the community organization is the *victim,* the blameless individual, whose difficulties are so clearly caused by the problems confronting the broader group. A sick child is the victim of toxic poisoning, a surgically mutilated house pet is the victim of insufficiently restrained medical experiments. During the Vietnam War era, peace movements were handed a dramatic symbol of the victim when television cameras recorded the agony of a young Vietnamese girl covered with burning napalm, running down the street.

A somewhat more dangerous personalized symbol is that of the *enemy,* "identifiable persons or stereotypes of persons to whom evil traits, intentions or attentions can be attributed" (Edelman, 1988, p. 87). Personalizing the symbol of the enemy has the cost of distracting attention from the social causes of problems, but it does provide focus to the immediate campaign. Thus, the Vietnam war became Johnson's war, the nuclear plant became Three Mile Island, slum housing can become Mr. Showstack's houses, and poor schools can be laid at the feet of the mayor.

An appropriate symbolization of the enemy can clarify the goals of the action campaign. In the civil rights campaigns, was the enemy the southern sheriff and police or the politician blocking passage of needed legislation? The choice defined the immediate campaign, though, fortunately, the campaign could be modified as it progressed.

The organization has to decide whether or not to focus on a specific individual as the enemy. Alinsky's classic advice is "pick the target, freeze, *personalize* it, and polarize it" (Alinsky, 1971, p. 128, emphasis added), but in doing so, there is the danger that the campaign focuses on the individual as enemy rather than the social structure that makes the enemy powerful or the tactics (of oppression) used (Edelman, 1988, p. 67).

There are cases in which particular individuals so represent the problem that symbolizing the issue through that person causes little difficulty. The southern governors who stood in the doorways of schools to (symbolically) block integration clearly were appropriate as symbolic enemies. When attacking corporate America, however, clear enemies are harder to find and portray. Company heads are often (intentionally) colorless individuals who provide a murky image as enemy, and too often, members of community organizations who hate corporate policies envy the wealth and life-style of the chief executive officers. Flamboyant union busters such as Lorenzo at Eastern Airlines make fine symbolic enemies, but such individuals are rare.

On the other hand, social action organizations often symbolize their causes in the person of a leader. The leader as symbol can legitimate new definitions of the problems group members face, and through his or her efforts can publicize sufferings and get the organization's issues on the public agenda.

Transform Symbols of Success and Failure.   In many campaigns, what is a victory and what is a defeat is inherently unclear; even the jailing or death of organizational activists can be turned into the victory of martyrdom. Antagonists in social action campaigns symbolically minimize their defeats and exaggerate their victories, while magnifying the defeats of their opponents and minimizing their successes. This is possible because

> beliefs about success and failure are among the most arbitrary of political constructions and perhaps the least likely to be recognized as arbitrary. The issue turns on which actions and which consequences are to be highlighted and which ignored. (Edelman, 1988, p. 43)

When immediate objectives have not been accomplished, symbolize the issue in terms of striving, battling against the odds, and the achievement of high levels of participation. The defeat is not denied but is transformed into a symbol of why the effort was needed. As Mansbridge concludes after describing the defeat of the Equal Rights Amendment (ERA):

> Because the ratification campaign raised consciousness, helped women organize politically, and stimulated legislative and judicial action, that campaign was worth the effort put into it. (Mansbridge, 1986, p. 188)

Handling symbols of victory can be trickier. Effective organizations celebrate past victories as symbols of the potential for future success and as motivation to continue to work together. Ineptly handled, however, such symbols suggest that all the victories were in the past, or that the great victories of the past are currently unachievable.

To summarize, to be successful, social action campaigns have to get their issues high on the list of public issues requiring action. Community organizations do this in part by thoughtful use of symbols, both to motivate their membership and to influence outsiders' perceptions. At the beginning of a campaign, it is important to use symbols to legitimate the campaign itself and its tactics. During the campaign, it is important to develop symbols of the problems that simplify the discussion yet create sympathy for the group and its goals—the sick child as the innocent victim of pollution. Toward the end of a campaign, the organization has to be able to symbolize successes and failures, both to keep up morale, and to win public approval. Symbols are extremely powerful and sometimes take on a life of their own outside members' control. The example of labeling feminists as "bra burners" shows how this can happen. Community organizers need to create and control symbols because symbolic speech is the language of most public dialogue.

Structuring the Bargaining

Symbolic dialogue is part of a bargaining process between those in power and those seeking justice or economic redistribution. As a campaign progresses, bargaining may then continue in a literal rather than figurative manner. The organization doesn't want symbolic concessions, it wants real ones. Organizers of social action campaigns need to think about how they can structure that bargaining to get the outcomes they want before they get to the bargaining table. To do so, community organizations can define the scope of conflict, frame the issues, and define the situation in ways that make it less difficult for the opponent to concede what the group wants.

Community organizations pick issues and formulate demands that define the *scope of conflict,* that is, how broad and how fundamental are the issues under dispute. Should the organization confine the scope of conflict to a very narrow issue (e.g., the improvement of an apartment building), or should it expand the scope to include broader questions of the power of property owners in American society? A picket sign saying that Joe Smith, a landlord, neglects 1000 Main Street sets a very different scope than a sign that argues that property-owning capitalists exploit renters.

A narrow-scope conflict is easier to resolve, but each case has to be raised separately. If the organization expands the scope of conflict, it has the potential of solving

Demands need to be
phrased in ways that compliance can be easily verified.
(Courtesy National People's
Action)

MORTGAGE BANKER'S ASSOC.

YES NO

1. PUT $25 MILLION A YEAR FOR NEXT FIVE YEARS INTO A POOL TO FIX UP FHA-DEVASTATED NEIGHBORHOODS.

SELF-POLICE YOUR MEMBERS TO DO THE FOLLOWING:

2. STOP BREAKING THE LAW BY IMPOSING MINIMUM LOAN AMOUNTS.

3. STOP CHARGING EXTRA FEES ON SMALLER LOANS.

4. STOP FINANCING ABOVE 91% LOAN-TO-VALUE.

5. STOP LOBBYING FOR HIGHER FHA LIMITS.

6. SUPPORT FHA CLEN-UP LEGISLATION.

many issues at once, but the stakes may then be so high that the opposition solidifies. A middle path is usually the best; expand the conflict beyond a very narrow issue, so that if a resolution is reached it will be meaningful, but do not make the issue so broad that the opponents feel threatened and unite to take countermeasures. For example, an environmental group might work to maintain a wilderness area for recreational instead of commercial use. This campaign need not raise broader questions of who owns natural resources: the lumber companies that have title or a lease to the property or the public. Raising the issue of ownership guarantees countermeasures from all lumbering companies, not just the one whose immediate plans are thwarted. While recreational environmentalists can reach accommodation with lumbering companies, such accommodations are rare between those working to preserve wilderness and logging firms. Sometimes there seems to be no middle ground.

Most campaigns begin with a narrowly defined issue, usually based on the concrete experiences of community members. In the initial stages of battle, the conflict will be seen as a *zero-sum situation* in which what one side wins the other loses. For instance, a neighborhood organization wants economic development funds to be spent to retrain individuals whose jobs have moved out of the city rather than on subsidies for larger businesses. The perception may be that either big business benefits from the money or the neighborhood workers do. One way out of this bind is to support *linked-development programs* in which government encourages those office developments downtown that receive government support to aid neighborhoods. The one-wins-and-the-other-loses structure of the original problem is transformed; it is possible for government to help both businesses and neighborhoods.

In many cases, a zero-sum situation can be translated into a cooperative one by framing the issues so that each side can get something it wants, frequently by expanding the number of items being bargained over. Suppose a community organization is concerned that a savings and loan is disinvesting from neighborhood housing, and the organization begins to pressure the bank to reveal its loans and devise a program of housing rehabilitation. The bank could then put on the table a request for the community organization's support for a government-backed mortgage program to be run by the bank. By putting the second item on the table, especially if such a mortgage program is a realistic option, both sides can get something they want at relatively little cost to the other. Such cooperative situations are possible when fundamental values are not in conflict.

In packaging such cooperative deals, though, the cautious (perhaps cynical) organizer makes sure that the entire package will be carried out. If the deal is to have both job training and downtown redevelopment, make sure the city provides the neighborhood with a training center and staff at the same time the redevelopment project is built, not afterward. Otherwise, the city may do something for big business and never get around to fulfilling its promise to do something for the neighborhoods.

In short, community organizations need to formulate their original campaign goals so that the organization resolves more than one tiny issue if it succeeds, but without raising any more than the minimum amount of opposition. It helps to phrase the goals in such a way that the opposition can see itself gaining something from conceding to the group's goals.

Keeping up Morale Over the Long Run

Campaigns that seek to bring about major structural changes that threaten those in power meet with much opposition and may not always be successful, especially in the short run. Campaigns for civil rights, gender equality, and unionization have lasted for generations. Victories followed defeats, but equally important, defeats followed victories. As campaigns stretch out, demoralization occurs, even when short-term victories are achieved. The elusiveness of victory can discourage activists. For example, in the antinuclear movement:

> The Clamshell experience of discouragement and collapse is far from unusual. Within a few years after achieving the goals of "take-off," every major social movement of the past twenty years has undergone a significant collapse, in which activists believed that their movements had failed, the power institutions were too powerful, and their own efforts were futile. This has happened even when movements were actually progressing reasonably well along the normal path taken by past successful movements! (Moyer, 1987, p. 1)

Part of the cause of this phenomenon is that people burn out. Gitlin describes the end of the 1960s:

> As the movement imploded, a good many New Left veterans, especially stranded men, went into retreat. We *were* overcome. . . . It was assumed that a healthy movement was going to be there to return to: a whole way of life, a church. When that assumption went up in smoke, political projects remained, reform institutions dug in, but not the movement itself as living, portable destination. If the movement no longer satisfied, if it made too many demands of a depleted self, what arrived was a full-blown crisis of faith. (Gitlin, 1989, p. 424)

How does an organization cope? In the short run, working to accomplish quick, reinforcing victories can be helpful. But even here there is a danger. A tactic of the opponent might be to grant smaller victories that postpone broader structural changes. Such concessions distract from the broader issues, and to the extent that they cause less committed members to withdraw, they create demoralization among those pushing for larger changes.

One response for long-term activists is to remind each other that an ebb and flow of social action campaigns is normal and that major goals are accomplished only over a long period of time. In moments of discouragement, have group members think of how many important changes in their lifetimes or their parents' lifetimes emerged from long-term struggles that reached fruition only recently. Federal recognition of the right to unionize only dates back half a century. We are less than a generation removed from legalized racial discrimination. The young women of today are the first generation who have legal access to birth control (for the unmarried and in some states the married). In each of these cases, rights that we now take for granted were obtained only after a long struggle in which temporary defeat was frequent. Maintain morale by reinforcing the lessons of such past victories.

Another approach is to step back and study the stages through which social movements pass. To this end, Moyer (1987) developed the *Movement Action Plan*, which models eight stages of progressive social movements. In Stage Five "Identity Crisis of Powerlessness," movement members frequently feel they have failed. Moyer emphasizes that this is wrong; rather, what is occurring is that the fatigue of the early battles and its victories has so overwhelmed the original activists that they cannot see the successes through their exhaustion. In such cases, the need is "to help activists become empowered . . . to catch up to their movement. They need to learn what the long road of success looks like" (Moyer, 1987, p. 9).

Leadership does burn out and lose its vision and must be replenished. With few exceptions, members of organizations with entrenched leadership lose their zeal as leaders' motivation burns out. To cope, most long-run, community-based organizations have fairly strict rules for leadership succession to ensure replacing older, tired individuals with newly enthused members.

Another source of demoralization occurs when separate organizations with similar goals compete for membership and for issue leadership. Such efforts distract organizations from fighting the targets, can split membership loyalty, and disperse limited funds too widely. Many of these problems can be overcome through carefully negotiated coalition strategies.

There is an optimistic side to the presence of competing organizations, especially those that have slightly different philosophical approaches. Competitive organizations enable a movement to survive after short-run defeats weaken some of the groups. Feminism, civil rights, and environmentalism, among others, are represented by competing organizations whose ideology and tactics range from mainstream to radical. The more militant groups make legendary forays against targets and the injustices they represent and often bring about dramatic changes. Such efforts are hard to sustain, and they collapse, either through burnout or repression. During such ebbs, the less militant organizations provide a home for the remnants of the collapsed groups. It is debatable how much social reform occurs under the aegis of the more mainstream groups, with their fear of undertaking structural changes. But such organizations keep the spirit alive, enabling the burned out to recover or to be replaced by a new generation. Later, those who reject the mainstream positions may spin off a new organization that again attempts structural reform.

Sometimes what is seen as defeat is adjustment of strategies and tactics to changing times. In recent years, conservatives have wiped out much of the financial support of the federal government for subsidized housing. Housing activists who had been pressuring the federal government shifted focus to work toward tenant-controlled housing. The shift to local control as an issue (through tenant's councils and Community Development Corporations that build, own, and manage affordable housing) should not be seen as a defeat.

Times change. If housing has fallen out of favor, the environment has fallen into favor, at least with the public. A generation ago, environmental concerns were held by a limited number of people but today

> polls show that more Americans identify themselves as environmentalists than as Democrats or Republicans and that eighty percent say environmental improvements must be made regardless of cost. (Steinhart, 1990, p. 20)

Such changes should make environmental organizing easier. It is important to look for current opportunities for organizing rather than lament that some issues used to be easier to organize on than they are today.

The Enemy Strikes Back.   Another source of discouragement is that when organizations go after important targets and big issues, the enemy almost always strikes back. In its mildest form, the response of targets may only be an attempt to deny the

Acquired immune deficiency syndrome (AIDS) is a relatively recent organizing issue.
(Ellen B. Neipris-ACT UP)

legitimacy of protests, as when one Harvard professor put down anti-war protesters as
merely [metaphorically] masturbating; that is, young, full of energy, and talking only to
themselves. Sometimes, however, those counterstrikes are brutal and may decimate the
membership. During the 1960s, police officials raided homes of African-American militants and killed them, supposedly in self-defense.

Protesters have to be prepared for the possibility of serious repression, the purpose
of which is to destroy those who dare to protest inequities. Goon Squads were used
against labor organizers, tactical police against peace protesters. Southern police as-
sisted local hooligans in beating up civil rights workers. Repression against African
American and Native American militants involved the use of "eavesdropping, bogus
mail, 'black propaganda operations,' disinformation, harassment arrests, infiltration,
snitch-jacketing—creating suspicion—through the spreading of rumors, manufacturing of evidence—that bona fide organization members . . . are FBI/police informers—,
fabrication of evidence and even assassination" (Churchill & Wall, 1988).

More recently, the FBI infiltrated Earth First! and ambushed the group when a
member was allegedly trying to cut down a power line tower. The FBI spent hundreds
of thousands of dollars "to investigate what was essentially a small band of environmental troublemakers" who held a garage sale to fund their activities (T. Atlas, 1990).

Repression does occur, organizations do get infiltrated, and people are sometimes
beaten and arrested. Repression does affect the strategy of social action campaigns. It
also affects recruitment, because a different sort of person is willing to get arrested (or

beat up) than is willing to circulate petitions. On the positive side, overt repression denies the enemy legitimacy and often grants it to protesters. Finally, evoking a response (even a highly negative response as with the use of excessive force) from the opposition is a sure indication that a direct action organization has reached and scared its target.

If a group is working on important issues, it should expect countermeasures. The community group should try to anticipate the opponent's countertactics. Assume, for example, that opponents will try to seize the organization's books, records, and mailing lists. They will search for financial irregularities in the organization's books and try to taint the organization with scandal. Keep the organization's finances squeaky clean; be especially careful of skeletons in the closet of organizational leaders; keep books and mailing lists in secure places, and watch what is put into writing that might appear incriminating to someone else.

Because the organization is trying to take the moral high ground, it must be very cautious to avoid the appearance of impropriety; what another organization might be able to tolerate would be terminally embarrassing to an organization that is trying to make people more ethical and mutually responsible. Members should also plan what to do if the leaders are arrested, or if the target tries to break the solidarity of the group by threatening some and bribing others. If a group is prepared for countermeasures, opponents are likely to do much less damage to the group and to its morale.

Perhaps most important when social action campaigns fail is the need to figure out why. What organizational tactics could have been changed? Was the timing of the campaign poor? Did the opponents capture the symbols that garner public support? Was there too much fragmentation in the organization to bring about a coherent effort? What should be done differently next time? Such analysis is not only forward looking, it also suggests that the next time success is more likely, because the group knows what it did wrong and how to avoid it.

Social action campaigns for democracy, capacity building, and rectification of social injustices are long-term efforts with both defeats and victories. If success were easy, the struggle would not be necessary. One way of keeping up morale is to keep in mind the philosophy with which Gitlin concludes his book on the struggles of the 1960s:

> "It was not granted you to complete the task," said Rabbi Tarfon nineteen hundred years ago "and yet you may not give it up." (Gitlin, 1989, p. 438)

VARIATION IN TACTICS

All social action campaigns have some common elements, such as the need to deal with temporary failures, to gain power and legitimacy, to get on the public agenda, and to structure the bargaining. But social action campaigns vary in the degree to which they emphasize political pressure, legal actions, or confrontations.

A campaign may begin with a confrontation to attract media attention, then proceed to political pressure tactics to make long-term changes. Or, it may begin with mild pressure tactics, and if success is not forthcoming, gradually apply more power, using first legal, and finally, confrontation tactics. Or the campaign may run several tactics simultaneously. Community organizations need to know how to combine tactics in an overall strategy to achieve desired effects. To do that, they need a good feeling for what each type of tactic accomplishes.

With pressure tactics, an organization recognizes the legitimacy of the opposition's rules and tries to play by them, attempting to defeat opponents at their own game. Legal tactics also use the opponents' rules, but the purpose is to force the opponents to abide by their own rules, which they seem to be ignoring. In contrast, with confrontation—protest—actions, the members of the organization have decided that the rules of the game are not fair and make their own rules.

Confrontations and demonstrations are vital for getting the attention of authorities and showing them the power of the community organization. Confrontations are the social explosion that yells "Pay attention! There is a problem here!" Suppose bankers ignore the requests of community members to invest money in their neighborhood; if organization members play by the rules, they lose, because the existing rules favor the banks. If members of the organization think those rules unfair, they must call attention to the problem by unorthodox tactics, like tying up the bank's services. Activists are no longer playing by their rules and applying for a loan; the suppliant role is gone.

Because pressure tactics use the opponents' own rules, if community members win, the opponents have to accept the legitimacy of the outcome. In contrast, in confrontations, organization members try to win while forcing the opponents to play by new rules. The opposition might concede the immediate issue but still not grant the legitimacy of the tactics or abide by the outcome in the long run. By themselves, confrontations do not politically institutionalize the changes needed. Authorities might concede the immediate issue yet fail to set up laws, regulations, or conventional patterns of behavior to carry out the agreement over longer periods of time.

To make lasting changes, organization members need to think about ways to change laws, regulations, and levels of enforcement. Tenants can't demonstrate each time a landlord turns off the heat in a building. Rather, a tenants' organization needs to have a city code adopted and enforced that guarantees warm apartments. These tactics require detailed knowledge of laws and regulations as well as of the power structure, interest groups, and the political process. While confrontation tactics force opponents to pay attention and make short-term changes, political pressure tactics are intended to change laws and enforce regulations that preserve the short-term victories.

Effective social action campaigns are built by skillfully blending confrontation, legal actions, and political pressure. If the goal of the organization is to increase the city's commitment to open housing, representatives of the organization might lobby to get a strong open-housing ordinance on the books (a political pressure tactic) and simultaneously seek a court injunction to halt the city's receipt of state development funds until its housing profile improves (a legal tactic), while conducting demonstrations in the plaza in front of city hall to publicize the difficulties facing the poor in finding clean, low-cost housing (a confrontation tactic).

Members of Communities Organized for Public Service (COPS) in San Antonio blended pressure and confrontation tactics (Sekul, 1983). COPS, an active coalition of neighborhood organizations in the Mexican-American sections of San Antonio, was formed in the 1970s by Ernesto Cortes, following techniques of the Alinsky Industrial

Areas Foundation. The organization worked to unite the Mexican-American neighborhoods, which received fewer government services and had less political representation and more problems (such as flooding) than other parts of the city. The actions of COPS were carefully orchestrated to directly affect government decision making and obtain the publicity needed to continue to pressure government. Much of COPS's success is based on knowledge of how to use government regulations and the electoral process.

For example, aware that federal regulations require public hearings, members of COPS appeared en masse at the hearings on the Community Development Block Grant Program, to ensure that their neighborhoods received funds. When the city manager disagreed with them on the use of Urban Development Action Grant funds, "a delegation of COPS people, led by president Carmen Badillo, paid [the city manager] a visit in his office. They demanded with TV camera present that the [city manager] meet with them" (Sekul, 1983, pp. 181–182). When that tactic was only partially successful, COPS made a direct appeal to the city council representatives, who understood the power of an organized coalition in the electoral process.

Classic confrontation tactics were used on the school board that COPS claimed neglected its neighborhoods.

> At first school board members proved unresponsive. COPS' initial demand . . . was merely to see a copy of the districts' budgets. They were refused, being told in one case that extra copies were unavailable. COPS persisted by staging confrontations with school board members at the board meeting: on cue from leaders, COPS members walked in en masse, ignored the agenda and speaker sign-up sheets, cheered friendly speakers, and congregated at the front of the room. Security guards were called to restore order on occasion. (Sekul, 1983, pp. 183–184)

These tactics were followed up by conventional political procedures, as COPS worked to elect school board members who supported their policies. Similarly, BUILD, the powerful Baltimore community organization, institutionalized its power by becoming a regular political actor with access to city hall. In Baltimore,

> Mary Pat Clarke, the president-elect of the City Council, and mayor-elect Kurt Schmcke both agreed to meet regularly with BUILD. . . . And, [now governor] Schaefer's campaign had been waged largely around BUILD Agenda issues. (Boyte, 1989a, p. 113–114)

Long-term effectiveness requires the political institutionalization of the goals and objectives of the community organization. Laws must be passed and bureaucrats made to carry them out. To do that, the community organization has to enter the political arena. This means that the community organization has to gain and use political power over a long period of time. Confrontations are translated into political power to obtain the aims of the community organizations. Politicians actively seek the votes of BUILD members, and COPS now is consulted on city urban development projects.

Community organizations need to get issues on the agenda, they need to demonstrate power and voting potential, and they need to ensure that opponents will do what they promise to do. Ideally, as a consequence of their victories, the community organization becomes a power to be reckoned with and one that is consulted when decisions are made concerning their issue or membership. To achieve all these aims, community organizations combine pressure, legal, and confrontation tactics in a single campaign.

12 | Influencing the Political System

T he purpose of political pressure campaigns is to pass new laws, gain resources for development and social service programs, and ensure that public policies are implemented in ways advocated by progressive organizations. Community members learn the conventional rules of politics and work within them. Protest is not enough; only political involvement ensures long-run responsiveness to the progressive agenda (Browning et al., 1984).

COMPLEXITY OF THE POLITICAL ENVIRONMENT

Learning about the political environment is time-consuming but necessary. The environment is complex because there are multiple levels of government, each with administrative, legislative, and judicial officials, many of whom (and on occasion all of whom) influence the policy area of concern. A second source of complexity is the difficulty of knowing when political compromise is appropriate. Is it better to work for the entire policy that the organization wants and chance complete failure or to ensure success for only part of the organization's agenda?

The Political Winnowing Game

At the federal level, there are sets of organizational actors—including business interests, labor, and community organizations—who are simultaneously trying to set the legislative agenda, to gain support of politicians, and to convince other organizations in the policy arena to lend their support. Even when a community group gets a bill introduced, the resulting legislation may bear little relationship to a proposal originally supported because

> an issue's policy options may have undergone considerable modification and reduction as proponents and opponents negotiate over terms. This process we refer to as *winnowing* the alternatives. (Laumann & Knoke, 1987, p. 17)

Determination can make politicians yield. (Courtesy National People's Action)

Controversial legislation emerges only after long-term contests between many strong organizations that represent contending interests. Outcomes reflect compromise rather than a "monolithic rationality and clarity of class interests" (Laumann & Knoke, 1987, p. 6). Housing policies, for example, result from differing pressures from progressive housing advocates, municipalities, realtors, bankers, developers, and building trades unions. It can be difficult to see where progressive interests lie within such elaborate compromises.

What bills community groups should support is often not clear. Should a community organization advocate tax subsidies to the rich to encourage them to invest in housing for the poor? Is it better to work with trade unions who insist on on-site construction (which is more expensive), or to advocate a program opposed by unions that will develop less expensive modular housing and provide more housing for the poor?

To participate in this winnowing game, progressive community organizations need to have staying power.

Without continual participation, progressive organizations might become involved in policy issues only after many of the options have been excluded and the choices unnecessarily narrowed.

Staying power is needed to combat the disproportionate influence business groups historically have had over government. For example, back in 1978, with a democratic president and Congress, an alliance of business groups, the Business Round Table, was able to beat back a

> bill creating a consumer protection agency [even though] legislation had already passed the House or Senate on five separate occasions; was backed by the president, the speaker of the house and 150 consumer, labor, and other groups, and it had been supported two to one by the public in surveys. (Gilbert & Kahl, 1982, p. 247)

The outcomes worsened under President Reagan, even though progressive organizations were better organized in Washington. At a time of increased homelessness and hardship among the disadvantaged, it wasn't the poor that received (at least) a $300,000,000,000 bail out from Uncle Sam, it was the Savings and Loans.

Matching Business Pressure

To match the effectiveness of organized business, community organizations must overcome four problems. First, political influence tactics require continuity. Second, community organizations should concentrate on influencing fundamental decisions. Third, community organizations have to convince officials that the interests of their agencies lie with democratic organizations rather than business consortiums. Fourth, activists from community organizations have to learn the skills of political influence.

The first problem is that community organizations often apply political pressure briefly, then retreat, while business organizations spend full-time monitoring political events and maintaining relationships. Though national coalitions now employ full-time lobbyists for progressive causes, many state and local community organizations still operate episodically. Instead, they should focus on maintaining contact with the government officials so that input from progressive organizations is expected even when the immediate interest of the organization is not at risk.

The second problem is that community organizations are most active when the stakes are small and on issues of immediate concern to their members, such as a bike path, stop sign, or shelter for the homeless. They are taking many small defensive actions. In the meantime, the business community might be proposing a downtown revitalization project involving tens of millions of dollars, providing profit for banks and businesses, glory for politicians, and promising more revenue and jobs for the city.

While individual community organizations have to focus on projects of immediate interest to their members, citywide or statewide coalitions can focus on broader programs. Successful organizations such as Baltimoreans United for Leadership Development (BUILD) or Communities Organized for Public Services (COPS) deal with a broader set of issues in addition to problems in their neighborhoods. Coalitions of progressive organizations can take the offensive by drawing up an agenda that has their major needs and projects on it, the accomplishment of which would bring glory to the city or the state and the agencies sponsoring the activities.

The third problem facing community organizations in battles for power with the business community is the perceived coincidence of interest between bureaucratic agencies and business. Public officials favor business interests because the demands of business are clearly defined and bureaucratically obtainable, providing officials with visible symbols of change—a new building, an expanded factory, a refurbished Main Street. In contrast, community organizations working to improve the economic conditions of the poor want government to provide job training and employment opportunities for the people who are the hardest to place in a changing economy. Such projects are less attractive to government officials because they are invisible and difficult to achieve. To combat this problem, community organizations need to work out projects that are clearly possible and for which bureaucrats can take credit. They can point to successful community projects such as the Nehemiah Project, which restored housing in a burned-out area in the Bronx.

The fourth problem is that community organizations lack extensive knowledge of how to gain political influence. Business groups start out with advantages: They know the elected officials, they have experts willing and able to testify, and they are experienced in providing the financial and electoral support for which politicians are grateful. Negotiating with business representatives over cocktails makes politicians feel more comfortable than dealing with community leaders under the threat of confrontations.

CHOOSING POLITICAL TACTICS

To match business's political influence, progressive groups have to pick the right political tactics for the situation, balancing problem solving and empowerment. In Table 12–1, we describe eight forms of political activity.

Political pressure campaigns often involve several of the tactics shown in Table 12–1.

Each tactic should be judged on five attributes. First, how narrowly does the tactic focus on a particular problem? Second, how effective is it likely to be in solving a particular problem? Third, how likely is the tactic to result in group members' adopting the opponents' perspective? Fourth, how much effort does it require? Fifth, how much will it empower the members?

Focus. Political tactics differ in the extent to which they allow an organization to focus on a specific interest. Campaigning for a candidate has low issue focus because getting a person elected replaces emphasis on specific projects to improve housing or obtain medical services for the elderly poor. Advocacy has high issue focus because it concentrates on the specific problem at hand to the exclusion of other issues.

Effectiveness. Political tactics differ in their effectiveness in solving particular problems. If a candidate supported by the group is elected mayor, he or she can propose laws that will probably get the necessary votes and solve the problem. The input from most citizen advisory boards is often ignored, so participation on boards has a low likelihood of solving problems.

TABLE 12–1
Eight Forms of Political Activity

Electing Office Holders	People supported by the progressive organization run for political office and the organization campaigns to help assure their election.
Policy Advocacy	Organizational leaders or staff lobby for specific organizational goals such as housing for the homeless. A policy advocate may work independently of the membership.
Informational Lobbying	Organizational members and leaders make sure that elected officials are aware of the preferences and problems of the membership as well as background facts and figures on the issue at hand.
Citizen Advisory Boards	Organizational members are appointed to boards to advise public officials in specific areas such as community-development programs.
Preparing Legislation and Regulations	Organizational members work with politicians to draft laws and with bureaucrats to prepare regulations.
Monitoring	Organizational members collect information on the actions of bureaucratic and regulatory agencies to make sure laws are carried out appropriately.
Referendum and Initiative	When legislatures refuse to pass needed laws, progressive organizations get proposals on the ballot and then work to convince people to vote for them.
Voter Registration	The organization persuades community members to register and vote. In so doing, it also tries to sign up more members.

Co-optation.   Political involvement risks *co-optation,* that is, group members adopting the attitudes of those in power. It is difficult not to be co-opted when holding office and working daily with others who have official positions. At the other extreme, policy advocates have little opportunity to be co-opted, because they are seen as outside gadflies.

Effort.   How much work does each tactic involve? Referendum and initiative campaigns are full-time efforts, but monitoring can usually be worked around other activities. Lobbying may be intensive when a desired or hated piece of legislation is being discussed but may take little or no time the rest of the year.

Empowerment.   Gaining a sense of empowerment is as important as solving problems. Policy advocacy rarely creates a sense of empowerment because there is little direct involvement of most of the membership. Monitoring and writing regulations, at least for those activists doing the work, are more empowering. In recent years, registering to vote and voting have not been very empowering, although they were during the civil rights era.

Table 12–2 summarizes the strengths and weaknesses of various political tactics with respect to focus, effectiveness, co-optation, effort, and empowerment.

Policy advocacy is appropriate when solving the problem is more important than empowerment. Getting homes for the homeless or food for the starving is more urgent than the need for empowerment. People have to eat and be kept warm now. Referendum campaigns and voter registration efforts are often better recruiting and teaching techniques for empowerment than they are ways of accomplishing immediate goals. For most organizations, the best combination of political activity is helping to design and implement legislation. These activities involve reasonably large numbers of organizational members in an empowering way and are effective in focusing on particular issues.

One success resulting from this approach was the Community Reinvestment Act of 1977. Gale Cincotta, a neighborhood leader working with a national coalition of neighborhood groups, helped pass the law to compel banks to reinvest some of their capital in their own communities and then monitored how well banks were complying. Using the clout created by the law,

> Philadelphia activists went across state lines to win an $85 million low-income neighborhood reinvestment package from New Jersey's Mid Atlantic Banks Inc. . . . The activists could prove that Mid Atlantic had made scarcely any loans in Camden, Newark, Passaic and Paterson—cities in which it had 19 branches and $470 million in deposits. (Neal Peirce, 1987, p. 1862)

TABLE 12–2
Evaluating Political Activities

Political Activity	Characteristics				
	Focus	**Effectiveness**	**Co-optation**	**Effort**	**Empowerment**
Electing organizational members to office	Modest	High	High	High	Modest
Policy advocacy	High	High	Low	Modest	Low
Informational lobbying	Modest	Modest	Low	Modest	Modest
Citizen's advisory boards	Modest	Low	High	Low	Low
Bill and ordinance preparation	High	High	Low	Modest	Modest
Monitoring regulation and implementation	High	High	Low	Modest	Modest/high
Referendum and initiatives	High	Modest	Low	High	High
Voter registration and involvement	Low	Modest	Low	High	Modest

Cincotta's group got results—the law was tailored for the benefit of community members. Many activists were involved. Moreover, making sure government and banks live up to the law keeps the organization in an oppositional mode, reducing the chance of co-optation.

TWO POLITICAL STYLES

The political tactics just described fit into two broad groupings, lobbying and direct involvement. In *lobbying,* members of community organizations persuade governmental officials to adopt policies they favor. If lobbying fails, community organizations can try *direct involvement,* in which the organization's supporters become political actors by running for political office or sponsoring referendum and initiative campaigns. Monitoring the implementation of programs and serving on citizen and neighborhood political boards merge elements of lobbying and direct involvement.

Lobbying and Political Pressure

The word *lobbying* connotes wealthy, cigar-smoking inside dopesters who use bribes and campaign contributions to make elected officials do their will. Such problems do occur, but most of the over 11,000 registered Washington lobbyists (Victor, 1987, p. 2727) and many others at the state and local levels are doing nothing more nefarious than seeking access to and petitioning their elected officials.

Lobbying means persuading elected officials. It involves gaining the trust of politicians so they will listen when the organization provides information. Successful lobbying requires a grab bag of technical skills, including digging up and laying out information in a readable way and using political symbols proficiently. Necessary skills also include figuring out whom to lobby and what kinds of arguments are likely to be successful with different actors.

Whom to Approach, Where and When?

To put pressure in the right place, organization members have to understand the decision points of the political system. Pay attention to the material described in Chapter 7 on how bills get passed in Congress and how ordinances are passed in cities. Offering an organization's viewpoint as a bill is coming up for the third (final) reading accomplishes little if most modifications take place before the second reading. Get involved as a bill is proposed, and stick with the bill as it moves through the different stages to fend off weakening amendments.

Alternatively, the organization can propose its own bill. If the elderly are being displaced by condominium conversions, obtain a model ordinance from a national housing coalition, and have a sympathetic city council person introduce it. There will be opposition from large real estate interests, but at least the organization's version will be on the floor.

The appropriate people to contact vary from city to city or state to state. Seeking out the support of professional staff is more effective in a reformed city than in a machine city, because the staff is likely to have more authority in a reformed city. The mayor is a more important ally in strong-mayor than in council-manager cities, because the mayor generally has more power in the strong-mayor structure. Regardless of the formal structure, some elected or appointed officials are powerful because of their personality and political skills or because they are old friends of the mayor, governor, or president. It is worth finding out the actual distribution of decision making power before deciding whom to lobby. Reporters covering city hall (or the statehouse) and League of Women Voters' members make good informants about who actually makes decisions. At the national level, news magazines are useful, as are the newsletters of interest groups.

What Level of Government to Pressure.   An early task is to find out what level of government has responsibility for the issues facing the action organization. This process is complicated because different levels of government often collaborate in designing, funding, or implementing a program. Since the early 1980s, problems of finding where to put pressure have become more complicated, especially in the community development and social service area, because many responsibilities shifted from the federal government to the states. At the same time, there has been a reshuffling of responsibilities between the state and local governments (W. J. Moore, 1987, 1988a, 1988b). The uncertainty over who has discretion in such a rapidly changing environment has been labeled *crazy-quilt federalism*.

With so much overlap and flux, who should the group pressure at what level of government? A group needs to be fairly specific about what it needs to accomplish and then figure out who has discretion (decision-making power) over that kind of decision. Suppose a local group is interested in increasing independence for the disabled. It could

Neighborhood organization addresses New Orleans Community Development Block Grant hearing. (Courtesy City of New Orleans)

try to persuade local employers or community colleges and universities to build entrance ramps and toilets accessible to the disabled. The employers might not own the buildings, however, and so have limited ability to respond to the demands. The universities might own their buildings, but not have much control over their budgets. In addition, the need to persuade one owner at a time might make the solution too slow. It might be more logical for the group to lobby city hall to pass a law requiring accessible facilities. Because local governments give building permits and establish standards for construction, they have considerable leverage over new construction.

If the group is working to increase financial support for disabled members, it could pressure the local branch of the state-operated welfare office. Such pressure would be especially appropriate if the group's concern is how the disabled are treated when they apply for benefits, because the office being pressured has discretion to change such treatment. But if the group's concern is for program design, such as whether the goal of a federal program is rehabilitation or independent living, then the group may need to agitate in Washington.

Picking Committees to Lobby.　Which committees to lobby depends on the issue. In federal programs for the disabled, there are three related policy approaches and hence three sets of committees to pressure. The first approach is to deal with disability through welfare. The second approach is rehabilitation. The third is guaranteeing the disabled their civil rights (E. Berkowitz, 1987). Welfare is part of the Social Security system, which is handled in Congress by the Ways and Means Committee in the House and by the Finance Committee in the Senate. Civil rights issues are the responsibility of the judiciary committees, while most issues having to do with health and rehabilitation are handled by the Committee on Education and Labor in the House, and Committee on Labor and Public Welfare in the Senate. Each have subcommittees that specialize in matters of the handicapped. In addition, Congress occasionally sets up special committees to deal with particular topics, such as aging and child welfare. A community organization would lobby these committees, keeping up contacts, and providing a stream of information.

What Agencies to Lobby.　Executive branch agencies affect policy in many ways. These agencies sometimes propose technical amendments to existing legislation; they draw up and implement regulations and often determine enforcement levels. Sometimes they have discretion over the awarding of grants.

For example, in the case of the disabled, 1978 legislation gave the Commissioner of Rehabilitation Services in the Department of Health and Human Services discretionary authority to award money to the states for independent living facilities, providing that "handicapped individuals were substantially involved in policy direction" (Berkowitz, 1987). The legislation also established direct grants to state vocational rehabilitation agencies to fund independent living services.

Other agencies also affect policy on the handicapped and can be lobbied. For instance, Social Security is also administered by the Department of Health and Human Services, but by a different agency, the Social Service Administration. Civil rights legislation is generally overseen by the Justice Department, which has an office of Civil Rights, but implementation of civil rights legislation can be delegated to a variety of agencies, including housing agencies and schools, so the implementation structure is more diffuse.

Organizers have to keep updating their knowledge of where responsibility and power lie. During the summer of 1990, Congress passed major civil rights legislation to protect the handicapped. Interest group organizers must learn who has discretion to enforce these new laws, especially because the new laws will be implemented through the civil rights structure.

As occurs in programs that affect the disabled, one level of government often funds the program and another level provides the services. When that happens, community organizations need to find out how much discretion the granting agency has given the recipient over how the money will be spent, in order to figure out which agency—the donor or the recipient—to pressure.

The easiest way to find out where discretion lies is to read the text of legislation and regulations and pay particular attention to the type of grant. *Categorical grants* provide money that can be used only for specified types of projects. A categorical grant to help localities build convention centers cannot be spent on other public facilities such as shelters for the homeless. *Block grants* allow the recipients to choose projects from several different programs. The Community Development Block Grant (CDBG) can be spent for sewer pipes, land clearance, or housing rehabilitation, but not for police patrol because that is outside of the purview of the CDBG. *Revenue sharing* allows recipients to use the money for virtually any legal purpose. The Federal Revenue Sharing program has ended, but many states still share revenue with their local governments.

Aiming at Bureaucrats or Politicians.   When targeting the executive branch of government, community groups must tailor separate arguments depending on whether they are lobbying politicians (elected officials and their appointees) or bureaucrats (career officials who carry on day-by-day business). The kinds of arguments likely to impress bureaucrats are less likely to impress politicians and vice versa. Politicians tend to have a short-run view, extending to the next election, while bureaucrats often think in longer terms. Politicians are more likely to think about the level of popular support for an issue, while bureaucrats are more likely to worry about administrative bottlenecks.

Most important, politicians are likely to respond to requests for favors or exceptions; bureaucrats tend to be more concerned with the appearance of equality of treatment and avoiding establishing precedents. With a politician, a community organization can ask for special treatment to escape from a hardship. With a bureaucrat, the organization should argue that their organization was treated differently and hence, unfairly. If an organization wants an exception from a bureaucrat, it has to find a reason why the exception does not establish an undesirable precedent.

Part of the technique for motivating politicians and bureaucrats to use their discretion in your group's favor is to figure out what they need to keep their careers going and make proposals that satisfy those needs. Politicians need monuments that demonstrate their success and help them win votes. Bureaucrats need tasks that provide clearly measurable outcomes so that they can demonstrate that they are doing their jobs. Giving politicians an opportunity to be filmed helping the needy is a good way of gaining their support. A group can win support from bureaucrats by showing them that if they work with your group they will look good, because your group gets dramatic projects completed on time and under budget.

When to Lobby.   Whom you contact at what level of government is important, but in political pressure campaigns, timing is crucial. Right after a convict on home leave rapes someone is a poor time to propose a work-release program. On the other hand, after a disaster like the Valdez oil spill is good time to propose stricter environmental controls.

Skillful community activists capitalize on unpredictable events, but they don't just wait for them and then think about what to do. Instead, they take advantage of the normal stages of policy making, preparing the way, so that when a triggering event occurs that makes a problem salient, they can take advantage of it.

At the local level, policy discussions begin when there is a vague sense that something is wrong. These general discussions sort out those parts of the problem that will receive attention. Proposed solutions become formalized as ordinances are proposed and then enacted into law. Bureaucrats may alter the policies as they try to implement them. A policy can be derailed at any stage; if the problem remains unsolved, the cycle can begin again (Waste, 1989, pp. 29–47).

Community organizations must intervene at different stages to keep the process going and to direct attention to the solutions the organization finds most helpful. Suppose a neighborhood is facing a flooding problem. In the *problem stage,* the organization focuses attention on the problem through getting newspaper coverage and calls to city council members. The flooding problem may be a long-term one that everyone knows about but does little to resolve. It takes a *triggering event* to activate people, for example, an 8-inch rain that forces people to abandon their houses. The trick is to turn the trigger event into an *agenda issue* that stays in the public awareness long enough to require action.

Turning trigger events into urgent agenda issues is vital because opponents are likely to delay until the pressure to act goes away. Developers might oppose an anti-flooding plan because it might force them to buy more expensive and better-drained land. These threatened developers might insist on hiring engineers to evaluate the problem and write a report. Delaying tactics must be anticipated and sidetracked or bypassed. The community organization can present an environmental study showing the extent of flooding before anyone else can suggest undertaking another study.

After the issue gets on the formal agenda, city council members seek possible solutions from the city staff and affected citizens. At this point, the community group should offer its advice: Seek state recreation funds to buy houses in the flood plain and strictly limit construction nearby.

Suppose the council ignores this sound advice and permits construction as long as new houses are built on stilts. At this stage the organization has two responsibilities. First, to make sure new construction follows the law. Second, to obtain evidence on whether the new standards do eliminate downstream flooding. If the city council adopted the stilts policy to sidetrack the community organization, the group should consider using confrontation tactics. But if the policy represented a good-faith effort that failed, the organization must come up with face-saving reasons why a new and stronger policy should be adopted.

Community organizations have to follow the issue for as long as it takes, sometimes years, because a shared understanding grows up between the community members and the city officials about past history, and that understanding constrains current and future possibilities. An organization that comes in at the 11th hour and proposes a solution outside that shared history will probably be ignored.

Coming in early and leaving early is not much more effective than coming in late. One of the reasons cited for the failure of the Equal Rights Amendment (ERA) was that many feminist organizations showed little staying power.

> In spite of the ERA activists' mottoes, "We won't go away," that was exactly what the state legislators expected them to do. The legislators expected, and often got, sporadic initiatives, intense one-time activity, and little follow-through. (Mansbridge, 1986, p. 158)

Community organizations have to stay with the issue through the implementation stage. That means making sure money is available to carry out the law and that staff are assigned to enforce it. Federal law prohibits discrimination against women, minorities, and the elderly, but the budgets of agencies that implement these laws have been cut drastically. Just getting a law passed isn't enough to ensure that it will be carried out.

Community organizations require binding agreement that political deals will be kept and laws carried out as intended. Vigilance is required to ensure that the law is carried out as intended. This is especially important if the issue was opposed by business interests or is inconsistent with the ideology of those in the executive branch (remember, laws are passed by the legislative branch).

For example, to bypass the Reagan administration's refusal to build public housing, Congress, with urging from community organizations, passed tax laws that encouraged private developers to help not-for-profits build lower income housing. The Department of Housing and Urban Development, which was responsible for implementing the law, delayed in certifying that the housing was suitable for the poor until the tax laws expired. Executive branch opposition killed the program in the implementation stage.

Following up to ensure implementation is particularly important with regulatory agencies. Such agencies are formed after a public outcry over some widely publicized abuse, such as a river that catches fire or huge jumps in gasoline prices. After it is established, the regulatory agency may be captured by the companies it is supposed to regulate. Staff from the regulated companies are hired by the regulatory agency, and the agency staff sometimes resign to take jobs with the regulated companies. The ideology and values of regulators may become indistinguishable from those of the regulated. Establishing a regulatory agency does little good unless community groups make it work.

Organizations such as Public Citizen hire as citizen advocates people with knowledge about technical issues to check that regulations are being enforced. These organizations sue to ensure openness of records and reports of regulatory agencies. Public openness reduces the power of the experts in government and in the regulated industries and allows for public influence over policy implementation (McCann, 1986, p. 99).

How to Pressure Public Officials

After determining where and when to put pressure, community organizations need to consider how to do it most effectively. The first piece of advice is to make it as easy as possible for elected officials to give the organization what it seeks by making politicians look good. Second, recognize the constraints they are under. Third, try reaching decision makers indirectly, through their friends, supporters, and staff. Fourth, concentrate primarily on passing information to decision makers, in conversation, through letter-writing campaigns, at meetings, and at legislative mark-up sessions.

Show Concern for the Image of Elected Officials.   Pressure campaigns on public officials require a careful balancing of power and reason. Power and the potential for disruption lie behind a political pressure campaign, and politicians might capitulate to force or the threat of force. But they will not admit that force is the reason for giving in, lest they destroy their image as tough-minded officials. As a result, political pressure tactics are often conducted under the shared pretense that force is not being applied. Action organizations have to present politicians with a *rationale*—a reason for supporting the organization—other than giving in to force.

A rationale can be cast in terms of broad principles: Support the community health center, because we all have a responsibility for caring for the young and the old. A rationale can be cast in terms of the facts of the matter: Don't rezone the empty lot for a commercial use because it will increase traffic flow through the neighborhood by 40% and endanger the children. The city council might agree to the demands because they fear that members of the neighborhood association will vote against them if they don't, but they have the face-saving rationale that children will be endangered if they do not take action. Rationales are the public excuse for taking actions supported by the pressure organization.

Realize the Constraints Faced by Public Officials.   Effective pressure tactics take into account the constraints elected officials face, and community members need to distinguish between constraints based on administrative or fiscal realities, and constraints stemming from political pressure from opponents of the organization. This knowledge allows the organization to plan tactics that accommodate to real constraints rather than the demands of opponents.

Political actions are limited by governmental resources and previous commitments made based on these resources. Before seeking funds, learn the size of the budget and the amount of intergovernmental grant revenue and how it has been used in the past. Uncommitted funds are the best target, because funding to ongoing projects is rarely discontinued without good cause. For example, a bond that is about to be paid off may release money to be spent on new projects. Don't assume that the contest is always between the good guys—Eliminate the Rats Association—and the bad guys—The Association for Redeveloping Downtown and Displacing Poor People. Two community organizations, each working to empower their members, can be contending for limited funds. Elected officials are put in the awkward position of leaving one organization or another dissatisfied. Keep in mind that an important role of a city council, or any legislative body, is to balance the needs of different constituencies.

Effective community organizations recognize the cross pressures politicians face and when possible try to find solutions that reduce those cross pressures. Suppose small manufacturers are opposing proposed middle-income housing nearby because they fear the new residents might complain about the noise their businesses make. A community organization that wants to improve the neighborhood might suggest that a portion of the newly proposed apartments have rents reasonable enough so that employees of nearby small factories can live there. Existing housing will be improved, middle-class people who want access to downtown can move into the more expensive apartments, yet, with their own employees living in the neighborhood, factory owners are less fearful of residential pressures that will hurt their businesses. What appeared to be a problem pitting businesses, middle-class residents, builders, and working class residents against each other can be resolved to nearly everyone's satisfaction. When community organizations come up with such solutions, they help frame the outcomes, and they get credit for helping the politician out of a difficult spot.

Approach Politicians Indirectly.   Politicians can be influenced through their social and political networks. Locate campaign workers or contributors, former colleagues and business associates, and friends (Alderson & Sentman, 1979, p. 221). Among this group of people, the community organization should seek out those who are most sympathetic to the organization's goals and try to motivate them to persuade the politician.

Another indirect way of reaching politicians is through their staff members, who do the ground work on legislation and provide the technical knowledge that might influence the positions legislators take on proposed bills. Staff members have more time to talk with members of the organization than do elected officials and often are insulted if the organization tries to bypass them. Staff members usually are knowledgeable about the history of an issue and can warn community groups when proposals will cause problems for the legislator. They can also suggest technical compromises to community members.

Don't approach staff with political threats; instead, come prepared with specific suggestions or detailed questions. If your organization has data on the problem, give them to staff members before presenting it to politicians. Staff can put the data in reports that politicians read; politicians are more likely to believe the data if their staff does.

In most cities, council members don't have personal staffs. The heads of the different governmental departments—the city manager, the police chief, fire chief, public works director, planner—sometimes serve as a council's staff, but the relationship is far more distant than the congressional staffs are to legislators. Department heads make recommendations to the council but are less concerned with the political fates of the council members. However, like congressional staff members, they are often extremely knowledgeable about issues.

In preparing a proposal to the city council, it is a good idea to work with the relevant departments. The administrative departments can be good sources of data for proposals. If an organization is concerned about traffic flow from a new project, ask the city engineer for traffic estimates. Administrative departments can also be important in supporting or defeating a proposal. Will city inspectors be upset if the organization wants to expand its own home-inspection program?

Sometimes an organization can work out a proposal that aids its cause and helps the administrative departments. In that case, the organization and the city department may present identical proposals to the council. In Waterloo, Iowa, an National People's Action (NPA) affiliate convinced the police to join with it in a preventative program against drugs. The department benefits by increased funding, and the community gets further support on solving its problems.

In some cities, community organizations are fortunate enough to be able to work with advocacy planners or progressive planners. Most planners gather information and respond to requests and plans from builders. In contrast, *advocacy planners* define as part of their role speaking for those in need, while insisting on open public hearings to get information about neighborhood preferences. *Progressive planners* recognize that what hurts community organizations is a lack of proper information or distorted information (Forester, 1989, p. 46). So progressive planners, such as Norman Krumholz in Cleveland, work with community organizations to try to offset the biased information that enters into the decision making. For example, in cost–benefit calculations, they include negative impacts of downtown development projects in the calculation of costs.

How to Provide Information

Above all else, lobbying is providing information to elected officials.

It is crucial to follow Ralph Nader's advice that

> communicating with legislators is your principal reason for perpetually haunting the capitol. *Talking frequently to legislators is the best way to persuade them of your position;* the importance of this simple method cannot be overstated. (Nader, quoted in Caplan, 1983, p. 126)

By presenting facts and figures, the organization conveys that it is helping politicians do their work. It is important to be sure that the facts presented are correct so that the politician will learn to trust the figures of the progressive group. Separate facts from conclusions. Don't just oppose a redevelopment project, provide information on the harm it will cause: the number of people displaced, the tax cost to the community of putting in new sewers and streets, the amount of increased traffic.

It is also important to provide information that inoculates politicians against the arguments of the opponents. For example, women's organizations have pressured government to adopt "comparable worth" salary policies. The goal is to eliminate the sexual discrimination in which jobs traditionally open to women, such as nurses, receive lower pay than jobs traditionally open to men, such as electricians. Opponents will argue that comparable worth policies cost too much money. Anticipate this argument by showing that higher salaries for women will reduce the need for publicly supported social services; the group can also argue that low pay and low status in traditional female jobs has created crisis shortages of able workers in such areas as nursing and teaching.

Effective political campaigns require understanding what resources both politicians and the organization have available. (Thom Clark)

In providing information, a lobbyist becomes the trusted policy advocate, a person whose beliefs and goals are known but who has sufficient respect for politicians not to lead them astray with faulty information. This has been achieved in some cities in which community organizations have set up political partnerships with council members that

> allow council members to receive information about needs of neighborhood residents and about the effects of city policies on the neighborhood directly from grass roots level . . . political partnerships thus provide those council members who are a bit wary of the completeness of the information supplied by the city administration with a source of information unfiltered by city departments. (Davidson, 1979, p. 26)

If politicians trust the information they get from community groups, they are more likely to see issues from the community perspective and frame legislation accordingly.

Providing information is also a form of direct social action. National progressive organizations and coalitions of neighborhood organizations prepare and release reports on problems of housing, acquired immune deficiency syndrome (AIDS), child abuse, and other situations crying out for social reform. In this more activist vein, Public Interest Research Groups (PIRGs) combine information-gathering techniques with direct political or legal tactics to try to ensure that information is turned into legislative or administrative action.

PIRGs have prevented transportation of hazardous waste, inspected streams for illegal runoff, and investigated work-related injuries. The basic pattern is to document a problem, publicize it, and then seek legislative or legal redress (Griffin, 1987). This pattern of documentation, publicity, and lobbying has also been used in different states by Citizens Utility Boards. They monitor utility costs, provide information to legislators (often through the mass media as well as personal contact), and advocate citizens' rights against the utilities.

PIRGs, Citizens Utilities Boards, and numerous Washington-based advocacy groups lobby by providing information to politicians and publicizing that information so that it cannot be ignored. There are other important ways of providing information to politicians. Progressive organizations use letter-writing campaigns to demonstrate their interest in a problem, and if the mailing is of significant enough size, to tacitly indicate to politicians the number of votes they can mobilize.

Letter writing, by itself, is too far removed from bill writing and the nuances of decision making to be effective in shaping the legislation. To handle these problems, activists attend public hearings and legislative markup sessions.

Run Effective Letter-Writing Campaigns.   A letter-writing campaign is often the only way for large numbers of people to contact public officials. To stimulate such campaigns, most national progressive organizations have lists of members whom the organization contacts—often with "Action Alerts"—to request letters be written to politicians. The ability to run such a campaign can be influential because it indicates that the organization can mobilize large numbers of people.

There is an art to running a letter-writing campaign. Elected officials appreciate clarity and brevity. Letters should focus on only one problem, because they are often sorted into piles, pro and con on an issue. The letter should show an understanding of what the official has already done on the issue and then inquire what the official is planning to do next. Be explicit in giving advice but don't threaten; the officials already know that if they let people down, they lose votes. After an issue has been decided, let politicians know that their support was appreciated. At all times, be courteous.

If the letter-writing task is made easy for the members, they are more likely to send in their letters. However, duplicate postcards, photocopies, and letter forms that people fill out are not treated as seriously by politicians as letters composed and written by individuals. The most effective letters are those that provide personal anecdotes that make problems real to a politician.

Some cities are beginning to experiment with hi-tech ways of encouraging individuals to communicate their opinions to politicians.

> Gone are the days in Santa Monica, Calif. when people who couldn't find time to attend City Council Meetings were shut out of city government. . . . The computer age has changed all that. . . . The city's Public Electronic Network . . . allows them to debate with officials in a kind of electronic town meeting. Residents simply input their opinions on their personal computers . . . or on one of 33 personal computers located in public areas in Santa Monica. (Fiordalisi, 1989, pp. 24–25)

Learn the Decorum for Public Meetings, Hearings, and Markup Sessions.   Many decisions are made as a result of information garnered at public meetings and hearings. It is important for members of community organizations to know how to present arguments at meetings and hearings in ways considered acceptable to elected officials. Though it might be necessary to use a public meeting as a setting for a social confrontation, this tactic is not normally a way of persuading decision makers.

City council meetings and legislative hearings are formal occasions, at which both the facts presented and the decorum shown are important. Public officials don't like rancor or rudeness at such meetings and appreciate respect shown to them and to the deliberative process.

Most elected officials do not spend much time reading reports, so much of what they learn is from what they hear at public meetings. In preparing these presentations, organization members may wish to draw from administrative records. These records are publicly available, although pressure organizations sometimes have to use the federal or state freedom of information laws to get the information. Table 12–3 describes information available from local government agencies that could be of use in preparing presentations to council members.

When presentations do not come from agency records, elected officials have little way of evaluating the factual content of the presentations made to them. Hence, they often judge on the appearance or attitude and manners of the presenter (Davidson, 1979, p. 74). The presentation should convince politicians that the facts presented are trustworthy. Watch the behavior of lawyers and highly paid business lobbyists at such meetings. They are calm, courteous, and factual. They understand that they'll win sometimes and lose other times. Little is to be gained if they infuriate officials to such an extent that the politicians ignore them the next time they make a presentation.

For most public meetings, arrangements can be made in advance to get a spokesperson for an organization on the agenda; don't just show up and expect to be heard (though many city governments reserve time at their meetings for citizens who want to speak on a subject not included elsewhere on the agenda).

Observe some meetings to learn what to expect. At legislative hearings, the order of speaking is usually fixed: the chairperson of the committee questions witnesses first, then members of the committee in order of seniority by political party. City councils are more variable: In some cities, citizens are heard, then staff, and council wraps up, but in others, citizens are scheduled later in the proceedings as each issue is heard.

Statements made at city council meetings and public hearings should be logical and brief. If an organization has 200 people showing up to pressure a city council, choose one or two of them to read a carefully prepared statement, and have the speakers ask the people in the audience whom they represent to stand up.

At public hearings, speeches are often restricted to 5 or 10 minutes, so each statement should contain (somewhat) different information. The first speaker should present the gist of the argument. Then several other organization members should present separate parts of the total argument in their 5-minute segments. For example, one person could describe the impact of airport noise on hearing and mental health; another could describe the danger from traffic congestion. At the end, have someone wrap up the arguments. This way, statements are kept short, yet the organization makes its case.

Facts and figures that are boring to hear can be shown on neatly prepared charts, referred to during the presentation. At the end of the presentation, the spokesperson for the organization asks that a typewritten version, including the factual material, be

TABLE 12–3

Sources of Data Available From Local Administrators Used by Community Organizations to Inform Local Officials

Source	Type of Data	Use in Pressure Campaigns
City planning department	Projections of the community's future	Can find statements by elected officials of community goals that can be quoted to them to force them to act consistently. Can find officially accepted figures on the consequences of different plans for redevelopment, rezonings, open space; planning departments tend to have current data on the social and economic conditions within a community.
Public works and engineering	Traffic counts	Indicates the consequences of new developments on noise and safety within the community. Indicates the distribution of work to improve community infrastructure in the different neighborhoods.
Community development department	Poverty and need statistics	Collects data on the location and amount of poverty, need for housing, and other indicators of social distress. Such information should be incorporated within arguments to increase services to poorer neighborhoods.
	Federal grant compliance	Might have records on how funds were targeted and whether or not such targeting was in accord with federal guidelines.
County clerk	Property ownership	Can (sometimes) determine who owns deteriorated property; also might be able to find out who owns property that will benefit from public programs.
	Property sales	Can check on block-busting activity or find data needed to argue for neighborhood preservation programs.
	Tax records	Can learn the tax payments for different properties to determine if there is favoritism toward large owners or undertaxing of business property.
	Campaign contributions	Can determine the names of active supporters of local elected officials to target indirect pressure.
Building department	Code violations	Can check reports of code violations by location and whether action was taken.
Police department	Incident reports	Can determine if crime rates differ by neighborhood to argue for increased police protection; can also check if there is a bias in who is arrested by race or area of the city.
	Traffic accidents	Can determine dangerous intersections to lobby for stop signs or lights; can argue when developments will increase traffic danger.
City clerks	Minutes of meetings	Records of votes and statements made by elected officials to find out where they stood. Sometimes can ferret out the types of arguments to which local officials are amenable.
	Bids received and asked	Records of which companies and individuals receive city contracts. Can check to see if contracts were awarded to lowest bidder.

placed in the record. Once it is part of the record, the testimony can be referred to in legal actions.

In the presentations, balance facts with more personal descriptions of why the outcomes are important: "I oppose the rezoning because as the engineering department figures show it will increase traffic by 40% near the Jefferson school. And I have two children attending the school." Add drama to the statement by having the children stand by the speaker. Other people can show how many people were displaced, describing briefly their experiences in trying to find affordable housing. Summary statements, however, should be phrased in terms of broad public interest, not personal impact, to help provide rationales for elected officials to justify their decisions.

At these meetings, opponents will fight vigorously for their side of the issue. Those presenting testimony for the community group should avoid public fights with opponents but should resist when opponents, sometimes represented by council members or legislators, twist statements in ways that change their meaning. Try to be tactful.

> If a legislator, while questioning you, asserts facts you know aren't correct, simply cite the source of your correct facts. You don't want to make an opponent lose face in a hearing but you do want to show that his facts are wrong. Present the correction, calmly and forthrightly, setting aside your emotions. (Alderson & Sentman, 1979, p. 282)

Sometimes opponents will toss loaded or hostile questions at spokespeople from community groups. Grasp the question, show that the premises are understood, and then correct the misunderstanding. Suppose an alderperson harshly questions a representative of a spouse abuse center. "Those women in the shelter can't be from our community, they must be coming from neighboring towns. Spouse abuse is what happens to poor people, when the men are out of work." One possible response might be, "Economic stress is a cause of violence, as the alderman indicates, but there are a number of other causes. Spouse abuse happens in all social classes, and more than 70% of our clients have local addresses."

Authoritatively, yet courteously, refute any arguments that the opponents are likely to make. This is somewhat tricky, because at hearings, one side does not directly debate the other, rather, each side makes separate presentations to the same committee or council. Spokespeople for the community organization have to find out what their opponents are likely to say. The opponents may have petitioned the government before and, if they have, there should be a formal record of their presentation. Read the record to anticipate what they will say this time and prepare evidence to counter their case. When possible, prepare a fact sheet that can be given to a legislator or city councilperson who supports the community organization and let him or her do the questioning. Disagreeing with the opponent's facts or interpretation is acceptable, but be cautious about casting doubt on an opponent's motives. Public officials are uncomfortable with such personal arguments.

Let's examine these strategies of arguing with an opponent in a case in which members of an organization that wants to preserve parks and open space are faced with a developer who wants to put up a large housing complex. Spokespeople for the environmental group can

1. **Disagree with the evidence the opponent presents.** The developer will describe the amount of green space to be left when the project is completed. The environmental organization argues that much of this green space will be in small front yards and won't be usable by most people.
2. **Point out inconsistencies in the opponent's arguments.** The developer describes how easily the city can accommodate the small increase in population, while describing how much more money the city will get in taxes from the increased population. The environmental organization argues that either growth is moderate or gain in taxes is moderate.
3. **Challenge the assumptions made by the opponent.** The developer argues that traffic and congestion will not be a problem. Action researchers examine the model used by the developer to estimate traffic and learn that the model assumes only one car per family. The spokesperson for the environmental organization presents evidence showing that suburban families average 1.8 cars.
4. **Challenge the priorities expressed by the opponent.** The developer argues the need for housing because people want to move to the city. Environmentalists argue that maintaining an uncongested environment is more important. If more people move in, everybody loses by an increase in urban sprawl.
5. **Challenge the track record of the opponents.** The environmental organization presents pictures of other projects built by the developer. These pictures show that the houses are already deteriorating.
(Modified from Alderson & Sentman, 1979, pp. 236–239)

Public hearings are just one stage in the development of a law or ordinance. The community group must make sure an appropriate bill is written and that key parts of it are passed. Assuming the organization has been persuasive, a legislative staff person will draw up a bill encompassing the organizational demands. To be doubly sure, write your own bill, at least on the state and local level, because

> A perpetual problem for part-time legislators is getting bills written. . . . A lawmaker who likes your proposal will be grateful to have a written bill—rather than just an idea—as a starting point. (Caplan, 1983, p. 31)

A written bill, however, even one supported by several legislators is just a starting point. Bills proceed through many committees and are marked up, that is, rewritten. Too often, wording is changed by lobbyists for the opposition, weakening the bill beyond repair. If the community organization representatives are present, they can often stop such efforts on the spot.

To summarize, it not only matters what the organization knows, but how it presents its case. Presence at hearings and legislative markups is important, and remaining calm and courteous in the face of provocation is also important. The need to maintain the dignity of the proceedings means that arguments with opponents are typically indirect, avoiding any semblance of name calling. Passion for the cause is allowed, if it is reasonable in tone, but not anger at opponents or disrespect for the decision-making process.

DIRECT-INVOLVEMENT POLITICS

There is another political option besides pressuring officials and bureaucrats to comply with organizational demands. The organization works to get laws passed through referendum or initiative, that is, a direct appeal to the electorate. A second approach is participation on advisory boards or various neighborhood governments. The third approach requires community organizations to support candidates, including their own members, for political office.

These strategies assume that winning an election or serving on an elected board brings meaningful control. Public service, however, imposes responsibilities and obligations that exceed the scope of interest of organizational members. Moreover, being in office requires compromises that can be destructive to community causes.

If participation in direct-involvement politics required an all-or-nothing decision, nothing might be the better choice. Short of revolutionary transformation, serving in conventional political offices separates leaders from organizational members and creates pressures to go-along-to-get-along, lessening the inclination to present the more radical alternative supported by the community organization. Fortunately, the choice is rarely all or nothing, and striving for public office can have benefits other than winning. Direct-involvement politics can be a useful part of a broader package of action-campaign tactics.

Direct Democracy Through Referenda and Initiatives

Referenda and initiatives require community organizations to run signature campaigns to place issues on the ballot. Every year, several dozen major referenda take place, on topics such as banning throw-away bottles, property tax limitations, the use of English as the sole official language, public funding of abortion, and nuclear power plant construction (Dresang & Gosling, 1989; D. Schmidt, 1989). Community organizations have sponsored neighborhood referenda to stop block busting in racially changing neighborhoods (Scheiber, 1987) and to oppose nuclear power and weapons (Zisk, 1989b).

Statewide referenda require the personnel and media resources of a large-scale campaign. They involve so much work, the organization can do little else. To get onto the ballot requires a large number of signatures, so the organization has to have members throughout the state. They have to be mobilized quickly, because there are usually strict time limitations on signature gathering (Dresang & Gosling, 1989, p. 180). Sometimes professionals are hired to collect signatures. One tactic used to collect signatures is *mall tabling,* which involves setting up a table at a shopping center and asking passersby to sign the petition (D. Schmidt, 1989, p. 43). Once referenda are on the ballot, battles can be fierce.

Because referenda affect powerful interests—a recent California referendum threatened insurance companies—they evoke large-scale and expensive responses. The opposition may spend millions of dollars in media blitzes to oppose progressive causes.

Referenda and initiatives enable organizations to get their issue heard and publicized. Even when issues don't pass, the campaign symbolizes the importance of the problem and serves as a mobilization technique:

> In . . . (the failure to pass the [Nuclear] Freeze, statewide in Arizona), a loss at the polls was accompanied by a major movement victory—the creation of an active peace movement in Arizona, even in the act of defeat, *because* of the electoral activity (unprecedented in Arizona in 1982). (Zisk, 1989b, p. 9)

Another plus is that referenda have forced community organizations to confront antiquated laws that limit political access. Organizations have battled and sometimes won to eliminate laws demanding unconscionably high numbers of signatures on petitions. And in certain cases they have won the right to collect petitions in shopping malls, even though such malls are technically private property.

It is arguable whether the disproportionate funding that the opposition can bring to bear on referendum battles increases the likelihood of their winning. There is some evidence that this need not be the case.

> Out of 72 city or county ballot measure campaigns that pitted poorly funded local residents and environmentalists against the overwhelming spending of developers, the developers *lost* two-thirds! (D. Schmidt, 1989, p. 36)

In referenda, progressive causes win as often as they lose. On the other hand, Cronin quotes studies that show that "campaign spending is the single most powerful predictor of who wins and who loses" (1989, p. 112). Community organizations can sometimes make up for a lack of money, but choosing a political arena in which money for advertisements is so important is not playing to the strengths of most progressive organizations.

Another problem with referenda is that to mount statewide campaigns, community groups have to work in coalitions with other groups they are not comfortable with.

> Many of the people who might have pushed strongly for a low keyed grassroots strategy were not only worried about opposition strength, but profoundly concerned about remaining respectable and disassociated with those who did civil disobedience or who insisted that racial justice, and Central American issues were part of the larger arms control problem. (Zisk, 1989b, pp. 18–19)

Such problems routinely occur in coalition activity, as opponents play up the differences in opinions among progressive organizations.

A third problem is that the most effective referendum campaigns have been those run by hierarchical organizations working with hired experts. Inherently, this creates a gulf between winning and building participatory, democratic organizations.

Finally, whenever an issue is presented simplistically (which it must be on a referendum) and requires a majority to vote yes or no, minority rights may be trampled (Cronin, 1989, p. 98). This is a problem with most yes–no voting procedures, but it takes on particular salience when one realizes that recent conservatively backed referenda have attempted to quarantine AIDS victims or mandate English only as the official language (Calderon & Horton, 1988). It doesn't take much imagination to come up with even more dangerous proposals, such as confiscation of goods of all those accused of a crime, or deportation of Jews (or Chicanos, or African Americans or New Yorkers).

It's not just that the opponents of community organizations can use the same tool with potentially frightening results, it is that no tradition or law suggests the breadth or appropriateness of an issue for a referendum. While it makes sense to ask the public whether they approve funding for a particular highway, and have the majority bind the minority, it makes less sense to ask the public whether abortion should be legal, or whether terminally ill patients should have the right to die. These are issues with many legitimate positions between yes and no. When there are only two positions, yes and no, moderates are forced to the extremes, and one extreme will win, and dominate the rest, even if no one really favors that extreme. What appears democratic may not be democratic at all. Referenda are tools that must be used carefully.

Whether they initiate referenda or not, progressive organizations must understand referendum tactics, because conservative groups are increasingly relying on referenda. Community organizations may have to fight to defend their principles. They have to be prepared to throw everything they have into a campaign and win it. That means figuring out good symbolic arguments, printing up literature, raising funds for ads, and going door to door to motivate the sympathetic and getting them to the polls on election day.

Community Boards and Neighborhood Governance

During the 1960s, many liberals believed that democratic representation could be obtained by setting up community boards or neighborhood governance, especially in poorer areas of the city. In addition, several federal programs required neighborhood consultation or citizens' advisory boards. Most scholars and activists have been critical of the effectiveness of such boards in promoting local democracy and capacity building. Community boards sometimes allowed officials to make a pretense of popular involvement but provided little in the way of effective participatory governance.

Progressive authors have found in most such boards:

1. Lack of representativeness of the participants. . . .
2. The most successful citizen inputs are found in programs which seem to require the least expertise.
3. Overall, the impact of citizens groups has been limited.
4. Most participatory programs are geared to intervention at the local administrative or service delivery level, leaving the vast reaches of agenda-setting and policy prescription relatively untouched. (Crosby et al., 1986, p. 170)

Some information is obtained from the public, but in the difficult areas, experts, rather than those affected by decisions, make the final determinations.

In addition, community boards sometimes pit neighborhood against neighborhood. The resulting rivalries permit the less fragmented business community to prevail. As described in New York City:

With a shrinking pie, a division of the city into separate community boards tended to place neighborhood interests in competition with each other. Neighborhoods were divided from each other, not united, by the arrangement. (Marcuse, 1987–1988, p. 281)

Even more fractious conflicts have appeared between communities over locally controlled school boards (M. Williams, 1989). Locally controlled school boards have created a "New American Dilemma" (Hochschild, 1984) in which issues of racial equality, access to schools, and local decisional autonomy pit one neighborhood against another.

Still, when federal support strongly encouraged neighborhood involvement, in certain issue areas, community and neighborhood boards were effective. The Health Systems Agencies, which had active citizen decision-making boards, were reported in 1979 to have turned down a total of $2.3 billion in proposals for hospital capital projects. Citizen committees were often able to take effective action when proposals for hospital expansion went against community desires (Mueller & Comer, 1982). Citizen boards inspired by CDBG, at least in some cities, contributed to more efficient and targeted administration of neighborhood programs (Thomas, 1986, p. 95). Some helped government agencies that benefited neighborhoods increase their budgets (J. C. Thomas, 1986, p. 96). They also contributed to a stronger sense of community identity (J. C. Thomas, 1986, p. 119). Most optimistically, setting up neighborhood boards

> has not detracted from the interests of the city as a whole. . . . By involving neighborhood representatives in defining citywide interests on crucial issues, City Hall has usually won neighborhood support for those interests. . . . More groups need not mean increased antipathy toward common interests, especially if the groups are treated as though they, too, share those interests. (J. C. Thomas, 1986, p. 153)

Neighborhood success in gaining resources and setting agendas occurs when city government both respects neighborhood concerns and is willing to work to teach members of neighborhoods about urban governance.

The more successful experiments have been led by public officials rather than citizens, but they have helped build capacity in neighborhood groups.

When a city government provides a supportive environment and treats neighborhood groups as a forum for teaching and expanding capacity, there is a potential for success. In Dayton, Ohio, neighborhood groups help allocate the city budget, especially the projects that affect the neighborhoods.

Dayton's budget process is designed so that when the preferences of the neighborhood groups differ from that of city government department heads, the public officials are put on the defensive and have to demonstrate reasons for disagreement. Cooperation between neighborhoods is encouraged because programs that have the support of multiple neighborhoods gain an even higher priority. In part, the system works because activists on these boards receive extended instruction on how budgets are formed and how local government works. Greater neighborhood power is a joint product of neighborhood groups and city government, with the shared goal of more stable and attractive neighborhoods. The potentials can be seen elsewhere:

> Across the city of Boston, residents are helping shape the future of their neighborhoods by participating in neighborhood-based rezoning efforts, affordable housing developments, and design review meetings with city officials and developers. (Devine, 1990, p. 1)

City commitment to such programs often depends on the support of the mayor. A board member of the Neighborhood Association of the Back Bay warned "This administration has tried to be responsive to neighborhood concerns, but this administration is not going to be around forever" (Devine, 1990, p. 17).

With political involvement, there is a perpetual tradeoff between gaining short-term power and effectiveness and being co-opted or at least becoming politically dependent on an elected official. These issues must be weighed before an organization decides to commit substantial energy to working in official neighborhood and community governing boards.

Electoral Campaigns

Should community organizations expend effort at winning political offices for their leaders? Generally not, because of the constraints imposed on successful candidates. The responsibilities of governing as well as the compromises needed to win political office distract from more basic goals of community organizing.

We are not arguing that progressive organizations should avoid electoral politics. Quite the contrary. The clout of neighborhood associations comes from their ability to get out the vote for the candidate they endorse. (Such candidates are often former activists from the organizations, but it is the individual making the decision to run for office, not the group pushing the person as representative of the organization.) Mayor Flynn of Boston, Mayor Goldschmidt of Portland, Mayor Washington in Chicago and others have won based on neighborhood support and have paid more attention to problems of concern to community groups.

Progressive and community organizations can tell their membership which elected officials voted in support of their group's agenda and which ones opposed it. Advertising a candidate with a positive score on the organization's issues is a form of endorsement. But endorsing a candidate is much less difficult, time-consuming, and potentially embarrassing than holding office. For a limited amount of effort, the organization might gain a friend at city hall or in the legislature. If the official is co-opted by the structure, the organization only needs to endorse someone else. When the organization runs one of its own leaders for office, the potential loss is far greater, as is the role stress for the official.

A good reason to participate in election campaigns is to dramatically symbolize the group's issues and get the issues on the agenda, regardless of the election outcomes. A campaign may symbolize that blacks, or women, or the handicapped, or the elderly are coming into their own, are beginning to exercise power, and are no longer on the outside looking in. It may symbolize that the public is discontent, that some changes will be made, or that downtown development or reallocation to the banks is no longer acceptable. Winning office may be secondary to the message.

Jesse Jackson's earlier runs for the presidency created the Rainbow Coalition, which symbolized the potential for a progressive alternative.

The Rainbow presence . . . provides a place to go. "Legislators tend to gravitate to the middle" [an activist] notes, "and we keep moving the middle. We've redefined the boundaries of what is acceptable in Vermont politics." (Ashkenaz, 1986, p. 14)

Redefining the boundaries of what is acceptable, giving left and liberal politicians a place to go, and legitimating their ideas are important political contributions that should outlast any one election or candidate. To be useful, however, such efforts have to elect some of the candidates running with the group's backing because "even committed activists eventually grow weary of putting their energies into progressive races that are clearly doomed from the start" (Ashkenaz, 1986, p. 17).

Endorsing candidates and running symbolic campaigns are generally more appropriate for community groups than winning and holding office. Here, the scorecard for the progressive organization is far more mixed.

The benefits from gaining office are real. Once in power, La Raza Unida and its local allies worked to reduce some of the blatant anti-Hispanic discrimination in Southwestern cities (Muñoz & Barrera, 1982; Shockley, 1974). The group created a much more supportive environment for other progressive actions. After progressives took over city government in Santa Monica, the rent control board was able to maintain and increase its power. More generally, minorities who moved from protest to political participation were better able to protect their gains because they were effectively represented in policy making (Browning et al., 1984, p. 25).

Clavel considers that "progressive governments did make a difference" (Clavel, 1986, p. 233). They empowered advocacy and progressive planners. They provided "*support for neighborhood organizations*" and "pressured local administrations to *depart from the traditional hierarchical models of government*" (Clavel, 1986, p. 215).

But if the gains of winning are real, so are the costs. The effort of gaining and holding political office in a generally nonsupportive social and political climate can distract from direct action, pressure campaigns, and building locally empowered organizations. In some cities in which neighborhood coalitions of one minority group have won, the result was distrust and accusations of racism (Falcon, 1988). To build community, to win an election, and then to escape from a history of racist conflict all at one time is asking a lot.

Without a supportive ideological environment, winning office may not be worth the costs in time and energy. After middle-class progressives took office in Santa Monica, California, expertise replaced skill development, and neighborhood input was seriously reduced (Kann, 1986, p. 128). The desire to win and to continue to hold office became strong enough among some council members to distract from the left-wing, participatory ideology.

Once in office, politicians have responsibilities for other people besides the members of progressive organizations who elected them. Elected officials cannot serve their community organizations by exploiting others. Filling the responsibilities of office in a fair fashion while supporting the platforms of progressive groups creates such tensions that office holding is best avoided.

In summary, getting involved in campaigns has its plusses, especially if the members keep in mind the tradeoff between the amount of work involved and the likelihood of success. Especially useful are endorsing candidates and running symbolic campaigns that get issues on the policy agenda. Running campaigns for referenda and initiatives are very time-consuming and require the kind of funds that many community organizations do not have. Nevertheless, referenda can be good opportunities for organizing.

Whether they want to or not, community organizations may have to get involved in referendum campaigns, because conservatives are running them more often, and the consequences of defeat for the more progressive organizations can be devastating. Running its own organization members for office is less rewarding than endorsements, symbolic campaigns, or referenda. The work is enormous, and the likelihood of real success only moderate.

13 Social Confrontations: From Legal Tactics to Direct Actions

Demonstrations, sit-ins, pickets, injunctions, and boycotts symbolize the failure of conventional politics to respond to popular demands. Confrontations get the attention of targets and communicate in no uncertain terms that social injustices must be addressed now. Confrontation tactics force those in power to solve problems and to take an action organization seriously as a contender for power. In addition, social confrontations publicize the severity of a problem. Having the homeless camp out at city hall calls public attention to the lack of affordable housing and virtually compels officials to find at least temporary shelter for those protesters.

Legal actions use the courts to force those in positions of power to live up to their own rules and agreements. Direct-action campaigns challenge the opponent's rules, demanding that problems be solved now.

LEGAL CAMPAIGNS

After persuasion and petitions to those in power have failed, legal tactics are one way of forcing a solution. Courts can order targets to stop evicting individuals from their homes; courts can mandate compensation for damages caused by toxic waste. Judges can give interpretations of poorly written legislation that clarify the responsibility of governmental agencies. For example, courts clarified the badly written environmental laws so that government regulators had to protect the environment (Sax, 1971, pp. 108–124). Legal tactics can force governmental officials to carry out laws. This has been a central focus of civil rights campaigns.

Benefits of Legal Campaigns

Legal campaigns enhance the organization's legitimacy, help create badly needed delays, and are a tool for obtaining information about the opponent. The threat of a lawsuit sometimes brings opponents to the bargaining table. Courts can help protect the organization from retaliation and preserve the speech rights that permit public dissent.

When a court recognizes the grievances of the homeless, the handicapped, or those harmed by pollution, both the issues and the protest are granted legitimacy. The opposition may think of organization members as destructive rabble rousers, but in court, the public face of the group is a neatly dressed lawyer whose willingness and ability to work through the court system suggests respectability.

A second advantage is that legal tactics can stall the opponents. If a government redevelopment authority issues dispossession notices to residents before they have a chance to react, sue. The minute papers have been served, the opponents must stop or risk being in contempt of court. A recent environmental campaign delayed lumbering in the Northwest with a lawsuit to determine the fate of an endangered owl. Damage was halted while the organization gained breathing space to plan its next actions and to rally its troops.

Sometimes the delay itself is a victory. Through lawsuits, elderly residents of single-room occupancy hotels held off eviction actions by the San Francisco Redevelopment Agency for half a decade. The action organization—TOOR—sued the Redevelopment Agency and the federal Department of Housing and Urban Development, claiming that decent housing was not being provided to people who were relocated. When government agencies delayed in fulfilling these legal requirements, a judge ordered a halt to all renewal activity until an agreement was reached about replacement housing (C. Hartman, 1974, pp. 123–157).

A third advantage of legal tactics is that they can provide information about opponents that can be used against them. Once a case has been filed, an action organization can gain information through discovery. *Discovery* is the legal procedure that allows lawyers to examine documents germane to the case even if the documents are in the possession of the opponent. Through discovery, community organizations found internal reports of the Department of Interior that showed that public water was being sold far below market costs to large-scale commercial farmers. These figures on the extent of subsidy can be used to pressure government to conserve water, to reduce the amount of tax money used to subsidize the well-to-do, or to increase subsidies to the poor.

A fourth advantage of legal tactics is that they are so expensive that sometimes the threat of suit alone can lead to negotiations. For example, a builder generally borrows money to buy land and build houses, only paying off the notes when the homes are sold. If a community group obtains an injunction against the builder, the construction is delayed, so the loan is producing no revenue. To avoid the squabble, a housing developer might be willing to provide some housing for the poor.

Legal actions can preserve and widen the legitimate scope for other forms of direct action.

The targets of direct-action campaigns may fight back by trying to stop assemblies or demonstrations. For example, they may require tremendous amounts of insurance before allowing use of a public park. To maintain the ability to act, progressive organizations then fight to preserve the constitutional guarantees of the right to assemble, petition, receive redress, and speak freely.

Free speech is not enough if access to an audience is precluded. In the past, people congregated on public sidewalks or in parks, where action organizations could present their case. At present, people are more likely to be found at privately owned shopping malls. Mall owners have sought to exclude action organizations, claiming they were trespassing on private property. Action organizations have fought back to defend speech rights. Though court decisions have been mixed, the trend has been to open malls for petitioning and issue advocacy (W. Freedman, 1988).

Legal Tactics

There are two major forms of legal action, injunctions and lawsuits. *Injunctions* are court orders to stop possibly harmful actions until additional facts are gathered. Environmental organizations commonly use injunctions to halt construction projects that might harm plants and animals. Neighborhood organizations use an injunction to prevent a developer from tearing down apartments until a court can rule on the developer's right to do so.

Suits are filed to right a wrong, to claim compensation for harm done, or to make a party perform as agreed. Suits filed to make somebody live up to a contract are called *performance suits*. For example, when the Reagan administration tried to trim the number of people receiving social security disability payments, the policy was carried out overzealously, so that many eligible people were denied aid. These unfortunate people had to sue to get the aid to which they were legally entitled.

Substantive suits include claims for compensation or redress from such problems as unsafe working conditions, illegitimate exclusion from welfare roles, and faulty work under a contract. When many people are affected by the same substantive problem, they may file a class action suit.

Class action suits are crucial when the overall societal damage is large but the damages suffered by any single person are relatively small, making individual suits prohibitively expensive. Both environmental and consumer activists have successfully fought business abuses through class action suits. Opponents have responded by pressuring government to make it more difficult to bring such a suit. They have insisted that before lawyers can represent people in court, they have to get their clients' permission in writing. This may be a nearly impossible task, if potential clients are scattered throughout the country. In response, advocacy organizations pressure governmental regulatory agencies, which do have legal standing, to bring the suits.

A *procedural suit* can be brought if a government or regulatory body does not follow its own bureaucratic procedures. Consumer organizations concerned about the safety of food additives and drugs sued for action after claiming that the Food and Drug Administration ignored the scientific evidence of product harm. In a zoning case, a procedural suit would be in order if the city's regulations state that abutters may testify and a zoning board refused to receive testimony from them. Procedural cases do not determine the correctness of outcomes but determine whether the rules were followed.

An action organization greatly improves its bargaining power if it can catch bureaucratic agencies in procedural errors. A housing agency that does not follow its own regulations for publicizing building code violations, a civil rights agency that holds closed hearings, or an environmental agency that ignores its rules that require businesses and governments to fill out environmental impact statements are all vulnerable to law suits. To avoid a loss in court, they might start enforcing the regulations.

Problems With Legal Tactics

Legal strategies can bring opponents to the bargaining table and are often necessary to maintain freedom of speech and assembly. But legal tactics have a number of drawbacks. For one thing, rather than intimidate opponents, they stimulate opponents to sue the organization or use the court system for their own ends. Second, when seeking legal redress at the state level, solutions in one state do not carry over into any other state. Third, even when the courts decide in the organization's favor, the solution may be only temporary. Most important, legal strategies are expensive in time and money and, because they require specialized expertise, might not provide an empowering experience for the membership of an organization.

Opponents Fight Back.   Progressive organizations can lose in court, and the opponents can fight back. In recent years, the courts have systematically limited access to abortion, while recent court rulings have greatly weakened the use of the Freedom of Information Act that had been used to gain information in civil rights suits (Evans, 1989, p. 3).

> Every year . . . hundreds, perhaps thousands, of civil lawsuits are filed that are aimed at preventing citizens from exercising their political rights or punishing those who have done so. . . . when the National Organization for Women organized a boycott of conventions in states whose legislators had not ratified the Equal Rights Amendment, the attorney general of Missouri sued NOW on behalf of affected local business. (Canan & Pring, 1988, p. 506)

Countersuits are becoming a real problem.

Variability From State to State.   Another problem of legal tactics is that laws differ from state to state. For example, the legal rights of tenants vary from Indiana, with weak pro-tenant laws, to Massachusetts, where tenants are protected by implied warranties that housing is habitable, tenants have a right to deduct repair costs from rents, and tenants cannot be evicted for taking action to promote tenants' rights (J. Joseph, 1983, p. 133). Rent strikes are feasible in New York City because strong laws protect the strikers; elsewhere rent strikes might not be a viable tactic.

Advocates for the homeless have won significant victories in some states, but the tools they have used do not apply in other states.

> Despite the strengths and recent victories of legal advocacy in behalf of the homeless, this tactic does contain inherent limitations. To begin with a number of states do not have statutes or administrative codes that parallel those which exist in New York or Connecticut. (Fabricant & Epstein, 1984, p. 16)

In the last several decades, civil rights and civil liberties organizations tended to rely on federal courts. Federal courts were more likely to escape parochial local interests—southern state judges came out of the same legal system that civil rights activists opposed. Also, the decisions of federal courts have a national rather than a local impact. Today, the choice of which court to use is less clear, because federal judges appointed by conservative politicians are less likely to rule in favor of progressive organizations. In some cases, state courts may be a better choice.

> The United States Supreme Court's civil liberties rulings have grown more restrictive. . . . New York's highest court has been battling this trend by basing its decisions increasingly on the New York State Constitution . . . to extend protections for individuals beyond those granted by the United States Supreme Court. (Kolbert, 1990, p. 12)

Short-Lived Victories.   In many cases, legal victories may only be temporary. If an action organization succeeds and obtains a new interpretation of a law, opponents may bring pressure to change the law itself. For example, consumers have been protected by liability laws that permit suits for negligence and product defects. Consequently,

> since 1981, most large companies . . . and their trade associations have been battering away at the Congress, trying to get a preemptive federal product liability law passed that would allow manufacturers and sellers to place dangerous products on the market with diminished liability to the people they injure. (Claybrook, 1988, p. 23)

More generally,

> A decade ago, legal victories seemed to outlast victories won by other means. Today, we are seeing environmental laws repealed and past legal actions revoked. A similar trend seems to be at work in the civil rights area. In the final analysis, the law is political and it changes as political events move to the left or the right over a period of years. (Midwest Academy, 1973, p. 64)

Lawsuits Are Expensive and Require Professional Staff.   Legal suits involve large expenditures of both time and money to hire lawyers, do research, and make presentations in court. Interest groups such as the National Sexual Harassment Legal Back-up Center of the Working Women's Institution, the Women's Legal Defense Fund, the National Organization for Women (NOW) Legal Defense and Education Fund (Deckard, 1983, p. 381) and the Environmental Defense Fund maintain lawyers on their staffs. Organizations such as the American Civil Liberties Union and Public Citizen employ their own lawyers. These organizations have limited resources and have to pick which cases to work on. Most of the time, the opponents of an action organization are better able to afford court costs than a voluntary organization.

Even when lawyers are available, it is questionable whether their use contributes to the capacity building and empowerment ideals of the community development ideology. When a community organization depends on outside experts, members of the organization might lose the sense that they can accomplish anything on their own; they might not even be aware of what is being accomplished.

> Trials are held during the day, which often precludes attendance by workers. The litigation time line is not controlled by members and can be lengthy. The role that members can play is extremely limited, so a litigation project does not facilitate leadership develop-

ment. It is difficult to recruit members around legal cases for these reasons, which means it is difficult to build the power of the organization. (Gaventa et al., 1990, p. 115)

The goal of capacity building can get shunted aside in the effort to win a case. For example, the costs of reliance on lawyers were evident in the anti-urban renewal campaigns in San Francisco.

> While the lawyers and litigation strategy . . . were crucial to [the community group's] success in fighting the . . . project, there can be no substitute for internal organizational strength. . . . When a community of poor people places its faith in outside professionals, it becomes dependent on individuals from a different social class who have their own agendas, reference groups, priorities, and styles. (C. Hartman, 1974, pp. 207–208)

To combat this problem, some organizations devise ways to involve their members in legal tactics. ACORN (Association of Community Organizations for Reform Now) activists describe how members of tenants' organizations and rural labor organizations serve legal papers on their opponents.

> [This] offers exciting opportunities: "I went right up to the door of that mansion. You should have seen the look on his face when he took the paper. I thought I was nothing compared to him, but he had to take the paper from me and see the medicine we had planned for him." (McCreight, 1984, p. 183)

Some organizations can involve their members in the information-gathering and detective work preparatory for court hearings. Chicago housing activists work with city housing inspectors to document problems, gather background data on tax delinquencies of unscrupulous landlords, and find out who owns certain buildings when ownership is hidden through blind trusts (R. Slayton, 1986b). This way, people in progressive organizations can improve their chances by gathering information that an overburdened court system is either unwilling or unable to get.

To summarize, legal tactics are varied and often effective, though slow and expensive. Injunctions gain time to prepare for a longer-term battle while finding procedural irregularities, which is a way of enforcing bureaucratic fairness. Yet, whether one wins or loses in court is a chancy proposition, and time spent in court often distracts from mobilizing large numbers of active members. Still as part of a general campaign, the threat of a court suit and the potential for carrying one out can give the target pause, and with luck, can force negotiations.

DIRECT ACTIONS

Direct action tactics vary from large-scale demonstrations complete with militant speakers and milling crowds to a silent vigil by candlelight. Direct actions include marches, sit-ins, rallies, boycotts, and rent strikes, as well as diverse forms of active nonviolence, such as lying in the path of a bulldozer to stop destruction of a park. Some direct action tactics involve mocking of opposition while others are illegal or even violent, such as the sabotage of industrial plants that are polluting the environment.

Preconditions for Direct Action Campaigns

Direct action campaigns must not be undertaken lightly; they require people's time and moral commitment to the issue, and sometimes they involve risk. Only try direct action after a conventional approach has failed, and then do so cautiously by engaging in testing actions that "continuously explore the protective armor of the power structure" (Jenkins, 1985, p. 6). The testing actions find the vulnerabilities of the opponent.

When planning campaigns, give thought to the symbolic meaning of the protest. A dramatic turning point occurred in the civil rights protests in Birmingham, Alabama, when the children began to march. The children put themselves in danger, symbolizing the depth of commitment of the civil rights marchers, as well as the meanness of the segregationists for arresting children.

> Reporters saw things they had never seen before. George Wall, a tough-looking police captain, confronted a group of thirty-eight elementary-school children and did his best to cajole or intimidate them into leaving the lines, but they all said they knew what they were doing. Asked her age as she climbed into a paddy wagon, a tiny girl called out that she was six. (Branch, 1988, p. 757)

The arrest of the young did not immediately resolve the issue, but the publicity dramatically illustrated the problems of segregation, while the eventual freeing of the children symbolized the freeing of all African-Americans.

The symbolism of direct action must catch the public eye. Organizations of office workers skillfully designed such tactics.

> Office worker groups . . . had developed an effective model of corporate campaigns, combining the elements of lively and imaginative public rallies (Heartless Awards on Valentine's Day, Scrooge of the Year at Christmas) with threats of investigations by federal

Catchy slogans create important organizing symbols. (Courtesy National People's Action)

anti-discrimination agencies and letters to boards of directors, stockholders, and customers. The organization relied on the eagerness of corporations to get out of the public eye and their willingness to make some policy compromises to keep a good public image on women's issues. (Gaventa et al., 1990, p. 207)

Philosophies of Direct Action

There are two approaches to direct action. The first—*Alinsky tactics*—is a pragmatic, do-what-you-have-to-do approach in which actions grow out of the situation at hand. The second philosophy is *active nonviolence,* in which the means are as important as the ends they seek to accomplish.

Alinsky Tactics for Direct Action Campaigns.   Saul Alinsky prepared a set of pragmatic rules for social action campaigns (Alinsky, 1971, pp. 127–130). The rules capitalize on the weaknesses of the opponent and are planned with an awareness of how far members of the action organization are willing to go in a campaign. They emphasize the threat of social disruption as well as the opponent's fear of bad public relations.

Tactics Must Receive Support From Within the Organization.   The tactics chosen by an organization must be those enjoyed by its members. Long campaigns fatigue members who want to see some immediate results.

In Alinsky's (1971, pp. 127–130) words

1. Never go outside the experience of your people.
2. A tactic that drags on too long becomes a drag.
3. A good tactic is one your people enjoy.

Use Direct Actions to Enhance the Image of Power of the Organization.   Usually, community groups are bargaining from positions of weakness. Accordingly, tactics should emphasize the potential for disruption. A city council might fear the bad publicity from a mob scene in the council chambers; an actual protest, though, could easily be dispersed by local police. Trying to carry out a threat risks displaying the weakness of the organization.

As Alinsky (1971, pp. 127–130) argued

4. Power is not only what you have but what the enemy thinks you have.
5. The threat is usually more terrifying than the thing itself.

Effective Tactics Show an Understanding of the Rules of the Game by Mocking Them.
Rather than presenting an alternative to the current system, Alinsky advocated mocking the rules set up by the opponent. Opening up numerous small bank accounts at the main office of a bank superficially is buying into the bank's rules; wise people save. But this tactic is threatening, because members of the organization are tying up the bank.

During the Vietnam war era, protesters flooded the Selective Service Office (draft boards) with mail describing each change in status, as required by the law. As one of the organizers explained

We want everyone to take this law so seriously that they inform their board of every single change, even if they're over age or have already completed their service. This means wives, mothers, and friends as well. They should submit documents attesting to any change in the status of the registrant. The Selective Service just cannot stand up, administratively, to absolute obedience to the draft law. (G. Sharp, 1973, p. 417)

Protest activities must be applied steadily. Keep it up long enough, and your opponents will weary, perhaps make mistakes, or be willing to negotiate with the action organization. An opponent might even laugh after one or two bank-ins, bathroom-ins, or mock press conferences at which they are satirized.

Alinsky was famous for outlandish tactics that wore down the resistance of the enemy. He advocated:

6. Whenever possible go out of the experience of the enemy.
7. Make the enemy live up to their own books of rules.
8. Ridicule is man's [sic] most potent weapon.
9. Keep the pressure on.
10. The major premise for tactics is the development of operations that will maintain a constant pressure upon the opposition.
(Alinsky, 1971, pp. 127–130)

Don't Fight Institutions.   Specific individuals rather than institutions should be the target of the campaign. Who can attack the telephone company or the government? If is far easier to attack the callousness of the president of the company, Mr. Smith, who won't let shut-in elderly people have affordable phones, while he has a telephone in his limousine. Community members might not fully understand how corporate power works. They can understand the good life of the head of a company and picture him or her as indifferent to the plight of the poor.

Alinsky's summary of this point is his most often quoted aphorism:

11. Pick the target, freeze it, personalize it, and polarize it. (Alinsky, 1971, pp. 127–130)

Be Patient Until Your Opponents Make a Mistake.   The purpose of continual pressure is to cause your opponents to make a mistake. Perhaps they will get impatient, call the police to break up a meeting, and create sympathy for the community group. Perhaps they will deny members of the action organization the right of free speech or assembly, leading to court suits that the organization will win. The goal is to make them make a mistake that strengthens the cause.

For example, Ralph Nader was able to successfully attack GM after they made the mistake of spying on his personal life. President Reagan's first Secretary of Interior, James Watt, a person unpopular among environmental groups, was replaced only after he publicly made comments that were interpreted as racist and antagonistic to handicapped people. Environmental organizations could not defeat the man on his policies.

Organizations can gain power by taking advantage of the opposition's fear of making a mistake. In one demonstration, the elderly intentionally acted boisterously at public hearings. Officials running such meetings normally would expel unruly people, but this tactic would have backfired if a young marshal were filmed throwing elderly, handicapped people out of the hall (Kleyman, 1974, p. 45).

As Alinsky argued,

12. If you push a negative hard and deep enough it will break through into its counter-side. (Alinsky, 1971, pp. 127–130)

Anticipate the Opponent's Reaction.   Opponents counterattack. Sometimes they will try to delay through setting up a committee to study the problem. Be realistic; if the problem really does need studying, make sure the organization has representatives on the committee, but be sure a deadline is set. If the opposition is simply stalling, continue with the direct actions until they accede to the demands.

A tactic frequently used by the enemy is to concede that the problems are real, then ask the organization to provide a solution. If the target is willing to provide the action organization with the technical and economic resources to solve the problem and is willing to accept the organization's solution with minimal change, accept its proposal. If not, tell the target it has the technical and financial means to solve the problem and should do so. However, it is a good idea to have an alternative proposal in mind. As Alinsky argued,

13. The price of a successful attack is a constructive alternative. (Alinsky, 1971, pp. 127–130)

Nonviolent Direct Action.   Alinsky's approach is the pragmatic one of finding a tactic that works. Alinsky tactics are not intended to be violent, but only because violence usually doesn't win the issue for community organizations. By contrast, the philosophy of nonviolence is based on a narrow set of powerful beliefs. Nonviolence involves a refusal to engage in physical violence even if assaulted, a willingness to be arrested and jailed but an unwillingness to concede on the principles of the matter.

The effectiveness of nonviolent direct action depends on weakening the opponent's legitimacy in the eyes of the public. *Civil disobedience* is a primary form of nonviolent direct action in which activists intentionally disobey a law and then accept without resistance the consequence of the disobedience. Underlying nonviolence is the belief that the means are as important as the end because the moral development of the participants is affected by the form of direct action. To win the battle through immoral tactics is to lose the war by destroying the integrity of the protesters.

Nonviolent tactics consider the consequences of actions on the opponent as well as the activist. While Alinsky set out to discomfort the opponent, those believing in nonviolence argue on the importance of their own suffering. By suffering, they avoid harming the opponent, and keep attention on the issue itself.

Nonviolence, however, must be tactically effective. In Chavez's words:

> We're nonviolent because we want to get social justice for the workers. If all you're inter-ested in . . . is saving your soul, at some point the whole thing breaks down—you say to yourself "Well, let them be violent, as long as I'm nonviolent. Or you begin to think it's okay to lose the battle as long as you remain nonviolent. *The idea is that you have to win and be nonviolent. That's extremely important! You've got to be nonviolent—and you've got to win with nonviolence!* (Chavez quoted in Cooney & Michalowski, 1987, p. 179, emphasis added)

Using nonviolent civil disobedience, members of a protest organization violate an unjust law or policy, putting themselves in a position to be beaten or arrested so they can symbolize the injustice. For example, black people sat in at segregated lunch counters and at the front of the bus during civil rights demonstrations, permitting themselves to be arrested for violation of Jim Crow laws. Their actions symbolized the injustice of racial segregation. The contrast between their stoic acceptance of arrest and the brutality of the southern police shifted public opinion to favor the protesters.

Nonviolent tactics include *sociodrama,* in which members of the organization act out the harm caused by the targets as the media records the events. Creating shanty housing in public squares to demonstrate lack of housing or having people lie down as if dead next to a nuclear reactor site are vivid forms of sociodrama. The symbolism of being nonviolent is meant to contrast with the underlying violence associated with nuclear energy and bombs (Downey, 1986, p. 369).

Nonviolent tactics are designed for symbolic impact. Environmentalists and antiwar activists sail ships into areas of the Pacific in which nuclear testing is to be done. Large groups of antiwar people hold silent vigils around an army base, as if to mourn the dead. During such times, the intent is often to persuade and bring over the opponents and, if possible, even the police.

At times, threats to the life of the nonviolent protester become the symbol of the movement. Hunger strikes in which the leader, as a symbol of the oppressed, refuses to eat until changes have been made vividly demonstrate such moral commitment. Environmentalists who sail into nuclear test zones are risking their lives to typify the danger to wildlife and to people. Civil disobedience makes a symbolic point, but that does not make the violence or danger less real. Nonviolent protesters in the civil rights movement were beaten, often viciously, and some were killed, but the televised image of police using water cannons and dogs to attack nonviolent young protesters cost the segregationists their moral position.

People must be trained for nonviolent tactics. Few people can be beaten and arrested without wanting to defend themselves. People who by temperament are not nonviolent must be kept out of the actions. During the Montgomery Bus Boycotts, there were training schools in nonviolence, and only people trained and experienced in nonviolence were allowed to become Freedom Riders (Branch, 1988, p. 438). Such training has to be done with care because "you don't push a person beyond their commitment" (Branch, 1988, pp. 471–472). During exercises in civil disobedience, those with the greatest experience in nonviolent tactics must be placed throughout the protest crowd, ready to intervene if, in the heat of the moment, tempers flare.

Training and Tactics Can Converge.   In Europe, the Women's Peace Movement held camps on nonviolence on the perimeter of Cruise missile bases. The opportunity for putting the lessons into practice was immediately available for those who were willing. Similar approaches have been followed by antinuclear activists in the United States.

While different from Alinsky tactics in a variety of ways, the tactics of nonviolence, like Alinsky's approach, are premised on building a sense of community or neighborhood commitment (Levene, 1985). Nonviolent tactics are usually found in members of closely linked affinity groups who are willing to put their bodies on the line and collectively suffer beatings or arrest to make the political point (Barkan, 1980). Facing such dangers together creates a long-lasting feeling of solidarity, even among strangers.

Characteristics of Direct Action Tactics

Alinsky tactics emphasize cleverness, having fun, and mockery. Nonviolent tactics emphasize suffering, endangerment of the self, and moral worth. Once an organizer has decided which of these two overall strategies to pursue, there are still a number of choices to be made. In picking tactics that make sense in a campaign, the goal is to play to the organization's strengths and the opponent's weaknesses. To do that requires knowledge of how tactics are supposed to work.

Direct action tactics can be grouped on three characteristics. The first characteristic is the extent to which the tactics are aimed to win support from public opinion. The second is the extent to which the tactics rely on the mistakes and weaknesses in the opponent. The third characteristic is the degree to which the tactic is a form of direct power to force change.

The goal of informational campaigns is to affect the broader climate in favor of the progressive organization. Public disruptions are most effective when they build on mistakes of the opponents, yet win broad public support by putting the bodies of the demonstrators on the line. Finally, economic pressures focus on an immediate target, to force a favorable outcome such as getting apartments repaired or getting specially equipped phones at low cost for the hearing impaired.

Informational Campaigns.   Information campaigns might be an outgrowth of the action research discussed in Chapter 8, in which the organization digs up facts and figures that embarrass the opponent. A second type of campaign involves teach-ins. Focused on students, teach-ins typically involve debates that elevate the level of awareness about a policy issue. The third type of informational campaign is aimed at the community at large, to tilt public opinion through open forums, door-to-door contacts, magazine or newspaper articles, or talk shows.

Dramatically presented information can force people in the public eye to live up to their promises to bring about improvements. The Nader Public Interest Research Groups specialize in using information as a weapon for reform. The California PIRG discovered that stores were intentionally misgrading meats; another PIRG did a report that showed that the conversion of military jobs to civilian employment would increase the number employed. Such reports contradict widely held myths and help bring about change. Moreover, they involve the membership in empowering ways.

> Equipped with hipboots, maps of streams, data sheets and a list of industries and their discharge permits, students would hike or canoe along stream beds and make systematic assessments of sources of pollution. Their findings . . . were used by local community and environmental groups, as well as understaffed county, state and federal agencies charged with monitoring industrial discharges. (Griffin, 1987, pp. 19–20)

The act of informing others can simultaneously mobilize people and pressure the opposition. Teach-ins mobilize people by informing them about the need for collective action. If members of the opposition show up, they may feel the pressure of the criticism and the embarrassment of questions they cannot answer. Teach-ins were a major part of the anti-Vietnam war movement:

Local experts would teach about Vietnam. . . . Some three thousand students attended Ann Arbor's all-night teach-in; the atmosphere was electric, and copies sprang up on campuses everywhere. . . . The State Department even agreed to send out speakers, most of whom got trounced. (Gitlin, 1987, pp. 187–188)

The use of teach-ins for the antiwar movement made sense because many of the college students were eligible for the draft and were the most likely to be activated. Teach-ins are effective if knowledgeable people can convey factual material in a charged atmosphere. A debate by well-known public figures may raise the level of interest of noncommitted students. This tactic makes sense for highly controversial topics that affect college campuses, perhaps abortion issues in states advocating more restrictive laws or racial discrimination on campuses torn with violent or emotional incidents.

Relatively few situations qualify for teach-ins, but many more qualify for community education. Community education programs, especially in the environmental movement, combine the Nader information-gathering-for-action approaches with some of the information-as-mobilization-and-as-pressure approaches of the teach-ins. Using the tools of action research, people learn about environmental problems and then hold community forums that inform concerned neighbors of the problem. A frequent side benefit is that when confronted by knowledgeable opponents the opposition shows itself to be ignorant of technical details, which makes them look foolish and denies them legitimacy.

Antinuclear activists have sometimes sponsored debates with representatives of the nuclear power industry. By inviting sympathetic scientists . . . the group can directly challenge corporate or government arguments. Many groups report that industry or government representatives are often so ill-informed or deceptive that they discredit themselves. An official of Dow Chemical, for example, testified at a California public hearing on [a pesticide] that despite animal research showing testicular damage from the pesticide, it had not occurred to Dow that it might also harm human male reproductive ability. (Freudenberg, 1984, p. 139)

These forums have the advantage of including opponents and deflating their arguments. Activists feel efficacious, and the target is discomforted.

Public Disruptions.   Public disruptions include rallies, marches, sit-ins, and vigils, as well as slow-downs of services, traffic blockages, and demonstrations. They bring about disarray by halting traffic flow, drawing large crowds, using loudspeakers, filling up parks with tent cities, and generally interrupting the normal flow of activity. They create news, imply the potential for violence, and tempt the opponents to retaliate in ways that may create a climate more sympathetic to the protesters. The fear of future social disorders might put some important questions on the public agenda.

Rallies

Rallies accomplish three purposes:

- Show the opposition that the action organization can mobilize large numbers of people for the cause

Congress is unlikely to ignore this rally. (Courtesy Department of Housing and Urban Development)

- Provide supporters and potential supporters with information and a sense that they are not alone in their cause
- Provide the mass media with information about why the organization is protesting and how important the issues are that are being raised

Care is required in balancing these objectives. Speakers should make strong enthusiastic statements meant to rally the troops, but they have to watch out that these statements aren't misconstrued by the press and television. The mass media should focus on the issues and not on the act of protest itself. The headlines should not read, "unruly mob lambasts city council" but "displaced people demand adequate housing."

The lore of social activism contains many examples of successful demonstrations. The 1963 March on Washington for Civil Rights is legendary for Dr. King's "I Have a Dream" speech and for the size and excitement of the huge rally. The whole nation (including the President and Vice President) were exposed to the power of King's speech. The rally was on national television and had an audience near the Washington Monument of between 200,000 and 500,000 participants. Just holding the rally was an accomplishment that demonstrated the participants' power to themselves and to the outside world.

More recently, in response to Supreme Court rulings weakening abortion rights, NOW arranged a rally in Washington, DC.

By all estimates— 300,000 according to the United States Park Police—it was a recordbreaking crowd for such an event. . . . People came from every state . . . and from 12 foreign countries. ("Aboard Bus D," 1989, pp. 1, 6)

Demonstrators who had fought the battles of a previous generation shared their hopes (and fears) with the young and future activists.

While few organizers plan huge national rallies, the chances are good that a community organizer will at some time stage a more modest public rally. Such events are difficult to run and require considerable attention to detail. The following are some guidelines for running such a rally (modified from Burghardt, 1982a; Cassidy, 1980; Midwest Academy, 1976/1981).

1. Look over the rally site. If it's a wide plaza, make sure cameras will be located in places that make the group appear larger. Place loudspeakers so everyone can hear. If the rally is taking place inside a building, make sure people can get in. It is a wise idea to plant somebody inside just in case the opposition tries to lock the organization out.
2. Slightly underestimate the size of the turnout. If leaders estimate that 100 people will appear, announce that 75 will show up, and plan a space for about 70 to 100 people. Don't grossly underestimate the size of the crowd, or some supporters might be discouraged and not show up.
3. Do the leg work to ensure that people turn out. Don't rely on general promises of support. One technique to turn people out is to set up a telephone network and call all the members of the organization before the rally to remind them to come.

   Make sure the rallies are held at a time convenient for the participants. If working with a neighborhood organization, provide transportation from schools or churches in the neighborhood to the site of the speeches. For issue-based organizations with a widely dispersed membership, collect information on how to get to the site and send the information to the participants. For example, if arranging a demonstration in the state capital, make sure the local organizations are aware of how to charter a bus to get their group to the site.
4. Explain to speakers and activists in the group in advance what is expected at the rally. The time for creative ideas is the planning sessions among members of the organization, not in front of the mass media. A call for revolution at a nonviolent rally or spontaneous civil disobedience can leave a group in disarray. The audience should show enthusiasm for the speakers but maintain general decorum to present a credible image of the organization.
5. To maintain crowd control, choose marshals from the active core of the organization and place them strategically throughout the site. Signals should be worked out for communicating with the marshals if disorder occurs.

   Crowd control can also be maintained in ways that emphasize the message of the rally. People do listen to music and will join in, so plan songs that will inspire the participants and provide a center of attention.
6. Arrange that speeches, messages on signs, and other communications be available in press-release form for the mass media. Tell media representatives what is planned. If the highlight of the demonstration is a flag burning and that is the image you want to communicate, make sure the media know where to point their cameras. Better yet, assign someone full-time to interpret the events for the media. Remember, the media will also be getting a statement from the opposition.

7. Balance speeches meant to stir up members of the opposition with those intended to intimidate opponents or appeal to public opinion. In dress and mannerism, try to present a "cooler"—less disruptive—image than the content of the messages might indicate. A neatly dressed person can get away with a militant speech without appearing so threatening on the 6 o'clock news that the message is ignored. Image management is especially important because the opposition tries to maintain control by putting down social protest groups—humorless feminists, disheveled college students—rather than paying attention to the issues they raise.

Paint slogans or complaints clearly; newspeople are likely to photograph them. If threats are to be voiced, try not to put them in easily photographable formats. The direct targets of the campaign will still hear the threats, but the broader public will pay them less attention. If the press picks up on the threats, it may create a negative image for the organization, win sympathy for the opposition, and perhaps force public officials into the role of "tough guys."

Symbolic actions can be quite effective for communicating a message without thoroughly alienating the uncommitted spectator. Mock funerals, for example, burying a civil rights law after the city has stopped enforcing it, make the point clearly yet maintain the culturally accepted solemnity of a burial.

Tying tactics to religious ceremonies is effective when moral values underlie the protest action. Much of the civil rights movement has been led by religious figures, who use prayer in the rallies. The same tactic has been followed in demonstrations and rallies among unemployed workers, especially in the steel towns of the rustbelt (Harrington, 1984).

8. Plan the end of the rally. It is a terrible idea to leave large numbers of inflamed people milling around without a purpose. Police raids often occur after the speeches are over, when the press has left and cannot take pictures.

One way to end the rally is to march out together singing solidarity songs. This kind of exit leaves participants with a good feeling and also quickly clears the demonstration site.

It is wise, though, to have lawyers on call in case of arrests. In addition, information should be spread among participants on how to handle suits for false arrest (J. Joseph, 1983, p. 192).

Moral Demonstrations

The teeming numbers at a rally or demonstration imply a threat of force. In moral demonstrations such as voluntary jailings and fasts, an individual, or at most a few individuals, become the focus of attention. Pressure results as the opposition (and often much of the entire nation) focus on the well-being of those in the moral demonstration. The opposition is stymied as it cannot use force to disrupt an action that is so openly nonviolent. But if the demonstration continues, the people who are fasting or languishing in jails may be hurt or die, with negative, possibly violent consequences.

While rare in American traditions, the hunger fast can be an effective moral demonstration that discomforts the enemy, calls attention to the cause, and rallies the supporters for further efforts. Cesar Chavez's famous fast during the grape boycott succeeded in getting national attention. Among the farm workers, it evoked admiration because "this is part of the Mexican culture—the penance, the whole idea of suffering for something, of self-inflicted punishment" (J. Levy, 1975, p. 277). The fast emphasized the need for nonviolence among strikers, whose patience with growers was wearing thin. The fast also provided a sense of solidarity among the different groups in the movement.

> Before the fast, there were nine ranch committees, one for each winery. The fast, for the first time, made a Union out of those ranch committees, because they had some common things to work on—what was happening there, and how they were going to organize to go down to the courthouse. Everyone worked together. (J. Levy, 1975, p. 283)

This moral demonstration emphasized to sympathizers across the nation the need to continue the grape boycott and brought in Senator Robert Kennedy on the side of the farm workers.

Another form of moral demonstration involves accepting jailing. Jail-ins combine both moral force with tactical advantage.

> Another [of those jailed] had written a letter . . . "Try to understand that what I'm doing is right. It isn't like going to jail for a crime like stealing or killing, but we are going for the betterment of all Negroes." . . .
>
> What made the Rock Hill action so timely, however, was that it responded to a tactical dilemma . . . how to avoid the crippling limitations of scarce bail money. The obvious advantage of "jail, no bail" was that it reversed the financial burden of protest, costing the demonstrators no cash while obligating the authorities to pay for jail space and food. (Branch, 1988, pp. 391–392)

The power of moral demonstrations becomes greater when those who go to jail do so to discomfort the opponents. For example, Dr. King refused bail and while incarcerated, he was able to focus the attention of the whole country on his plight (and call attention to the threat of riots or worse that could occur if he were harmed). Yet King was free to prepare eloquent moral statements such as his *Letter From a Birmingham Jail*. The violence of the opposition in forceably jailing a pacifistic man of the cloth was highlighted. (The circumstances under which King wrote this letter are described in Branch, 1988, p. 742.)

Prayer is another form of moral demonstration that focuses attention on a cause. People opposing abortion have combined picketing of abortion clinics with prayer vigils. Unlike the more militant antiabortion protesters, those supporting "Peaceful Prayer Walks" do not argue with opponents or interfere with the use of the clinic. They are trying to symbolize suffering in silence for the unborn (Ginsberg, 1989, p. 95).

Picketing and Marches

In a rally, members of an organization get together to hear speeches about a problem and make appeals that seek broad support; picketing focuses attention on the target of the opposition. In either case, there is the danger that the disruptions will create public anger against the protest organization rather than the target.

Picketing gives the image of potential force. Protesters have picketed nuclear reactors to protest the dangers of nuclear energy, the Love Canal Homeowners Association picketed the governor of New York and President Carter, and demonstrators against the war in Vietnam picketed Vice President Humphrey, who traveled more than did President Johnson, and so was an easier target. Picketing also can show the breadth of public support for the protest group. When Fair Share in Massachusetts picketed then-Governor Dukakis, "firefighters and police, small businesspeople and homeowners joined with black tenants and homemakers" (Boyte, 1980, p. 74).

Picketing is intended to achieve immediate political solutions. Harrington (1984, p. 51) describes how members of the Mon Valley Unemployment Committee stopped the sheriff's sales of the possessions of unemployed workers.

> Eventually, this persuaded the sheriff—who it is said, might run for higher office in the near future—to refuse to go on with this unpopular process, an action supported by a sympathetic judge, who, it is said, might run for higher office in the near future. (Harrington, 1984, p. 51)

ACT-UP, the AIDS Coalition to Unleash Power, uses confrontational picketing at political meetings, at appearances of the Cardinal (whose support for AIDS victims is seen as flagging), in front of pharmaceutical companies, and at bureaucratic offices responsible for helping AIDS victims. Their dramatic efforts gain publicity. They have crumbled a communion wafer in a church and put themselves in a symbolic concentration camp in a Gay Pride parade (DeParle, 1990, p. 11). ACT-UP aims at bringing about an immediate change of policy, and with some success:

> "There's no doubt that they've had an enormous effect," said Dr. Stephen C. Joseph, the New York City Health Commissioner who himself has been a target of ACT-UP's ire. "We've basically changed the way we make drugs available in the last year." (DeParle, 1990, p. 11)

The crucial issue to the success of picketing and marching is the proper recruitment and training of those on the line. For picketing, volunteers must be willing to carry signs and walk endless miles around a plant or an office. Of equal importance, picketers must be trained not to respond to taunts or unpleasant distractions. Giving in to taunts makes the picketers look disorderly and thereby lose legitimacy.

In planning picketing, organizers must consider many details. Some cities have laws about the physical material with which picket signs can be made, to prevent them from being used as weapons. Picketers should be located where they get attention, but if they obstruct traffic or violate private property, they may anger the public and risk arrest. Organizers need to work out a plan to get picketers out of jail.

The amount of planning required for a successful march is enormous. The logistics are formidable, and getting people to the site can overwhelm transportation systems. When Dr. Martin Luther King, Jr., led marches in Chicago during the summer of 1966, months of negotiation were required to determine which groups would participate and to ensure that King's overall philosophy of nonviolence would be observed. The choice of which streets to march down were argued over for weeks because some streets showed the deterioration of housing but other streets better illustrated the effects of discrimination. Whether to ask for police protection became a major tactical decision.

Sit-ins

Sit-ins are more disruptive than most marches. They inconvenience the opponent by taking over offices, highways, lunch counters, stairways, lobbies, or other public places. A sit-in puts protesters eyeball-to-eyeball with the opponent on the opponent's turf. Sit-ins often lead to arrest, because those involved are trespassing.

Some sit-ins seek immediate gains. In the welfare rights movement in Massachusetts, protesters sat-in while demanding services to which the law entitled them (Bailis, 1974, pp. 47–54). The directors of the offices had the authority to grant these demands and often did. Other sit-ins are meant to symbolize a broader issue. When state laws abrogated the fishing rights of Native Americans (which were guaranteed by treaties), they staged a fish-in, catching fish (illegally, according to state law) in full view of the game warden (Sharp, 1973, p. 318). The Native American "capture" of Alcatraz was a symbolic sit-in to emphasize the abnegation of Indian Treaty Rights (G. Sharp, 1973, p. 389).

A successful sit-in inconveniences the opponent, earns press attention, and avoids violence. Environmentalists chaining themselves to trees that are going to be cut down typify such actions. Blocking construction vehicles is a frequent form of sit-in. For example, to stop construction of the Seabrook Reactor in New Hampshire, the Clamshell Alliance conducted a sit-in of over 2,000 individuals.

An unsuccessful sit-in is one that inconveniences lots of people other than the target, has little possibility of bringing about immediate solution to problems, and makes no symbolic case. Even if the intent is to call attention to some broader problem, unless the sit-in and the problem are logically linked, the technique does not work well.

> Perry thought that a traffic jam would be a good way to force people in St. Louis to confront the violence and brutality then being directed against the civil rights movement in the South. . . . Steering the truck onto the Highway 40 exit [the main road] . . . Ivory Perry eased it at an angle across the traffic lane, stepped on the brake, and turned off the ignition. He left the vehicle and locked its doors, pausing only to remove the distributor cap. . . . At about the same time that Perry . . . blocked the . . . exit, other civil rights demonstrators stalled vehicles at two congested locations in other parts of St. Louis. (Lipsitz, 1988, pp. 86–88)

The blockade—a motorized sit-in—got attention, but it did not symbolize the broader issues very well.

In a different type of sit-in, employees take action against their employer. An ordinary sit-in doesn't work in this situation, because it doesn't look very dramatic sitting at your desk, not doing any work. Moreover, if not working jeopardizes public health and safety, workers may lose their legitimacy. A firefighter who allows someone to be killed in a fire is not helping the cause.

Instead, protesters employ a variation of sit-in tactics called *working to the rule.* Employees precisely follow each bureaucratic rule, so that the normal work load of the organization is no longer accomplished. For example, in a protest over low salaries and underfunded facilities, doctors at Boston City Hospital held a "heal-in." They admitted every patient that could benefit from hospital care and provided the best medical service possible. The facility was soon overcrowded, and serious negotiation with the hospital administration began (G. Sharp, 1973, p. 394).

An important part of planning for a successful sit-in is making sure the media has pictures or film that convey the symbols the organization wants to communicate to the public. A picture of an elderly woman waiting in a crowded shelter for the homeless is far more convincing than that of an older teenager. A shot of a mother with her children sitting-in at the health department offices to find out about the medical effects of a chemical dump is far more dramatic than one of a scientist examining chemicals in the water. Such pictures play on deeply held values of the politicians and the public: "Don't kick an elderly mother out in the street" and "a mother should be able to protect her children."

Because the plan is to bring about some immediate concession, members of the protest organization must be available to negotiate with representatives of the target group. Skill and experience are needed to determine when the point of the sit-in has been made and serious negotiations can begin. Giving up the sit-in too early weakens the leverage of the protest organization; too late, and the organization appears unwilling to negotiate and is labeled publicity crazy.

Although the organization is after concessions, not all concessions are equally useful. A concession to end the confrontation that does not touch on the issues that caused the problem in the first place—lack of power, unjust laws, low-paying jobs—is a minor rather than a major victory. Preserving an apartment building occupied by the poor from commercial redevelopment is a victory, but it would be better if the negotiations led city hall to consult with leaders of neighborhood organizations on the overall need for new, affordable housing. Ideally, the consequences of a social action campaign should go beyond the immediate short-term issue on which the campaign focuses.

Monkey Wrenching

When organizers try to bring about larger changes, progress may seem excessively slow. Frustration with the slow rate of change may lead to violence. The Weather faction broke off from the Students for a Democratic Society to implement a strategy of violent sabotage. Some civil rights groups have taken up arms. An absolute pledge of nonviolence is sometimes impossible. Still, community actions should not be based on tactics of preemptive violence.

Monkey wrenching, at least as practiced by some militant environmental organizations, is at the border between the acceptable and the unacceptable. Protesters create economic costs to the opposition, sometimes through clever symbolism, sometimes through dangerous sabotage. Monkey-wrenching tactics were developed by people in such organizations as Earth First! that split off from nonviolent direct-action groups like Greenpeace in frustration over their inability to stop companies from destroying land and animal habitats (D. Russell, 1987, p. 30).

Some monkey-wrenching tactics are symbolic and humorous. They inconvenience the opponent with minimal potential for physical harm.

> In Yellowstone National Park . . . members dressed in bear suits to protest a new hotel smack in the middle of traditional grizzly bear feeding ground. When asked to leave, several members checked into the hotel and ordered berries from room service. (Savage, 1986, p. 36)

More often, tactics are meant to immediately stop the actions of the opponent. Earth First! members have chained and tied themselves to trees. If the lumbering company were to cut down the tree, the protester would be hanged. This is a rather dramatic form of moral demonstration. But the tactics get more extreme with the introduction of direct sabotage, such as "spiking" trees. If a lumberperson hits the spike with a saw, the saw breaks. This can effectively halt lumbering but also might kill a worker. Because of their potential violence, we oppose such tactics.

Still, such groups are gaining in popularity, with 10,000 subscribers claimed by the radical environmental journals. Primers on monkey wrenching have gone into multiple printings (D. Russell, 1987, p. 31). Why? In part, people do get frustrated by the recalcitrance of opponents, especially when government seems to side with the opposition. Also, people feel involved and achieve at least short-term successes: Trees with spikes are not cut down. Groups that encourage radical sabotage create a feeling among large numbers of participants that further success is possible. This approach to direct action contrasts with the controlled, symbolic, and nonviolent actions of Greenpeace, which gain publicity but often neglect the need to involve supporters and make them feel efficacious (D. Russell, 1987, p. 40).

The lesson is that frustration can create violence.

Economic Pressures.   Economic pressure campaigns are meant to accomplish an immediate solution by causing financial hardship to the targets of the protest. Boycotts rely on the support of a wider public while tenants' strikes depend on the determination and unity of the tenants' organization.

Boycotts mean refusing to purchase from a company or to buy a particular form of merchandise in order to pressure a protest target. Targets of boycotts have ranged from specific companies, such as companies owning the nonunionized grape farms, to specific products, such as tuna fish that are caught in ways that endanger dolphins, to entire countries, such as in Greenpeace's efforts to pressure whaling nations to stop killing a nearly extinct animal.

Probably the most famous boycott in recent times was associated with Chavez's efforts to organize farm labor. To pressure commercial farmers to yield to union demands, Chavez and his supporters organized a national grape boycott until the union was recognized. Today, a similar tactic is being used to force farmers to show concern about the health implications for farm workers of spraying fields with toxic chemicals.

Boycotts directly affect the economic interests of the opponents, interests that are often protected through strict laws that an organization must know and learn how to circumvent. For example, it is perfectly legal to encourage people not to buy a particular product. However, to organize a boycott against a store that sells the product is an illegal secondary boycott. In the grape boycott, activists could tell people not to buy the grapes, but they could not tell people not to shop in stores that sold the grapes.

There are ways around such obstacles, though some are of marginal legality and ethics. In

> the "shop-in" . . . a respectable-looking housewife entered the store, filled her basket and then suddenly discovered that these were scab grapes. She demanded to see the manager. How could he put scab grapes on the shelves when some farm worker's children were starving? The drama became the center of attention. With the eyes of the checkers and customers riveted on the front of the store, the housewife lectured the grocer and then triumphantly marched from the store with children in tow. (Jenkins, 1985, pp. 168–169)

Most protest organizations are too small to affect the finances of the targets, so it is vital to gain the cooperation of others over the wider geographic area in which a product or service is marketed. The grape boycotts were greatly aided when the Teamsters refused to ship nonunion-grown grapes. In addition, liberal organizations and student groups worked nationally to promote the boycott by picketing near grocery stores (Jenkins, 1985, p. 167).

The choice of boycott target can also help. For example, Chavez initially targeted farms owned by the liquor conglomerate Schenley, which cared more about the negative publicity than it did the tiny earnings produced by the wineries. More generally, in boycotts, negative publicity is often as effective a tool as the economic costs. For example, INFACT led an international boycott against Nestles for marketing baby formula in poor countries in which breast feeding was healthier for the child. The direct economic impact was minor compared to the negative publicity that implied a food company was not concerned about the health of children.

Boycotts are most successful when they result in lasting solutions to the original problem. Nestles did change its marketing strategy, and commercial farmers reluctantly accepted unions as representatives of the farm workers.

A tenants' strike is another form of direct economic pressure. In this case, tenants refuse to pay rent until the landlord makes some changes, such as providing adequate heat or eliminating roaches (Lawson, 1986). During the 1960s, there were large numbers of coordinated tenants' strikes, with the most notable in New York City and St. Louis. Though private owners were often struck, the city public housing authority was frequently the target because it housed the poor in inadequate facilities.

In planning a rent strike, an organization must be concerned about the strike's legality, unless the organization has decided to symbolize the issue by letting people get evicted or arrested for nonpayment of rent. In some states, tenants who claim inadequate services can place funds in an escrow account while engaged in a battle with the landlord, but they must pay money to that account every month. In other states, it's illegal to withhold rent no matter what the landlord is doing.

There are tactics that test the waters on the willingness of tenants to participate and stay within the law about the payment of rent.

> Some organizers promoted what they called the "rent slowdown." This was not really a strike, but a strategy in which all tenants held back their rents until the middle of the month, when the tenant leader handed them all to the landlord at the same time. It was an eloquent demonstration of tenant solidarity, and therefore, also a warning to the land-lord, who often responded to tenant grievances at this point. For the tenants, it was in fact an organizational and emotional preparation for a strike should the landlord ignore the warning. (Lawson, 1986, pp. 227–228)

Maintaining organizational solidarity is vital during rent strikes because individual tenants are economically weak compared to the landlord and fear losing their apartments. During most rent strikes, the landlord will try to divide the tenants by pressuring or bribing them to break ranks with co-strikers. A worthy counterstrategy is the rolling rent strike in which only selected landlords are struck but tenants living in other houses support and encourage the strikers. This can divide landlord against landlord rather than tenant against tenant. The task of the organizer is to keep on top of these efforts and constantly reassure the tenants that the ranks are holding (Brill, 1971; Lipsky, 1970; Worthy, 1976).

Tenant strikes can bootstrap to greater power. In St. Louis, the tenants strikes led to eventual tenant management of public housing (Lipsitz, 1988, p. 163) and later involvement of tenants' associations in the committees planning urban redevelopment (Lipsitz, 1988, p. 171). In New York City, the strikes encouraged the courts to be more willing to handle landlord-tenant disputes. Concern with tenants' rights and powers instigated ACORN to conduct squatters campaigns in which those without housing or with poor housing marched in and took over abandoned homes and started upgrading them for habitation (Borgos, 1986).

Problems With Confrontation Tactics

Confrontation tactics can be risky. They may provoke the opposition to strike back more harshly than expected. They may distract from efforts to build the organization. And they may fail to achieve long-term gains.

The Opposition Responds.   Protest organizations walk a thin line between intimidating the opposition into compliance and encouraging them to organize for a counterthrust. Long-term and continuous disruption may well bring forth countertactics that overwhelm the protest groups.

The opposition can use force to destroy protest groups. Those in power can turn one group against another, exploiting tensions between groups. Opponents can accuse the group's leader of being communist, homosexual or lesbian, an embezzler, or a philanderer. Opponents charge that protest is un-American. They may also mount their own campaigns against social change. Jerry Falwell of the activist religious right, Phyllis Schlafly of the antifeminists, and David Duke, a former Ku Klux Klan leader who was elected to the Louisiana legislature, have lead such campaigns.

In response to the gains of feminists, strong and effective opposition arose paralleling the organizing tactics of progressive movements.

> [Phyllis Schlafly] established a national movement STOP ERA, and immediately began to mobilize the loyalists she had attracted. . . . Within months, Schlafly had constructed a minutely organized campaign which could respond immediately where action was necessary. (Hartman, 1989, p. 136)

Similar efforts have been made to oppose abortion rights and to attack the progress made by gay-rights activists (Adam, 1987).

Another tactic is the *pseudo-solution,* in which a board or a committee is established to handle the problem that caused the confrontation in the first place. Some Human Relations Committees become forums for masking racial, sexual, and gender discrimination. More generally, grievance committees can distract from organizing efforts, because "grievance systems are often used by management to delay and derail resolution of grievances" (Fantasia, 1988, p. 115). Even when grievance systems work, they focus on the individual's problems rather than the structural causes of problems. They distract from the need to build organizations and create a countervailing power.

Distracts From Organization Building.   While confrontations are required in the battle for power, power is maintained by building progressive organizations and not by glorying in short-term victories. Cesar Chavez, whose leadership ability in confrontations was apparent, still emphasized that

> a movement with some lasting organization is a lot less dramatic than a movement with a lot of demonstrations and a lot of marches and so forth. The more dramatic organization does catch attention quicker. Over the long haul, however, it's a lot more difficult to keep together because you're not building solid. (Chavez, 1984, p. 28)

Specific complaints should lead to a better organized community and not get sidetracked into grievance systems. (*City Limits*)

Does Not Ensure Implementation.   In the excitement of carrying out a confrontation, a group might neglect to ensure that gains are implemented. It is easy for officials of a business or governmental agency to yield during a demonstration and renege after everyone has gone home. The result of direct actions must be enforceable agreements.

To summarize, direct actions are emotionally charged. They involve the whole membership. They display power. They are often effective in calling attention to problems and are sometimes effective in bringing about solutions to problems. Yet they have to be carefully planned, and they have some built-in problems. For example, they do not necessarily build community organization, and they are not always tightly enough linked to implementation strategies. However, when the rules of the game are biased against the members of the organization, direct actions are the way to begin to solve the problems.

14 | Extending Power: Coalitions, Publicity, and Negotiating Tactics

Skills in building coalitions, obtaining publicity, and in bargaining increase the likelihood that social action campaigns will succeed. Coalitions extend the geographic and political reach of a progressive organization, while publicity campaigns gain community support. Concessions made by opponents in campaigns have to be translated to longer-lasting changes by skillful bargaining and negotiations.

WORKING WITH OTHER ORGANIZATIONS

Progressive organizations remain small, so that they can be responsive to their membership, but small groups have difficulty in tackling major problems. A neighborhood association can carry out a housing fix-up campaign by itself but can do little to force a bank to give loans to community members. To change the bank's behavior, pressure has to be put on city, state, and federal governments. For such a campaign, a community group needs allies.

As obvious as the need is to work with other organizations, doing so can be difficult. Coalition work threatens the autonomy of each group that participates. Potential allies may have different philosophies or may disagree about specific tactics. One may be more or less militant, more or less revolutionary, or more or less honest than another. Or members may be embarrassed to be associated with other groups that favor different forms of social action. For example, in the antinuclear campaign:

> Many of the people who might have pushed strongly for a low keyed grassroots strategy were not only worried about opposition strength, but profoundly concerned about remaining respectable and disassociated with those who did civil disobedience. (Zisk, 1989b, pp. 18–19)

Tensions may be aggravated by competition over money, membership, or credit claiming. Ethnic and racial rivalries extend from neighborhoods to the organizations representing them (Bennett, 1987).

321

Coalitions are necessary when issues cross many different groups. (Thom Clark/*Neighbor-hood Works*)

Yet coalitions have many advantages. They can help provide expertise when local organizations join national coalitions that provide scientific and technical information. Greenpeace and state-level Public Interest Research Groups (PIRGs) provide local environmental groups with information about the consequences of toxic wastes; National Peoples' Action gives advice on how to handle housing laws and regulations. In Illinois, rural action organizations associate with the statewide Illinois Public Action Coalition, which furnishes information on the political vulnerabilities of Illinois legislators (Frank, 1989).

Coalitions allow groups to build on each other's strengths. The more radical groups can test the waters on issues, while other organizations can stand back and see how receptive the public and the targets are to such campaigns (Zwier, 1987). The Equal Rights Amendment (ERA) movement illustrates this strategy:

> One organization within the movement would attract a more conservative membership, another a more radical one. Internally, this decentralization let members of each group feel more comfortable with one another. Externally, the division of labor made possible a "Mutt and Jeff" (or "good cop/bad cop") act, in which the more conservative organization could tell relevant power holders that if certain concessions were not forthcoming it could not hold back the radicals much longer. (Mansbridge, 1986, p. 184)

Because working in coalitions is useful, but difficult, a variety of structures have grown up to deliver what the organizations want from the coalitions while minimizing the inevitable stresses.

Working Together Through a Variety of Structures

Separate organizations work together in cooperative efforts, formal coalitions, alliances, and networks. Each form of collaboration allows organizations choices about the intensity of the relationship. Table 14–1 summarizes the scope of problems, the commitment required, and the governance structure for each form of joint operation.

Cooperative Efforts.   Cooperative efforts are the least structured form of joint activity. Progressive organizations just help each other out on a particular issue. For example, labor unions volunteered not to handle "scab grapes" to support the grape pickers attempt to organize.

With cooperative efforts, there is no long-term commitment between the organizations; agreements are reached case-by-case. For example, two neighborhood associations may agree to jointly put on a demonstration to protest poor city services. Leaders of the cooperating organizations meet once or twice to hammer out tactics and decide when to picket and what signs to carry. Both groups enhance their power by getting more people to the demonstration, and the groups lose almost no autonomy because they have made minimal commitment to each other.

Formal Coalitions.   Formal coalitions are organizations within a geographic area that share complementary goals and decide to work together. Alinsky organizers bring the organizations together to explore how working together might help to accomplish their goals. Alinsky coalitions contain block clubs, church groups, social service organizations, tenants' associations, and business organizations. The members of three Alinsky coalitions are listed in Table 14–2.

The advantage of formal coalitions is that they provide the strength of numbers without committing each organization to all activities. The member organizations continue to perform smaller scale projects independently.

> SECO [Southeast Community Organization] is a coalition organization: a federation of block clubs, improvement and civic associations, senior citizens groups, church groups, and planning councils. By 1980, member groups numbered over 70 and reflected a multiplicity of interests and population within Southeast Baltimore. Each member organization handles its own small issues, but looks to SECO for help on larger issues. (Cunningham & Kotler, 1983, p. 20)

The participating organizations develop a long-term commitment to share ideas. Yet any individual organization need not get involved in any particular campaign of which it disapproves.

In Alinsky coalitions, most decisions are made at the annual meeting. Between the annual meetings, joint actions are proposed by a steering committee, consisting of elected representatives from the different member organizations. Members of the steering committee discuss which issues require joint action and negotiate over strategies. Major decisions made by the steering committee are then brought back to the component organizations for approval.

TABLE 14–1
Separate Organizations Working Together

Scope of problems	
Cooperative efforts	Focuses on narrow immediate problems
Formal Coalitions	A diversity of separate problems considered within one geographic area
Networks	A wide variety of problems shared by different organizations throughout the country
Alliances	Longer-term commitment to specific problem area
Extent of commitment of local organizations	
Cooperative effort	Ad hoc commitment for single campaign
Formal coalitions	Longer-term commitment to joint action but extensive bargaining over which problems to focus on in the joint actions
Networks	Longer-term commitment to a philosophy of organizing; degree of participation variable depending on the immediacy of the problem in the local area
Alliances	Longer-term commitment to a narrow problem area; degree of participation depends on local needs and local tactics
Coordinating agency or governing board	
Cooperative efforts	No formal board; information exchanged between leaders of the different organizations
Formal coalitions	Elected steering committees that might appoint their own staff, but committee members are first of all leaders of their separate organizations
Networks	Permanent board and staff emerge out of local organizations with similar philosophies
Alliances	Permanent board and staff provide information or services to local organizations but work independently of such organizations

Networks.   Formal coalitions are made up of organizations working in a single geographic area. Networks are more likely to be composed of organizations that share a common philosophy or approach, though the individual organizations might be working on a variety of separate issues. Four examples of networks are ACORN (Association of Community Organizations for Reform Now), Citizen Action, National People's Action, and the Industrial Areas Foundation (G. Delgado, 1986, pp. 26–27). Each contain many

TABLE 14–2
The Composition of Alinsky-Style Coalitions

Type of Member Organization	OBA % of All Groups	NCO % of All Groups	SCC % of All Groups
Block clubs	56.5	1.3	3.7
Organization committees	.8	0.0	0.0
Church groups	22.6	56.8	61.0
Association of block clubs	3.2	0.0	0.0
Social service	1.6	7.8	11.0
Public education and youth	5.6	15.5	19.5
Business	0.0	1.3	0.0
Tenants	1.6	0.0	0.0
Miscellaneous	8.1	2.0	2.4
Ethnic	0.0	14.0	0.0
Civic and fraternal	0.0	1.3	2.4
	100%	100%	100%
	N = 124	N = 155	N = 82

NCO, Northwest Community Organization; OBA, Organization for a Better Austin; SCC, Southwest Community Congress.
Source. From *Radicals in Urban Politics: The Alinsky Approach* (p. 53) by R. Bailey, 1974, Chicago: University of Chicago Press. Copyright 1974 by University of Chicago Press. Reprinted by permission.

multipurpose local organizations located in many different cities. The members of each of the networks share a common belief in how to get people mobilized, are more likely to cooperate on some issues than others, and often share a common training program. There is, however, minimal attempt to impose a common set of tasks on the organizations within a network.

A network is likely to support a permanent staff that gathers information, organizes affiliates, and reinforces particular action philosophies through training and technical assistance. The intent is to build strong local organizations regardless of whether they are pursuing similar issues. Integration is maintained through conventions and through frequent interaction between staff and component organizations. The strength of networks emerges from continuing relationships between groups with common action philosophies.

Alliances. Like networks, alliances tend to bring together geographically dispersed organizations. But unlike networks, alliances focus on particular issues, such as supporting the handicapped, protesting toxic waste, or providing information for community-based economic development.

Relationships within alliances ebb and flow according to need. A neighborhood organization might get advice from a toxic waste alliance while working to close a waste site, and later seek advice from a community economic development alliance on how to increase the number of jobs for the poor. During campaigns for the ERA, alliances between feminist organizations were close; after the ERA defeat, these alliances waned but have been recently reinvigorated by the battle over abortion rights.

An alliance often maintains a permanent professional staff in Washington or a state capital to lobby. Unfortunately, alliances do not have much to do with the day-to-day issues that face most groups, and members of the local organization may not participate in national or state lobbying efforts and feel little elation over victories. As a result, the relation between local groups and alliance leadership can become tenuous.

Establishing Cooperation, Coalitions, Networks, and Alliances

How does a group establish cooperation, coalitions, networks or alliances? The first step is to look at the *structural conduciveness* of the environment. That is, is the environment favorable for joint ventures? The second step is to find other organizations that the group is likely to get along with, and set up *interorganizational linkages* between people in different organizations who know each other. The third step is to *cut the issue,* that is, find common interests with other organizations.

Structural Conduciveness.   First examine the conditions in the action environment that encourage or discourage joint work. If the conditions are favorable, even two dissimilar organizations may be able to work together. If conditions are highly unfavorable, even similar organizations may find the costs of working together greater than the benefits.

When financial resources are shrinking, organizations compete more, trust each other less, and are less likely to form coalitions. Under these circumstances, two radical environmental organizations are likely to be rivals, but a radical group might find it easier to work with a more mainstream organization because they are appealing to a different membership base or funding sources. Similarly, organizations whose interests only occasionally overlap may find it easy to cooperate because they are not in competition with each other.

While increased competition over shrinking resources discourages coalitions between rival organizations, other forms of shared adversity encourage cooperation. For example, if police are cracking down on militant environmentalists or if court decisions are eroding civil liberties, environmentalists and civil liberties groups are more likely to join together.

Studies of coalition formation among pro-choice feminist organizations show that changing conditions affect their ability to work together.

> When there are clear indications that victory is possible . . . organizations have a real incentive to combine resources. . . . The pro-choice movement experience suggests that . . . threats provide an even greater incentive for cooperation as the first major countermovement victory, passage of the Hyde Amendment, led to the formation of the most successful pro-choice coalitions. . . . Once exceptional . . . conditions subside, ideological conflicts and organizational maintenance needs of individual movement organizations are likely to cause conflicts within coalitions which may lead to their dissolution. (Staggenborg, 1986, p. 388)

If lack of resources combines with either great opportunity for success or great threat from the opposition, organizations that would normally compete or disagree can often work together.

Interorganizational Linkages.   Under more ordinary circumstances, the more similar organizations are in structure, training, and goals, the more likely that they will be able to cooperate successfully. Also, the more frequent the contact between members of different organizations, the greater the likelihood of successful coordination (Rogers & Whetten, 1982, pp. 54–94).

Coordination is more likely to work if two organizations are compatible on ideology and structure. One organization can be somewhat more militant than the other, but if members of one organization see government as enemies while members of the other organization see government as allies, it may be difficult to work out common strategies. Coordination is most effective when the activists in each group have the same degree of professionalism and commitment. Otherwise, one group will be frustrated at the lack of ability of the other, and the less professional group will fear dominance by the more professional group. Also, coordination is simpler between organizations that choose their leaders in a similar way and have comparable ways of reaching decisions. Groups that make decisions by consensus are unlikely to work easily with groups that deferently follow a charismatic leader, no matter how similar the organizations are in their goals (Rogers & Whetten, 1982, pp. 54–72).

Interpersonal linkages can overcome many of the forces that divide one progressive organization from another. Cooperative work can occur because leaders in one organization know one another and have shared experiences (Galaskiewicz & Shatin, 1981, p. 435). Overlapping membership also encourages cooperative work. If members or leaders meet with each other regularly, they can work out shared understandings of each other's limits and capacities that might otherwise generate resentment.

To summarize, long-term cooperation, without the pressure of outside threats or opportunities, is easier when there is similarity in ideology, structure, and professionalism between organizations. Once cooperation has begun, frequent contacts are required to maintain it and handle the stresses of competition, personality conflict, and compromise.

Cutting the Issue.   Organizations have to perceive that benefits will result from working with other organizations. To bring about this impression, organizers need to define or *cut* the issues in a way that appeals to the interests of each organization separately.

Take the issue of public transportation. Senior citizen groups could support it because most seniors either don't drive or don't have the income to own cars and they need access to services throughout the city. Unions might support it because it would mean additional jobs in construction and in operating an improved mass transit system. Women's organizations might support it if there were particular guarantees written into the program to assure safety at night for women using it. Minority organizations might support a plan which assured service between their neighborhoods and places where jobs were available. (Kahn, 1982, p. 279)

Cutting an issue to attract other organizations might involve a reordering of organizational priorities. To gain another group's support for a neighborhood revitalization campaign, a neighborhood group might have to work with the other group on their project to stop a highway. In addition, to successfully cut an issue, it is important to avoid issues over which the organizations compete. For example, a neighborhood organization pressuring for better city services should not define the issue as one of allocation, in which some neighborhoods will get less and others more. Rather, it should emphasize issues on which the whole pie will be expanded and every participating neighborhood will be better off.

An issue can be cut in such a way that a group facing a particular problem might gain support from a larger ideological movement. For example, in New York City

> The Women's Housing Coalition was created two years ago to advocate the female point of view on housing—changing the stereotype of homelessness as a male phenomena, linking the need for low income housing for women and children with broader feminist concerns like day care and providing a support network for women who are working on these issues. (Babb, 1989, p.8)

In this coalition, homeless women can gain support from the stronger networks of women's groups.

Sometimes coordination is possible only on narrowly defined issues on which the organizations agree. The skill in coalition building is finding this basis of agreement. Even in cities with racial tension over schools, community organizations representing black and white neighborhoods of the city have been able to work together on issues of school quality.

In many places, labor, civil rights organizations, and environmentalists have been at loggerheads.

> Although there has been considerable overlap between the agendas of civil rights advocates and those of economic boosters, these agendas often conflict with those of environmentalists. . . . The "jobs versus environment" argument has held black Southerners captive to a system that often forces them to choose between employment and a clean work environment. (Bullard, 1990, pp. 192–193)

Organizers have to cut the issues in such a way as to bridge these gaps, for example, by pointing out that the toxins are most likely to affect the poor living near polluting plants.

To summarize, when the issue an organization is working on requires cooperation from other groups in a city, or the ability to lobby state or federal government, or requires more expertise or greater numbers than the group can muster by itself, coalitions may be the answer. They are difficult to manage but not impossible.

For long-term coalition work, it is easier to work with groups that are similar in values and structure, but for short-term cooperation, by cutting the issue properly, several groups that don't generally agree can find common ground. And sometimes circumstances are conducive to coalition formation and submerge temporarily the differences between groups. Groups can maintain their autonomy in coalition activity by limiting their participation to issues they agree on and by working with other groups that have similar levels of professionalism so that neither group is dominated by others.

REACHING OUT TO OBTAIN PUBLICITY

Publicity grabs the attention of opponents and the public. Effective publicity symbolizes the problems facing people and helps to set the political agenda. Publicity efforts enhance the image of the power of an organization, increasing the chance of victory. Publicity helps mobilization and recruitment efforts. Potential members learn about a group and its accomplishments, increasing the chance of their joining, and those already in the group are encouraged by its successes. Publicity efforts spread information about issues of concern to the action organization. Publicity helps convey to opponents the commitment of an organization. A publicized event has more credibility than a private threat, because opponents know that the action organization would lose face if it failed to perform.

Most well-planned publicity campaigns accomplish several of these tasks simultaneously. Television coverage of the plight of the homeless symbolizes the issue, using the image of a homeless mother with several children. The story forces politicians to explain why no action has been taken, encourages concerned individuals to join advocacy groups for the homeless, and educates people about the causes of homelessness, such as the lack of affordable housing, widespread long-term unemployment, and the emptying of mental hospitals onto the streets.

Symbolization

A symbol is an easily recognized and transmitted representation of a problem. Pictures are common symbols of a cause. Animal rights groups circulate pictures of trusting baby seals about to be bludgeoned to death for their coats. Abortion rights groups use a coat-hanger to symbolize botched abortions; antinuclear protesters use pictures of the cooling towers of nuclear plants to remind people of the dangers with which they live. Images of civil rights marchers washed against a wall by a police water cannon symbolize passive resistance to terrible injustice.

Some actions are planned specifically to create a symbol and get it publicized. Lying down in front of bulldozers to stop urban renewal actions or tying oneself to a branch to stop tree harvesting gains press coverage (especially if announced in advance), stalls the opponent until the protesters are carted away, and leaves a dramatic visual image of the courage of the protesters and the bullying physical force of the opponents. With proper publicity, the symbolic threat replaces the need for potentially dangerous direct actions involving large numbers of people.

It is important to pick an appropriate symbol. Stopping traffic on a major highway may not convey much symbolism to most commuters. When the women's movement burned bras to indicate personal liberation, the press misinterpreted their action to mean sexual license.

Control the media to set an action agenda. (Courtesy VISTA)

Setting the Political Agenda

Publicity efforts define the broader political agenda by forcing political leaders to pay attention to problems. In Massachusetts, an advocacy organization ranked each school in the state on how well it was complying with a law to serve handicapped students. They released the study to each of the 400 local newspapers in the state, and "every one of them ran the story on their own school system's rating" (L. Brown, 1984, p. 223). The advocacy group set an action agenda by evoking the competitiveness between school districts.

Publicity on the potential for disruption worries people other than the target. During the civil rights movement, many cities changed their policies after local business people witnessed on television protest actions that took place in other cities.

Elected officials supported racist policies until they were pressured by their supporters in the business community who feared a reputation for racial strife would result in a loss of trade.

Mobilization, Recruitment, and Organizational Bonding

The best form of mobilization is direct canvassing and learning about felt needs, but only so many people are willing to canvass, and they can reach only a limited number of community members. Newspaper stories, telecasts, and word-of-mouth publicity about an organization's successes draw in members, as supporters see the potential for success.

People join as they learn of successes. Let the neighborhood know that the community organization founded the new community center and was responsible for rerouting traffic away from the elementary school. Potential organization members without sufficient courage to join demonstrations still feel pride when the television news describes a successful march, rally, or teach-in. Mailings and publicity increase solidarity among geographically dispersed organizations. Greenpeace runs an Adopt a Whale Campaign to let members symbolically join with those activists blocking whaling boats. People for the American Way periodically sends out press clippings, letting members enjoy the successes and recognition of the group around the country.

If the organization did it, flaunt it. Public success increases mobilization.

Information and Education

Publicity efforts should spread factual information about the problem facing people: for example, the number of homeless, the body count of otters killed by an oil spill, the comparative salaries of black men and white men with the same education, the size of the reduction in federal funding to aid the poor. Information campaigns challenge the complacency of authorities with dramatic evidence about social failure.

To appeal to a large number of people, education campaigns, especially those conducted through the mass media, must be simple and concise. Six hundred pages of data, no matter how accurate or shocking, don't communicate. Activists should follow the education strategy of environmentalists who

> choose the few key messages that will form the core of the community education campaign. Two criteria determine the choice of message. On the one hand, educators want to alert people to the most serious dangers the hazards possess. . . . On the other hand, they want to present information that will address the neighborhood concerns. (Freudenberg, 1984, p. 137)

Information campaigns should be not only factual but also grounded in the experiences and understanding of the intended audience.

Factual information should be presented in ways that communicate to nontechnical audiences. The advice we provided on pages 181–186 on how to present data should be followed as part of an information campaign. Particular attention is required to drawing the action conclusions from the information.

Mass Media Campaigns

Publicity depends on effective use of mass media. The first thing to remember is that the public is bombarded with messages all the time, most of which are ignored. The second is that messages have both an overt component and also a subtext, a symbolic message. The third point is that people do not come to the media with an open mind, they select the messages they want to pay attention to based on their preconceptions, and they interpret what they hear according to those preconceptions.

Any message an organization puts out is just one of hundreds received by the public for whom the mass media presents a jumble of stories, opinions, and impressions that blur into each other. Part of the reason for the jumble is that messages have not only an explicit but also an implicit or latent content (McLuhan, 1967). For example, people in an organization might be engaged in a sit-down demonstration at city hall to protest poor housing in the neighborhood and feel that they are reaching the broader public with information about their intolerable living conditions. Unfortunately, viewers see only the discontent, unhappiness, and threat of civic unrest. The explicit message of poor sanitary conditions is obscured by the "hot" (emotional) subtext.

Not only must the organization pay attention to designing its own messages so that they communicate the right facts and the right feeling but, in doing so, they must combat the message of their opponents that there is no problem (Edelman, 1988, pp. 115–119) or that the problem is being solved. When television portrays arrests of drug dealers as being the solution to the drug problem, community organizations may have a difficult time communicating that the economy of the community needs to be rebuilt before drugs can be controlled. The organization has to figure out how to communicate that arresting drug offenders has had little impact on the problem before they propose their own solution.

The progressive organization should realize that media campaigns are unlikely to change basic beliefs. Instead, the group tries to frame an issue so that more people can accept it. Rather than getting involved in the fetus-is-alive-or-not debate, the pro-choice movement framed the issue in terms of whether women can control their own bodies and whether women have privacy rights. Framed in that way, the issue can garner widespread support of those who believe in individual autonomy on personal issues.

In short, messages not only have to be cast to get through a barrage of half-observed and partly digested material, they also have to be designed to fit with people's existing values lest they be rejected or misinterpreted. In addition, progressive messages must counter the images put forth by those in power without at the same time creating a harmful emotional tone for their own message.

Getting Attention.   Given the barrage of information available, community organizations must interest reporters in following their story and must convince the media that the story will capture public attention. To do so, organizers must learn what newspapers and television consider newsworthy and must design media events and press conferences accordingly. Second, it is important to find out how the news media work—their rhythms, their needs, their deadlines—and when possible, gear publicity efforts to fit their patterns. Third, community organizations should establish good relations with individual reporters.

Newsworthiness.   Publishers want their newspapers to sell, and television stations want people to watch their programs, so they focus on stories that attract an audience. Stories are newsworthy if they involve large numbers of people or are unusual, or both. A mass demonstration at city hall would probably attract media attention because of the number of people involved. If residents of a public housing complex tied up the elevators at city hall to protest the lack of elevator service at a 20-story public-housing building, the story might get attention because of the unusual focus.

Stories become newsworthy when they involve famous people. One reason to picket high government officials is that they guarantee media coverage. If a celebrity such as Jane Fonda shows up at a demonstration, the chances are good that the media will cover the event. They may, however, pay more attention to the celebrity than to the group's message.

Media people need a hook or a peg for a story. Make sure something is happening. An organization demonstrates to call attention to a problem. It announces scandalous information about the opposition. It opens a community center for recycling waste materials. It marches to protest a decision made by the city council. People milling around or making calls for general social improvement rarely make good stories: It's action that counts in providing a hook for a story.

Cleverness is important in finding a hook for a story. For example, a rent strike was called against the owner of an apartment building, a Catholic hospital, that wanted to demolish the building to expand the hospital. The strike groups sent a petition, in Latin, to the Pope, requesting aid. The Latin language petition provided a good peg for news stories (Worthy, 1976).

Sometimes courage and boldness help create a hook. Imagine the image communicated on film by the following action that occurred during a protest of police indifference to reports of police brutality:

> Ivory Perry immediately walked out of the police station into the street and organized the demonstrators into a circular picket line designed to obstruct traffic. A little red car got caught inside the circle and its driver guided it slowly toward the demonstrators in order to get away. Ivory Perry threw himself onto the asphalt in the path of that car, and when it stopped, he stretched out in front of the wheels. Police officers rushed over to drag him out from under the automobile, but demonstrators encircled the policemen and tried to prevent them from reaching Perry. (Lipsitz, 1988, p. 119)

Perry caught the attention of the media, but the symbolism wasn't very clear.

Appropriate symbolism helps the group get its message across, but to catch media attention, the tactic has to be clever and fresh:

1. Protesting the lack of rat-control measures in poor neighborhoods in Washington, DC, activist Julius Hobson threatened to trap large numbers of rats and release them

in Georgetown, a posh residential area. He then drove through Georgetown with cages of rats atop his car to make the threat more dramatic.

2. To bring home the importance of water pollution, one community organization collected a bucketful of foul-smelling effluent from a factory outflow pipe at the river's edge and poured the effluent over the plush carpeting at corporate headquarters.

3. To demonstrate the hazards of radiation escaping from nuclear power plants, Californians released 2,000 helium-filled balloons at a power plant site, with the attached message: As easily as this balloon reached you, so could the radiation from Diablo Canyon Nuclear Power Plant if the plant goes into operation. (Examples 1 to 3 adapted from Alderson & Sentman, 1979, pp. 214–215.)

4. Herbert and Irene Rubin received front-page coverage in a local paper as they brushed their teeth on the steps of city hall. They were symbolizing the inadequate sewer system in their neighborhood that caused sewer backups and made home plumbing unusable (Zech, 1987).

5. In reaction to the firing of a secretary for not making coffee for her boss, Women Employed arrived en masse (followed by TV cameras) to a Chicago law firm. While the cameras whirled, they taught the lawyers how to make coffee (Boyte, 1980, p. 111).

6. When a representative of *Playboy* was speaking on the campus of Grinnel College, students publicly took off their clothes. They were protesting the portrayal of women in *Playboy* (Deckard, 1983, p. 339).

In each case, the media was forewarned about a dramatic visual opportunity, the actions themselves symbolized the problem, and each event showed either humor or personal daring.

Such tactics must be carefully planned and paced so that reporters or editors do not become bored. Even mass demonstrations lose their news interest if media events are repeated too frequently. When possible, humorous or mocking events should alternate with confrontation and protest activities.

To interest the press in facts and figures, numbers should be put in human terms. An estimate that a community needs $22 million in mortgage money doesn't communicate the impact of the shortage, but a picture of people standing in the cold without houses makes an appropriate hook. The number of deaths from chemical pollution is a less exciting story than a picture of a child made sick from the pollution.

Human interest stories are most successful if they can create dramatic and easily understood symbols of the cause:

> The redlining issue is hooked to an attractive young couple with five kids who can't get a mortgage. The expressway issue is hooked to a particularly handsome church which would be torn down. The zoning violation is hooked to a rich absentee landlord who lives in the suburbs. (Cunningham & Kotler, 1983, p. 175)

Think of what kind of pictures an action creates. A proposed expressway does not make a front-page picture, but a before-and-after shot of a church demolished by construction crews does. Film of a truck unloading illegal chemicals is more dramatic than a still of the dump site. The least preferred story in television involves a *talking head,* that is, the reporter looks at the camera and reads a story. For national news, like rumors from the White House, or court cases in which cameras are restricted, the press has no choice but to use the talking head. With action campaigns, the press has a choice. If it's not visually attractive, it probably won't run. Find somebody with a wide-angle camera or a Camcorder and focus on the action, then decide if the shot would look good on television or on the front page of the paper.

Learn the Rhythms and Patterns of the Media World. Learn to time stories to fit into media rhythms. An event that is ignored on a busy news day might make the front page on a less busy occasion. Stories released on a Friday are more likely to be covered in the paper but less likely to be read. An event scheduled midmorning can make the afternoon papers and evening news, but an evening event usually will not get reported until the next day. An event scheduled too close to a camera or press deadline will get ignored: why should reporters kill themselves to make a deadline when other stories are available?

By paying close attention to timing, activists improve not only the chances of coverage at rallies, demonstrations, and press conferences but also their ability to get on radio and television talk shows. Producers of talk shows want to fill air time, especially with controversial issues, but also need flexibility to cover big stories as they break. They ignore the representatives of an action organization, especially a local group, at a time when everyone is talking about a national story, but may be more than willing to talk about local issues when the national story has quieted down. Persistence and willingness to appear at the drop of a hat can gain the organization greater visibility.

Potential speakers let talk shows know that they are available and describe the issues they'll raise. After an organization has done something newsworthy, call the talk show, then write a letter, then call the producer again. Find the producer's name from the station's operator or the show's credits and personalize all letters and calls. Be persistent.

Establish Good Relations With Individual Reporters. Reporters need good informants, and organizations want top-notch coverage. For example, good press relations helped in a protest against an expressway in North Carolina.

> It was the good personal relationships with the press that were primarily responsible for two extremely favorable items; a banner headline and a long story on the local page of the *Durham Morning Herald* reporting the contents of the position paper followed by a lead editorial endorsing [the action organization's] call for a city council study of alternatives. (Luebke, 1981, p. 259)

Over time, organizations can develop good press relations, which generally result in more favorable coverage. Organizations can give the best stories as exclusives to reporters who sympathize with their cause and are most likely to give the story good play. An organization can also earn good will by giving reporters stories that are not about the organization, but that the group knows about. For example, a housing coalition provides information on real estate developments that is of use to reporters.

Keep in mind that a responsible journalist, even one sympathetic to the action organization, should be covering both sides. Don't try to persuade a reporter that the other side is wrong, just provide a good story. Make sure the stories are complete and reliable. If reporters get caught using misinformation, the action organization loses a potential ally.

It can be useful for the leaders of the group to chat with reporters, to give them background on stories, and convince the reporters that they are not dangerous revolutionaries. A reporter who is willing to dig into the background of the issues eventually will write good stories.

Stories can break quickly, especially during an action campaign, so it is best to designate someone as the press relations person. In the crush of events, the reporter knows whom to call. Between campaigns, the press relations person can work to build good relations with reporters.

> The PIO [Press Information Officer] should make a point to meet new people and public service directors at local radio and television stations. A good way to initiate such contacts is to mail each of them a one- or two-page description of the organization, its purposes and goals, plus a personal letter introducing yourself as the new PIO. The letter should be no more than one page long and should say that you will call in a few days to arrange for a meeting to inform the editor or public service director about your work and to ask his [sic] advice on how to best work with him [sic]. (Kleyman, 1974, p. 156)

Thereafter, try to funnel most press contact through the PIO. When a story is breaking, especially one in which the opposition has the initiative, a good reporter will want to learn the community organization's side of the story. Having a PIO who is known, trusted, and accessible can determine whether the story of the action organization is told or not.

Distortion-Proof Messages.   Getting attention is a major problem in media campaigns, but once a group is fairly certain it can catch the media's attention, it has to think more about the content of the message and how it will be interpreted. An offhand statement to a reporter in the heat of a confrontation may end up as a headline, or documentation of a problem may end up garbled. One way of increasing the chance that the organization's carefully thought-out message is the one actually reported to the public is for the organization members to write the story themselves in the form of news releases.

News releases can be delivered to papers and read at press conferences, where reporters can ask follow-up questions and take pictures. Inform the local offices of the wire services of the time of your press conference. Send personalized letters to the city editors of local newspapers and producers of television and radio news programs. Then assume the mail wasn't delivered and follow up with a telephone call. Try hard to provide several days' notice, so that attendance at the press conference can be scheduled.

Don't hold a press conference without hard news to release. Strongly encourage members of the organization to attend the press conference, because a full room makes reporters feel that something important is happening. Balance the presentation between those describing hard facts on the problem and those personally affected. For example, the press conferences on the Love Canal dispute balanced technical discussions of the effects of waste chemicals with the reactions of individuals who were made ill from the chemical pollution.

Make a complete, neatly typed copy of any statement available at the door, so reporters can take a copy on the way into the room. Facts and figures about projects or community problems should also be available as part of an information package for the press, along with background descriptions on the action organization.

If someone in the organization is good with a camera, have 8 × 10 glossies ready for press distribution. Especially with local papers in smaller cities, if the organization provides pictures to reproduce, it has a better chance of communicating the image it wants. Make sure the pictures follow the rules for media interest, either showing dramatic actions or exchanges between organization members and notables. A city council member refusing to receive the organization's petition opposing the new land fill makes a good action picture.

Preparing a press release is relatively easy. Get a book like Seitel's (1980) *The Practice of Public Relations* and copy the formats. Do not be creative with the format of the press release. Press releases should answer the questions: Who? What? When? Where? Why? and How? In Figure 14–1, we have included a sample press release. The format of a release should follow this one, but the statement can be longer.

Note the funnel writing style. The most important news is reported first; more details are given later. The hope is that the press will use the whole story as written. The story may have to be cut to fit the available space. This story can be cut at the end of any paragraph and still coherently communicate the message. While reporters will sometimes dig for a story, they are often pressed for time and will use the news release (perhaps in a slightly rewritten format). Because this is ideal, make it easy for them.

FIGURE 14–1
Neighbors Against Child Abuse

Press Release	January 5, 1992

[When, who, what] **[Where]**	Today, Neighbors Against Child Abuse opens a 24 hour-a-day hotline for parents who fear they may be abusive and neighbors who suspect a child is being abused. Calls to 000-9999 will be answered by trained counselors.
[Why and Hook]	Last year, Sandy Jones died of a concussion. He fell against a table after his stepmother hit him. He was 4 years old. Neighbors Against Child Abuse began as a community response to Sandy's death.
[How]	The service is funded by a start-up grant from the State Department of Children and Family Services. Later in the year, Neighbors Against Child Abuse will sponsor a children's marathon to raise funds to keep the hotline going.
[Another hook]	Wilbur Jones, Sandy's father, described his wife as a "good woman." "She loved Sandy," he explained at the inquest, "but we quarreled a lot after I got laid off. When Sandy cried, I guess it was too much for her."

Contact Person: For more information, call Jim at 999-0000

First, enclose background data so that they feel they could get more details or check out the story if they choose. Make sure a contact person is listed on the release. This person should know the details of the story, should be able to answer or quickly find answers to reporters' questions, and should be available (Seitel, 1980, pp. 95–101).

Second, write the press release so that it can be easily edited. Use wide margins and type double-spaced on only one side of the paper. Third, keep sentences and paragraphs short; that's the newspaper writing style. Write grammatically and spell correctly. Sloppiness means more work for the reporter and chances losing the credibility of the organization. Reporters may well wonder, if they can't spell, how good can their facts and figures be?

Distribute the press release to editors and reporters who were not able to attend the press conference. The local-section editor, or perhaps the editor of the family page, might be interested in the plight of a displaced family, while the political or city editor might be the one interested in a protest against reductions in job-training programs.

A more modern version of a press release is a video or video commercial that the organization produces. Big businesses have been producing their own videos for some time, and often television stations play them without indicating that they were paid for by large companies. Tony Schwartz produces videotapes such as "Guerrilla Media: A Citizen's Guide to Using Electronic Media for Social Change," (Varied Directions Inc., of Camden, ME) that show how progressive organizations can make their own tapes (Shales, 1988). Michael Pertshuk, from the Advocacy Institute in Washington, argues "The concept of turning the ordinary citizen-activist into a media advocate has the potential to be revolutionary" (Shales, 1988, p. 8).

Public Information Campaigns Without Mass Media

Neighborhood organizations can carry out low-cost publicity efforts that do not require the aid of the mass media. Use bumper stickers, displays in public libraries, and wall posters to increase awareness of the organization. Members can talk to people at home or phone neighbors to describe the cause and some of the organization's victories. T-shirts with the name and the cause of the group can earn money for the organization and become walking billboards for the organization. In some neighborhoods, the message of the group can be taken to the streets by rap groups. For example, a number of rap stars

> came together to produce a record called "Self-Destruction," They picked the National Urban League to receive their royalties. . . . On the Streets, "Self-Destruction" plays on boom boxes . . . as something of a national anthem among young, black teenagers tempted by the lure of quick money, drugs and gangs. (Curry, 1989, p. 6)

If the organization has an office or can get space in a community center or city hall, it can set up a display showing its accomplishments. Pictures of deteriorated buildings that have been turned into decent housing or garbage-strewn lots that have been turned into vest-pocket parks can make a dramatic impact. With a little equipment, an automatic slide show of the successes of the organization or a television hooked up with a video of the group's accomplishments provides inexpensive but catchy publicity. Some shopping malls make space available to community organizations for such purposes.

Though presenting the organization in a favorable light, the content of these exhibits must be honest and accurate. People can take a walk around a block or two and see what is claimed in the exhibit. If they find graffiti covering the rehabilitated house in the pictures, the organization loses credibility.

Newsletters can keep the membership informed about the actions in a campaign and provide a constructive activity for supporters who are not involved in the direct action. For example, during a strike, activists

> began publishing their own newspaper, the *Voice of Labor.* . . . The paper would "report the facts about the *workers'* plight truthfully and without prejudice." The *Voice of Labor* was read by virtually all the strikers and their families and was handed out at factory gates and in certain taverns throughout the city. (Fantasia, 1988, p. 199)

The newsletter publicized the dispute to others and of perhaps greater importance reinforced the sense of shared solidarity among people in the action campaign.

Campaign newsletters are most important when the campaign is a long-run effort carried out by only a few people, such as the technical negotiations over an economic or housing development project. Large numbers of people might have participated in the rent strikes or picketing to pressure for more housing, but only a few are needed as the city and the organization try to implement the agreements. In such situations, newsletters let community members know the organization is still alive and active.

For national organizations representing widely scattered communities of interest, such as environmental organizations, peace groups, or alliances of the elderly, newsletters are the only practical way of maintaining contact. A typical issue has an informational article—background on housing funding, or on the effects of a particular pollutant; an indignation article—a violation of the antiwhaling treaties, or some blatant form of sexism or racism; as well as summaries of action campaigns being conducted by the group. The newsletter shares the information, indignation, and successes that motivate direct-action campaigns.

A successful newsletter is realistic in its descriptions of the problem but shows the progress being made. Some newsletters spend so much space documenting the magnitude of the problems and the perfidiousness of the enemy that the less dedicated reader might feel overwhelmed. Indignation is important, but without a sense of movement, of the potential for successes, people will lose interest.

Organizations must avoid the temptation to run out and begin a newsletter as one of their first tasks. A sloppily produced newsletter or one virtually devoid of content is an embarrassment to the group. For the nuts and bolts of putting one out, read booklets like Nancy Brigham's *How to Do Leaflets, Newsletters and Newspapers* (cited in Cassidy, 1980, p. 120) or John McKinney's (1977) *How to Start Your Own Community Newspaper.* With desk-top publishing programs for personal computers, it is within the financial and technical reach of all except the smallest organizations to produce nearly professional-quality publications.

In short, community organizations can extend their reach and get the public on their side by using publicity. Events need to be planned to catch media attention and designed to convey the appropriate symbolic message. Good relations with reporters and awareness of the work rhythms of the media can help get favorable stories covered. But community organizations don't always need mass media to publicize their events and successes. They can use bumper stickers and T-shirts, and send out snappy newsletters.

BARGAINING AND NEGOTIATIONS

The results of action campaigns are determined through negotiations between the action organization and the target. The negotiations should resolve the immediate problem. For example, the negotiations at the end of a sit-in to hire more minority group members at a department store may result in an agreement to hire 10 minorities a year for 5 years. In addition, negotiations should aim to produce longer-term settlements that resolve some of the conditions that led to the problem in the first place. In the employment example, the agreement could include a change in recruitment practices, increased promotion from entry-level positions, and an extended trial period, so that people with little prior experience can be judged on their accomplishments.

Negotiations can be traps for the unwary. If negotiations are poorly structured, the opponents may take a slice and divide approach to the underlying problems. Each circumstance is handled separately, and compromises are worked out on the small piece while the larger issues are obscured. Or the inexperienced bargainer might accept unenforceable agreements or none at all because there is so much posturing that the opponent finds it impossible to make concessions.

To avoid some of these pitfalls, the organization needs to plan before negotiations on how to structure the bargaining and carry out the negotiations with skill, knowing when to give in, and how much, and when to hold out.

Planning for Negotiations

Often, the entire social action campaign is preparation for negotiations. Part of the purpose of the campaign is to end up

> where issues are clearly defined, the various sides perceive the existence of a balance of power, and they perceive that their objectives cannot be achieved without negotiations. (Talbot, 1983, p. 91)

Besides clarifying issues, community organizations have to convince their opponents to come to the bargaining table.

Suppose that the neighborhood organization accuses the police of brutality, slow response times, and indifference to black-on-black crimes. Such accusations are likely to create a lot of anger, and are not designed to bring police to the bargaining table. To bring the police to the bargaining table, ways are needed to make the police department dependent on maintaining a good relationship with the neighborhood group. Producing an annual report comparing anticrime activities by neighborhood might show the police department that supportive neighborhoods can make their work safer and make them look better. Or, the group could suggest local cooperation with the police through a Neighborhood Watch Program in exchange for a faster response rate to calls from the neighborhood.

Make Opponents Afraid of What Your Group Will Do

During the campaign, the action group should make the target afraid of the consequences of direct actions. Hopefully, they will make concessions to avoid future protests. For example, the decision not to promote a woman worker to a managerial position might be reversed to end sit-ins by feminists. The sit-ins might create terrible publicity for the targeted organization.

There are several ways in which direct action campaigns increase the opponent's dependence on the action organization.

Create an Image of the Group's Power. The solidarity shown during a campaign communicates an image of power to the group's opponents. The number of people the group can turn out for demonstrations, the ability of the group to get favorable press coverage, and personal contacts with important or well-known people all convey an image of power. Such an image can be as effective as real power in cowing opponents.

Demonstrate Commitment. A second strategy for increasing the group's bargaining power involves making a firm commitment to a course of action so that the organization appears to be absolutely locked into a position. Chaining people to a house to block demolition equipment is one such tactic. The opponent either has to concede or use force—wire cutters and people to cart off organization members.

Commitment creates strength from weakness. Commitment requires

> some voluntary but irreversible sacrifice of freedom of choice. [It] rest[s] on the paradox that the power to constrain an adversary may be dependent on the power to bind oneself; that, in bargaining, weakness is often strength . . . and to burn bridges behind one may suffice to undo an opponent. (Schelling, 1960, p. 22)

Creating the appearance of commitment need not involve dramatic displays such as lying in front of a bulldozer. Commitment can be made through public communications. When an organization's leadership describes its absolute minimal requirements to the mass media, it commits both to its opponents and to its membership. Commitment is more credible when opponents realize that the people with whom they are negotiating have little flexibility. For example, the negotiator for an organization who can convincingly claim to be bound by a vote that would be difficult to retake appears committed. This is one of the reasons that lawyers and other hired negotiators are used in conflicts. The lawyer states that his or her (unreasonable) clients will not budge, and opponents know they are bargaining with somebody who has minimal flexibility. Furthermore, if organization members carefully monitor the actions of their negotiators, the negotiators are slower to make concessions (Pruitt, 1981, p. 44).

Avoid Being Trapped by Your Opponents' Commitment. In the bargaining game, the opponents can use the same tactics of commitment and nonnegotiable stances as the action organization. A construction firm can begin to build a project before protest tactics are organized and then argue that they are committed by the costs already sunk into the project. Environmental groups face this problem, when the Army Corps of Engineers begins work on a water project before getting citizen approval. To strengthen their commitment, city officials and politicians may claim to be bound by regulations and argue they lack flexibility to concede.

If a group can show that city officials have not uniformly enforced the laws, it can show they are not really bound by their own laws. For example, if a business group was allowed to overspend its budget, it should be possible to argue that the neighborhood redevelopment group should be allowed the same variation from the regulations. In prebargaining positioning, it is important for the organization to figure out what the real constraints of the opponent's are as opposed to the ones they claim.

Structuring the Bargaining

The legal, political, and confrontation tactics that occur before the bargaining begins make opponents dependent on the community organization and bring them to the bargaining table. Once the opponents have agreed to bargain, the community organization has to try to structure the negotiations so that it will be relatively easy for the opponents to concede. The most common way of dealing with such situations is to split the difference. Everyone gets something, but not as much as they want. An alternative to compromise is to put enough issues on the table so that both sides can win all of something important to them (win–win bargaining).

Reaching a compromise is easiest when there is a mutually prominent alternative that both sides accept. A *mutually prominent alternative*

> must stand out in both parties' thinking either because it embodies some standard of fairness or reasonableness or because it enjoys perceptual "uniqueness, simplicity, precedent or some rationale that makes [it] qualitatively differentiable from the continuum of possible alternatives. (Schelling, 1960, p. 70)

In many negotiations, the idea of splitting the difference provides a mutually prominent alternative. For example, the community organization needs 200 new apartment units, the city says it can afford only 100. If the difference is split, the city will agree to provide an extra 50 units. From the city's perspective, it reduced the demand by 50; from the community organization's perspective, it got 50 more units than it would have. Each side can claim a victory. When organizations from separate neighborhoods are arguing over how community-development funds should be divided, a mutually prominent alternative might be to allocate the money in proportion to the population below the poverty level.

In many circumstances, splitting the difference will not work. For one thing, the difference has to be splittable. If the organization is requesting a whole something—a health clinic, a fire station—getting half of it may not make sense. Also, real compromise means never getting what you need or want, so, like Xeno's frog, who jumps half the distance to the well in each hop and never arrives at the well, splitting the difference may not be an efficient way to get anywhere when what is needed is a major change.

In these circumstances, another technique is to break up issues into their component parts, so that each organization can claim victory on some issues. Perhaps the city is unwilling to commit capital funds for new housing projects but is willing to spend more to maintain existing houses. If the issue is phrased as *new housing,* the answer will be no; if the issue of housing for the poor is broken into new construction and repairs, a mutually agreeable solution can be found. This process is called *fractionating* the issue, that is, dividing the issue into individually negotiable parts as a way of reaching solutions (Fisher, 1972). The protest organization gets something it wants, and the opponent has found an area that is easier for it to concede on.

Another approach involves *linking* issues together. Linking involves combining different issues into one larger package. For example, cities, developers, and neighborhood organizations are often at loggerheads over how to link expansion of downtown office space with housing for new workers and those displaced by office development. In some cities, permits for new office space have been directly tied to building new housing for lower-income people, but developers balk at this requirement. It solves the city's problem but at the direct expense of the builders, who have no motivation to comply.

Community organizations have come up with alternative proposals that are more readily seen as win–win situations by developers and city officials. Businesses need suitable employees, but the existing work force cannot afford the available housing if the downtown is cleared for office development. Instead of asking the developers to pay for new lower-income housing, these community organizations suggest providing job training so that some of those displaced can earn enough to pay the higher rents. The city benefits from the resolution of the neighborhood–central business district conflict; developers and employers get needed labor; and the poor get new and needed job skills (Pennsylvania Economic League, 1989). The trick in structuring the bargaining is not to just increase the number of issues being bargained over but to find the issues that make all parties feel they are coming out ahead.

Some Tactics of Negotiations

When the community organization has forced its opponents to the bargaining table, there may be more of a feeling of opposition than cooperation when the bargaining starts. Even in a friendlier atmosphere, opponents may be determined to give as little as possible. Once the bargaining has begun, what tactics can negotiators use that will increase the chances of achieving organizational demands?

Preparing for the Negotiating Sessions. First, prepare for the negotiating session by simulating the negotiations with members of the organization. Have some members take the other side and try to out-negotiate each other. Perhaps the simulation will uncover different ways of linking issues that both sides will find acceptable.

Use these simulations to learn which organization members are the best negotiators and make the best impression, especially if there will be media coverage of negotiations.

Choosing negotiators is not simply choosing the best individuals but the best team that has individuals with complementary skills.

Who is quickest on his or her feet? Who can tactfully sum up a situation, appear conciliatory to the opposition, yet not concede on fundamental issues? Who has the facts and figures at his or her fingertips and can catch the opponents' deceptions? Who can stick with the negotiations if the bargaining drags on?

While choosing negotiators, also think of what other members of the organization should be doing. For longer-term negotiations, organizational members should maintain the pressure campaign outside the negotiating sessions. Actual discussions should be carried out by a limited number of negotiators who report back to the organization.

Before the negotiation session begins, make sure the negotiators have mastered the facts of the situation. When trying to get your opponents to spend resources on local communities, learn how much they have to spend. Examine their budgets to see where money can come from. For example, environmentalists have pointed out the extent to which the U.S. Forest Service subsidizes logging companies, shaming the government into increasing efforts to preserve natural woodlands. When publicly announced, these facts put the Forest Service on the defensive.

Make sure the negotiating team can put the facts in a broader context. For example, if defenders of the status quo argue that employment has increased in downtown areas so government intervention is not required, the organization's negotiators can respond that while overall employment has increased, it has worsened for people with a poor education. Such a response demonstrates that the organization has done its homework, while expanding the scope of the argument from job training to improving the schools.

Another activity in preparing for negotiations is to come up with *specific verifiable demands* before going into the negotiating session. For example, suppose the group is agitating for street improvements in a particular part of town. They should aim for an agreement from the negotiations such as the following:

> The City Department of Streets and Roads will resurface Maple Street from Main to Mary Lane, and Alpine Street from Juneau Blvd to Raleigh. The contracts for the work are to be let no later than June 1, 1993, for work to be completed no later than December 31, 1993.

There is no ambiguity about what is to be done, who is responsible, or when the work is to be completed. The acceptance of bids for work is normally done in public, so the group can check that the contracts were let on time. Because the street work is so easily visible, the organization should have no difficulty verifying that the work was completed as promised.

Tactics at the Negotiating Table.   Tactics that improve the group's chances at the negotiating table include showing firm commitment to a position, knowing when to make concessions, being prepared for counterproposals, revealing just the right amount of information, and managing the flow and timing of the negotiations. Negotiators have to know, too, when the bargaining has reached an impasse and when a mediator needs to be called in.

Be Firmly Committed to a Position

Showing firm commitment to a position will result in the other side being more likely to concede a point.

> The other [side] will make larger concessions to the extent that the actor seems unlikely to move far in their direction. Hence, high initial demands, slow concession making and positional commitments are useful for eliciting unilateral concessions. This is especially true when the other [side] is under high time pressure. (Pruitt, 1981, p. 74)

Because the opposition needs to get the community group off of its back, it may respond to firm demands by quickly conceding especially when the organization members are keeping up the pressure by lobbying, legal tactics, and direct actions.

Learn When and How to Make Concessions

The community organization has to make some concessions too. But when making concessions, careful timing is needed: Too fast, and the negotiator is seen as weak by the opponent; too slow, and the opponent refuses to reciprocate (Pruitt, 1981, p. 20). Before deciding what to concede on, redefine the issue, fractionating it into component parts or linking it with other issues of import to the opposition. Concede some of the linked issues, especially those of import to the opposition and of less concern to your organization.

Be Very Careful in Responding to Counterproposals

In practicing for negotiations, your team should have a good idea of counterproposals the opposition is likely to make and should have a response in mind. If the opponents surprise the group's negotiating team with an unanticipated counterproposal, take the time to evaluate it.

> Let's say that we're members of a tenants' organization negotiating with the landlord over a rent increase. The landlord has announced a 20 percent increase. In our planning sessions prior to the negotiations, we agreed that we would demand no increase but that we would actually be willing to accept 7½ percent increase in rent. . . . The landlord comes up with a totally different sort of suggestion . . . he will agree to no rent increase but that instead of a month-by-month rental, there should be year-long leases with a one-month security deposit for damages. This is a possibility that we had not thought of. Rather than trying to think this through in front of the landlord, the thing to do is to call for a "caucus." This means we take a break to discuss the new offer. (Kahn, 1982, pp. 164–165)

Examine counterproposals for possible deceit, but remember, the more the opponent fears the future actions of the community organization, the greater his or her incentive to also come up with a win–win agreement. An established neighborhood association that has carried out successful confrontation actions can trust the local merchants association more than can a group formed to solve a one-time problem.

Decide How Honest to Be With the Opponent

It is the perception of power as much as real power that affects outcomes. But how far should negotiators go in deceiving opponents at the bargaining table? There are both ethical and practical implications of deceptive behavior. Lying may help in the short-term, but if the lies are discovered, the organization's power will be reduced (Lewicki, 1983).

There are different levels of lying. Asking for more than the group really needs is a normal part of bargaining. A bluff, for example, a threat to walk out of the negotiations, is a mild and expected deception. Making opponents feel that the organization's negotiators are dependent on a determined membership is a necessary deception. However, to lie on facts, such as the cost of housing or the number of people willing to join a neighborhood health plan, is foolhardy. Such deception can discredit the group and it is easy to catch.

Keep the Negotiations Moving

Sometimes minor concessions can enable both sides to move toward mutually prominent alternatives. Such concessions are particularly important if the negotiations seem to be breaking up for irrelevant reasons.

Suppose that in negotiations with city officials about housing subsidies, the negotiators were close to achieving agreement, but then someone raised the question of socialized housing. At this point, the session deteriorated. Leaders of the action organization got angry with the "reactionaries," while the city wanted to break off discussions with "that bunch of revolutionaries." In such circumstances, the organization's negotiators might suggest some minor concessions to reduce the tension.

In the negotiations with the city over housing, an appropriate concession to get the negotiations back on track might be a reduction in the requested number of subsidized units the city will build. Members of the action organization know the city doesn't have the money to build all those units anyway.

Impose a Time Limit on the Negotiations

A deadline increases the possibility that the negotiations will be broken off, magnifying costs to all concerned. To reach a timely conclusion, each side may be more willing to make some concessions. While the threat of termination of negotiations can be useful, generally, the action organization does not want the negotiations to stop before a resolution is reached. To convey the threat while not risking actual termination, it makes sense to have one member of the negotiating team act touchy, "quick to anger when frustrated" (Pruitt, 1981, p. 78). The quick-tempered person jumps up and leaves the negotiations and is called back by people on his own side.

Mediation and Third-Party Intervention

On occasion, negotiations do get stuck and require the services of a mediator who can reduce the chances of negotiations breaking down over minor misunderstandings. There are two types of mediation, *process* and *content*.

> Process mediation seeks to develop conditions and skills that will facilitate concession making and problem solving. By contrast, content mediation deals with the substance of the issues under discussion, with the third party developing suggested solutions or trying to persuade the bargainers to move in particular directions. (Pruitt, 1981, p. 203)

Mediators can ensure that negotiating sessions are held with sufficient civility that people listen to one another. If sessions seem to be getting out of hand, mediators can call a break. When negotiations get touchy, mediators can carry ideas back and forth between the two sides and present their own ideas on how the conflict can be settled. It is easier to agree with ideas presented by a mediator (even if they are only warmed-over versions of the opponent's ideas) than with ideas presented by the opponent.

In the last decade or so, mediation has become increasingly popular, especially in disputes involving government, business and environmentalists (Amy, 1987; Forester, 1987; Talbot, 1983). Mediation is seen as a less expensive and often quicker approach than litigation. But there are some concerns about mediation.

Most mediators are part of the established political and social structure, and hence may tilt away from the goals of community and protest groups. The essence of mediation is to tone down the edge of conflict, dulling "the fighting edge of some participants" (Amy, 1987, p. 114). When this occurs, solving a dispute and reaching an agreement may displace the community group's concerns with social or economic equity.

To handle such problems, the mediator needs to be trusted by and accepted by both sides. Also, the mediator's role should be specified. The mediator can be a fact finder, so neither side has to rely on the facts and figures provided by the other. The mediator can meet with both parties before formal negotiations to communicate to each the concerns of the other and encourage informal meetings away from the negotiating table. Showing a builder the flooded basements of new homes can do more for mutual understanding than days of picketing over run-off problems. A good mediator can perform shuttle diplomacy, probing and advising both sides, sometimes suggesting possible concessions (Forester, 1987, pp. 306–309).

To summarize, community organizations that engage in social action campaigns need to have good bargaining skills. Direct actions are of little use if the organization cannot get opponents to agree to enforceable settlements. The negotiating team has to know how to frame the issues so that it is relatively easy for opponents to concede. It has to create an illusion of power yet be willing to concede on less important issues. The team has to be in command of the facts and be able to anticipate opponents' counter-proposals or be able to evaluate them during the bargaining. If the organization can learn to bargain skillfully, it can lock in improvements stemming from the power shown by demonstrating in the streets, lobbying in the capitol, and litigating in the courts.

VI | The Development Model

Developmental organizations manage social and economic programs to solve problems that handicap the poor and the disempowered: They offer shelter to battered women; comfort the dying in community hospices; combat crime in the neighborhood; and provide quality housing at reasonable cost. More recently, they have turned their attention to providing jobs and job training while encouraging the growth of community businesses.

> *Developmental actions are successful when people build and maintain their own organizations that provide a community-based capacity for problem solving.*

Success grows out of a willingness to work together to combat shared problems, but it also requires that the participants have sufficient technical knowledge to make projects work. In a cooperative apartment building, somebody must know how to fix a broken furnace, caulk windows, and put aside money to pay real estate taxes. Those working in neighborhood development corporations learn to package financial deals, combining investments from community members, local businesses, government, and community foundations.

In the following chapters, we introduce future organizers to the technical skills that underpin successful development work. Chapter 15 presents a model of the different paths toward democratic development, as well as numerous examples of community-based social and economic projects. It contains an overview of requisite managerial skills for successful project implementation. Chapter 16 describes the internal aspects of running an organization democratically, while Chapter 17 focuses on project management, including planning, funding, implementing, and evaluating.

Chapter 18 examines how community-based organizations work to promote economic projects to benefit the poor. Traditional approaches to economic development disempower and virtually rout the poor; community-based economic development tames capitalism and makes it serve those most in need.

15 | An Introduction to Development Campaigns

D evelopmental organizations are those community-based groups that provide economic and social services. They sponsor neighborhood-based health care, sell fresh fruits and vegetables in consumer cooperatives, administer shelters for the homeless, maintain homes for battered women, build and manage moderately priced housing, teach job skills, and provide the seed funds for starting new businesses.

Developmental organizations enable people to gain control over social and economic changes that affect them. Such organizations contest the right of businesses to abandon a city without helping those left behind. They insist that business profits must be balanced against the harm to people, to neighborhoods, and to environments.

The developmental model demonstrates that by participating in economic and social projects people gain skills and confidence that lead to even more empowering activities. A tenants' group, formed to protest an indifferent landlord, learns to manage its housing complex. With financial support from progressive foundations, this increasingly confident group buys, builds, or rehabilitates apartments for the poor. In the course of maintaining the housing, members of the developmental organization learn needed skills and form their own profit-making businesses.

Development is about solving problems and improving living conditions. But it is also a battle for control over economic and social decisions. It represents an important step in a broader societal transformation.

WHAT DEVELOPMENTAL ORGANIZATIONS DO

Community-development organizations work to benefit the disempowered by providing needed services, increased income, and expanded capacity to control economic and social outcomes. They are, however, highly variable in scale and function, from a small fresh fruit and grain cooperative to a multimillion dollar community-development corporation. More systematically, developmental organizations differ in three ways— their respective emphasis on social services or economic expansion; the degree to which

351

they remain independent of government or conventional businesses; and the extent to which they accept conventional social and economic values.

Developmental organizations differ on whether they supply a social service or concentrate on economic development.

A community-sponsored day-care center is a typical social service, while financing a local mall that employs community members is a form of economic development. Housing, when managed by tenants, fits in between, both as a needed service to the tenants and a source of jobs and job training to resident employees.

The second dimension is the extent to which the developmental organization is dependent on established businesses or government to accomplish its tasks. Most neighborhood rehabilitation projects are done through extensive partnerships with business and government. In contrast, small community-controlled enterprises, food cooperatives, for example, intentionally avoid government, although they may be dependent on other co-ops. Community crime patrols are in between, staffed primarily by community volunteers but succeeding only with the cooperation of the police.

The third dimension is the extent to which the organization supports conventional social or economic values. Shelters for battered women scrap the conventional value that women should be subservient to men. Community crime patrols accept conventional social values on law and order. Cooperatively owned businesses fall in between, because the firm rejects capitalist ownership, yet competes in a capitalist marketplace.

Table 15–1 lists examples of community-based developmental organizations and the types of projects that they have undertaken.

The projects shown in Table 15–1 vary in where they fit in our typology. The widowed persons support group (1) is independent of government, provides a service and accepts mainstream social values. Both the employment training of women (7) and the cooperatives (10–14) are undertaken independent of government and provide an economic service but only partly accept conventional social and economic values. Land trusts (4) sometimes receive money from government, putting them in the middle of the dependence scale; they also play both a social and economic function by enabling poor and moderate-income people to remain in communities with rapidly increasing land values. Yet, in promoting common ownership of land, they reject conventional economic values. Most of the community development corporations (21, 24–26, 28) work in partnership with government and sponsor profit-making capitalist firms.

HOW SUCCESSFUL ARE COMMUNITY-BASED DEVELOPMENT ORGANIZATIONS?

Against the odds, many community-development groups are succeeding. Focusing on housing and economic activities, The National Congress for Community Economic Development (NCCED) pointed out that the 2,000 or so community-development organizations

operate under difficult circumstances—in distressed areas, with limited capital and shallow pockets, buffeted by changing public and private policies. (NCCED, 1989, p. 3)

Yet, these organizations

> . . . have built nearly 125,000 units of housing, over 90% for low-income occupants
> . . . have developed 16.4 million square feet of retail space, offices, industrial parks and other industrial developments in economically distressed communities
> . . . have made loans to 2,048 enterprises, equity investments in 218 ventures and own and operate 427 businesses
> . . . have accounted for creation and retention of close to 90,000 jobs in the 1st five years
> . . . [and] are engaged in numerous other activities—such as community organizing, advocacy, assistance to the homeless and housing counseling. (NCCED, 1989, pp. 1–2)

Other studies of community development corporations are also optimistic about their potential for success (Neal Peirce & Steinbach, 1987; Task Force, 1987). Studies of cooperatives show them to be financially successful, while some worker-owned plants have also done extremely well.

> In April 1985 the workers became owners of the Seymour plant and renamed the company Seymour Speciality Wire. Last year's sales topped $30 million, and today it is the largest, most successful democratically owned company in the country. (Turner, 1987, p. 71)

Even more impressive, in the face of banking failures, the community-controlled South Shore Bank in Chicago was maintaining profitability (Taub, 1988, p. 103).

Consumer-owned and -managed cooperatives provide better food at reasonable prices. (Courtesy TTB)

TABLE 15-1
Examples of Community-Based Developmental Organizations and Their Projects

Organization	Projects
1. Widowed Persons	A self-help group, in which people adjust to widowhood; teaches those newly widowed how to cope and handle problems.[a]
2. San Francisco Community Board	Residents in two San Francisco neighborhoods set up local conciliation boards to arbitrate neighborhood controversies without involving the public criminal justice system. Cases range from burglaries to consumer disputes.[b]
3. East Boston Community News	A community-based newspaper founded to report local events. Run by a volunteer staff, the paper is financed by business advertising and printing jobs done for others.[c]
4. Brattleboro Area Community Land Trust	A land trust that purchases homes that are then sold as co-ops. "The trust will continue to hold the land in perpetuity, keeping prices low and controlling property transfers." Funds are from Vermont Housing Conservation and HUD.[d]
5. Common Ground Community Economic Development Corporation	A land trust founded by a coalition of Dallas neighborhood groups. Has acquired land and rehabilitated property for over 65 units. Funds are from donations and grants.[e]
6. Illinois Neighborhood Development Corporation	An inner city development corporation that owns the South Shore Bank, a commercial bank with a socially conscious investment policy. Runs a Neighborhood Institute that manages development and social projects and a Neighborhood Fund that provides equity capital for local businesses.[f]
7. Coalition for Women's Economic Development	A Los Angeles self-help group that teaches unemployed women entrepreneurial skills. Also sponsors a revolving loan fund for start-up business capital.[g]
8. South Minneapolis Federal Credit Union	Three community members, along with a community-development organization, organized low-income neighborhood to form a credit union. The credit union has 420 members and $150,000 in assets and has started making loans to community members.[h]
9. Cabrillo Economic Development Corporation	"This group evolved from a farm worker cooperative into a county-wide economic development organization that does housing construction and rehabilitation and operates a cabinet shop and retail store, a 7,200 square foot office building and a light industrial park."[i]
10. Philadelphia Association for Cooperative Enterprise	Organization set up to establish worker-owned supermarket cooperatives in the Philadelphia area.[j]

TABLE 15–1

continued

Organization	Projects
11. East End Food Co-op	A food cooperative operating in a low-income neighborhood in Pittsburgh that now does over $250,000 a year in business. Seed money to expand the cooperative was obtained from the East End Cooperative Ministries.[k]
12. Cheeseboard Cooperative	This worker-owned and -controlled food store specializes in cheese and bread. Located in San Francisco, the cooperative is actively involved in social activities in the Bay Area.[l]
13. Hoedad Co-op	This 300-member cooperative in Eugene, Oregon, provides democratically controlled employment to individuals involved in reforestation.[m]
14. Southwest Detroit Construction Cooperative	A cooperative that both trains and employs local workers in construction. Workers become certified as licensed builders.[n]
15. Philadelphia [Housing] Model	In response to the lack of moderate-income housing in Philadelphia, ACORN led a squatters campaign to force city and HUD officials to agree to sponsor housing rehabilitation programs for the homeless.[o]
16. Mid Bronx Desperados	A Local Initiatives Support Corporation (LISC) grantee helped fund MBD's involvement in a neighborhood crime prevention program. The intent was both crime reduction and increased positive publicity for the community-development organization.[p]
17. Terrace Gardens Block Association	Members of three adjacent apartment buildings in Brooklyn contribute funds, matched by the city, to support anticrime activities. Crime prevention hardware is added to the building, and elected floor captains encourage individuals to take security precautions.[q]
18. Bishop Co-op	A cooperative housing project for the elderly funded by HUD. Special services are provided to check on the physical well-being of the elderly in the building.[r]
19. Seattle, Washington Park Projects	"The city of Seattle, Washington has contracted with established community groups for partial maintenance of 15 vest pocket parks. . . . The groups themselves negotiate with neighborhood residents for performance of specific tasks."[s]
20. New York City Cooperative Conversion Program	"New York City cooperative conversion program, the emphasis is on training tenants to assume management functions . . . involves direct management . . . if three-fifths of the residents sign a petition requesting it. After an eleven-month trial period, tenants are offered an opportunity to assume ownership as a cooperative."[t]

TABLE 15–1
continued

Organization	Projects
21. Whittier Neighborhood Revitalization	A partnership between a foundation, community groups, and the city of Minneapolis, whose goal is to bring about overall neighborhood improvement including housing rehabilitation, economic redevelopment, local business revitalization, and the formation of housing cooperatives. The project involves many millions of dollars and is run by a professional staff.[u]
22. Pittsburgh Neighborhood Services	A partnership to improve neighborhood housing in Pittsburgh. It provides technical information on housing repair and access to below market-rate loan funds to community members. Some of the seed money for the project was granted by HUD, while the city provides technical knowledge and increased enforcement of the building codes.[v]
23. Cochran Gardens Tenant Management Council	"Cochran Gardens is one of four public housing projects in St. Louis managed by tenants. It is the centerpiece of extensive housing developments, businesses, and services owned and operated on a nonprofit basis by the Tenant Management Council: A catering service, health clinics, day-care centers, a vocational training program."[w]
24. BUILD—Bronx United in Leveraging Dollars	A not-for-profit organization in the Bronx that rehabilitates housing in poor neighborhoods and sets up housing management. Much of the funding is obtained either from the city or from a complicated system that allows corporations that aid BUILD to obtain tax credits.[x]
25. Community Development Corporation—Kansas City	A community-controlled developmental organization in a deteriorated area of Kansas City. Among other activities, it has sponsored an inner-city shopping center, relocated manufacturing businesses, and aided a construction company. Successfully packages funds from the city, federal grants, and the LISC as well as conventional loan money from insurance companies.[y]
26. West Oak Lane Community Development Corporation	An outgrowth of an older Alinsky-style group that was fighting redlining. West Oak Lane worked "to rehabilitate the neighborhood's 600 abandoned houses . . . with its own construction crew . . . broadened its focus to business development opening its own Dunkin Donuts franchise."[z]
27. Bethel New Life	The not-for-profit Bethel New Life "will take over responsibility for Illinois's welfare-to-work program." The goal is to have a community-based social service program.[aa]

TABLE 15–1
continued

Organization	Projects
28. Bedford-Stuyvesant Restorations Corporation	A federally sponsored development corporation supervised by a prestigious board of nationally known individuals, it works on projects to improve housing and build businesses in poor areas in New York City. It has loaned money to entrepreneurs, worked on physical redevelopment projects, and set up a local professional theater.[bb]
29. West Contra Costa Community Health Care Corporation	Organized to provide a community-based approach to health care in a neighborhood from which doctors were exiting. Serves 100 patients a day. Originally dependent on federal money as well as manpower training programs, it is trying to become a self-supporting Health Maintenance Organization.[cc]
30. Citizens United to Reform Education	One of many different organizations that worked to get community-based school-board authorities authorized in Illinois. These boards can hire and fire principals and provide oversight to local schools.[dd]
31. Dudley Street Neighborhood Initiative	An outgrowth of the neighborhood planning movement in Boston that is authorized by the city redevelopment authority to "use the eminent domain power to acquire vacant land in its community." Land acquired will be owned by a community-controlled land trust.[ee]
32. South Armour Square Neighborhood Coalition	A pressure group to ensure that the community benefits from the state-funded reconstruction of a baseball stadium.[ff]
33. Renegades Housing Movement	Members of the Renegades Housing Movement in Spanish Harlem provide their own labor—"sweat equity"—to improve local housing conditions. As buildings are repaired, they are turned over to a housing cooperative that neighborhood people can join. Seed money was provided by not-for-profit sponsors of cooperatives, and later funding came from HUD.[gg]

[a]Silverman, 1980; [b]Stewart, 1979; [c]MacGregor, 1979; [d]Keese, 1989, p. 21. [e]White & Matthei, 1987, pp. 45–46; [f]Taub, 1988; [g]D. Smith, 1989, p. 3; [h]U.S. Office of Consumer Affairs, no date, p. 6; [i]Local Initiatives Support Corporation, 1982, p. 9; [j]Whyte, 1986; [k]U.S. Office of Consumer Affairs, no date. [l]Jackall & Levin, 1984; [m]Jackall & Levin, 1984; [n]Turner, 1987, p. 75; [o]Borgos, 1986; [p]Vidal et al., 1986, p. III-4; [q]Washnis, 1976; [r]U.S.D.H.U.D., 1979, p. 7; [s]International City Manager's Association, 1983; [t]Bratt, 1989b, p. 177; [u]Hanson & McNamara, 1981; [v]Ahlbrandt & Cunningham, 1979; [w]Boyte, 1989a, p. 3; [x]Finder, 1990, p. 23; [y]Task Force, 1987, p. 14–16; [z]Neal Peirce & Steinbach, 1987, p. 34; [aa]Reardon, 1989; [bb]Berndt, 1977; [cc]U.S.D.H.U.D., 1987, p. 13; [dd]M. O'Connell, 1988, p. 5; [ee]Girard, 1989, pp. 1, 21; [ff]Barry, 1987a, 1987b; [gg]U.S. Office of Consumer Affairs, no date.

The extent to which community-controlled social services are used is indicative of their importance and success. For example, over 3% of the island's population had stayed in one Hawaiian shelter for battered women during a 10-year period (Rodriquez, 1988, p. 239). Success can also be measured by how well these organizations do in reducing economic inequities. Here too, development organizations are doing a good job. For example, in employee-owned firms, black–white and male–female salary differences still exist, but the gaps are dramatically less than in conventional firms (Squires, n.d.).

The NCCED has suggested some of the reasons for the success of these organizations:

> As grassroots organizations, [they] understand their communities—the needs, opportunities, resources.
>
> They operate with a clear mission and a comprehensive, strategic approach to community revitalization; they are involved in a long-term process, with each project building on the last and toward the next.
>
> They forge partnerships with local developers, lenders, businesses, foundations, religious institutions, other nonprofit organizations and government at all levels. . . .
>
> They have the political and technical skills, and tenacity needed to pull together a complex array of resources needed to get projects done. (NCCED, 1989, pp. 3–4)

These organizations achieve success because they have integrated a developmental ideology with managerial skills.

Community organizations can provide needed social services. (Courtesy TTB)

DEVELOPMENT PRINCIPLES AND DILEMMAS

Successful developmental organizations combine a concern for the community and local empowerment with service delivery and economic growth. However, balancing empowerment and community building with service delivery can be difficult. To minimize problems, it helps to keep a few principles of balanced development in mind and be able to reconcile the tensions that result.

Three Principles of Balanced Development

While development should help those in need, it is vital that benefits occur as a result of an expansion of the economic pie rather than a contentious redistribution of current resources. Second, to succeed at development, organizations must start modestly and let one success spawn and fund other activities. The third principle is to make sure that developmental projects have a firm community base.

Distribution Versus Redistribution.   Redistributive projects in which resources are taken from one group to benefit another are far more controversial than projects that expand overall resources. Unfortunately, much of the establishment wisdom in urban economic development assumes that programs that benefit the poor do so by taking from the middle class and the wealthy, and, at best, share the wealth.

Those who accept this perspective claim that wealth expands only through projects that support conventional businesses. They assume the poor will benefit from a trickling down of new jobs. However, successful community-based developmental activities have demonstrated that projects targeted at the poor can expand overall economic resources. Successful community groups challenge the self-serving belief that only the established businesses deserve economic development subsidies.

For example, the Mississippi delta region is one of the poorest areas in the country, but even there, progressive community organizations expanded the economic pie in ways that benefited the poorest. By building on local pride, Mississippi Action for Community Education (MACE) and the Delta Foundation increased people's job skills and created new sources of employment.

> We wanted to develop the abilities of people who already regard this part of Mississippi and Arkansas as their home and who therefore could realize what they did or did not do would affect their friends, relatives and neighborhoods as well as themselves. (Task Force, 1987, p. 32)

MACE formed the Delta Foundation, whose "bottom line, through the buttressing and creation of for-profit local businesses, was decent jobs and incomes for area residents" (Task Force, 1987, p. 33). The Delta Foundation helped to set up plants to manufacture blue jeans, electrical components, and attic stairs and provided seed capital through its venture capital subsidiaries. With MACE, it assists in training entrepreneurs and worked with cities for commercial redevelopment. It has spread out to provide better housing for people in the area and today "MACE and the DELTA Foundation have combined assets of about $40 million" (Task Force, 1987, p. 35).

Bootstrapping.   The second principle of participatory development is to start with small projects that a single group with limited resources can achieve and let those successes generate more funding, more members, more hope, and more projects.

> Chicanos Por La Causa (CPLC) began as an advocacy and protest group . . . by some young men and women of Mexican descent. . . . As naturally as it expanded from advocacy to housing development and services, CPLC enlarged its range of operations . . . to build an emergency medical clinic. . . . A dramatic shift both financially and programmatically, took place . . . [that] enabled Chicanos Por La Causa to become designated as a statewide, nonprofit community development corporation. (Task Force, 1987, pp. 19–21)

Development organizations bootstrap by combining services to the community with pressure tactics. In Chicago, Voice of the People (VOP) is a major actor in housing rehabilitation that gets foundation and government funds to "maintain Uptown as a decent neighborhood for low-income families" (Vidal, 1986, p. III-5). Voice of the People used its services to build community organizations and was able to use that organization to strengthen its pressure tactics to provide further resources for rehabilitation projects.

> In addition to becoming a skilled development organization, VOP has developed a strong grassroots tenants organization. The residents of each building meet monthly to review the building's finances and to select new tenants. Each tenant council is represented on VOP's board. . . . VOP has also hired a community organizer to build organizations of other neighborhood tenants. . . . Building on its existing track record and assets . . . it has ambitious plans for additional rehabs. (Vidal, 1986, p. III-8)

Development supports pressure tactics that, in turn, support development.

Bootstrapping works, in part, because pride created through successful projects increases people's willingness to participate in future projects. For example, in cooperative workplaces, there is a

> small yet statistically significant increase in the level of worker-shareholder participation. . . . This finding . . . suggests that participation tends to breed more participation and that the act of participation plays an educative role stimulating further participation. (E. Greenberg, 1986, pp. 77–78)

Another reason why efforts bootstrap is that those who care enough to work in one progressive effort are likely to work in others as well. Cooperative members, for example, are likely to be active in environmental causes. In his book on worker cooperatives, Gunn describes that

> much of the energy of the co-op members goes not into building the co-op, but into developing the community where most members live. Community projects have included a food co-op and building both a free school and a combined community center, health clinic, and co-op office. Members have a reputation for being ardent environmentalists who strongly oppose the use of herbicide and are willing to take direct action against their use. (Gunn, 1984b, p. 85)

In addition, a small amount of money can be bootstrapped into a variety of projects.

> Boston's Roxbury Action Program (RAP) . . . began in 1969 with a few thousand dollars diverted from a regional church group that felt it ought to encourage black self-reliance instead of just administering programs for needy black people. With this seed money, RAP went on over the years to lever private investment capital for a multi-million dollar housing rehabilitation and construction program for its mostly low-income black neighborhood. (S. E. Perry, 1987, p. 54)

Sometimes the steps required to complete one project show the need for undertaking another. For example, to obtain Housing Trust Funds from a city agency, development organizations are required to conduct a needs-assessment study to document problems in their communities. These studies emphasize the interdependence of problems of housing, jobs, day care and other social needs, thereby stimulating further developmental action.

While one successful project encourages other ventures, there are potentially serious problems created by such spin-offs.

> New ventures are frequently launched by a small, tightly knit group of people . . . new ventures may create few jobs at first and thus they may cause resentment in the larger group. . . . New operations may also diminish the original group's cohesiveness. (Gunn, 1984b, p. 89)

One way to handle this problem is to create offshoot groups that are only loosely linked to the original organization. To minimize resentment among members of the

Partnerships between cities and community groups can be an effective way of providing housing. (*City Limits*)

original organization, the group might wait until its own survival is secure before risking money on new ventures.

A Firm Community Base.   Developmental organizations succeed because of the strength of community support. The world's largest group of worker-owned coopera- tives, the Mondragon Cooperatives, are located in the Basque region of Spain. The Basque communities provide them broad cultural support (Whyte & Whyte, 1988). Closer to home, the success of tenant-management organizations is also dependent on community support.

> A successful RMC [resident management council] is not only, or even first, a good prop- erty manager. It is a good community organizer. Those RMCs that are reported to have trouble achieving or sustaining an acceptable level of performance as a property manager are those that have trouble or no interest in keeping the community well organized. (Monti, 1989, p. 49)

Building community integration is an important prelude to successful develop- mental efforts, and successful developmental and community-based social service ef- forts build community. In describing a mall sponsored by a community-development corporation in the impoverished Liberty City area of Miami, Neal Peirce and Carol Steinbach found:

> "There is a real sense of pride in what has happened here," says Otis Pitts, the ex-cop who is Tacolcy's executive director. "It's not like people just coming to shop in a store. It's like they're coming to something that is a vital part of the community." Says a local merchant . . . "We don't only look good, we are good. Now everybody is committed to staying in the neighborhood. Why leave now? We sweated out the worst. Ain't nothing to do but look forward now." (Neal Peirce & Steinbach, 1987, p. 37)

A community crime watch set up to fight a crime wave in Cambridge, Massachu- setts did reduce crime. Equally important, participation in the crime watch provided people with a better sense of community, both as a territory to protect and as an area that has a shared history, shared problems, and shared accomplishments (M. D. Levine, 1986).

In short, successful developmental organizations build on existing community integration, and contribute to building a sense of community, which helps bridge the gap between service and economic growth on one hand, and community development on the other.

Developmental Dilemmas

Balancing democratic involvement with the skills needed to solve problems creates some inevitable dilemmas. The first is in balancing routine organizational tasks with the types of activities people find empowering. The second dilemma is in obtaining needed expertise without destroying the empowerment that occurs when members control their own projects. The third dilemma involves obtaining resources from gov- ernment and businesses without losing organizational autonomy. These tensions cannot be easily resolved, but organizers must recognize them, lest they succumb to pressure to go off in contradictory directions.

Empowerment Versus Routinization. Should the emphasis of the organization be more on its effectiveness in providing social or economic needs or in building an empowered community? Portrayed narrowly, no dilemma is apparent. If an organization wants to provide a service—day care, rape crisis counseling, recycling, job training—it provides such a service and sets up procedures to do so in an efficient manner. If its members are more concerned with establishing a general capacity for problem solving, the organization works in that direction.

A problem arises if routinization reduces the empowerment ideal. For example, some shelters for women,

> embody many features of custodial systems (e.g., rule-ordained, overcrowded, limited resources, exclusionary, and we–them authority structures). How, then, can a basically authoritarian model of service delivery yield democratic results, including the empowerment of victims, which enables them to assume control over their own lives? (N. J. Davis, 1988, p. 403)

The opposite problem can also occur. An organization can be so concerned with empowerment that it fails to establish any administrative routines and has to spend all its time inventing solutions to recurring problems.

Organizations are more likely to become rule bound if they depend for their survival on the profitability of whatever business they sponsor. In these circumstances, there is a temptation to concentrate on profit and to devise administrative forms that focus on efficiency rather than empowerment. This worry has plagued Community Development Corporations (CDCs).

> For the CDCs emerging in the 1980s, the dearth of funding for operating expenses has obliged many to become so project-oriented that some longtime CDC supporters fear they may be giving short shrift to such traditional CDC goals as developing minority leaders or empowering poor residents. (Neal Peirce & Steinbach, 1987, p. 32)

Organizations that were originally protest groups are more likely to have the opposite problem and to become so fixated on providing local empowerment that they cannot routinize any task. There is a risk that they will continue to demonstrate at city hall about the lack of jobs, when the appropriate action is to create their own employment and training agency and begin to fund their own enterprises.

Community organizations have to find a balance between empowerment and problem solving that works for them. Sometimes recognition of the problem can suggest some ways to combat it. While some women's shelters simply provide a social service, other

> collectives remind themselves that if a commitment to democracy and participation is to be lived, then the criteria for success is not just the accumulation of programs and money. They recognize how quickly efficiency replaces participation and build in mechanisms to challenge the abuse of authority and power. They encourage many women to get involved in committee and house meetings. (Schechter, 1982, p. 103)

Another approach is to divide the tasks between two related organizations.

> Some of the most successful community organizing and development have occurred with a division of labor between an advocacy, action oriented coalition, and its more pragmatic neighborhood development partner. It does, however, require that the development group subordinate its plans to the organizing agenda. (Lenz, 1988, p. 27)

It may also be helpful to divide up the organization's task into those that really must be routinized and those that can be done more informally or episodically. For example, many skills of financial management are necessarily routine. Collecting fees for services and paying bills for lights, heat, telephone, rent, and insurance have to be done regularly, on time, or activities are likely to grind to a halt.

Obtaining funds and paying bills is not very interesting, but if money does not come in regularly, the organization may ricochet from crisis to crisis. Crisis management may be exciting, but people get weary of the constant heavy demands on them. The routine activities to make sure bills are paid can be supplemented by more creative fund-raising events that give everyone a chance to participate.

In short, development organizations can maintain a balance between routinization and flexibility by selecting interesting tasks for members to do that encourage participation and a sense of empowerment without draining members with perpetual crises.

Broad Participation or Professional Effectiveness.   Developmental organizations may succeed by hiring experts to do some of the work; but if organizational members do not participate and expand their confidence to handle new tasks, the organization is not achieving developmental ideals.

Avoiding dependence on experts and professionals is difficult. Social service programs run by and for community members are often in direct competition with governmental social service agencies staffed by professionals who want to serve the same clients. Competition over who should help battered women illustrates this problem.

> As professionals established "family violence" as their realm of expertise, their feminist colleagues were discredited as "not professional enough" and labeled irrelevant. . . .
>
> Shelters had to lay their claim to expertise in order to ward off competition from more traditional agencies and obtain funding. . . . Adding more difficulties, funding agencies, boards and some staff advocated or demanded the hiring of professional directors or counseling staff in order to acquire the expertise needed to survive and help battered women. (Schecter, 1982, pp. 107–108)

Workers in community-based service organizations have to be expert enough to satisfy funding agencies and compete with traditional service providers but not so expert as to alienate themselves from people in need. Experts generally demand deference, the wrong message to give clients who need to develop self-confidence.

Difficulties can occur whenever community participation collides with a need to maintain a professional staff. In one case, a health center was set up in a minority community and jointly supervised by a government agency and a citizens' board. The professionals running the center felt that local citizens should only be advisers and the administrators should run the center. As a consequence, citizens had little involvement in establishing policies, and the resulting conflicts between the professionals and citizens' groups led to the withdrawal of financial support (Hessler, 1977; Hessler & Beavert, 1982).

To avoid such problems, experts should be treated as hired labor who work for the community organization. Their job is to find out how to do what the members of the organization want to do. A consultant provides technical advice, while the members of the organization make decisions on goals and targets. Suppose a community organization is working to promote neighborhood economic development. The organization hires a consultant who describes the options for project financing and then disappears as organization members decide what to do with the information. Another approach is to have professionals develop expertise among community members. Consultants who understand the importance of local autonomy are available from the progressive coalition organizations.

A third response is to resist professionalization unless it is absolutely necessary. Sometimes specialized technical skills are less important than experience and sympathy, as a particularly successful women's shelter illustrates.

> Because the staff selects its new members from former residents, residents do not confront social service "experts" in the [shelter], but rather women much like themselves. The staff and residents not only share a history of battering and shelter residence, but also generally belong to the same social class. (Rodriguez, 1988, p. 248)

At that moment of their lives, the residents of the shelter needed to know that other women like them were able to get out, to support themselves, and to rebuild their lives. Overly sensitive to domination, they needed role models more than they needed professionally trained experts to advise them. Because the organization does its own training, it is simultaneously increasing the capacity of individuals and providing good advice.

To summarize, in progressive organizations, there is a tension between the effectiveness that comes with professional skill and broader democratic participation. The tension can be eased in several ways. Organizations can hire experts but keep a close rein on them, or the organization can emphasize a teaching model, in which experts pass on their knowledge to organization members, who in turn combine their own experiences and training to develop a self-maintaining local capacity.

The Third Dilemma: Power Versus Dependence.   Almost by definition, locally controlled organizations are small and poorly financed. They need more resources to successfully carry off projects, but if they give up some decision-making autonomy to get that additional support, it may become impossible for their members to continue to make policy decisions.

For example, suppose a small neighborhood cooperative joins with other cooperatives to purchase goods in bulk to get a cheaper price. One coop might want to buy blue cheese while the other wants to buy cheddar. All of a sudden, the choice of which cheese to purchase has to be negotiated, the members of each group no longer having an automatic say. In this case, the slight autonomy lost is far more than made up in the increased economic power.

The loss of autonomy is likely to be greater if an organization seeks funding from government. The group is likely to be co-opted; that is, their goals and objectives may change to match what the government is willing to fund. The members of a community organization cannot make major policy decisions if the funding agency determines the projects and the way they will be carried out.

Government funding is likely to make a group less oriented to community solutions and more oriented toward traditional social services carried out for clients. Critics argue that this is what happened to the old Mobilization for Youth Program. That program changed "from a nonbureaucratic, nontraditional social work agency to a reform organization concerned with institutional change," and then it became a heavily bureaucratized organization providing services directed to individual adjustments (Helfgot, 1981, p. 131). When those forcing changes are also those providing the funding, it can be very difficult to resist the pressures.

The problems of resource limitations are endemic to poor people's organizations. Even though the initiative for action comes from the local group, funding is likely to come from government, the business community, and the philanthropic sector (Task Force, 1987, p. 39). As such, organizations become dependent and vulnerable to any cutoff in funds. Organizational survival becomes the goal rather than the means of accomplishing community goals. Goals change just to keep the organization alive.

Though the problem of maintaining independence while working with other organizations will always be present, there are some ways to prevent it from becoming destructive. If there is a danger that funding agencies will derail the goals of a community organization, one solution is to keep the budget small. Small budgets preserve organizational independence because the

> hardest organizations to kill off are those with modest budgets which raise their own funds from inside the neighborhood. . . . They get along without high-paid organizers. They may borrow organizers, hire them at modest prices, or have volunteer leaders do the job. (Cunningham & Kotler, 1983, p. 158)

This solution might work for social service providers but is unlikely to be effective when investment capital for economic projects is required. For economic projects, a better approach is to fund one project from the profits of earlier projects. Alternatively, the group can rely on community-controlled or cooperatively maintained banks. The Mondragon cooperatives in Spain own their own banks and use profits from one progressive organization as seed money for other cooperatives (Whyte & Whyte, 1988). Closer to home, Chicago's South Shore Bank is community controlled and supports local projects.

Ultimately, there is a tradeoff between doing what can be done with limited funding and the loss of autonomy that occurs with increased outside support. Organizers have to try to find a middle ground that balances autonomy and resources if they are going to make democratic development a reality.

To summarize, developmental organizations attack problems directly. They provide social services or economic programs that are controlled by and benefit community members. Their goal is not only to solve problems such as unemployment but also to empower the community and increase the capacity of individuals. They must be democratically run to achieve these goals. If, in their efforts to solve problems, they set up too many boring routines that do not attract the membership, they cut themselves off from the community. If they rely too heavily on technically trained outsiders, they may defeat the goal of local empowerment and community development. If, in their efforts to get funds, they lose community control, they fail as developmental organizations, even if they get projects off the ground.

Tensions between technical success and community control are endemic to community-developmental organizations, but there is a middle way. Organizers can provide interesting tasks for members without burning them out with continuing crises. Leaders can teach members technical skills and learn to treat experts as hired help. The group can stay small and independent or maintain enough autonomy to be responsive to members.

PROJECT-MANAGEMENT SKILLS

To provide a service or product while teaching community members skills and a can-do attitude, progressive managers adapt conventional administrative skills so they fit in a democratic organizational setting. Figure 15–1 portrays six groups of administrative and managerial techniques that can successfully transform community goals into completed projects and community-controlled services.

- *Planning* includes determining an organization's goals and priorities and deciding the steps to be taken to accomplish these goals.
- *Organizational development* involves getting people to work together, building the skills to handle technical tasks, and establishing the minimal bureaucratic structures needed to ensure democratic participation and organizational continuity.
- *Environmental scanning* encompasses coordinating with other organizations that are working on the project and determining which projects will work best in current political, economic, and social circumstances.
- *Project implementation* entails scheduling work and coordinating activities needed for project completion and adjusting assignments and timing as the project environment changes.
- *Fiscal control* means ensuring that money is available when needed and recording income and expenditures so clearly that organization members, funding agencies, and the public can see where money came from and how it was spent.
- *Evaluation* examines whether or not the goals of the organization and its membership have been accomplished.

Each of these skills is important. Without adequate planning, an organization moves from one task to another without achieving the organization's goals. Failure to build a lasting organization makes it difficult to monitor project implementation over time, and failure to set up a structure that allows for participation defeats the goals of community empowerment. If a group doesn't accommodate to changing environmental circumstances, it may respond to minor rather than major problems, or run into overwhelming unanticipated opposition. Careful financial management allows organizational members to concentrate on activities that have a high impact on the community.

In the next two chapters, we'll discuss these project-management skills in the light of the tensions between project success and democratic participation and control.

FIGURE 15–1

Administrative and Managerial Techniques to Successfully Transform Community Goals into
Completed Projects and Community-Controlled Services

16 | Organizational Development and Administration

Success at solving community problems requires not only the enthusiastic participation of organizational members but also skills at managerial tasks. If projects are underfunded and out of control, if supervision is heavy handed, the projects will fail, no matter what the original enthusiasm of community members. Familiarity with administrative procedures is empowering because it eliminates many unnecessary obstacles to successful project completion.

For example, successful neighborhood development organizations (NDOs) have a range of administrative skills, including

> assembling a complete and harmonious staff team; preparing effective proposals and reports . . . getting productive participation from the organization's board of directors; effectively dividing project responsibilities and managing that division; and providing accurate financial accounting of expenditures while making these expenditures only according to funder rules. (N. S. Mayer, 1984, p. 98)

In democratic-collectivist organizations, conventional management techniques can be modified to allow for both administrative efficiency and democratic participation. To do so, a participatory organization maintains only a minimum bureaucratic structure so as not to overwhelm individual members. Project supervision has to encourage growth in the capacity of participants. Even fund raising and fiscal control can be empowering if they give people new skills and help members feel that contributions are being used appropriately and effectively.

This chapter provides only the briefest of introductions to the details of administration. The future organizer may wish to take courses in social service administration or enroll in programs that teach managerial skills to organizers. Those with a specific interest in progressive forms of ownership and worker control can find information from the National Center for Employee Ownership (Rosen, 1989), the Industrial Cooperative Association, or the Philadelphia Association for Cooperative Enterprise (Jackall & Levin, 1984, p. 287).

ESTABLISHING THE STRUCTURE

A formal administrative structure can facilitate development projects. Most project-oriented community organizations should incorporate as not-for-profits and set up a board of directors. Being a not-for-profit allows many financial advantages while a good board of directors facilitates linking with other organizations. In addition, a working board can provide the organization with needed skills, resources, and external legitimacy.

Incorporate as a Not-for-Profit Corporation

Once community members form an organization and have decided on its overall purposes, it makes sense to *incorporate* as a *not-for-profit corporation.* Incorporation turns the organization into a legal person that can sue, be sued, receive money, contract debt, and sign contracts. It is no longer Mary Jane who is responsible for the phone bill, but the East Side Neighborhood Development Association.

Incorporation is a relatively simple matter, handled by the state government, most often by the office of the Secretary of State. It's usually inexpensive. In the application, the founders specify the purpose of the organization, give an address, and provide the names of the Board of Directors and officers. Incorporation papers can also include the bylaws, that is, the rules to be followed in running the organization.

Apply for a Tax-Exempt Status.   At some time during the first year, many community organizations are eligible to apply for a tax-exempt status with the Internal Revenue Service (IRS) under Section 501 (c)(3) of the Internal Revenue Code. One advantage of the tax-exempt status is that the organization does not have to pay federal taxes on income collected for legitimate tax-exempt purposes. The organization can also apply to the state government for an exemption from sales taxes. Most important, tax exemption allows people who want to donate money to the organization to get a tax deduction for doing so.

Wealthy people and large businesses are more likely to make donations to organizations that can give them a tax break. Private foundations, such as the Ford Foundation, are largely restricted to giving their money to other tax-exempt organizations, and many federal programs only give grants to not-for-profit groups. Finally, some lawyers who do free public service work prefer to work only for not-for-profit organizations.

There is an important catch: A tax-exempt organization is not allowed by law to spend a substantial amount of its activity lobbying, that is, trying to influence legislation.

> This means that the 501 (c)(3) group may not advocate the adoption or rejection of legislation, or urge its members to contact members of Congress with the purpose of suggesting that they support or oppose bills before them [but] 501(c)(3) groups . . . are able to advocate positions before administrative agencies and initiate litigation . . . they [tax-exempt groups] can give Congress information that is pertinent to current or proposed legislation. (J. Berry, 1977, pp. 46–47)

Political pressure groups are not eligible, but most self-help groups are eligible for tax-exempt status. The status of some groups is unclear because they provide services, but they lobby to keep their funding. To further complicate matters, what constitutes lobbying and how much lobbying is considered substantial are ambiguous. Trying to persuade legislators is treated as lobbying whereas pressuring bureaucrats and suing in court is not. But a tax-exempt group is allowed to work with legislators in an educational capacity, that is, providing technical information and background facts.

Recently, the IRS has issued rulings clarifying how much lobbying a not-for-profit is permitted and specifying in greater detail what constitutes lobbying. Since such rules do change, it is wise to check with an attorney, but the new rules seem to be quite generous. Smaller not-for-profits can spend up to 20% of their budget on lobbying with an additional allowance permitted for encouraging organization members themselves to lobby. To be considered as lobbying, at least by the IRS, the organization must make direct references to specific pieces of legislation. General discussions or background discussions about the issues of concern are not considered as lobbying. Finally, foundations are allowed to contribute money to not-for-profits that lobby, so long as the grant is not directly earmarked to pay for the lobbying (At long last, 1991).

Even with these changes, both not-for-profits and foundations that fund such groups should be cautious in claiming exemptions for actions that appear to constitute lobbying. To bypass this legal confusion, an organization that both lobbies and provides a service might want to form two groups, one that concentrates on unambiguously tax-exempt activities and the second that concentrates on lobbying. Housing organizations form not-for-profit affiliates that receive and spend the large grants and loans needed for their projects. They also set up a second organization, usually funded by dues, that lobbies and conducts protest campaigns. So long as both groups are incorporated and have their own boards, this separation of activities is legal.

Choosing a Board of Directors

As part of the incorporation procedure, the not-for-profit organization sets up a board of directors, a set of individuals legally responsible for the organization. Most community organizations must strive to set up an active board. Active board members can help solicit donations of goods and services, they can contribute their professional expertise and experience, and they may even contribute money. Lawyers and accountants sometimes make good board members. If the organization is engaged in community redevelopment, it might want builders, bankers, and artisans on the board. Skilled board members can provide advice for free that might otherwise be too expensive to obtain.

When the organization represents different constituencies, it must be cautious not to get board members from only one faction lest organization members of the other faction resign. Representing each constituency on the board may prevent destructive conflicts or at least permit problems to be worked out before the separate factions commit themselves to contending positions.

When coordination between different organizations is important, the board should have representatives from each of the organizations. Figure 16–1 portrays the structure of the board of directors of the Whittier Alliance, a neighborhood redevelopment group.

FIGURE 16–1

Whittier Alliance Organization Framework. *(Source. From* Partners *(pp. 94–95) by R. Hanson and J. McNamara, 1981, Minneapolis: Dayton Hudson Foundation. Copyright 1981 by Dayton Hudson Foundation. Reprinted by permission.)*

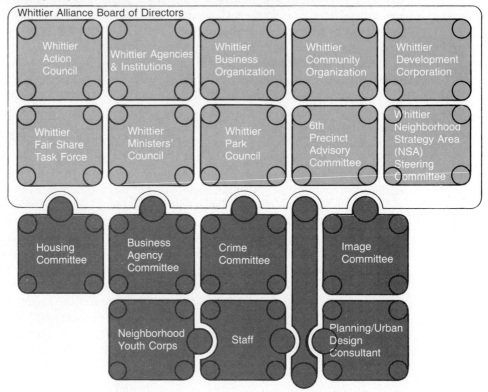

Note that the board includes representatives of the participating organizations in a structure that parallels that of an Alinsky organization.

Boards should reflect the democratic nature of an organization. As an example, worker cooperatives in the reforestation industry are divided up into work crews, each of which chooses its own leader. These leaders meet as a board to make decisions on everyday matters. To further accentuate this democratic orientation, important decisions are left to an annual meeting at which all the members meet, socialize, and decide on the direction of the organization (Gunn 1984b, pp. 144–152).

The board should include some of the activists who originally founded the organization. In recruiting other board members, make a list of people who could help the organization. Approach them, telling them what the organization wants to accomplish and why they might be interested and helpful. Make it clear that the organization requires a working board, and indicate how much work will be required. Keep the size of the board small. A decision-making group should not be much more than 10 or 12 people to get anything done.

In setting up a board, make sure its members really support the beliefs of the organization. Ideological motivations are important because, at least in cooperatives, with the exception of psychic rewards of prestige, status, and a sense of involvement, membership on the board of a cooperative does not present an attractive package of rewards and perquisites . . . members receive no compensation or reward for the long hours . . . which probably helps explain why more people do not run for the board and why turnover is so high. (E. Greenberg, 1986, p. 54)

Fortunately, studies of why people join boards of directors of not-for-profit organizations indicate that individuals willing to work hard for a cause are precisely the ones most likely to join a board. People join for community service or civic duty, as advocates of a cause, and because of "commitment to a program or an agency" or to an "ideology or movement" (Widmer, 1985, pp. 11–12).

It is especially important to check for ideological agreement when recruiting people with high prestige who might subvert the organization by trying to implement their own goals. Representatives from government or business might seek to temper the activities of the organization. Still, people with very different ideas can be won over to the community organization's views through interactions on the board. For some members of the establishment, being on the board of a community organization will be their first experience with the problems ordinary people face.

In setting up an active and involved board, organizers should keep the following questions in mind:

1. Is the person really interested in the organization and willing to spend time to help? A local state representative who will never show up to a meeting is useless.
2. Does the person have some skills or resources that are badly needed by the organization? An organizer may want to recruit a lawyer for the board to help with legal problems or a journalist to help with publicity.
3. Is there a possible conflict of interest? Don't have a banker on the board if the organization is planning to borrow from his or her bank.
4. Will the proposed board member lend legitimacy and visibility to the effort? The mayor or some other prominent citizen on the board may add a respectability to the organization that appeals to contributors. But make sure this individual will work for the group.
5. Is the board representative of racial, geographic, or interest communities involved in the work of the organization?
6. Does the board contain people whose support and opinions are necessary for the organization to accomplish its goals? For example, if the organization is running a shelter for battered spouses, it might be a good idea to have a formerly battered spouse on the board, to ensure that those running the organization always keep in mind how those receiving services feel.

After putting in a lot of effort to get the right people on the board, it is important to make sure the board members actually show up at meetings. Pick locations for meetings that minimize travel. If some members have to travel long distances, try to reduce the number of meetings required, and let them know how many meetings they will have to come to before they decide to become board members. If the meeting time means an overnight stay, be sure to find out if prospective board members can stay overnight, and try to pay for the accommodations, or else arrange meetings in more convenient places.

An effective board must be willing to ask hard-nosed questions about the administration of the organization, particularly regarding the appointment of key officials and how money is being spent. Even more important, the board has to be willing to force staff members to explain how what they are doing leads to the accomplishment of the organization's goals. With these questions, the board can counteract the tendency on the part of staff to focus on immediate problems and lose sight of major goals.

In the best possible circumstances, the board

> provides an opportunity for shared wisdom. Ideally, it places at the disposal of an institution the knowledge, insights, and personal contacts of a group of unusually able people who have wide-spread spheres of influence. . . . *Most of the time that members devote to a board is spent in aiding and supporting the institution, not in controlling it* [emphasis added]. (Houle, 1989, pp. 7–8)

ADAPTING MANAGEMENT TOOLS FOR A DEMOCRATIC ORGANIZATION

To balance participation with effective management, project leaders need to assign work and set up systems of supervision so that each participant can feel he or she is contributing to the project. Experts should not be allowed to take over policy making from the members of the organization. Conflicts over limited resources and decision-making power should be minimized. Differences of opinion should be discussed and resolved, rather than buried. Conflict should be on substantive issues, not personalities.

Managing People to Enhance Personal Capacity

Community organizations should take as part of their mission increasing the skills and experience of those working for the organization. This takes more time than hiring those who already have good skills, but it is a means of empowerment that increases loyalty to the organization.

Supervision can be reduced to a minimum and should always be light-handed. When workers are involved in what they are doing and feel that they control the work setting, they need less supervision. For example, worker-owned cooperatives have fewer supervisors than capitalist work places (Jackall & Levin, 1984, p. 7).

In community organizations, supervising with a punishment and control orientation is not appropriate. Good management is largely skillful negotiation, reconciling individual goals and values to organizational needs. There is no need to give anyone direct orders. Supervision is the means to enable individuals to hone their skills to accomplish a common goal. As one worker in a cooperative stated when asked to describe supervisors

> They're there to help us. They're there to make our job easier. They're not there as bosses. (E. Greenberg, 1986, p. 47)

Supervisors help members rather than boss them. Again, in workers' cooperatives

> the shareholder's role as an owner and not a wage laborer transforms the function of supervision from the exercise of control in the name of distant capital and management to the coordination of production. (E. Greenberg, 1986, p. 47)

Recruitment of workers should revolve around locating people who find working for the goals of the organization an intrinsically rewarding experience. It is the project leader's responsibility to set up work tasks so that the participants can see how their activity leads to the accomplishment of the organization's goals. If people cannot see how folding fliers and licking envelopes builds housing in poorer neighborhoods, they will lose their motivation to participate.

Motivating People Through Training

In development organizations, leaders should emphasize training, from classroom instruction to on-the-job activities. The objective is to get tasks done while teaching people how to handle new situations.

Training should be fun. Most people enjoy learning through doing, so use simulations to teach. Through such simulations, people learn they need to acquire additional technical skills. For example, in bargaining with business and government, the ability to read and interpret budgets and economic forecasts is central to the outcome. After several simulated sessions, community members catch on that acquiring these technical skills is the way to win.

Another technique in training for empowerment is to make sure the organization has backup people for crucial jobs. For example, the director of a drug abuse hotline might want to train a large number of operators and have a standby system so that if someone is ill or doesn't show up, a substitute can be contacted quickly. This training is often done by the people who are already on the job, because sharing knowledge in this way increases the sense of community. In addition, training backup people increases the number of organizational members who can play glamour roles and makes being an active member of the organization more attractive.

Training activities bridge the gap between expanding the skills of individuals and accomplishing organizational goals. The organization benefits as greater skills are brought to bear on the problem at hand while individuals benefit as they learn useful skills. People sometimes participate in local developmental organizations because they see it as a way to gain skills that will help them get back into the job market.

Assigning and Scheduling Work

Organizational leaders decide who is going to do what work when. Effective assignment and scheduling require thinking about what skills are necessary to perform which tasks and who is best suited for each task. Especially when working with volunteers, project directors should try to balance the glamorous work with the boring. Carting crates of food to the shelves is hard work without much glory. When there is a lot of boring work

Organizing creates paper work. (Macmillan photo)

that has to get done, it is usually better for morale to create a temporary work group to do the task in one burst. People in the work group can talk to each other, sing, compete with each other, and otherwise motivate one another, and the task is done much more quickly.

Supervision Is Supportive

Even with a democratic ethos, supervision is important. People want assistance when they begin new tasks, and supervisors have to coordinate different activities. Yet supervision has to be done with a light touch to avoid making people feel uncomfortable. Those in charge should look for ways to solve problems rather than complain about sloppy work. A particular person who does not show up on Saturday nights might be much more reliable on a Monday night. If changing the time slot works, it is a much better approach than yelling at the person for not coming in. If volunteers come to work late or are often absent, find out why. Part of the solution may be to improve day-care services.

Supervision involves some evaluation of work, but such evaluations should recognize and encourage good performance rather than criticize poor work.

In motivating people to work, even on simple, boring tasks, it is important that they be able to see how their task contributes to the achievement of the long-run goal, and it is important that they can see progress toward that goal.

Indicate to organization members personally that everyone appreciates how hard they are working. Try to show how particular contributions brought about observable accomplishments. People feel good if they believe they are contributing to the accomplishment of a goal they value. Project leaders can show progress toward goals with visual symbols, like the thermometer that measures advancement toward fund-raising goals, or a time line that shows what tasks have been done and which ones remain before the goal is reached.

Such performance evaluations formalize goals for each work team and then report on what proportion of the goals have been achieved. These techniques not only allow individuals to see how their activities are contributing to the overall goal, but they also help pinpoint the work teams that are advancing more slowly and where more people, more training, or more stimulating tasks are needed.

Conflict Resolution

Organizational leaders should try to channel conflicts toward productive ends.

> Conflict is a central feature of democratic decision making, since democratic forms of participation are designed to allow the routine expression of different interests and values. The question that faces democratic workplaces is how to treat such conflict as a normal part of the decision-making process by using it as a productive way to explore and select among alternatives. (Z. Gamson & Levin, 1984, p. 235)

When a conflict is brewing, the skillful manager should set up meetings among those who are disagreeing to explore the alternatives. In this way, conflicts over issues become an opportunity to discuss ways of improving organizational performance. The trick is to use conflict to improve the organization, without letting people waste their time battling one another.

Conflict is endemic to project implementation. People quarrel about who will get limited resources; they disagree about priorities; and they may resent others who they think are not carrying out their share of the work. Especially in neighborhood-based organizations, conflicts can be exacerbated by differences in ethnic, racial, or religious background.

People sometimes fight with each other because they don't like one another or because they are prejudiced against other ethnic groups. It is foolish to waste time on fights like this.

In conventional organizations, conflict often occurs because higher-level managers keep information from organizational participants, creating jealousy and uncertainty among workers. In democratic organizations, more people share knowledge about how resources are distributed and what the constraints are. This knowledge should persuade people to curtail some of their demands and thus help prevent some conflicts.

Face-to-face relationships improve coordination. (Macmillan photo)

Organizations can also reduce conflicts by working out rules and letting people know what they are in advance. For example, if quarrels over resources are likely, the rule might be: Whoever brings in a grant gets to spend it; or section x of the organization will get more money this year, but section y will get more next year. The particular solution is less important than working out a system in advance to help defuse competition over resources.

If the organization is large enough to have several competing sections, the possibility of conflict can be reduced by structuring the work flow appropriately.

> Avoid placing groups in direct win–lose situations. . . . Direct the conflict toward enabling both groups to be partial winners. When negotiating, do not place representatives in the dilemma of choosing between loyalty to their group or loyalty to the best interests of the [organization]. (Daft, 1983, p. 452)

The work should be structured and resources allocated so that members of one part of the organization do not feel that another group's gain is their loss. If the success of one part of the organization results in a few extra dollars, perhaps those dollars should be spread around, so that one group's victory directly benefits the entire organization. Or if one work group finishes a task early, it joins with others to help them finish. Incentive systems that put people or units in direct competition with each other, in which some win and some lose, are likely to aggravate the level of conflict.

Reduce conflicts between people working in specific projects or parts of the organization by rotating personnel. Members working on a unit or project become loyal to each other and come to see those working on separate projects as competitors. To defuse this insider–outsider mind set, rotate participants among different projects or work teams. In this way, people develop a sense of the whole organization and the contribution of each part to the whole.

The more the democratic-collectivist ideal is realized, the lower the level of harmful conflict. Disruptive conflict is lowest when people feel a sense of group solidarity. Conflict is most functional when it encourages people to express their values and ideas in an atmosphere of mutual respect.

ORGANIZATIONAL FUND RAISING AND FISCAL ADMINISTRATION

The major purpose of fund raising is to pay for running the organization. In addition, some fund-raising activities allow members an opportunity to contribute to and work for the organization.

Fund Raising for Organizational Commitment

Fund raising not only provides the money needed to keep an organization going but helps increase commitment to the organization. After they have paid dues, people are more likely to think the organization is worthwhile. Also, those who pay dues are more likely to join in the activities of the organization.

There are two ways to solicit funds, person to person, or through direct mail. Progressive organizations favor door-to-door fund raising rather than direct mail campaigns because such canvassing lets organizers talk to people, find out what they feel, and dramatically increases the likelihood that people will respond favorably.

> Though direct mail can reach much larger audiences, the response rate is just a fraction of the rate for a canvass campaign. . . . Perhaps 1–4 per cent of the people who get a direct-mail solicitation will send back a contribution while "good canvassers will get financial contributions from 15–35% of their cold contacts," according to a paper written by leaders of ACORN. (A. Cooper, 1985, p. 2647)

The following are some hints for successful fund raising:

1. People give to people. Ask in person.
2. The best people you can ask for money are those who already have given money. Keep complete records of your donors.
3. People cannot respond unless you tell them what you want. Always ask for a specific amount or item. Be enthusiastic, optimistic, and bold. You get what you ask for.
4. People who ask for money become better givers. People who give money become better askers.
5. People want to back a winner. Be proud of your organization, what you do, and how you do it. Success breeds success!
6. More people mean more money and more funds. Find a job for every volunteer. Make it more fun to be on the inside and participating than on the outside and looking in.
7. People want recognition. Send thank-you notes! (Flanagan, 1981, pp. 170–171)

More details on how to raise funds while increasing commitment to the organization can be found in publications put out by the Foundation Center and the Fund-Raising Institute.

In a door-to-door presentation, the canvasser should present his or her own name, the organization's name, its purpose, its accomplishments, the nature of the problem, and the way that the potential donor can contribute to the solution. All this information has to be presented briefly:

> [Name and identification] My name is Deanne Sassafras and my family and I live around the corner on Elm Street. [Organization's name] I'm working with the Working Mother's Association, [Accomplishments] the group that stopped the closing of the Medical Clinic. [Current Problem] This time we are fighting to keep the Community Day-Care Center open near the south-side office complex. [What the donor can do] To help us put out fly-ers and pay for the legal fees to fight the city's decision, [Amount of contribution] we're asking each family to contribute $10. Will you help us?

The purpose is to describe the group and the issues, motivate people to join, and get a commitment (in the form of a contribution), all in a short presentation.

Mail solicitations are necessary for organizations whose supporters are located throughout a city or throughout the country. As they get started, organizations try to obtain mailing lists from similar organizations. For example, the Sierra Club maintains a nationwide list of people who are known to donate to environmental causes, while Co-op America maintains mailing lists of people interested in an alternative, cooperative economy.

Written appeals for funds should include descriptions of what the organization is doing and why, ways of obtaining more information, the organization's name and address, and directions on how to send money. A neighborhood-based organization might send out the following letter.

> [Statement of the Problem] What is happening in our neighborhood? Garbage is accumu-lating in the alleys, litter is blowing through the streets. Recently, packs of dogs have be-gun prowling the alleys, threatening children. [Who] Your neighborhood organization, *Better Neighborhoods for Us,* wants to solve these problems.
>
> [What the organization is doing] We are proposing a two-part solution, In the first part, we in the neighborhood will have an outdoor cleanup day on October 15. Then, *Bet-ter Neighborhoods* will pressure the city to improve street sweeping and garbage pick up and to catch the wild dogs.
>
> [Accomplishments] We have never yet lost a campaign, and we have been active since 1965. We fought the city over street lights and got new lights. We got the city to close the open drainage ditch behind the school, and we got a new heating system for the school. We can win this one too, but we need your support.
>
> [What the donor can do] We need your help to rent equipment for the cleanup day. [Use of the money] It costs $300 a day to rent a truck with a sweeper, if we staff the truck with volunteers, and it will cost about $250 to buy rakes and brooms to sweep out alleys and empty lots. [How much] With a donation of $5, you can join our effort to clean our neighborhood.
>
> [Instructions on how to give the money] Please send your donation to *Better Neigh-borhoods,* 1001 MacClean Blvd., Big City, 00000. Or drop your donation off in person. We would like to meet you and tell you how the campaign is going.

More details on how not-for-profits have successfully used direct mail campaigns can be found in Torre and Bendixen, *Direct Mail Fund Raising: Letters That Work* (1988). The book emphasizes how to build effective mailing list by incorporating information from prior responses to solicitation letters.

No matter what technique is used, good fund raising campaigns publicize the activities of the organization, for example, by sending out posters that show the group's accomplishments. Fund-raising events themselves can highlight an organization's program and successes:

> The Amnesty International (AI) adoption group . . . sponsored an Argentine Concert Series. . . . AI works to free prisoners of conscience and to stop the death penalty. . . . Each local group "adopts" prisoners in one prison, then works to persuade the government in question to release the prisoners. . . . The . . . group had adopted prisoners and their families in Argentina, so they combined concerts featuring Argentine mimes and musicians with discussions about the issue. (Flanagan, 1982, p. 145)

In a similar vein, a historical preservation society might hold an open house in a restored mansion, serving food on the lawn, for a few dollars, to show how preservation enriches a community. Or a wildlife preservation group can collect fees for leading a canoe tour down a lonely river, to enhance respect for the wilderness.

Special events can be set up to create a sense of community integration, which may be one of the goals of neighborhood-based organizations. For example, a street fair with booths containing ethnic foods, jewelry, or art can symbolize the cultural richness and integration of community life. The annual food festival in the Hill area of St. Louis creates community solidarity while raising funds for the neighborhood organization (Schoenberg 1980).

Community organizations sometimes use a wide variety of special events to raise funds and involve volunteers. These events vary from luncheons, to selling ad books, award dinners, art fairs, and virtually any other activity that enables community members to participate, is fun, and has a reasonable chance of collecting money. Such events give volunteers a sense of accomplishment.

Good Fiscal Management Practices

No matter how money is obtained, it is important that it be wisely managed by following sound fiscal practices. While the business management techniques described here may not sound like the proper tasks of community organizers (though the job ads request such skills), they are very important for keeping an organization alive.

> *No matter how dedicated the membership and how worthy the cause, without proper fiscal management, community organizations will collapse.*

A community organization with good financial records appears efficient and honest to potential lenders, to donors, and to its own membership. Donors want to know that the organization will spend the money in accordance with their specifications. They often require that a recipient organization has the proven capacity to track funds and does not mix money earmarked for different purposes. Members want to know that their money is being spent as they intended. It is very discouraging to members to discover that no one can account for the money they have been setting aside for a project.

Missing money at best makes members feel that their efforts have been wasted; at worst, it suggests corruption.

Good financial practices actually save money. The dollar savings come from three places. First, an organization that is financially well managed needs to borrow less, so less money is spent for interest charges. If the organization does need a loan, it is more likely to get one if it appears fiscally responsible. The ability to borrow may mean the difference between survival and collapse, especially when grant money is coming in after project expenses have occurred. Second, a financially well-managed organization can earn interest on revenue by careful cash management. Third, organizations that pay bills on time get discounts from vendors.

The financial management techniques of program budgeting and cost accounting help identify areas in which the community organization's costs are too high, allowing the group to reduce costs and increase efficiency. Another reason to pay attention to financial management is that it enables the organization to survive fluctuations in revenues and have something put aside for unexpected expenses.

Budgeting and Accounting.   The heart of good financial management is a two-step process of budgeting and accounting. Together, budgeting and accounting link revenues to plans for projects, allowing the organization to prove money was spent appropriately and wisely. In addition, budgeting and accounting ensure that enough money is on hand when needed, while providing information that helps organizations get good value for the dollars spent.

A budget is a statement that balances estimates of both revenues and expenditures and allocates money to accomplish what the membership wants to do. Budgeting ensures that revenues and expenditures match, which prevents expensive emergency borrowing and possible bankruptcy.

Making good estimates of revenue and expenditures is difficult the first year, because members do not yet know how much things cost, what they will use, or how much revenue they will receive. Instead of relying on past experience, estimates have to be built step by step by figuring out the costs for everything required to run a program. First, think of the projects planned, and list all the activities associated with those projects: putting out a newsletter, busing people to the demonstration, providing day care for children. Then estimate what expenditures each of these activities will entail, for example, by calling the bus company to see how much renting a bus will cost. Then think of the continuing and routine costs: paying rent, light, heat, insurance, and office supplies.

For an organization planning a community day-care center, costs will include operating expenses (such as rent, heat, light, insurance and personnel) and supplies (such as toys, paper towels, and lunches). Personnel include both teachers and administrators for the center.

Budgets are built up in *service levels* or cost packages; that is, the organization plans a given amount of service or a certain number of projects at a given cost. Some services can be increased a little at a time, but others have to be increased in whole units. You can usually add one more child to a day-care center at a fixed additional cost, but it is hard to think how one can successfully start half a community-owned store or rehabilitate only half of a deteriorated building. Additional children in the day-care center may require additional room. More space requires larger heating and electricity bills. More children may also require more instructors, but probably won't require more people to administer the program unless the center gets very large.

Estimating revenues is more difficult than estimating expenditures because no one knows in advance how many people will contribute how much money. Each potential source of revenue should be forecast separately. Revenues from dues can be approximated by multiplying the estimated number of members by the amount of dues. For contributions, estimate the number of fund raisers in the organization, and use information from other organizations to anticipate how many people they can reach and how much each person reached is likely to contribute. Information about the payoffs from special events can also be obtained from other groups. After the first year, the estimates should improve.

When estimating revenue, be sure to subtract the anticipated costs of fund raising. Thus, the cost of printing a leaflet needs to be subtracted from the revenue obtained from door-to-door solicitation; the costs of hiring a band and a hall need to be subtracted from the revenues from a benefit dance.

How well original revenue estimates and planned expenditures balance are shown in a budget. If they are out of whack in the original budget document, either expenditures have to be cut or other sources of revenue found. Table 16–1 shows a simple sample budget.

The expenditure items in the sample budget are grouped into programs, and the programs are in turn broken into *line items*. In Table 16–1, the programs are emergency shelter, financial counseling, psychological counseling, nursery, and administration. The line items are groups of similar costs, such as personal services or supplies.

If there is question about any of the budget lines, they can be broken down further. Thus, if a board member wants to know whether the director or instructional staff are getting benefits, the personnel line can be broken out into wages and benefits. Although the budget is built up from detailed estimates, there is generally no need to put all the detail in the document, unless there is a question of cost or accountability. For example, the supplies line item might be made up of letterhead stationery, yellow legal pads, pens, and typewriter ribbons for the administration program, and toys, construction paper, paper towels, diapers, and disinfectant for the nursery, but they appear only as "supplies" in the budget.

Note that the sample budget is balanced; that is, estimated revenues equal or exceed estimated expenditures. Ideally, a larger amount would be reserved for contingency, that is, unexpected expenses like a boiler or roof repair. The small size of the contingency fund and the low amount of the salaries indicate this group is operated partly on donated labor, for example, to staff the emergency shelter project, and is running on a very low budget for what it is trying to accomplish. Any unexpected drop in revenues could throw this organization into a deficit and force it to borrow to stay afloat.

Balancing Revenues and Expenditures

Community organizations should avoid deficits. Once an organization starts spending more than it is taking in, leaders spend all their time trying to raise funds, and organizational objectives get lost in the shuffle. An organization may become so des-

TABLE 16-1
Spouse Abuse Center Budget, 1991

Revenue Source	Revenue Estimates ($)	
	Amount	Total
Grant revenue		
City donation	5,000	
Title XX	40,000	
Family Service	7,500	
Foundation	10,000	
Contributions		
Individual	5,000	
Corporate	10,000	
Total		77,500

Program	Expenditure Estimates ($)		
	Nonpersonal Services	Personal Services	Total
Emergency shelter program			
Rent	12,000		
Utilities	3,600		
Laundry	1,200		
Insurance	2,400		
Security	10,000		
Subtotal	29,200		
Financial counseling			
Personal services		6,000	
Psychological counseling			
Personal services		6,000	
Nursery			
Supplies	2,000		
Furniture	3,000		
Personal services		6,000	
Subtotal	5,000	6,000	
Administration			
Salaries/benefits		22,200	
Telephone	2,000		
Postage	500		
Photocopy	300		
Supplies	200		
Contingency	100		
Subtotal	3,100	22,000	
Total	37,300	40,200	77,500

perate that it modifies what it is trying to accomplish to please funding agencies, thereby reducing local empowerment.

In planning to balance a budget, fiscal conservatism is a wise tactic. Fiscal conservatism means being careful with money. (It doesn't have anything to do with being politically or socially conservative.) The most fiscally conservative approach to balancing a budget is to plan fixed and recurring expenditures not to exceed income that is virtually certain. Fixed and recurring expenses are costs that have to be paid every month, like salaries, rent, electricity, heat, telephone, and duplication costs. Only after paying these expenses should the organization plan to spend money on nonrecurring items, such as the purchase of special equipment.

If the organization is fiscally conservative, it will never run a deficit; it won't miss any pay days; it will pay bills on time; and it won't have to borrow very often. However, sometimes the urgency of social problems makes members willing to accept more financial risk. Shelters for battered women are now overcrowded and the number of homeless people has dramatically increased. A group may decide to commit the money now, before it is in hand, to alleviate misery, and hope that additional revenue will show up by the time the bills are due.

Spending money for urgently needed community services is laudable, but don't throw caution to the winds. Look at the variable sources of revenue and make a conservative estimate of what they will yield. It is fairly safe to take the lowest yield in the past and bet that this year's revenue won't be worse than that figure.

When the pressing need for the services or projects requires a more risky strategy, organizations should try to compensate by making sure that expenditures are a little flexible and there is something that can be cut if revenue does not show up. For example, if the project funded with uncertain revenue requires hiring people for temporary tasks, make sure the personnel policy permits giving a short notice to lay off people in case of funding shortages. Or consider the possibility of salary reductions or furloughs (mandatory, unpaid leaves) to save money without firing people. These are unpleasant choices, but the more uncertain the funds that the revenue managers commit to recurring expenses like salary, the more they have to think about ways to recoup in case the revenue does not appear. Organization leaders have to keep paying bills if the organization is to keep going.

Accounting.   Some kind of bookkeeping system is necessary to record money received and money spent. Such a system should be started as soon as the organization is set up. It can be very simple, based on check stubs, or it can be quite elaborate with different accounts and double-entry bookkeeping.

For organizations that are running several programs at the same time, a more complicated bookkeeping system is required, perhaps necessitating hiring an accountant to set up the books. A good accounting system can *track* dollars, reporting on when they came in and where they went. When receiving funds from granting agencies and governmental bodies, it is very important to be able to demonstrate that grant money was spent as promised. A city housing department frowns on the grant for housing they provide being used to pay for a day-care center until the community organization receives the state funds to pay for the day care, especially if the organization couldn't prove which dollars had been spent for what.

The accounting system lets people stay on top of how well revenues are matching expenditures by providing information on cash flow. *Cash flow* is the relation of revenues and expenditures at any one time. An annual budget might be balanced for the whole year, because a grant is coming in during the fourth quarter. But the expenses are continuous throughout the year. How do organizers pay bills during the first three quarters of the year? For those three quarters, revenue is likely to be less than expenditures, a real management problem. This kind of problem, not having the cash on hand to pay bills when due, is called a *cash-flow problem*.

One technique to handle cash-flow problems is to pay all recurring expenses and postpone commitments for nonrecurring expenditures until cash is at hand. Be cautious about borrowing to handle cash-flow problems, and when borrowing is necessary, try to find a sympathetic lender. Sometimes, profitable cooperatives will invest funds in other community-based activities, and there has been a recent increase in the number of alternative funding sources for progressive organizations (Bruyn, 1987).

Cost Control and Cost-Effectiveness

Detailed accounting data help establish the actual costs the organization faces and the proportion of total budget spent on particular items or programs. Such information focuses attention on problems that are causing increased expenses and where the organization is making or losing money.

Records of the costs and returns can help save an organization that is in financial trouble by pinpointing its less profitable parts. A food cooperative that is losing money each month is in trouble. If a detailed analysis of accounting data shows that it is making money on grains and nonperishables but losing it on fresh produce, the cooperative board has several options: go out of business, improve the profitability of fresh produce, or drop that area of activity.

Accounting data permit cost comparisons with other organizations. For example, in an apartment cooperative, board members may try to compare how much owners of privately owned buildings are paying for heat, water, or maintenance. However, while cost comparisons between for-profits and community-controlled organizations are useful, they have limits. For example, in a cooperative, many expenses are paid for collectively (that is, everyone pays), so the incentive for individuals to reduce expenses is reduced. The following exchange at a board meeting of a cooperative illustrates this point.

> **Member:** I asked about the increase in my rent ("carrying charge"). The explanation was that it was the fuel bill. I looked at our fuel bill and was shocked. I wonder why we don't have storm windows to cut down the bill.
> **Management:** Little can be done other than the storm windows, which according to the rules, any member can put up.
> **Member:** If I put them up, and nobody else does, it costs me money and there are no heat savings. (H. J. Rubin, 1981, p. 169)

The obvious solution to such problems is to build cooperatives with individual metering for heat and electricity. But if too many expenses are individualized, the cooperative spirit evaporates.

Keeping costs down is especially important when dealing with poor people or trying to attract new members. Yet progressive organizations are more than simply businesses trying to reduce expenses. In the housing cooperative example, the co-op was trying to teach people to work together within a residential community even if it meant higher costs for heating. The cooperative spirit is worth something, but overall costs still have to be kept down, or the project will not be able to serve those of moderate means.

Risk Management.   Community organizations, especially those working with volunteers on controversial issues, must be prepared for problems caused by accidents, malevolence, or lawsuits. Anticipating such problems is termed *risk management.* Because the potential losses resulting from an accident—a fire in the workplace—or from an unplanned event can seriously disrupt operations, the organization must make allowances for those risks. One way of buffering the organization against such losses is insurance.

Insurance against loss of services and property is a vital part of prudent financial management, though the precise form of insurance depends on the activity. For example, if the community organization plans to take the elderly shopping, vehicle insurance and driver liability insurance are essential. Almost every organization needs fire and theft insurance and protection against a lawsuit if someone trips and falls in the office and sues.

Those organizations performing health or counseling services should carry malpractice insurance. What if a counselor advised a woman to return to her husband after he had beaten her, and she followed the advice, only to be beaten again and hospitalized? Can the organization be successfully sued for malpractice? If there is even a chance that this could occur, the organization ought to get malpractice insurance.

If some members of the organization handle large amounts of money, especially from government or foundation funds, they should be bonded. Bonding is a guarantee that if someone runs off with the organization's money, the insurance company will make up the loss. Before someone is bonded, they must be approved by the insurance company, so a person with a record for embezzlement is not likely to be bonded.

How much insurance is needed depends on the dollar value of the property and the risk inherent in the operations (a shelter for the abused is more risky than a food cooperative.) Talk over these issues of coverage and cost with an insurance broker and with a representative of a state or national coalition of community organizations. If the estimated expense of needed coverage is too great for the budget to bear, consider joining an insurance pool. This is an alternative to commercial insurance, created by several community organizations that contribute to a fund to be used in emergencies ("Nonprofits Pool Resources for Liability Coverage," 1989).

If developmental organizations are not well managed, they will fail. But good management should not take precedence over community empowerment and enhanced individual capacity. Rather, the management of project-oriented community groups needs to blend the needs of democratic participation and training for capacity with good managerial techniques. Light and helpful supervision, fund raising that builds commitment, and financial management that understands the press of social problems merge community-building ideals with prudent management practices.

17 Project Management: Planning, Funding, Implementation, and Evaluation

The successes of developmental organizations have been limited because they get the toughest of problems and often get them only after other approaches have failed. The police have been unable to hold down crime rates, so why should a community group be able to do any better? If banks and businesses have decided to withdraw investment from deteriorating neighborhoods, where can local people obtain the money to make up the loss? Private supermarkets are only marginally profitable; how can a group of neighbors, without food handling or marketing experience, hope to keep a food cooperative afloat?

With firms that workers have bought from failing companies, the problems are even more acute.

> When a community or a group of workers joins together to purchase a firm and operate it according to democratic principles, the firm is almost always in dire economic straits. In fact, community or employee purchase is often a last-ditch effort to stem economic failure and closure. (Z. Gamson & Levin, 1984, pp. 220–221)

But it is not simply the complexity of the problems facing the developmental organizations that sometimes leads to failure. In part, it is lack of knowledge among enthused, yet inexperienced, participants on how to run a firm or provide a service. To increase the chances for project success, members of developmental organizations have to learn project-management skills—planning, funding, implementation, and evaluation. With these skills, the organization can anticipate and correct problems that, if ignored, may lead to project failure.

Without adequate planning, an organization may end up going off in all directions at once and failing to focus on those problems that can be solved. With inadequate funds, a community group can only try small projects that have minimal community consequences. Botched project implementation can throw off schedules, increase costs, and demoralize participants. Organizations that fail to evaluate their actions can neither correct mistakes nor adapt to changing conditions.

PROJECT PLANNING

Planning means working out what to do before action is taken. Why plan? Why not let things happen spontaneously? Planning has several advantages. It forces people to explore a range of problems and alternative solutions. Planning ensures that before a task is undertaken it is shown to be a means for accomplishing the long-term objectives determined by organization members.

Too often, community members see a problem and want to solve that problem immediately, for example, eliminating a crack house in a deteriorated building. They might rush right out to try to shut down the building. Such shoot-from-the-hip responses to an immediate problem prevent a group from thinking about more fundamental causes and might preclude consideration of longer-lasting solutions.

The first stage of planning involves agreement on the goals community members want to achieve. Is it the elimination of one crack house? Or is it the elimination of the visible consequences of drugs from the streets, such as drug deals and shootings? Or does the group want to address safety in the community more broadly? Was the original problem that bothered people drugs or abandoned housing? Without a consensus on overriding goals, achieved through a participatory planning process, a group might work on several unconnected activities or chase crack dealers from one abandoned building to another, without improving the community. There is no possibility of success unless the goal is clearly stated and widely agreed on.

Sometimes people agree on the goal—reduce crime, improve housing, fight gentrification—but have little sense of the intermediate steps they need to take to achieve these goals. Good planning forces people to link *goals* to more narrowly defined *objectives* and to specific, measurable *tasks* that accomplish these objectives. To reduce crime (a goal), one objective might be to improve lighting, a task easily measured by counting the number of functioning street lights and the number of ordinary lights replaced by bright sodium vapor lamps. To reduce fear of crime (a goal), an objective might be to increase the police presence on the street; success can be measured by asking residents whether they are willing to go out at night. Before undertaking a task, organization members must determine both how that task relates to a broader goal and how to judge the success of that task.

Planning forces people to think about the order in which activities are undertaken. It is tempting to focus on more manageable tasks first, rather than figuring out what must be done first. An environmental group might start fund raising to acquire ownership of a nesting site for migratory birds, a goal that pleases its members and has clear steps for accomplishment. Yet, if a major highway is going to expand near the site, a more immediate task should be to fight the highway, because the highway will claim land and pollute the area, destroying the project. Planning calls attention to the need to put tasks in priority order.

Planning is also useful because it increases the range of problems and alternatives examined. Planning relies on information gathered through action research to determine the problems people feel most strongly about, and to lay out possible solutions that are most compatible with community goals. Because planning is based on systematic inquiry, it often shows that what appears to be a single problem, say housing for the

Community projects require careful planning. (Courtesy Department of Housing and Urban Development)

poor, turns out to be several problems, including bank redlining and gentrification. Having identified several problems, planning can then lay out some possible solutions to each.

> Much of the not-for-profit community-based housing movement is linked to neighborhood struggles against both disinvestment and gentrification. Success has depended on the ability of nonprofit groups to juggle a number of conflicting goals—confronting the land-use policies of local governments and at the same time getting access to publicly-owned land; fighting inappropriate tax abatements for luxury development while seeking city and state subsidies for low-income housing; obtaining low-interest loans and mortgages while challenging banks' redlining policies. (Dreier & Atlas, 1989, p. 35)

Undertaking these tasks simultaneously is difficult but is much more likely to lead to success than taking only one approach and ignoring the other problems.

Planning encourages a search for different solutions and a comparison of their effectiveness. Planning involves determining whether others have tried to solve the problem, what was tried, and what was successful. Planning forces community organizations to compare proposed solutions by posing three questions:

1. Is the solution worth the effort? Even if the organization has the money and personnel, it might not be worth the effort to set up its own day-care center if the city or local businesses can be pressured into running the same projects.
2. Do alternative solutions produce more benefits at less cost? Building a neighborhood center and building housing for the elderly are both important, but one may cost less and be more welcome in the community.
3. Who gets the benefits and who pays the costs? Gentrification projects may improve the physical neighborhood by bringing in new housing and stores to serve upscale tenants. But if the projects displace residents and eliminate affordable stores, poor or moderate-income people pay while the well-to-do benefit.

In comparing projects, costs and benefits should include not only the dollars spent, but also the value of opportunities foregone, the value of political credit, and the social effects that are not easily translated into dollars.

First, consider monetary costs and benefits. The dollar costs of setting up and running a community day-care center include space rental, personnel costs, insurance, and supplies. Monetary costs should also include lost opportunity costs, that is, the value of projects not undertaken because the group was working on this project. These costs can be compared to the expected monetary benefits; that is, the income people can earn because they have a safe place to leave their children. Another benefit easily expressed in dollars is the reduction in payments to welfare mothers because some of them will be able to get a job if someone else watches their children. A third monetary benefit is the increased tax payments that parents can make because they can work instead of being on welfare.

Less tangible and immediate benefits and costs also need to be included in the calculation. A project that gains the group political credit with an important politician might have a value beyond the immediate economic payoff; a project that makes a politician mad at a group might not be worth doing even if its financial benefits are substantial and outweigh the financial costs. A project that increases the legitimacy of the group so that its opinions will be taken into account in other projects, may be very valuable to a group; a project that reduces the group's credibility may be avoided, regardless of the ratio of financial benefits to financial costs.

When deciding between possible projects, be sure to include the social consequences that are difficult to measure in economic terms. How does one estimate the value of the increased personal efficacy that community members feel when they learn their actions helped lower the crime rate? Or the sense of well-being of the elderly who can continue to live in their familiar community?

In weighing alternative solutions to community problems, it is helpful to draw up informal *benefit–cost* comparisons, such as those illustrated in Table 17–1. Such displays also indicate that the perception of costs and benefits might differ, depending on whether a project is considered from the perspective of a particular neighborhood or the entire city. A sports stadium might be a benefit to a city as a whole, but its construction might destroy a socially integrated neighborhood. On the other hand, in trying to get governmental support for a neighborhood project, the group must recognize that

TABLE 17–1
Illustrative Benefits and Costs of Community Projects

Project or Program	From the Perspective of the Local Neighborhood		From the Perspective of the Overall City	
	Benefits	**Costs**	**Benefits**	**Costs**
Partnership with police on neighborhood patrol	Increased surveillance of neighborhood	Time costs of volunteers in the program	Reduction in community alienation	Increases in time for community relations
	Development of contacts at precinct	Social costs of neighbors informing on other neighbors	Increased crime clearance	Pressures to provide service elsewhere
	Publicity moves criminals away	Personal danger involved in crime patrol	Reduced costs per hour of effective patrol	Operating costs of such programs, such as extra radios
	Reduction in insurance rates	Liability for false accusations		Increased crime elsewhere
	Crime reduction			
	Increased sense of security			
Neighborhood crafts festival held by closing down streets leading into small neighborhood park	Increases in community solidarity	Time and energy to organize	Enhances image of city as place with cultural diversity	Traffic management problem around festival site
	Monetary benefits to organization and participants	Loss of business for other stores in area	Provides a forum for political talks	Increase in street litter
	Publicity for the organization as a recruitment effort	Possible ethnic tensions as strangers enter the neighborhood		Pressure on city to subsidize festivals elsewhere
	Increase in street activity reduces crime	Encouraging people to spend money that could better be used for necessities		
Managing subsidized home rehabilitation program that also helps fund mortgage guarantees for new residents	Improved housing quality	Housing becomes too expensive for current inhabitants	Increases in local taxes	Increase in service demands from new residents
	Influx of new community members	Antagonisms between those subsidized and others	Slowing of migration out of the city	Pressure to house the homeless
	Increase in property values		Reduction in fire calls	Time-consuming negotiations with banks

activities that might have overwhelming benefits for a neighborhood might be seen by the city as too costly.

Planning helps to lay out and analyze possible solutions to problems, then suggests the appropriate order for undertaking tasks while highlighting the deadline before which they must be accomplished. It warns that concrete must be poured before the weather gets too cold; and grant proposals have to be written and sent to the state capital or Washington before the cutoff date. Planning also points out when resources will be needed and where bottlenecks can occur if there is insufficient personnel or money. Planning guides the scheduling and coordination of project implementation.

While planning is indispensable to community groups in carrying out their own projects, governmental bodies sometimes use planning as a means of sidetracking community input. Government sets up community-planning organizations that produce ideas that are ignored. The likely outcome is wasted time and lost enthusiasm, unless the organization has already shown those in government that the organization has political clout and cannot be ignored.

In "progressive cities" (Clavel 1986), community planning is taken seriously because the support of neighborhood organizations is crucial to politicians seeking office. With political support, some neighborhood groups actually undertake planning for the city within their own communities. This has occurred to some extent in Boston, Massachusetts, in which planning groups have a say in local zoning, and in Dayton, Ohio, in which neighborhood groups help set budget priorities.

With these two exceptions—having progressives in office who owe political support to the neighborhood and having established an independent planning capacity— planning in partnership with power is dangerous. It too easily becomes a pattern in which neighborhood goals are sought by city experts and then tossed together into a large heap of suggestions and requests from other neighborhoods. City experts maintain the decision-making power over which suggestions, if any, will be implemented and when.

> *Only when governmental bodies are willing to delegate the choice of project and its implementation to communities—a condition that occurs after neighborhood organizations have established their power—is planning with government or business likely to be useful.*

OBTAINING PROJECT FUNDS

A major problem of progressive organizations is their relative lack of funds for carrying out projects. Neighborhood organizations can hold a bake sale to pay for a microwave oven for the community center. Small efforts like this are useful because they raise funds for a needed purchase and give members a sense of participation and efficacy. However, larger ongoing projects, such as maintaining a day-care center, purchasing a neighborhood shopping center, or buying apartments, cannot be funded by a sequence of bake sales. Generally, community organizations have to combine income from several different sources to fund these projects.

As grant funding has devolved more to the states and local governments, the need to piece together funding has increased. Catherine Lovell observed that

> hundreds of community-based organizations are piecing together various sources of funds to fill out their budgets . . . opportunities for meshing the various funding sources to implement programs have been enlarged . . . by the fact that the local jurisdiction rather than the federal government now has control over allocation. Most of the community-based organizations do not depend on federal grants alone but combine the federal, state and local funds, private donations, and fees from clients. (Lovell, 1979, p. 436)

The increasing scarcity of federal funds has reinforced this trend toward multiple sources of funding.

The general pattern has been to fund ongoing expenditures, such as those for day care, with fees and donations, and perhaps an annual special event. Large projects are funded by combining money from federal or state programs, foundation grants, and special events. A housing project, for example, might get support from the city to repair adjacent streets and sewers, receive title to the property from the Department of Housing and Urban Development (HUD), and get a loan (as well as technical expertise) from Local Initiatives Support Corporation (LISC) to rehabilitate the building.

A technique to increase money for larger projects involves *leveraging,* in which a group obtains small contributions from organization members to convince potential donors of larger grants that a project is worth their investment. Another technique of increasing money is through *matching,* which occurs when a granting agency contributes a dollar (or some other amount) for every dollar of locally collected funds. Foundations particularly like this approach because they consider the ability of the local group to raise its own funds as an indication of community support for the project.

A third technique to fund larger projects is to establish a *revolving loan fund.* With a revolving loan fund, the development organization provides loans to community members or community businesses at low interest rates. As the loans are paid back, the same money is used to fund similar projects. The original funding can come from donations, foundation grants, or government programs. In this way, organizations spend the same dollar many times.

Many of the accomplishments of the Neighborhood Housing Services (NHS), an organization set up to stop the decline in deteriorating neighborhoods through housing rehabilitation, are achieved with revolving loan funds. To keep the revolving loan fund intact, NHS tries to ensure that people pay back the loans. To do so, it helps community members buy building materials at cost, provides training in building techniques, and refuses to loan recipients more than they can afford to pay back. For those too poor to borrow money, NHS supplies grant money from foundations.

The key question in all of this is how we get the money in the first place. One way is to sell goods and services. Another way is to apply for grants from government agencies, foundations, and businesses. A third approach is to set up a business, initially borrowing some of the funds, and later recycling recovered loans and profits into new projects. The fourth approach is to lobby local government to design programs that funnel some development expenditures into the neighborhoods.

Selling Goods and Services

For ongoing services, community organizations need to have a continuing source of funding, such as a fee for service or a government contract for service delivery. Day-care centers pay for their daily costs through fees charged to parents, and the basic costs of tenant-managed housing are met from rental payments, though both parents and tenants may receive support from government programs to help pay costs.

Community organizations can also get income by working under contract to governmental agencies. Local governments contract for health services and day care, often with not-for-profits, and occasionally with neighborhood organizations (Hatry & Valente, 1983). By providing needed services paid for by a government contract, the community organization can tailor the services to community needs.

There are, however, some disadvantages of contract work. Contracted services are often those considered most marginal by local government and the first to be dropped when money is scarce; a community organization might hire staff to carry out a service contract only to have to fire these employees when government funding dries up. Another problem is that the contract might not cover all costs, leaving the community organization in a financial bind. In either case, service recipients are likely to blame the community organization for poor service rather than the agency that cut the funding. These potential drawbacks suggest some caution in writing up the contract to ensure that the level of service is specified and that the full costs for that level of service are covered. The group might ask for a multiyear contract to provide some protection against the ups and downs of municipal budgets.

Applying for Grants

Seed money and capital funding for large projects often come from grants from governmental agencies, foundations, and corporations. Depending on the source of the grant, different techniques for applying for funds should be followed.

Governmental Grants.   To find out what projects are eligible for federal grants, consult the *Catalogue of Federal Domestic Assistance* (1987), which describes program conditions and who is eligible to receive the money. However, don't be deterred if a program seems to be restricted to other governmental agencies. In many cases, a state or city agency can apply, receive the money, and maintain legal responsibility for the project, while the community organization actually carries out the activity.

Foundations.   With the reduction in federal efforts, foundations are playing an increasingly important role in funding community development and community action. Foundations vary in size from the giant Ford Foundation to small community foundations. The types of projects they fund vary from social action campaigns to research on wildlife in South America. A group should look for those foundations willing to fund the type of projects group members want to undertake.

One way to find the appropriate foundations is to look through publications put out by the Foundation Center (79 Fifth Avenue, New York, NY 10003) such as *The Foundation Directory, Foundation Directory Supplement* (supplements appear in *Foundation Center Information Quarterly*), and the *Foundation Grants Index Annual.* These books describe lists of foundations, their location, their objectives, how much money they have, and how to make contact with them. Another resource is the Grantsmanship Center, headquartered in Los Angeles. The Grantmanship Center publishes the *Grantsmanship Center News,* which provides information on deadlines for application, new funding sources, and advice on grants management and accounting. Both organizations sell books with information on how to apply for a grant.

Examine the goals of the foundations and the types of projects they have already funded. Foundations don't want to bother with frivolous applications, so they are forthright in their descriptions of what they will fund. If a community group has questions about whether a foundation might consider some particular kind of project, group members can inquire by phone or by letter.

Money for more radical projects can sometimes be found from the Funding Exchange. This exchange is funded by the children and grandchildren of the wealthy who prefer to use their inheritances for social causes:

> Instead of giving to Hampshire College, where he graduated in 1983, Mr. Collins [the great-grandson of Oscar Mayer] donated his entire $300,000 inheritance to disarmament groups, minority-leadership projects, and a variety of grassroots organizations supporting liberal causes in the South. (Greene, 1989, p. 27)

Overall, the Funding Exchange in 1989 gave away $5.5 million

> for battered women and abused children, the homeless and disabled, homosexuals, lesbians, minority members and a range of neighborhood groups that could not attract help from conventional donors. (Teltsch, 1990, p. A10)

Another potential source of grant money is from community foundations, locally based foundations meant to improve a specific geographic area. Today, 319 of them control assets of almost $5 billion. Many of these foundations not only distribute funds but also conduct research to pinpoint community problems. Their goals are often compatible with those of progressive community organizations, to help poor neighborhoods, house the homeless, and improve inadequate schools (Neil Peirce, 1989a, p. 690). As an example, in 1988

> over $11 million in grants were made to Chicago's community organizations, while the MacArthur Foundation established a several-year $11.3 million grant program for community development. (Denney & Brown, 1989, p.1)

Another increasingly important source of funding, especially for housing and community-based economic development projects, is LISC,

> a national nonprofit lending and grantmaking institution funded by private corporations and foundations. Through a network of local advisory committees . . . it helps independent, community-based development organizations to improve the physical and economic

conditions of their areas while also strengthening their management and financial capability. (Local Initiatives Support Corporation, 1982)

A recent LISC news release reported that "nearly 600 major corporations and foundations have committed more than $300 million to LISC-supported [Community Development Corporation] CDC projects in more than 30 cities. Those funds have attracted an additional $1.3 billion from public and private sources, leading to the creation of more than 21,000 housing units and nearly six million square feet of commercial and industrial space" (LISC, news release, 1989). Some of LISC's support has been in the form of outright grants, some in the form of loans, and some in the form of technical assistance.

Some early LISC projects included a $250,000 grant in Salinas, California, to open mini-mart stores, a $100,000 loan to a Hispanic Housing Development Corporation in

Housing funded by Local Initiatives Support Corporation being built by community organization in Chicago. (Courtesy of Local Initiatives Support Corporation)

Chicago for industrial development, and an $85,000 loan to the Voice of the People in Chicago for rehabilitating a 24-unit apartment building (Local Initiatives Support Corporation, 1983). Since 1980, LISC has invested nearly $5 million in the South Bronx, in support of 36 CDC-sponsored projects. LISC gave $115,000 in grants and loans to the Metropolitan Organization in Houston for housing rehabilitation and training. And LISC provided a $40,000 loan to the Hispanic Association of Contractors and Enterprises, Inc. (HACE) in Philadelphia for a commercial redevelopment project (LISC, 1988). All these projects are community run, are intended to improve conditions and increase jobs in poor communities, and require that some of the money be spent to provide training to people in the neighborhoods.

Corporations.   Especially for visible, noncontroversial housing or social service projects, corporations are a good source of funding. Recently, British Petroleum has been advertising in the business pages of newspapers that it has helped nonprofit organizations rehabilitate housing and historic buildings. They use rhetoric that should sound familiar to organizers: "symbols of urban despair turned into symbols of pride."

To trace down the businesses most likely to help, ask other community organizations which corporations have given them money in the past. Or think about which companies have the largest stake in the community and therefore want to maintain goodwill. Banks and savings and loans are likely candidates, especially because they are pressured by the Community Reinvestment Act. Major universities, especially church-related institutions, are investing money in housing programs in their community (Nicklin, 1990, p. A29). Other businesses that are dependent on community goodwill might help. For example, a car dealer might donate a van to a group transporting the elderly (Flanagan, 1982, pp. 79–80).

Some corporations are more comfortable contributing money to community groups indirectly by supporting groups such as LISC. For example, the BankAmerica Foundation has provided LISC with $10 million for low-interest loans to community groups involved in renewal efforts.

Sometimes local businesses don't think they have enough money to contribute to community organizations. If that is what they say when solicited, ask them if they have surplus furniture or equipment. Community organizations can often use tables, desks, and chairs, and from a tax perspective, giving away old equipment can be beneficial to a corporation. A company might be quite willing to give away a small office computer as it upgrades its own equipment.

Preparing a Proposal.   Leaders of community organizations have to convince government, foundations, and corporations to fund their projects. To find out who is a likely source of funding, first check the directories of grant support. Then write a preliminary letter of inquiry that briefly describes the proposed project. Most foundations and many governmental agencies will respond to such a letter indicating whether or not further work on the applicant's part is worthwhile.

Once an appropriate funding source has been located, the organization prepares a formal written proposal explaining the problem faced, the ways in which the project will solve the problem, how much it will cost, and precisely how the money will be spent. Proposals indicate who in the organization will actually run the project and their experience in managing funded projects. A proposal must convince donors that the particular project is a good one and that the organization is capable of carrying it out.

There is no surefire way of writing a proposal that will be funded, but the following advice should help:

Preface the proposal with a **brief** overview of the project's goals, its budget and procedures for evaluation. Though staff members of a foundation will carefully read the entire document, board members who make the final decisions are busy and appreciate a concise summary.

Early in the proposal, discuss the objectives of the project and the plans for achieving those objectives. Provide evidence documenting the problem that the organization intends to solve, but place detailed findings from technical studies in an appendix to the proposal. Part of the art of writing a proposal is showing that the problems are serious enough to merit a grant but not so overwhelming that the organization cannot provide a solution.

In the proposal, describe the organization, its membership, what it has accomplished, and who has benefited. Carefully relate organizational resources and experience to the particular problem at hand. Having picketed city hall is not the appropriate experience for managing a large housing rehabilitation grant, but rehabbing several small buildings might be.

Be precise in explaining exactly how the requested resources will be used by including a detailed project budget. If the foundation or governmental agency accepts the ideas and thinks that the organization has the capacity to implement them, the budget becomes the central focus of their evaluation. Too big a budget will make them nervous about the percentage of their funds going to one organization. Too small a budget, and they will worry about whether those proposing the activity understand the realities of running projects.

Use the budget to indicate the enthusiastic involvement of the organization in the project. For example, present the contributions of equipment, labor, and cash that the community and members of the organization will provide. *Sweat equity* — the voluntary contribution of community members' labor — is an important concept that funding sources like to see in proposals from poorer communities. Also, most funding organizations like to leverage their funds, so the proposal has a better chance of getting the grant it is applying for if another granting agency, bank, or foundation has already committed itself to the project.

Finally, describe how the organization will evaluate the success or failure of the project. Specifying evaluation procedures pleases the agencies, as it shows a responsibility in handling funds. Planning an evaluation also has a side benefit of making the community organization think about what members can learn from the project so future projects will accomplish even more.

On occasion, a proposal is presented orally to a selection panel or the board of a foundation or a corporation. In such personal presentations, plan to describe the idea briefly. Even if the organization has forwarded a written proposal, assume that the people hearing the presentation have not yet had the time to read it. Make sure to describe not only the importance of the project for the community but also why it fits within the mission of the foundation or agency. If they are at all interested, they'll question those making the presentation on the ideas in the proposal and the accomplishments of the organization.

The first few times an organization tries to get funding, it probably will not be successful. But sometimes the foundations or agencies will not refuse outright. Instead, they may want to negotiate. For example, they may refuse to fund the proposal as it is but may be willing to fund a demonstration project, to see if the idea will work. If the proposal is rejected outright, but members of the organization still like the idea, submit the proposal to other foundations and agencies.

Borrowing and Investing

Community organizations sometimes undertake large developmental projects—major shopping complexes, community-based industries, and neighborhoodwide housing rehabilitation programs. The costs of such projects cannot possibly be met from fees, and granting agencies rarely are willing to provide the large sums required. To accomplish these large projects, community groups often set up Community Development Corporations (CDCs) (also known as Neighborhood Development Organizations, NDOs) that piece together grants and loans from a variety of sources.

Neighborhood economic development projects depend heavily on leveraging money. A small grant is obtained to fund a staff person who then goes out and gets community contributions and promises of city support, such as donation of land or city-owned housing. Money for site improvement might be obtained from a grant from HUD or a state housing agency, while money for rehabbing of the housing is borrowed from LISC. The costs of the project are kept down by community members' contribution of their time and energy to improve the housing units.

To maintain their fiscal soundness, CDCs and banks supporting CDCs are careful to invest in developmental activities that seem likely to make a profit. But for CDCs, profit is not enough; they encourage people to learn new skills and to be more confident and competent citizens. For example, CDCs that run profit-making businesses sometimes set up not-for-profit affiliates that provide employment training, advocate tenants' rights, and put pressure on the local schools. These affiliates receive money directly from the CDC and, as not-for-profits, can accept funds from government employment programs and foundations that won't give money to for-profit businesses (Taub, 1988, pp. 116–117).

Lobbying for Financial Support

Using the Community Reinvestment Act, banks can be pressured to contribute to neighborhood redevelopment. City governments can be lobbied to design linked-development programs that give community organizations funds to compensate for the pressure that downtown development puts on housing markets. In addition, community groups can pressure local governments to set up housing trust funds to help build and rehabilitate units for the poor.

Linked-Development Financing.   Linked-development programs are government programs that resulted from community pressure to ensure that the entire city and not just the downtown area benefits from downtown office construction. Linkage programs have been adopted in Santa Monica, Boston, Jersey City, San Francisco, and Berkeley (Keating, 1989).

When linkage programs are in place, community housing programs receive contributions from developers for neighborhood housing projects. The contributions are based on a formula depending on the square footage of downtown developments. The amount of money received rarely fully compensates for the increased pressure on the housing market created by the new office complexes, but the amounts involved are still substantial. For instance, in Boston:

> By the end of 1987, more than $45 million in linkage funds had been committed by downtown developers. At least another $20 million was projected to come from projects in the development pipeline. As of the end of 1987, $17 million had been approved for allocation, primarily for "gap financing" of housing developments, encompassing about 2,000 units. A Neighborhood Housing Trust now allocates the funds, with priority given to nonprofit developers. (Dreier, 1989, p. 47)

The program has damped down conflict between supporters of downtown renewal and members of neighborhood groups. In Boston, neighborhood groups did not object to the large International Place office–hotel complex because they would receive "$6 a square foot that goes into a fund the city uses to build low-cost housing and train residents for jobs" ("Boston: Office Complex," 1990, p. 35).

Housing Partnerships and Housing Trust Funds.   Housing trust funds are "pots of money committed to constructing or rehabilitating affordable housing or providing related housing services, such as helping poor people find an apartment" ("Housing Trust Funds," 1988). Neighborhood nonprofits pressured local governments to set up such funds, and though the money is controlled by trust officials rather than neighborhood groups, community housing groups are often the recipients of the funds.

There are also other less stable sources of money for housing development. Some housing activists have suggested that tax-delinquent properties be turned over to community groups, and more recently, as part of the bailout deal for the Savings and Loan Industry, banks were mandated to target an increasing share of their profits into programs for affordable housing (Lehman, 1990, p. 2d). Such programs continue efforts by neighborhood organizations to pressure local banks to invest in the same areas of cities that their prior redlining policies harmed economically. In Baltimore:

> In less than one year, the Maryland Alliance for Responsible Investment (MARI) has built a coalition representing 17 organizations . . . won a $50 million lending agreement from Maryland's largest bank [and] introduced state community reinvestment legislation. (Chalkley, 1987, p. 1)

Similar efforts have been successful in Chicago and Washington, DC. Through legal and pressure tactics, community organizations force banks to return some of the investment funds previously extracted from urban neighborhoods.

PROJECT IMPLEMENTATION

Successful projects balance scheduling and adaptation. *Scheduling* provides direction to project implementation and helps anticipate problems, while *adaptation* implies mid-course corrections. If too much emphasis is put on adaptation, the group can get stuck in *firefighting,* that is, case-by-case solutions to immediate problems, without regard to a long-run remedy to the problem.

Scheduling and Adaptation Rather Than Firefighting

Effective developmental organizations anticipate what steps must be taken to finish a project but allow for unanticipated problems. Sometimes firefighting is unavoidable, as when a new crack house opens up in a block being renovated or a cold-wave wipes out the fuel budgets of tenant-managed housing. The community must focus police attention on the crack house, and the management team must seek additional fuel allowances.

The best way to avoid firefighting is to anticipate problems that could occur and work out solutions in advance. It won't always be possible to come up with an empowering solution, but any solution that considers the long-term implications is better than firefighting.

Another way to avoid firefighting is to draw up flowcharts and time charts that show what steps need to be taken in what order. Such charts can help group members anticipate and reduce problems while providing a sense of direction for projects. Figure 17–1 is a planning chart taken from work done by the Whittier Alliance—a neighborhood development organization in Minneapolis.

These planning charts must accommodate to both the uncertainty of some tasks and the difficulties in predicting how long each might take. Designing an intake procedure for a spouse-abuse center should be a fairly straightforward task and can rely on the experiences of other community organizations. However, if the task to be accomplished is "obtain funding for the housing project," the outcome is not so clear. State and federal funding programs may be under debate and funding levels uncertain; interest rates may be fluctuating, so the expense and availability of loans may be unpredictable. Accomplishing the task of finding funding may take more time than the time line suggests, and it may not be possible at all.

The timing of projects has to be planned around such unpredictable tasks. If a particular grant comes through, the purchase date for equipment may be pushed up, or if the grant fails to come through on time, the purchase may be delayed. If interest rates go up, the whole project may be delayed or canceled; if interest rates go down, there may be a flurry of activity to take advantage of the lower rates.

The relationship between one outcome and the next decision is termed *sequential interdependence.* Effective planning for project implementation requires thinking about the sequences of interdependent tasks, perhaps by working out diagrams such as Figure 17–2 that highlight the relationship between the different stages of pressuring the city to drop an unwanted city-sponsored development project.

FIGURE 17–1

Year 1 Activities Timing. (*Note. From Partners (p. 69) by R. Hanson and J. McNamara, 1981, Minneapolis: Dayton Hudson Foundation. Copyright 1981 by Dayton Hudson Foundation. Reprinted by permission.*)

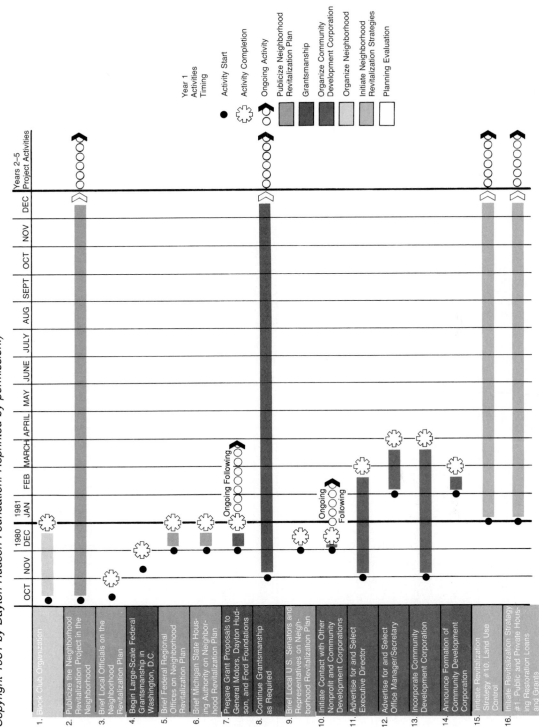

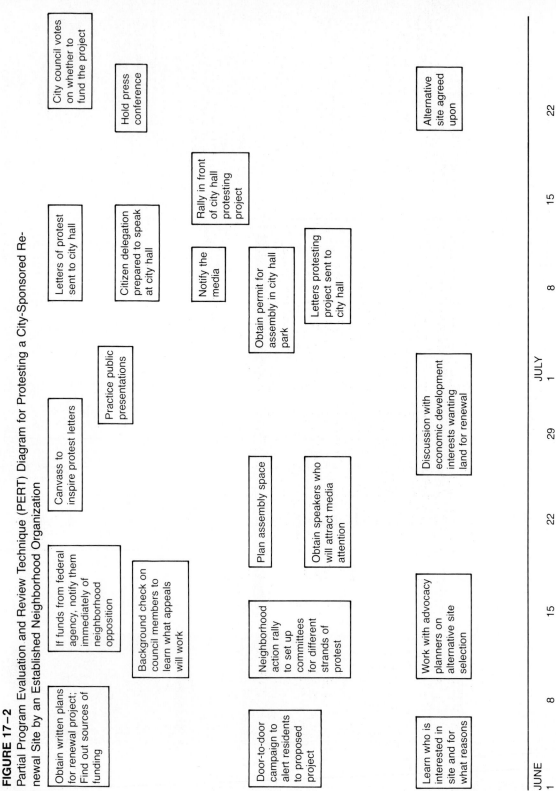

FIGURE 17–2

Partial Program Evaluation and Review Technique (PERT) Diagram for Protesting a City-Sponsored Renewal Site by an Established Neighborhood Organization

Think about a project in the following way:

1. Break up tasks into *separable action steps*. For example, break up a program to revitalize housing into the separate subtasks of evaluating the condition of the building, obtaining financing, purchasing the building, planning repairs, purchasing building materials, and carrying out the repairs.
2. Examine tasks to see if together their completion will accomplish the overall goal. If something important has been left out, the project may fail.
3. Estimate the length of time to complete each task. It is especially important to know which tasks can be speeded up with more effort and which take a relatively fixed amount of time. For example, a grant will or will not arrive on a given date—a task that cannot be hurried with more effort—whereas 20 people can gut a house in a rehabilitation project faster than 10.
4. Note the *interdependencies* among tasks. Then plan the order in which tasks are to be accomplished. For example, legal title to property must be ensured before community groups invest money to revitalize a block.
5. Prepare a *chart,* sometimes known as a Program Evaluation and Review Technique (PERT) chart, in which the timing and relationship among the tasks is laid out. The bottom line of the chart is marked with a calendar. Each task is represented by a line starting at one date and continuing to another date. Group members can see when each task starts and how long it will take. The chart portrays diagrammatically which tasks must be completed before others can be begun.
6. The schedules for different tasks are worked out to isolate those tasks that can be done almost any time from those tasks that provide a vital step in the project completion. Different contingencies are examined for the unpredictable tasks.
7. The chart is examined for critical events, that is, tasks that must be performed or the goal cannot be reached. Winning a suit to stop the city from destroying older housing might be one such event. Once the housing is destroyed, rehabilitation is impossible. The trick in planning implementation is to schedule the tasks in ways that minimize such critical events.
8. Possible roadblocks and delays are noted, and when possible, resources are shifted to reduce the extent of such delays. In a neighborhood redevelopment program, funds might be shifted from park cleanup to housing rehabilitation. Without good housing, people won't stay in the neighborhood long enough to use the park.

Planning for project implementation need not be carried out in a lock-step fashion so long as organization members recognize the contingent nature of different parts of a developmental project. Developmental projects that rely on uncertain funding and respond to an unpredictable political environment must be treated as a set of contingent steps; that is, when key events do not occur as planned, many other activities may be affected, and the group should have some other options prepared.

One example of adaptation during a project occurred in the Milton-Park neighborhood of Toronto. Starting out in the late 1960s, community activists sought to stop developers from demolishing a city neighborhood. During the course of two decades, the protest action slowly evolved into an effort by the community group to take over the development itself. By the end of the 1980s, the neighborhood organization had rehabilitated a large number of apartments and set them up as cooperatives. In the course of the extended project, the organizers had to change from a protest to a development focus while coping with markedly different political and economic environments (Helman, 1987).

The Toronto example is rather extreme in its scope and duration. More often, smaller changes are made in the way goals are carried out, but the goals remain the same. For example, suppose a community organization wants to set up a crime patrol. Community members are enthusiastic; they imagine themselves duplicating the successes in Boston in which such a group solved a rash of arson cases (Brady, 1982). Neighborhood crime patrols require police cooperation, but the police are unwilling to cooperate because they are worried about civilian competence. Group members had planned to provide their own training, but because of police skepticism about their abilities, they decide to ask the police to train them to patrol their neighborhood and phone in reports of crimes. When the police are confident about the training level, they provide radio equipment to summon help. A slight adjustment was made in program implementation to gain police support.

Successful planning for implementation requires activists to think of both backward and forward scheduling. Forward scheduling is required as a result of unpredictable contingencies. If a grant doesn't arrive, how can the group fund the next stage? On the other hand, scheduling requires working backward from each key event that has a deadline. Thus, if the house has to be ready for occupancy by a certain date, then the interior painting must be finished before that, and the wallboard must be up before it can be painted, and the wiring, plumbing, and heating ducts must be in before the wallboard can go up. A group that can think both forward and backward will not be stymied by changes in the environment and is unlikely to paint itself into a corner.

Implementation That Depends on Others

Sometimes developmental projects turn out to be more difficult than expected. An organization can find that it is suddenly dependent on the vagaries of the financial market, and bewildered members call in a financial consultant. Or an old building that members were going to rehabilitate turns out to have dry rot, so the group calls in an experienced restorer to advise them how to proceed. Sometimes major projects by government and business affect the neighborhood and require the participation of the developmental organization. Coordinating projects with others without sacrificing the developmental ethos can be difficult.

Contracting for Services.   Sometimes, to carry out a project, the development organization needs to hire people from outside of the organization, such as auditors or financial or legal consultants. When a group becomes dependent on someone else to provide key information or to carry out portions of the task, members may lose some confidence in their own ability. The group is vulnerable to project failure if an outside expert does not carry out a crucial task on time. Most such problems, however, can be handled by finding responsible and sympathetic contractors and consultants and by writing contracts that legally bind those providing services to comply with the group's requirements.

Ask leaders of other community organizations which contractors they found satisfactory. In most big cities, these tend to be firms of younger, more idealistic professionals who do work for community groups, understand their problems, and sympathize with their goals.

Put everything in writing.

Draw up a *contract* that describes what the person or firm hired is to do, at what cost, and the responsibilities of the community organization to the contractor. Make sure to specify:

1. The scope, quantity and quality of work expected.
2. The community organization's responsibilities, for example, to remove debris from an apartment before the professional electricians and carpenters begin their work.
3. The time when the contract is to begin and when the contractor is to complete the work and submit the results.
4. The form in which the contractor's work is to be submitted, such as blueprints, reports, or completed buildings.
5. The standards that must be followed in completing the contract. Spell out who judges whether these standards have been met and what happens if they are not met.
6. The amount and timing of the payment. Some contractors want a down payment for materials. If moderate, such requests are reasonable. More often, the first payment may be made on the submission of the first *deliverable*—that is, the first product done by the contractor—and the remainder may be paid as each step of the project is completed.
7. The conditions under which one or both parties can back out of the contract.

Be especially cautious to work out the group's requirements before writing the contract, because changes made later are likely to be expensive, and the consultant or contractor may not be able to adapt. Try to anticipate any difficulties that might occur. For example, ask the contractor if he or she could give several additional days or weeks to the project if it takes more time than estimated. Set aside a bit of extra money in case it's needed to finish a project.

Developmental Partnerships.   Increasingly, community-based developmental organizations are involved in partnerships with government and business to carry out developmental projects. The assumption is that through partnerships community members will have more say over which economic development projects receive government support, and community organizations will receive more funding for projects they want.

To effectively implement partnership projects requires a willingness on the part of government to lend some of its powers to the community group. One of the most important of these powers for development organizations is *eminent domain,* the power

City councilperson in Cleveland addresses a neighborhood group concerning new projects for the neighborhood. (Courtesy Warner Thomas/City of Cleveland)

that allows government agencies to force owners to sell their land to the government for some public purpose. In some cases, the government has delegated this power to community organizations to help them purchase land for development:

> A community organization in the North Dorchester section of Boston, the Dudley Street Neighborhood Initiative (DSNI), is working to reshape its future using one of the most powerful tools available for community development: eminent domain. The Boston Redevelopment Authority in November 1988 authorized DSNI to use the eminent domain power to acquire vacant land in its community. Thus the same power that inspired the term "urban removal" in the large redevelopment schemes of the 1960s and 1970s will now be used by and for the benefit of a low-income community. (Girard, 1989, p. 1)

Other powers that local governments can delegate include the planning and budgeting authority for implementing partnership projects. If government does not delegate some power to the community group, the partnership is likely to be too frustrating and disempowering for the group to participate in.

Working in partnership with business can be especially disempowering, because business people often feel they know what is best for the public good. Action research can help solve this problem if group members look for documentation of economic successes of other community groups. They can show, "our way works." It also helps if the mayor is able to say "no" to some business requests and is not him or herself taken with the mythology of business infallibility. In Boston,

> the Flynn administration redefined the politics of growth and the relationship between the public and private sectors . . . to get private firms to further the "public interest"— defined in terms of benefits to poor and working-class residents. It did not accept the private sector's terms concerning what was reasonable or feasible, nor did it back down when business leaders claimed that policies like linkage [and] the resident jobs policy would undermine the city's economic growth. (Dreier, 1989, p. 56)

If the organization does not get control in the partnership situation, there is a real danger that the resulting development will not serve the poor. Another danger is that the community group might be a formal participant but not really be included in the decision making. Business groups often dominate public–private partnerships.

> There is perhaps a fine line between the public–private cooperative activities and dominance by a city's business community, particularly in cities where there is a substantial overlap between the business and political elites. (Wolman & Ledebur, 1984, p. 31)

Another serious problem that can threaten successful implementation from the community organization's perspective is that public officials are credit claimers. Government officials may exaggerate their own role and minimize the role of neighborhood groups in achieving community goals (Gratz, 1989, p. 142). If a group cannot successfully claim its own successes, it cannot bootstrap and build its own power. Fortunately, credit is stretchable, and a group can provide good publicity for politicians while taking credit for itself, but it may have to take the public relations lead to get its perspective across.

In short, a community group has to have enough power, recognition, and respect in the community to hold effective power before participating in partnership efforts. Otherwise, working with more powerful partners is likely to reduce the group's sense of efficacy even if the project achieves some of its goals.

Equally troublesome are the problems that occur in partnerships with federal agencies. The Department of Housing and Urban Development (HUD) supposedly set up a program to help the homeless find housing, with the intent of working with nonprofit community organizations. The unpleasant consequence was that the nonprofits became entangled in red tape—60 or 70 pages of regulations had to be complied with to get some funds. Even after the requirements were met, there were frustrating, long delays in getting the money.

Housing advocate Michael Fabricant put together a deal to renovate an old building to provide shelter for the homeless and found an owner willing to wait for governmental approval. However, he ended up in difficulty when he

> discovered that it would take several months more for the government to release the check even if the project were approved . . . "I've given up on H.U.D.," [Mr. Fabricant] said. ("Bush's Promise," p. A16)

When a community group works in a partnership with government or business, it loses control over the timing of the crucial tasks, which increases the potential for project failure. Bills may not get paid when due. Try to work with agencies that have a reputation for on-time payment. Some agencies cannot control the timing of their disbursements, but almost always make good on their commitments eventually, or will tell those working with them that the money may not come through. It is a completely legitimate question to ask partners how certain they are that they can come up with funds or make key decisions on time, and it is just as reasonable to check out if they have been able to deliver on such promises in the past. It is not worth working with partners who have a track record of previous failed projects.

It is also worth following the political environment so that activists can make their own judgments about the ability of government agencies to come through on their promises. Is a program about to come up for renewal? If so, its funding may be highly unpredictable, and earlier program guidelines may suddenly change. Is a major contested election about to occur? If so, bureaucrats may feel they cannot make any obligations that may constrain a new chief executive. Or they may try to make such obligations, only to have them revoked by the new mayor, governor, or president. In short, a group can make its own predictions about the reliability of an agency's promises and act accordingly.

There are no simple solutions to ensuring that partnership projects will be implemented in ways consistent with the community-development approach. Enter the relationships gradually, and if a little bit works, try some more. Successful partnerships emerge when separate parties recognize that their actions are interdependent. Leaders of these different organizations then gradually test each other to see who can be trusted. Each party brings different definitions of the problem to the partnership, which are part of the negotiations leading to agreement to work together on a particular solution (Waddock, 1989, pp. 83–87).

PROJECT AND PROGRAM EVALUATION

When community projects succeed, organizers across the country are eager to know what went right and how the lessons can be used in other places; when community projects fail, organizers have to be prepared to learn from their failures and do better the next time. In this way, community development becomes a reflective and adaptive process.

Has the food cooperative lowered the costs of obtaining nutritious food? Has the number of crimes decreased since the organization started the crime patrol? Did the Neighborhood Housing Services improve housing quality while enabling those already in the community to keep their houses? To answer these and related questions, developmental organizers rely on evaluation research (Patton, 1990; P. H. Rossi & Freeman, 1985).

Evaluations force organization members to question whether they are progressing toward the goals they intend. Evaluations should also pose the question of whether the goals are still appropriate. In addition, evaluations enable the organization to determine whether some programs are working better than others and to compare several techniques for accomplishing the same goal to determine which is more cost-effective. As the final stage in project development, self-reflective evaluations help direct future organizational effort to where it will do the most good.

Evaluations

- Provide the information to improve ongoing programs.
- Permit developmental organizers to monitor how well programs and projects are being implemented.
- Enable organizations to choose between programs in terms of which is providing more benefit for the organization and its members.

- Provide information on what works and what doesn't, so that organizations can learn from each others' performances.
- Show community members that their support of the organization has been worthwhile.
- Satisfy legal requirements from granting agencies, who often require evaluations.

Although evaluations provide useful data, they are only worth the effort if the people making the evaluation can make changes that will improve programs and projects.

Program Monitoring or Impact Analysis

Evaluations monitor how a program is being conducted and they assess the impact; that is, they measure what the program has accomplished. To use a medical analogy, *monitoring* is the daily measurement of vital signs, while *impact analysis* determines if a treatment is effective.

Some large-scale evaluations monitor and evaluate impacts. For example, LISC contracted with the Kennedy School of Government at Harvard to evaluate how well LISC is doing in funding different community-renewal projects (a form of monitoring) and whether such projects have been accomplishing their goals (a type of impact assessment). The book-length evaluation report describes the different types of funding LISC has used, examines the types of projects funded, and isolates the circumstances most likely to lead to project success (Vidal, Howitt, & Foster, 1986).

In the LISC evaluation, the researchers also pointed out secondary effects of the projects. They noted that LISC projects added resources to community projects over and above money already available (people feared LISC money would replace rather than add to government grants); facilitated cooperation between local community development organizations; and encouraged other funding organizations to increase their contributions to community development efforts (Vidal, Howitt, & Foster, 1986). This broad evaluation not only showed that LISC is succeeding in its immediate goals, but also dramatically illustrated how a modicum of funds to activist community groups can trigger the bootstrapping process that builds development capacity.

The LISC evaluation is exceptional in its scope, but it provides a model of the sort of information that organizations should seek as they conduct program monitoring or impact-assessment evaluations.

Program Monitoring.   Program monitoring allows those who have set up a program to learn what a program is doing while it is underway.

- **How much of a service is produced?** How much money has the community credit union lent out and how much repaid each year, for home repairs, for small businesses? How many code violations are found in buildings, and how many are corrected?
- **How many people are served and who are they?** How many people come to the homeless shelter each night? Is it primarily families who show up, or single men? What is the income level of people borrowing from the Neighborhood Housing Service?

- How do the people working on the projects spend their time? Are project administrators publicizing Crimewatch or helping people catch crooks? Are people rehabilitating homes or filling out reports to federal funding agencies?

Program monitoring helps a group identify and shore up weaknesses in programs or services. If those who are better off economically are the prime beneficiaries from Neighborhood Housing Services programs, perhaps more effort needs to be made to inform and interest the poor. If the group reports many building code violations but the city ignores the reports, activists may have to supplement their code violation reports with political pressure campaigns.

As part of program monitoring, the organization prepares *efficiency measures,* which determine how much of an activity is being accomplished for how much cost. Cost is measured in terms of both money and effort. A program to keep the elderly in their own homes may be too expensive if it includes refurbishing the building for handicapped access, 24-hour on-call emergency staff, a communal kitchen, and recreational facilities. Could more people be served for the same amount of money if the program were structured differently? Perhaps a program that combined delivery of prepared hot meals and a service to clean and cook would help more people be independent.

Careful program monitoring distinguishes between measures of effort and measures of program outcome. *Effort* measures the energy or money spent by the organization to accomplish its goals: dollars put into rehabilitation; number of hours a day that an emergency hot line is maintained. *Outcomes* measure the changes brought about by the program: How much did the quality of housing improve as a result of the rehabilitation? Did the reported rate of child abuse decline in the area served by the hotline? Were there fewer hospital admissions of children with puzzling injuries? People work hard on projects and want to be praised for their efforts, but hard work at activities that are poorly conceived or implemented is of little benefit to the community. Evaluations must measure both outcome as well as effort.

Impact Evaluation.   Project monitoring provides descriptions of what is happening; impact evaluation measures the outcomes that affect the community. Have the overall objectives of the development project been accomplished?

Some measures of program success are based on observable outcomes, such as changes in claims for unemployment, results of medical testing, or amount of housing space that is heated. In the LISC evaluation, visible outcomes included the number of people living in improved housing, the increase in capital investment, and the increased profits of community-owned businesses.

Other measures of program success rely on reports of personal satisfaction. The question "Do they feel more secure in the neighborhood?" is a satisfaction measure for a community crime watch, while the question "Are people more or less satisfied with their apartments?" might be a satisfaction measure for a rehabilitation program.

People may report higher satisfaction levels even when the observable measures of program outcome do not improve. For example, community crime patrols may make people feel more secure without reducing crime rates (S. Bennett & Lavarakas, 1989).

If the goal of the program were to make people feel more secure, it is a success even if crime rates do not decrease.

Impact evaluation asks, What were the goals of the program, and were they achieved? Program goals usually specify who is supposed to benefit. A job-retraining program may be targeted to the chronically unemployed but actually serve those who have been out of work only a short time. The program might be successfully placing hundreds of the unemployed at minimum dollar costs but still be a failure because it is serving the wrong clientele.

Handling Unfavorable Findings.   The purpose of an evaluation is to get information that will help improve community services and programs. Evaluation is potentially the most useful when it shows that the program is not accomplishing its objectives. Rather than ignoring the findings or blaming someone or something else for the failure, members of an organization should rethink whether the program is worthwhile. If they cannot make the program function more effectively, they should consider dropping it and finding a better solution.

More often, evaluations find both strengths and weaknesses in ongoing programs. Perhaps the evaluation will point out that a particularly costly part of the program is not producing many benefits and show that funds are better spent on other tasks. Mixed evaluations may be able to highlight why some programs are working better than others and hence may help in the redesign of those that are working less well. Mixed evaluations are easier to accept, because they offer some hope and some acknowledgment of success. When carrying out evaluations, group members should strive to find the positive as well as the negative, because such reports improve the likelihood that a group will be able to reflect on its performance and fix itself, with renewed energy and increased certainty that they know what the solutions to community problems should be.

Community organizations are generally composed of volunteers who, when they join, may know little about technical solutions to community problems. In solving problems, people gain knowledge of these technical skills, a personally empowering outcome. Development is more than solving problems. Development also occurs when people learn to do projects themselves without too much reliance on experts.

Successful projects result when the organization spends time trying to anticipate where difficulties are likely to occur, and sequences steps to avoid creating problems for itself. A developmental organization has to allow time for its members to catch their own mistakes and correct them before the organization collapses with frustration or misplaced effort.

Economic Development for Social Change

For industrial workers in older, central cities, the economic outlook appears bleak. Decent-paying jobs are harder to find, as manufacturing firms move out to the suburbs. Capitalizing on the despair of the working class, companies play worker off against worker, lower wages, and take back previously granted benefits. Cities pay attention to the service sector downtown but give short shrift to workers in poorer neighborhoods. City officials have often tried

> to revive downtown commercial centers but little, if any, serious attention has been paid to the benefits that might flow to the less fortunate urban residents or to their neighborhoods. (Shearer, 1989, p. 289)

To counteract these tendencies, progressive organizers have increasingly emphasized development projects that combat the economic problems of workers and poorer neighborhoods. Community economic development battles against the failings of capitalism that hurt the poor, encourage the ruin of cities, and allow the physical environment to deteriorate (Giloth, 1988, p. 347). The objective is to help workers and community residents control their own economic fate.

This chapter describes the goals of community economic development, the role of the organizer, and some of the skills involved in accomplishing those goals.

THE GOALS OF PROGRESSIVE ECONOMIC DEVELOPMENT

The twin goals of community economic development are to create more good-quality jobs for poor people and to provide workers with more control over the workplace. Though there are many ways of achieving these goals, each approach shares some common values. Community economic development looks beyond net profits to examine the impacts of projects on people, neighborhoods, and on the environment. It rewards the ideas and efforts of workers, independent of how much capital they may have invested in a company. Community economic development directly addresses the hopelessness that affects economically declining areas by trying to generate sustainable, community-controlled growth.

Approaches to Achieving the Goals of Community Economic Development

Each of the three different approaches to community economic development offers hope for a better future. With the first approach, *advocacy,* organizations pressure government for new or improved programs or additional funds, or protest unwanted development or plant closings. Organizations that take the second *quasi-capitalist* approach, help start new firms, sponsor job training, and generally do the same things that capitalist businesses do, but they direct the benefits to poor communities and individuals. The third approach is *alternative development,* which involves challenging or withdrawing from the capitalist market in favor of self-help, mutual aid, worker ownership, and cooperative enterprises.

Table 18–1 shows different types of community-based economic development efforts grouped by target and approach.

All three approaches to community economic development—advocacy, quasi-capitalist, and alternative development—are appropriate and can be effective in some settings. The more desperate the situation becomes, and the fewer other options are available, the more radical the solutions that group members are willing to consider. When a plant is shutting down, and employees can see no other possibilities for employment, they may consider buying the plant and running it themselves.

Advocacy Approaches.   Advocacy relies on protest, political lobbying, and publicity to benefit workers and their communities. For example, advocacy groups organize workers to report violations of industrial health and safety laws and insist that workers receive proper medical care. Coalitions of community organizations pressure governments to establish *set-aside programs,* which guarantee that a fixed percentage of government contracts will be issued to firms owned by women or minorities. Sometimes advocacy organizations pressure state government to provide funds to finance low-income housing or help pay for start-up costs of community development corporations. Community groups have successfully lobbied for support for housing in Ohio, Michigan, Florida, and Indiana (Neal Peirce & Steinbach, 1990, p. 25).

Economic advocacy organizations pressure cities to sponsor industrial or commercial parks in poor communities. They also argue for linked-development programs in which funds for housing in poor communities are obtained from fees imposed on downtown developers. Other advocacy organizations concentrate their efforts on discouraging firms from abandoning cities, a difficult and frustrating effort because owners have a legal right to move, and no legal obligation to pay for the social costs resulting from their move. In Chicago:

> The Coalition to Keep Stewart-Warner Open was formed to work to keep the plant open. They were joined in their efforts by the Northwest Community Organization . . . the Lo-

TABLE 18–1
Types of Community Economic Development

Target	Approaches		
	Advocacy	**Quasi-Capitalist**	**Alternative Development**
Individuals	Worker health and safety measures	Community controlled job-training programs	Urban farming
			Labor exchanges
	Minority or gender set-asides	ESOPS—workers on boards of directors	Other forms of self-reliance
		Feminist/minority entre-preneurial training	
Firm	Plant closing legislation	Community Development Corporations set up com-panies by providing ven-ture capital or becoming sponsors of incubators Neighborhood community-controlled mall develop-ment	Worker-owned cooperatives
Neighbor-hood	Stadium protests	Community-based plant buyouts	Neighborhood self-reliance
		Neighborhood shopping mall development	Linked-housing develop-ment programs
		Neighborhood markets	Tenant-managed housing
		Fighting neighborhood blight, especially with housing-renovation programs	

ESOPS = employee stock ownership plans.

gan Square Neighborhood Association . . . and some twenty other groups interested in maintaining the economic vitality of the area. (Hudson, 1990, p. 15)

The strategy has been to threaten companies with bad publicity while pressuring government to take legal actions. A toy company in Chicago received a large subsidy from the city to keep its plant open and hire more employees; within a short time, the conglomerate that owned the firm announced it was shutting the plant, abandoning the city, and leaving 700 employees jobless. In response, the Midwest Center for Labor Research (MCLR)—an advocacy organization—worked with community groups and

organized a nationwide boycott of Playskool Toys. . . . While the boycott and the threat of a city suit against the company did not stop Playskool from moving, it did delay the shut-down by one year and helped force the company to provide $300,000 to support a job-placement program for the dislocated workers. (Squires et al., 1987, p. 59)

Partnership programs stimulated by advocacy organizations can create community housing and jobs. (Courtesy Joan Vitale Strong/City of New York)

To obtain more clout in battles with firms intent on abandoning communities, progressive economic development organizations persuaded Congress to require companies to provide advance notice of plant closings. "WARN, Worker Adjustment and Retraining Notification Act—permits affected workers, unions or local governments to sue and collect damages if an employer fails to give notice" (Moberg, 1989, p. 1). As with most advocacy actions, follow-up is required to ensure implementation. There is the possibility that plant owners will satisfy the letter but not the intent of the WARN Act by maintaining a permanent announcement that they might move.

A generation ago, those protesting against projects that would negatively impact their communities either stopped the project or lost the fight. Today, when it appears impossible to stop a development, economic advocates work to modify the project to provide some community benefit. For example, neighborhood groups have battled vigorously to ensure that plans for rebuilding stadiums for the professional sports teams provide some benefit for the impacted communities. One group's report on a proposed stadium concluded

> mechanisms must be established to tap into the money that it will generate. One mechanism, a surcharge on tickets, has already been proposed. Other possible mechanisms are impact fees and land banks. Linkage mechanisms should be designed to meet the needs of the area by increasing local ownership, developing local businesses and training local residents for the new jobs. (Steinhoff, 1988, p. 25)

Quasi-Capitalist Approaches.   Community-development organizations frequently use the tools of capitalism to promote the development of new firms and to help community members learn the skills needed for the modern workplace. Often working in loose partnerships with government, business, or foundations, developmental organizations redirect the benefits of mainstream capitalism toward members of poorer communities. The goal of such organizations is to treat people as important, rather than as interchangeable components for achieving a profit.

Quasi-capitalist projects range from providing job training (often paid for by government) for people in poor communities, to helping workers in ongoing firms set up employee stock ownership plans (ESOPS) in which employees slowly buy out a conventional firm by becoming stockholders (Rosen, 1986, 1989). Other quasi-capitalist development projects seek to bring the deprived into the economic mainstream. For example, some groups teach technical business skills to chronically unemployed women who want to form their own firms (O'Neill, 1988, p. 3), while other groups encourage minority entrepreneurs (S. Green & Pryde, 1990).

Most quasi-capitalist projects are undertaken by *Community Development Corporations (CDCs)*, which are not-for-profit organizations set up in poorer communities to encourage economic improvement. The first batch of CDCs was formed in the early 1960s. Recently,

> there has been another proliferation of CDCs, with estimates of 1,000 to 2,000 CDCs throughout the United States. . . . In a period of nearly twenty years, CDCs have become firmly entrenched in low-income communities as a mechanism for promoting economic opportunities that benefit low-income residents. (Zdenek, 1987, p. 115)

Community Development Corporations establish profit-making firms, own, manage or rehabilitate housing, and sometimes deliver social services. They provide capital and expertise to help small businesses in poorer communities and arrange entrepreneurial and marketing training for those in the community who might like to set up a business but don't know how. They employ experts to help local start-up companies become profitable or act as a conduit for start-up capital from government, foundations, and private investors. Enterprises started by CDCs are owned and run by community residents, a step toward the empowerment ideal.

A Kansas City CDC built a major inner-city shopping center (Task Force, 1987 p. 17); in Boston, a CDC recycled an old brewery into an office complex for community-based businesses (Neal Peirce & Steinbach, 1987, p. 25); and in rural areas, the Northern Community Investment (a CDC)

> is credited with having created or saved 1,931 area jobs; its investment portfolio is worth some $8 million. More important [it] has leveraged an additional $54 million in financing for its firms. . . . NCIC carefully monitors the management capacity of the firms it invests in, enlisting when needed experts from the federal Small Business Administration or universities to provide technical assistance. (Neal Peirce & Steinbach, 1987, p. 31)

Though quite active in setting up companies, the major effort of CDCs is in housing development. Community Development Corporations learn which buildings to buy and rehab and where cooperative housing will work better than rental housing. They set up training programs so tenants can form their own management teams. The funding for such programs and often the original donation of property come from governmental agencies, progressive foundations, and linked development programs.

The Community Development Corporation of Kansas City transformed an abandoned hospital site into a modern 80,000-square-foot inner-city retail complex. (Courtesy Community Development Corporation of Kansas City)

Alternative Development Approaches.   The third approach to progressive economic development—alternative business development—questions two premises of capitalism. It argues against the notion that ownership and share of the profits must be based exclusively on the amount of an individual's financial investment. Second, it questions the disproportionate emphasis on financial growth that is characteristic of conventional economic development. Alternative business development balances growth with concerns for the quality of life and personal empowerment.

One way to build an alternative economy is to encourage people to withdraw from the conventional marketplace. For example, developmental organizers might encourage people to set up roof-top gardening, or labor-exchanges between those with different skills. They organize neighborhood-controlled consumer cooperatives in which people volunteer labor in exchange for less-expensive groceries. In a small way, these activities echo the communitarian approaches of the past, which argued for escape from society to a life of reflection and self-sufficient farming.

The self-reliance approach combines economic concerns with a search for personal empowerment. For example, women in Appalachia formed a small firm to process and market products from the mayhaw tree, a local fruit tree. Starting with little more than their willingness to work, they built a profitable business, using local products and training local labor (Hils, 1990). They showed the sexist business community that firms owned by women could make a profit.

The most significant efforts to create an alternative economy are cooperatively owned companies. Cooperatives are employee-owned firms that provide a product or service that is sold in the marketplace. Cooperatives, like all firms, require capital—for buying plants and investing in machinery—but in a cooperative, capital is a tool that aids labor, not a separate, dominating contribution.

In conventional firms, control is determined by the amount of money invested in stock ownership. Conventional firms get their capital from individuals and financial institutions that invest money and receive shares of stock; the more shares owned, the greater the control over the company and the more profits received. In large conventional firms, share owners appoint professional managers to run the company. The managers are accountable to the stockholders, who judge success mainly by the size of the dividends (share of profits) they receive.

In contrast, ownership in a cooperative assumes equality of investors. Each member has one vote, regardless of the contribution of capital. Both ownership and management are the responsibility of the workers. In cooperatives, human effort is the crucial investment; capital is a means for accomplishing collective goals.

How to Achieve Community-Based Economic Development

All three approaches to community economic development try to achieve the same goals—dignity, empowerment, and economic uplift. There is widespread agreement on appropriate means to achieve these goals. Developmental organizations rely on government, business, and foundations for financial support; they advocate participatory organizations and work settings; and they encourage projects that build confidence, momentum, and community pride.

Developmental organizers work with government to bring about community-based economic development. They set up partnership efforts—CDCs or linkage programs between office development and housing—that rely on governmental financial, legal, and programmatic support. Organizers reject the ideological belief that economic success occurs only because of individual effort. Government already subsidizes contractors, developers, and other business firms; why not direct some of the benefits from economic development to the poor?

Activists in local economic development assume that projects and jobs should be run on a democratic and participatory model. They reject the assumption that a successful firm must control decisions and obtain obedience from workers through a strict hierarchy of authority. As the history of work organizations shows, strict hierarchy in a firm is no more related to economic efficiency than dictatorship is related to governmental efficiency. In worker-owned cooperatives, important decisions are made collectively with minimal hierarchy and with far fewer supervisors than in conventional firms. Yet many cooperatives are economically profitable. Clearly, participation and profitability are compatible.

Workplace democracy encourages political and social democracy. In worker-owned firms, people not only earn a living, they feel empowered. Workers feel more competent and committed. The more workers believe that their opinions count and that work should be done cooperatively, the stronger their commitment to the firm (Wetzel & Gallagher, 1990).

> Workers' control and self-management are most consistent with a society that would take as fundamental people's right to be fully involved in the decisions that affect their lives. Such a society would encourage open, nonhierarchical and nonbureaucractic economic, social and political organizations . . . it would locate those characteristics in a larger economic and political setting that also balanced collective needs with individual and group autonomy. (Gunn, 1984b, p. 204)

The choice of projects should reflect the goal of reducing feelings of defeatism. Fear of job loss encourages passivity among employees who fear to talk back to exploitative bosses and are unwilling to contribute ideas to improve the company they work for. Those facing economic deprivation blame themselves and lack the confidence to work together to overcome the shared problems. Economic development gives people the confidence that they can change the local economy, improve their own jobs, and escape from poverty and dependency.

Projects should enhance people's sense of dignity and pride. Dignity comes from holding a productive job, doing skilled work, and creating useful and healthful products. Dignity also comes when workers have a say about how work will be carried out.

Showing the world that people whom others define as failures can succeed economically creates a sense of pride. The story of the mayhaw firm described earlier is about more than jobs; it is about the ability to fight back and succeed. It eloquently demonstrates that poor women could carry off a tricky entrepreneurial effort. The example showed

> the refusal of these women to accept paralyzing negative perceptions of either their community or themselves. . . . When they realized that the male leadership had bought into the fatalistic perception that the community was the victim of unmovable economic forces, they decided to take the initiative themselves rather than spend energy fruitlessly in trying to persuade the men to do something. (Hils, 1990, p. 163)

Alternative economic development simultaneously emphasizes capacity building and economic success.

Development projects that help individuals without providing a demonstrable community uplift are only partly successful. Community economic change must address the psychology of economic decline. Empty apartment houses, stores, and factories are vivid symbols of previous community defeats; lack of food stores and retail businesses is a visible sign of economic distress (Bendick & Egan, 1989, p. 9).

A new or upgraded neighborhood shopping center directly defies this negative image, symbolizing pride, energy, and economic possibilities. It provides jobs and higher-quality merchandise, while demonstrating that the community is still alive. In general, projects started by CDCs provide a hope for community renewal. In the poor but improving South Bronx, CDCs have created a new optimism.

> Chunks of territory once staked out by rival gangs . . . have been rechristened with the names of community development organizations. The Banana Kelly Community Improvement Association, the Mid Bronx Desperados . . . the NW Bronx Community Clergy Coalition, BUILD. Cumulatively, they represent a dynamic force for economic regeneration.
>
> In 1977 the South Bronx symbolized death. In 1987 it mirrors life. (Neal Peirce & Steinbach, 1987, p. 88)

By helping start new firms and creating jobs, CDCs restore communities.

Part of the goal of community economic development is to create sustained growth. The psychology of success is achieved by creating a feeling of possibility and momentum, by encouraging firms to help each other, and by picking projects that build off existing firms (Meehan, 1987, p. 144). By increasing the amount of money earned within the community that is spent in the community, the number of local jobs can be stabilized. Often, dollars leak out of the community that could feed the local economy if there were more local businesses and if local residents patronized them. In Miami:

> It has been estimated that each $1,000 of goods or services sold . . . in the Cuban community generates $1,630 in total community earnings; the comparative figure in the Black community is only $1,140. (Bendick & Egan, 1989, p. 17)

In nonminority communities, the figure is far higher, suggesting the potential of the strategy of keeping local dollars in the community. Economic-development organizations can encourage firms to purchase goods and services from other local firms to help expand the local economy.

The strategy of encouraging local businesses to depend more on each other is shown by recycling businesses, where one company's waste products become another company's raw materials. Recycling businesses provide local job opportunities and reduce pollution. Earthcare, one of the largest firms in the recycled paper business, began as a community-sponsored enterprise in Madison, Wisconsin, and now employs many people from a poor community.

What differentiates community economic development from traditional economic development is the effort to blend financial success with a concern for community problems. The appropriate balance is not always easy to maintain. A group can go overboard in either direction. The history of the South Shore Bank in Chicago illustrates the problem and shows how it was resolved in one case.

The South Shore Bank was set up to halt local economic decline by ensuring that funds saved in the community were reinvested there. It tried to serve a social mission while making money to stay afloat. The bank encouraged people to set up accounts even if the accounts were too small to be profitable because the poor had no other place to keep their money. In response to the lack of consumer credit, the bank lent funds to people in the area for their consumer needs but ended up with many defaults (Taub, 1988, p. 60).

Eventually, the bank shifted to larger development projects, such as shopping centers and housing. It tried to ensure that each project was located in the community and employed people from the neighborhoods. The bank provided community services through promoting economic development. As one observer describes, the

> South Shore Bank has kept community organizations at arm's length and, by so doing, has gained a heightened capacity to act. . . . If a bank is working with the community on a daily basis, it has some idea about what residents think. . . . Provided with adequate credit and some guidance, these small locally grown operations become self-sustaining, producing new wealth and better housing for South Shore residents. This is economic, as compared to political, mobilization. (Taub, 1988, pp. 136–137)

The sponsors of the bank did not abandon their social mission. Instead, they provided funds to separate organizations, many run by an associated neighborhood development institute, for important activities that are not economically profitable. To help businesses get off the ground, the bank refers local entrepreneurs to training centers (some of which the bank partially funds) until they learn enough to be eligible for a developmental loan.

There is a thin line between concentrating too much on economic development in lieu of social transformation and concentrating so much on social transformation that the firms fail to survive economically. The problem is widespread.

> An executive director [of a CDC] reflects the continually compromised position in which many CDCs find themselves. Because of their community service mission, they do not operate solely on the basis of profit maximization. At the same time, if they totally disregard the need to be profit conscious, they will cease to be in business at all. (Cummings & Glaser, 1986, p. 58)

To gain resources, CDCs become less confrontational (Vidal, 1989, p. III–6). As a result, community groups may lose their vision of more radical change. For example, the large and successful Bedford-Stuyvesant Restoration Corporation "has been hailed as a model for progressive community development. But some charge it has diffused protest and stymied more sweeping changes" (Louis & Mims, 1987, p. 16).

One solution is to set up coalitions with more- and less-militant groups. A coalition can put pressure on government for more funds and better programs, while some of its constituent groups run economic-development projects and others run protests. As an example, the Chicago Association of Neighborhood Development Organizations (CANDO), a coalition that focuses on community economic development, pressures the mayor to concentrate on neighborhood redevelopment and investment projects. The influence of CANDO stems, in part, from its being a coalition, some of whose constituent organizations are protest groups (UIC, 1987, p. 26).

Another approach is for alternative economic-development organizations to maintain a close association with sister groups that are still involved in service or protest actions. For example, CDCs that spin off commercial businesses also support social services and are often active in housing. In Arizona, Chicanos Por La Causa moved from protest, to housing, to community-based economic development. As a CDC, it provided help and managerial assistance to small businesses in the communities it served, opened a community-based credit union that concentrated loans on neighborhood needs, and established a revolving loan fund for local businesses (Task Force, 1987, pp. 19–21). More recently, La Causa established for-profit subsidiaries that make money and help to fund and provide quarters for nonprofit services and programs (Task Force, 1987, p. 21). Other profitable CDCs funnel money into nonprofit community-service activities (S. Perry, 1987, p. 111).

Observers report that advocacy and development organizations are improving their relationships with each other.

> It appears that the development and advocacy factions have begun to move closer together . . . although tensions remain. "We now see that groups can fail by putting too much emphasis on one or another end of the spectrum" said Andrew Baker of the Institute for Community Economics. . . . "You've got to have both tree shakers and jam makers to make community development work." The bricks and mortar organizations require the additional resources that advocacy groups have been able to pressure financial institutions and local and state government to provide. At the same time, advocacy groups need development organizations to use the concessions they have won and translate them into real housing and jobs. (Neal Peirce & Steinbach, 1990, p. 22)

THE ROLE OF THE ORGANIZER

What is the role of the organizer in community economic development? Generally, he or she plays a linking role. This means knowing where to go for technical support. Sometimes it means bringing various interested parties together, or packaging a deal by getting smaller commitments from some actors and leveraging them into larger commitments from others. It might mean operating as a cultural translator for a minority community.

For members of poor communities, obtaining information on starting and running a business can be difficult. Though people can learn business skills from formal courses, most business knowledge is gained while working for others. Specialized knowledge and start-up funding are obtained from networks of friends and acquaintances already established in the business community. It is precisely this linkage to information, advice, and funding sources that is missing in poor communities. To whom do you turn to learn how to repair a house when skilled crafts people have moved elsewhere? How do you learn which sources of funding are available when your community is ignored by traditional investors? With little or no budget to hire a lawyer or planner, how do you work with a city in planning land development?

A few years ago, there were no good answers. Small firms in poor communities might die from lack of information on how to handle relatively simple problems. Small firms and housing projects were constantly starved for money to get started and to survive temporary economic setbacks. Fortunately, today there is an expanding network of progressive organizations that provide information, advice, connections, and aid in obtaining funding.

Sit-ins by neighborhood organizations led to the development of Tent City, affordable housing for low- and moderate-income people in Boston. (Courtesy Boston Redevelopment Authority)

Some of these helping organizations were formed by coalitions of successful neighborhood development groups. Others are technical groups funded by progressive foundations and staffed by those who believe in community development. The variety of help available can be seen in the appendix to *Community Economic Development Strategies* (UIC, 1987), which describes half-a-dozen sources of information on alternative forms of ownership, three organizations that teach about job training, two pressure organizations that hold workshops on how to retain businesses, six groups that specialize in how to get capital, one group that shares information on how to establish incubators, and six entrepreneurial training centers.

The first and most important rule for successful community economic development is to make contact with these developmental intermediaries and seek advice from them.

Developmental intermediaries (Neal Peirce & Steinbach, 1990) facilitate community based development in three ways. Intermediaries lobby for laws that facilitate local economic development. Second, they provide technical, legal, and financial information to member organizations. Third, intermediaries work with neighborhood organizations to design projects that foundations and government agencies are most likely to fund. The participation of an intermediary organization encourages government and foundations to fund a project because the intermediary can pick projects likely to succeed and provide the technical assistance that increases the likelihood of success.

Table 18–2 (summarized from Neal Peirce & Steinbach, 1990, pp. 25–32) describes the best-known national organizations, as well as two locally focused intermediary groups.

Recently, the Council for Community Based Development was launched in Washington DC, to disseminate information on the availability of funding for neighborhood economic development projects and to publicize successful community endeavors (Neal Peirce & Steinbach, 1990, p. 64). In several large cities, successful neighborhood organizations have joined to form their own networks, such as the Neighborhood Development Support Collaboration in Boston and the Fund for Community Development in

TABLE 18–2
Illustrative Economic Development Intermediaries

National Congress for Community Economic Development	Gathers and disseminates information on the entire neighborhood community-development movement; a central clearinghouse of available technical assistance.
Local Initiatives Support Corporation	A major source of funding for community-based economic development projects. Acquires funds from corporations and foundations and provides them to community groups, usually through loan programs. Central to community-based housing programs. On occasion, funds organizing efforts.
Neighborhood Reinvestment Corp/ Neighborhood Housing Services	Sets up local development partnerships concentrating on home repair and rehabilitation. Provides technical assistance. Combines federal money with local sources.
Enterprise Foundation	Helps housing construction efforts and low-income job placement. Helps finance low-income housing. Provides technical assistance and its own research on housing rehabbing.
The Community Builders	A regional organization working in the Northeast that focuses on aid in housing construction as well as property acquisition while helping community groups negotiate with local government.
Neighborhood Progress, Inc.	A group based in Cleveland that helps corporations and foundations target funds for neighborhood development projects. Also provides technical assistance to established neighborhood organizations.

Source: Summarized from Neal Peirce & Steinbach, 1990, pp. 25–32.

Chicago (Vidal, 1989, p. I–2). In addition, some city governments have assigned staff to work as intermediaries with community groups (Neal Peirce & Steinbach, 1990, p. 43).

Some support networks specialize in information for particular types of economic activity. Corey Rosen runs a center for information on employee stock ownership plans (Rosen, 1989). National networks provide information on cooperatives, such as the Industrial Cooperative Association in Somerville, Massachusetts. Current information on both worker-owned and consumer cooperatives is provided by the magazine *Building Economic Alternatives,* published by Co-op America.

Sometimes intermediary organizations lobby in support of neighborhood organizations. A state coalition in Ohio is lobbying for legislative changes that would allow cities more flexibility to support community-based housing programs. A coalition in Cincinnati, Ohio, is pressuring the city government to ensure that neighborhood groups receive prompt payment for projects funded by government grants.

Networks and intermediaries allow local development organizations to learn what others have accomplished and, equally important, where others have failed. Some intermediaries conduct studies to provide technical information, such as cost-effective ways of rehabbing a house. Other intermediaries share information on the types of products and firms that might succeed in a given locale. Providing this kind of information is called *technical assistance.*

Technical assistance means teaching the nuts and bolts skills that make the difference between project success and failure. How does a new housing organization determine if the purchase cost of an old building is too high? Technical assistance in property assessment may help. Can a community group lure in investors for a neighborhood rehabilitation project if it can designate the area as a historical landmark? Technical assistance from a group specializing in historic preservation might help. What is the best time to make a bid for a plant that is threatening to close? Some intermediary organizations actually specialize in information about how to handle plant closings.

Intermediaries bridge the psychological and knowledge gap between government, large foundations, or banks on one hand and neighborhood organizations on the other. Government, banks, and wealthier foundations find it irritating to work with local organizations whose projects and leadership can rapidly change, but they have little knowledge about what types of community-based economic projects are likely to succeed. So they use intermediaries to help them choose and monitor projects. They may also use intermediaries as conduits for funding, so the intermediary, rather than the community organization, is responsible for the money. Those in the conventional economy feel that their funds are more likely to produce successful projects if they are spent and monitored in this way.

By helping projects funded by others succeed, intermediary organizations are better able to pressure government, banks, and foundations to continue to invest their money in poorer communities. Community housing groups can build apartments at costs far below those of conventional developers, and so increasingly, housing funds are funneled through CDCs. In 1979, LISC began with a $9.25 million dollar grant. By 1989

> The $250 million LISC raised from 515 corporations and foundations . . . had leveraged over $1 billion in direct investment in projects of more than 525 community groups. (Neal Peirce & Steinbach, 1990, p. 27)

The advice to community organizers is to seek assistance from intermediary organizations and join coalitions of state and local development groups. The costs are nominal, often under $200 a year. Then use the technical assistance offered and be prepared to teach it to others. Linking the community organization to all these sources of information and help is a key part of the role of the organizer in community economic development.

Once the organizer has become more knowledgeable, he or she can play a somewhat different linking role, that of *packaging deals*. Packaging deals involves putting together the separate pieces needed to accomplish a project while at the same time modifying the individual pieces to better fit into an overall scheme. To do this well requires considerable knowledge of what kinds of projects are feasible, what the community group wants to do, and who might provide the resources if the project is framed properly.

For example, a neighborhood organization might want to rehab housing for the poor adjacent to downtown but can't find funding. In packaging a deal, the staff person learns that city officials want housing for the elderly near the downtown to provide more life in the area. The organizer might package the following deal: The city provides land at low costs, puts in new sidewalks, and reroutes a bus line. The community group changes its project to include a mix of lower-income and lower middle-income families, including some elderly people. With the city's support, they apply jointly for funding from a state housing program. The city clears more land than is needed for the housing project, so a small mall can be built. The city looks for possible tenants, who borrow on conventional bank mortgages, but at low rates because the city subsidizes the interest rates. The mini-mall serves the elderly and generates revenue for the city to reduce the costs of the project.

Part of the art of packaging deals is putting the people with money together with the people who have the ideas. Organizers can broker economic-development deals by putting community development corporations in touch with local entrepreneurs and introducing each to managers of progressive investment funds.

Besides linking community organizations to sources of information, and linking projects and funding agencies, organizers sometimes play a third linking role, as *cultural translator*.

> In Los Angeles, a number of entrepreneurs of Asian background have opened small businesses with strong general business skills but limited knowledge of American laws and cultural practices. Community based organizations have assisted some of them by mediating disputes which resulted from misunderstandings and by counseling them on "doing business the American way." (Bendick & Egan, 1989, p. 43)

Through activities such as these, the developmental organizer facilitates the rebuilding of communities.

SKILLS

Carrying out community economic development requires some special skills over and above the skills discussed in earlier chapters. These include piecing together funding and choosing development projects that will succeed financially, empowering local community members, and helping restore neighborhoods and communities.

Piecing Together the Money

Paying the salaries of those in start-up companies, purchasing property, repairing apartments, or building community shopping malls requires money. For groups working in poorer communities, obtaining such funds can be quite difficult.

In part, how to get money depends on the intended uses. Six somewhat overlapping ways in which money is used in development efforts are summarized in Table 18–3.

The ease of getting money depends on the amount of risk for the investor. Investments in start-up overhead or product development are the riskiest. The most secure are investments backed by tangible assets—a saleable building or movable manufacturing equipment other firms could use. Almost all conventional investments from

TABLE 18–3
Funding for Economic Development Projects

Type of Money	Description
Operating expenses for CDC staff	Money for salaries and overhead expenses of the staff members of Community Development Corporations who package deals, provide technical assistance and encourage community members to start firms.
Predevelopment funds; seed money	Money with which to do original planning. In housing projects, predevelopment funds pay for architectural fees, site surveys, inspections of old buildings to see if they can be rehabbed. In businesses, seed money funds preliminary market studies or product design.
Venture capital	Money invested in risky projects usually after some product design or market analysis has been accomplished. Money is provided in the hope that the company will be profitable but with little or no security. Can be turned into equity investments if firm succeeds.
Operating expenses	Money for paying ongoing salaries and overhead expenses such as heating, lighting, rent for a store, taxes, routine repairs, and other expenses that are relatively fixed. Money is needed to cover these expenses until they can be covered by income from sales.
Equity investment	Ownership in ongoing firms or housing units.
Investments in mortgageable assets	Property owned by groups for which conventional lenders (might) provide mortgage money. Buildings, saleable machinery, and land (at least in some locations) are mortgageable assets. Product technology, expertise of companies, and customer goodwill are not.

banks and insurance companies are secured by mortgageable assets. If projects fail, those that provided the funding might end up owning a building or a plant that has resale value. That way, they can get some or all their money back.

Unfortunately, the money that is needed first—for start-up salaries, predevelopment work, or site design—is the hardest to obtain. Many companies with good ideas never reach the stage of needing equity investments or property mortgages because they die from lack of funds before they get that far. This problem is especially acute for firms in poor areas. At best, foundations, commercial banks, insurance companies, or government agencies will jointly share the risk.

What CDCs often do is to package financial deals from a variety of investors so no one's risk is too high. For example, a CDC in a poor, minority area in Kansas City put together over $5 million for a shopping center.

> Public monies included a $500,000 grant from the U.S. Department of Health and Human Services, $270,000 from the city's Community Development Block Grant allotment . . . and a $925,000 HUD Urban Development Action Grant.
>
> Private funds came from the Local Initiatives Support Corporation ($25,000), the Hall Family Foundation ($150,000) and a critical 25-year loan from the Prudential Insurance Company, for $2.5 million at 8% interest. This financing enabled the rents to be reduced to a competitive level to attract tenants to the project. Local lending institutions participated in the form of a $3 million loan from Centerre Bank and a $500,000 letter of credit from the First National Bank of Kansas City.
>
> Some of the equity also was furnished directly by CDC-KC. Two half-acre parcels were sold to the restaurant franchises who would be locating at the corner of the project. And a syndicate was formed for 17 individuals to invest in Linwood Shopping Center. The investors purchased units at $5,000 with each unit securing a loan of $25,500 from local banks. (Task Force, 1987, pp. 16–17)

Describing a CDC run by the Bethel New Life, Peirce and Steinback ask

> Where does Bethel New Life's money come from? From foundations large and small, with AMOCO, First National Bank of Chicago, MacArthur, Kellogg, Joyce and Harris Bank Foundations prominent on the roster. From churches—predictably the national Lutheran Church, but also the Catholic Church's Campaign for Human Development. . . . From government and a long list of private contributors. (Neal Peirce & Steinbach, 1987, p. 71)

The effectiveness of limited capital investments is increased when CDCs set up revolving loan funds, which lend money for new projects as money borrowed for older projects is returned. Before such loans are made, most CDCs carefully investigate the financial potentials of the firm and provide technical assistance to ensure the money will be paid back. The idea is to turn a one-time grant into a sustaining pool of investment money. For example, North County Investment Corporation (NCIC), a CDC,

> gained access to $10.2 million in public sector dollars, notably from the federal Office of Community Services Secretary's Discretionary Fund, that has helped leverage an additional $43.1 million in private dollars for a number of economically distressed counties in northern Vermont and New Hampshire. (Zdenek, 1987, p. 117)

These funds were successfully invested over a decade, so that "about 90% of NCIC's annual investment now comes through recycled funds, rather than from grants" (Task Force, 1987, pp. 24–25).

A current controversy is whether it is better for a CDC to set up revolving loan funds or own firms itself. This is a difficult tradeoff, with little research indicating which way to go. Firms owned by CDCs are usually responsive to their communities, but putting all its capital in a single firm limits the good a CDC can do. CDCs can do more with revolving loan funds, but staff may concentrate so intently on keeping the fund solvent that they lose sight of their community mission. The Local Initiatives Management Assets Corporation provides a reason for favoring the loan route. This Local Initiatives Support Corporation (LISC) affiliate purchases loans from CDCs, so rather than waiting 5, 10, or more years before recovering enough of the loaned money to loan to someone else, the CDCs can get their money back right away (Wiewel & Weintraub, 1990, p. 170).

Urban banks, probably in response to the pressures created by the Community Reinvestment Act, are setting up their own development finance corporations. Some of these efforts may be manipulative attempts by the banks to assuage community activists, but there is increasing evidence that bank-owned CDCs actually invest in inner-city entrepreneurial projects (Wiewel & Weintraub, 1990, p. 171). For example, large banks in New York City, such as the Chemical Bank, have set up CDCs, some with a capitalization up to $10 million. In addition, Chemical Bank's CDC

> deposited $250,000 to local development-oriented credit unions at no interest. The credit unions, in turn, lend the funds to people who would otherwise be unable to get a bank loan. (Louis, 1989, p. 21)

The Center for Community Change has published a handbook that details how to use the Community Reinvestment Act to encourage bank investments (Center for Community Change, 1987).

Another approach is to obtain funds by selling tax credits, a provision in the federal tax code that encourages for-profit businesses to help community development corporations. The for-profit firms provide investment capital for neighborhood projects, and, in turn, are allowed important deductions on their income tax. This provision of the tax code requires annual renewal by Congress and could expire at any time.

Gaining start-up money is difficult enough for capital projects, but it is even more difficult to get money to pay for predevelopment work and staff salaries. To governmental agencies, commercial investors, or even the large foundations, this money shows little visible return. Yet, this money is vital, especially when training and research are needed to get a business off the ground. The problem is especially complicated for CDCs, because they often link their development and training activities.

Some older CDCs collected predevelopment funds through community solicitations in which people contributed $10 a month for 36 months, until a capital fund was built up (S. E. Perry, 1987, p. 148). In other cases, progressive unions provided the seed money. For TELACU, a Los Angeles CDC, the "intimate relationship with the United Auto Workers Union has been critical" (S. E. Perry, 1987, p. 142) for providing start-up money. The amount of money needed for these early and risky expenses can be kept down by using aid provided by intermediaries. For example, in Boston, Community Builders, a nonprofit developer, has refurbished an old warehouse near the downtown and will rent space to nonprofits at $23 a foot, compared to downtown rents of $35 a foot ("Office Space," 1989, p. 33).

Money for staffing and predevelopment activities is tight, but there are some sources for this purpose. In Boston, a coalition supporting neighborhood work provides some money for operating support (Neal Peirce & Steinbach, 1990, p. 68), and a handful of cities fund staffing for CDCs. Fortunately, LISC is starting to make some money available for predevelopment work (Neal Peirce & Steinbach, 1990, p. 28), and a few community foundations support staff salaries.

Finally, start-up costs are often covered through personal contributions of those who will benefit from the project. People contribute their sweat equity—work in lieu of capital investments—in housing projects. Local entrepreneurs with a good idea often invest all their personal assets in a proposed firm and solicit investments from family and friends.

Choosing Projects

Following the goals of community economic development, organizers should look for projects that are nonexploitative, that help those in need, and that have a chance of surviving in the marketplace. Ideally, these projects should symbolize the energy and capacity of the participants and the pride and renewal of the community.

Several families of projects are especially appropriate. Housing-development projects and neighborhood malls fill a need and symbolize community regeneration. Projects that generate jobs by taking advantage of unsatisfied markets or by capitalizing on the geographic location of a neighborhood are also suitable. So is job creation by nurturing young businesses. Finally, cooperatives can be economically successful, serve people's needs, and provide a source of community pride.

Housing and Shopping Malls.   Almost any project employing the poor in a nonexploitative fashion is a victory for a community economic development organization. But both housing redevelopment activities and community-owned (or at least sponsored) shopping centers are exemplary types of activities that can accomplish many important economic development goals. Housing combines social services with a potential for economic profit. When housing is tenant managed, it provides an opportunity for skill enhancement. Shopping centers and malls keep wealth in the community and sometimes attract new money. Both are visible signs of community rehabilitation. Bratt comments,

> as a community development initiative, housing is more satisfying than the often invisible "economic development." A CDC-supported venture that creates a handful of jobs does not have the same visual impact as watching a formerly vacant lot become the site of newly constructed housing or an abandoned building being renovated. (Bratt, 1989b, p. 271)

But housing is more than a visible sign of progress. It enables community organizations to recycle land that cities and federal agencies are willing to donate to not-for-profits. With less need for profit and more understanding of the need for housing, community organizations convert vacant land into housing for the poor, more effectively than do either private developers or governmental agencies.

Members of the community can provide the labor needed to rehabilitate deteriorated property, reducing dramatically the costs of construction. Tenant-managed housing encourages people to learn job skills, such as budgeting and home repair. It provides an affordable home for people who work nearby and symbolizes that the community is no longer physically deteriorating.

Housing improvements are the start of a bootstrapping process in which the upgrading of the value of one parcel of land encourages more productive uses for adjacent properties. This is the same kind of process that occurs with renewal that is managed by big business, except that people from within the community benefit when community groups do the renewal.

Community-controlled malls and shopping centers provide jobs, job training, and a visible indication of community improvement. In Philadelphia, a coalition of community groups kept a supermarket open, turning it into a worker-controlled cooperative. The new store was a visible demonstration of confidence in the neighborhood. The Linwood Shopping Center built by a CDC in a deteriorated rubbish strewn area of Kansas City

> by any measure . . . is a success, a model of commerce. It also is a matter of neighborhood pride. (Task Force, 1987, p. 14)

It is busy enough to constantly fill up its 375 parking spaces and it provides employment to many inner-city residents.

CDCs often act as the commercial developer for malls. Advocacy and pressure groups have also influenced commercial redevelopment efforts. The Pike Place Market in Seattle was a victory for community groups that wanted to preserve neighborhood integrity (Frieden & Sagalyn, 1989; Seattle Saves, 1988, p. 1).

The original redevelopment plan for Pike Place Market was to build an upscale mall with small shops, to attract wealthier people to a historically interesting area. Such upscale malls do little for the people in the community and are often too expensive for older, neighborhood businesses. Community groups pressured city officials to work with them in redesigning Pike Place. Together, they restored historically significant property and avoided building barriers to separate the marketplace from the surrounding community. Unlike other projects that created sanitized, though often architecturally appealing, inner-city marketplaces, Pike Place maintains the vibrant characteristics of its neighborhoods.

> Activists across the political spectrum have considered Pike Place Market not so much as a real estate project as a crusade. . . . After the renovated market was open for business, it meant many things to many people: help for the poor, treats for the tables of the gourmets, entertainment for the family on a Saturday afternoon, and a boost for tourism. (Frieden & Sagalyn, 1989, p. 185)

Pike Place successfully lures the tourists, yet it has provided a base for community preservation. Pressure from community groups preserved a local market, kept small shop owners in business, and helped provide an economic lift to an inner-city neighborhood.

The Niche Economy.   Poorer communities are often physically close to the upgraded business-shopping-gentrified areas of the city and can profit from their location. In Chicago, an affiliate of the Hull House established a home-delivery service for advertising flyers, while elsewhere, communities profit from recycling businesses. Filling such niches produces jobs and profits.

If the niche that is filled involves the provision of inexpensive labor or unglamorous services for the wealthy community, such jobs can have a negative effect on community pride. But not all niches are unglamorous or involve dead-end jobs. For example, in New York, entrepreneurs in Harlem produce luxury spices and other exotic hot-house foods for sale to downtown restaurants. In Chicago, community developers are helping those in the printing industry update their equipment so they can serve businesses in the central business district.

Another approach to a niche-economy involves setting up firms that reinforce a sense of community solidarity while luring in funds from elsewhere. In Liberty City, in Miami, a specialized bookstore sells materials on African-American subjects. There is a local market for such books and magazines, but to be profitable, the business needs a larger market than the local community. The bookstore has expanded its sales through a catalogue that is distributed nationwide (Bendick & Egan, 1989, p. 37).

Incubators and Business Development Centers.   To help reduce costs for new firms, some CDCs set up *incubators,* or business-development centers.

An incubator is usually an old factory or a warehouse that has been fixed up to provide inexpensive space for start-up businesses. Community entrepreneurs with ideas for a new business approach a CDC and request space in the incubator. A well-managed CDC will insist that such start-up firms have a carefully worked out business plan before gaining entry into the incubator. Usually, business plans contain a market analysis for the proposed product and service, descriptions of how much funding will be required and where it will be obtained, and estimates of when the firm will turn profitable.

Firms allowed into the incubator usually have access to an office pool so that small businesses can have secretarial help, photocopying, faxing, and mailing without the overhead expense of hiring full-time employees. Many CDC-sponsored incubators have accountants and lawyers on call to provide advice at reduced cost to start-up firms. Sometimes, CDC-run incubators require that firms contract with accountants and other technical support people because their advice can spell the difference between success and failure. Most incubators allow a firm to occupy the subsidized space for only a limited number of years. By then, most firms will have moved on to their own space or collapsed.

Some CDCs provide business services and technical support to start-up firms without setting up an incubator facility. For example, Coastal Enterprises, a development corporation in Maine maintains

> a small business development center, offering advanced technical assistance and training to over 1500 current and aspiring business owners. (Neal Peirce & Steinbach, 1990, p. 21)

The Cooperative Approach.   In the United States, there are many small worker-owned cooperatives. Most are involved in manufacturing, but some provide services. For example, a free clinic provides medical services to almost 500 patients; *Community News,* a progressive cooperatively owned local newspaper, provides an alternative slant to the news; and a law collective is a source of community legal services and a training site for future lawyers (Rothschild & Whitt, 1986, pp. 31–41).

Although there are many smaller, middle-class purchasing and service cooperatives, the primary beneficiaries of cooperation are the working class and the poor. In California, developmental organizers worked with the poorest Chicano farm workers to set up cooperatively owned farms (Rochin, 1986). Most of these 10 cooperatives were small, with a membership ranging from 2 to 75 families. Their success rates were mixed, though those that controlled their own marketing outlets survived. In Philadelphia, when an A&P was about to shut down a major supermarket, workers cooperatively purchased the store. They preserved jobs and continued to provide a needed service in the community (Whyte, 1986). The advocacy organization supporting the endeavor, Philadelphia Association for Cooperative Enterprise (PACE) has now founded several other stores, though not all have been successful ("Worker Ownership," 1987). A local CDC financed the cooperatives, and a government program supported training for workers in the management and technical skills needed to run a food store.

Many U.S. cooperatives are flourishing middle-sized businesses that provide jobs and maintain worker control. The Hoedad cooperative in Eugene, Oregon, has employed over 300 members (Jackall & Levin, 1984). Large-scale lumbering cooperatives are able to pay their members more than capitalist firms (Gunn, 1984b), and cooperative lumber workers are far less alienated than conventional employees in the same industry (E. Greenberg, 1986). A cooperatively owned scavenger business in San Francisco pays its workers more than similar companies. Sometimes CDCs sponsor industrial cooperatives as well as the more common housing cooperative.

In short, cooperatives not only work in the economic marketplace and provide jobs when they may be desperately needed, they also provide worker participation and increase workers' control over their economic lives.

TOWARD A HUMANE ECONOMIC DEVELOPMENT

Community groups carry out projects that produce jobs and housing to benefit the poor, help improve declining neighborhoods, and encourage democratic involvement. Community economic development expands wealth and increases workplace democracy while recognizing the importance of improved community spirit and enhanced worker dignity. It rejects many aspects of capitalism, but it is far from an advocacy of state socialism. Both capitalism and socialism

> are seriously flawed . . . there is another alternative waiting to be recognized, one that is not characterized by either the competitive market or the regulatory state. (Bruyn, 1987, p. 5)

Guiding the tactics of economic development are several assumptions. First, those that provide capital should not and need not determine the fate of locales. Second, the capitalist goal of maximizing profit need not prevail over a fairer distribution of wealth. Third, being pro-worker or pro-community development is part of the historic American impetus for community improvement.

The humane approach to economic development offers a constructive way of taking control of declining economies at the local level. Many of the tactics described—community-sponsored firms, worker ownership, self-reliance—are compatible with smaller and localized production, which can survive almost independent of international economic events. Firms that are small and firms with a responsibility to a locale need not be economically backward. Such firms are increasingly linked to each other through the supportive networks of the alternative economy, networks that share information on successful and unsuccessful approaches to economic change.

These efforts to bring about democratic economic development bridge the trenches between home and neighborhood on one hand, and work and income on the other. They help span the gap between labor solidarity and community harmony. They simultaneously see individuals both as workers and as citizens and thereby create a solid foundation for democracy. The ideals of developmental organizations are not utopian; each approach has been used and been successful. In fact,

> the failure of the community development movement . . . is unthinkable. In an age of social fragmentation and indifferent bureaucracies, the movement promises a personalized, neighborhood-based renewal for the most disadvantaged Americans. If the active participation of millions of poor and minority citizens will be required for a strong, competitive national economy, then community development organizations are not just a minor local phenomenon. They are an absolute national necessity. (Neal Peirce & Steinbach, 1990, p. 73)

Community economic development works and can be made to work even better.

Epilogue: Toward an Empowering Future

The approach taken by community organizers to solving problems differs dramatically from that of either political conservatives or liberals. Conservatives blame the poor, the alienated, and the discouraged for the difficulties they face. Conservatives respond to social problems with neglect or repression, or at the very best, charity. They fear the empowerment of the have-nots. Liberals accept public responsibility for alleviating inequity and injustice; their answers to social problems include government welfare programs along with social legislation. They combat problems by doing things for those in need. Their approach suggests they may also fear the empowerment of the have-nots.

In contrast, in the organizing model, people work together to solve the problems they collectively face and, by doing so, become empowered. People learn about political, social, and economic roots of their shared problems. They form organizations that enable them to combat social inequities and overcome future difficulties.

Success encourages future collective efforts. Through a protest, a community organization stops a property owner from converting an empty factory into loft-housing for the upper-middle class. The organization finds ways of using the loft space to attract new businesses and creates additional jobs for community members. Collective capacity is increased as protest is combined with development to lock in long-term benefits.

Pressure tactics steer government and business in directions that benefit neighborhoods, the poor, women, the handicapped, minorities, and the environment. Social action organizations organize the handicapped to demand their rights as citizens. Coalitions of community groups force local banks to invest in deteriorating neighborhoods, while women's organizations form their own banks. Neighbors join together to battle the effects of toxic waste.

Community groups buy abandoned plants and set up new industries to be owned and run by the formerly unemployed. Community-based development organizations create food cooperatives, purchase and refurbish housing, and train the unemployed for new positions in the marketplace. Worker-owned cooperatives provide employees control over their workplace, while community development corporations and resident-

437

A neighborhood group in St. Louis absorbs the children as well as the adults. (King Schoenfield)

managed housing spin off new businesses that employ community members. Accomplishments in the alternative economy show that financial success and community benefit are compatible. Organizing bolsters people's control over the market and over government, enhancing the dignity and power of individuals.

Community organizers must continue to work for social change and to fight political and social inequality. They must continue to work with the dispossessed and the downtrodden, seeking the source of social problems in economic changes and political decisions. Future community development must create a sense of personal empowerment while emphasizing the jointness of the communities to which we all belong.

A BEACON FOR THE FUTURE

In this country, where the response to drug use is to bring in the army, where comparable worth and job equality for the sexes are disparaged as too expensive, where children no longer have the prospect of living better than their parents, community organizing is needed to remind people that there are alternatives. Repression is not the only or the best solution for government and the upper classes; passivity in the face of unemployment and degrading work is not the only or the best solution for the working classes.

Community organizers present an image of a more democratic society, a less exploitative economy. The ideals of personal empowerment and creative community problem-solving provide a vision for the future. Community organizing creates a vocabulary of responses, a range of choices other than the simple, authoritarian, and impoverishing ones. Community organizing offers an attractive model for those not yet convinced of the possibility of collective action.

THE THREE PILLARS FOR FUTURE ORGANIZING

Three pillars should guide future organizing:

Maintain democracy in the community organization.

Encourage democracy in the workplace.

Expand democracy in the overall society.

In democratic organizations, people can see the relationship between the decisions they make and collective outcomes. Democracy in the workplace increases the control that ordinary people have over their livelihoods. Democracy in the society keeps government accountable and helps avoid repressive actions when people make legitimate demands. Democracy keeps government open to the less well off and reduces the bias toward business and wealthy. Most important, it communicates the ideals of community empowerment to the whole society.

Democracy is achieved in community organizations when decisions are arrived at after full and frank discussions that encourage people to actively participate. Participants learn through continued experience in the group that their opinions are valued and valuable, that they influence action, and that the ideas of the group can be translated into successes.

With sensitivity and experience, community members can fully participate in their community organizations. In the workplace, it is more difficult to achieve democracy because hierarchical control is the norm in big businesses (Bowles & Gintis, 1986). In response, progressive groups develop alternative businesses—cooperatives and community-based corporations. The responsibility for and benefits from such businesses are in the hands of the employees.

If people learn democracy in the workplace, they are more likely to use it in political actions, for example, to actively oppose policies that encourage businesses to swallow each other for profit and to ignore the consequences on the communities. Empowered individuals will resist bureaucratic assumption of authority; they are less likely to tolerate abridgment of anyone's rights. Such actions not only facilitate future organizing, but help bring about a more equal and tolerant society.

A more democratic society presumes a strong sense of community and an obligation and willingness to participate and help others. Boyte calls such a shared and supportive community a *commonwealth*. To create this sense of community obligation means overcoming the narrow focus of much of present-day organizing.

> Much of citizen activism . . . has addressed itself to fairly narrow issues. Activists have not often asked what their work "means" in a larger sense, where they are going in the long run, or how their particular efforts might add up to more than the particular or localized campaigns they engage in . . . much of grass-roots activism has spoken a thin, sometimes cynical language of narrow interests and protest detached from any enlarged social and political vision. (Boyte, 1989a, p. 12)

A goal for future organizing involves creating and implementing an "enlarged social and political vision." To the extent that problems are systemic and structural—for example, an unjust distribution of wealth and resources—solving immediate problems will have an impact only if the effort is part of a broader struggle for structural reform. People need to see that the difficulties they face are shared by others elsewhere and that what appear to be separate issues may stem from the same underlying source.

Ultimately, a democratic community is more than a set of rights. It must be a set of actions, of shared involvement by many people, who recognize that their self-interest includes the well-being of the broader community. People learn that by working to help others with their problems, they may help themselves.

Building consensual democracy, exploring alternative economies, and working to create a sense of commonwealth share a common thrust. Each effort is part of the struggle against the disabling sense of political, economic, and social alienation. Small victories can help overcome this sense of helplessness. Learning to work in coalitions helps to teach that problems are shared. Successes that are achieved together help forge a sense of community and commonwealth. Many such successes viewed together create a tantalizing glimpse of a better society and show how that society can be achieved.

THE VALUE OF SELF-REFLECTION

But how can we get from the present to an empowered future? First, we must take stock of where we are and make sure community organizations stay focused on major goals. Reflection allows organizers to question whether a solution to one problem makes another more difficult to solve. And reflection helps activists to accommodate their tactics to a changing political and social environment.

Keeping Community Organizations on Course

To realize the vision of the empowered society, community members must repeatedly ask themselves, are we accomplishing the goals we wish to accomplish, and are these goals still appropriate?

> Supporters of community organizations must be willing to devote sufficient time to *reflect on their experience* . . . the lessons to be learned, and the midcourse corrections that will strengthen people's power and capacity to bring about change. (Mott, 1986, p. 12)

When caught in the immediacy of a task, community groups can too easily forget their longer-run goals. Managing and owning an apartment complex is meant to provide better housing for the poor and give them an opportunity to learn skills. A community group should not become just another landlord.

A self-evaluation that reminds the organization that its purpose is to empower women and not simply to protect them from abusive husbands prevents it from becoming just one more social service agency. Reflecting that the goal is to build a more democratic society prevents an organization that owns a community business from reasserting hierarchical controls in a misguided effort to increase business profits.

Evaluating current actions and looking for midcourse corrections may be threatening to those who have contributed their time to the organization. Activists may balk at suggestions that changes are needed. But an organization that is incapable of asking where it is going and whether the means for getting there are appropriate is likely to get far off the track. When organization members routinely ask themselves if daily tasks are leading them toward their goals, they can detect and correct mistakes quickly.

Avoiding Making Problems Worse

Organizers should use periods of reflection to explore the systemic basis of social problems. They should pay particular attention to knotty issues for which solutions to one problem exacerbate another. Helping native Alaskans, among the poorest people in the country, earn a living, even in cooperatively owned companies, can create severe environmental destruction (Egan, 1990). Affirmative action programs that alleviate employment problems for women and minorities may reinforce the prejudices of dominant-group men who are suffering shrinking opportunities and incomes because of the decline of U.S. manufacturing.

At first glance, contradictory actions seem to be called for. Damn the pristine Alaskan land, people must eat; or damn the native Alaskans, there is no other suitable habitat for the polar bear. Affirmative action must be supported as a response to discrimination; affirmative action must be opposed because it destroys worker solidarity.

Rather than having labor against feminists and the poor against the environment, progressive organizers must develop a shared vision of broader, longer-term solutions. The tension between affirmative action and fears of white men that they will not be hired if minorities and women are hired can be resolved if people understand why there are not enough jobs for everyone and learn how to design programs to increase the number of jobs. Employment and environmental preservation are in conflict so long as the society allows those who benefit from environmental degradation to escape paying for the damage they do. If companies had to pay for the damage, they would find cleaner ways to do business. The problem lies in the capitalist belief that maximizing short-term profits justifies raping the environment and getting away with it; there is no intrinsic conflict between native Alaskans and polar bears.

Adapting to a Changing Environment

As the political and social climate changes, peoples' understandings of why problems occur take on a new meaning (Sarason, 1986; Seidman & Rappaport, 1986). Effective strategies for mobilizing to gain support depend on these problem definitions. To adapt tactics to a changing environment, community organizers have to reflect on these evolving definitions of social problems.

Historically, the unemployed were considered lazy and unwilling to work, a problem that suggested state or private provision of food and shelter in exchange for labor, such as sewing or chopping wood. The only acceptable community action was personal charity. Over the years, the relationship between cycles of the economy and unemployment became clearer, and the public came to define the problem of unemployment as socially caused and not the fault of individuals. Community groups then pressured government to change labor laws and create unemployment insurance. Today, the formation of large conglomerates has been identified as a source of job loss. Forming community businesses is seen as an appropriate community response.

As recently as two decades ago, the homeless were viewed as a few unfortunate individuals, requiring modest shelter; gradually the perception changed as the numbers of homeless people increased. The homeless are now seen as victims of a housing industry that cannot make a profit on inexpensive homes and a government that gave up responsibility to house the needy. The definition of the problem may come to include all those who are inadequately housed as well as the homeless. Acceptable solutions include private housing rehabilitation programs carried out with the labor of those seeking shelter.

The Evolving Political Environment.   The twists and turns within the political arena are central to understanding the changing definitions of social problems. After more than a decade of conservative national politics, federal programs supportive of progressive causes are in disarray. People harmed by economic changes blame each other instead of government policies. The need for collective action is increasing, as the poor become poorer and the rich richer, but potential activists are distracted by the conservative agenda.

While hundreds of billions of dollars are being spent to bail out failed savings and loans, money is increasingly scarce for redistributive social or educational programs. The political right has organized a powerful anti-tax movement. They have joined with those working in anti-feminist causes, especially the anti-abortionists, and have attacked civil rights. They have sought to curtail the rights of acquired immune deficiency syndrome (AIDS) victims, censored art displays, and attacked symbolic speech.

Conservatives distract from the sins of bankers who steal by ranting about pornography and claiming it is corrupting the society. Sex is condemned as immoral, while the wizards who arrange leveraged buyouts (which reduce the number of jobs) are praised as heroes of capitalism. Conservatives erode the spirit of the commonwealth with manipulative praise of self-reliance and distract people from their problems with the false patriotism of anti–flag-burning campaigns.

Those in power have restricted the actions that can be taken by progressive, community organizations. They have made it more difficult to file a class action law suit. They have weakened unions that might mount a successful response to plant closings or at least help people cope with job loss. They have permitted large companies to underfund retirement plans. They have abandoned programs that funded community groups directly and terminated or severely restricted public programs that engaged in community organizing.

Conservative politicians have supported workfare, a throwback to the 19th century definition of the unemployed as lazy, able-bodied people. Today, the jobs for unskilled people often don't exist; those on welfare often lack the education to take available jobs. Welfare is no substitute for community organizing, but it does provide needed sustenance. Conservative politicians campaign on anti-welfarism, playing on the resentments of economically threatened working and middle-class people who do not want to use their shrinking resources to pay someone else's bills.

Conservatives advocate localism and voluntarism, but their idea of voluntarism is a reduction in federal transfer payments, and their idea of localism is to put the burden of providing social services on local governments that have limited revenues and tax systems that burden the poor more heavily than the rich. Further, voluntarism means a revival of a paternalistic society in which people who accept charity must be humble and passive. Self-help translates as the freedom of those who have money to do what they want with it and the freedom of those who have no money to send their children to school hungry.

The shift from manufacturing jobs to service jobs has meant less pay and less-dignified work for many people. Making a product for a fair wage provides more dignity and status than flipping hamburgers or delivering advertising flyers. In their humiliation, workers often blame their job loss on others who also want to obtain one of the limited number of decent jobs, turning worker against worker, whites against blacks, and men against women. Rather than responding collectively to structural changes in the economy, workers become resentful of the gains of others. Filled with self-pity, they become harder to organize.

People want to maintain and restore the good life they used to know; as individuals and as a nation, they borrow without the wherewithal to repay their debts. Students choose the earnings of the corporate lawyer rather than the satisfaction of defending the poor. As MBAs, they manipulate stocks and bonds for short-term profits rather than encourage companies to improve long-term profitability and stabilize the communities in which their plants are located.

Responding to the Political Environment.   Organizing over the next few years will have to respond to these changes in the political climate. It will need to address directly the needs and fears of the downwardly mobile and those who are just hanging on to middle-class life-styles. It will need to defuse the increasing tendency to blame economic ills on other groups just as badly off and to help focus attention on the underlying economic problems and on solutions that serve not just neighborhoods and community groups but large segments of society (B. Ehrenreich, 1989).

Community groups may have to battle tax limitation movements that prevent the funding of social programs; they may have to confront the conservative myth of the lazy welfare cheats with counterimages of the deserving and sometimes desperate poor. Because localities are becoming increasingly responsible for social services, community members may have to help recreate a sense of community responsibility, building on people's belief that it is okay to help a neighbor.

Ironically, the next decade may be a good time to try to build commonwealth. For the first time in many years, people who thought poverty or unemployment could never happen to them, who were certain that those who were poor were responsible for their own condition, have lost their jobs through no fault of their own. That experience is likely to make them more sympathetic to programs to help those thrown out of work.

The timing may also be good in the sense that as more responsibility is placed on the local government, people are more likely to know the poor, to think of them as our poor, and feel a responsibility they do not feel when the federal and state governments are running programs. Local taxpayers can help design programs to aid the poor, answering their own objections to federal programs. The changing economy and political environment have created many opportunities for organizing and suggested some of the appropriate directions to take.

Creating Opportunities for Reflection

To plan for future success, periods of reflection are vital. Yet activists in the middle of projects are unlikely to pause and think about the progress being made or speculate about the underlying causes of social problems and the direction that organizing ought to take. Today's crises are urgent and cannot be set aside. How, then, can organizers step back and analyze what has been accomplished and where to go?

Reading the publications of national advocacy groups and organizing networks and attending the meetings of national umbrella organizations provide an opportunity for such reflection. Conveners of such meetings and publishers of newsletters should schedule open forums in which questions of direction and purpose are posed and debated.

Second, it is the responsibility of academics to reflect on organizing issues and work more closely with activists. Academics can gather and organize the background information needed to analyze trends and can translate research on economic and social change into terms that can guide community action. Our own work, for example, has described the harm done to communities by misguided economic development policies (I. S. Rubin & Rubin, 1987). Such information can help community groups figure out what policies to push for and which ones to oppose.

Implementing a closer relationship between academics and activists in the communities has been difficult. As Terry Mizrahi points out, there is "resistance from community practitioners who see research as inimical to or diverting social action" (Mizrahi, 1989, p. 1). But research need not be inimical to practice, and a closer set of ties should be part of the future agenda for organizing.

As the relationship between academics and practitioners improves, practitioners gain the ability to set a research agenda for academics. Academics can learn from practitioners what is happening in the neighborhoods and use this knowledge to challenge the research community to discover more about the structures of social power or to investigate alternative forms of economic enterprise. A continuing exchange between academics and practitioners helps define what knowledge is required to keep community organizations adaptive and successful.

A third opportunity for reflection occurs during schooling. Students whose class assignments involve observing those in need and thinking about what they see can come up with insights that will help shape their future strategic choices:

> By spending time observing a soup kitchen . . . the researcher discovers that, in addition to meeting a basic need, the food service also created a positive sense of community among the recipients. (Mizrahi, 1989, p. 8)

Time spent in courses not only provides a respite from action on the streets, it provides material to reflect on, including the history of organizing, its successes and failures, and proposed directions.

RESOLVING TENSIONS BETWEEN VALUES

One of the most important reasons that organizers have to find time for periods of reflection is to understand and resolve some of the basic tensions between values that underlie organizing. Four value tensions repeatedly appear throughout this book.

First, organizing aims to *empower individuals,* and it does so through actions that build and enhance a sense of *community solidarity.* However, too much community solidarity can destroy individuality and discourage personal efficacy. Next, there is a continuing tension between achieving *successful projects and protests* and *encouraging democratic participation* in the organization. The third tension is between *organizational autonomy* and *the need for joint activities* with other organizations. The fourth tension is between *protest* and *development* activities. The long-term patience and concern required for successful developmental work differs markedly from the need for immediate success that is part of the mobilization process for protests.

An unwillingness to face and resolve these tensions precipitates battles among people who ought to be working together in progressive causes. The more militant protesters cry "sell-out" to those who work with city officials on development projects. Even more disconcerting, neighborhood activists attack economically successful minority group members who move away from the ghetto for not staying to build an ethnically based local economy. If organizers take the time to think about these tensions, they can sometimes avoid and often reconcile them.

Individual or Community Success

At its very best, a united and supportive community encourages people to develop the capacity to help themselves. By providing a source of pride and demonstrating that others like themselves can succeed, community integration helps individuals overcome their (shared) problems. But tensions can develop between individual capacity building and community growth, tensions that are illustrated in Figure E–1.

When community and individuality have been reconciled, the strengths of each helps build the other. Community solidarity provides social support that increases personal efficacy. The entrepreneurs who receive help from community-based development corporations profit from being part of the collectivity. In turn, individual success

FIGURE E–1
Tensions That Can Develop
Between Individual Capacity
Building and Community
Growth

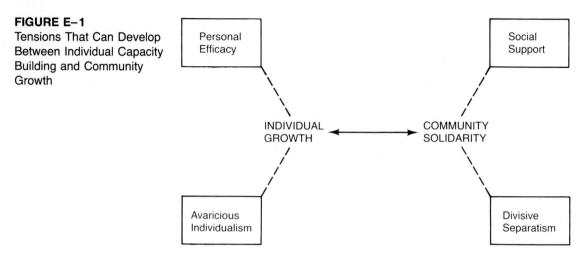

benefits the community. The local entrepreneur hires others from the neighborhood, contributing to the fight against local poverty.

If the tension has not been sufficiently well worked out, two different kinds of problems can emerge. When solidarity is overemphasized, the result can be a divisive separatism that feeds ethnic antagonisms. Black fights Hispanic rather than the poor working with the poor. Or, people glory in the symbols of an exclusive community, rather than build a broader community as a foundation for collective action. If individual growth is overemphasized, the result can be avaricious individualism in which people join a movement or organization and work together only until they can achieve their immediate self-interested goals.

Reconciling Community With Individualism.   To reconcile individualism and community, organizers show how a united community provides psychological support and social networks that enable individuals to succeed. Pride in community can reinforce a desire to succeed because people want to be a credit to the community. On a more pragmatic level, advice and material aid that help achieve economic success are passed along community networks. Empowered communities are built up from *liberated networks* in which people are willing to work together because they share multiple overlapping interests and not simply a geographic or an ethnic affinity.

Future organizing should portray community as a shared environment rich with the possibility for progressive groups to build on each others' successes. A small victory for one group can be bootstrapped into subsequent community change by other organizations, as successful groups teach others how they succeeded. The idea should gradually become widespread that within communities, the success of individual projects is linked.

An important step in forging a broad-based progressive movement is to bring disparate interests into this rich community of cooperation. Part of the task of future organizing is to help people learn that while they face different problems and have

Join together for collective action. (Courtesy TTB)

separate interests they are united in a struggle for change. In McKnight's grandiloquent language this

> approach is the *community vision*. . . . It understands the community as the basic context for enabling people to contribute their gifts. It sees community associations as contexts to create and locate jobs, provide opportunities for recreation and multiple friendships, and to become the political defender of the right of labelled people to be free from exile. (McKnight, 1987, p. 57)

Democratic Participation or Successful Project Outcomes

In progressive organizing, it is important to complete a project, but equally important to act with concern for individual dignity and democratic involvement. Figure E–2 portrays some of the tensions involved.

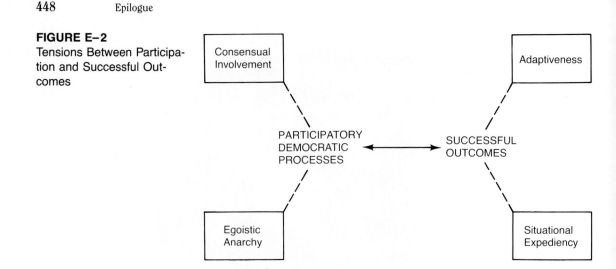

FIGURE E–2
Tensions Between Participation and Successful Outcomes

It is tempting to bypass democratic procedures to obtain successful outcomes, that is, to act in a "situationally expedient" way, for example, by hiring workers at poor pay to make a cooperative economically more profitable. Activists have to be cautious to strive for balance between success and democratic involvement.

This can be done step-by-step. It isn't necessary to withdraw support for a community-controlled local business that provides jobs in a poor community just because the firm is not being run democratically. Support the company, but work to increase democratic involvement, for example, by pointing out that firms that encourage worker participation are more efficient and profitable than are other companies.

Democratic involvement is not inefficient unless it is taken to extremes such as the *egoistic anarchy* that passed for democracy with the Students for a Democratic Society. Uncurtailed participation under the guise of participatory democracy generated long, unfocused discussions, seriously harming organizing efforts. Potential members were frustrated with all the blathering.

Democratic processes might conflict with successful outcomes in two other ways. In the first, the rules necessary to provide needed services efficiently conflict with broad participation. In the second, dependence on experts discourages those seeking democratic involvement.

Institutionalization or Participation.   *Institutionalization* refers to the rules and bureaucratic structures that make it possible to accomplish routine organizational tasks. Without institutionalization, people must "rediscover the wheel" to solve each problem. But too many rules or a rigid structure can discourage people from participating.

Some activists, fearing that formalized structures will result in managers making all the decisions, avoid establishing any formalized structures. However, rather than encouraging broad participation, lack of structure creates its own problems that can reduce the chance of organizational success.

Using the term *tyranny of structurelessness*, Joreen (1973) described some of the pathologies that arose from resistance to structure in the early years of the women's liberation movement. Fear of power and reluctance to exercise authority led to a variety of troubles which sometimes undermined the very existence of the organization. Under such conditions, rumormongers, narcissisms, and petty thieves flourished in counter-cultural cooperatives and collectives. The tendency was to refrain from doing anything until it was often too late or to address these problems with such ambivalence that a destructive factionalism was generated among members. (Z. Gamson & Levin, 1984, p. 226)

Avoiding all structure clearly does not work. Moreover, under normal circumstances, structure gradually evolves. Bureaucratization (rules and procedures) and specialization (expertise) seem to be inevitable consequences of successfully implementing many projects. For example, in East Boston, community members tried to create a neighborhood-controlled community newspaper in which the

> basic structure allowed real decision-making in the *Community News* by almost anyone in East Boston who wants to participate. Residents can attend a staff meeting and speak their piece, or they can join the staff, become a member of the corporation, and eventually run for election to the board of directors.
>
> In practice, however, the structure has been less than perfect. Access, for example, does not guarantee participation, and less than a dozen or so people have contributed to the production of the *Community News* at any one time. Moreover, most decision making gravitates to a few hands. . . . When the paper's budget climbed from a few thousand dollars to over $25,000 a year, full-time staff were needed to raise funds, handle business matters such as taxes, accounting and billing and coordinate volunteers to ensure efficient participation. Those who spend more time on the paper inevitably make more decisions. (MacGregor, 1979, pp. 5, 13)

Structure slowly increased, and, as it did, participation was gradually reduced. The trick in a situation like this is to find a stable and appropriate balance between routinization and participation.

It is desirable to have some structure, so long as it doesn't become rigid or result in excessive control from the top. The purpose of structure is to get the job done effectively, at the lowest cost, and in a timely manner. Supervisors must coordinate many activities, but they need not be domineering. Their purpose is to make things run smoothly, not to assert their authority.

Sometimes simple changes will make an inflexible and domineering structure more flexible and participatory. Some manufacturing companies have moved from an assembly line with extreme division of labor and strict hierarchical supervision to work teams, each of which is responsible for a complete product. Each team sets its own pace and is responsible for how the job gets done. Structure is used to increase involvement.

Excessive structure can destroy the motivation of people to participate. The answer is not to avoid all structure but to find a middle ground in which there is sufficient structure to encourage participation and routinize appropriate tasks, but not so much that it encourages top-down decision making and overly narrow specializations.

Expert Leadership Versus Broad Participation.   Another tension is between relying on expert leadership and encouraging broad participation. Community members cannot afford to reject the skills used by experts; they need technical knowledge to solve complicated economic, legal, and organizational problems. The trick is to avoid creating a group within the organization that dominates others because it has needed skills. For example, a small member-owned food cooperative in Hyde Park in Chicago hired experts to purchase meat and vegetables and hired dietitians to help people get good nutrition. Community members probably got better-quality foods and more services than from a commercial supermarket, but membership in the coop was not a democratic, empowering experience. The difficulty with experts is not that they know too much, but that they disregard the opinions of others.

The tension between expert control and effective participation is not just a battle between organization members and outsiders. Over time, as people work in an organization, some become good at particular activities and develop expertise that would be difficult to replace. For example, cooperative housing is usually run by an elected board of directors, who learn managerial and technical skills, such as preparing an annual budget, purchasing equipment, and contracting for maintenance. Almost any conscientious cooperative member can learn these skills, but most do not have the time, so the board members come to be seen by other residents as the "bosses," and democratic involvement disintegrates. But if such expertise in housing management were not developed, the complex would rapidly deteriorate into a slum (H. J. Rubin, 1981).

Activities in which paid experts work with community volunteers can also create problems in project implementation. Volunteers may insist on being paid, thus destroying the sense of participation. Or the volunteers may feel they have a right to boss the hired experts. That's asking for trouble: Telling a carpenter what to build causes no problems; telling him or her how to hold the hammer is asking for stress.

The resolution of the tension between experts and members involves several strategies. The main one is to hire experts who like to teach and who see their role as teacher and enabler, not as boss. Second, technical knowledge should be spread widely throughout the organization. Train several people in press relations, in newsletter production, in bookkeeping, and in purchasing. Rotate board members, so that old members can train new ones, and many people get to make the rules without spending inordinate amounts of time learning. Third, though the group might delegate technical decisions to experts, it should maintain control over policy.

Bottom-Line Profit or Community Aid.   Making a profit sometimes seems to clash with helping the community. It is easy to slip into an overemphasis on profit making:

> In an effort to attract more consumers and increase their income—and survive—many food co-ops have felt compelled to compromise or even forsake their original goals . . . many co-ops have badly exploited their *own* workers in a desperate effort to keep costs down. (Zwerdling, 1979, p. 104)

A financially bankrupt cooperative is a failure, but a cooperative that metamorphoses into a supermarket and underpays its workers is equally a failure. It there is not enough money, members should modify their original goals to ones they can afford rather than give up the goals to make a profit.

It is just as easy to err in the opposite direction, to overemphasize doing good for the community, threatening the financial viability of the project. For example, the leaders of an apartment cooperative wanted to help the poorer members, so they let people in financial trouble defer their monthly payments. Soon the word got around, and a very high percentage of individuals were in arrears. The cooperative could not survive financially and defaulted on its debt.

Fortunately, it is possible to balance financial viability and community benefits. A community-controlled firm that makes money by providing gainful employment for the welfare poor, or a financially successful tenant-managed housing complex that acts as a cornerstone for a reawakened community balances democratic involvement and profit making. The community investments of the South Shore Bank in Chicago (Taub, 1988) and those of some forestry cooperatives show that profit and social responsibility are compatible. The forestry cooperatives

> put liquid assets more directly to work in the Eugene Community. Funds were loaned to Starflower, a feminist collective and regional food distribution company, on a short term note at 2.5 percent above passbook interest rates. . . . Placing the funds with community-based organizations and receiving some premium over passbook interest rate satisfies the co-op's desire for both more economically astute and more socially desirable cash management. (Gunn in Jackall & Levin, 1984, p. 160)

Organizational Autonomy or Dependent Partnerships

If the problems people face are straightforward and local, community organizations may be able to achieve success on their own. Often, however, the kinds of problems that inspire the creation of community organizations are complicated and interdependent and require more concerted attacks than a single organization can launch. Larger development projects are possible if more financial resources are available. In pressure campaigns, coalitions increase the number of supporters on the community organization's side of the issue.

A community organization that wants to attack complex issues must extend its power, through coalitions, through co-production activities with government and business, and through the use of large sums of money. Each approach creates the possibility that people outside the organization will set the key goals and that group members will be co-opted by those they ask for help. The dilemma is illustrated in Figure E–3.

There are several responses to this problem. One is to opt out of the modern world because the organization is so afraid of having its goals distorted. Those joining isolated communes achieve self-direction but at a cost of being ineffective in bringing about needed social changes.

Another response to preserving organizational autonomy is to remain small and work only on those problems for which the organization has adequate resources. Much of the self-help movement—community hospices, aid to the bereaved, neighborhood conflict resolution—appropriately fits within this model (Hutcheson & Dominquez, 1986; Lieberman et al., 1979; Milofsky, 1988; J. A. Rivera, 1987; Silverman, 1980). Small self-help actions can accomplish much good and rarely require much cooperation from other organizations.

When joint work requires governmental resources, the danger of being co-opted or manipulated is real. An organization might end up serving city hall, or taking the blame

FIGURE E–3
The Dilemma of Dependent
Partnerships

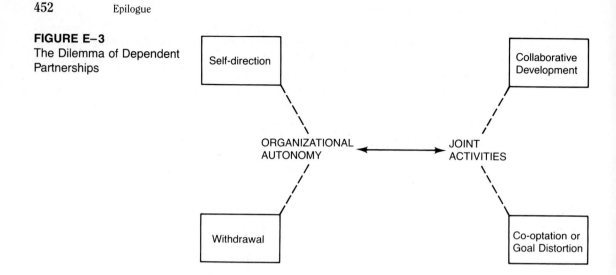

for poor services, or carrying out the goals of funding agencies rather than fulfilling the goals of its members. Although the possibility of cooptation is present in any joint work, it is most likely when community groups join projects initiated by others. To avoid cooptation, community organizations must plan ahead to set the agenda for other organizations.

The fear of having to follow some else's goals is not unreasonable when dealing with those in positions of power. Unfortunately, this same distrust characterizes relations between community organizations, neighborhood groups, and progressive interest groups. This fragmentation has seriously handicapped efforts for social change.

> ACORN and other Alinskyite groups have usually avoided forming coalitions with other progressive organizations, such as peace efforts and women's groups. . . . But building bridges with other groups may, in the long run, aid in breaking down the feelings of powerlessness and isolation which often accompany the difficult task of grassroots organizing. By explicitly identifying themselves with a tradition of organizing for social justice, and by acknowledging goals shared with other progressive organizations now active, Alinskyite groups could present a vision of ordinary people making history and thereby work toward sustaining greater membership solidarity and commitment. (Stein, 1986, p. 110)

To become a force for broader societal change, to present "a vision of ordinary people making history," progressive organizations must link up with each other, subdue the rivalries between different groups, and replace them with a common mission. Even groups that fear working too closely together can support progressive, national clearinghouses that provide technical information on problems and campaign strategies. Through widely read newsletters, such clearinghouses can help groups form common images of possible futures.

Activists working in progressive interest groups and those working in neighborhoods need to build stronger linkages to each other, rather than perceive each other as irrelevant and possibly wrongheaded. For a high-school dropout from a minority community whose economic opportunities are limited, worrying about the fate of a Western owl seems frivolous. From the point of view of the environmentalist, workers' willing acceptance of jobs that will kill them with chemicals and poison the local water supplies seems incomprehensible. But the underlying problems faced by both the dropout and the environmentalist are not that different.

When business no longer needs semi-skilled labor, it reduces its support of public education for the poor. The lumber industry sees the endangered owl as an obstacle to profitable timbering. In both cases, business considers maximizing economic profit as the goal and discards people or owls if they get in the way or if they are no longer needed. In both cases, hungry people facing unemployment (lumberjacks and the urban unemployed) discount the harm to the environment of any business that will employ them. Why are there so few jobs? What can be done? Training programs and alternative, pollution-free businesses might be helpful in both cases.

Overcoming isolation between interest-based and neighborhood-based groups is a major problem for future organizing. Organizers have to find the common strands and the solutions that might unite groups with different organizing philosophies and goals.

Future Actions: Protest or Development?

Many activists still feel an antagonism between developmental projects and head-on confrontations. At the extremes, developmental organizers label those who promote protest as rebellious anarchists. Those who champion protests argue that only a few benefit from development work, while the community, still handicapped by social injustice, gains little.

Both concerns are legitimate. Anarchistic rebellion and selective benefits threaten the protest and developmental models, respectively. But protest and development strategies can be integrated, if their central themes, rather than their perversions, are thoughtfully examined.

In protest, the resolution of individual grievances is not enough. People must also confront the social bases of inequality.

Protest is a search for collective redress of shared injustices.

It is not simply an emotional release based on the expression of collective anger. Protest is a dramatic questioning of structural inequality. A protest that benefits only those immediately involved does not contribute to social change and hence is not truly successful.

A parallel argument holds for those engaged in developmental work. Successful development has to be more than encouraging one or two or even a thousand entrepreneurs from poor communities. Helping individuals in the development model must be the means toward accomplishing a social redistribution. The success of some must symbolize the possibility of others doing the same.

So long as activists remember that the purpose of organizing is to rectify social injustices, protest and development are complementary. A search for collective redress through protest is totally compatible with development as the means to bring about social redistribution.

The tension and its resolution are summarized in Figure E–4.

Advocacy and development remain compatible. (Courtesy TTB)

Capture the Social Agenda Through Shared Symbols.   To accomplish this synthesis of protest and development, activists need to ensure that the projects they undertake contribute to social change. They also need to symbolize this message of social change, so that those not involved in progressive organizing can see how joining the movement can lead to a better society.

Both protests and development efforts should highlight fundamental questions about political and economic power and in doing so set the social agenda to which the establishment responds.

> *Controlling the social agenda is a major step toward empowerment that both protest and development activities can accomplish.*

Establishing community-based alternative businesses, promoting comparable worth, protesting and then lobbying to protect endangered animals, working to redraw the boundaries of election districts to enfranchise minority group members, all take the initiative to establish a new agenda to which those in power must react.

Working to build alternative businesses questions the need for capitalistic exploitation. Comparable worth disputes the right of business to perpetuate sexual inequality and challenges business's role in keeping women dependent on men by paying them too little to support themselves and their children. The defense of animal species asks whether people have the right to exploit and destroy nature and raises the issue of long-term survival of the human species. Enfranchising the poor, that is, giving them

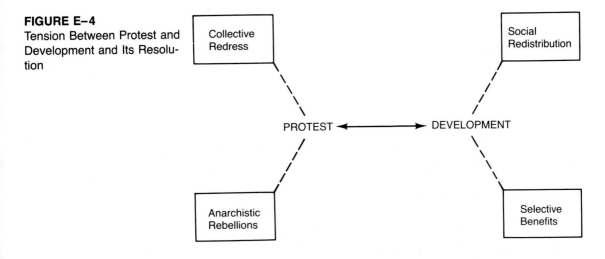

FIGURE E–4
Tension Between Protest and Development and Its Resolution

a real chance to elect political representatives, raises the possibility of using the political system to blunt the negative effects of economic restructuring.

To succeed at such activities, progressive community groups must capture and mold symbols of oppression and myths of social change. Such myths help shape the public's perception that the goals of community groups are just. Taking control of the public agenda means shaping and controlling those myths that help define public problems.

> For a problem definition to get widespread popular appeal, it must reflect a shared image of what is wrong in the present and how the future might be different. A myth provides such an image. It serves as a common metaphor for all to make similar sense of events. It allows people to say, "this new and unfamiliar situation is really an example of this other familiar situation." Moreover, its shared moral allows leaders to justify that an issue is worthy of concern. It permits them simply to refer to known stories and to communicate a way of seeing an issue quickly to a wide audience, while also delivering a complex and emotionally charged message. (deNeufville & Barton, 1987, p. 183)

Protest communities share such myths, including the oppression of racism, cruel bosses, sexually abusive men, and callous hunters. To mobilize people for action, organizers repeat these stories of shared exploitation. But many of these myths do not communicate to the broader society. For example, African Americans sometimes argue that the inequities they face are the result of slavery, and current society needs to make up for the terrors of slavery. This shared symbol creates a reaction among dominant-group members who are appalled by slavery and equally appalled that they should be blamed for the consequences of historic injustice. Similarly, most men agree that abusing their positions to get sexual favors from female subordinates is abhorrent behavior, but they know they are not guilty of it and resent being tarred with that brush.

In the future, to create acceptance among a broader, as yet unmobilized public, community groups must formulate and agree on a different set of myths. Boyte's (1989a) evocation of a possible commonwealth in which people share common responsibilities is one attempt to create such a myth. Community groups can draw on David and Goliath stories or turn the myth of rugged individualism into a justification for community self-determination and control. The myth of the American West may be useful, because it evokes simultaneously the images of rugged individualism and collective endeavor, as settlers overcame poor land, locust plagues, horse thieves, drought, illness, and terminal loneliness. In the Western myth, people learned to do things by themselves—they were empowered—but many of the community-building efforts were collective, including defense, firefighting, harvesting, and barn construction. These myths, and others that community groups will invent in the future, are especially useful because they resonate with the whole society, not just with a particular group.

TOWARD AN EMPOWERING FUTURE

By reflecting on their experiences, community organizers can create a template for change in the broader society. Community well-being and individual empowerment bolster each other as increased community solidarity brings about a future in which individual capacity can develop. Success at developmental projects encourages individuals to have the confidence to attempt more on their own. Both protest and development cry out for collective redress and a fairer allocation of resources.

Continued success for organizing lies in defining the issues that society must confront rather than reacting to the agendas of others. These items on the social agenda are steps in building a society in which power is broadly shared. Helping individuals who are unemployed is important, but confronting the system that instills in workers a fear of losing their jobs is even more important. Issues of economic justice must be near the top of a community-defined action agenda.

The future agenda must merge concerns with social issues with those of economic change. Community organizations must actively promote civil rights and civil liberties. Without the respect for human dignity that such rights represent and without the First Amendment protections that enable community groups to vociferously argue for their causes, the process of community organizing become much more difficult, and economic victories, if obtained, might be hollow.

A better society will come about gradually. Shared power comes from the successes of many individual democratic organizations, each working to accomplish their part of a societal transformation. Change will occur because people learn from many small, collective successes that their self-interest is served by joining with others.

Changes occur as immensity in businesses and government become suspect and are opposed, not because big is innately bad, but because big is distant from the control of ordinary people. This rejection of distant bigness holds as much for centrally, planned socialistic governments as it does for privately controlled international business cartels.

Small size creates the potential for people to control the institutions that affect them. Small is not powerless.

Just as individuals gain power by joining together, many small, alternative, progressive organizations collectively working on a common problem can bring about large change.

"The Hope of the Future" (on bulletin board of neighborhood organization). (Courtesy TTB)

In accomplishing their agenda, progressive organizations must emphasize their willingness to work together for societal change. Activists must prevent those in government or business from turning organizations representing one minority against another, or organized labor against feminists, environmentalists against the unemployed, or neighborhood activists against those more concerned with improving the quality of work life. Activists must overcome the divisive tensions within the progressive movement, and share a common vision and a mutual respect.

In addition, the advantage of a movement with many small components is that a failure of a part does little to affect the whole. As the long history of organizing has shown, the movement is resilient in the face of adversity. Because so many organizations are trying different approaches, organizers can find many new and effective approaches to choose from. If organizing can learn from its trials and errors, it will become more and more successful.

The goal of societal transformation is broad and far-reaching, but it can be achieved a little at a time. The impact of each organization's successes often goes far beyond the members of that group. An employee-owned plant that increases profits and introduces new and improved products as a result of the democratic involvement of its workers provides a standard for the traditional economy to follow. Successful Community Development Corporations set up supportive models of entrepreneurship. Fights for civil rights and civil liberties apply not only to minorities, but to society as a whole.

It is not simply achieving a better future that counts, but getting there in a way that is empowering for the individual. Respectful listening to the opinions of others and broad participation in decision making lead to more effective actions. Getting people to participate in democratic organizations at home, at work, and in government, is an end worth achieving. Democratic institutions are the manifestation of a society that believes in human equality and individual dignity. They must be cherished and strengthened.

In sum, there is much to be done. The need is increasingly urgent. We know the way. Let us continue our proud march.

Bibliography

Abbott, C. (1981). *The new urban America: Growth and politics in Sunbelt cities.* Chapel Hill, NC: University of North Carolina.

Aboard bus D. (1989, April 30). *Chicago Tribune,* Tempo, pp. 1, 6.

Adam, B. D. (1978). *The survival of domination: Inferiorization and everyday life.* New York: Elsevier.

Adam, B. D. (1987). *The rise of a gay and lesbian movement.* Boston: Twayne Publishers, G. K. Hall & Co.

Adams, D. E., & Goldbard, A. (1980, Spring). The Neighborhood Art Program National Organizing Committee. *Journal of Alternative Human Services, 6,* 9–15.

Adamson, M., & Borgos, S. (1984). *This mighty dream: Social protest movements in the United States.* Boston: Routledge & Kegan Paul.

Ahlbrandt, R. S., Jr. (1986). Using research to build stronger neighborhoods: A study of Pittsburgh's neighborhoods. In R. Taylor (Ed.), *Urban neighborhoods: Research and policy* (pp. 285–309). New York: Praeger.

Ahlbrandt, R. S., Jr., & Cunningham, J. (1979). *A new public policy for neighborhood preservation.* New York: Praeger.

Alderson, G. & Sentman, E. (1979). *How you can influence Congress: The complete handbook for the citizen lobbyist.* New York: E. P. Dutton.

Aldrich, H. (1979). *Organizations and environments.* Englewood Cliffs, NJ: Prentice-Hall.

Alinsky, S. D. (1969). *Reveille for radicals.* New York: Random House.

Alinsky, S. D. (1971). *Rules for radicals.* New York: Random House.

Amidei, N. (1987, Summer). The new activism picks up steam. *Public Welfare, 45,* 21–26.

Amy, D. (1987). *The politics of environmental mediation.* New York: Columbia University Press.

Angevine, E. (Ed.). (1982). *Consumer activists: They made a difference.* Mount Vernon, NY: Consumers Union Foundation.

Argyris, C., Putnam, R. S., & McLain, D. (1985). *Action science: Concepts, methods, and skills for research and intervention.* San Francisco: Jossey-Bass.

Arias, M. (1988, August–September). Beyond shelters: Making homes for battered women. *City Limits, 13,* 18–20.

Ashkenaz, J. (1986, May). Grassroots organizing and the Democracy Party—the Vermont Rainbow experience. *Monthly Review,* pp. 8–21.

Atlas, J., & Dreir, P. (1986). The tenants' movement and American politics. In R. G. Bratt,

C. Hartman, & A. Myerson (Eds.), *Critical perspectives on housing* (pp. 378–397). Philadelphia: Temple University Press.

Atlas, T. (1990, March 2). FBI tactics questioned in probe of activists. *Chicago Tribune,* pp. 1, 12.

At least give the IRS credit for persistence. (1990, June 12). *Washington Post Weekly,* p. 14.

At long last: Lobbying rules we can live with. (1991, Winter/Spring) *Community Change,* *24,* 5–6.

Auletta, K. (1982). *The underclass.* New York: Random House.

Avery, M., Auvine, B., Streibel, B., & Weiss, L. (1981). *Building united judgment: A handbook for consensus decision making.* Madison, WI: Center for Conflict Resolution.

Axinn, J., & Stern, M. J. (1988). *Dependency and poverty: Old problems in a New World.* Lexington, MA: Lexington.

Ayres, B. D., Jr. (1989, August 20). Neighbors unite and score a victory in capital's drug war. *New York Times,* p. 14.

Babb, S. (1989, April). Women's coalition: New voices for affordable housing. *City Limits,* *14,* 8–9.

Babbie, E. (1989). *Survey research methods* (2nd ed.). Belmont, CA: Wadsworth.

Bacharach, S., & Lawler, E. (1981). *Bargaining.* San Francisco: Jossey-Bass.

Bachelor, L., & Jones, B. (1981). Managed participation: Detroit's neighborhood opportunity fund. *The Journal of Applied Behavioral Science, 17*(4), 518–536.

Bachrach, P., & Baratz, M. S. (1963). Decisions and non-decisions: An analytical framework. *American Political Science Review, 57*(3), 632–642.

Bailey, R. (1974). *Radicals in urban politics: The Alinsky approach.* Chicago: University of Chicago Press.

Bailis, L. (1974). *Bread or justice: Grassroots organizing in the welfare rights movement.* Lexington, MA: Lexington.

Baltimore alliance wins state's first CRA agreement. (1987, May). *The CRA Reporter: Center for Community Change,* pp. 2–5.

Barkan, S. E. (1980, October). Strategic, tactical and organizational dilemmas of the protest movement against nuclear power. *Social Problems, 27,* 19–37.

Barkan, S. E. (1986). Interorganizational conflict in the southern civil rights movement. *Sociological Inquiry, 56*(2), 190–205.

Barnes, D. A. (1987a). Organization and radical protest: An antithesis? *The Sociological Quarterly, 28*(4), 575–594.

Barnes, D. A. (1987b). Strategy outcomes and the growth of protest organizations: A case study of the Southern farmers' alliance. *Rural Sociology, 52*(2), 164–186.

Barry, P. (1987a, July). Deal-making begins as west side stadium gets nod. *The Neighborhood Works, 10,* 9–11.

Barry, P. (1987b, April). Residents seek role in stadium shuffle. *The Neighborhood Works, 10*(1), 8–10.

Batra, R. (1987, May 3). An ominous trend to greater inequality. *New York Times,* section F, p. 2.

Beeghley, L. (1989). *The structure of social stratification in the United States.* Boston: Allyn & Bacon.

Beer, J. E. (1986). *Peacemaking in your neighborhood: Reflections on an experiment in community mediation.* Philadelphia: New Society Publishers.

Bellah, R. N., Madsen, R., Sullivan, W. M., Swidler, A., & Tipton, S. (1985). *Habits of the heart: Individualism and commitment in American Life.* New York: Harper & Row.

Bendick, M., Jr., & Egan, M. L. (1989). *Linking business development and community development: Lessons from four cities.* Presented at the Community Development Research Center. Washington, DC.

Bennett, L. (1986, December). Beyond urban renewal: Chicago's North Loop Redevelopment project. *Urban Affairs Quarterly, 22,* 242–260.

Bennett, L. (1987). The dilemmas of building a progressive urban coalition: The linked development debate in Chicago. *Journal of Urban Affairs, 9*(3), 263–276.

Bennett, L. (1989). Postwar redevelopment in Chicago: The declining politics of party and the rise of neighborhood politics. In G. D. Squires (Ed.), *Unequal partnership: The political economy of urban redevelopment in postwar America* (pp. 161–177). New Brunswick, NJ: Rutgers University Press.

Bennett, S. F., & Lavrakas, P. J. (1989). Community-based crime prevention: An assessment of the Eisenhower Foundation's Neighborhood Program. *Crime & Delinquency, 35*(3), 345–364.

Bensman, D., & Lynch, R. (1987). *Rusted dreams: Hard times in a steel community.* New York: McGraw-Hill.

Berger, P., & Neuhaus, R. J. (1977). *To empower people.* Washington, DC: American Enterprise Institute for Public Policy Research.

Berkowitz, B. (1987). *Local heroes.* Lexington, MA: Lexington Publishers.

Berkowitz, E. D. (1987). *Disabled policy: America's programs for the handicapped.* Cambridge, England: Cambridge University Press.

Berkowitz, W. (1982). *Community impact: Creating grassroots change in hard times.* Cambridge, MA: Schenkman Publishing.

Berndt, H. (1977). *New rulers in the ghetto: The community development corporation and urban poverty.* Westport, CT: Greenwood Press.

Berry, J. (1977). *Lobbying for the people.* Princeton, NJ: Princeton University Press.

Berry, P. (1989, December). No time to waste. Special Issue. *The Neighborhood Works,* pp. 1–31.

Betten, N., & Austin, M. J. (Eds.). (1990). *The roots of community organizing, 1917–1939.* Philadelphia: Temple University Press.

Biklen, D. (1983). *Community organizing: Theory and practice.* Englewood Cliffs, NJ: Prentice-Hall.

Bingham, G. (1986). *Resolving environmental disputes: A decade of experience.* Washington, DC: The Conservation Foundation.

Bishop, K. (1989, September 11). Tent cities are front lines in battle over homelessness. *New York Times,* pp. 1, 8.

Blasi, J. (1988). *Employee ownership: Revolution or ripoff?* Cambridge, MA: Ballinger.

Blood-Patterson, P. (Ed.). (1988). *Rise up singing.* Bethlehem, PA: Sing Out Publication.

Bond, D. (1988). The nature and meaning of nonviolent direct action: An exploratory study. *Journal of Peace Research, 25*(1), 81–88.

Bookman, A. & Morgen, S. (1988). "Carry it on": Continuing the discussion and the struggle. In A. Bookman & S. Morgen (Eds.), *Women and the politics of empowerment* (pp. 314–321). Philadelphia: Temple University Press.

Borgos, S. (1986). Low-income homeownership and the ACORN squatters campaign. In G. Bratt, C. Hartman, & A. Myerson (Eds.), *Critical perspectives on housing,* (pp. 428–446). Philadelphia: Temple University Press.

Boston: Office complex gets big loan. (1990, February 25). *New York Times,* p. 35.

Boucher, D. (1987). *Radical citizenship: The new American activism.* New York: Schocken.

Bowles, S., & Gintis, H. (1986). *Democracy & capitalism: Property, community, and the contradictions of modern social thought.* New York: Basic Books.

Boyte, H. C. (1980). *The backyard revolution: Understanding the new citizen movement.* Philadelphia: Temple University Press.

Boyte, H. C. (1984). *Community is possible: Repairing America's roots.* New York: Harper & Row.

Boyte, H. C. (1989a). *Commonwealth: A return to citizen politics.* New York: The Free Press.

Boyte, H. C. (1989b, January). Moving into power: Reinvigorating public life for the 1990s. *Community Renewal Press: Occasional Papers, 1,* unpaged.

Boyte, H. C., Booth, H., & Max, S. (1986a). *Citizen action and the new American populism*. Philadelphia: Temple University Press.

Boyte, H. C., & Riessman, F. (Eds.). (1986b). *The new populism: The politics of empowerment*. Philadelphia: Temple University Press.

Bradford, C. (1987, January–February). Building a development engine. *The Neighborhood Works, 10*(1), 7–11.

Brady, J. P. (1982, April). Arson, fiscal crisis and community action. *Crime & Delinquency, 28*, 247–274.

Branch, T. (1988). *Parting the waters: America in the King years 1954–1963*. New York: Simon & Schuster.

Bratt, R. G. (1989a). Community-based housing in Massachusetts: Lessons and limits of the state's support system. In S. Rosenberry, C. Hartman, & A. Myerson (Eds.), *Housing issues in the 1990s* (pp. 277–306). New York: Praeger.

Bratt, R. G. (1989b). *Rebuilding a low-income housing policy*. Philadelphia: Temple University Press.

Brill, H. (1971). *Why organizers fail: The story of a rent strike*. Berkeley: University of California Press.

Brilliant, E. L. (1986, December). Community planning and community problem solving: Past, present and future. *Social Service Review, 60*, 568–569.

Brooks, M. E. (1989a). *A citizen's guide to creating a housing trust fund*. Washington, DC: Center for Community Change.

Brooks, M. E. (1989b). *A guide to developing a housing trust fund*. Washington, DC: Center for Community Change.

Brower, S. (1986). Planners in the neighborhood: A cautionary tale. In R. Taylor (Ed.), *Urban neighborhoods: Research and policy* (pp. 181–214). New York: Praeger.

Brown, C. R. (1984). *The art of coalition building: A guide for community leaders*. New York: The American Jewish Committee.

Brown, L. (1984). The good advocate needs troops. In J. Ecklein (Ed.), *Community organizers* (2nd ed., pp. 217–225). New York: John Wiley & Sons.

Brown, L. H. (1985, January). Organizational consistency in new wave food co-operatives: The challenge of congruence. *Sociological Focus, 18*, 49–67.

Browne, D. (1986). *Resident management of public housing*. Chicago: The Natalie P. Voorhees Center for Neighborhood and Community Improvement.

Browning, R. P., Marshall, D. R., & Tabb, D. H. (1984). *Protest is not enough: The struggle of blacks and Hispanics for equality in urban politics*. Berkeley: University of California Press.

Bruyn, S. T. (1987). Beyond the market and the state. In S. T. Bruyn & J. Meehan (Eds.), *Beyond the market and the state: New directions in community development* (pp. 3–27). Philadelphia: Temple University Press.

Buechler, S. M. (1989). *Organization and community in women's movements: An historical overview*. Presented at the Annual Meeting of the American Sociological Association, San Francisco.

Buffum, C. (1989, September 10). My life with crack. *New York Times*.

Bullard, R. D. (1990). Environmentalism, economic blackmail, and civil rights: Competing agendas within the black community. In J. Gaventa, B. E. Smith, & A. Willingham (Eds.), *Communities in economic crisis: Appalachia and the South* (pp. 190–199). Philadelphia: Temple University Press.

Bullard, R., & Wright, B. H. (1987). Environmentalism and the politics of equity: Emergent trends in the black community. *Mid-American Review of Sociology, 12*(2), 21–38.

Burby, R., & Rohe, W. M. (1989). Decentralization of public housing: Effects on residents' satisfaction with their living arrangements and their fear of crime. *Urban Affairs Quarterly, 25*(1), 117–141.

Burghardt, S. (1982a). *Organizing for community action.* Beverly Hills, CA: Sage.

Burghardt, S. (1982b). *The other side of organizing: Resolving the personal dilemmas and political demands of daily practice.* Cambridge, MA: Schenkman.

Burghardt, S., & Fabricant, M. (1987). *Working under the safety net: Policy and practice with the new American poor.* Newbury Park, CA: Sage.

Burnham, M. A., & Koegel, P. (1988, April). Methodology for obtaining a representative sample of homeless persons: The Los Angeles Skid Row Study. *Evaluation Review, 12,* 117–152.

Burns, J. M., Peltason, J. W., & Cronin, T. (1981). *State and local politics.* Englewood Cliffs, NJ: Prentice-Hall.

Bush's promise to the homeless: A "Godsend" or much ado about nothing? (1990, February 12). *New York Times,* p. A16.

Buursma, B. (1989, March 19). In Santa Monica, activism enters the computer age. *Chicago Tribune,* p. 5.

Cable, S., Walsh, E. J., & Warland, R. H. (1988, June). Differential paths to political activism: Comparisons of four mobilization processes after the Three Mile Island accident. *Social Forces, 66,* 951–969.

Calderson, J., & Horton, J. (1988). *The English only movement: Sources of support and opposition in California.* Paper Presented at the Annual Meeting of the American Sociological Association, Atlanta.

Camacho, E., & Joravsky, B. (1989, August 20). Retreat from Chicago. *Chicago Tribune,* section 4, pp. 1, 4.

Campbell, D. (1986). *Organizing grassroots power: Transcending Alinsky-style leadership.* Presented at the 1986 Annual Meeting of the American Political Science Association. Washington, DC.

Canan, P., & Pring, G. W. (1988, December). Strategic lawsuits against public participation. *Social Problems, 35,* 506–519.

CANDO. (1989). *CANDO'S 10th anniversary conference: The next decade for neighborhood economic development* [advertising brochure] Chicago: Author.

Caplan, M. (1983). *Ralph Nader presents a citizens' guide to lobbying.* New York: Dembner Press.

Carson, R. (1962). *Silent spring.* Boston: Houghton Mifflin.

Cassidy, R. (1980). *Livable cities: A grassroots guide to rebuilding urban America.* New York: Holt, Rinehart & Winston.

Castells, M. (1983). *The city and the grassroots: A cross-cultural theory of urban social movements.* Berkeley: University of California Press.

Center for Community Change. (1987). *The Community Reinvestment Act: A citizen's action guide.* Washington, DC: Center for Community Change.

Center for Popular Economics. (1987). *A field guide to the U.S. economy.* Prepared by N. Falbre. New York: Pantheon Books.

Chalkley, T. (1987, June). Coalition capitalizes on financial revolution. *The Neighborhood Works, 10*(1), 14–15.

Champagne, A., & Harpham, E. J. (Eds.). (1984). *The attack on the welfare state.* Prospect Heights, IL: Waveland Press.

Changing shares. (1988, December 18). *New York Times,* section E, p. 5.

Chavez, C. (1984). La Causa and La Huegla. In J. Ecklein (Ed.), *Community organizers* (pp. 15–27). New York: John Wiley & Sons.

Chavis, D. N., & Wandersman, A. (1986). Roles for research and the researcher in neighborhood development. In R. Taylor (Ed.), *Urban neighborhoods: Research and policy* (pp. 215–249). New York: Praeger.

Checkoway, B. (1981). The politics of public hearings. *The Journal of Applied Behavioral Science, 17*(4), 566–580.

Checkoway, B., & Norsman, A. (1986, October). Empowering citizens with disabilities. *Community Development Journal,* pp. 270–277.

Checkoway, B. (1985). Neighborhood planning organizations: Perspectives and choices. *The Journal of Applied Behavioral Science, 21*(4), 471–486.

Chell, E. (1985). *Participation and organization: A social psychological approach.* London: Macmillan.

Christrup, J., & Schaeffer, R. (1990, January/February). Not in anyone's backyard. *Greenpeace, 15,* 14–19.

Churchill, W., & Vander Wall, J. (1988). *Agents of repression: The FBI's secret wars against the Black Panther Party and the American Indian Movement.* Boston: South End Press.

City of Chicago. (1989). *The President's proposed 1990 budget: Impact on Chicago.* Budget director, Thomas J. Elzey. Chicago: City of Chicago.

Clark, G. L., & Dear, M. (1984). *State apparatus: Structures and language of legitimacy.* Boston: Allen & Unwin.

Clark, T. (1988a, December). Tenants and neighbors battle HUD and ComEd. *Illinois Issues, 14,* 20–24.

Clark, T. (1988b, May–June). Who controls South Lakefront redevelopment? *The Neighborhood Works, 11*(1), 18–20.

Clavel, P. (1986). *The progressive city: Planning and participation, 1969–1984.* New Brunswick, NJ: Rutgers University Press.

Claybrook, J. (1988, January–February). Another assault on our liability laws. *Public Citizen, 8,* 23.

Clegg, S. R. (1989). *Frameworks of power.* Newbury Park, CA: Sage.

Cohen, J. L. (1985, Winter). Strategy or identity: New theoretical paradigms and contemporary social movements. *Social Research, 52,* 663–716.

Cohen, M. (1988). *The sisterhood: The true story of the women who changed the world.* New York: Simon & Schuster.

Collins, A., & Pancoast, D. (1976). *Natural helping networks: A strategy for prevention.* Washington, DC: National Association of Social Workers.

Committee on National Urban Policy. (1988). Committee report—Overview. In M. G. H. McGeary & L. E. Lynn Jr., (Eds.), *Urban change and poverty,* (pp. 3–64). Washington, DC: National Academy Press.

Community Change. (1989, Summer).

Cooney, R., & Michalowski, H. (Eds.). (1987). *The power of the people: Active nonviolence in the United States.* Philadelphia: New Society Publishers.

Cooper, A. (1985, November 23). Liberal groups go door-to-door for dollars, Will conservatives follow? *National Journal,* pp. 2647–2649.

Cooper, T. (1980). Bureaucracy and community organization. *Administration & Society, 11*(1), 411–444.

Costain, A. N. (1988). *Activists, agitators and issues: Mobilizing a women's movement in America.* Presented at the Annual Meeting of the American Political Science Association, Washington, DC.

Costner, P., & Rapaport, D. (1990, January–February). What works: An oral history of five Greenpeace campaigns. *Greenpeace, 15,* 9–13.

Crenshaw, E., & St. John, C. (1989, March). The organizationally dependent community. *Urban Affairs Quarterly, 24,* 412–434.

Crenson, M. (1971). *The unpolitics of air pollution: A study of nondecision making in two cities.* Baltimore: John Hopkins University Press.

Crenson, M. (1980). Social networks and political processes in urban neighborhoods. *Journal of Political Science, 22,* 578–594.

Crenson, M. (1983). *Neighborhood politics.* Cambridge, MA: Harvard University Press.

Cronin, T. E. (1989). *Direct democracy: The politics of initiative, referendum, and recall.* Cambridge, MA: Harvard University Press.

Crosby, N., Kelly, J. M., & Schaefer, P. (1986, March–April). Citizen panels: A new approach to citizen participation. *Public Administration Review,* pp. 170–178.

Cruz, W. UNO: Organizing at the grass roots. *Illinois Issues, 14,* 18–22.

Cummings, S., & Glaser, M. (1985). Neighborhood participation in community development: A comparison of strategic approaches. *Population Research and Policy Review, 4,* 267–287.

Cummings, S., & Glaser, M. (1986). Selecting sound investments for community development corporations: Some practical advice from executive directors. *Journal of Applied Sociology, 3,* 51–62.

Cunningham, J. V., & Kotler, M. (1983). *Building neighborhood organizations: A guidebook sponsored by the National Association of Neighborhoods.* Notre Dame, IN: University of Notre Dame Press.

Curry, G. E. (1989, August 27). Rappers take Urban League's message to the streets. *Chicago Tribune,* p. 6.

Daft, R. L. (1983). *Organization theory and design.* St.Paul, MN: West Publishing.

Danielson, M. (1976). *The politics of exclusion.* New York: Columbia University Press.

Darden, J. T., Hill, R. C., Thomas, J., & Thomas, R. (1987). *Detroit: Race and uneven development.* Philadelphia: Temple University Press.

Davidson, J. (1979). *Political partnerships: Neighborhood residents and their council members.* Beverly Hills: Sage.

Davis, L. V., & Hagen, J. L. (1988, December). Services for battered women: The public policy response. *Social Service Review, 62,* 649–667.

Davis, N. J. (1988). Shelters for battered women: Social policy response to interpersonal violence. *The Social Science Journal, 25*(4), 401–409.

de Neufville, J. I., & Barton, S. E. (1987). Myths and the definitions of policy problems. *Policy Sciences, 20,* 181–206.

Deckard, B. (1983). *The women's movement: Political, socioeconomic and psychological issues.* New York: Harper & Row.

Delbecq, A., Van de Ven, A. H., & Gustafson, D. (1975). *Group techniques for program planning: A guide to nominal group and Delphi procedures.* Glenview, IL: Scott, Foresman.

DeLeon, D. (1988). *Everything is changing: Contemporary U.S. movements in historical perspective.* New York: Praeger.

Delgado, G. (1986). *Organizing the movement: The roots and growth of ACORN.* Philadelphia: Temple University Press.

Delgado, M., & Scott, J. (1979). Strategic intervention: A mental health program for the Hispanic community. *Journal of Community Psychology, 7*(2), 187–197.

Denney, V., & Brown, J. (1988–1989, December–January). Mixed picture on neighborhood funding. *The Neighborhood Works, 11,* 1, 4.

DePalma, A. (1988, December 28). Newark struggles to recreate itself. *New York Times,* p. 9.

DeParle, J. (1990, January 3). Rash, rude and effective, Act-Up helps change AIDS policy. *New York Times,* section B, p. 1.

Deutschman, I. E. (1988). *Feminist theory and the politics of empowerment.* Presented at the 1988 Annual Meeting of the American Political Science Association, Washington, DC.

Devine, K. S. (1989–1990, December–January). Boston gives residents voice on local decisions. *The Neighborhood Works, 12*(1), 17–19.

Dill, B. T. (1988). "Making your job good yourself": Domestic service and the construction of personal dignity. In A. Bookman & S. Morgen (Eds.), *Women and the politics of empowerment* (pp. 33–52). Philadelphia: Temple University Press.

Dillman, D. (1978). *Mail and telephone surveys: The total design method.* New York: Wiley.

Dionne, E. J., Jr. (1989a, July 21). Abortion rights backers adopt tactics of politics. *New York Times,* p. 7.

Dionne, E. J., Jr. (1989b, August 8). States spending fastest on jails. *New York Times.*

Downey, G. L. (1986, June). Ideology and the Clamshell identity: Organizational dilemmas in the anti-nuclear power movement. *Social Problems, 33,* 357–373.

Dreier, P. (1987, Fall). Community-based housing: A progressive approach to a new federal policy. *Social Policy,* pp. 18–24.

Dreier, P. (1989). Economic growth and economic justice in Boston: Populist housing and job policies. In G. D. Squires (Ed.), *Unequal partnership: The political economy or urban redevelopment in Postwar America* (pp. 35–58). New Brunswick, NJ: Rutgers University Press.

Dreier, P., & Atlas, J. (1989, Winter). Grassroots strategies for the housing crisis: A national agenda. *Social Policy,* pp. 25–38.

Dresang, D. L., & Gosling, J. J. (1989). *Politics, policy & management in the American states.* New York: Longman.

Druckman, D. (Ed.). (1977). *Negotiations: Social-psychological perspectives.* Beverly Hills, CA: Sage.

Dugger, W. M. (1987, March). Democratic economic planning and worker ownership. *Journal of Economic Issues, 21,* 87–99.

Duncan, W. A. (1986, Spring). An economic development strategy. *Social Policy,* pp. 17–24.

Durrance, J. C. (1984). *Armed for action: Library response to citizen information need.* New York: Neal-Schuman Publishing.

Eckberg, D. Lee. (1988, December). The physicians anti-abortion campaign and the social bases of moral reform participation. *Social Forces, 67,* 378–397.

Ecklein, J. (1984). *Community organizers.* New York: John Wiley & Sons.

Edelman, M. (1971). *Politics as symbolic action: Mass arousal and quiescence.* Chicago: Markham Publishing.

Edelman, M. (1988). *Constructing the political spectacle.* Chicago: University of Chicago Press.

Edsall, T. (1984). *The new politics of inequality.* New York: W. W. Norton.

Egan, T. (1989, April 27). U.S. stand on owl is seen saving trees in West. *New York Times,* section I, p. 18.

Egan, T. (1990, June 1). Mired in poverty, Alaska Natives ponder how much land to spend. *New York Times,* pp. 1, 11.

Ehrenreich, B. (1989). *Fear of falling: The inner life of the middle class.* New York: Pantheon.

Ehrenreich, J. H. (1985). *The altruistic imagination: A history of social work and social policy in the United States.* Ithaca, NY: Cornell University Press.

Elzey, T. J., Budget Director. (1989, December 12). *The president's proposed 1990 budget: Impact on Chicago.* Chicago: Bureau of Budget.

Evans, D. (1989, December 12). Ruling limits access to document. *Chicago Tribune,* p. 3.

Fabricant, M. (1988, Spring). Empowering the homeless. *Social Policy, 19,* 49–55.

Fabricant, M., & Epstein, I. (1984). Legal and welfare rights advocacy: Complementary approaches in organizing on behalf of the homeless. *The Urban and Social Change Review, 17*(1), 15–19.

Fagan, J. (1987, November). Neighborhood education, mobilization, and organization for juvenile crime prevention. *Annals, AAPSS, 494,* 54–70.

Fainstein, S., Fainstein, N., Hill, R. C., Judd, D., Smith, M. P., & Armistead, J., with Keller, M. (1983). *Restructuring the city.* New York: Longman.

Falcon, A. (1988). Black and Latino politics in New York City: Race and ethnicity in a changing urban context. In F. C. Garcia (Ed.), *Latinos and the political system* (pp. 171–195). Notre Dame, IN: University of Notre Dame Press.

Fantasia, R. (1988). *Cultures of solidarity: Consciousness, action, and contemporary American workers.* Berkeley, CA: University of California Press.

Feagin, J. R. (1988). *Free enterprise city: Houston in political and economic perspective.*

New Brunswick, NJ: Rutgers University Press.

Feagin, J. R., & Parker, R. (1988). Economic troubles and local state action: Some Texas examples. In M. Wallace & J. Rothschild (Eds.), *Research in Politics and Society: Vol. 3. Deindustrialization and the restructuring of American industry* (pp. 127–154). Greenwich, CT: JAI Press.

Feagin, J. R., & Smith, M. P. (1987). Cities and the new international division of labor: An overview. In M. P. Smith & J. R. Feagin (Eds.), *The capitalist city: Global restructuring and community politics* (pp. 3–34). New York: Basil Blackwell.

Fear, F. A., Carter, K. A., & Thullen, M. (1985). Action research in community development: Concepts and principles. *Research in Rural Sociology and Development, 2,* 197–216.

Feins, J., Peterson, J., & Rovetch, E. (1983). *Partnerships for neighborhood crime prevention.* Washington DC: U.S. Department of Justice: National Institute of Justice.

Ferraro, K. (1989, February). Policing woman battering. *Social Problems, 36,* 61–74.

Finder, A. (1990, March 11). Nonprofit groups rebuilding housing for the poor. *New York Times,* p. 23.

Fiordalisi, G. (1989, October 9). Computers link residents, city hall. *City & State,* pp. 24–25.

Fischer, C. (1982). *To dwell among friends: Personal networks in town and city.* Chicago: University of Chicago.

Fischer, C. (1984). *The urban experience.* New York: Harcourt, Brace, Jovanovich.

Fischer, C., Jackson, R., Stueve, C. A., Gerson, K., Jones, L. M., & Baldassare, M. (1977). *Networks and places: Social relations in the urban setting.* New York: The Free Press.

Fisher, R. (1972). Fractionating conflict. In R. Fisher (Ed.), *International conflict and behavioral science* (pp. 91–109). New York: Basic.

Fisher, R. (1984). *Let the people decide: Neighborhood organizing in America.* Boston: Twayne G. K. Hall.

Fisher, R., & Kling, J. M. (1987, January–February). Leading the people: Two approaches to the role of ideology in community organizing. *Radical America, 21,* pp. 31–45.

Fisher, R., Romanofsky, P. (Eds.). (1981). *Community organization for urban social change: A historical perspective.* Westport, CT: Greenwood Press.

Fisk, J. H. (1973). *Black power/white control: The struggle of The Woodlawn Organization in Chicago.* Princeton, NJ: Princeton University Press.

Flanagan, J. (1981). *The successful volunteer organization: Getting started and getting results in non-profit, charitable, grass-roots, and community groups.* Chicago: Contemporary Books.

Flanagan, J. (1982). *The grass roots fund raising book: How to raise money in your community.* Chicago: Contemporary Books.

Ford Foundation Project on Social Welfare and the American Future. (1989). *The common good: Social welfare and the American future.* New York: The Ford Foundation.

Fordham, C. C., III. (1986). Shantytown protests: Symbolic dissent. *The Atlantic Community Quarterly,* 244–247.

Forester, J. (1987, Summer). Planning in the face of conflict: Negotiation and mediation strategies in local land use regulations. *Journal of the American Planning Association, 53,* 303–314.

Forester, J. (1989). *Planning in the face of power.* Berkeley, CA: University of California Press.

Foundation Center. (1988). *The foundation grants index* (17th ed.). New York: Author.

Foundation library center (1960). New York: Russell Sage.

Fox, W. M. (1987). *Effective group problem solving: How to broaden participation, improve* decision making, and increase commitment to action. San Francisco: Jossey-Bass.

Fox-Genovese, E. (1986, January, March). Women's rights, affirmative action, and the myth of individualism. *The George Washington Law Review, 54,* 338–374.

Frank, C. (1989, June). Community organizing downstate: Conflicts and coalitions. *Illinois Issues, 15,* 18–25.

Frankel, A. J. (1989). *Clinical social work and community organization: A re-marriage made in heaven.* Presented at the CSWE Community Organizing and Administration Symposium. Chicago.

Freedman, W. (1988). *Freedom of speech on private property.* New York: Quorum Books.

Freeman, J. (1983). A model for analyzing the strategic options of social movement organizations. In J. Freeman (Ed.), *Social movements of the sixties and seventies* (pp. 193–210). New York: Longman.

Freudenberg, N. (1984). *Not in our backyards! Community action for health and the environment.* New York: Monthly Review Press.

Frieden, B. J., & Sagalyn, L. B. (1989). *Downtown, Inc.: How America rebuilds cities.* Cambridge, MA: MIT Press.

Fuller, A. (1989). *The women's peace movement: An assessment of social movements theory.* Paper presented at the Annual Meeting of the Society for the Study of Social Problems. Berkeley, CA.

Friere, P. (1990). M. B. Ramos (Trans.), *Pedagogy of the oppressed.* New York: Continuum.

Fulton, W. (1987, August). "Off the barricades into the boardrooms." *Planning,* pp. 11–15.

Galaskiewicz, J. (1979). *Exchange networks and community politics.* Beverly Hills, CA: Sage.

Galaskiewicz, J. & Stein, D. (1981). Leadership and networking among neighborhood human service organizations. *Administrative Science Quarterly, 26*(3), 434–448.

Gale, D. E. (1987). *Washington, D.C.: Inner-city revitalization and minority suburbanization.* Philadelphia: Temple University Press.

Gamson, W. A. (1968). *Power and discontent.* Homewood, IL: Dorsey.

Gamson, W. A. (1975). *The strategy of social protest.* Homewood, IL: Dorsey.

Gamson, W. A., Fireman, B., & Rytina, S. (1982). *Encounters with unjust authority.* Chicago: Dorsey.

Gamson, Z., & Levin, H. (1984). Obstacles to the survival of democratic workplaces. In R. Jackall & H. Levin (Eds.), *Worker cooperatives in America* (pp. 219–244). Berkeley: University of California Press.

Gans, H. (1988). *Middle American individualism: The future of liberal democracy.* New York: The Free Press.

Garland, A. W. (1988). *Women activists: Challenging the abuse of power.* New York: The Feminist Press at the City University of New York.

Garofalo, J., & McLeod, M. (1989, July). The structure and operations of neighborhood watch programs in the United States. *Crime & Delinquency, 35,* 326–344.

Gaventa, J., Smith, B. E., & Willingham, A. (Eds.). (1990). *Communities in economic crisis: Appalachia and the South.* Philadelphia: Temple University Press.

Gaziano, C. (1985, October). Neighborhood newspapers and neighborhood leaders: Influences on agenda setting and definitions of issues. *Communication Research, 12,* 568–594.

Gentry, M. E. (1987, Fall). Coalition formation and processes. *Social Work With Groups, 10,* 39–54.

George, M. (1987, August). Housing development squeezes out industry. *The Neighborhood Works, 10,* 3–5.

Geschwender, J. A. (1983). The social context of strategic success: A land-use struggle in Hawaii. In J. Freeman (Ed.), *Social Movements of the Sixties and Seventies* (pp. 235–251). New York: Longman.

Gilbert, D., & Kahl, J. (1982). *The American class structure: A new synthesis.* Homewood, IL: Dorsey.

Gilkey, B. (1989, July). Come see what I'm sayin': The tenants are turning public housing around. *Community Renewal Press: Occasional Papers, 1,* unpaged.

Giloth, R. (1985, Winter). Organizing for neighborhood development. *Social Policy,* 37–42.

Giloth, R. (1988, November). Community economic development: Strategies and practices of the 1980s. *Economic Development Quarterly, 2,* 343–350.

Ginsburg, F. D. (1989). *Contested lives: The abortion debate in an American community.* Berkeley, CA: University of California Press.

Girard, A. (1989, April–May). Boston group pioneers use of eminent domain. *The Neighborhood Works, 12*(1), 20–21.

Gitlin, T. (1987). *The sixties: Years of hope, days of rage* (hardcover ed.). New York: Bantam.

Gitlin, T. (1989). *The sixties: Years of hope, days of rage* (paperback ed.). New York: Bantam.

Glaberson, W. (1988, June 19). Coping in the age of "Nimby." *New York Times,* section 3, pp. 1, 25.

Glazer, L. (1989a, August–September). On the road with air pollution. *City Limits, 14,* 16–19.

Glazer, L. (1989b, October). The powers to be. *City Limits,* 24–28.

Glynn, T. J. (1986, October). Neighborhood and sense of community. *Journal of Community Psychology, 14,* 341–352.

Goering, J. (1979). The national neighborhood movement: A preliminary analysis and critique. *Journal of the American Planning Association, 48*(4), 506–514.

Goetze, R. (1979). *Understanding neighborhood change: The role of expectation in urban revitalization.* Cambridge, MA: Ballinger.

Goldberg, S. B., Green, E. D., & Sander, F. E. A. (1985). *Dispute resolution.* Boston: Little, Brown.

Golden, S. (1983). *Driving the drunk off the road: A handbook for action.* Washington, DC: Acropolis.

Golden, S. (1988, January). Single women: The forgotten homeless. *City Limits,* pp. 12–16.

Goldfield, D. (1980). Private neighborhood redevelopment and displacement. *Urban Affairs Quarterly, 15*(4), 453–468.

Goldstein, H. (1987, January). Toward community-oriented policing: Potential, basic requirements, and threshold questions. *Crime & Delinquency, 33,* 6–30.

Goodman, M. R. (1988, November). Crafting urban partnerships: Implementing neighborhood assistance programs. *Administration & Society, 20,* 251–274.

Goodwin, C. (1979). *The Oak Park strategy: Community control of racial change.* Chicago: University of Chicago Press.

Gottlieb, B. (Ed.). (1981). *Social networks and social support.* Beverly Hills, CA: Sage.

Grady, R. C. (1987). *Workplace democracy and political democracy.* Paper presented at the Annual Meeting of the American Political Science Association. Chicago.

Gramsci, A. (1973). In Lynn Lawner (Ed. and Trans.), *Letters from prison.* New York: Harper & Row.

Granovetter, M. (1973). The strength of weak ties. *American Journal of Sociology, 78*(6), 1360–1374.

Gratz, R. (1989). *The living city.* New York: Simon & Schuster.

Green, C. (1986, July). The professional ideology and grassroots community organizations: New York's South Bronx community in perspective. *Afro-Americans in New York Life and History,* pp. 29–44.

Green, P. M. (1988, May). SON/SOC: Organizing in white ethnic neighborhoods. *Illinois Issues, 14,* 24–28.

Green, S., & Pryde, P. (1990). *Black entrepreneurship in America.* New Brunswick, NJ: Transaction Publishers.

Greenberg, E. S. (1986). *Workplace democracy: The political effects of participation.* Ithaca, NY: Cornell University Press.

Greenberg, S. W., & Rohe, W. (1986). Informal social control and crime prevention in modern urban neighborhoods. In R. Taylor (Ed.), *Urban neighborhoods: Research and policy* (pp. 79–118). New York: Praeger.

Greene, E. (1989, May 24). Some young philanthropists shun gifts to alma maters in favor of support for direct social-action projects. *The Chronicle of Higher Education,* pp. A27–28.

Gricar, B., & Brown, L. D. (1981). Conflict, power and organization in a changing community. *Human Relations, 14*(10), 877–893.

Griffin, K. (1987). *Ralph Nader presents more action for a change.* New York: Dembner Books.

Gross, J. (1989, August 10). One man organizes pollution patrol. *New York Times,* p. 8.

Gross, M., & Warshauer, W., Jr. (1979). *Financial and accounting guide for nonprofit organizations.* New York: John Wiley & Sons.

Grossman, L. (1984). Organizing tenants in low-income public housing. In J. Ecklein (Ed.), *Community organizers* (pp. 139–149). New York: John Wiley & Sons.

Guest, A. M. (1986, June). Informal social ties and political activities in the metropolis. *Urban Affairs Quarterly, 21,* 550–574.

Gunn, C. E. (1984a). Hoedads Co-ops: Democracy and cooperation at work. In R. Jackall & H. Levin (Eds.), *Worker cooperatives in America* (pp. 140–170). Berkeley: University of California Press.

Gunn, C. E. (1984b). *Workers' self-management in the United States.* Ithaca, NY: Cornell University Press.

Hall, G. W. (1987). (Eds.). *Advocacy in America: Case studies in social change.* Lanham, NY: University Press of America.

Hall, R. (1982). *Organizations: Structure and process.* Englewood Cliffs, NJ: Prentice-Hall.

Hammerback, J. C., Jensen, R. J., & Gutierrez, J. A. (1985). *A war of words: Chicano protest in the 1960s and 1970s.* Westport, CT: Greenwood Press.

Hanson, R., & McNamara, J. (1981). *Partners.* Minneapolis: Dayton Hudson Foundation.

Hardy-Fanta, C. (1986, March–April). Social action in Hispanic groups. *Social Work, 31,* 119–123.

Harrington, M. (1962). *The other America: Poverty in the United States.* New York: Macmillan.

Harrington, M. (1984). *The new American poverty.* New York: Holt, Rinehart & Winston.

Harrington, M. (1989). *Socialism: Past & future.* New York: Arcade Publishing.

Harrison, B., & Bluestone, B. (1988). *The great U-turn: Corporate restructuring and the polarizing of America.* New York: Basic Books.

Hartman, C. (1974). *Yerba Buena: Land grab and community resistance in San Francisco.* Berkeley, CA: University of California Press.

Hartman, C. (1984a). San Francisco's International Hotel: Case study of a turf struggle. In J. Ecklein (Ed.), *Community organizers* (pp. 150–160). New York: John Wiley & Sons.

Hartman, C. (1984b). *The transformation of San Francisco.* Totowa, NJ: Rowman & Allanheld Publishers.

Hartman, S. M. (1989). *From margin to mainstream: American women and politics since 1960.* Philadelphia: Temple University Press.

Hatry, H., & Valente, C. (1983). Alternative service delivery approaches involving increased use of the private sector. In International City Management Association, *The municipal yearbook* (pp. 188–217). Washington, DC: International City Management Association.

Helfgot, J. (1981). *Professional reforming: Mobilization for youth and the failure of social science.* Lexington, MA: Lexington.

Helman, C. (1987). *The Milton-Park affair: Canada's largest citizen-developer confrontation.* Montreal: Vehicule Press.

Henig, J. (1981, November–December). Community organizations in gentrifying neighborhoods. *Community Action,* pp. 45–55.

Henig, J. (1982). *Neighborhood mobilization: Redevelopment and response.* New Brunswick, NJ: Rutgers University Press.

Hessler, R. (1977). Citizen participation, social organization and culture: A neighborhood health center for Chicanos. *Human Organization, 26*(2), 124–134.

Hessler, R., & Beavert, C. S. (1982). Citizen participation in neighborhood centers for the poor: The politics of reform organization change 1965–1977. *Human Organization, 41*(3), 245–255.

Hicks, F., & Borkman, T. (1988). *Self-help groups and political empowerment.* Paper presented at the Annual Meeting of the American Political Science Association, Washington, DC.

Hilgartner, S., & Bosk, C. L. (1988, July). The rise and fall of social problems: A public arenas model. *American Journal of Sociology, 94,* 53–78.

Hils, R. (1990). The mayhaw tree: An informal case study in homegrown rural economic development. In J. Gaventa, B. E. Smith, & A. Willingham (Eds.), *Communities in economic crisis: Appalachia and the South* (pp. 158–174). Philadelphia: Temple University Press.

Hinds, M. deC. (1989, September 15). 50% Cutback in funds for homeless in Philadelphia is fiercely protested. *New York Times,* p. 8.

Hirsch, E. L. (1986). The creation of political solidarity in social movement organizations. *The Sociological Quarterly, 27*(3), 373–387.

Hirsch, E. L. (1990, April). Sacrifice for the cause: Group processes, recruitment, and commitment in a student social movement. *American Sociological Review, 5*(2), 243–254.

Hochschild, J. L. (1984). *The new American dilemma: Liberal democracy and school desegregation.* New Haven: Yale University Press.

Holli, M. G. (1969). *Reform in Detroit: Hazen S. Pingree and urban politics.* New York: Oxford University Press.

Holloway, M. (1989, December). The toxic avengers take Brooklyn. *City Limits,* pp. 8–9.

Hooks, B. (1989). *Talking back: Thinking feminist, thinking black.* Boston: South End Press.

Horwitt, S. D. (1989). *Let them call me rebel: Saul Alinsky—His life and legacy.* New York: Alfred A. Knopf.

Houle, C. O. (1989). *Governing boards: Their nature and nurture.* San Francisco: Jossey-Bass.

Housing bill calls for big change, more $s, but administration says no. (1991, Winter/Spring). *Community Change, 24,* 7–10.

Housing trust funds fast becoming new sources of $s. (1988, Summer). *Community Change,* p. 5.

Huckfeldt, R. (1986). *Politics in context: Assimilation and conflict in urban neighborhoods.* New York: Agathon.

Hudson, R. (1989, December–1990, January). Stewart-Warner coalition fights plant shutdown. *The Neighborhood Works, 12,* 15–16.

Hula, R. C. (1989). *Alternative community development strategies; privatization in Baltimore.* Presented at the Annual Meeting of the American Political Science Association, Atlanta.

Hunter, A., & Riger, S. (1986, January). The meaning of community in community mental health. *Journal of Community Psychology, 14,* 55–71.

Hunter, A., & Staggenborg, S. (1986). Communities do act: Neighborhood characteristics, resource mobilization, and political action by local community organizations. *The Social Science Journal, 23*(2), 169–180.

Hunter, F. (1980). *Community power succession: Atlanta's policy-makers revisited.*

Chapel Hill, NC: University of North Carolina Press.

Hutcheson, J. D., & Dominguez, L. H. (1986, October–December). Ethnic self-help organizations in non-barrio settings: Community identity and voluntary action. *Journal of Voluntary Action Research, 15,* 13–21.

Hutcheson, J. D., Jr., & Prather, J. E. (1988, March). Community mobilization and participation in the zoning process. *Urban Affairs Quarterly, 23,* 346–368.

Hyde, C. (1987, March). *The inclusion of a feminist agenda in community organization curriculum.* Paper presented at the CSWE Community Organizing and Administration Symposium, St. Louis.

Iannello, K. (1988). *A feminist framework for organizations.* Paper presented at the Annual Meeting of the American Political Science Association, Washington, DC.

International City Management Association. (1983). *The municipal yearbook 1983.* Washington, DC: Author.

Issac, J. C. (1987). *Power and Marxist theory: A realist view.* Ithaca, NY: Cornell University Press.

Jackall, R. (1984a). Paradoxes of collective work: A study of the Cheeseboard, Berkeley, CA. In R. Jackall & H. Levin (Eds.), *Worker cooperatives in America* (pp. 3–15). Berkeley, CA: University of California Press.

Jackall, R. (1984b). Work in America and the cooperative movement. In R. Jackall & H. Levin (Eds.), *Worker cooperatives in America* (pp. 277–290). Berkeley, CA: University of California Press.

Jackson, K. T. (1985). *Crabgrass frontier: The suburbanization of the United States.* New York: Oxford University Press.

Jacobs, B. (1981). *The political economy of organizational change: Urban institutional response to the War on Poverty.* New York: Academic Press.

Jacobs, R. (1980). Portrait of a phenomenon— The Gray Panthers: Do they have a long run future? In E. Markson (Ed.), *Public policies for an aging population* (pp. 93–102). Lexington, MA: Lexington.

Janis, I. (1982). *Groupthink: Psychological studies of policy decisions and fiascoes.* Boston: Houghton Mifflin.

Janowitz. M. (1967). *The community press in an urban setting: The social elements of urbanism.* Chicago: University of Chicago Press.

Jaynes, G. D., & Williams, R. M., Jr. (1989). *A common destiny: Blacks and American society.* Washington, DC: National Academy Press.

Jenkins, J. C. (1983). Resource mobilization theory and the study of social movements. *Annual Review of Sociology, 9,* 527–553.

Jenkins, J. C. (1985). *The politics of insurgency: The farm worker movement in the 1960s.* New York: Columbia University Press.

Jenkins, J. C. (1987). Nonprofit organizations and policy advocacy. In W. Powell (Ed.), *The nonprofit sector* (pp. 296–318). New Haven, CT: Yale University Press.

Jenkins, J. C. (1989). *Mainstreaming the movements: Elite patronage and professionalization.* Paper presented at the Annual Meeting of the Society for the Study of Social Problems, San Francisco.

Jenkins, J. C., & Eckert, C. M. (1986, December). Channeling black insurgency: Elite patronage and professional social movement organizations in the development of the black movement. *American Sociological Review, 51,* 812–829.

Jenkins, J. C., & Perrow, C. (1977). Insurgency of the powerless: Farm worker movements 1946–1972. *American Sociological Review, 42*(2), 249–268.

Johnson, J. (1989, August 14). 2 approaches to rebuilding women's movement. *New York Times,* p. 7.

Jones, B., Bachelor, L., & Wilson, C. (1986). *The sustaining hand: Community leadership and community power.* Lawrence, KS: University of Kansas Press.

Jones, S. E., Barnlund, D. C., & Haiman, F. S. (1980). *The dynamics of discussion: Com-*

munication in small groups. New York: Harper & Row.

Joravsky, B. (1988, January). Community organizing: Alinsky's legacy. *Illinois Issues, 14,* 10–14.

Joreen, J. (1973). The tryanny of structurelessness. In A. Koedt, E. Levin, & A. Rapine (Eds.), *Radical feminism* (pp. 285–299). New York: Quadrangle.

Joseph, B. (1986, March). Taking organizing back to the people. *Smith College Studies in Social Work,* pp. 122–131.

Joseph, J. (1983). *How to fight city hall . . . the IRS, banks, corporations, your local airport and other nuisances.* Chicago: Contemporary Books.

Judkins, B. M. (1983). Mobilization of membership: The black and brown lung movements. In J. Freeman (Ed.), *Social movements of the sixties and seventies* (pp. 35–51). New York: Longman.

Kahn, S. (1970). *How people get power: Organizing oppressed communities for action.* New York: McGraw-Hill.

Kahn, S. (1982). *Organizing: A guide for grassroots leaders.* New York: McGraw-Hill.

Kann, M. E. (1986). *Middle class radicalism in Santa Monica.* Philadelphia: Temple University Press.

Kantor, P., & David, S. (1988). *The dependent city; The changing political economy of urban America.* Glenview, IL: Scott, Foresman.

Kaplan, M. (1986, October–December). Cooperation and coalition development among neighborhood organizations: A case study. *Journal of Voluntary Action Research, 15,* 23–34.

Karpik, L. (Ed.). (1978). *Organization and environment: Theory, issues and reality.* Beverly Hills, CA: Sage.

Kasarda, J. D. (1988). Jobs, migration, and emerging urban mismatches. In M. G. H. McGeary & L. E. Lynn, Jr. (Eds.), *Family structure, poverty and the underclass* (pp. 148–199). Washington, DC: National Academy Press.

Kasarda, J. (1989, January). Urban industrial transition and the underclass. *The Annals of the American Academy of Political and Social Science, 501,* 26–47.

Katz, J. (1982). *Poor people's lawyers in transition.* New Brunswick, NJ: Rutgers University Press.

Katzenstein, M. F. (1987). Comparing the feminist movements of the United States and Western Europe: An overview. In M. F. Katzenstein & C. McC. Mueller, (Eds.), *The women's movements of the United States and Western Europe* (pp. 3–20). Philadelphia: Temple University Press.

Katznelson, I. (1981). *City trenches: Urban politics and the patterning of class in the United States.* New York: Pantheon.

Keating, W. D. (1989). Linkage: Tying downtown development to community housing needs. In S. Rosenberry & C. Hartman, (Eds.), *Housing issues in the 1990s* (pp. 211–222). New York: Praeger.

Keese, S. (1989, May 14). Brattleboro, Vt.: Renewed hope in a poor area. *New York Times,* section 10, p. 21.

Kessler, M. (1987). *Legal services for the poor: A comparative and contemporary analysis of interorganizational politics.* New York: Greenwood Press.

Klandermans, B. (1984, October). Mobilization and participation: Social-psychological expansions of resource mobilization theory. *American Sociological Review, 49,* 583–600.

Klandermans, B. (1988). Union action and the free-rider dilemma. In L. Kriesberg, B. Misztal, J. Mucha (Eds.), *Research in social movements, conflicts and change: A research annual: Social movement as a factor of change in the contemporary world* (pp. 77–92). Greenwich, CT: Jai Press.

Klandermans, B., & Oegema, D. (1987, August). Potentials, networks, motivations, and barriers: Steps towards participation in social movements. *American Sociological Review, 52*, 519–531.

Klein, K. J., & D'Aunno, T. A. (1986, October). Psychological sense of community in the workplace. *Journal of Community Psychology, 14*, 365–377.

Kleyman, P. (1974). *Senior power: Growing old rebelliously.* San Francisco: Glide Publications.

Klor de Alva, J. J. (1988). Telling Hispanics apart: Latino sociocultural diversity. In E. Acosta-Belen (Ed.), *The Hispanic experience in the United States: Contemporary issues and perspectives.* (pp. 107–136). New York: Praeger.

Knoke, D.(1987). *Incentives in collective action organizations.* Paper presented at the 82nd Annual Meeting of the American Sociological Association, Chicago.

Knoke, D., & Wood, J. (1981). *Organized for action: Commitment in voluntary organizations.* New Brunswick, NJ: Rutgers University Press.

Knopp, L. (1987, June). Social theory, social movements and public policy: Recent accomplishments of the gay and lesbian movements in Minneapolis, Minnesota. *International Journal of Urban and Regional Research, 11*, 243–261.

Knox, P. (1982) *Urban social geography,* New York: Longman.

Kolbert, E. (1990, January 8). In civil liberties cases, New York's Court leans on the State Constitution. *New York Times,* p. 12.

Kolodny, R. (1986). The emergence of self-help as a housing strategy for the urban poor. In R. G. Bratt, C. Hartman, & A. Myerson (Eds.), *Critical perspectives on housing* (pp. 447–462). Philadelphia: Temple University Press.

Kornblum, W. (1974). *Blue collar community.* Chicago: University of Chicago Press.

Korrol, V. S. (1988). Latinismo among early Puerto Rican migrants in New York City: A sociohistoric interpretation. In E. Acosta-

Belen (Ed.), *The Hispanic experience in the United States: Contemporary issues and perspectives* (pp. 151–162). New York: Praeger.

Kowitz, A., & Knutson, T. (1980). *Decision making in small groups: The search for alternatives.* Boston: Allyn & Bacon.

Kozol, J. (1988). *Rachel and her children: Homeless families in America.* New York: Crown.

Kraft, D. (1987, August). Consumer, community groups block ComEd deal. *The Neighborhood Works, 10,* 12–13.

Kraft, M. E., & Clary, B. B. (1988). *Assessing citizen participation in environmental policy: The NIMBY syndrome and radioactive waste disposal.* Paper presented at the annual meeting of the American Political Science Association, Washington, DC.

Krauss, C. (1988). Grass-roots consumer protests and toxic wastes: Developing a critical political view. *Community Development Journal, 23*(4), 258–265.

Krumholz, N. (1982). A retrospective view of equity planning. *Journal of the American Planning Association, 48*(2), 163–174.

Kweit, M. G., & Kweit, R. (1981). *Implementing citizen participation in a bureaucratic society: A contingency approach.* New York: Praeger.

Kwong, P. (1987). *The new Chinatown.* New York: Hill & Wang.

Ladd, H. F., & Yinger, J. (1989). *America's ailing cities: Fiscal health and the design of urban policy.* Baltimore: John Hopkins University Press.

Lancourt, J. (1979). *Confront or concede: The Alinsky citizen-action organizations.* Lexington, MA: Lexington.

Lauer, R. H. (1989). *Social problems and the quality of life* (4th ed.). Dubuque, IA: William C. Brown.

Lauffer, A. (1982a). *Assessment tools: For practitioners, managers and trainers.* Beverly Hills, CA: Sage.

Lauffer, A. (1982b). *Getting the resources you need.* Beverly Hills, CA: Sage.

Laumann, E. O., & Knoke, D. (1987). *The organizational state: Social choice in national policy domains.* Madison, WI: University of Wisconsin Press.

Lavrakas, P., & Herz, E. (1982). Citizen participation in neighborhood crime prevention. *Criminology, 20*(3–4),479–498.

Lawrence, K. (1987, January–February). NAP: Rule or ruin. *Radical America, 21,* 22–24.

Lawson, R. (1986). Tenant response to the urban housing crisis, 1970–1984. With the assistance of R. B. Johnson, III. In R. Lawson & M. Naison (Eds.), *The tenant movement in New York City, 1904–1984* (pp. 209–278). New Brunswick, NJ: Rutgers University Press.

Lehman, H. J. (1990, March 18). S & L bailout plan aids low-income housing. *Chicago Tribune,* section 16, p. 2D.

Lenz, T. J. (1988, Spring). Neighborhood development: Issues and models. *Social Policy, 19,* 24–30.

LeVeen, D. (1983). Organization or disruption? Strategic options for marginal groups: The case of the Chicago Indian Village. In J. Freeman, (Ed.), *Social movements of the sixties and seventies* (pp. 211–234). New York: Longman.

Leveillee, J., & Leonard, J. F. (1987, December). The Montreal citizens' movement comes to power. *International Journal of Urban and Regional Research, 11,* 567–580.

Levene, S. (1985). Civil disobedience begins at home: The nuclear free Cambridge campaign. *Radical America, 19*(1), 7–24.

Levine, A. (1982). *Love canal: Science, politics, and people.* Lexington, MA: Lexington.

Levine, M. D. (1986, October). Working it out: A community re-creation approach to crime prevention. *Journal of Community Psychology, 14,* 378–390.

Levine, M. V. (1988). Economic development in states and cities: Toward democratic and strategic planning in state and local government. In M. V. Levine, C. MacLennan, J. J. Kushma, C. Noble, & J. Faux (Eds.), *The state and democracy: Revitalizing America's government* (pp. 111–146). New York: Routledge.

Levine, M. V. (1989). The politics of partnership: Urban redevelopment since 1945. In G. D. Squires (Ed.), *Unequal partnership: The political economy of urban redevelopment in postwar America* (pp. 12–34). New Brunswick, NJ: Rutgers University Press.

Levitan, S. A. (1985). *Programs in aid of the poor.* Baltimore: John Hopkins University Press.

Levitan, S. A., & Shapiro, I. (1987). *Working but poor: America's contradiction.* Baltimore: John Hopkins University Press.

Levitan, S., Morgan, G., & Pines, M. (1989, July 10). Government aid should invest in the self-sufficiency of poor families. *Northeast Midwest Economic Review, 2,* 6–9.

Levy, F. (1987). *Dollars and dreams: The changing American income distribution.* New York: Russell Sage Foundation.

Levy, J. E. (1975). *Cesar Chavez: Autobiography of La Causa.* New York: W. W. Norton.

Lewicki, R. J. (1983). Lying and deception: A behavioral model. In M. H. Bazerman & R. J. Lewicki (Eds.), *Negotiating in organizations* (pp. 68–90). Beverly Hills: Sage.

Lewis, D. A., Grant, J. A., & Rosenbaum, D. P. (1988). *The social construction of reform: Crime prevention and community organizations.* New Brunswick, NJ: Transaction Books.

Lewis, G. H. (1987, December). Style in revolt: Music, social protest, and the Hawaiian cultural renaissance. *International Social Science Journal, 66,* 168–177.

Lieberman, M., Borman, L., & Associates. (1979). *Self-help groups for coping with crisis.* San Francisco: Jossey-Bass.

Liebschutz, S. F., & Taddiken, A. J. (1986). The effects of Reagan administration budget cuts on human services in Rochester, New York. In G. E. Peterson & C. Lewis, (Eds.), *Reagan and the cities* (pp. 131–154). Washington, DC: The Urban Institute Press.

Lindgren, H. E. (1987). The informal-intermittent organization: A vehicle for successful citizen protest. *The Journal of Applied Behavioral Science, 23*(3), 397–412.

Lipsitz, G. (1988). *A life in the struggle: Ivory Perry and the culture of opposition.* Philadelphia: Temple University Press.

Lipsky, M. (1968). Protest as a political resource. *American Political Science Review, 62*(4), 1144–1158.

Lipsky, M. (1970). *Protest in city politics: Rent strikes, housing and the power of the poor.* Chicago: Rand McNally.

Local Initiatives Support Corporation. (1982). *Annual report 1982.* New York: Author.

Local Initiatives Support Corporation. (1983). *Annual report 1983.* New York: Author.

Local Initiatives Support Corporation. (1988). *Annual report 1988.* New York: Author.

Logan, J. R., Molotch, H. (1987). *Urban fortunes: The political economy of place.* Berkeley, CA: University of California Press.

Louis, E. T. (1989, November). When banks open community development corporations. *City Limits, 14,* 21.

Louis, E. T., & Mims, R. E. (1987, October). Bed-Stuy restorations: False promises? *City Limits, 12,* 16–19.

Lovell, C. (1979). Coordinating Federal grants from below. *Public Administration Review, 39*(5), 432–439.

Lowe, S. (1986). *Urban social movements: The city after Castells.* New York: St. Martin's Press.

Luebke, P. (1981). Activists and asphalt: A successful anti-expressway movement "New South City." *Human Organization, 40*(3), 256–263.

Luker, K. (1984). *Abortion and the politics of motherhood.* Berkeley: University of California Press.

Lukes, S. (1974). *Power: A radical view.* London: Macmillan.

Luttrell, W. (1988). The Edison school struggle; the reshaping of working-class education and women's consciousness. In A. Bookman & S. Morgen (Eds.), *Women and the politics of empowerment* (pp. 136–156). Philadelphia: Temple University Press.

MacGregor, D. (1979). Managing and financing community newspapers. *Self-Reliance, 20*(4), 5, 13.

Majka, L. C., & Majka, T. J. (1982). *Farm workers, agribusiness, and the state.* Philadelphia: Temple University Press.

Majka, T. J., & Donnelly, P. G. (1988). Cohesiveness within a heterogeneous urban neighborhood; Implications for community in a diverse setting. *Journal of Urban Affairs, 10*(2), 141–160.

Manikas, P., & Protess, D. (1979). *Establishing a citizen's watchdog group.* Washington, DC: U.S. Department of Justice.

Mansbridge, J. J. (1980). *Beyond adversary democracy.* New York: Basic Books.

Mansbridge, J. J. (1986). *Why we lost the ERA.* Chicago: University of Chicago Press.

Marciniak, E. (1981). *Reversing urban decline: The Winthrop-Kenmore corridor in the Edgewater and uptown communities of Chicago.* Washington, DC: National Center for Urban Ethnic Affairs.

Marcus, I. (1981). *Dollars for reform: The OEO neighborhood health centers.* Lexington, MA: Lexington.

Marcuse, P. (1987–1988, Winter). Neighborhood policy and the distribution of power: New York City's community boards. *Policy Studies Journal, 16,* 277–289.

Maris, R. W. (1988). *Social problems.* Chicago: Dorsey.

Marquez, B. (1985). *Power and politics in a Chicano barrio: A study of mobilization efforts and community power in El Paso.* Lanham, MD: University Press of America.

Marullo, S. (1988, Fall). Leadership and membership in the nuclear freeze movement: A specification of resource mobilization theory. *The Sociological Quarterly, 29,* 407–428.

Marx, G. (1979). External efforts to damage or facilitate social movements: Some patterns, explanations, outcomes and complications. In M. Zald & J. McCarthy (Eds.), *The dynamics of social movements: Resource mobilization, social control and tactics* (pp. 168–189). Cambridge, MA: Winthrop.

Massey, D. S., & Eggers, M. L. (1990, March). The ecology of inequality: Minorities and the concentration of poverty. *American Journal of Sociology, 95,* 1153–1188.

Mayer, M. (1978). *The builders.* New York: W. W. Norton.

Mayer, N. S. (1984). *Neighborhood organizations and community development: Making revitalization work.* Washington, DC: Urban Institute Press.

Mayer, R. N. (1989). *The consumer movement: Guardians of the marketplace.* Boston: Twayne.

McAffee, K. (1986). Socialism and the housing movement: Lessons from Boston. In R. G. Bratt, C. Harman, & A. Myerson (Eds.), *Critical perspectives on housing* (pp. 405–423). Philadelphia: Temple University Press.

McCann, M. W. (1986). *Taking reform seriously: Perspectives on public interest liberalism.* Ithaca, NY: Cornell University Press.

McCarron, J. (1988, December 18). Unionleader unlikely hero in house-building crusade. *Chicago Tribune,* section I, p. 5.

McCarron, J. (1989, April 5). Goose Island plan prompts a lawsuit. *Chicago Tribune,* section 2, p. 12.

McCarthy, J. D., & Zald, M. N. (1987). Resource mobilization and social movements: A partial theory. In N. Zald & J. D. McCarthy (Eds.), *Social movements in an organizational society: Collected essays* (pp. 15–42). New Brunswick: Transaction Books.

McCreight, M. (1984). Lawsuits for leverage. In *Roots to power: A manual for grassroots organizing* (pp. 181–187). New York: Praeger.

McGeary, M. G. H., & Lynn, L., Jr. (Eds.) (1988). *Urban change and poverty.* Washington, DC: National Academy Press.

McHenry County Defenders (1987). Reorganization of the board and staff.

McKinney, J. (1977). *How to start your own community newspaper.* Port Washington, NY: Meadow Press.

McKnight, J. L. (1987, Winter). Regenerating community. *Social Policy, 12,* 54–58.

McLanahan, S., Garfinkle, I., & Watson, D. (1988). Family structure, poverty and the underclass. In M. G. H. McGeary & L. Lynn, Jr., (Eds.) *Urban change and poverty* (pp. 102–147). Washington, DC: National Academy Press.

McLuhan, M. (1967). *The medium is the massage.* New York: Bantam.

McMillan, D. W., & Chavis, D. M. (1986, January). Sense of community: A definition and theory. *Journal of Community Psychology, 14,* 6–23.

Meehan, J. (1987). Working toward local self-reliance. In S. T. Bruyn & J. Meehan (Eds.), *Beyond the market and the state: New directions in community development* (pp. 131–151). Philadelphia: Temple University Press.

Meenaghan, T., & Washington, R. (1980). *Social policy and social welfare: Structure and applications.* New York: Free Press.

Melvin, P. M. (Ed.). (1986). *American community organizations: A historical dictionary.* New York: Greenwood.

Melvin, P. M. (1987). *The organic city: Urban definition & community organization 1880–1920.* Lexington, KY: The University Press of Kentucky.

Members of Project 2000. (1987, Spring). The emerging American progressive ideology. *Social Policy, 12,* 23–33.

Meryash, P. (1988, July–August). The anger that ignited Gallaudet. *Public Citizen,* p. 22.

Midwest Academy. (1981). Rallies. In *Midwest Academy organizing manual* (pp. 173–178). Chicago: Author. (Original work published 1976)

Midwest Academy & Booth, H. (1973). Part III. In *Midwest Academy organizing manual.* Chicago, Midwest Academy.

Midwest Academy & Max, S. (1977). *Midwest Academy organizing manual* (5th ed., revised). Chicago: Midwest Academy.

Milbrath, L. (1977). *Political participation.* Chicago: Rand McNally.

Miller, J. (1987). *"Democracy is in the streets": From Port Huron to the siege of Chicago.* New York: Simon & Schuster.

Miller, S. N. (1985, Summer). Challenges for populism. *Social Policy, 10,* 3–6.

Milofsky, C. (1988). Structure and process in community self-help organizations. In C. Milofsky (Ed.), *Community organizations: Studies in resource mobilization and exchange* (pp. 183–215). Yale Studies on Nonprofit Organizations. New York: Oxford University Press.

Mitchell, J., & Stallings, C. (Eds.). (1970) *Ecotactics: The Sierra Club handbook for environmental activists.* New York: Trident Press.

Mitford, J. (1963). *The American way of death.* New York: Simon & Schuster.

Mizrahi, T. (1989). *The future of research utilization in community practice.* Paper presented at the conference on research utilization sponsored by Boysville of Michigan, Inc., and Wayne State University School of Social Work, Detroit.

Moberg, D. (1987, May). The next four years: Neighborhood agendas. *The Neighborhood Works, 10*(1), 4–8.

Moberg, D. (1989, August–September). Organizing to make plant closing law work. *The Neighborhood Works, 12*(1), 4–6.

Mohai, P. (1985, February). Public concern and elite involvement in environmental-conservation issues. *Social Science Quarterly, 32,* 820–838.

Molotch, H. (1972). *Managed integration: Dilemmas of doing good in the city.* Berkeley, CA: University of California Press.

Molotch, H. (1976). The city as a growth machine: Toward a political economy of place. *American Journal of Sociology, 82*(2), 309–322.

Monti, D. J. (1989). The organizational strengths and weaknesses of resident-managed public housing sites in the United States. *Journal of Urban Affairs, 11*(1), 39–52.

Moore, C. M. (1987). *Group techniques for idea building.* Applied Social Research Methods Series. Newbury Park: Sage.

Moore, W. J. (1987, April 11). Cutoff at town hall. *National Journal,* pp. 862–866.

Moore, W. J. (1988a, November). Crazy-quilt federalism. *National Journal, 26,* 3001–3005.

Moore, W. J. (1988b, December 17). Local-level losses. *National Journal,* pp. 3180–3184.

Morgan, D. L. (1988). *Focus groups as qualitative research.* Qualitative Research Methods Series. Newbury Park, CA: Sage.

Morgen, S. (1988). "It's the whole power of the city against us!": The development of political consciousness in a women's health care coalition. In A. Bookman & S. Morgen (Eds.), *Women and the politics of empowerment* (pp. 97–115). Philadelphia: Temple University Press.

Morgen, S., & Bookman, A. (1988). Rethinking women and politics: An introductory essay. In A. Bookman & S. Morgan (Eds.), *Women and the politics of empowerment* (pp. 3–29). Philadelphia: Temple University Press.

Morris, D., & Hess, K. (1975). *Neighborhood power: The new localism.* Boston: Beacon Press.

Mott, A. H. (1986, Spring). The decades ahead for community organizations. *Social Policy, 11,* 11–16.

Moyer, B. (1987). *The movement action plan: A strategic framework describing the eight stages of successful social movements.* San Francisco: Social Movement Empowerment Project.

Mueller, K. J., & Comer, J. C. (1982). *Participation and independence of consumer mem-*

bers in a health system agency. Paper presented at the annual meeting of the American Society for Public Administration, Honolulu.

Munoz, C., Jr., & Barrera, M. (1982, April). La Raza Unida Party and the Chicano student movement in California. *The Social Science Journal, 19,* 101–118.

Murray, C. A. (1984). *Losing ground: American social policy 1950–1980.* New York: Basic Books.

Nachmias, C., & Palen, J. J. (1982). Membership in voluntary neighborhood associations and urban revitalization. *Policy Sciences, 14*(2), 179–193.

Nader, R. (1972). *Unsafe at any speed: The designed-in dangers of the American automobile.* New York: Grossman.

Naison, M. (1986). From eviction resistance to rent control: Tenant activism in the Great Depression. In R. Lawson (Ed.), *The tenant movement in New York City, 1904–1984* (pp. 94–133). New Brunswick, NJ: Rutgers University Press.

Naparstek, A., Biegel, D., & Spiro, H. (1982). *Neighborhood networks for humane mental health care.* New York: Plenum.

Naples, N. A. (1987). *The importance of community for women workers in anti-poverty programs, 1964–1984.* Paper Presented at the annual meeting of the American Sociological Association, Chicago.

National Citizens' Monitoring Project of the Working Group for Community Development Reform. (1981a). *Citizen monitoring—A how-to manual.* Washington, DC: Author.

National Citizens' Monitoring Project of the Working Group for Community Development Reform. (1981b). *Community development versus poor peoples's needs: Tension in CDBG.* Washington, DC: Author.

National Commission on Neighborhoods. (1979). *People building neighborhoods: Final report to the President and the Congress of the United States.* Washington, DC: Author.

National Congress for Community Economic Development. (1989). *Against all odds: The achievements of community-based development organizations.* Washington, DC: Author.

National Training and Information Center. (1977). *Neighborhoods first: from the 70s into the 80s.* Chicago: Author.

Nelson, K. P. (1988). *Gentrification and distressed cities: An assessment of trends in intrametropolitan migration.* Madison, WI: University of Wisconsin Press.

Nes, J., & Iadicola, P. (1989, January). Toward a definition of feminist social work: A comparison of liberal, radical, and socialist models. *Social Work, 34,* 12–21.

Newman, S. J., & Schnare, A. B. (1989). Reassessing shelter assistance: The interrelationship between welfare and housing programs. In S. Rosenberry and C. Hartman (Eds.), *Housing issues in the 1990s* (pp. 121–148). New York: Praeger.

Nicklin, J. L. (1990). More colleges are making investments in projects that deal with problems of their communities. *The Chronicle of Higher Education,* A29–30.

Nissenbaum, D. (1988, Summer). INFACT: Bringing GE to light. *SANE/FREEZE Focus, 27,* 12–15.

Nonprofits pool resources for liability coverage. (1989, August 6). *Chicago Tribune,* section 7, p. 10.

O'Connell, M. (1988, August–September). Organizing effort pays off for schools. *Neighborhood Works, 11,* 3–6.

O'Connell, M., Bernstein, S., Hallett, S., Perkins, S., & Tholin, K. (1986, July–August). Working neighborhoods: Taking charge of your local economy. Insert. *The Neighborhood Works, 9,* 1–33.

O'Neill, M. (1988, March–April). Breaking barriers to women's self-employment. *The Neighborhood Works, 11,* 3–5.

Obama, B. (1988, August–September). Why organize? Problems and promise in the inner city. *Illinois Issues, 14,* 40–43.

Office of Management and Budget. (1987). *Catalogue of federal domestic assistance* (21st ed.). Washington, DC: U.S. Government Printing Office.

Office space for nonprofits. (1989, October 15). *New York Times,* section X, p. 21.

Oliver, M. (1988). The urban black community as network: Toward a social network perspective. *The Sociological Quarterly, 29*(4), 623–645.

Oliver, P. (1984, October). "If you don't do it, nobody else will": Active and token contributors to local collective action. *American Sociological Review, 49,* 601–610.

Olsen, M., Perlstadt, H., Fonseca, V., & Hogan, J. (1989, February). Participation in neighborhood associations. *Sociological Focus, 22,* 1–17.

Olzak, S. (1985). Ethnicity and theories of ethnic collective behavior. In L. Kriesberg (Ed.), *Research in social movements, conflicts and change* (pp. 65–86). Greenwich, CT: Jai Press.

Opp, K-D. (1988, December). Grievance and participation in social movements. *American Sociological Review, 53,* 853–864.

Ortiz, I. (1981). Chicano community organizations and the idea of ethnic coalitions: A case study. *Journal of Voluntary Action Research, 10*(3–4), 85–98.

Ostendorf, D., & Levitas, D. (1987). Education for empowerment and social action in rural America. *Mid-American Review of Sociology, 12*(1), 55–64.

Padilla, F. M. (1987). *Puerto Rican Chicago.* Notre Dame, IN: University of Notre Dame Press.

Page, B. (1983). *Who gets what from government.* Berkeley, CA: University of California Press.

Palmer, P. J. (1990, January). Scarcity, abundance and the gift of community. *Community Renewal Press: Occasional Papers, 1,* 1–5.

Patton, M. Q. (1990). *Qualitative evaluation and research methods second edition.* Newbury Park, CA: Sage.

Peirce, Neal R. (1987, July 18). Neighborhood challenges to big bank mergers. *National Journal,* p. 1862.

Peirce, Neil R. (1989a, March 18). Community foundations as the New Paul Reveres. *National Journal,* p. 690.

Peirce, Neil R. (1989b, April 4). Housing the poor without Uncle Sam's money. *National Journal,* p. 1068.

Peirce, Neal R., & Steinbach, C. F. (1987). *Corrective capitalism: The rise of America's Community Development Corporations.* New York: Ford Foundation.

Peirce, Neal R., & Steinbach, C. F. (1990). *Enterprising communities: Community-based development in America, 1990.* Washington, DC: Council for Community Based Development.

Pennsylvania Economic League, Inc. (1989). *Prospects for linking commercial and community development in Philadelphia.* Philadelphia: Pennyslvania Economic League.

Perlman, J. E. (1976). Grassrooting the system. *Social Policy, 7*(2), 4–20.

Perlman, J. E. (1979). Grassroots empowerment and government response. *Social Policy, 10*(2), 16–21.

Perruci, C. C., Perruci, R., Targ, D. B., & Targ, H. R. (1988). *Plant closings: International context and social costs.* New York: Aldine De Gruyter.

Perry, D. (1987). The politics of dependency in deindustrializing America: The case of Buffalo, New York. In M. P. Smith & J. Feagin (Eds.), *The capitalist city: Global restructuring and community politics* (pp. 113–137). New York: Basil Blackwell.

Perry, S. E. (1987). *Communities on the way: Rebuilding local economies in the United States and Canada.* Albany, NY: State University of New York Press.

Peterman, W. (1988, October–November). Race and economics in city Neighborhoods. *The Neighborhood Works, 11*(1), 8–9.

Petersen, G. E. (1986). Urban policy and the cyclical behavior in cities. In G. E. Peterson & C. Lewis, (Eds.), *Reagan and the cities* (pp. 11–36). Washington, DC: Urban Institute Press.

Pilisuk, M., & Minkler, M. (1980). Supportive networks: Life ties for the elderly. *Journal of Social Issues, 36*(2), 95–116.

Pines, S. (1986, April). Minorities, others organize against toxic threat. *The Neighborhood Works, 9,* 5–6.

Piven, F. F., & Cloward, R. (1977). *Poor people's movements: Why they succeed, how they fail.* New York: Pantheon.

Piven, F. F., & Cloward, R. (1978). Social movements and societal conditions: A response to Roach and Roach. *Social Problems, 26*(2), 172–178.

Piven, F. F., & Cloward, R. (1982). *The new class war: Reagan's attack on the welfare state and its consequences.* New York: Pantheon.

Plotkin, S. (1983). Democratic change in the urban political economy: San Antonio's Edwards aquifer controversy. In R. Johnson, J. A. Booth, & R. J. Harris (Eds.), *The politics of San Antonio: Community, progress & power* (pp. 157–174). Lincoln, NE: University of Nebraska Press.

Podolefsky, A., & DuBow, F. (1981). *Strategies for community crime prevention: Collective responses to crime in Urban America.* Springfield, IL: Charles C. Thomas.

Pratt, H. (1976). *The Gray lobby.* Chicago: University of Chicago Press.

Prestby, J. E., & Wandersman, A. (1985). An empirical exploration of a framework of organizational viability: Maintaining block organizations. *Journal of Applied Behavioral Science, 21*(3), 287–305.

Pruitt, D. (1981). *Negotiation behavior.* New York: Academic Press.

Public housing under siege: A special issue. (1989, Winter–Spring). *Community change,* pp. 1–20.

Quimby, E., & Friedman, S. (1989, October). Dynamics of black mobilization against AIDS in New York City. *Social Problems, 36,* 403–415.

Ramati, R. (1981). *How to save your own street.* Garden City, NY: Dolphin Books.

Randall, R., & Wilson, C. (1989, May). The impact of federally imposed stress upon local-government and nonprofit corporations. *Administration & Society, 21,* 3–19.

Ranney, D. (1986, December). Are organizations more important than people? *The Neighborhood Works, 9,* 3–6.

Rappaport, J. (1985, Fall). The power of empowerment language. *Social Policy,* pp. 15–21.

Rasky, S. (1989, September 17). How disabled sold Congress on a new Bill of Rights. *New York Times,* section E, p. 5.

Rathke, W., Borgos, S., & Delgado, G. (1979). ACORN: Taking advantage of the fiscal crisis. *Social Policy, 10*(2), 35–36.

Reardon, P. (1989, July 17). Community taking over jobs program. *Chicago Tribune,* section 1, pp. 1, 6.

Redburn, F. S., & Buss, T. F. (1986). *Responding to America's homeless: Public policy alternatives.* New York: Praeger.

Redburn, F. S., & Buss, T. F. (1987, February). Beyond shelter: The homeless in the USA. *Cities,* 63–69.

Reinarman, C. (1988). The social construction of an alcohol problem. *Theory and Society, 17,* 91–120.

Reisch, M., & Wenocur, S. (1986, March). The future of community organization in social work: Social activism and the politics of profession building. *Social Service Review, 60,* 70–93.

Reitzes, D. C., & Rietzes, D. C. (1982). Alinsky reconsidered: A reluctant community theorist. *Social Science Quarterly, 60*(2), 265–279.

Reitzes, D. C., & Rietzes, D. C. (1987). *The Alinsky legacy: Alive and kicking.* Greenwich, CT: JAI Press.

Rewriting the social contract for America's have-nots. (1987, April 12). *New York Times,* section E, p. 5.

Riessman, F. (1986). The new populism and the empowerment ethos. In H. C. Boyte & F. Riessman (Eds.), *The new populism: The politics of empowerment* (pp. 53–63). Philadelphia: Temple University Press.

Rivera, J. A. (1987). Self-help as mutual protection: The development of Hispanic fraternal benefit societies. *Journal of Applied Behavioral Science, 23*(3), 387–396.

Rivera, R. (1988, December). When communities tell it to the judge. *City Limits, 13,* 12–15.

Robert, H. M. (1984). *Robert's rules of order.*

Rochin, R. I. (1986). The conversion of Chicano Farm Workers into owner-operators of cooperative farms, 1970–1985. *Rural Sociology, 51*(1), 97–115.

Rodrigues, N. M. (1988). A successful feminist shelter: A case study of the family crisis shelter in Hawaii. *The Journal of Applied Behavioral Science, 24*(3), 235–250.

Rogers, D., Whetten, D., & Associates. (1982). *Interorganizational coordination: Theory, research and implementation.* Ames, IA: Iowa State University.

Rosen, C. M. (1989, August). Employee ownership: Promises, performance and prospects. *Economic Development Quarterly, 3,* 258–265.

Rosen, C. M., Klein, K. J., & Young, K. M. (1986). *Employee ownership in America: The equity solution.* Lexington, MA: Lexington.

Rosenthal, B. B., & Mizrahi, T. (1990, Spring). Coalitions: Building strength from diversity. *NY Ragtimes, 1,* 3–4.

Rossi, P. H., & Freeman, H. E. (1985). *Evaluation: A systematic approach* (3rd ed.). Beverly Hills, CA: Sage.

Rossi, P., & Wright, J. (1989, January). The urban homeless: A portrait of urban dislocation. *The Annals of the American Academy of Political and Social Science, 501,* 132–142.

Rothschild, J. (1987). *Do collectivist-democratic forms of organization presuppose feminism? Cooperative work structures and women's values.* Paper presented at the Annual Meeting of the American Sociological Association, Chicago.

Rothschild, J., & Whitt, J. A. (1986). *The cooperative workplace: Potentials and dilemmas of organizational democracy and participation.* Cambridge, England: Cambridge University Press.

Rothschild-Whitt, J. (1979). The collectivist organization: An alternative to rational bureaucratic models. *American Sociological Review, 44*(4), 509–527.

Rubin, H. J. (1981). Rules, collective needs and individual action: A case study in a townhouse cooperative. *Environment and Behavior, 13*(2), 165–188.

Rubin, H. J. (1983). *Applied social research.* Columbus, OH: Merrill.

Rubin, H. J. (1984). The meshing organization as a catalyst for municipal coordination. *Administration and Society, 16*(2), 215–238.

Rubin, H. J. (1986). Local economic development organizations and the activities of small cities in encouraging economic growth. *Policy Studies Journal, 14*(3), 363–388.

Rubin, H. J. (1987). Community economic development: The role of the applied sociologist. *Journal of Applied Sociology, 4,* 31–46.

Rubin, H. J. (1988). Shoot anything that flies; claim anything that fall: Conversations with economic development practitioners. *Economic Development Quarterly, 2*(3), 236–251.

Rubin, H. J. (1989). Symbolism and economic development work: Perceptions of urban economic development practitioners. *American Review of Public Administration, 19*(3), 233–248.

Rubin, H. J. (1990). Working in a turbulent environment: Perceptions of urban economic development practitioners. *Economic Development Quarterly, 4,*(2), 113–127.

Rubin, H. J., Rubin, I. S., Grush, J., & Dobson, D. (1987). Evaluation for cutback management in small cities. In T. Busson & P. Coulter (Eds.), *Policy evaluation for local government* (pp. 167–182). New York: Greenwood.

Rubin, I. S. (1985). *Shrinking the federal government.* New York: Longman.

Rubin, I. S. (1990). *The politics of public budgeting: Getting and spending, borrowing and balancing.* Chatham, NJ: Chatham.

Rubin, I. S., & Rubin, H. J. (1987, September). Economic development incentives: The poor (cities) pay more. *Urban Affairs Quarterly, 23,* 37–62.

Russell, D. (1987, Fall). The monkeywrenchers. *The Amicus Journal,* pp. 28–42.

Russell, R. (1985). *Sharing ownership in the workplace.* Albany, NY: State University of New York Press.

Sabatier, P., & Mazmanian, M. (1980). The implementation of public policy: A framework for analysis. *Policy Studies Journal, 8*(4), 538–559.

Sampson, R. J. (1987, September). Urban black violence: The effects of male joblessness and family disruption. *American Journal of Sociology, 93,* 348–382.

Sarason, S. B. (1986). The nature of social problem solving in social action. In E. Seidman & J. Rappaport (Eds.), *Redefining social problems* (pp. 11–28). New York: Plenum.

Savage, J. A. (1986, Summer). Radical environmentalists: Sabotage in the name of ecology. *Business and Society Review, 58,* 35–37.

Sax, J. (1971). *Defending the environment: A strategy for citizen action.* New York: Alfred A. Knopf.

Schecter, S. (1982). *Women and male violence: The visions and struggles of the battered women's movement.* Boston: South End Press.

Scheiber, M. S. (1987, April). Home equity plan put before local voters. *The Neighborhood Works, 10,* 6–7.

Schein, E. H. (1985). *Organizational culture and leadership.* San Francisco: Jossey-Bass.

Scheisl, M. J. (1977). *The politics of efficiency: Municipal administration and reform in America, 1800–1920.* Berkeley, CA: University of California Press.

Schelling, T. (1960). *The strategy of conflict.* New York: Oxford University Press.

Schillinger, E. (1988, January). Dependency, control, and isolation: Battered women and the welfare system. *Journal of Contemporary Ethnography, 16,* 469–490.

Schlozman, K. L., & Tierney, J. T. (1986). *Organized interests and American democracy.* New York: Harper & Row.

Schmidt, D. D. (1989). *Citizen lawmakers: The ballot initiative revolution.* Philadelphia: Temple University Press.

Schmidt, R. J. (1988, June). Cultural pluralism and public administration: The role of community-based organizations. *The American Review of Public Administration, 18,* 189–202.

Schmidt, W. E. (1989, October 25). Projects link inner cities, jobless to suburban work opportunities. *New York Times,* section I, p. 13.

Schoenberg, S. P. (1980). *Neighborhoods that work.* New Brunswick, NJ: Rutgers: State University of New Jersey.

Schuck, P. (1983). *Suing government: Citizen remedies for official wrongs.* New Haven, CT: Yale University Press.

Schumacher, E. F. (1973). *Small is beautiful: Economics as if people mattered.* New York: Harper & Row.

Schwab, J. (1987, August). Brass roots. *Planning,* 6–10.

Scotch, R. K. (1988). Disability as the basis for a social movement: Advocacy and the politics of definition. *Journal of Social Issues, 44,* 159–172.

Sealander, J., & Smith, D. (1986, Summer). The rise and fall of feminist organizations in the 1970s: Dayton as a case study. *Feminist Studies, 12,* 321–341.

Seattle saves market, saves neighborhood. (1988, January–February). *The Neighborhood Works, 11,* 1, 7–8.

Seidman, E. (Ed.). (1983). *Handbook of social intervention.* Beverly Hills, CA: Sage.

Seidman, E., & Rappaport, J. (1986). Framing the issues. In E. Seidman & J. Rappaport (Eds.), *Redefining social problems* (pp. 1–8). New York: Plenum.

Seitel, F. (1980). *The practice of public relations.* Columbus, OH: Merrill.

Sekul, J. D. (1983). Communities organized for public service: Citizen power and public policy in San Antonio. In D. R. Johnson, J. A. Booth, & R. J. Harris (Eds.), *The politics of San Antonio: Community, progress and power* (pp. 175–190). Lincoln, NE: University of Nebraska Press.

Shales, T. (1988, March 14–20). Media power to the people. *Washington Post National Weekly Edition,* 8–9.

Sharp, E. (1978). Citizens organizations in policing issues and crime prevention: Incentives and participation. *Journal of Voluntary Action Research, 7*(1–2), 45–58.

Sharp, E. (1981). Organizations, their environments and goal definition: An approach to the study of neighborhood associations in urban politics. *Urban Life, 9*(4), 415–439.

Sharp, E., & Elkins, D. (1989). *Public and private models of economic development.* Paper presented at the annual meeting of the Midwest Political Science Association, Chicago.

Sharp, G. (1973). *The politics of non-violent action.* Boston: Porter Sargent Publisher.

Shearer, D. (1989). In search of equal partnerships: Prospects for progressive urban policy in the 1990s. In G. D. Squires (Ed.), *Unequal partnership: The political economy of urban redevelopment in postwar America* (pp. 289–308). New Brunswick, NJ: Rutgers University Press.

Shelton, B. A., & Feagin, J. R. (1987). *The impact of community based movements on the physical environment: The case of Houston.* Paper presented at the annual meeting of the American Sociological Association, Chicago.

Shockley, J. S. (1974). *Chicano revolt in a Texas town.* Notre Dame, IN: University of Notre Dame.

Sierra Club. (1989). *The Sierra Club: A guide.* Washington, DC: Author.

Silverman, P. (1980). *Mutual self-help groups: Organizations and development.* Beverly Hills, CA: Sage.

Simpson, D., & Gentile, A. (1986, Spring). Effective neighborhood government. *Social Policy,* pp. 25–30.

Skogan, W. G. (1988). Community organizations and crime. *Crime and Justice, 10*(1), 39–78.

Skogan, W. G. (1989, July). Communities, crime and neighborhood organization. *Crime & Delinquency, 35,* 437–457.

Skogan, W. G., & Maxfield, M. (1981). *Coping with crime: Individual and neighborhood reactions.* Beverly Hills, CA: Sage.

Slaton, C. D. (1989). The politics of symbolic consistency: Being green while organizing greens. Paper presented at the Annual Meeting of the American Political Science Association, Atlanta.

Slayton, R. A. (1986a). *Back of the yards: The making of a local democracy.* Chicago: University of Chicago Press.

Slayton, R.A. (1986b, October). Making housing court work for you. *The Neighborhood Works, 9,* 14–15.

Smith, D. (1989, December). Self-employment project targets Latino women. *Neighborhood Works, 12,* 3–4.

Smith, D. H., Macaulay, J., & Associates. (1980). *Participation in social and political activities: A comprehensive analysis of political involvement, expressive leisure time, and helping behavior.* San Francisco, Jossey-Bass.

Smith, D. H., Reddy, R., & Baldwin, B. (1972). *Voluntary action research.* Lexington, MA: Lexington.

Smith, D. H., Reddy, R., & Baldwin, B. (Eds.). (1980). *Participation in social and political activities.* San Francisco: Jossey-Bass.

Smith, M. P. (1979). *The city and social theory.* New York: St. Martin's Press.

Smith, M. P. (1988). *City, state & market: The political economy of urban society.* New York: Basil Blackwell.

Smith, P. B., & Peterson, M. F. (1988). *Leadership, organizations and culture: An event management model.* Newbury Park, CA: Sage.

Solo, P. (1988). *From protest to policy: Beyond the freeze to common security.* Cambridge, MA: Ballinger Publishing.

Sommer, R., & Nelson, S. (1986). The use of survey results by democratically controlled organizations. *The Journal of Applied Behavioral Science, 22*(2), 113–125.

Squires, G. (no date). *Employee ownership and equal opportunity: Ameliorating race and gender wage inequalities through democratic work organizations.* Unpublished manuscript, University of Wisconsin–Milwaukee.

Squires, G., Bennett, L., McCourt, K., & Nyden, P. (1987). *Chicago: Race, class and the response to urban decline.* Philadelphia: Temple University Press.

Staggenborg, S. (1986, June). Coalition work in the pro-choice movement: Organizational and environmental opportunities and obstacles. *Social Problems, 33,* 374–389.

Staggenborg, S. (1987). *Organizational and environmental influences in the development of the pro-choice movement.* Paper presented at the Annual Meeting of the American Sociological Association, Chicago.

Staples, L. (1984). *Roots to power: A manual for grassroots organizing.* New York: Praeger.

Steggert, F. (1975). *Community action groups and city government.* Cambridge, MA: Ballinger.

Stein, A. (1986). Between organization and movement: ACORN and the Alinsky model of community organizing. *Berkeley Journal of Sociology, 31,* 93–115.

Steinbach, C. F., & Peirce, N. R. (1987, June 6). Picking up hammers. *National Journal,* pp. 1464–1468.

Steinhart, P. (1990). Bridging the gap: Can Earth Day unite Greens and mainline conservationists? *Audubon, 92*(1), 20–23.

Steinhoff, S. (1988). *Making the link: Directing economic benefits of the proposed west side stadium to local neighborhood development.* Research Note No. 1-88. Chicago: Natalie P. Voorhees Center for Neighborhood and Community Improvement.

Stewart, D. (1979, May–June). Neighborhood solutions for crime prevention. *Self-Reliance, 19,* 1, 4–5.

Stewart Mott Foundation. (1987). *Community policing: Making the case for citizen involvement.* Flint, MI: Charles Stewart Mott Foundation.

Stone, C. (1976). *Economic growth and neighborhood discontent: System bias in the urban renewal program of Atlanta.* Chapel Hill, NC: University of North Carolina Press.

Stone, C. (1986). Power and social complexity. In R. J. Waste (Ed.), *Community power: Directions for future research* (pp. 77–113). Newbury Park, CA: Sage.

Stone, C. (1989). *Regime politics: Governing Atlanta, 1946–1988.* Lawrence Kansas: University Press, of Kansas.

Struyk, R. J., Turner, M. A., & Ueno, M. (1988). *Future U.S. housing policy: Meeting the demographic challenge.* Urban Institute Report 88-2. Washington, DC: The Urban Institute Press.

Study questions whether subsidies for business produce benefits for the poor. (1989, Summer). *Community Change,* pp. 1–3.

Sumka, H. (1979). Neighborhood revitalization and displacement: A review of the evidence. *Journal of the American Planning Association, 45*(4), 480–487.

Susser, I. (1988). Working-class women, social protest and changing ideologies. In A. Bookman & S. Morgen (Eds.), *Women and the politics of empowerment* (pp. 257–271). Philadelphia: Temple University Press.

Susskind, L., & Cruikshank, J. (1987). *Breaking the impasse: Consensual approaches to resolving public disputes.* New York: Basic Books.

Susskind, L., & McMahon, G. (1985). The theory and practice of negotiated rulemaking. *Yale Journal on Regulation, 3,* 133–165.

Suttles, G. (1968). *The social order of the slum.* Chicago: University of Chicago Press.

Suttles, G. (1972). *The social construction of communities.* Chicago: University of Chicago Press.

Swack, M. (1987). Community finance institutions. In S. T. Bruyn & J. Meehan (Eds.), *Beyond the market and the state: New directions in community development* (pp. 79–96). Philadelphia: Temple University Press.

Swanstrom, T. (1985). *The crisis of growth politics: Cleveland, Kucinich, and the challenge of urban populism.* Philadelphia: Temple University Press.

Talbot, A. R. (1983). *Settling things: Six case studies in environmental mediation.* Washington, DC: The Conservation Foundation and the Ford Foundation.

Task Force on Community-Based Development. (1987). *Community based development: Investing in renewal.* Washington, DC: Author.

Taub, R. P. (1988). *Community capitalism.* Boston: Harvard Business School Press.

Taylor, C. D. M. (1990). Worker organizing in South Carolina: A community-based approach. In J. Gaventa, B. E. Smith, & A. Willingham (Eds.), *Communities in economic crisis: Appalachia and the South* (pp. 108–122). Philadelphia: Temple University Press.

Teitz, M. B. (1989, May). Neighborhood economics: Local communities and regional markets. *Economic Development Quarterly, 3,* 111–122.

Teltsch, K. (1990, January 30). Founded by rich idealists, group thrives on helping needy. *New York Times,* section A, p. 10.

Thomas, J. (1988). *Prisoner litigation: The paradox of the jailhouse lawyer.* Totowa, NJ: Rowman & Littlefield.

Thomas, J. C. (1986). *Between citizen and city: Neighborhood organizations and urban politics in Cincinnati.* Lawrence, KS: University of Kansas Press.

Timberlake, M. (1987). World-system theory and the study of comparative urbanization. In M. P. Smith & J. R. Feagin (Eds.), *The capitalist city: Global restructuring and community politics* (pp. 37–65). New York: Basil Blackwell.

Torre, R. L., & Bendixen, M. A. (1988) *Direct mail fund raising: Letters that work.* New York: Plenum.

Tourigny, A., & Miller, J. (1981). Community based human service organizations: Theory and practice. *Administration in Social Work, 5*(1), 79–86.

Trapp, S. (1976a). *A challenge for change.* Chicago: National Training and Information Center.

Trapp, S. (1976b). *Dynamics of organizing.* Chicago: National Training and Information Center.

Trapp, S. (1979). *Who, me a researcher?* Chicago: National Training and Information Center.

Trenholm, S. (1989). *Persuasion and social influence.* Englewood Cliffs, NJ: Prentice-Hall.

Tropman, J. (1980). *Effective meetings: Improving group decision making.* Beverly Hills, CA: Sage.

Turk, H. (1977). *Organizations in modern life: Cities and other larger networks.* San Francisco: Jossey-Bass.

Turner, C. (1987). Worker cooperatives and community development. In S. T. Bruyn & J. Meehan (Eds.), *Beyond the market and the state: New directions in community de-*

velopment (pp. 64–78). Philadelphia: Temple University Press.

Tygart, C. E. (1987). Participants in the nuclear weapons freeze movement. *The Social Science Journal, 24*(4), 393–402.

U.S. Conference of Mayors. (1986). *Rebuilding America's cities.* Cambridge, MA: Ballinger Publishing.

U.S. Department of Housing and Urban Development. (1989). *New directions in housing and urban policy: 1981–1989.* Washington, DC: Author.

U.S. Department of Housing and Urban Development, Office of Community Planning and Development. (1987). *Outstanding local partnerships in community development programs and projects.* Washington, DC: Author.

U.S. Department of Housing and Urban Development, Office of Neighborhoods, Voluntary Associations and Consumer Protection. (1979). *Neighborhoods: A self-help sampler.* Washington, DC: Author.

U.S. Department of Housing and Urban Development, Office of Neighborhoods, Voluntary Associations and Consumer Protection. (1980). *Neighborhood planning primer.* Washington, DC: Author.

U.S. Department of Housing and Urban Development, Office of Policy Development and Research. (1982). *An impact evaluation of the Urban Development Action Grant Program.* Washington, DC: Author.

U.S. Department of Housing and Urban Development, Office of Policy Development and Research. (1988). *An evaluation of the neighborhood development demonstration.* Washington, DC: Author.

U.S. Office of Consumer Affairs. (no date). *People power: What people are doing to counter inflation.* Washington, DC: Author.

University of Illinois, Circle Campus, Center for Urban Economic Development. (1987). *Community economic development strategies: A manual for local action.* Chicago: Author.

VanGundy, A. B. (1987). *Creative problem solving: A guide for trainers and managers.* New York: Quorum Books.

Vellela, T. (1988). *New voices: Student political activism in the '80s and '90s.* Boston: South End Press.

Victor, K. (1987, October). New kids on the block. *National Journal, 31,* 2726–2730.

Vidal, A. C., Principal Investigator. (1989). *Community economic development assessment: A national study or urban community development corporations—Preliminary findings.* New York: Community Development Research Center, Graduate School of Management and Urban Professions, New School for Social Research.

Vidal, A. C., Howitt, A. M., & Foster, K. P. (1986). *Stimulating community development: An assessment of the Local Initiatives Support Corporation.* A Report Submitted to the Local Initiatives Support Corporation, June 1986. Cambridge, MA: The State, Local and Intergovernmental Center, John F. Kennedy School of Government, Harvard University.

Waddock, S. A. (1989, May). Understanding social partnerships: An evolutionary model of partnership organizations. *Administration & Society, 21,* 78–100.

Wagner, D. (1989, June). Radical movements in the social services: A theoretical perspective. *Social Service Review, 63,* 264–284.

Walsh, E. J. (1981, October). Resource mobilization and citizen protest in communities around Three Mile Island. *Social Problems, 29,* 1–22.

Walsh, E., & Warland, R. H. (1983). Social movement involvement in the wake of a nuclear accident: Activists and free rides in the TMI area. *American Sociological Review, 48*(6), 764–780.

Wandersman, A. (1981). A framework of participation in community organizations. *The Journal of Applied Behavioral Science, 17*(1), 27–58.

Warcquant, L. J. D., & Wilson, W. J. (1989, January). The cost of racial and class exclusion in the inner city. *The Annals of the American Academy of Political and Social Science, 501,* 8–25.

Warren, D. (1975). *Black neighborhoods: An assessment of community power.* Ann Arbor: University of Michigan Press.

Warren, D. (1977). The functional diversity of urban neighborhoods. *Urban Affairs Quarterly, 13*(2), 151–179.

Warren, D. (1981). *Helping networks.* Notre Dame, IN: University of Notre Dame.

Warren, R. (1978). *The community in America.* Chicago: Rand McNally.

Warren, R., Rose, S., & Bergunder, A. (1974). *The structure of urban reform.* Lexington, MA: Lexington.

Warren, R. B., & Warren, D. (1977). *The neighborhood organizer's handbook.* Notre Dame, IN: University of Notre Dame Press.

Washnis, G. (1976). *Citizen involvement in crime prevention.* Lexington, MA: Lexington.

Waste, R. J. (1989). *The ecology of city policy making.* New York: Oxford University Press.

Weatherford, M. S. (1982). Interpersonal networks and political behavior. *American Journal of Political Science, 26*(1), 117–143.

Weicher, J. (1984). *Maintaining the safety net: Income redistribution programs in the Reagan administration.* Washington, DC: American Enterprise Institute for Public Policy Research.

Weick, K. E. (1979). *The social psychology of organizing.* Reading, MA: Addison-Wesley Publishing.

Weisman, A. (1989, July 30). For breath. *New York Times Magazine,* pp. 15–16.

Weisner, S. (1987, June). Comments on "the future of community organization in social work." *Social Service Review, 61,* 365–366.

Weitzman, P. (1988, October). State of the stock. *City Limits,* pp. 12–15.

Wellman, B., & Leighton, B. (1979). Networks, neighborhoods, and communities: Approaches to the study of the community question. *Urban Affairs Quarterly, 14*(3), 363–390.

Wells, M. (1987). Power brokers and ethnicity: The rise of a Chicano movement. *Aztlan, 17*(1), 47–73.

Wenocur, S., & Reisch, M. (1987, June). Author's reply. *Social Service Review, 61,* 367–368.

Wenocur, S., & Reisch, M. (1989). *From charity to enterprise: The development of American Social work in a market economy.* Urbana, IL: University of Illinois Press.

Wertheim, E. (1976). Evolution of structure and process in voluntary organizations: A study of thirty-five consumer food cooperatives. *Journal of Voluntary Action Research, 5*(1), 4–15.

West, G. (1981). *The national welfare rights movement: The social protest of poor women.* New York: Praeger.

Wetzel, K. W., & Gallagher, D. G. (1990, February). A comparative analysis of organizational commitment among workers in the cooperative and private sector. *Economic and Industrial Democracy, 11,* 93–109.

Wharton, C. S. (1987, Summer). Establishing shelters for battered women: Local manifestations of a social movement. *Qualitative Sociology, 10,* 146–163.

White, K., & Matthei, C. (1987). Community land trusts. In S. T. Bruyn & J. Meehan (Eds.), *Beyond the market and the state: New directions in community development* (pp. 41–63). Philadelphia: Temple University Press.

Whyte, W. F. (1986, March–April). Philadelphia story. *Society, 23,* 36–45.

Whyte, W. F., & Whyte, K. K. (1988). *Making Mondgragon: The growth and dynamics of the worker cooperative complex* (p. 317). Ithaca, NY: ILR Press, New York State School of Industrial and Labor Relations.

Widmer, C. (1985, October–December). Why board members participate. *Journal of Voluntary Action Research, 14*(14), 4.

Wiewel, W., & Weintraub, J. (1990). Community development corporations as a tool for economic development finance. In D. Bingham, E. W. Hill, & S. B. White, (Eds.), *Financing economic development: An institutional response* (pp. 160–176). Newbury Park, CA: Sage.

Williams, B. (1988). *Upscaling downtown: Stalled gentrification in Washington, D.C.* Ithaca, NY: Cornell University Press.

Williams, M. (1984). Two models of community organizing: Book review essay. *Urban Affairs Quarterly, 19*(4), 568–573.

Williams, M. (1989). *Neighborhood organizing for urban school reform.* New York: Teachers College Press, Columbia University.

Wilson, W. J. (1987). *The truly disadvantaged: The inner city, the underclass, and public policy.* Chicago: University of Chicago Press.

Wireman, P. (1984). *Urban neighborhoods, networks, and families: New forms for old values.* Lexington, MA: Lexington Books.

Withorn, A. (1987, January–February). Socialist analysis and organizing: An interview with Richard A. Cloward and Frances Fox Piven. *Radical America, 21,* 21–30.

Wolman, H. (1988). Local economic development policy: What explains the difference between policy analysis and policy. *Journal of Urban Affairs, 10*(1), 19–27.

Wolman, H., & Ledebur, L. (1984). Concepts of public–private cooperation. In C. Farr (Ed.), *Shaping the local economy: Current perspectives in economic development* (pp. 25–32). Washington, DC: International City Management Association.

Worker ownership goes to the supermarket. (1987, July). *The neighborhood works, 10,* 6–7.

Worthy, W. (1976). *The rape of our neighborhoods.* New York: William Morrow.

Wright, L. E. (1989). *Participatory research: A study of empowerment in public housing through resident management.* Unpublished doctoral dissertation, Northern Illinois University, DeKalb.

Wright, P. A. (1989, October–November). "Is community control a thing of the past?" *The Neighborhood Works, 12,* 3–5.

Yarrow, M. (1990). Voices from the coalfield: How miners' families understand the crisis of coal. In J. Gaventa, B. E. Smith, & A. Willingham (Eds.), *Communities in economic crisis: Appalachia and the South* (pp. 38–52). Philadelphia: Temple University Press.

Yin, R., Vogel, M., Chaiken, J., & Both, D. (1976). *Patrolling the neighborhood beat: Residents and residential security.* Rand Corporation publication no. R-1912-DOL. Santa Monica, CA: Rand.

Yukl, G. A. (1989). *Leadership in organizations.* Englewood Cliffs, NJ: Prentice-Hall.

Zald, M. N. (1987). The future of social movements. In M. N. Zald & J. D. McCarthy (Eds.), *Social movements in an organizational society: Collected essays* (pp. 15–42). New Brunswick, NJ: Transaction Books.

Zald, M. N. (1988). The trajectory of social movement in America. In L. Kriesberg, B. Misztal, & J. Misztal (Eds.), *Research in social movements, conflicts and change: A research annual: Vol. 10. Social movement as a factor of change in the contemporary world* (pp. 1–18). Greenwich, CT: JAI Press.

Zald, M. N., & McCarthy, J. D. (Eds.), (1979). *The dynamics of social movements: Resource mobilization, social control and tactics.* Cambridge, MA: Winthrop.

Zald, N., & McCarthy, J. D. (1987). Social movement industries: Competition and conflict among SMOs. In M. N. Zald & J. D. McCarthy (Eds.), *Social movements in an organizational society: Collected essays* (pp. 161–

180). New Brunswick, NJ: Transaction Books.

Zander, A. (1985). *The purposes of groups and organizations.* San Francisco: Jossey-Bass.

Zdenek, R. (1987). Community Development Corporations. In S. T. Bruyn & J. Meehan (Eds.), *Beyond the market and the state: New directions in community development* (pp. 112–127). Philadelphia: Temple University Press.

Zech, T. (1987, August). Flooding problems continue. *The Daily Chronicle, 26,* 1.

Zigas, B. (1987, Summer). A growing loss of subsidized housing. *Community Change,* 1–2.

Zisk, B. H. (1989a). *Coalitions among peace and environmental groups: A comparative study of the impact of local political culture.* Paper presented at the annual meeting of the American Political Science Association, Atlanta.

Zisk, B. H. (1989b). *Green agenda-setting and the consensus process: A comparative study of local and national Green organizing efforts in America.* Paper presented at the annual meeting of the American Political Science Association, Atlanta.

Zisk, B. H. (1988). *Movement politics, voter education, and the electoral process: Referenda campaigns of peace and environmental activists.* Paper presented at the Annual Meeting of the American Political Science Association, Washington, D.C.

Zwerdling, D. (1979). The uncertain revival of food cooperatives. In J. Case & R. Taylor (Eds.), *Co-Ops, communes & collectives: Experiments in social change in the 1970s* (pp. 89–111). New York: Parthenon.

Zwier, R. (1987). *Coalition strategies of religious interest groups.* Paper presented at the annual meeting of the American Political Science Association, Chicago.

Index